Pastor Hatfield

May you enjoy this version along with others in your studying.

Arlo Swanson

GOD'S NEW COVENANT

GOD'S NEW COVENANT

A New Testament Translation

by

Heinz W. Cassirer

WILLIAM B. EERDMANS PUBLISHING COMPANY
GRAND RAPIDS, MICHIGAN

Published by William B. Eerdmans Publishing Company
255 Jefferson Avenue, SE, Grand Rapids, Michigan 49503

Printed in the United States of America

Library of Congress Cataloging-in-Publication Data

Bible. N.T. English. Cassirer.
God's new covenant.

I. Cassirer, H. W. (Heinrich Walter), 1903–1979.
II. Title.
BS2098.C37E47   1989   225.5'209   89–23653
ISBN 0–8028–3673–9

FOR
OLIVE

Contents

CONTENTS

*The Emotional and Spiritual Categorical Headings
under Which the Translator Initially Divided
the Content of St. Paul's Letters*

List of Abbreviations
of Old Testament and Apocryphal Books
in Alphabetical Order

appearing as references at the feet of the pages of this translation

Am	Amos	Lv	Leviticus
1 Ch	1 Chronicles	1 M	1 Maccabees
2 Ch	2 Chronicles	2 M	2 Maccabees
Dn	Daniel	Mal	Malachi
Dt	Deuteronomy	Mic	Micah
Ec	Ecclesiastes	Nah	Nahum
Ec'us	Ecclesiasticus	Neh	Nehemiah
Est	Esther	Nm	Numbers
Ex	Exodus	Obd	Obadiah
Ezk	Ezekiel	Pr	Proverbs
Gn	Genesis	Ps	Psalms
Hab	Habakkuk	Rt	Ruth
Hg	Haggai	1 Sm	1 Samuel
Hos	Hosea	2 Sm	2 Samuel
Is	Isaiah	Sg	Song of Songs
Jl	Joel	Tb	Tobit
Jg	Judges	Wis	Wisdom of Solomon
Jnh	Jonah	Zc	Zechariah
Job	Job	Zp	Zephaniah
Jos	Joshua		LXX—The Septuagint (Greek
Jr	Jeremiah		version of Old Testament and
1 K	1 Kings		Apocrypha)
2 K	2 Kings		[ ]—Allusions to Old Testament
Lm	Lamentations		passages

Introducing the Translation
and Its Translator

This New Testament translation was made by a philosopher who had not read a word of the Bible before he had reached the age of 49. The experience of discovering these texts was of such magnitude that he was to devote the next twenty-one years of his life to their study. His Jewish heritage took on new meaning, while God's ultimate self-revelation in Jesus Christ became to him a profound reality which in turn led to his full acceptance of the truth of the Christian message. In 1955 he was baptized into the Anglican Church. Although he now referred to himself as a 'Jewish Christian', he would not permit anyone to attempt to classify him in a way that went beyond this basic description of what he now truly was: he was ever wary of an ignominious trail over the ages of insincere conversions—frequently enforced, sometimes opportunistic—and thus expressed overt hostility towards anyone who would go out with the aim of converting the Jews to Christianity. There is no denominational bias, no ulterior motive, to sway the integrity of this translation, which must be allowed to speak for itself. The classicist and philosopher approached these texts with fresh eyes and a sense of wonder, eager to find out for himself exactly what they were saying.

The translation arose from this need for personal clarity and was well under way before Cassirer realized it could be read to advantage by others. The result is now offered to laymen, priests, and scholars, while the translator's unusual history, with its absence of religious preconditioning, will make the work particularly accessible to those coming to these texts for the first time, to Jews interested in Christianity, and to members of the Christian Church who are ready to explore further the Jewish roots of their religion.*

* The theologian Thomas F. Torrance has remarked challengingly: "How can we see Jesus the Jew from Bethlehem, Nazareth and Jerusalem, without the use of Jewish eyes? . . . I was looking through lenses of Gentile spectacles which distorted what was there, so that I had to learn to take off the spectacles I did not even know I was wearing." From

The Cassirers were a Jewish family who had moved to Germany from eastern Europe. Many of them were endowed with exceptional intellectual and artistic gifts. They had considered themselves sufficiently enlightened and sophisticated to abolish circumcising their male offspring well before the closing decades of the nineteenth century, having declared the symbol to be of no special importance. It was only when Heinrich (Heinz) Walter Cassirer had reached the depths of an intellectual despair he had come to know in the climate of British philosophical thinking in the years immediately following the Second World War that he decided to turn to the scriptural writings, with a view to finding out if they might have anything valuable to say about human freedom. The consequences were dramatic, forcing him to begin afresh and to reconsider many of the conclusions he had attempted to formulate first as a classical scholar and then as a leading commentator on the philosophy of Immanuel Kant.

Heinz Cassirer had been among the very few Jews in Germany who had foreseen, in its staggeringly horrific fullness, the 'solution' that Hitler had in store for the Jews of Europe. When Hitler established his dictatorship in March 1933, Cassirer announced that he would not spend another night in the country. He left for Switzerland with his family, and in January 1934 arrived in Britain, where he joined his father, Ernst Cassirer, in Oxford. At that time he spoke no English; but he learnt it rapidly, spent more than a quarter of a century teaching philosophy at the Universities of Oxford and Glasgow, and published his commentaries on Kant's *Critique of Judgment* and *Critique of Pure Reason*.

When he came to realize that there was something missing in Kant's nevertheless unsurpassed philosophical efforts to solve the question of moral freedom, he began seriously to ask himself whether this was a matter for the human intellect at all—a most unusual and uncomfortable position for a professional philosopher to admit to: it is necessary at this point to stress that he never in fact abandoned his firm belief that Kant was the greatest of all the philosophers; indeed, after completing his translation of the New Testament, he was to translate Kant's *Critique of Practical Reason*, as well as Sophocles' last play, *Oedipus at Colonus*, before planning to investigate what the Early Church Fathers had to say about moral freedom (a plan which was cut short by his sudden death in February 1979).

While his Kantian upbringing had originally made him scorn the idea that any kind of 'supernatural' help could be called upon to assist a human being in solving a moral predicament, he had since

"The divine vocation and destiny of Israel in world history," in *The Witness of the Jews to God*, edited by D. W. Torrance (Handsel Press, Edinburgh, 1982).

childhood shown himself uncomfortably aware of the existence of a radical evil which, he observed, had its source in human nature. Such an awareness, it should be pointed out, he shared with as austere and rational a philosopher as Kant himself.

It was on reading the epistles of St. Paul that Cassirer experienced a collapse, a total inward paralysis. The record of this period of his life, as well as his detailed analysis of human sinfulness, is to be found in his book *Grace and Law: St. Paul, Kant, and the Hebrew Prophets* (published 1988). Working his way backwards, from the New Testament to his discovery of the Old Testament (which he was subsequently to describe as 'my language'), he became more profoundly aware of his own Jewish roots and realized that he was understanding Paul's writings in a completely new light.

Withdrawing from academic life, which had grown increasingly burdensome to him, he immersed himself in these texts, while putting into operation his acute powers of judgment as he set about selecting and rejecting commentaries and—most important to his way of working—concentrating on the Arndt & Gingrich *Greek-English Lexicon of the New Testament* (and the German original by Walter Bauer), a wide range of English dictionaries, as well as biblical and theological dictionaries. He decided, for the sake of his own clarification, to make a translation of St. Paul's letters. The cornerstone of this endeavour was to set the greater portion of Paul's writings under 40 Spiritual and Emotional Categorical Headings, an exhaustive and original venture which was to fill 272 pages of foolscap paper. (The headings appear on the last two pages of this book.)

It was in 1957/58 that he worked on these categories. Not until the spring of 1972, however, did he feel fully prepared to translate the New Testament in its entirety. In actual fact, however, the translation had already firmly shaped itself in his mind; and all that remained was to set it down on paper, a task which he accomplished over a period of thirteen months (from July 1972 until August 1973). During this time he totally revised his translations of Paul's letters, the Letter Addressed to Readers of Hebrew Descent, the Apostles and Their Deeds (Acts), as well as the first draft of the books he had come to at a somewhat later stage of his pilgrimage, namely, the Gospel Story as Told by St. John and the shorter epistles.

Regarding the translation itself, Cassirer aimed for a clarity that would be sensitive to every inflection of the original Greek. His style does not water down or reduce meaning; on the contrary, its probing is often assisted by his own musical sensitivity, and this allows the spiritual processes of these texts to unfold at their own tempo. In the case of Paul's letters, there is a focussing on the unimpeded, spiral manner in which the apostle's thought-processes operate. There is always to be discerned a sensitive, observant response to the different voices of each document that makes up the canon of the New Testament, be it in the unfolding of narrative (Luke's literary style, for example, allowing him a wide range of expressive freedom to which this translation is very much alive) or in the expounding of doctrine.

As indicated, Cassirer was intent on translating in depth; as such he made it clear that *God's New Covenant* should in no way be considered a paraphrase. Yet if the subtlety of the Greek warranted it, and if by so doing this would draw out the meaning with greater spiritual accuracy (bearing in mind the oral tradition out of which the scriptures grow), he would not hesitate, within disciplined boundaries, to call upon an extra word or group of words.

A response which is alert to every emotional nuance of the text lies at the heart of this translation. Insights that come from a developed literary and artistic imagination must of necessity work in partnership with meticulous scholarship: this tenet of Cassirer's is all-pervasive. It is valuable to read *God's New Covenant* out loud. One immediately becomes aware of points of emphasis in these texts which can be overlooked. In being true to the original Greek, the translator showed a natural preference towards an English style grounded in a long and rich literary tradition, and with which he had made himself thoroughly familiar. This tradition is brought together with a keen, contemporary, idiomatic use of the language. He trusted that imaginative scholars who so wished would be able to find a firm foundation implied within the context itself for any challenging and unexpected choices of word or phrase. I well recall his response when I first reacted to the translation of the line in the Lord's Prayer which reads, "And do not bring us to the point of being put to the final test" (Matt. 6:13)—the last two words returning in this translation when Jesus, at Gethsemane, urges his disciples to pray that they might be spared from having to undergo the final test (Matt. 26:41; Mark 14:38). Notwithstanding the absence of the definite article in the Greek, Cassirer rejected the familiar 'lead us not into temptation' in the Lord's Prayer, and he pointed out that 'do not put us to the test' was meaningless on the ground that God, in both Old and New Testaments, is ever testing us. "No," he chuckled, using the symbolic vocabulary which came to him so naturally, "this is the driving test which nobody can pass."

St. John's gospel had been a stumbling block for a long time—and Cassirer's decision to translate the New Testament came only when he was satisfied in his own mind that the passages that have long fuelled anti-Semitic reactions had been disastrously distorted and misinterpreted over the centuries, and were not in themselves anti-

Semitic. Indeed, it was to become his favourite gospel and later he was to advocate strongly its essentially Jewish character. It is unambiguous in this translation that 'the Jews' of the text frequently refer to the Jewish authorities whose influence holds sway (though Cassirer thought it lacking in subtlety to expand, except in a couple of instances, on the two-syllable 'the Jews'). As for the disturbing seventh and eighth chapters, the reader suddenly realizes that Jesus' manner of retort to his *own* people is very much in keeping with the prophetic tradition.

The tone of the translation of the Gospel Story as Told by John is established immediately with the rendering of the Greek preposition *pros:* "The Word was *by the side of* God, and the Word was the very same as God." The crucial importance of this drawing out of the spatial, that is, the intimately *personal* Father-Son relationship, at the very same time is illuminating the full extent of the 'oneness' of that relationship: "No one has ever seen God. It is his only Son, who rests on the breast of the Father, who has made him known" (1:18). Linked with this, of course, is the translation of *paraklētos* in the fourteenth chapter, the promise of the coming of the Holy Spirit—"The one who will stand by your side." Mention should also be made of Cassirer's feeling for the rhythmical shaping in a gospel which is imbued with its own sense of poetry, for this in turn releases the very *process* involved in coming to understand the gospel's message: "Even though you should not believe me, base your belief on the deeds I perform, so that you may learn and come to believe that the Father dwells in me, and I dwell in the Father" (10:38).

Cassirer was in no doubt that the intellectual backbone of Christianity was to be found in Paul's letters, and that Christianity could not be understood without them. In The Apostles and Their Deeds, the translator is not only intent on capturing the spiritual fervour and intellectual force behind Paul's words: he aims to make the reader aware of the struggle Paul himself has to undergo in order to communicate the truth and originality of what has been revealed to him after the experience on the road to Damascus. And when Paul is eventually able to express his insights with the confidence of a 'man united to Christ Jesus', the mockery of the authorities swiftly turns to unbridled fury —and Paul can offer the following retort to the High Priest Ananias: "God will strike you in return, you, the very image of a wall daubed over to deceive" (KJV: "God shall smite thee, thou whited wall") (Acts 23:3).

Throughout the Pauline letters themselves, the reader will be aware of how Paul's language reverberates with a tone which parallels the Hebrew Prophets, most notably in his unflinching diagnosis of the spiritual disease within the human soul. ("Who is enticed into sin, and I am not in a furnace of distress?" [2 Cor. 11:29]). Paul's penetrating intellect is driven forward by an unhindered outpouring of emotion, and the translation's intent is to carry the reader unerringly through every stage of Paul's argument by way of connecting Paul's thought-process to the complex thread of his emotions. Cassirer would often remark that one of the secrets of accurately translating these letters lay in the ability to have a thorough grasp of how Paul used prepositions—a fact well known to scholars who set out to interpret Paul.

This introduction attempts to pinpoint just a few distinctive features of *God's New Covenant*. It is not the place to outline how Cassirer viewed each part of the New Testament. Suffice to mention that, as he embarked on each section, that section would in turn become the consuming force. At one stage, for instance, his intent on 'getting the theology right' in both letters of Peter dominated every moment of his thinking. But it was the symbolism embedded within the Letter Addressed to Readers of Hebrew Descent and in The Revelation Which John Received that, along with Paul's letters, understandably held a place specially close to Cassirer's heart.

Since he is of Hebrew descent himself, there is an attentiveness to Jewish sensibilities present in the most subtle of ways in these texts— to take but one example, there is a firm, natural instinct that makes one aware of the continuous construction of the spoken Aramaic, in places where the literal following of the Greek present tense cannot be insisted upon: The most obvious instance is in the first Beatitude: "A blessing rests on those whose spirit makes them think but poorly of themselves: the kingdom of heaven shall be theirs" (Matt. 5:3; cf. Luke 6:20).* Cassirer was endlessly absorbed in observing how the English language could be used to reach an understanding of a truth. As for the use of exclusive expressions, such as 'man' and 'men' to describe both members of the human race, he had more than a glimmer of the day approaching when there would be a hue and cry for them to be banned. But in a text such as the New Testament—especially in a translation in which the Jewish patriarchal spirit makes itself felt so strongly—they cannot always be responsibly or intelligently expunged; and Cassirer resisted what he saw as an encroachment upon the English language and which fatally undermines its poetic force. (Echoing Paul, he would not 'conform to the fashion of this present world' [Rom. 12:2]; subsequently, the editorial decision has been

---

* "The tense of *estin* must not be pressed: it is timeless, and in Aramaic the connecting verb would not be used" (A. H. M'Neille, *The Gospel according to St. Matthew*).

to respect his wish in most instances, only permitting change, with caution and trepidation, where this could be made without tampering with interpretation or weakening the translation's stylistic distinctiveness.* The temptation to pepper the book with explanatory footnotes has likewise been largely resisted in accordance with the translator's explicit injunction, for he believed that a translation should be its own commentary.)

In Cassirer's original manuscript, Old Testament quotations (whether direct or paraphrased by the New Testament writers) appeared in capitals. The publishers have taken pains to ensure that these now appear in a slightly bolder typeface, the references appearing at the feet of the pages. Many of these are to be found in the Greek editions Cassirer used;† he added others as he explored and re-explored the Old Testament texts. (Discovering some more, I considered it right to add them.) These references are by no means exhaustive, but this important feature of *God's New Covenant* will serve to remind the reader of the New Testament's inextricable dependence on the Hebrew Bible, and the latter's emphasis on God's everlasting covenant. (There is no change to the typeface where an Old Testament passage is alluded to, and the reference appears at the foot in square brackets.)

The swift intensity with which Cassirer set down the translation, and made revision to earlier drafts, while at the same time pondering the choice of each word and responding to the rhythmic flow and shape of every phrase, has already been referred to. During this period I assumed the role of amanuensis, and was responsible for producing a clean typescript. There were times when a word or a subclause would be missing. A phone call would produce the correct translation within seconds. When I began to prepare the typescript for publication, four years after Cassirer's death, it was necessary of course to check the text, verse by verse, alongside the original. Inevitably a few omissions were discovered, but it was possible to reconstruct the exact wording carefully by referring to an earlier draft; and in the case of the Pauline letters, by consulting those all-important 40 emotional and spiritual categories which he had drawn up at the start of his enterprise.

Cassirer showed no desire to see this translation published in his lifetime. He expressed confidence that it would have its day, and was

---

* The problems of exclusive language in biblical translation have been helpfully set out and discussed by Paul Ellingworth in "Translating the Bible Inclusively," *Meta*, XXVII, 1 (1987).

† Nestle and Kilpatrick, *New Testament* (British & Foreign Bible Societies, 1958); Nestle, *Novum Testamentum Graece* (Stuttgart, 1952); Aland, Black, Metzger, etc., *The Greek New Testament* (United Bible Societies, 1966).

content to say, "Now it is up to the Holy Spirit." He then made preparations to begin translating Kant's major ethical work, *The Critique of Practical Reason*.

At this point I should like to thank the Very Rev. Professor Thomas F. Torrance, who revealed exceptional insight at the outset into very important aspects of the translation, and who played an indispensable part in bringing about its publication.

Rev. Dr. Paul Ellingworth, translations consultant in the United Kingdom to the United Bible Societies, was asked by the publishers to check the typescript, and he generously gave of his time and knowledge when queries arose, making valuable suggestions. I also wish to acknowledge the vital spiritual support we received from the late Very Rev. Dr. Eric Abbott (for many years Dean of Westminster), and from Father Aelred Stubbs of the Community of the Resurrection. Of those who helped with checking the typescript and proofs, Hugh Pyper of Glasgow University and the Religious Society of Friends in particular gave to this task many hours of his perception and time. Dr. Michael Weitzman of the Department of Hebrew and Jewish Studies at University College, London, kindly shared his knowledge where questions arose relating to the occasional use of Aramaic in these texts. Bill Eerdmans' recognition of the translation's qualities has been accompanied by a publisher's insistence on thoroughness, by continuous patience, and by a rare sense of humour which reveals true generosity of spirit: these attributes have been reflected in the cooperation and professionalism shown by his staff.

There is no way in which this work could have been accomplished without the unceasing support given to the translator by the very presence of his wife Olive. After his death, Olive Cassirer spent many a memorable day with me making a careful check through her husband's work, regularly offering firm and wise guidance.

Cassirer entrusted me with overall editorial supervision; and during the long period when the volume was being prepared for publication my responsibility has been to keep firmly in mind Cassirer's purpose, and to make every effort to preserve in all its essentials the integrity and style of this single-handed translation.

RONALD WEITZMAN
London, August 22, 1988

GOD'S NEW COVENANT

THE GOSPEL STORY
AS TOLD BY MATTHEW

1 A record of the descent of Jesus Christ, offspring of David, himself an offspring of Abraham.

²Abraham became father of Isaac; Isaac became father of Jacob; Jacob became father of Judah and his brothers; ³Judah became father of Perez and Zerah (their mother being Tamar); ªPerez became father of Hezron; Hezron became father of Ram; ⁴Ram became father of Amminadab; Amminadab became father of Nahshon; Nahshon became father of Salmon; ⁵Salmon became father of Boaz (his mother being Rahab); Boaz became father of Obed (his mother being Ruth); Obed became father of Jesse; ⁶and Jesse became father of King David.

David became father of Solomon (his mother having been the wife of Uriah); ⁷Solomon became father of Rehoboam; Rehoboam became father of Abijah; Abijah became father of Asa; ⁸Asa became father of Jehoshaphat; Jehoshaphat became father of Joram; Joram became father of Azariah; ⁹Azariah became father of Jotham; Jotham became father of Ahaz; Ahaz became father of Hezekiah; ¹⁰Hezekiah became father of Manasseh; Manasseh became father of Amon; Amon became father of Josiah; ¹¹and Josiah became father of Jeconiah and his brothers. This was at the time of the deportation to Babylon.

¹²After the deportation to Babylon Jeconiah became father of Shealtiel; Shealtiel became father of Zerubbabel; ¹³Zerubbabel became father of Abiud; Abiud became father of Eliakim; Eliakim became father of Azor; ¹⁴Azor became father of Zadok; Zadok became father of Achim; Achim became father of Eliud; ¹⁵Eliud became father of Eleazar; Eleazar became father of Matthan; Matthan became father of Jacob; ¹⁶Jacob became father of Joseph, the husband of Mary. It was of her that Jesus was born, the one who is called God's anointed.*

¹⁷Thus there are fourteen generations, all told, from Abraham to

ª[Rt 4:18-22]

* [Gk. = '(the) Christ'; Heb. = 'Messiah'.]

David; fourteen generations from David until the time of the deportation to Babylon; and fourteen generations from the deportation to Babylon until the time of God's anointed.*

[18] This is the story of how Jesus, God's anointed, came to be born. Mary his mother was promised in marriage to Joseph when it was found, at a time when they had not as yet come together, that she was to be a mother, and that by the power of the Holy Spirit. [19] Joseph, her partner in marriage, who was a man good and true and who did not wish her to suffer public disgrace, was planning to send her away secretly. [20] However, while he was still debating the matter with himself, all of a sudden one of God's angels appeared to him during a dream and addressed him in the following words: "Joseph offspring of David, do not hesitate about taking Mary your wife into your home. For it is by the power of the Holy Spirit that she has conceived what is in her womb. [21] She will give birth to a son, and Jesus, that is to say, Saviour, is the name you shall give him, because he is the one who is to save his people from their sins." [22] (Now all this happened so as to bring to fulfilment these words which the Lord spoke by the mouth of his prophet: [23] [b] **This is what is to happen: the virgin shall be with child and give birth to a son, and the name they shall give him will be Emmanuel'** (which, correctly translated, means [c] **God is with us'**). [24] On waking from his dream, Joseph acted in conformity with the order which had been given him by the angel. He took his wife to his home [25] while yet refraining from being on terms of intimacy with her until after she had given birth to her son. And the name he gave him was Jesus.

2 After Jesus had been born at Bethlehem in Judaea, during the reign of King Herod, it happened one day that certain men skilled in the magical arts,† who had come from the east, made their appearance in Jerusalem. [2] And this is what they asked: "Where is he who has been born to be king of the Jews? We have observed his star as it rose and we have come to pay him homage." [3] King Herod was greatly perturbed when he heard this, as was the whole of Jerusalem. [4] And so he called a meeting of all those who held the position of chief priests or that of experts in the law among the people, enquiring of them where God's anointed was to be born. [5] "At Bethlehem in Judaea," was their reply; "for this is what the prophet wrote: [6] [d] **And you, Beth-**

[b] Is 7:14   [c] Is 8:8.10 LXX   [d] Mic 5:2; 2 Sm 5:2

* [Gk. = '(the) Christ'; Heb. = 'Messiah'.]
† [Or 'skilled in reading the stars'.]

lehem, in the land of Judah, are by no means **least in the sight of those that bear rule over Judah, for out of you a leader shall come forth, a man who is to be shepherd of my people Israel.'"**

7 At that, Herod called the Magi secretly to himself and ascertained from them the precise time at which the star had appeared. 8 He then told them to go to Bethlehem, addressing them in these words: "Be on your way and make careful enquiries about the child. When you find him, let me have word of this so that I, too, may pay homage to him."

9 On hearing the words of the king, they set out, and this is what happened to them: the star which they had seen at its rising went right ahead of them, coming to a standstill just over the place where the child was. 10 At the sight of the star they were beside themselves with joy, 11 and on entering the house they saw the child with Mary his mother. At that they threw themselves to the ground and paid homage to him. Moreover, opening their treasure chests they presented their offerings to him, *e*offerings of gold, of frankincense, and of myrrh. 12 And having received warning in the course of a dream that they were not to return to Herod, they went back to their own country by another way.

13 Some time after the Magi had left, it happened that one of the Lord's angels appeared to Joseph during a dream. And this is what he said: "Rise up, taking the child and his mother with you, and make your escape into Egypt, staying there until I give you word. For Herod intends to make a search for the child and to have him put to death." 14 So Joseph rose up and, taking the child and his mother with him at dead of night, took refuge in Egypt, 15 remaining there until the death of Herod. These things happened so that fulfilment might be brought to this proclamation of the Lord made by the mouth of his prophet: *f*'**It was out of Egypt that I summoned my son'.**

16 Herod, for his part, on realizing that the Magi had made a dupe of him, flew into a great rage and gave the order that all children of two years or under at Bethlehem and in the surrounding districts were to be done away with, the time of this corresponding with the accurate information he had received from the Magi. 17 And so it was that this utterance made by the prophet Jeremiah was fulfilled: 18 *g*'**A voice has been heard in Ramah; there has been wailing and great lamentation. It was Rachel crying over her children, and refusing to be comforted because these children are no longer.'**

19 No sooner had Herod died than God's angel appeared to Joseph in Egypt in the course of a dream, 20 addressing these words to him: "Rise up and, taking the child and his mother with you, go to the land

e[Ps 72:10.15; Is 60:6]   *f*Hos 11:1   *g*Jr 31:15

of Israel, for those who were out for the child's life are dead." 21So Joseph rose up, took the child and his mother with him, and made his way into the land of Israel. 22However, when he learned that Archelaus was reigning over Judaea in the place of his father Herod, he was afraid to go there. And so, having been given a warning in the course of a dream, he took refuge in the district of Galilee, settling there in a town called Nazareth. 23This came about in order that the words uttered by the prophets, 'He shall be called a Nazarene', should come to be fulfilled.

3 At that time John the Baptist made his appearance, proclaiming his message in the Judaean desert. 2"Repent," he exclaimed; "the kingdom of heaven is drawing near. 3As for him of whom I am speaking, he is the very man mentioned by the prophet Isaiah in these words: *h*'**A voice of one crying out in the desert: Prepare a way for the Lord; straighten out the paths** which he is to tread.'"

4John's clothing consisted of a garment made of camel's hair and of a leather belt round his waist; and the food he ate was locusts and wild honey. 5People came flocking to him at that time from Jerusalem, from all Judaea, and from all the districts adjoining the Jordan, 6being baptized by him in the River Jordan while making confession of their sins. 7When John became aware that many of the Pharisees and Sadducees were coming forward to have baptism administered to them, he said to them, "A brood of vipers that you are! Who has given you warning to take flight from the retribution to come? 8What you must do is act in such a way that the fruit borne by what you do is in keeping with a state of repentance. 9And do not imagine that you can say to yourselves, 'We have Abraham as father.' For what I have to declare to you is this: God has the power of creating children for Abraham out of these very stones. 10Why, even now the axe lies poised at the root of the trees; and so it will happen that every tree failing to yield good fruit will be cut down and cast into the fire. 11I am baptizing you with water, the goal of this being that you should come to repent. But another is to come after me, endowed with much greater power than I have, a man so great that, as regards myself, I shall not even be worthy to carry his shoes. The baptism he will administer to you will be one by the Holy Spirit and by fire. 12His winnowing shovel will be in his hand. He will clean out his threshing floor, and his wheat he will gather together into his granary. The chaff, however, he will burn up in a fire never to be extinguished."

13Some time after this Jesus arrived at the Jordan, coming from

*h*Is 40:3

Galilee, and went to John with the intention of being baptized by him. [14]But John sought to prevent him, remarking, "It is I who stand in need of being baptized by you, and you come to me!" [15]"Let it be so for the present," was Jesus' reply; "it is no more than seemly that we should allow the requirements of righteousness to be brought to the fullest possible expression." So John yielded to him. [16]As for Jesus, having received his baptism, he came up from the water at once. All of a sudden the heavens opened up, and he saw the Spirit of God descending after the fashion of a dove and resting upon him. [17]Moreover, there was a voice speaking from heaven saying, "This is [i]**my Son,** my **dearly-loved** one; **it is he on whom my favour rests.**"

4   Some time after this Jesus was led away by the Spirit into the desert, that he might be put to the test by the devil. [2]He fasted for forty days and forty nights, and in the end he was plagued by hunger. [3]Then the tempter drew near and said to him, "If it be true that you are the Son of God, order these stones to turn into loaves of bread." [4]"This is what is written in scripture," was Jesus' reply, [j]"'**Man cannot live with bread as his only support; what he stands in need of is every word which proceeds from the mouth of the Lord.'**" [5]After this the devil took Jesus with him into the Holy City, placed him on the summit of the temple, [6]and said, "If it be true that you are the Son of God, throw yourself down. For as scripture has it, [k]'**He will give his angels a commission concerning you. They will bear you up on their hands, that there may be no fear of your striking your foot against a stone.'**" [7]"This is what is written in turn," was Jesus' reply, [l]"'**You must not put the Lord your God to the test.'**" [8]Next the devil took him up a very high mountain and showed him all the kingdoms of the world and the splendour which goes with them. [9]And this is what he said: "I shall give you all this if you will fall to the ground and pay homage to me." [10]"Away with you, Satan," answered Jesus, "for this is what stands written: [m]'**You shall do homage to the Lord your God, and you shall worship** no one but **him.'**"

[11]At that the devil left his company; and all of a sudden, angels appeared, drawing near him and taking care of him.

[12]On hearing that John had been committed to prison, Jesus withdrew to Galilee. [13]Moreover, leaving Nazareth he settled at Capernaum, which is a lakeside place situated in the region of Zebulun and Naphtali. [14]This came about in fulfilment of these words spoken by the prophet Isaiah: [15]"[n]**Land of Zebulun, land of Naph-**

[i]Gn 22:2; Ps 2:7; Is 42:1   [j]Dt 8:3   [k]Ps 91:11f   [l]Dt 6:16   [m]Dt 6:13   [n]Is 9:1f

tali, **the sea road beyond the Jordan, Galilee of the Gentiles.** ¹⁶**The people who spent their days shrouded in darkness have seen a great light; and on those that dwelt in a land overshadowed by death a light has dawned.'**

¹⁷From that time onwards Jesus began to proclaim his message in these words: "Repent, for the kingdom of heaven is drawing near you."

¹⁸One day when he was walking by the shore of the Sea of Galilee, his eyes fell on two brothers, Simon, also called Peter, and his brother Andrew. Being fishermen, they were occupied with throwing their nets out into the lake, ¹⁹when Jesus addressed these words to them: "To my side, follow me; fishers of men is what I shall be making out of you." ²⁰At that they left their nets immediately and followed him. ²¹When he had gone on some distance he saw two other men who were also brothers. These were James son of Zebedee, and his brother John; they were in their boat with their father Zebedee, mending their nets. Jesus called them to his side; ²²and they, leaving their boat and their father, followed him immediately.

²³Jesus himself went from place to place all over Galilee, teaching in the synagogues there and proclaiming the good news of the kingdom. And since he went among the people and engaged in healing all sorts of diseases and infirmities, ²⁴the tale of him spread all over Syria. There were brought to him all those who found themselves afflicted: sufferers from various diseases, those racked by pain or possessed by demonic spirits, the victims of epilepsy and the paralyzed, and he brought healing to them. ²⁵Moreover, he was followed by large crowds composed of people coming from Galilee, from the Decapolis, from Jerusalem, from Judaea, as well as from the districts beyond the Jordan.

5　When Jesus saw the crowds, he went up the hill. He sat down, and his disciples drew near him. ²Then, opening his mouth, he gave them his teaching in the following words:

³ ⁰"A blessing rests on those whose spirit makes them think but ᵖ**poorly** of themselves; the kingdom of heaven shall be theirs.

⁴"A blessing rests on those whose lives are full of ᵍ**sorrow;** they shall find themselves ʳ**comforted.**

⁵"A blessing rests on those who are of a ˢ**gentle** spirit; they shall be the ones to **possess the earth.**

⁶"A blessing rests on those who hunger and thirst that right may be done; they shall have their satisfaction.

ᵒ[Ezk 44:30]　ᵖIs 57:15; [Ps 51:17]　ᵍPs 126:5　ʳIs 61:2f　ˢPs 37:11

⁷"A blessing rests on those who are compassionate; they shall have compassion shown them.

⁸"A blessing rests on those whose ᶠhearts are full of **innocence**; they shall see God before their very eyes.

⁹"A blessing rests on those who are bent on establishing peace; 'Sons of God' is the name that shall be given them.

¹⁰"A blessing rests on those who suffer persecution in defence of the right; the kingdom of heaven belongs to them.

¹¹"A blessing rests on you when they revile you, when they persecute you, when they speak evil of you in every way, when they tell falsehoods against you, and all on my account. ¹²Be glad, be full of joy. It is a rich reward that awaits you in heaven. And indeed, in just the same way they made the prophets before you suffer persecution.

¹³"You are the ones that serve as salt for the world. But if the salt itself becomes insipid, what is there to give it back its salty flavour? In fact, it is no longer good for anything, and all that can be done is throw it out altogether, letting it be trodden on by human feet.

¹⁴"You are the men who bring light into the world. If there be a city built on the top of a hill, there is no way of keeping it hidden. ¹⁵Moreover, no one, on lighting a lamp, then places it under a grain measure. On the contrary, people put it on a lampstand, letting its light shine on everybody in the house. ¹⁶In the same way the light which is in you should shine forth in the sight of men so that, on witnessing the noble deeds performed by you, they may come to give praise to your Father in heaven.

¹⁷"Do not suppose that, if I have appeared, that was with the intention of abolishing the teaching of the law and the prophets. I have made my appearance not to abolish it, but to give full expression to it. ¹⁸Indeed, I can give you solemn assurance of this: it is not till heaven and earth are removed that anything shall be removed from the law, be it but one letter, but one flourish. What is necessary first of all is that all its purposes should be accomplished. ¹⁹And so, whoever seeks to do away with one of the law's commandments, even though it may be counted among those of the least significance, and teaches others to do the same, that person will be of least significance in the kingdom of heaven. But he who keeps the commandments, and teaches them, will be esteemed to stand high in the kingdom of heaven. ²⁰And one more thing. Unless the righteousness of conduct found in you surpasses that found in the experts in the law and the Pharisees, you will never gain entry into the kingdom of heaven.

²¹"You have heard what was said to the men of old: 'You shall do ᵘ**no murder.** If, however, anyone does commit murder, he shall be

ᶠPs 24:4; 51:12; 73:1   ᵘEx 20:13

9

answerable for this to a court of law.' 22 Yet what I am saying to you is this: anyone who gives vent to anger against his brother will be answerable for this before a court of law; anyone who calls his brother 'Fool'* will be answerable for this before the High Council; and anyone who says to his brother, *v*'You rebel against God',† will be answerable for this to the extent of being consigned to the fire of hell.

23 "So then, when you are taking your offering to the altar, and come to recall there that your brother has some ground of complaint against you, 24 you must leave your offering in front of the altar, going back and becoming first of all reconciled to your brother. And after that you should return and present your offering.

25 "Come to terms speedily with your opponent while you are still on the way to court with him. Otherwise there is danger that your opponent will hand you over to the judge, the judge handing you over to the law officer, and that you will be thrown into prison. 26 Indeed, I can give you solemn assurance of this: you will not come out of there till you have paid the very last penny.

27 "You have heard how they were told, *w*'**You must not commit adultery**'. 28 But what I say to you is this: anyone who looks at a woman in such a way that desire for her is aroused in him has already committed adultery with her in his heart.

29 "If your right eye should provide you with an occasion for sinning, tear it out and fling it away from yourself. It is better for you to suffer the loss of one part of your body than to have the whole of your body thrown into hell. 30 And if your right hand provides you with an occasion for sinning, cut it off and fling it away from yourself. It is better for you to suffer the loss of one part of your body than to have the whole of your body making its way into hell.

31 "This is what was said to them: *x*'**Anyone who sends his wife away must provide her with a writ of dismissal**'. 32 But I tell you this: anyone who sends his wife away, except on the ground of fornication, makes an adulteress of her, and anyone marrying a woman sent away after this fashion commits adultery.

33 "Again, you have heard what was said to the men of old: *y*'**You must not perjure yourselves**', and '**You must keep the oaths which you have sworn in the sight of the Lord**'. 34 But what I am saying to you is this: you are not to swear at all: not by *z***heaven**, for it is **God's throne**; 35 nor by the earth, for it is *a***the footstool on which he rests his**

v[Dt 21:18.20; 32:6; Is 32:6; Ec'us 50:26]   *w*Ex 20:14; Dt 5:18   *x*Dt 24:1   *y*Lv 19:12; Ex 20:7; Nm 30:2; Dt 23:21   *z*Is 66:1   *a*Lm 2:1; Is 66:1; [Ps 99:5]

* ['Blockhead', 'empty head' (alt. translation). The original is in Aramaic: *Raca*.]
† [I.e., a far worse insult.]

feet; nor by Jerusalem, for it is *b***the city of the great King.** ³⁶Nor should you swear by your own head, because it is not in your power to turn a single hair of it either white or black. ³⁷A simple 'Yes' and 'No' is all you ought to say. Anything that goes beyond that comes of the evil one.

³⁸"You have heard what was said to them: 'An *c***eye for an eye** and a **tooth for** a **tooth'.** ³⁹But what I am saying to you is this: offer no resistance to one who does you evil. Should a man strike you on the right cheek, turn towards him and offer him the other cheek as well. ⁴⁰Should anyone wish to go to law with you with a view to obtaining your tunic, let him have your coat as well. ⁴¹Should anyone seek to compel you to walk one mile, walk two miles with him. ⁴²If a man asks you for anything, give it to him, and if he wishes to borrow from you, do not turn him away.

⁴³"You have heard what has been said: '*d***Love your neighbour** but hate your enemy'. ⁴⁴Yet what I am saying to you is this: love your enemies and pray for those who persecute you, ⁴⁵so that you may be the true sons of your heavenly Father. After all, he makes his sun rise on good and bad alike, and his rain falls on the just as well as the unjust. ⁴⁶If you love only those who love you, what credit is that to you? Is it not true that even the tax collectors do the same? ⁴⁷And if you limit your love to those who are brothers of yours, what is remarkable about that? Do not the Gentiles do the very same thing? ⁴⁸What you must strive for is *e***to be perfect;** your heavenly Father is perfect.

6   "Make certain that you do not perform your acts of piety in the sight of men with a view to being observed by them. If you do that, you have no claim to a reward from your Father in heaven. ²Well then, if you perform an act of charity, do not put a trumpet in front of your mouth proclaiming the deed, and acting after the fashion of the hypocrites in the streets and in the synagogues whose one aim is to win men's approbation. Indeed, I can give you solemn assurance of this. All the reward due to them they have already had in full. ³Instead of this, you should, when you perform an act of charity, proceed in the following manner. Your left hand must, as it were, be left in ignorance of what your right hand is doing, ⁴your aim being that your charitable deed should be one hidden from sight. Then you shall have your requital from your Father, who has the power of seeing what is done in a place hidden from sight.

⁵"Moreover, when you pray, you must not take the hypocrites for your model, the men who, when they wish to engage in prayer, love

*b*Ps 48:2   *c*Ex 21:24; Lv 24:19f   *d*Lv 19:18   *e*Lv 19:2; Dt 18:13

to take up their stand in the synagogues and at the street corners, their purpose being to attract the notice of their fellow men. Indeed, I can give you solemn assurance of this. All the reward due to them they have already had in full. [6]Instead of this, the way in which you are to act at the time of prayer should be that you *f*withdraw to the innermost room of your house, close your door, and offer prayer to your Father, who dwells in a place hidden from sight. Then you shall have your requital from your Father, who has the power of seeing what is done in a place hidden from sight.

[7] "And one more thing. When you offer prayer, you must not give way to babbling, as is the custom among the Gentiles. They imagine that by stringing words together they will secure a hearing. [8]You must on no account become like them. For your Father knows, before you have ever asked him, what it is that you stand in need of. [9]This, then, is the way in which you ought to pray:

'Father of ours, you who have your dwelling in heaven:
*g*may your very name be treated as holy.
[10]May your kingdom appear.
May your will be accomplished on earth as it is accomplished in
   heaven.
[11]*h*Provide us this day with the bread that is needful to us.
[12]*i*Remit us the debts we have incurred against you
   as we have done to those who owed us a debt.
[13]And do not bring us to the point of being put to the final test.
On the contrary, come and rescue us from the evil one.'

[14] "And indeed, if you forgive your fellow men the wrongs they have done, your heavenly Father will forgive you; [15]whereas if you do not forgive your fellow men their wrongs, neither will your heavenly Father forgive you your wrongs.

[16] "Again, when you fast, do not take the hypocrites for your model, sullen creatures that they are. For men such as these disfigure their faces so as to be seen by their fellow men to be fasting. Indeed, I can give you solemn assurance of this. All the reward due to them they have already had in full. [17]But this is what you must do when you are fasting. Pour oil on your head and wash your face, [18]so that it may not be your fellow men by whom you are seen fasting, but your Father who dwells in a place hidden from sight. Then that Father of yours, who has the power of seeing what is done in a place hidden from sight, will give you your reward.

[19] "Do not store up treasure for yourselves on earth, where moth or rust does its work of destruction, and where thieves break in and steal.

*f*2 K 4:33; Is 26:20   *g*[Ezk 36:22f]   *h*[Pr 30:8]   *i*[Lv 4:26ff; Dt 15:1ff; Ec'us 28:2ff]

20 Store up treasure for yourselves in heaven, where no moth, no rust, does its work of destruction, and where no thieves break in and steal. 21 And indeed, where your treasure is, there also will your heart be.

22 "The body has the eye for its lamp. Well then, when your eye is sound, your whole body will be full of light; 23 while when it is in poor condition, your body will be shrouded in darkness. And if that in you which brings you light becomes darkness, what profound darkness it will be!

24 "No one can be the servant of two masters. If he is, he will either love the one and hate the other, or treat the one with respect and the other with contempt. You cannot be servants of both God and money.

25 "I would entreat you, therefore," he said, "not to bestow anxious care on the food by which you sustain your life or on the clothes with which you cover your bodies. Does not life mean more than nourishment, the body more than clothing? 26 Fix your gaze on the birds of the air: take note how they neither sow nor harvest, nor gather their goods into storehouses. And yet your heavenly Father nourishes them. Are you not worth much more than they are? 27 Which of you, by being anxious, can add a single cubit to his stature? 28 And why are you anxious about your clothing? Consider the lilies in the fields, how they grow. They do not toil or spin. 29 And yet, this I can assure you of: even Solomon in all his splendour was not arrayed as one of these. 30 But then, if this is how God clothes the grass, which grows in the field today and is thrown into the furnace tomorrow, how much more will he be ready to clothe you, you men of little faith. 31 Do not be anxious, therefore, asking, 'What are we to eat? What are we to drink? What are we to wear?' 32 For these are things which the Gentiles strive for. Your heavenly Father knows that you stand in need of all these things. 33 It is his kingdom and the righteous way in which it is governed which you must be in pursuit of first of all; and if you are, you will have all these things bestowed upon you as well. 34 And do not be anxious about what tomorrow will bring. Tomorrow will have itself to be anxious about. Each day has enough trouble of its own.

7 "Pass no judgment on others, so as to have no judgment passed on yourselves. 2 For whatever standard of judgment you employ, you will find yourselves judged by the very same standard. And whatever measure you deal out, the same will be dealt out to you. 3 How is it that you can observe the speck of dust in your brother's eye, while yet you are not aware of the piece of wood in your own? 4 Or by what right will you say to your brother, 'Brother, give me leave to take the speck of dust out of your eye', when all the time there is this piece of wood in your own eye? 5 Dissemblers that you are, first take the piece

of wood out of your own eye, and then you will see clearly enough to be able to take the speck of dust out of your brother's eye.

[6] "You must not let the dogs have meat which has been consecrated. Neither must you, should you be the owners of pearls, throw them in front of swine, for fear that they may trample them down with their feet, then turn and tear you to pieces.

[7] "Ask for something, and you will be given it; look for something, and you will find it; knock, and the door will be opened to you. [8] And indeed, everyone that asks receives; everyone that looks finds; he who knocks will have the door opened to him.

[9] "If there be one among you whose son asks him for a loaf of bread, is it to be supposed that he will offer him a stone; [10] or if he asks for a fish, that he will offer him a snake? [11] Well then, if you who are evil know how to make good gifts to your children, how much readier will your Father in heaven be to bestow good things upon those who ask him for them.

[12] "Whenever there is something you wish other people would do for you, it is your duty that, acting in the same way, you should do it for them. This is the very meaning of what is taught by the law and the prophets.

[13] "Let it be the narrow gate through which you make your entry. There is a spacious road and a wide gate, but what it leads to is perdition, while many make their entry that way. [14] But narrow is the gate and confined the road leading to what is truly life, and there are but few that find it.

[15] "Be on your guard against false prophets, those who come to you dressed up as sheep while inwardly they are rapacious wolves. [16] By the fruit which they bring forth you will be able to recognize them. Do people gather grapes from a thornbush, or figs from thistles? By no means. [17] In the same way every healthy tree yields good fruit, while a decayed tree yields worthless fruit. [18] It is impossible that a healthy tree should bear worthless fruit, just as it is impossible that a decayed tree should bear good fruit. [19] Every tree failing to yield good fruit will be cut down and cast into the fire. [20] Well then, by the fruit which they bring forth you will be able to recognize them.

[21] "Not everyone addressing me with the words 'Lord, O Lord' will find entry into the kingdom of heaven. Such entry will be found only by those whose actions are in conformity with my heavenly Father's will. [22] Many will be saying to me on that day, 'Lord, O Lord, [j]**have we** not **prophesied in your name?** Have we not driven out demonic spirits in your name? Have we not performed many a miracle in your name?' [23] And this is what I shall tell them to their faces: I never knew

[j]Jr 14:14; 27:15

14

you at all. *k* **Depart from my presence, you perpetrators of lawless deeds!**

24 "What, then, is the nature of the person, whoever he may be, who hears these words of mine and acts on them? He is like a man of prudence who has built his house on a rock. 25 The rain descended, the floodwaters rose, the winds blew and hurled themselves against that house. But it did not fall because it was on rock that its foundations were laid. 26 And what is the nature of the person, whoever he may be, who hears these words of mine and does not act on them? He is like a foolish man who has built his house on sand. 27 The rain descended, the floodwaters rose, the winds blew and beat against that house. Then it fell, and the fall of it was indeed a great one."

28 Now what happened when Jesus had come to the end of this discourse of his was that the crowds were astounded at his teaching. 29 This was because his way of teaching was like that of a man invested with authority, and quite unlike anything done by their own experts in the law.

8 After he had come down from the hill, he was followed by large crowds. 2 Then it happened that a man who was a sufferer from leprosy drew near, threw himself at his feet, and exclaimed, "Lord, you have the power of cleansing me, if only you wish to!" 3 Upon this, Jesus stretched out his hand, touched him, and called out, "Be cleansed; it is my wish that you should be." At that he was at once cleansed of his leprosy. 4 Then Jesus said these further words to him: "Be sure not to tell anybody about this. However, you must be on your way and *l***show** yourself **to the priest,** and present the offering which Moses has prescribed. This will suffice as evidence for them."

5 On making his entry into Capernaum he came upon a certain centurion who made an appeal for help to him in these words: 6 "Sir, I have in my house a servant who lies bedridden, paralyzed and cruelly tortured by pain." 7 "I shall come and heal him," said Jesus, 8 the centurion making this reply: "Sir, I do not deserve to have you entering my house. However, let the word of command be spoken, and then my servant will find healing in this way. 9 For I know what it means to be placed under authority; and I myself have soldiers who are subject to me. I say to one of them, 'Go', and he goes; and to another, 'Come', and he comes. I tell my servant to do this or that, and he does it." 10 When Jesus heard this he was amazed; and this is what he said to those who were following him: "Indeed, I can give you

*k*Ps 6:8   *l*Lv 13:49; 14:2.32

solemn assurance of this. I have not found faith as great as this in anyone in Israel. [11] And there is one more thing I will tell you: Many will come *m*from both **east and west** to recline at the banquet in the kingdom of heaven in the company of Abraham, of Isaac, and of Jacob. [12] Yet, as for those born to the kingdom, they will find themselves expelled from it and cast out into a place in which darkness reigns, where there shall be weeping and gnashing of teeth." [13] And to the centurion Jesus spoke thus: "Go on your way, and may that be done for you which your faith has deserved." And it was at that very moment that the servant's health was restored.

[14] After that, Jesus went to Peter's house, and there he found Peter's mother-in-law lying prostrate on a sickbed, suffering from a fever. [15] He touched her hand and the fever left her. So she rose up and waited on him. [16] When evening came, they brought into his presence many who were beset by demonic spirits, and he expelled the spirits by a word of command. Moreover, he brought healing to all those who were ill. [17] Certain words of the prophet Isaiah had to find their fulfilment: *n*'**He has taken away our infirmities, and as for our diseases, he has lifted them from us'.**

[18] At the sight of the crowds surrounding him, Jesus gave the order that they were to cross over to the other side. [19] Now an expert in the law approached him there and said, "Master, I shall follow you, no matter where you are going." [20] Jesus made him this reply: "Foxes have their holes to go to, and the birds of the air have their nesting places. Yet the Son of Man has no place where to rest his head." [21] Another man, one of his disciples, said to him, "Give me leave first of all to go and bury my father." [22] "Follow me," replied Jesus, "and let those who are dead bury the dead who belong to them."

[23] He got into the boat, followed by his disciples. [24] All of a sudden, a storm broke over the lake which was so violent that the boat was covered all over by the waves. But he was asleep. [25] So they went to the place where he was, wakened him, and exclaimed, "Lord, save us; we are perishing!" [26] "Why are you such cowards, you men of little faith?" was his reply. Thereupon he rose to his feet and administered a rebuke to the winds and to the sea; and a great stillness arose. [27] His companions were amazed, and said to each other, "What kind of man is this? Why, even the winds and the sea obey his commands."

[28] When he arrived on the other side in the country of the Gadarenes, he encountered two men beset by demonic spirits who were coming out from the tombs. They were very violent men, so much so that no one had sufficient strength to summon up the courage to pass that way. [29] And all of a sudden, they shrieked out these words:

*m*Is 49:12; 59:19; Mal 1:11; Ps 107:3   *n*Is 53:4

"What do you want with us, you Son of God? Have you come here to torture us before the time is ripe?" 30Now, some way off, a herd of swine was grazing; 31and the demons pleaded with Jesus, saying, "If you drive us out, send us forth into the herd of swine." 32"Begone," Jesus said to them, upon which they came out and went into the swine. And then it happened that the whole herd rushed headlong down the slope of the mountain into the lake, finding their death in its waters.

33As for those in charge of the swine, they took to flight, went off into the city, and reported the whole story there, including what had happened to the men possessed by demons. 34Thus it came about that the whole of the city turned out, desirous of encountering Jesus; and when they saw him, they made the urgent request that he withdraw from their territory.

9 He got into the boat, crossed over to the other side, and arrived at his home town. 2There it was that they brought into his presence a paralyzed man who was lying on a bed. When Jesus perceived the faith that was in them, he addressed these words to the man who was paralyzed: "Have courage, my friend, your sins are forgiven you." 3At that, certain of the experts in the law said to themselves, "This fellow utters blasphemies." 4Jesus, for his part, who well knew what thoughts they were harbouring, addressed them in these words: "Why is it that such evil thoughts are in your mind? 5After all, which of these is more easily said, 'Your sins are forgiven you,' or 'Rise up and walk'? 6The truth is that, if things turned out the way they did, this was so that you should be made to realize that the Son of Man, while he is on earth, has the authority granted to him to forgive sins." Then he said to the paralyzed man, "Rise to your feet, lift up your bed, and be on your way home." 7So the man rose up and went off to his home. 8On witnessing this, the crowds there were filled with awe and gave praise to God for granting to men power such as this.

9When Jesus had gone on a little way from that place, his eyes fell on a certain man by the name of Matthew, who was occupying his place in the tax office. "Follow me," Jesus said to him. And he, rising up, followed him. 10So it was that, when Jesus was reclining at table in the house, there reclined in his company and that of his disciples many men who were tax collectors or were given over to some other kind of sin.* 11On seeing this, the Pharisees addressed these words to Jesus' disciples: "Why is it that your master eats and drinks with tax collectors and other sinful men?" 12And Jesus, on hearing these

* [Usually understood as those who were less observant of the dietary and other Jewish laws, and who were treated as pariahs.]

words, made them this rejoinder: "It is not those who are strong and healthy that are in need of a physician; it is those who are in bad health. [13] Moreover, there is one thing you had better do: go and learn what is meant by the words, *o'***It is mercy I delight in, not sacrifice'.** And as for myself, I have made my appearance among men to hold out an invitation, not to people of virtue, but to sinners."

[14] Some time after this, John's disciples approached him with these words: "Why do we and the Pharisees fast, while your disciples do not fast?" [15] Jesus replied to them thus: "Is it conceivable that the friends of the bridegroom should be grieving while the bridegroom is still in their company? However, time will come when the bridegroom is taken away from them, and it will be then that they will be fasting.

[16] "No one puts a patch made of unshrunk cloth on an old coat. If this is done, the patch will take something off the coat, and there will be a worse tear than before. [17] Neither do people pour new wine into old wineskins. Otherwise the result will be that the wineskins burst, the wine is poured out, and the wineskins are ruined. No, people pour new wine into fresh skins; and so both are preserved."

[18] While Jesus was still addressing his audience in this way, a man holding an influential position suddenly approached him, threw himself down at his feet, and exclaimed, "My daughter has just died! But come to my house, laying your hand upon her, and she will come back to life!" [19] At that, Jesus rose up and followed him, his disciples doing the same. [20] And then a woman who had been a sufferer from constant bleeding for twelve years suddenly came up from behind and touched the fringe of Jesus' cloak. [21] This she did because she had been saying to herself, 'If I but touch his garment, I shall have my health restored.' [22] As for Jesus, he turned round, and when he saw her, he addressed her thus: "Courage, my daughter, it is by your faith that your health has been restored." And from that very moment the woman had her health given back to her.

[23] When Jesus arrived at the house of the man of influence he saw flute players there, and the crowd in a state of great commotion. [24] "Be off," he exclaimed, "the girl is not dead, only resting in sleep!" But they only laughed at him. [25] After the crowd had been removed, he went inside and took her by the hand; at that, the girl rose to her feet. [26] So it was that the tale of him spread all over that district.

[27] As he was going on from that place, two blind men were following him and shouting out, "Son of David, have pity on us!" [28] When he reached the house for which he was making, the blind men drew near him. Jesus asked them this question: "Do you believe that I have

*o*Hos 6:6

the power of accomplishing this?" 29"We do, Lord," was their reply. Thereupon Jesus touched their eyes, exclaiming, "May that be done for you which your faith has deserved!" 30At that their sight was restored to them, while Jesus gave them this stern warning: "Make sure that no one gets to know about this." 31However, they had no sooner left than they spread the tale of him all over that district.

32They had only just gone when a dumb man, who was possessed of a demonic spirit, was brought into his presence; 33and when the demon had been driven out, the dumb man regained his power of speech. The crowds were full of astonishment at this and exclaimed, "Nothing like this has ever been seen in Israel!" 34But there were the Pharisees, and what they said was this: "It is with the help of Beelzebub, the prince of demonic spirits, that he is casting the demonic spirits out."

35So Jesus went round all the cities and villages, teaching in the synagogues of the people and proclaiming the good news of the kingdom, while at the same time he engaged in healing all sorts of diseases and infirmities. 36Moreover, when he saw the crowds he was filled with compassion for them because they were being harassed and thrown to the ground *p*like sheep that have no shepherd. 37Then he addressed these words to the disciples: "The harvest is indeed plentiful, but of labourers there are few. 38So turn to the man who owns the harvest, requesting him to send out labourers to bring in his harvest."

10 One day he called the twelve disciples to his side and invested them with authority over the *q*tarnished spirits, thus enabling them to drive them out and to heal every kind of illness and infirmity.

2These are the names of the twelve apostles. First there was Simon, also called Peter, and his brother Andrew. Then James the son of Zebedee, and his brother John. 3Then there were Philip and Bartholomew, Thomas, and Matthew the tax collector, James son of Alphaeus, Thaddaeus, 4Simon, a member of the party of the Zealots, and Judas Iscariot, the one who became his betrayer.

5These twelve Jesus sent forth, giving them the following instructions: "Do not take any road leading you to the Gentiles, nor make your entry into a town inhabited by Samaritans. 6But instead make your way to the sheep that belong to the house of Israel and have gone astray. 7And as you are on your way, proclaim this message: 'The kingdom of heaven has drawn near.' 8Heal the sick; raise the dead to life. Cleanse the lepers; drive out the demonic spirits. You have

*p*Nm 22:17; Ezk 34:5; 1 Sm 22:17   *q*[Zc 13:2]

received what you have without charge; let it be without charge that you bestow your gift. [9]You must not acquire anything to fill your purses with, be it gold, silver, or copper; [10]no knapsack for the journey, no spare tunic, no footwear, no staff. After all, he who labours has a right to be provided with his keep.

[11]"Whenever you enter a city or a village, look out for some worthy person in it; then make your home there until you are obliged to leave the place. [12]When you make your entry into a house, give it your salutation. [13]And if the house is worthy, may the peace you have been wishing it descend upon it. If not, then let that peace return to yourselves. [14]Whenever people will not receive you or listen to your words, you must make your departure from the house or city where you are, shaking off the dust that clings to your feet. [15]Indeed, I can give you solemn assurance of this: what will befall Sodom and Gomorrah on the Day of Judgment will turn out to be more bearable than what will befall that house. [16]Mark my words: in being sent out by me you will find yourselves in the position of sheep that are thrown right in the midst of wolves. Well then, make of yourselves men as shrewd as serpents and as guileless as doves.

[17]"Be on your guard against what men will do to you. They will hand you over to their councils and have you flogged in their synagogues. [18]You will be dragged before governors and before kings, all on account of me, and you will have to bear testimony before them and the Gentiles. [19]However, do not be anxious, when they hand you over in this way, about what you are to say or how to say it. For when the time comes, the power of saying what you ought will be granted to you. [20]And that will be so because it is not you yourselves who will be speaking, but the Spirit of your Father speaking in you.

[21]"Brother will hand over brother to have him put to death, and fathers will act in the same way towards their children. **[r]Children will rise up against their parents** and bring death upon them. [22]As for yourselves, you will be hated by everyone because of your allegiance to the cause which bears my name. Yet if a man remains steadfast to the last, salvation shall be his. [23]If you are persecuted in one town, take flight and turn to the next. Indeed, I can give you solemn assurance of this: before you have come to the end of your journey through all the towns of Israel, the Son of Man will have made his appearance.

[24]"It is impossible that a pupil should be his teacher's superior, or a servant be his master's superior. [25]A pupil should be satisfied with becoming the equal of his teacher, a servant with becoming the equal of his master. If Beelzebub is the name they have affixed to the master

[r]Mic 7:6

of the house, how much more will they be ready to affix it to the members of his household!
26"Well then, do not be afraid of them. For there is nothing,
however carefully hidden away, that will not be revealed, nothing
kept concealed that will not be made known. 27Indeed, as regards
yourselves, you must tell in broad daylight that which I say to you in
the dark, and that which is whispered into your ears you must
proclaim from the housetops. 28And one more thing. Do not be afraid
of those who put the body to death but have no power of bringing
death to the soul. Rather, be afraid of him who has the power of
destroying both body and soul in hell.
29"Is it not a fact that one copper coin buys two sparrows? Yet
without your Father's consent not one of them will fall to the ground.
30As for yourselves, why, the very hairs on your head have been
counted. 31Cease feeling anxious, therefore: there is more in you than
in many sparrows.
32"Well then, everyone who acknowledges me before men I will
acknowledge before my Father in heaven; 33and anyone who
repudiates me before men I will repudiate before my Father in heaven.
34"Do not suppose that, if I have appeared, that was to bring peace
to the earth. I have not appeared to bring peace but a sword. 35Indeed,
this has been the purpose of my appearing: to turn a man [s]**against his
father, a daughter against her mother, and a daughter-in-law against
her mother-in-law.** 36Moreover, it is **the members of a man's
household** who will be his **enemies.**
37"He who loves his father and mother more than he loves me is
not worthy of me; he who loves his son and daughter more than he
loves me is not worthy of me; 38and he who does not take his cross
upon himself, following in my footsteps, is not worthy of me. 39He
who gains possession of his life will lose it; and he who loses his life
will gain possession of it.
40"He who gives a welcome to you gives a welcome to me, and he
who gives a welcome to me gives a welcome to him who has sent me
forth. 41He who gives a welcome to a prophet, because he is a prophet,
will receive the reward due to a prophet. He who gives a welcome to
an upright man, because he is an upright man, will receive the reward
due to an upright man. 42As for him who offers something to drink
to one of these little ones, though it be only a cup of cold water, and
does so because he is a disciple of mine, I can indeed give you solemn
assurance of this: he will on no account suffer the loss of the reward
due to him."

[s]Mic 7:6

11 When Jesus had come to the end of his instructions to the twelve disciples he left the place where he was, for the purpose of teaching and preaching in the people's cities.

2 As for John, when he learned in prison about the wondrous deeds performed by Christ, he made an approach to him by way of sending certain of his disciples to him with this message: 3 "Are you the one of whose coming we have been told, or are we to wait for some other man?" 4 And this is the reply Jesus made them: "Go on your way and report to John the things which you are seeing and hearing: 5 how *t*the **blind recover their sight,** the lame can walk, the leprous are cleansed, the deaf can hear, the *u***dead** are **raised to life,** and *v***the poor are having good news proclaimed to them.** 6 And one more thing: a blessing rests on all those who take no offence at me."

7 No sooner had the envoys departed than Jesus took the opportunity of talking about John to the crowds. "When you went out into the desert," he asked, "what did you expect to encounter? One having the character of a reed which the wind moves to and fro? 8 What kind of man, then, did you expect to meet when you went out? Someone clothed in soft, silky garments? Why, those wearing soft apparel are to be found in the palaces of kings. 9 What, then, did you expect when you came forth? Did you expect to see a prophet? Yes, indeed, you can have my assurance that he is something much greater than a prophet. 10 In fact, it is he of whom it is written in scripture, *w***Take note of this: I am sending my herald ahead of you; and it is he who will make ready the way** for your **coming'.** 11 And indeed, I can give you solemn assurance of this. Among all the sons of women no one greater than John has ever appeared. Yet he who holds the lowest place of all in the kingdom of heaven is greater than he. 12 From the time when John the Baptist appeared up to the present day the kingdom of heaven has been subjected to violence, and violent men are seeking to seize it by force. 13 Indeed, the task which occupied all the prophets as well as the law, up to the time of John, was to foretell things to come. 14 But John, if you will but accept it, is none other than Elijah of whom it was said that he was to return. 15 Let him who has ears, listen.

16 "To whom am I to compare this generation? It is like children sitting in the market place, calling out to one another and exclaiming, 17 'We have played the flute for you, and you would not dance; we have sung dirges to you, and there has been no beating of breasts.' 18 John the Baptist appears, refraining from eating and drinking, and they say, 'He is a man possessed of a demon'; 19 the Son of Man ap-

---

*t*Is 35:5f; Is 29:18   *u*Is 26:19   *v*Is 61:1   *w*Mal 3:1

pears, eating and drinking like any other man, and they say, 'Look at this glutton ˣ**gulping down wine,** this man who befriends tax collectors and sinners.' Yet, for all that, wisdom found the rightness of her ways acknowledged by virtue of the deeds she has accomplished."

²⁰ After that Jesus set about reprimanding the cities in which most of his miracles had been performed, because they had not been led to repent their ways. ²¹ "How pitiful is your condition, Chorazin," he exclaimed; "how pitiful is your condition, Bethsaida! For, truth to tell, if miracles such as have been performed in your midst had taken place in Tyre and Sidon, the people there would long since have come to repent in sackcloth and ashes. ²²Still, I am telling you this: even as things are, what will befall Tyre and Sidon on the Day of Judgment will turn out to be more bearable than what will befall you. ²³ And as for you, Capernaum, is it to be supposed that ʸ**you will be lifted up as high as heaven?** Far from it: ᶻ**you will have to make the descent to Hades* itself.** For if miracles such as have been performed in your midst had taken place in Sodom, it would have remained standing to this very day. ²⁴Still, I am telling you this: what will befall the land of Sodom on the Day of Judgment will turn out to be more bearable than what you will have to endure."

²⁵ At that moment Jesus gave utterance to these words: "Father, Lord over heaven and earth, here I am giving praise to you for concealing these things from those possessing wisdom and cleverness, while revealing them to the children. ²⁶ Yes, Father, that was the very thing which it was your good pleasure to accomplish. ²⁷ My Father has committed everything into my hands. Moreover, no one knows the Son but the Father, and no one knows the Father but the Son, as well as all those to whom the Son chooses to reveal him.

²⁸ "To my side, all of you who toil and carry a heavy burden. I will refresh you. ²⁹ Take my yoke upon your shoulders and learn from me. For I am gentle and humble of heart. ᵃ**You will find refreshment for your souls.** ³⁰For the yoke I put upon men is a kind one, and the burden I put upon their shoulders is lightly borne."

12 At this time, one Sabbath day, Jesus was making his way through fields of corn. And his disciples, feeling hungry, began to pluck ears of corn and eat them. ²When the Pharisees saw this, they said to him, "Look at that, your disciples are doing something that is forbidden on the Sabbath day." ³ And Jesus made them this rejoinder:

ˣPr 23:20   ʸIs 14:13.15;   ᶻEzk 26:20   ᵃIs 28:12; Jr 6:16

* Heb. = *Sheol;* 'the pit' or 'world below'.

"Have you never read what David did when he and his companions were plagued by hunger; [4]how he entered the house of God, and how they ate *b*the Loaves of Presentation; this being something which neither he nor his companions were entitled to do, the priests being the only men having that permission? [5]Besides, have you never read in the law that *c*on the Sabbath day the priests profane the Sabbath in the temple and are none the less held to be innocent? [6]And I am saying this to you: what is here now is something greater than the temple. [7]Moreover, if you had come to understand the meaning of the words, *d***'It is mercy I delight in, not sacrifice'**, you would not have condemned the innocent. [8]And indeed, the Son of Man exercises his lordship even over the Sabbath."

[9]Upon this he left the place and went to their synagogue. [10]There he encountered a man one of whose hands had withered away. So they put to him this question: "Is it permissible to perform a work of healing on the Sabbath day?" They talked in this way so that they might have something to accuse him of. [11]And he made them this reply: "Is there a man among you who, if he were the owner of one sheep, and that sheep fell into a pit on the Sabbath day, would fail to catch hold of it and pull it out? [12]Well then, how much more there is in a man than in a sheep! And from this it follows that it is permitted to do good on the Sabbath day." [13]Then, turning to the man, he said, "Stretch out your hand." He stretched it out, and it was restored, becoming as sound as the other one. [14]As for the Pharisees, after they had made their exit, they held a consultation directed against him, their purpose being to plot his destruction.

[15]Jesus, however, who was aware of this, withdrew from the place. Large numbers of people followed him; and they, every one of them, were healed by him; [16]at the same time he warned them sternly not to make it known that it was he who had done it. [17]Now all this happened so that fulfilment should be brought to these words spoken by the prophet Isaiah: [18]*e***'Here he is, my servant whom I have chosen, my dearly-loved one in whom my soul has found delight. I shall make my spirit rest on him, and he will proclaim justice for the Gentiles. [19]He will not engage in quarrelling or shouting, nor will anyone hear his voice in the streets. [20]A bent reed he shall not break and a smouldering wick he shall not extinguish until the time when he leads justice to victory. [21]Upon his name the Gentiles shall rest their hope'**.

[22]They then brought into his presence a man possessed of a demonic spirit who was both blind and dumb. Jesus healed him, the man formerly dumb being able both to speak and to see. [23]Everyone

*b*Lv 24:5-9; 1 Sm 21:1-6　　*c*[Nm. 28:9f; Zp 3:4]　　*d*Hos 6:6　　*e*Is 42:1-4

in the crowd was astounded at this, and they said, "Can it be that this man is the Son of David?" 24But the Pharisees, when they heard these words, spoke thus: "It is with the help of Beelzebub, the prince of demonic spirits, that this man is casting out the demonic spirits."

25But Jesus, who knew full well what thoughts they were harbouring in their minds, said to them, "Every kingdom in which there are internal divisions is doomed to fall into a state of desolation, and no city or household which is internally divided shall ever be able to stand firm. 26So then, if it is Satan that drives out Satan, it follows that he is internally divided. In that case how do you suppose that his kingdom could stand firm? 27Moreover, if it is with Beelzebub's help that I cast out demons, what of those who are of your turn of mind? With whose help do they cast them out? Why, if you resort to that kind of argument, they themselves will be found to play the part of judges condemning you. 28But if it is in reliance on the finger of God that I cast out the demons, then there is only one safe conclusion: the kingdom of God has already made its appearance in your midst.

29"Or again, how can anyone enter the house of a strong man and rob him of his goods unless he has first put the strong man in fetters? It is only after he has done this that he enters the house and plunders it thoroughly.

30"He who is not on my side opposes me; and he who gathers in his store without having me by his side scatters his goods.

31"And so I tell you this. Whatever sin men commit, whatever slander they utter, they can find forgiveness for them. But slander against the Holy Spirit will not be forgiven. 32Anyone who speaks against the Son of Man can find forgiveness, while he who speaks against the Holy Spirit will not be forgiven, either in this order of things or in the order to come.

33"Suppose a tree is good, then its fruit will be good; suppose a tree has fallen into decay, then its fruit will be worthless. By its fruit each tree is known. 34A brood of vipers that you are! How can you say what is good if you yourselves are evil? For what the mouth utters comes from what the heart is full of. 35A good man brings forth what is good out of the good which is in him, while an evil man brings forth what is evil out of the store of evil which is in his heart.

36"I tell you this: men will be held accountable on the Day of Judgment for every careless word they utter. 37It is according to the words you have spoken that you will be acquitted. It is according to the words you have spoken that you will be condemned."

38At that certain of the experts in the law and of the Pharisees addressed themselves to him, saying, "Master, what we want is to witness a sign from you." 39Jesus replied to them thus: "How wicked, how disloyal a generation this is! It eagerly demands to have a sign vouchsafed to it, but it shall have none except such a sign as the prophet Jonah was. ⁴⁰For just as *f***Jonah was in the belly of the sea monster for three days and three nights,** so the Son of Man will be in the bowels of the earth for three days and three nights. ⁴¹The men of Nineveh will make their appearance at the time of the Judgment, this generation being brought face to face with them, and they will show it up as deserving of condemnation. For when Jonah preached to them, they were led to repentance. And what is here now is one greater than Jonah. ⁴²The queen of the South will come forward at the time of the Judgment, this generation being brought face to face with her, and she will show it up as deserving of condemnation. For time was when she came from the very ends of the earth to listen to Solomon's wisdom. And what is here now is one greater than Solomon.

⁴³"This is what a tarnished spirit does when it comes out of a man. It roams through waterless tracts, looking for a place where it may find rest; and when it cannot find one, ⁴⁴it says, 'I shall make my way back to the house I came from'. When it gets there, it finds the house unoccupied, swept clean, and neatly kept in order. ⁴⁵Then it goes off and brings along with it seven other spirits worse than itself. They enter and settle down; and so the man's condition is in the end worse than it was at first. This is how things will be with this present wicked generation."

⁴⁶While Jesus was still addressing the crowds, his mother and his brothers came and stood outside, wishing to speak to him. ⁴⁷Somebody said to him, "Here are your mother and brothers standing outside and wishing to speak to you." ⁴⁸And this is what he said to the man bringing him the message: "Who is my mother; who are my brothers?" ⁴⁹Then he stretched out his hand, pointing to his disciples, and said, "Look; here is my mother; here are my brothers. ⁵⁰And indeed, if there be anyone whose actions conform to the will of my Father in heaven, it is that person who is brother, who is sister, who is mother to me."

13 On the same day Jesus left the house in which he was and sat down by the lakeside. ²A large crowd of people gathered round him. And this made him get into the boat and take his seat there, while the crowd remained standing on the shore. ³He spoke to them at length and addressed them by means of parables.

"A man," he said, "whose business it was to sow, went on his way for that purpose. ⁴Now note what happened in the course of his

*f*Jnh 1:17

sowing. Some of the seed fell by the roadside, the birds coming and eating it up. [5]Other seed fell on rocky ground, where there was not much soil for it. And so it sprang up straightaway because it lacked soil reaching far down in depth. [6]It was scorched when the sun rose, and, having no root, it withered away. [7]Other seed fell among the thistles, and the thistles came up and choked it. [8]Again, some seed fell on good soil, and brought forth fruit, some yielding a hundredfold, some sixty, some thirty. [9]Let him who has ears, listen."

[10]Upon this his disciples approached him, asking, "Why is it that you are speaking to them in parables?" [11]And this is the reply he made them: "To you has been granted the privilege of knowing the very secrets of the kingdom of heaven, but to them no such privilege has been granted. [12]The truth is that he who already has something, gifts will be made to him and he will have means in abundance, while he who is without means, even what he has shall be taken from him. [13]Moreover, there is this reason why I am speaking to them in parables: though they look, they do not see anything; though they listen, they do not hear anything or understand anything. [14]And indeed, what finds its fulfilment in them is this prophecy of Isaiah's: [8]'**You will hear with your ears, but understand you never will; you will look, but never will you see anything. [15]For the minds of these people have become gross. Their ears are hard of hearing; and their eyes they have closed. And all this they have done to make sure that they would see nothing with their eyes, hear nothing with their ears, understand nothing with their minds, and that they might not return to me, and I become their healer'.**

[16]"However, as for yourselves, your eyes have a blessing resting upon them because they see, and your ears likewise because they hear. [17]Indeed, I can give you solemn assurance of this: many prophets and many upright men have longed to see what you are seeing, and have not seen it, and to hear what you are hearing, and have not heard it.

[18]"Well then, listen to the parable of the sower. [19]What happens whenever people hear the word that tells of the kingdom but fail to understand is that the evil one comes along, carrying off what has been sown in their hearts. This is what is represented by the seed sown by the roadside. [20]As for the seed sown on rocky ground, it signifies the person who, on hearing the word, immediately gives it a joyful welcome. [21]However, since he is a person without roots, one with whom nothing ever lasts for any length of time, he immediately falls away once he is made the victim of affliction or persecution on behalf of the word of God. [22]As for the seed sown among the thistles, it signifies the person who gives God's word a hearing; but then the anxiety

[8]Is 6:9f

caused by this world of ours, as well as the seduction which comes from wealth, have the effect of stifling the word, and that person fails to yield any such harvest. ²³Again, there is the seed sown in good soil, and what it signifies is the person who listens to God's word and understands it. He it is who yields a plentiful harvest, producing now a hundredfold, now sixty, now thirty."

²⁴He put another parable before them, his words being as follows: "The kingdom of heaven may be compared to a man sowing good seed in his field. ²⁵But when all the world was asleep, his enemy made his appearance, sowed poisonous weeds* right among the wheat, and then made off. ²⁶When the new wheat began to sprout, the weeds likewise appeared. ²⁷Thereupon the servants of the man who was the owner of the property approached him, and said to him, 'Sir, was it not good seed which you sowed in your field? How is it to be explained, then, that there are weeds in it?' ²⁸'This must have been done by a man hostile to me,' was the master's reply. 'Is it your wish, then,' his servants asked him, 'that we should go off and collect the weeds?' ²⁹'By no means,' he replied, 'for there would be a risk, then, that in collecting the weeds you might at the same time pull the wheat out by the roots. ³⁰What you must do is let them both grow up side by side. And when the time of the harvest has come, I shall give this order to the harvesters: "First of all collect the weeds, tying them in bundles, and then burning them. As for the wheat, you are to collect it into my granary." ' "

³¹He put before them still another parable, and this is what he said: "The kingdom of heaven is like the seed of a mustard plant which a man took and put down in his garden. ³²It is the smallest of all seeds, but when it grows it is larger than any garden herb. In fact, it becomes a tree, and what happens is that *h*the birds of the air come and nest in its branches."

³³Another parable he told them was the following: "The kingdom of heaven is like a quantity of yeast brought along by a woman which she buried away in three measures of flour until the whole batch was leavened all through."

³⁴All these things Jesus would say to the crowds in parables. In fact, he said nothing to them except by means of parables. ³⁵Fulfilment had to be brought to this utterance made by the prophet: *i*'I will open my mouth, speaking in parables. I shall unfold things kept hidden ever since the foundation of the world.'

---

*h*Dn 4:12.21; Ezk 17:23; 31:6; [Ps 104:12]   *i*Ps 78:2

* [Gk. = zizanion. Lolium temelentum, a poisonous annual plant at first indistinguishable from wheat (Fauna and Flora of the Bible, p. 194; UBS, London).]

36Some time later he sent the crowds away and returned to the house, when his disciples drew near him and said, "Be good enough to expound to us the parable about the weeds in the field." 37And he made them this reply: "The sower of the good seed is the Son of Man. 38The field is the world. The good seed signifies those born to the kingdom. The weeds signify those born of the evil one. 39The enemy that sows them signifies the devil. The time of the harvest signifies the end of the world. The harvesters signify the angels. 40And indeed, just as the weeds are collected and burned in fire, so things will be when the end of the world comes. 41The Son of Man will send forth his angels. They will collect together, and separate from his kingdom, all *j*those who put temptation in other men's way, all the perpetrators of lawless deeds. 42They will be *k*thrown into the blazing furnace, where there will be weeping and gnashing of teeth. 43And then it shall be that *l*the righteous will shine forth in the kingdom of their Father like the sun. Let him who has ears, listen.

44"The kingdom of heaven is like a treasure lying hidden in a field which a man found and hid again. He then went off and, for the joy which was in his heart, sold everything he possessed and bought that field.

45"Yet again: the kingdom of heaven puts one in mind of a trader looking out for beautiful pearls. 46When he found a pearl which was most precious, he went off, sold everything that he possessed, and bought that pearl.

47"And yet again: the kingdom of heaven is like a dragnet cast into the sea and gathering up a haul of all kinds of fish. 48When it was full, the men to whom it belonged pulled it on to the beach. Then they sat down, gathering the good fish into pails and throwing out those that were worthless. 49So it shall be when the end of the world comes. The angels will be coming forth, separating off the wicked from the upright. 50And they will *m*throw the wicked into the blazing furnace, where there will be weeping and gnashing of teeth.

51"Have you understood all this?" he asked, their reply being, "Yes, we have." At that he made this further remark to them: 52"And so it is that, when a teacher of the law becomes a learner in the kingdom of heaven, he resembles the master of a household who draws forth from his treasure new things as well as old."

53Having completed the telling of these parables, Jesus took his departure from the district. 54When he reached his home town, he gave instruction in the synagogues of the people, so that, in their amazement, they exclaimed, "How does that man come to have such wisdom and such powers? 55Is he not the carpenter's son? Is his

*j*Zp 1:3   *k*Dn 3:6   *l*Dn 12:3   *m*Dn 3:6

mother's name not Mary, and are his brothers' names not James, Joseph, Simon, and Judas? 56Do we not have all his sisters in our midst? From where then did he get all these things?" 57And so it was that they took great offence at him. But Jesus made them this reply: "There is only one place where a prophet is not honoured—in his home town and in his own family." 58And he performed but few miracles there by reason of their want of faith.

14 It was at this time that Jesus' fame came to the ears of Herod the tetrarch. 2"This is John the Baptist," he said to his attendants. "He has been raised to life, and that is why these wondrous powers are at work in him." 3For this was what had happened. Herod had had John arrested, putting him in fetters and depositing him in prison, all on account of Herodias, the wife of his brother Philip. 4For John had said to him, 'The law does not permit you to make her your wife.' 5Herod's own wish was to put John to death, but he was afraid of what the people might do, since they looked on John as a prophet.

6Now it happened that, at the celebration of Herod's birthday, Herodias' daughter danced right in the midst of the throng. Herod was charmed at this, 7and so it was that he made her a promise, accompanied by an oath, that he would give her anything she might ask for. 8And she, urged on by her mother, addressed these words to him: "Give me in this very place the head of John the Baptist placed on a dish." 9The king was distressed at this, but bearing in mind the oath he had sworn, as well as the guests reclining with him at table, 10he gave the order that her request was to be acceded to. 11Thus it came about that John's head placed on a dish was brought in and given to the girl, who in turn took it to her mother. 12The next thing that happened was that John's disciples appeared, removing the body and burying it; and having done this, they reported the matter to Jesus.

13On hearing of this, Jesus withdrew from the place where he was, getting into a boat and making for a solitary place where he could be alone with his friends. When word of this got around, the crowds emerged from the various towns and came after him on foot. 14When he stepped out of the boat he saw a large crowd, and being moved by pity for the people he brought healing to those who were beset by ill health. 15When evening came, the disciples approached him and addressed these words to him: "This is a solitary place, and it is already past the accustomed hour. Well then, dismiss the crowds so that they may make their way to the villages and be enabled to buy food for themselves." 16"There is no need that they should go away," said Jesus; "give them something to eat yourselves." 17"All we have here," they replied, "is five loaves of bread and two fish." [18]"Bring them here to me," he replied. [19]Next he gave the order that the crowds were to sit down on the grass. He then took the five loaves and the two fish into his hands, looked up towards heaven, invoking a blessing upon them; and breaking the food into pieces, he handed it to his disciples so that they, for their part, might hand it to the crowds. [20]And so all ate, and all had their fill. In fact, when the pieces left over were removed they were enough to fill twelve baskets. [21]Moreover, the number of those sharing in the meal was about five thousand men, women and children being left out of account.

[22]Immediately after this he made the insistent demand that the apostles were to cross over to the other side ahead of him, while he would engage in the task of sending the crowds away. [23]Having done this, he went up into the hills by himself to pray. And when evening came, there he was all alone. [24]As for the boat, it was already a considerable distance away from the land, being harassed by the waves because the wind was contrary. [25]Then, in the course of the fourth watch of the night, there was Jesus, making his way towards them, walking on the water of the lake. [26]When the disciples saw that he was walking on the lake they were dismayed, saying to each other, "It is an apparition!" And in their fear they cried out. [27]Jesus, however, spoke to them at once. "Be of good courage," he exclaimed, "it is I; cast off all fear." [28]At that, Peter said to him, "If it is you, Lord, then give me the order to come over to you on the water." [29]"Come," said Jesus; and Peter, leaving the boat, walked on the water and came towards Jesus. [30]However, on observing how strong the wind was, he was gripped by fear, and as he was beginning to go under he cried out, "Save me, Lord!" [31]Jesus stretched out his hand, immediately caught hold of him, and said, "How weak your faith is: why is it that such doubts arose in your mind?" [32]Then they got into the boat, and thereupon the wind ceased. [33]The men in the boat fell down at Jesus' feet, exclaiming, "In very truth, you are the Son of God!" [34]Completing the crossing, they came ashore at Gennesaret. [35]The inhabitants of the place recognized him and sent messengers all over the adjoining districts, while bringing into his presence all that suffered from ill health. [36]They appealed to him to grant them one wish only—to let them touch the fringe of his coat. And all who touched it found themselves restored to perfect health.

15 It was at this time that Jesus was approached by certain Pharisees and experts in the law who came from Jerusalem. [2]"Why is it," they asked, "that your disciples act contrary to the traditions handed down to us by the men of old? Thus they omit to wash their

hands when they sit down at table." [3]And this is the answer Jesus made them: "Why, indeed, do you act contrary to God's commandment on behalf of that tradition of yours? [4]For what God said was this: [n]'Pay honour to your father and to your mother,' and 'He who speaks evil of his father or his mother shall be punished by death'. [5]But this is what you say: 'If a man declares to his father or his mother, "Any gift of mine from which you might have benefited has in fact been set apart as an offering to God," [6]surely this exempts him from the duty of paying honour to his father and his mother.' And so it is that, on behalf of that tradition of yours, you have, in point of fact, made the word of God null and void. [7]Dissemblers that you are! It was about you that Isaiah prophesied, and how aptly, when he uttered these words: [8][o]'This people pays honour to me with their lips. But as for their hearts, they are far away from me. [9]Their worship of me is to no purpose; and the precepts found in the doctrines they teach have their source in mere men.'"

[10]He then called the crowd to his side and spoke to them thus: [11]"Attend to me, and come to understand. It is not what goes into a man's mouth that defiles him. What defiles him is that which comes out of his mouth." [12]Upon this his disciples drew near and asked him, "Are you aware that when the Pharisees heard what you said, they were offended at it?" [13]He made them this reply: "Wherever there is a plant not of my heavenly Father's planting, it will be pulled out by the roots. [14]Let them go on their way. Blind guides of blind men is what they are. But then, when one blind man acts as guide to another blind man, this is what will happen: they will both fall into the ditch."

[15]Peter responded thus: "Be good enough to explain this parable!" [16]"Are you, too," Jesus said, "men that even yet have no comprehension? [17]Do you not know that whatever goes into the mouth makes its entry into the stomach, and so passes into the place set up for drainage? [18]But the heart is the source of whatever things come out of the mouth; and it is these things which defile a man. [19]Indeed, among the things which have the heart for their source are these: evil thoughts, murder, adultery, fornication, theft, false testimony, and slander. [20]It is these that defile a man. Yet to sit down at a meal with hands unwashed does not defile a man."

[21]Jesus then left the place where he was and withdrew to the districts in the neighbourhood of Tyre and Sidon. [22]Here it happened that a woman, a Canaanite, who belonged to that region, came forth and cried out, "Take pity on me, sir, you Son of David; my daughter finds herself cruelly tormented by a demonic spirit!" [23]He, however,

[n]Ex 20:12; 21:17; Lv 20:9; Dt 5:16   [o]Is 29:13 LXX; [Ps 78:36f]

would not say one word in reply. His disciples then drew near him and appealed to him in these words: "Make her go on her way; she is following us, screaming loudly." 24 And this is the reply Jesus made: "I have been sent forth to the lost sheep of the house of Israel, and to no one else." 25 But the woman came close to him, fell down at his feet, and exclaimed, "Sir, come to my aid!" 26 "It is not right," replied Jesus, "to take the children's bread away from them, throwing it to the dogs." 27 "How true that is, sir," said the woman; "and yet even the dogs eat of the morsels of food that fall from their masters' tables." 28 And this is what Jesus said in response: "What firm faith you have, my dear woman! May your wish be granted to you." And from that very hour her daughter found that she was healed.

29 On leaving the district, Jesus reached the shore of the Lake of Galilee and then went up the hillside. He was sitting down in some place there 30 when a large crowd drew near him. They had brought with them many who were lame, deformed, blind, dumb, as well as many others who were suffering in some other way. These they laid down at his feet, and he healed them, 31 this having the effect that the crowds were amazed as they witnessed that the dumb were speaking, the deformed in possession of sound limbs, the lame walking, and the blind having their sight restored to them. And so it was that they gave praise to the God of Israel.

32 As for Jesus, he called his disciples to his side and spoke to them thus: "I am moved by pity for this crowd because they have already been with me for three days and they have nothing to eat. I have no wish to send them away hungry because then there is the risk that they may be overcome by weakness during their journey." 33 "From where in this solitary place could we possibly obtain a sufficient number of loaves," the disciples asked him, "to enable us to feed a crowd as large as this?" 34 "How many loaves of bread do you have?" asked Jesus, their reply being, "Seven, and a few fish." 35 So he gave the order that they were to sit down on the ground. 36 He himself took the seven loaves and the fish into his hands. Then, after having given thanks to God, he broke the food into pieces and handed it to his disciples, they in turn handing it to the crowds. 37 Then they all ate and all had their fill. In fact, when the pieces left over were removed, they were found to be enough to fill seven baskets. 38 Moreover, the number of those sharing the meal was four thousand men, women and children being left out of account. 39 He himself got into a boat, after dismissing the crowds, and made his way to the district of Magadan.

16 The Pharisees and the Sadducees came to him, with a view to putting him to the test, and requested that he should show forth a sign from heaven. [2] And this is the reply he made them:* "[In the evening you say, 'The weather will be fine, for the sky is red.' [3] And in the morning you say, 'Today will be stormy. The sky is red and has a threatening look'. You know how to interpret the appearance of the sky. Have you no power of interpreting the signs providing the key to these decisive times?] [4] How wicked and disloyal this generation is! It eagerly asks for a sign, but it shall have none except such a sign as Jonah was." Upon this he left their presence and went away.

[5] It turned out that the disciples, crossing to the other side, had forgotten to take any bread with them. [6] Jesus remarked to them, "Look out; be on your guard against the leaven there is in the Pharisees and the Sadducees." [7] At that they reasoned the matter out among themselves, concluding, "It is our not having brought any bread that he has in mind." [8] Yet Jesus, who was aware of it all, spoke to them thus: "Why do you reason with one another in this way, you men of but little faith, while imagining that what I had in mind was your not having brought any loaves of bread? [9] Do you still not understand? Do you fail to remember the five loaves of bread for the five thousand, and how many basketfuls you collected? [10] Or the seven loaves for the four thousand, and the number of baskets you collected? [11] How is it that you fail to grasp that I was not talking to you about loaves of bread? Be that as it may, you must be on your guard against the leaven there is in the Pharisees and the Sadducees." [12] It was then that they understood that he had not told them to be on their guard against leaven in the sense of bread, but against the teaching of the Pharisees and the Sadducees.

[13] After he had reached the district of Caesarea Philippi, Jesus asked this question of the disciples: "Who do men say that the Son of Man is?" [14] "Some," they replied, "say that he is John the Baptist, others Elijah, others Jeremiah or one of the prophets." [15] "But you yourselves," he asked, "who do you say that I am?" [16] And Simon Peter made him this reply: "You are God's anointed, the Son of the living God." [17] And Jesus answered him thus: "A blessing rests on you, Simon son of Jonah. Indeed, it is not any man of flesh and blood who has disclosed this to you, but my Father in heaven. [18] And what I am saying to you is this: you are Peter, the man called the Rock; and it is upon this rock that I shall build my church, all the forces of hell itself having no power to win a victory over it. [19] To you I shall give the keys opening up the kingdom of heaven. Whatever you bind on earth shall be considered bound in heaven; whatever you loose on earth shall be considered loosed in heaven." [20] Having spoken these words, he gave them stern warning not to tell anyone that he was God's anointed.

---

* Vv. 2b-3 may not be part of the original text.

21 From that time onwards Jesus began to explain to his disciples that he was destined to proceed to Jerusalem, that he would undergo many sufferings at the hands of the elders, chief priests, and experts in the law, that he would be put to death, and that on the third day he would be raised to life again. 22 At that, Peter took him aside, began to remonstrate with him, and exclaimed, "God forbid, Lord, that shall never be!" 23 But Jesus, turning round, spoke thus to Peter: "Out of my sight, Satan, get right behind me. You are seeking to entice me into sin because the thoughts you harbour are not those of God but those of men."

24 After this Jesus addressed these words to his disciples: "If anyone is desirous to walk in my steps, he must set his own self at nought, take up the burden of my cross,* and follow me. 25 In fact, anyone desirous to save his life will suffer the loss of it, while if there be someone losing his life, and that for my sake, he will save it. 26 Indeed, what advantage will a man reap if he gains the whole world, yet suffers the loss of his true self? Or what is there a man can offer in exchange for his self?

27 "It is decreed that the Son of Man shall appear invested with his Father's glorious majesty and accompanied by his angels; then *p***he will requite each man in accordance with what his deeds have deserved.** 28 Indeed, I can give you solemn assurance of this. There will be some among those standing in this place who will still be strangers to death when they shall see the Son of Man coming to inaugurate his royal reign."

17 Six days later Jesus took with him Peter, James, and James's brother John, and led them up a high mountain, where they were all by themselves. 2 There, before their eyes, Jesus was transformed, his face shining forth like the sun and his clothes turning a brilliant white like light itself. 3 Then, all of a sudden, there appeared to them Moses and Elijah, engaged in conversation with him. 4 Whereupon Peter addressed Jesus thus: "Lord, how good it is to be here. If you wish it, I shall set up three places of shelter right here, one for you, one for Moses, and one for Elijah." 5 He was still speaking when, all at once, there was a cloud that shone brightly, casting its shadow over them, and a voice coming from the cloud and calling out the words, "This

---

*p*Ps 62:12; Pr 24:12

* [Lit. " 'He must take up his cross', i.e., 'as a disciple of mine he must share *my* suffering and death' . . . [editor's italics]. Some way should be found of restoring, if possible, the original shock . . . of the phrase" (R. G. Bratcher's exegesis of Mk. 8:34 in *A Translator's Handbook on the Gospel of Mark;* UBS, Leiden). Cf. Mt. 16:24 and Lk. 9:23.]

is my ⁹**Son, my dearly-loved one; it is he on whom my favour rests: lend your ear to him**." ⁶When they heard this, the disciples fell on their faces, being greatly frightened. ⁷But Jesus came close to them, touched them with his hands, and exclaimed, "Rise to your feet and cast off all fear!" ⁸And when they looked up, there was no one to be seen but Jesus only.

⁹As they were coming down the mountain, Jesus gave them this order: "Do not talk to anyone of this vision until the time when the Son of Man has been raised up from the dead." ¹⁰The disciples, for their part, put this question to him: "Why do the experts in the law maintain that it is preordained that Elijah must appear first of all?" ¹¹Jesus replied to them thus: "ʳ**Elijah** is indeed to appear; and it is he who will bring the **restoration** of everything. ¹²Yet what I am saying to you is that Elijah has already appeared, and that, not giving him any recognition, they did with him just as they chose. In the same way the Son of Man is destined to suffer at their hands." ¹³At that the disciples realized that he was talking to them of John the Baptist.

¹⁴After they had rejoined the crowd, a certain man drew near him, fell on his knees, ¹⁵and exclaimed, "Lord, take pity on my son! He is plagued by epilepsy, and his condition is wretched indeed. Many a time he falls into the fire, many a time into water. ¹⁶Moreover, I brought him into the presence of your disciples, and they lacked the power to bring him healing." ¹⁷And this is what Jesus said by way of reply: "What an unbelieving and perverted generation you are! How long shall I have to remain in your company? How long shall I have to bear with you? Bring the boy here to me." ¹⁸Jesus then administered a rebuke to the demonic spirit, and when he did, it came out of the boy, who was healed from that very hour.

¹⁹Some time after that, when they were by themselves, Jesus' disciples came up to him and asked, "Why were we unable to drive the spirit out?" ²⁰"It was because of your want of faith," he replied. "And indeed, I can give you solemn assurance of this. If you had faith, even though it were no more than the size of a mustard seed, you could say to this mountain, 'Move away from here to some other place', and it would move. Nothing in fact will in that case be beyond your powers. ²¹Besides, as regards this sort of spirit, there is no other means of casting it out of a person apart from prayer and fasting."*

²²One day when they were together in Galilee, Jesus said to them, "The Son of Man is destined to be given over into the power of men.

ⁱGn 22:2; Ps 2:7; Is 42:1; Dt 18:15.19   ʳMal 4:5

* [V. 21 is found in the majority of manuscripts, though many scholars consider it to be a scribal assimilation to Mk. 9:29.]

23 They will put him to death, and on the third day he will be raised to life." And they were deeply distressed.

24 As they arrived at Capernaum, Peter was approached by one of the men whose business it was ˢto collect the half-shekel for the temple. "Why," he asked him, "does your master not pay the half-shekel?" 25 "It is true that he does not," replied Peter. When Peter reached home, Jesus forestalled him and said, "What is your opinion? Those who rule as kings on this earth, whom do they collect customs and taxes from—from those of their own kind or from aliens?" 26 When Peter replied, "From aliens," Jesus said, "Surely it follows from this that those who are of their own kind go free. 27 However, to prevent our giving any offence to them, go down to the lake and throw out a fishhook. Take along the fish which comes up first and open its mouth. You will find a silver coin in it. Then take that coin and give it to them. It will do for you and for me."

18 It was just then that Jesus' disciples approached him and asked, "Who, then, stands highest in the kingdom of heaven?" 2 At that he called a child to his side, placed it right in their midst, and said: 3 "Indeed, I can give you solemn assurance of this. Unless you suffer a change of heart, becoming like children, you will never find entry into the kingdom of heaven. 4 It is the person who makes little of himself, as this child makes little of himself, who stands highest in the kingdom of heaven. 5 Moreover, whoever gives a welcome to such a child, and does so for my name's sake, gives a welcome to me. 6 And again, if anyone provides an occasion for sinning to one of these little ones who believe in me it would be better for him that he should, with a millstone hung round his neck, be made to drown in the depths of the sea. 7 What wretchedness there lies upon the world by reason of the occasions for sinning it provides! That occasions for sinning should arise is indeed wholly inevitable. Still, what wretchedness there is in store for any person providing such an occasion!

8 "If your hand should provide you with an occasion for sinning, cut it off and fling it away from yourself. It is better for you to find entry, crippled or lame, into the place where true life is to be found than, possessing two hands and two feet, to be thrown into everlasting fire. 9 Again, if your eye should provide you with an occasion for sinning, tear it out and fling it away from yourself. It is better for you to find entry into the place where true life is to be found with only one eye than, possessing two eyes, to be thrown into the fire of hell.

10 "Make sure that you do not treat any of these little ones with con-

ˢ[Ex 30:13ff; Neh 10:32ff]

tempt. There is one thing I can tell you. The angels in heaven who have them in their charge are ever fixing their gaze upon the face of my Father in heaven.*

12 "What opinion do you have to offer about this? Suppose a man is the owner of a hundred sheep, and one of them goes astray. Will he not leave the other ninety-nine to themselves and go off into the hill country searching for the one that went astray? 13 Indeed, I can give you solemn assurance of this: should he find it, he will feel greater joy about it than he ever did about the other ninety-nine which never did go astray. 14 In the same way it is wholly contrary to the will of your Father in heaven that one of these little ones should get lost.

15 "Should a man do something wrong, go to him and convict him of the wrong, keeping the matter entirely between you and him. What will happen, if he pays attention to you, is that you have gained a brother for yourself. 16 But if he pays no attention, then take with you another man or two, so as to establish the truth of the saying, *'**Every issue shall be decided by the voice of two or three witnesses'**. 17 If he refuses to listen to them, report the matter to the congregation; and if he refuses to listen to the congregation, then look on him as being on the same level as a Gentile or a collector of taxes. 18 And indeed, I can give you solemn assurance of this. Whatever you bind on earth shall be considered bound in heaven; whatever you loose on earth shall be considered loosed in heaven. 19 And there is one other thing I have to tell you. If two of you come to an agreement on earth about a request you wish to make, whatever it may be, you will have it granted to you by my Father in heaven. 20 Indeed, in whatever place two or three of you are gathered together, to pay honour to my name, there I shall be right among you."

21 Some time later Peter approached him with this question: "How many times should I let my brother do me wrong, and yet forgive him? As often as seven times?" 22 "What I am saying to you," replied Jesus, "is this: not seven times but as often as seventy-seven times.

23 "And so it was that the following comparison was made with the kingdom of heaven. It was compared with a king who wished to settle his accounts with his servants. 24 Now as he was about to make the settlement, there was brought to him at the start a man who owed ten thousand talents, 25 but at the same time did not have the means of repayment. So the master gave the order that he, along with his wife and his children, as well as all his possessions, should be sold, and the proceeds paid to him. 26 Thereupon the servant fell at his feet and ex-

*Dt 19:15

* V. 11 is probably not part of the original text.

claimed, 'Have patience with me! I shall pay everything back!' [27]What happened next was that the master of that servant took pity on him, letting him go and remitting the debt. [28]No sooner had he left than the servant came upon one of his fellow servants who owed him a hundred pieces of silver. He caught hold of him, attempted to strangle him, and exclaimed, 'Pay back what you owe me!' [29]At this, his fellow servant threw himself down at his feet and implored him, saying, 'Have patience with me, and I shall pay you back.' [30]But he would not have it, went off, and had him thrown into prison until the time when he would have paid back his debt. [31]The other servants, greatly distressed on witnessing these happenings, went to their master, and gave him a clear account of everything that had happened. [32]Then the master called the servant to him and addressed him in these words: 'You scoundrel of a servant! I remitted to you the whole of your debt because you appealed to me to do so. [33]Was it not your duty to take pity on your fellow servant as I took pity on you?' [34]And the servant's master, flying into a rage, handed him over to the men whose business it was to exact debts by way of inflicting torture, until the day that he would pay him back everything he owed. [35]In the same way my heavenly Father will deal with you unless each of you forgive your brothers from your very heart."

19 When Jesus had come to the end of these discourses, he took his departure from Galilee and made his way towards that part of the country of the Jews which is situated beyond the Jordan. [2]Large numbers of people were following him, and he brought healing to their sick there and then.

[3]Certain of the Pharisees approached him, intending to put him to the test, and this is what they asked him: "Is it permissible for a man to send his wife away on any ground, no matter what?" [4]And this is the answer he made them: "Have you never read the words, 'From the beginning their creator [u]**made them male and female**'? [5]Moreover, there are the words, [v]**For this reason a man will leave his father and mother and be joined to his wife, the two of them becoming a single body**'. [6]So it is that they are no longer two bodies but a single one. Well then, let no man separate those whom God has joined together." [7]"Why then," they asked, "did Moses lay it down that men might [w]**send** their wives **away,** first **letting them have a writ of dismissal**?" [8]"Because of the coldness of your hearts," said Jesus, "Moses gave you permission to send your wives away. It was not so at the beginning. [9]And what I am saying to you is this: any man who sends

[u]Gn 1:27; 5:2   [v]Gn 2:24   [w]Dt 24:1

his wife away—the ground of fornication being left out of account—and marries another woman commits adultery."

¹⁰Upon this his disciples said to him, "If this is how things stand between a man and his wife, it is better not to marry at all." ¹¹And this is the reply he made them: "What I have said is incapable of being accepted by just anybody, but only by those to whom a special privilege has been granted. ¹²In point of fact, some eunuchs have been so from their birth; other men have been made eunuchs by human agency; and others have made eunuchs of themselves for the sake of the kingdom of heaven. Let him who has the power of accepting this do so."

¹³Some time after that, certain people came and brought children into his presence, their aim being that he should touch the children with his hands and say a prayer over them. His disciples administered a rebuke to them. ¹⁴But this is what Jesus said to them: "Let the children come to me, and do not prevent them. For it is to such as these that the kingdom of heaven belongs." ¹⁵Then he laid his hands upon the children and went on his way.

¹⁶Then it happened that he was approached by a certain man with this question: "Master, what good deed must I do to secure for myself possession of everlasting life?" ¹⁷And this is what Jesus said to him: "Why do you ask me a question concerning what is to be considered good? There is only one who is good. But if you wish to know how to find entry into the realm where true life is to be found, the answer is: keep the commandments." ¹⁸Upon this the man asked, "Which of them?" and Jesus made him this answer: ˣ" 'You shall not do murder; you shall not commit adultery; you shall not steal; you shall not give false testimony; ¹⁹pay honour to your mother and to your father'. And then this: ʸ'You shall love your neighbour as you love yourself.' " ²⁰"All these I have ever kept," replied the youth; "what is it I am still short of?" ²¹"If what you desire," Jesus said to him, "is to be a man making completeness his aim, then you must go on your way, selling everything that you have, and giving the proceeds to the poor. Then a treasure shall be yours, a treasure in heaven. And after that, come to my side and follow me." ²²When the youth heard this, he went on his way full of sorrow, for he had great possessions.

²³Jesus thereupon addressed these words to his disciples: "Indeed, I can give you solemn assurance of this. Great obstacles are placed in the way of a rich man when it comes to finding entry into the kingdom of heaven. ²⁴Again, I will tell you this: it is easier for a camel to pass through the eye of a needle than it is for a rich man to enter the kingdom of God." ²⁵When the disciples heard this, they felt completely overwhelmed and exclaimed, "Who, then, is there capable of ob-

ˣEx 20:13-16; Dt 5:16-20   ʸLv 19:18

taining salvation?" 26 And Jesus, fixing his gaze upon them, made them this reply: "Such a thing is indeed impossible for men, but ᶻ**for God everything is possible.**"

27 At that, Peter said to him in reply: "Here we are, having given up everything we possessed and become your followers. What, then, will happen to us?" 28 And this is what Jesus said to them: "Indeed, I can give you solemn assurance of this. At the time of the restoration of all things, when the Son of Man is seated in his state of glory, you, the men who have been my followers, will, for your part, be seated on twelve thrones, acting as judges over the twelve tribes of Israel. 29 Anyone who has given up houses, brothers, sisters, father, mother, children, or fields for the sake of the cause bearing my name will find himself repaid many times over and, moreover, will obtain possession of everlasting life. 30 And indeed, many that took first place will be last; many that took last place will be first.

20 "The kingdom of heaven puts me in mind of the following tale. There was once a landowner who went forth one day very early in the morning to hire labourers to attend to his vineyard. 2 Having agreed with them that their wage would be a silver coin a day, he sent them out into his vineyard. 3 About the third hour of the day he went forth again and saw other men standing about in the market place with nothing to do. 4 And he said to them, 'You, too, be on your way to my vineyard, and the wage I shall give you will be whatever fairness demands.' Off they went, 5 while the landowner went forth once again about the sixth hour of the day, and then the ninth hour, doing the very same. 6 On going forth about the eleventh hour, he came upon other men standing there, and said to them, 'Why are you standing about there the whole day with nothing to do?' 7 'Because no one has hired us,' was their reply. So he said to them, 'You, too, be on your way to my vineyard.' 8 When evening came, the owner of the vineyard said to his manager, 'Call for the labourers and let them have their wages, beginning with the men that came last and ending up with those that came first.' 9 When those who had come about the eleventh hour appeared, they received a silver coin each. 10 As for those who had come first, they expected to get more, but when their turn came, it was found that they, too, received a silver coin each. 11 They took it, but then fell to grumbling against the landowner in these words: 12 'All that these fellows who came last did was to work for one hour, yet you have seen fit to make no difference between them and ourselves who, in this heat, have been bearing the whole burden of the day.'

ᶻGn 18:14; Job 42:2

¹³But this is how the landowner replied to one of the men: 'My friend, I am doing you no injustice. Did you not make an agreement with me that you would have one piece of silver? ¹⁴So take what is yours and be on your way. It is my wish to give the one who came last the same as I gave you. ¹⁵Have I no right to do what I like with my own? Or is it that my being generous accounts for your having an envious nature?' ¹⁶And so it shall be: those that took last place will be first; those that took first place will be last."

¹⁷As Jesus was going up to Jerusalem, he took the twelve disciples aside, and this is what he said to them while they were on their way there: ¹⁸"Here we are, on our way up to Jerusalem, and what will happen is that the Son of Man will be handed over to the chief priests and to the experts in the law; they will condemn him to death, ¹⁹and they will hand him over to the Gentiles to be sneered at, flogged, and crucified. And on the third day he will be raised to life again." ²⁰Some time after that the mother of the sons of Zebedee came to him, in the company of her sons, and, wishing to make a request of him, she fell at his feet. ²¹"What is it you want?" Jesus asked her; and she replied, "Give the order that these two sons of mine are to take their seats in your kingdom, one sitting on your right side and the other on your left." ²²And this is what Jesus said to the sons in reply: "You do not know what you are asking. Do you have enough strength to drink the cup which I am about to drink?" "We do have it," was their reply. ²³"Drink it you shall," he said. "But as to having seats on my right or on my left, it is not for me to bestow this; they will be granted to those destined for this by my Father." ²⁴On learning about this, the remaining disciples were filled with indignation against the two brothers. ²⁵But Jesus, calling them to himself, addressed them thus: "You know that those who bear rule over the Gentiles lord it over them, and that their great ones act in a tyrannical way. ²⁶This is not how things stand as regards yourselves. On the contrary, if anyone among you should wish to rank high, he must be your servant; ²⁷and if he wishes to come first, he must be your slave. ²⁸This is how things are with the Son of Man, who has made his appearance not to be served but to serve, offering up his very life as a ransom paid on behalf of a multitude of men."

²⁹As they were coming out of Jericho, they were followed by a large crowd. ³⁰And then it happened that two blind men who were sitting by the roadside, when they heard that Jesus was passing by, exclaimed in a loud voice, "Lord, take pity on us, you Son of David!" ³¹The crowd rebuked them, seeking to make them hold their peace. But they cried out all the louder, "Take pity on us, you Son of David!" ³²At that, Jesus stopped, called them to himself, and asked, "What

would you have me do for you?" ³³"Make us regain our sight, Lord,"
was their reply. ³⁴And Jesus, taking pity on them, touched their eyes,
and all at once they could see again; and they followed him.

21 As they were drawing near Jerusalem and reached Bethphage
at the Mount of Olives, Jesus sent two of his disciples on an errand,
²giving them these instructions: "Go to the village that lies opposite
you, where you will immediately find a tethered donkey and her colt
with her. Untie them and bring them to me. ³And if anyone says anything to you, let your answer be this: 'The master has need of them.'
Then the man will let you have them without further ado." ⁴All this
happened so that fulfilment should be brought to this utterance of the
prophet: ⁵ᵃ**'Proclaim to Zion's daughter: look, your king is coming
to you, full of gentleness, seated on an ass, seated on the foal of a
beast of burden.'**

⁶The disciples went on their way and did what Jesus had instructed
them to do. ⁷They brought the donkey and the foal and spread their
cloaks over them. Then Jesus mounted. ⁸A large crowd of people
spread their cloaks on the road, while others cut branches off the trees,
spreading them in his path. ⁹The crowds, both those who went on
ahead and those who were following on behind, burst forth, shouting, "Hosanna to the Son of David! ᵇ**A blessing rests on him who appears in the name of the Lord! Hosanna** to him who is in the highest
heaven!" ¹⁰When he made his entry into Jerusalem, the whole city was
stirred up. ¹¹"Who is this man?" people asked, the crowd replying,
"It is the prophet Jesus, the man from Nazareth in Galilee."

¹²Jesus then went into the temple, driving out all those who bought
and sold goods there, overturning the tables of the money changers
and likewise the seats of those selling pigeons. ¹³And he said to them,
"This is what stands written in scripture: ᶜ**My house shall be known
as a house of prayer'**; but you are turning it into a ᵈ**robbers' den."**

¹⁴It was then that certain people who were blind and lame came
up to him in the temple, and he brought them healing. ¹⁵On witnessing the wondrous things which he accomplished and how the children in the temple were calling out loudly, 'ᵉ**Hosanna** to the Son of
David', the chief priests and the experts in the law were full of indignation. ¹⁶And this is what they said to him: "Do you hear what these
people are saying?" Jesus answered them thus: "Indeed I do. But then,
have you never read the words, ᶠ**It is from the lips of infants, from
the lips of those that feed at the breast, that you have made sure of**

ᵃZc 9:9; Is 62:11   ᵇPs 118:25f   ᶜIs 56:7   ᵈJr 7:11   ᵉPs 118:25   ᶠPs 8:2 LXX; [Wis
10:21]

praise for yourself'?" [17]At that he left their presence and went out of the city to Bethany, where he spent the night.

[18]The next morning, when he was on his way back to the city, he was feeling hungry. [19]And when his eyes fell upon a fig tree which was growing by the roadside, he went up to it. Yet all he found on it was leaves and nothing else. So he addressed the tree in these words: "May fruit never again come forth from you!" At that the fig tree withered away in an instant. [20]When the disciples saw this, they were amazed and enquired of him, "How is it that the fig tree withers away in an instant?" [21]And this is the reply Jesus made them: "Indeed, I can give you solemn assurance of this: if you had faith, a never doubting faith, what has been done regarding this fig tree would by no means be all you could accomplish. Why, if you said to this mountain here, 'Lift yourself up and throw yourself into the sea,' that is what would happen. [22]Moreover, whatever you ask for with confident hearts, while you are at prayer, will be granted to you."

[23]When he had gone into the temple, the chief priests and the elders of the people came up to him while he was giving instruction. And this is the question they put to him: "What kind of authority makes you act in this way, and from whom does that authority derive?" [24]"I, too," was Jesus' retort, "will ask you a question, and if you answer it properly, I in turn will tell you by whose authority I am acting in this manner: [25]Where did the baptism administered by John come from; did it have its source in God or in men?" At that they set about reasoning the matter out with one another, their words being these: "If we say, 'In God', then he will ask us, 'Why then, did you refuse to trust him?' [26]And if we say, 'In men', then we cannot but be afraid of the people, seeing that they all look on John as a prophet." [27]And so, by way of replying to Jesus, they said, "We do not know," his response to them being, "Neither shall I tell you by whose authority I am acting the way I do.

[28]"What opinion do you have to offer on this tale? There was a man who had two sons. He came up to the first, saying to him, 'My son, be on your way and work in my vineyard this very day.' [29]'I shall do so, sir,' was the son's reply. But he did not go. [30]Then the father went up to his other son, speaking to him in the same way. 'I have no wish to do so,' was the reply he received. Later, however, the man changed his mind and went. [31]Now which of these acted in conformity with his father's wishes?" "The second," they exclaimed; and Jesus spoke to them thus: "Indeed, I can give you solemn assurance of this. Tax collectors and prostitutes take precedence over you in the kingdom of God. [32]For when John made his appearance, showing you the way to where true righteousness was to be found, you would not trust him, while the tax collectors and the prostitutes did trust him. Yet you

yourselves did not, even on witnessing this, change your minds at a later time and trust him.

[33] "Give your attention to another parable. There was once a man who was a landowner. [g]**He planted a vineyard, put a fence round it, dug out a winepress in it, and built a tower.** Then he hired it out to certain vinegrowers and went off to another country. [34]When the proper time for the fruit to ripen was drawing near, he sent out his servants to the vinegrowers, that they might collect the portion of the fruit due to him. [35]However, the vinegrowers caught hold of his servants, giving a thrashing to one, putting another to death, and stoning a third. [36]Next he sent out other servants of his, a larger number than before, but the vinegrowers dealt with them in exactly the same way. [37]Then, finally, he sent out his son to them, saying to himself, 'They will be moved by respect for him.' [38]However, when the vinegrowers saw the son, they said to each other, 'This man is the heir. Come on then, let us kill him, so that we may obtain possession of the inheritance.' [39]So they got hold of him, threw him out of the vineyard, and did away with him. [40]Now what do you think the owner of the vineyard will do to these vinegrowers when he comes?" [41]"Evildoers that they are, he will bring them to an evil end!" they exclaimed. "He will hire out a vineyard to other vinegrowers, who will hand over to him the fruit at the time when it is ripe." [42]And this is what Jesus said to them: "Have you never read these words in scripture: [h]**'The very stone which the builders rejected has become the cornerstone. This was the Lord's doing, and how wonderful it is in our eyes.'**? [43]Well then, what I have to tell you, in view of this, is that the kingdom of God shall be taken away from you and given into the hands of a nation which, through what it does, brings forth such fruit as is in keeping with that kingdom.* [[44]Indeed, if a man falls on that stone, he will be dashed to pieces, while if the stone falls on him, it will grind him to powder.]"

[45]When the chief priests and the Pharisees heard him tell these parables of his, they knew well enough that he was speaking of them. [46]Their own wish was to seize him by force, but they were afraid of the people because they considered John† to be a prophet.

---

[g]Is 5:1f   [h]Ps 118:22f

---

* V. 44 may not be part of the original text.
† [The Greek does not give the proper name. 'Jesus' is usually understood to be implied here. The translator, however, understands this as referring back to v. 26. Cf. Mk. 11:32; Lk. 20:6.]

22 Jesus' response to this was once again to address the people by telling them parables. ²"The kingdom of heaven," he said, "may put one in mind of the following tale. There was once a king about to give a feast in honour of his son's wedding. ³He sent out his servants to summon the guests who had been invited to the wedding feast. But they refused to come. ⁴So in turn he sent out other servants, saying to them, 'This is the message you must give to those who have been invited: "Attend to my words. I have completed my preparations for the meal. My oxen and my fattened cattle have been slaughtered, and everything is ready. Well, be on your way to the wedding banquet." ' ⁵However, those to whom this was said paid no attention to it but went off, one to a field which he owned, another to engage in some business deal. ⁶And there were others who caught hold of the servants, treating them outrageously or putting them to death.

⁷"As for the king, he flew into a rage, despatched his troops to make an end of these murderers, and set their city on fire. ⁸Having done this, he said to his servant, 'The wedding banquet is all ready, but those invited as guests have proved unworthy of it. ⁹Well then, go forth into the main thoroughfares and invite to the wedding everyone you may come across.' ¹⁰So the servants went forth into the streets and collected everyone they could find, evil men as well as good; and the wedding hall was crammed with people sitting at table. ¹¹When the king entered to have a look at those sitting at table, his eyes fell on a man who was not wearing a wedding garment. ¹²And this is what he said to him: 'My friend, how is it that you have come in here without a wedding garment?' The man was reduced to silence. ¹³At that the king gave this order to his attendants: 'Bind him hand and foot and cast him out into a place far away in which darkness reigns, where there shall be weeping and gnashing of teeth.' ¹⁴And so it is. Many have been invited as guests, but only a few are chosen."

¹⁵Some time afterwards the Pharisees got together to hatch a plot, their aim being to entrap Jesus through one of his own utterances. ¹⁶They despatched to him disciples of their own as well as adherents of Herod's party. And they addressed the following words to him: "Master, we know how sincere you are, that you teach the way of life required by God with complete honesty, and that you court no man's favour, never showing any undue preference for anyone. ¹⁷Well then, tell us what your opinion is: is it permissible or is it not to pay tax to the Emperor?" ¹⁸And this is what Jesus, who was well aware of their wicked intentions, said to them: "Why are you putting me to the test, dissemblers that you are? ¹⁹Let me see a coin such as is used for the tax." They handed him a piece of silver, ²⁰and upon this, he asked them, "Whose head and whose inscription is this?" ²¹"The Emper-

or's," they replied. And at that, he said, "Well then, pay the Emperor what is due to the Emperor, and pay God what is due to God." 22When they heard this, they were taken aback and, leaving his presence, they went on their way.

23On the same day a number of Sadducees—the men who maintain that there is no such thing as a resurrection of the dead—approached him and asked him a question. 24"Master," they said, "Moses has laid down this precept: '*i***When a man dies without leaving any children, his brother,** as next of kin, is to marry the widow, **raising up offspring on his brother's behalf'**. 25Now there were seven brothers in our midst. The first died, having married, and since there was no offspring, he bequeathed his wife to his brother. 26The same befell the second brother, and then the third, and in the end all seven. 27And finally, the woman also died. 28So whose wife will she be at the resurrection, seeing that she was married to all of them?" 29And this is what Jesus said to them in reply: "You are in error because of your failing to have proper comprehension of either the scriptures or the power of God. 30The fact is that at the resurrection men and women neither marry nor are joined together in marriage. Indeed, their nature is like that of the angels in heaven. 31As for the resurrection of the dead, have you never read the words spoken by God himself, 32*j*'**I am the God of Abraham, the God of Isaac, and the God of Jacob**'? Now God is God not of the dead, but of the living." 33When the crowds heard this, they were astounded at the teaching he was offering.

34When the Pharisees learned that he had reduced the Sadducees to silence, they gathered together in one place. 35One of them, who was a lawyer, asked him this question, intending to put him to the test: 36"Master, which commandment of those contained in the law is the greatest?" 37And this is the reply Jesus made him: "*k*'**You are to love the Lord your God with all your heart, with all your soul, and with all your mind.'** 38This is the greatest and the first commandment. 39And there is another commandment that resembles it: *l*'**You are to love your neighbour as yourself'**. 40The whole of the law, and the prophets likewise, hinge on these two commandments."

41At one time when the Pharisees were assembled together, Jesus asked them this question: 42"What is your opinion concerning God's anointed? Whose descendant is he?" "David's descendant," was their reply. 43"How then is it," remarked Jesus, "that David, under the impulse of the Spirit, calls him his Lord, 44saying, *m*'**The Lord said to my Lord, "Take your seat at my right hand until I make your enemies a footstool for your feet"** '? 45Well then, if David calls him Lord, how

*i*Gn 38:8; Dt 25:5f   *j*Ex 3:6.15   *k*Dt 6:5   *l*Lv 19:18   *m*Ps 110:1

can he be a descendant of his?" ⁴⁶There was no one capable of offering a single word in reply to this; neither had anyone the courage, from that day, to ask him any further question.

23 Some time after this, Jesus addressed himself to both the crowds and to his disciples, ²his words being the following: "The experts in the law and the Pharisees are installed in the seat which Moses used to occupy. ³So you must do everything they tell you to do and observe all their teaching. You must not, however, model your conduct on their actions. For they say one thing and do another. ⁴They tie up heavy burdens and put them on men's shoulders, but they themselves will not move as much as a finger to shift them. ⁵As for their actions, the sole purpose these men have is to be observed by other men. They broaden the phylacteries they wear, and the tassels on their garments they make longer. ⁶They have a fondness for securing the places of honour at banquets, for obtaining the best seats in the synagogues, ⁷and for exchanging greetings in the market place. Moreover, their wish is that men are to address them as 'Rabbi'.

⁸"Yet as regards yourselves, you must not let anyone address you as 'Rabbi'. There is only one who is your Master, and you are all brothers alike. ⁹Further, do not address anyone on earth as 'Father'. You have only one Father, the one in heaven. ¹⁰Neither must you allow yourselves to be called leaders. There is one who is your leader, God's anointed. ¹¹Again, he who ranks highest among you is your servant. ¹²The truth is that he who exalts himself will find himself humbled, while he who humbles himself will find himself exalted.

¹³"Woe upon you, you experts in the law and you Pharisees, dissemblers that you are! For what you do is shut the door to the kingdom of heaven right in men's faces. You yourselves do not enter it, and just as others are about to enter you will not let them.* ¹⁵Woe upon you, you experts in the law and you Pharisees, dissemblers that you are! For you travel all over sea and land to win one convert, and when you succeed, you make him twice as worthy to be consigned to hell as you are yourselves. ¹⁶Woe upon you, blind guides that you are! What you say is this: 'If someone swears an oath by the temple, it goes for nothing. But if he swears by the gold of the temple, he is bound by his oath.' ¹⁷How foolish and how blind you are! Which is the greater: the gold or the temple which sanctifies the gold? ¹⁸And there is another thing you say: 'If someone swears an oath by the altar, it goes for nothing. But if someone swears by the offering that lies on the altar, he is bound by his oath.' ¹⁹Blind men that you are! Which is the

---

* V. 14 is probably not part of the original text.

greater: the offering on the altar or the altar which sanctifies it? [20] Well then, he who swears by the altar swears at the same time by everything that lies on it. [21] He who swears by the temple swears by it, and at the same time by him whose dwelling place it is. [22] And he who swears by heaven swears by the throne of God, and at the same time by him who is seated upon it.

[23] "Woe upon you, you experts in the law and you Pharisees, dissemblers that you are! You pay tithes for mint, for dill, and for cummin, but those points in the law which are of much greater weight—justice, mercy, and faith—you have let fall by the wayside. The truth is that you ought to do these things, while not letting the others fall by the wayside. [24] Blind guides that you are, straining out the gnat yet gulping down the camel!

[25] "Woe upon you, you experts in the law and you Pharisees, dissemblers that you are! The outside of the cup or dish you do indeed keep clean, but as for the inside, it is full of what comes of your rapacity and self-indulgence. [26] You blind Pharisee, see to it first of all that the inside of your cup is kept clean, so that the outside may become clean as well.

[27] "Woe upon you, you experts in the law and you Pharisees, dissemblers that you are! You bear a resemblance to tombs which have been whitewashed, which from the outside look fair enough, yet as regards the inside are full of dead men's bones and every kind of corruption. [28] In the same way, you appear to your fellow men from the outside to be men good and true, while inside you are full of dissimulation and lawlessness.

[29] "Woe upon you, you experts in the law and you Pharisees, dissemblers that you are! You are the builders of the graves of the prophets, and you occupy yourselves with adorning the tombs of men of piety. [30] And this is what you say: 'Had we lived in the times of our forefathers, we should not have made common cause with them in shedding the blood of the prophets.' [31] And so you testify of yourselves that you are the descendants of the men who murdered the prophets. [32] Well then, go on with the task you have set yourselves, to finish the work that your forefathers began.

[33] "You who have the natures of serpents, you brood of vipers! In what way could you escape a judgment condemning you to a life in hell? [34] Indeed, it is in consideration of this—attend to my words—that I shall be sending to you prophets, men of wisdom, and some versed in the law as well. Some of them you will put to death and crucify, some you will flog in your synagogues, and some of them you will persecute from city to city. [35] So it will happen that, wherever innocent blood has been shed on earth, it shall come upon your own head—from the time when the blood of Abel, that upright man, was

shed until the time of the shedding of the blood of Zechariah son of Berachiah, the man you murdered between the sanctuary and the altar. [36] And indeed, I can give you solemn assurance of this, it will all come down upon this generation.

[37] "Jerusalem, O Jerusalem, the city that puts the prophets to death and stones the messengers who have been sent to her. How often have I longed to gather together your children, as a hen gathers her brood under her wings; but you would not have it! [38] Look out, God [n]**is abandoning your house** of worship, **leaving it to you.** [39] Moreover, I tell you this: you shall not see me again until the time comes when you say, [o]**'A blessing rests on him who appears in the name of the Lord'**".

24 Jesus left the temple and was going on his way when his disciples approached him so as to draw his attention to the various buildings which made up the temple. [2] And this is the answer he made them: "You are gazing at all this, are you not? But I can give you my solemn assurance that there is not one stone here which will be left standing upon another. It will all be thrown down."

[3] When he was on the Mount of Olives, sitting down, his disciples approached him, no one else being present, and addressed these words to him: "Will you tell us when these things will happen, and what will be the sign signifying your Coming and the consummation of the age?"

[4] And this is the answer Jesus made them: "Take care that no one leads you astray. [5] Indeed, many will appear, making use of my name, and will say, 'I am God's anointed'. And they will lead many astray. [6] You will be told of wars and of rumours of wars. Make sure that you are not thrown into a panic. [p]**It is preordained that these things should happen,** while it is true at the same time that the end does not come immediately after that. [7] [q]**One nation will rise up in arms against another nation, and one kingdom against another kingdom.** [8] There will be famines and earthquakes in place after place. This is how the birth pangs of the new age will begin.

[9] "Then they will give you into the power of others, to suffer affliction or to be put to death. You will be hated by all the Gentiles because of your allegiance to the cause that bears my name. [10] Moreover, it will be at that time that [r]**many will take offence** and fall away; they will betray each other and hate each other. [11] Many false prophets will appear and lead many astray. [12] By reason of the increase of lawlessness the love of a multitude of men shall grow cold. [13] And yet if a man remains steadfast to the end, salvation will be his. [14] This happy news

[n]Jr 22:5; 12:7; 7:14; 1 K 9:7f   [o]Ps 118:26   [p]Dn 2:28   [q]Is 19:2; 2 Ch 15:6   [r]Dn 11:41

of the kingdom will be proclaimed all over the world, testimony being borne to all the Gentiles. And then the end will come.

¹⁵ "So when you see ˢ**the detestable thing of which the desolation comes,** the thing spoken of by the prophet Daniel, taking up its stand in the ᵗ**holy place**—let him who reads this ponder it—¹⁶ those who find themselves in Judaea should flee into the hills; ¹⁷ he who finds himself on the roof must not come down to fetch his possessions from his house; ¹⁸ and he who finds himself in the field must not turn back to collect his cloak. ¹⁹ Alas for women with child in those days and for those who have infants at the breast! ²⁰ Pray that your flight will not take place in winter time, or on the Sabbath day. ²¹ Indeed, there will be such dire ᵘ**affliction as there never has been from the beginning of the world to the present day,** nor ever shall be again. ²² In fact, but for those days being shortened no creature of flesh and blood would be able to survive. Yet, on behalf of God's chosen ones, those days will be shortened.

²³ "If anyone says to you at that time, 'Look, here is God's anointed', 'There he is', do not believe it. ²⁴ False Christs and ᵛ**false prophets** will appear, **showing forth** powerful **signs and portents,** and doing so to such an extent that, were it possible, they would succeed in misleading even God's chosen ones. ²⁵ Mark my words: I have given you warning. ²⁶ When they say to you, 'Look, he is in the desert', do not go forth there. Or if they say, 'Look, he is in one of the inner rooms', do not believe it. ²⁷ For like lightning proceeding from the east and, flashing forth, then seen in the west, so will be the coming of the Son of Man. ²⁸ Where the carcass is, there the vultures will gather together.

²⁹ "No sooner will these days of affliction have passed than this will happen. ʷ**The sun will be darkened, and the moon will not send forth her light. The stars will fall** from the sky, **and the celestial hosts will be made to totter.** ³⁰ And then the sign heralding the Son of Man will appear in the sky. Then, too, ˣ**all the nations of the earth will make lamentation** as they see ʸ**the Son of Man coming on the clouds of heaven,** equipped with great power and majesty. ³¹ He will send forth his angels ᶻ**at the sounding of a mighty trumpet call;** ᵃ**and they shall gather** his chosen ones **from the four corners from which the winds blow, from one end of heaven to the other.**

³² "Let the fig tree serve you as a simile teaching you a lesson. When its branches have become tender and it puts forth leaves, you know that summer is near at hand. ³³ In the same way, when you see all these things coming about, you may be certain that he is close to you, standing at the very doors. ³⁴ Indeed, I can give you solemn assurance that

ˢDn 9:27; 12:11; 11:31   ᵗDn 9:24   ᵘDn 12:1; Jl 2:2   ᵛDt 13:2   ʷIs 13:10; 34:4; Am 8:9   ˣZc 12:10.12   ʸDn 7:13f   ᶻIs 27:13; Jl 2:1   ᵃZc 2:6; Dt 30:4

this generation will not have passed away before all this has taken place. [35]Heaven and earth will pass away, but my words will not pass away.

[36]"As for the day or the hour when these things will be, no one knows about this, neither the angels in heaven nor the Son. It is the Father alone that knows.

[37]"Just as things were in the time of Noah, so they will be at the coming of the Son of Man. [38]In those days, before the deluge, men were eating, they were drinking, they married and joined others in marriage, up to the day when [b]**Noah entered the ark.** [39]They knew nothing until the deluge came and swept them all away. So things will be at the coming of the Son of Man. [40]At that time there will be two men in the same field. One will be taken and the other left. [41]There will be two women grinding with the handmill. One will be taken and the other left. [42]As for yourselves, then, be on the alert. You do not know on what day your Lord will be coming.

[43]"But there is one thing you can be sure of. Had the master of the house known at what time of night the burglar would be coming, he would have kept his eyes open and would not let his house be broken into. [44]This being so, you must likewise stand ready; for the Son of Man will be coming at a time when you least expect him.

[45]"What then is to be said of the servant, reliable and prudent, whom his master has put in charge of his household, to hand out the food at the proper time? [46]How blessed is that servant should his master, on coming home, find him performing this task! [47]Indeed, I can give you solemn assurance of this, that his master will put him in charge of all his property. [48]But if that man be a bad servant, saying to himself, 'My master is taking a long time coming home,' [49]and if he then proceeds to beat his fellow servants, giving himself over to eating and drinking in the company of drunkards, [50]the master of that servant will return on a day when he least expects him and at an hour which he does not know. [51]He will cut the servant to pieces and apportion to him the place which has been assigned to him, that by the side of the hypocrites. And then there will be weeping and gnashing of teeth.

25 "Time will come when the kingdom of heaven will be compared to ten virgins who, taking their lamps with them, went forth for a meeting with the bridegroom. [2]Five of them were foolish and five sensible. [3]And so it was that, when they took their lamps, the foolish ones failed to take any oil with them, [4]while the sensible ones,

[b]Gn 7:7

when they took their lamps, took oil as well, putting it in flasks. [5]When the bridegroom was a long time in coming, they all began to feel drowsy and fell asleep. [6]However, right in the middle of the night, someone was heard shouting, 'Here is the bridegroom; go forth to meet him!' [7]By this all the virgins were wakened, and they set about trimming their lamps. [8]But the foolish ones then said to the sensible ones, 'Let us have some of your oil; our lamps are on the point of going out.' [9]At that the sensible ones made them this reply: 'There would certainly never be enough to serve both us and you. You had better be on your way to those who sell oil and buy some for yourselves.' [10]While they were still on their way to do their buying, the bridegroom made his appearance. Those who were ready went inside with him for the celebration of the wedding. And then the door closed. [11]Some time later the other virgins likewise made their appearance. 'Lord, O Lord,' they exclaimed, 'open the door to us!' [12]But he made them this answer: 'I never knew you: I can give you solemn assurance of that.' [13]As for yourselves, then, keep on the alert. For you are ignorant of both the day and the hour when he will come.

[14]"Another instance: things are as though a man, about to go to a foreign country, had called his servants together, leaving all his possessions in their hands. [15]To one he handed five talents, to another two, and one he handed to a third, to each according to the ability he had. And immediately after having done this, he went on his way to the foreign country. [16]The man who had received the five talents went off without delay, traded with them, and gained another five. [17]The man who had received the two talents acted in the same manner and gained another two. [18]However, the man who had received one talent set off, dug a hole in the ground, and hid his master's money from sight. [19]When, after a long time, the master of these servants returned, he began to settle his accounts with them. [20]The one who had received the five talents made his appearance, brought another five talents with him, and said, 'Sir, you have entrusted me with five talents; look, here are another five talents which I have gained.' [21]'Well done, excellent and trustworthy servant that you are,' was the master's reply. 'You have shown yourself deserving of trust in small things. I shall put you in charge of great ones. Come and share your master's joy.' [22]Then the one who had had the two talents appeared, saying, 'Sir, you have entrusted me with two talents; look, here are another two talents which I have gained.' [23]'Well done, excellent and trustworthy servant that you are,' was the master's reply. 'You have shown yourself deserving of trust in small things. I shall put you in charge of great ones. Come and share your master's joy.' [24]After that the man who had received the one talent likewise made his appearance, and this is what he said: 'Sir, I knew well that you are a man of great harshness,

harvesting where you never sowed and gathering in from a field where you never scattered any seed. 25So I was afraid and went off, hiding your talent in the ground. Look, here it is; receive what is your own.' 26And this is the reply the master made him: 'Worthless and slothful servant that you are! You knew that I harvest where I never sowed, that I gather in from a field where I never scattered any seed. 27What you ought to have done is to put my money into the hands of the bankers. Then I could have collected it on my return along with the interest that had accrued. 28Well then, take the talent from him and give it to the man with the ten talents. 29The truth is that to everyone who already has something, gifts will be made and he will have means in abundance; while he who is without means will have taken away from him even the little that he has. 30And as for this worthless servant, cast him into a place far away in which darkness reigns, where there shall be weeping and gnashing of teeth.'

31"When the Son of Man ccomes in his state of glory, **all the angels** being **with him,** he will take his seat on the throne which is his in his glorified state. 32All the nations will be assembled in his presence, and he will separate people one from another as the shepherd separates sheep from goats. 33The sheep he will place on his right hand and the goats on his left. 34Then the King will say to those on his right hand, 'Come to me, you who have my Father's blessing resting upon you. Obtain possession of the kingdom which has been prepared for you from the very beginning of the world. 35I was hungry and you gave me food to eat; I was thirsty and you gave me something to drink. I was a stranger and you made me welcome. 36I was but poorly clad and you clothed me. I was sick and you took care of me. I was in prison and you came to see me.' 37Then those leading an upright life will in return say to him, 'Lord, when did we see you hungry and give you nourishment, or see you thirsty and give you something to drink? 38When did we see you as a stranger and make you welcome; when but poorly clad and clothe you; 39when did we see you sick or in prison and visit you?' 40And the King will reply to them thus: 'Indeed, I can give you solemn assurance of this: inasmuch as you have done these things for any of my brothers, and be it the least significant among them, you have done them for me.' 41Then he will address himself also to those standing on his left, and this is what he will say: 'Leave my presence, you who have ever been accursed, and make your way into the everlasting fire prepared for the devil and the angels that serve him. 42I was hungry and you gave me no food to eat; I was thirsty and you gave me nothing to drink; 43I was a stranger and you did not make me welcome; I was poorly clad and you did not

cZc 14:5

clothe me; I was sick and in prison and you did not visit me.' [44]Then they in turn will answer him, saying, 'Lord, when did we see you hungry, or thirsty, or as a stranger, or poorly clad, or sick, or in prison, and did not come to your aid?' [45]Then he will reply to them thus: 'Indeed, I can give you solemn assurance of this: inasmuch as you have failed to do these things for one of these, and be it the least significant, you have failed to do them for me.' [46]Then [d]**these people** shall go forth to suffer **everlasting** punishment, **while the** upright shall go where **everlasting life** is to be found."

26 When Jesus had come to the end of all these discourses, he addressed these words to his disciples: [2]"You know that the feast of the Passover is coming in two days' time, and that they will then hand over the Son of Man to be crucified." [3]Some time after this there was an assembly of the chief priests and the elders of the people in the palace of the High Priest—his name was Caiaphas — [4]and it was resolved that they were to catch hold of Jesus by way of trickery and put him to death. [5]However, this is what they said to one another: "It must not be during the festival, to prevent there being an uproar among the people."

[6]One day when Jesus found himself at Bethany in the house of a certain man by the name of Simon, who was a sufferer from leprosy, [7]he was approached by a woman who had with her a small flask containing oil of myrrh of the most precious kind, which she poured on his head while he was reclining at table. [8]The disciples were full of indignation when they saw this, and this is what they said: "Why that waste? [9]It would have been possible to sell this at a high price, the proceeds being given to the poor." [10]Yet Jesus, well aware of all this, addressed them thus: "Why are you causing trouble for the woman? She has done a noble work on my behalf. [11]As for the poor, there never will be a time when you will not have them with you, but me you will not always have. [12]What the woman did when she was pouring the oil of myrrh over my body was to prepare me for burial. [13]Indeed, I can give you solemn assurance of this. All over the world, wherever this gospel is proclaimed, her deed will be spoken of as a memorial offered to her."

[14]Some time after this, one of the twelve disciples, the man Judas—the one surnamed Iscariot—went off to the chief priests, [15]saying, "What are you prepared to give me if I should hand him over to you?" [e]**They fixed** the price they would pay him at **thirty pieces of silver.** [16]And from that day onwards he looked out for an opportunity of betraying him.

[d]Dn 12:2   [e]Zc 11:12

¹⁷On the first day of the Feast of Unleavened Bread the disciples approached Jesus, saying to him, "Where do you want us to make the preparations for eating the Passover meal?" ¹⁸"Make your way into the city," he said, "and go to a certain man, saying to him, 'This is the Master's message: "The time appointed for me is close at hand, and it will be in your house that I shall be having the Passover meal in the company of my disciples."'" ¹⁹The disciples did what Jesus had ordered them to do and prepared the Passover meal.

²⁰When evening came, he reclined at table in the company of his twelve disciples and, while they were partaking of their food, he spoke to them thus: ²¹"I can indeed give you solemn assurance of this, that one of you will betray me." ²²Being greatly grieved at this, they, each of them, exclaimed one after the other, "Surely it is not I, Lord?" ²³And this is what he said to them in reply: "It is the man who dips his hand into the dish at the same time as I do who will be my betrayer. ²⁴And so the Son of Man, as has indeed been foretold about him in scripture, goes on his way. And yet, woe upon the man by whom the Son of Man is being betrayed. It would be better for that man if he had never been born." ²⁵And then Judas, his betrayer, spoke to him thus in reply to this: "Surely, Rabbi, it is not I?" "The words are yours," said Jesus.

²⁶While they were partaking of their food, Jesus laid hold of some bread and, having spoken a blessing over it, he broke it into pieces, handed it to the disciples, and said, "Take this and eat it. This is my body." ²⁷Moreover, having seized a cup with his hand, he gave thanks to God, handed it to them, and said, "Drink of this, all of you. ²⁸For this is the *f***blood** sealing the **covenant**, my blood that is being poured out on behalf of multitudes, that they might find forgiveness of their sins. ²⁹And indeed, I have to tell you this. Never again, from this time onwards, shall I drink of this produce of the vine until the day comes when I drink it in your company, as something altogether new, in the kingdom of my Father."

³⁰Then, after the hymn singing,* they made their way to the Mount of Olives. ³¹And it was at that time that he addressed these words to them: "You will all take offence at me and fall away during this night. For this is what stands written in scripture: *g***'I shall strike down the shepherd, and the sheep of his flock shall be scattered far and wide'.** ³²However, after I have been raised to life again, I shall make my way into Galilee ahead of you." ³³And Peter said this to him in reply: "Even though they should, one and all, take offence at you and fall away, I

---

*f*Ex 24:8; Zc 9:11   *g*Zc 13:7

* [At the Passover meal, this is likely to have been the *Hallel*, i.e., Pss. 115–118.]

shall never take offence at you." [34]Jesus answered him thus: "Indeed, I can give you solemn assurance that this very night, before the cock crows, you will disown me three times." [35]"Even if I had to suffer death by your side," exclaimed Peter, "I shall never disown you!" And all the other disciples spoke in the same way.

[36]Some time after this, Jesus and the disciples with him reached a certain place called Gethsemane. "Stay here," he said to them, "while I go over there to give myself up to prayer." [37]He took Peter and the two sons of Zebedee with him. However, a feeling of great distress and desolation began to fill his mind, [38]and he spoke to them thus: "[h]**My soul is sadly distressed;** it feels as though I were dying. Stay with me here and be wakeful by my side." [39]Then he went on some distance further, fell on his face, and gave utterance to these words by way of a prayer: "My Father, if it be possible, may this cup of misery pass me by. And yet make everything happen as you, not as I, would have it."

[40]At that he went back to his disciples and found them asleep. So he addressed these words to Peter, "Is it true, then, that you lacked the strength to remain wakeful by my side, and be it only for an hour? [41]Do remain wakeful, while uttering a prayer to be spared from having to undergo the final test. As for the spirit, it is indeed eager enough; it is the flesh that makes us weak."

[42]Upon this he went away a second time and exclaimed by way of uttering a prayer, "My Father, should it be impossible for this cup to pass me by without my drinking of it, it is your will that is to be accomplished." [43]Then he went back once more and found them asleep, for their eyes were weighed down by drowsiness. [44]So he left them, went away again, and prayed a third time, his words being the same as before.

[45]Then he drew near his disciples, addressing these words to them: "From now on *do* sleep and take your rest. And take note of this: the hour appointed for the Son of Man has come, and he is being delivered into the hands of men given over to sin. [46]Rise to your feet and let us go. Here he is; my betrayer is drawing near."

[47]And while he was still uttering these words, there was Judas, one of the twelve disciples, making his appearance. And with him was a large crowd, equipped with swords and with cudgels, men who had been sent out by the chief priests and the elders of the people. [48]The betrayer, for his part, had arranged a signal with them, saying, "Whomsoever I shall be greeting with a kiss: he is the man himself. Lay hold of him." [49]So he went up to Jesus immediately, calling out, "My greetings to you, Rabbi." And then he kissed him. [50]"My

[h]Ps 42:5f; 43:5

friend, do what you have come to do," replied Jesus. Thereupon the others drew close to Jesus, laid their hands on him, and made him a prisoner.

[51] And then it happened that one of Jesus' companions reached for his sword and drew it, striking out at the High Priest's servant and cutting off his ear. [52] Yet Jesus called out to him these words: "Put your sword back where it belongs. And indeed, those who draw the sword shall, one and all, be destroyed by the sword. [53] Do you suppose that I could not make an appeal to my Father, and that he would not furnish me in an instant with twelve legions of angels, and more than that? [54] However, if I did act in this way, how could fulfilment be brought to the passages from scripture which declare that things are destined to happen in this way?"

[55] It was just then that Jesus addressed these words to the crowds: "It is with swords and cudgels in hand that you have set out, as though you had to deal with a brigand. Why, there I was sitting in the temple giving instruction, day after day, and you did not seize me. [56] However, all this has happened so that the words of the prophets set down in the scriptures should be brought to fulfilment." No sooner had he said this than all his disciples left him and took to flight.

[57] Those who had apprehended Jesus led him off to Caiaphas the High Priest, in whose house the experts in the law and the elders were assembled. [58] As for Peter, he followed him at some distance as far as the High Priest's courtyard, and then, going in, he sat down right among the attendants to await the outcome.

[59] The chief priests and the whole of the High Council were endeavouring to secure false testimony against Jesus, with a view to obtaining the means for having him put to death. [60] However, although many false witnesses did in fact come forward, they were unable to find what they were looking for. However, two false witnesses came forward, some time later, [61] and made this assertion: "That fellow said, 'I have the power of destroying God's temple and of building it up again within three days.'" [62] At that the High Priest rose up and said to Jesus, "Is there no reply you have to make to the charges which these men are bringing against you?" [63] Jesus, however, said nothing. And so the High Priest addressed him thus: "I adjure you, in the name of the living God, to tell us whether you are the Anointed One, the Son of God." [64] And this is the reply Jesus made to him: "The words are yours. Still, I have one more thing to say to you: from this time onwards you will see *the Son of Man sitting on the right side of the God of all power* and **coming down in the clouds of heaven.**" [65] The High Priest rent his clothing [j] when he heard this, and exclaimed, "He

[i] Ps 110:1; Dn 7:13   [j] [Lv 10:6; 21:10; 2 K 18:37]

has uttered blasphemy! What need of further witnesses do we have? Here it is, right before you. You have heard the blasphemy with your own ears. 66What is your opinion?" And the others answered, "He deserves to die." 67And then it was that they spat in his face and struck him with their fists. 68And there were others who exclaimed as they were buffeting him, "Play the prophet for us, you Anointed One! Who is it that has struck you?"

69Meanwhile, Peter was sitting outside in the courtyard when a certain servant girl came up to him and said, "You, too, were in the company of Jesus the Galilean." 70But Peter, denying it in front of them all, said, "I do not know what you are talking about." 71Later, when he had gone out into the gateway, another girl saw him and said to those present there, "That fellow was in the company of Jesus of Nazareth." 72Peter made a denial once again, confirming it with an oath, and said, "I have no knowledge of the man." 73A little while after that the men who were standing about there came up to Peter, saying, "No doubt whatever; you, too, are one of them. Indeed, your manner of speech gives you away." 74Peter thereupon began calling down curses upon himself and swearing, "I have no knowledge of the man." And immediately upon this, a cock was heard to crow. 75And Peter called to mind the words which Jesus had spoken to him: 'Before the cock crows you will disown me three times.' And going outside, he burst into bitter tears.

27   When morning came all the chief priests, and the elders of the people as well, resolved to take action against Jesus, being determined to have him executed. 2So they put him in fetters, led him away, and handed him over to Pilate, who held the office of Governor.

3Then Judas, the man who had betrayed him, when he realized that Jesus had been condemned, was filled with remorse over what he had done. So he took the thirty pieces of silver back to the chief priests and the elders, 4and said to them, "I have done wrong betraying an innocent man and bringing him to his death." "What is that to us?" replied the others, "That is your affair." 5At that, Judas, throwing down the money in the sanctuary, left their presence, went off, and hanged himself. 6The chief priests had the money picked up, but this is what they said: "Seeing that this is the price paid for a human life, it is not lawful to put it in the temple treasury." 7So they debated the matter and decided to buy the Potter's Field with the money to serve as a place of burial for people of alien descent. 8And this is how that field has come to be called the Field of Blood up to this day. 9Moreover, it was when these things were happening that fulfilment was brought to these words of the prophet Jeremiah:

'*k*And they took the thirty pieces of silver, which is the price of the man on whom a price had been set—estimating the man's worth at the hands of certain of Israel's sons—10and they gave the money for the potter's field. This was just what the Lord had ordered me to do.'

11Now as for Jesus, he was standing in the presence of the Governor. The Governor asked him, "Are you the king of the Jews?" "It is you who say that I am," was Jesus' reply. 12Moreover, while he was being accused by the chief priests and elders, Jesus refrained from making any reply. 13So Pilate asked him, "Do you not hear how many charges they are bringing against you?" 14But still Jesus would not say one word to him in reply, with the result that the Governor was greatly surprised.

15Now it was the Governor's practice, every year as the festival came along, to pardon one prisoner, whichever they might choose, as a favour to the people. 16On that occasion he was holding a notorious prisoner whose name was Barabbas. 17So when the people were assembled, Pilate asked them, "Which of them do you want me to pardon as a favour to you: Barabbas, or Jesus who is also spoken of as the Anointed One?" 18In point of fact, he knew that it was out of spite that they had handed Jesus over.

19Moreover, while he was occupying his seat on the judicial bench, he had this message from his wife: "Have nothing to do with that innocent man. I was greatly distressed on his account in the course of a dream which I had last night."

20Meanwhile the chief priests and the elders had persuaded the people to ask for Barabbas, making sure in this way that Jesus would have to perish. 21So when the Governor asked, "Which of these two am I to pardon as a favour to you?", they replied, "Barabbas." 22At that, Pilate enquired, "What then am I to do with Jesus, the one who is also spoken of as the Anointed One?" "Let him be crucified!" they exclaimed, one and all. 23"Why, what crime has he committed?" asked Pilate. But they cried out all the louder, "Let him be crucified!" 24When Pilate realized that he was accomplishing nothing and that the turmoil was growing worse and worse, he had some water fetched and washed his hands in the sight of the people. And this is what he said: "I am free from guilt, so far as this blood is concerned. It is your affair." 25At that all the people cried out, "May his blood come upon us and upon our children." 26And it was then that he pardoned Barabbas as a favour to them, while, as for Jesus, he had him scourged first of all and then handed him over to be crucified.

27After that, the soldiers of the Governor took Jesus along with them to the Governor's place of residence, where they gathered the

*k*Zc 11:12f; Jr 19:1; 32:6-9

whole of the cohort round him. [28]They divested him of his clothing, dressed him up in a scarlet cloak, [29]placed a crown which they had woven out of thorns upon his head, and put a staff in his right hand. And having fallen on their knees right in front of him, they sneered at him and exclaimed, "Hail to you, you king of the Jews!" [30]Then they spat at him and, taking the staff from him, struck his head with it. [31]Moreover, when they had done with their sneering, they took the cloak off him and put his own clothes on him.

And then they led him away to be crucified. [32]Having gone some distance, they came upon a certain man by the name of Simon, who was a native of Cyrene. It was this man whom they pressed into service, making him carry the cross of Jesus.

[33]So they came to a place called Golgotha—the meaning of this name being 'The Place of a Skull'. [34][l]**They gave** him a **drink** of wine mixed with **gall.** But after he had tasted of it, he refused to drink.

[35]So they crucified him, [m]**dividing** his **clothes** among themselves by way of **casting lots** over them; [36]and there they sat, keeping guard over him. [37]They also placed above his head the charge which had been made against him, written out in these words: 'THIS IS JESUS, THE KING OF THE JEWS.' [38]Moreover, two men who were brigands were crucified with him, one on the right and one on the left.

[39]Now those who passed by poured abuse upon him. [n]**Shaking their heads,** they exclaimed, [40]"You, the destroyer of the temple, the one who builds it up again in three days: if you are the Son of God, deliver yourself and come down from the cross!" [41]In the same way the chief priests, as well as the experts in the law and the elders, sneered at him and said, [42]"He came to the rescue of others but has no power to rescue himself. He is the king of Israel, is he not? Let him come down from the cross, and we shall believe in him. [43][o]**He has put his trust in God; let God rescue him if he finds any joy in him.** After all, he said that he was the Son of God." [44]Besides, even the brigands who were crucified with him reviled him after the same fashion.

[45]From the sixth hour to the ninth, darkness fell over the whole land. [46]At about the ninth hour Jesus cried out in a loud voice, *"Eli, Eli, lema sabachthani?"* which means, [p]**'My God, my God, why have you abandoned me?'** [47]Certain of those present there heard him and said, "That man is calling for Elijah." [48]One of them ran off quickly to get hold of a sponge, soaked it in [q]**sour wine**, and, fixing it on a reed, **gave** it to Jesus **to drink.** [49]But the others said, "Let us see whether Elijah will come to rescue him."

[l]Ps 69:21   [m]Ps 22:18   [n]Ps 22:7; 109:25; Lm 2:15   [o]Ps 22:8 [Wis 2:12-20]   [p]Ps 22:1
[q]Ps 69:21

[50]But Jesus, crying out again in a loud voice, breathed his last. [51]And it was there and then that the curtain in the temple was torn in two, from top to bottom. The earth was shaken and the rocks were split. [52]The tombs opened, and many of the consecrated ones who had already gone to their rest had their bodies raised to life again. [53]And after their resurrection they came out of their graves and entered the holy city, being seen plainly by many.

[54]The centurion and those with him who were keeping guard over Jesus were filled with awe when they witnessed the earthquake and the other happenings. And this is what they said: "In very truth this man was a son of God!" [55]Many of the women who had accompanied him from Galilee, looking after his needs, were also there, watching from afar. [56]Among them there was Mary of Magdala, Mary the mother of James and Joseph, and the mother of the sons of Zebedee.

[57]When evening came, a certain man called Joseph made his appearance. He was a man of great wealth and a native of Arimathaea. He, too, had become one of Jesus' disciples. [58]And so he approached Pilate, asking that he should let him have the body of Jesus, Pilate thereupon giving the order that it was to be handed over to him. [59]Joseph took it, wrapped it in a clean linen cloth, [60]and deposited it in a tomb belonging to him which was new and had been fashioned by being cut out of the rock. He rolled a large stone against the entrance of the tomb and then took his departure. [61]Mary of Magdala and the other Mary were present, sitting right opposite the grave.

[62]The next day, that is to say, the one following the Day of Preparation, the chief priests and the Pharisees gathered together for an approach to Pilate. [63]And they said to him, "Sir, we have called to mind the words of this impostor when he was still alive: 'After three days I shall rise to life again.' [64]Well then, give the order that the grave is to be kept secure until the third day. Otherwise there is a risk that his disciples will come along, steal the body, and say to the people, 'He has been raised from the dead.' If things turned out that way, the deception would in the end be more insidious than when it first began." [65]And this is the reply Pilate made to them: "You can have a guard. Be on your way, making everything as secure as you know how." [66]So they went and made the grave secure by putting a seal on the stone. And they had the guard as well.

28 The day after the Sabbath, as the first light of another week began to dawn, Mary of Magdala and the other Mary went forth to look at the grave. [2]Then all at once the earth was shaken violently, and that was because one of God's angels was coming down from heaven, and, on drawing near, rolled the stone away and sat upon it.

[3] His appearance was as brilliant as a flash of lightning, and his clothing was as white as snow. [4] As for the men who were keeping guard, their fear of the angel made them shake, and their appearance changed so that they looked like dead men.

[5] The angel, however, turned to the women and addressed them in the following words: "Throw off all fear. I know that you are looking for Jesus, the man who has been crucified. [6] He is no longer here, but has been raised up as he said he would be. Come here, and look at the place where his body was laid. [7] And after that make haste and go to his disciples with this message: 'He has been raised from the dead and is now making his way into Galilee ahead of you. There you will meet him.' Attend to my words. I have told you all."

[8] And so it was that the women took their departure from the grave in great haste, their minds being filled with awe and great joy at the same time. And as they were running to announce all this to the disciples, [9] there was Jesus, coming to meet them and saying, "My greetings to you." At that the women drew near him, caught hold of his feet, and did homage to him. [10] Thereupon Jesus addressed these words to them: "Throw off all fear. Be on your way and instruct my brothers to make their departure for Galilee. And there they will see me."

[11] While the women were still on their way, certain members of the guard, when they reached the city, reported to the chief priests everything that had happened. [12] And after a meeting with the elders, during which they consulted with them on this matter, they handed a considerable sum of money to the soldiers, [13] while addressing these words to them: "What you are to say to the people is this: 'This man's disciples made their appearance during the night, while we were asleep, and they stole the body.' [14] And if the Governor comes to hear of this, we shall provide a satisfactory explanation and make certain that you are kept out of trouble." [15] As for the soldiers, they took the money and acted on their instructions. Indeed, the story, as told by them, has spread widely among the Jews, being accepted by them up to this day.

[16] The eleven disciples, for their part, set out for Galilee, and made for the mountain where Jesus had arranged that they were to meet. [17] When they saw him, they did homage to him. Still, there were some who were doubtful. [18] But Jesus drew near and addressed them in the following words: "All authority in heaven as well as on earth has been given into my hands. [19] Well then, go forth and make people in every nation into disciples of mine, baptizing them in the name of the Father, of the Son, and of the Holy Spirit, [20] instructing them at the same time that they must observe all the commandments which you have had from me. And indeed, here I am by your side, any day and every day, until the very close of the present age."

63

THE GOSPEL STORY
AS TOLD BY MARK

1 The Good News concerning Jesus Christ, the Son of God, begins thus: ²This is what is written in the prophet Isaiah—ᵃ"**Take note of this: I am sending my herald ahead of you; it is he who will make ready the way** for your **coming.** ³ ᵇ**A voice of one crying out in the desert: Prepare a way for the Lord; straighten out the paths** which he is to tread.' ⁴There was John the Baptist in the desert proclaiming a baptism which was to have its source in repentance and which was to result in people having their sins forgiven them. ⁵The whole Judaean countryside and all the inhabitants of Jerusalem came flocking to him, being baptized by him in the River Jordan while making confession of their sins.

⁶John was clothed in a garment made of camel's hair, and he had a leather belt round his waist. The food he ate was locusts and wild honey. ⁷And this is the proclamation he made: "Another is to come, endowed with much greater strength than I have. He will be such a man that, as regards myself, I shall not even be worthy to bend down to unfasten the straps of his shoes. ⁸I have been baptizing you with water, but the baptism he will administer to you will be one with the Holy Spirit."

⁹It was at this very time that Jesus came from Nazareth in Galilee, being baptized by John in the Jordan. ¹⁰And as he was coming up from the water, he all at once saw the heaven split wide open and the Spirit, having the appearance of a dove, descending upon him. ¹¹At the same time a voice was heard from heaven which said, "You are my ᶜ**Son, my dearly-loved one. It is upon you that my favour** rests." ¹²Immediately after that the Spirit led him forth into the desert. ¹³And there he was in the desert for forty days, being put to the test by Satan. The wild beasts were his company, and God's angels looked after his wants.

¹⁴After John had been committed to prison, Jesus departed to

ᵃMal 3:1   ᵇIs 40:3   ᶜPs 2:7; Is 42:1

Galilee, where he proclaimed God's Good News. 15 And this is what he said: "The fulfilment has come. The kingdom of God is drawing near you. Repent and put your trust in the Good News."

16 One day when he was proceeding on his way by the shore of the Sea of Galilee, his eyes fell on Simon and Simon's brother Andrew who, being fishermen, were casting their nets into the lake. 17 And this is what Jesus said to them: "To my side; follow me; fishers of men is what I shall be making out of you." 18 At that they left their nets immediately and followed him. 19 When he had gone on a little way he saw James, the son of Zebedee, and his brother John; they were in their boat, mending their nets. 20 He summoned them at once; and they came after him, leaving their father Zebedee as well as the hired servants in the boat.

21 When they reached Capernaum, he immediately proceeded to go to the synagogue on the Sabbath day and to teach there. 22 The people were astounded at his teaching, because the way he taught was like that of a man invested with authority and quite unlike anything done by the experts in the law. 23 No sooner had he entered their synagogue than there appeared a man possessed of a *d*tarnished spirit 24 who cried out and exclaimed, *e*"**What do you want with us,** Jesus of Nazareth? Have you come to bring ruin upon us? I know who you are. You are God's Holy One!" 25 Jesus administered a rebuke to him, exclaiming, "Be silent and come out of him!" 26 At that the tarnished spirit threw him into convulsions and, crying out in a loud voice, it came out of him. 27 They were all astounded, so much so that, debating the matter with one another, they exclaimed, "What does this mean? This is a new kind of teaching, that of a man invested with authority! He gives orders to the tarnished spirits, and they obey his commands!" 28 So it was that the story about him spread swiftly all over the surrounding districts of Galilee.

29 On making their departure from the synagogue, Jesus made straight for the house of Simon and Andrew in the company of James and John. 30 Now Simon's mother-in-law lay sick, suffering from a fever, so they immediately told him about her. 31 Jesus went up to her, touched her hand, and raised her up. At that the fever left her and she waited on them.

32 When evening came and the sun was setting, they brought to him all those who were ill or were possessed of demonic spirits. 33 The whole town was there, crowded together at the door. 34 He brought healing to many who were sufferers from various illnesses, expelled many demonic spirits, and at the same time would not allow the demonic spirits to speak because they knew who he was.

d[Zc 13:2]   *e*Jg 11:12

[35] Very early in the morning Jesus rose up and left, making his way to a solitary place, where he devoted himself to prayer. [36] Simon and his companions went out to search for him, [37] and when they found him they said, "They are all looking for you!" [38] And this is the reply he made to them: "Let us go elsewhere to the neighbouring country towns, so that there, too, I may proclaim my message. This is the very thing I have come out to do." [39] Thus he went all over Galilee, proclaiming his message in the people's synagogues. And he likewise occupied himself with driving out demonic spirits.

[40] On one occasion a leper came up to him, begged for his help, and, falling on his knees, exclaimed, "You have the power of cleansing me if only you wish to!" [41] Jesus took pity on him, stretched out his hand, touched him, and exclaimed, "Be cleansed; it is my wish that you should be!" [42] At that the leprosy departed from him all at once, and he was cleansed. [43] As for Jesus, he immediately bade him go, warning him sternly [44] and addressing these further words to him: "Be sure not to tell anybody about this. However, you must be on your way and [f]show yourself to the **priest.** Moreover, you must make the offering in token of your cleansing, in accordance with what has been laid down by Moses. This will suffice as evidence for them." [45] However, no sooner had the man left than he proceeded to make it all public, causing the tale of Jesus to spread everywhere, with the result that Jesus could no longer go into any town openly but had to stay outside in places that were deserted. But even so, people flocked to him from all sides.

2 After an interval of a few days Jesus returned to Capernaum. When the news of his being home again spread, [2] a large number of people gathered together, with the result that even in the vicinity of the door there was no longer enough room to hold them. He proclaimed his message to them. [3] Then certain people appeared, bringing a paralyzed man to him. Four men were carrying him, [4] but when these were unable to get him close to Jesus on account of the crowd, they proceeded to open up the roof of the place where Jesus was. And having made a hole, they let down the stretcher on which the paralyzed man was lying. [5] When Jesus perceived the faith which was in them, he addressed these words to the man who was paralyzed: "Your sins are forgiven you, my friend."

[6] Now certain of the experts in the law were sitting there, reasoning in this way: [7] "Why is it that that fellow is talking like this? He is uttering blasphemies. Who except God alone has the power of forgiv-

[f]Lv 13:49

ing sins?" [8] As for Jesus, he recognized at once, by virtue of his spirit, that they were reasoning in this way within themselves, and so he spoke to them thus: "Why are you reasoning in your minds in this way? [9] After all, which is more easily done—to say to this paralyzed man, 'Your sins are forgiven you,' or to say, 'Rise up; lift up your stretcher and walk'? [10] This has happened so that you should be made to realize that the Son of Man, while he is on earth, has the authority granted to him to forgive sins." Then he addressed himself to the paralyzed man, saying, [11] "This is what I am telling you to do: rise up, lift up your stretcher, and be on your way home." [12] At that he rose up immediately, lifted up his stretcher, and made his departure in front of them all, with the result that everybody was astounded, giving praise to God and exclaiming, "Never at any time have we witnessed anything like this!"

[13] He went forth once more, walking by the side of the lake. The whole of the crowd was flocking to him, and he engaged in teaching them. [14] While he was on his way, his eyes fell on Levi the son of Alphaeus, who was occupying his place in the tax office. "Follow me," Jesus said to him. And he, rising up, followed him.

[15] One day it happened that Jesus reclined at table in Levi's house, and many who were tax collectors or were given over to some other kind of sin* reclined in his company and that of his disciples. For many among those were Jesus' followers. [16] Now when the experts in the law and the Pharisees became aware that he was having a meal with men given over to sin and with tax collectors, they said to his disciples, "Why is it that your master eats and drinks with tax collectors and other sinful men?" [17] On hearing this, Jesus replied to them thus: "It is not the strong and healthy who are in need of a physician; it is those who are in bad health. Indeed, I have made my appearance among men to hold out an invitation, not to people of virtue, but to sinners."

[18] On one occasion when John's disciples and the Pharisees were fasting, people came to him and asked him this question: "Why is it that John's disciples and those of the Pharisees fast, while your disciples do not fast?" [19] And he made them this reply: "Is it conceivable that the friends of the bridegroom should fast when the bridegroom is still in their company? So long as they have the bridegroom still with them, it is inconceivable that they should fast. [20] However, time will come when the bridegroom is taken away from them and, when that day comes, they will fast.

[21] "No one sews a patch of unshrunk cloth on an old coat. If that is done, the new patch will take something off the old coat, and there

---

* [Usually understood as those who were less observant of the dietary and other Jewish laws, and who were treated as pariahs.]

will be a worse tear than before. [22]Neither do people pour new wine into old wineskins. Otherwise this will make the skins burst, and both the wine and the skins are ruined. No, people pour new wine into fresh skins."

[23]One day it happened that he was making his way through fields of corn on the Sabbath day, and as his disciples were going on their way, they began to pluck ears of corn. [24]At that the Pharisees said to him, "Look, they are doing something that is forbidden on the Sabbath day." [25]And Jesus replied, "Have you never read what David did when he found himself in need, and he and his companions were going hungry; [26]how he entered the house of God in the time of the High Priest Abiathar, and how they ate [8]**the Loaves of Presentation,** those being the loaves which no one has any right to eat, only the priests being entitled to do so; and how he went so far as to give some of them to his companions?"

[27]Then he said another thing to them: "The Sabbath was made for the sake of man, not man for the sake of the Sabbath. [28]And the conclusion to be drawn from this is that the Son of Man exercises his lordship even over the Sabbath."

3 He went into the synagogue once again and there he met a man who had a withered hand. [2]They put a close watch on Jesus to ascertain whether he would heal the man on the Sabbath day, their desire being that they might have something to accuse him of. [3]"Rise up and come out into the middle," he said to the man with the withered hand. [4]Then he said to the others, "Which of these is permitted on the Sabbath: to do good or to do evil, to save life or to destroy it?" They did not say a word. [5]And he, looking angrily round at them and being grieved on account of the callousness of their minds, said to the man, "Stretch out your hand." He stretched it out, and his hand was restored to its former soundness. [6]Upon this, the Pharisees and the adherents of Herod's party made their exit and immediately began to hatch a plot against him, their purpose being to put him to death.

[7]As for Jesus, he withdrew to the lake in the company of his disciples. A large crowd followed him, people that came from Galilee, from Judaea, [8]from Jerusalem, from Idumaea, from the region beyond the Jordan, as well as from Tyre and Sidon. This large crowd, hearing of his deeds, came flocking towards him. [9]And because of the crowd, Jesus gave the order to his disciples that a boat was to be held in readiness for him, to avoid the risk of being crushed by them. [10]He brought healing to many; and so it was that those suffering from bodily affliction of any

[8]1 Sm 21:6; Lv 24:9

kind pressed about him in their eagerness to touch him. [11]Moreover, whenever the tarnished spirits saw him, they fell at his feet and cried out, "You are the Son of God!" [12]And many times he gave stern warning to the people not to make known what he had done.

[13]After that he went up the hillside and called to himself those of his choice, and they joined themselves to him. [14]He appointed twelve men that they might be his companions, that he might send them forth to proclaim his message, [15]and that they might have the power to drive out the demonic spirits. [16]And so he appointed the Twelve. He gave to Simon the surname of Peter. [17]Then there were James the son of Zebedee and his brother John, whom he surnamed Boanerges, the meaning of this being 'Sons of Thunder'. [18]Then there were Andrew, Philip, Bartholomew, Matthew, Thomas, James the son of Alphaeus, Thaddaeus, and Simon, a member of the party of the Zealots. [19]And there was Judas Iscariot, the man who betrayed him.

[20]When Jesus returned home, so large a crowd was gathering together once again that it was not possible to eat. [21]When those related to him heard of this, they went off to get hold of him, for people said that he was out of his mind.

[22]The experts in the law had come down from Jerusalem, and this is what they said: "He is possessed of Beelzebub; moreover, it is with the help of Beelzebub, the prince of demonic spirits, that he is casting out the demonic spirits." [23]So Jesus called them together and, by having recourse to figurative language, addressed these words to them: "How is it conceivable that Satan should cast out Satan? [24]Indeed, if there are internal divisions in a kingdom, it is impossible that such a kingdom should stand firm. [25]And if there are internal divisions in a household, it is impossible that such a household should stand firm. [26]So if it were true that Satan was in a state of rebellion against himself, and that he was internally divided, it would then be impossible for him to stand firm, and there would have to be an end of him. [27]Or again, no one has the power to enter the house of a strong man and plunder his goods unless he has first put the strong man in fetters. Only after he has done this will he enter his house and plunder it thoroughly.

[28]"I can give you solemn assurance of this. Whatever sins members of the human family may commit, whatever slanders they may utter, they can find forgiveness for them. [29]But he who slanders the Holy Spirit will never find forgiveness: he has incurred a guilt which is everlasting." [30]It was on account of their saying that he was possessed of a tarnished spirit that he spoke like this.

[31]At this point his mother and his brothers arrived and, standing outside, they sent a message to him asking him to come out to them. [32]Now a crowd was sitting round him, and they said to him, "Here

are your mother, your brothers, and your sisters standing outside and looking for you." ³³And Jesus made them this reply: "Who is my mother, and who are my brothers?" ³⁴Then, looking round at those who were sitting in a circle about him, he said, "Look, here is my mother; here are my brothers. ³⁵And indeed, if there be anyone whose actions are in conformity with the will of God, it is that person who is brother, who is sister, who is mother to me."

4 On another occasion he set out to teach by the lakeside. Such a large crowd gathered round him that he had to get into a boat on the lake. There he sat down, while the whole of the crowd was by the water's edge on dry land. ²He taught them many things by way of parables, and in the course of his teaching he spoke these words to them:

³"Attend to my words: there was a man whose business it was to sow seed. And he went on his way to sow. ⁴Now in the course of his sowing some of the seed fell by the roadside, the birds coming and eating it up. ⁵Other seed fell on rocky ground, where there was not much soil for it. And so it sprang up straightaway because it lacked soil reaching far down in depth. ⁶It was scorched when the sun rose and, having no root, it withered away. ⁷Other seed fell among the thistles. When the thistles came up, they choked it, and it failed to bring forth fruit. ⁸Again, some seed fell on good soil. It came up, grew, and bore fruit, some yielding thirty, some sixty, some as much as a hundredfold." ⁹And he added the words, "Let him who has ears, listen."

¹⁰When his companions, the twelve disciples among them, found themselves alone with him, they set out to question him about the parables. ¹¹And this is the reply he made them: "As for yourselves, you have had the very secret of the kingdom of God committed into your hands, while everything comes by way of parables to those others who stand outside. ¹²And the point of it all is that, ʰ**while looking indeed, they should see nothing, and while hearing indeed, they should understand nothing, to make it certain that they should not turn towards God and have their deeds forgiven them**."

¹³Then he spoke to them thus: "Do you not understand this parable? How then can you comprehend any of the parables? ¹⁴It is God's word that the sower sows. ¹⁵The seeds that fall by the roadside signify the case where God's word is sown, yet people have no sooner heard it than Satan appears, carrying off the word which has been sown in them. ¹⁶Similarly, what the seed sown on rocky ground rep-

ʰIs 6:9f

resents is people who, when they first hear the word of God, give it a joyful welcome. [17] Yet, being without roots, with them nothing ever lasts for any length of time; when they are made the victims of affliction or persecution on behalf of the word of God, they at once take offence at it and fall away. [18] The seeds sown among the thistles represent others: the people who have given a hearing to the word of God. [19] However, the anxieties caused by this world of ours, the seduction which comes from wealth, as well as other appetites, stifle the word of God and prevent it from proving fruitful. [20] But the seeds sown in good soil represent the people who lend their ear to the word of God and bid it welcome. They yield a plentiful harvest, some producing as much as thirty, some as much as sixty, and some as much as a hundredfold."

[21] He said another thing to them: "Do people have a lamp brought in to place it under a grain measure or a bed? Surely what they intend is that it should be put on a lampstand. [22] Indeed, nothing is kept hidden except with the intention that it should come into the open, nothing kept secret except with the intention that it should be brought to light. [23] He who has ears to hear with, let him listen."

[24] And he addressed these further words to them: "Take care to understand the meaning of that which you hear. Whatever measure you deal out the same will be dealt out to you—and you will even receive something more besides. [25] And indeed, he who already has something, gifts will be made to him; while he who has nothing, even what he has shall be taken from him."

[26] He also spoke these words: "This is what the kingdom of God is like: as though a man had scattered seed over the land, [27] then slept during the night, and rose again the next day. Meanwhile the seed sprouts and grows—how, he does not know. [28] For the earth bears her fruit of her own accord. There is first the blade, then the ear, then the ripe grain in the ear. [29] When the crop is ready, the man at once [i]**puts in the sickle, because harvest time has come.**"

[30] And this is another thing he said: "How can we best find a comparison with the kingdom of God, and what kind of parable is there by which its nature may be suitably expressed? [31] It is like a mustard seed which, when it is sown in the soil, is smaller than all the other seeds on earth. [32] However, after it has been sown, it springs up and becomes larger than any garden herb. It puts forth branches of great size, so that [j]**the birds of the air** can find **shelter** in it."

[33] He had recourse to many other parables of this kind in proclaiming God's word to them, in so far as they were capable of comprehending it. [34] In fact, he said nothing to them except by means of parables.

[i]Jl 3:13   [j]Dn 4:12.21; Ezk 17:23; 31:6; [Ps 104:12]

As for his own disciples, on the other hand, he explained everything to them when they were alone.

[35] It was on the very same day that he said to them, as evening came, "Let us cross over to the other side." [36] At that, taking leave of the crowd, they took him, just as he was, along with them in the boat. Moreover, other boats were accompanying him. [37] Now a violent gale sprang up, and the waves beat upon the boat with such force that it was on the point of sinking. [38] And there he was in the stern sleeping, with his head on a pillow. They roused him, and said, "Master, are you not concerned that we are perishing?" [39] And he, being roused from sleep, administered a rebuke to the wind and said to the sea, "Silence; be still!" At that the wind ceased and a great stillness arose. [40] And these were his words to them: "Why are you such cowards; how is it that you have no faith?" [41] A feeling of great awe seized them, and they said to one another, "What kind of man is this, that even the wind and the sea obey his commands?"

5 On the other side of the lake they came to the country of the Gerasenes. [2] No sooner had Jesus got out of the boat than he encountered a man coming out of the tombs who was possessed of a tarnished spirit. [3] The man lived among the tombs. No one was able to keep him bound, not even by using a chain. [4] In fact, on many an occasion he had been bound by fetters or chains. Yet he tore the chains apart and broke the fetters in pieces. Thus no one had the power to gain the mastery over him. [5] There he was, night and day, among the tombs and in the hills, screaming and cutting himself with stones. [6] When he saw Jesus from a distance, he ran towards him, fell down at his feet, [7] and shouted out in a loud voice, [k] "**What do you want with me,** Jesus, Son of God Most High? In the name of God I adjure you not to torture me." [8] (It was Jesus' saying the words, "Come out of that man, you tarnished spirit," which made him act in this way.) [9] Then Jesus asked him what his name was, and this is what he answered: "My name is Legion, for there are many of us." [10] Besides, he made strong entreaty of Jesus that he would not send them out of the district. [11] Now in that place by the mountainside a large herd of swine was grazing. [12] The spirits made entreaty of Jesus, saying, "Send us into the swine; let us go into them." [13] He granted their request. So the tarnished spirits came out and went into the swine. The herd rushed headlong down the slope of the mountain into the lake, being about two thousand in number. And in the lake they were drowned.

[14] Those in charge of the swine took to flight, spreading the story in

[k] 1 K 17:18

the city and the surrounding country. And so people came out to see what had been happening. [15]They went up to Jesus, and saw that the man possessed of demons—the very man who had had the Legion in him—was sitting there properly clad and in his right mind. And they were terrified. [16]Those who had witnessed the scene related to the others what had befallen the man possessed of demons, and also what had happened to the swine. [17]At that they began to entreat Jesus that he depart from their district. [18]Moreover, as Jesus was getting into the boat, the man who had been possessed of demons appealed to him that he might let him go with him. [19]But Jesus would not let him, speaking to him thus: "Go back home to your own people and report to them what great things the Lord has done for you and how he took pity on you." [20]The man went off and began to spread throughout the Decapolis the news of what great things Jesus had done for him. And everybody was amazed.

[21]When Jesus had once again crossed over in the boat, a large crowd gathered together and came towards him. And as he was there by the lakeside, [22]one of the leaders of the synagogue, whose name was Jairus, came to him. When he saw Jesus, he threw himself at his feet [23]and made an urgent appeal to him in these words: "My little daughter is near to death. Come with me and lay your hands on her, so that she may regain her health and live." [24]So Jesus went, a large crowd following and pressing closely against him.

[25]Now in the crowd was a certain woman who had been suffering from continual bleeding for twelve years. [26]She had had much to bear at the hands of a large number of physicians and had spent all the money she had. However, instead of deriving benefit from this in any way, she had got worse. [27]She had heard what was being said about Jesus, so she came up behind him out of the crowd and touched his cloak. [28]For this is what she had been saying to herself: "If only I can touch his clothes with my hands, I shall have my health restored." [29]Instantly, the source of her bleeding dried up and, by a feeling she had in her body, she knew that she was healed of her affliction. [30]And Jesus, who immediately became assured in his mind that power had gone out of him, turned round in the crowd and said, "Who has touched my clothes?" [31]"You are aware," his disciples replied, "that the crowd is pressing closely on you. And yet you ask, 'Who touched me?'" [32]Jesus, however, kept looking round to see who had done it. [33]As for the woman, she was frightened and trembled all over, knowing full well what had happened to her. So she went towards him, fell at his feet, and told him the whole truth. [34]And this is what Jesus said to her: "My daughter, it is by your faith that your health has been restored. Go on your way in peace, and be rid of your affliction."

[35]While he was still speaking, certain people came from the house

of the leader of the synagogue with this message: "Your daughter is dead. Why should you trouble the master any longer?" 36But this is what Jesus, who had heard the words as they were being spoken, said to the leader of the synagogue: "Banish all fear; all you need is to have faith." 37Now he would not permit anyone to accompany him except Peter, James, and James' brother John. 38When they arrived at the house of the leader of the synagogue, Jesus became aware of a great commotion there, with people weeping and lamenting unrestrainedly. 39Going in, he said to them, "Why are you making such a commotion, and why are you crying? The child is not dead; only resting in sleep." But they just laughed at him. 40However, he removed them all and took with him only the child's father and mother as well as his own companions. And so he went to the place where the child was. 41He took the child by the hand and said to her, *"Talitha cum"*, which, correctly translated, means 'Little girl, I am telling you to rise up.' 42At that the little girl got up, immediately beginning to walk about, for she was twelve years old. People were quite beside themselves with amazement. 43As for Jesus, he gave them strict orders that nobody was to make this known, at the same time insisting that the girl was to be given something to eat.

6 He then left the place and went to his home town, being accompanied by his disciples. 2When the Sabbath came round, he set about teaching in the synagogue. The large company listening to him were filled with amazement, saying, "How do these things come to this man? What kind of wisdom has been granted to him? And what is to be made of miracles such as are performed by his hands? 3Is this not the carpenter, the son of Mary and the brother of James, Joseph, Judas, and Simon? Do we not have his sisters in our midst?" And so they took offence at him. 4And this is what Jesus said in reply: "There is only one place where a prophet is not honoured—in his home town, among those related to him, and in his own house." 5So it was that he lacked the power to perform miracles there, except that he healed a few of those beset by ill health through laying his hands on them. 6Furthermore, he was amazed at the people's want of faith.

The next thing he did was to go round from village to village to teach. 7Then he called the twelve disciples to his side, sent them forth in pairs, and invested them with authority over the tarnished spirits. 8Moreover, he instructed them to take nothing for the journey, a staff being the one exception: no bread, no knapsack, no money for their purses. 9They were to wear sandals, but they were not to take with them a second coat to put on. 10And he addressed these further words to them: "Whenever you enter a house, stay there until the time has come for you to leave the place. [11]And whatever place will not bid you welcome, and where people will not listen to you, take your departure from there, shaking off the dust from under your feet as a testimony against them." [12]The disciples went on their way proclaiming to the people that they were to repent. [13]Moreover, they cast out a large number of demonic spirits and anointed with oil many people who were beset by ill health, and brought them healing.

[14]Now King Herod heard about all this, since Jesus' name had by then become publicly known. Some people said, "John the Baptist has been raised from the dead, and that is why these wondrous powers are at work in him." [15]Some said he was Elijah, while others again said that he was a prophet like the prophets of old. [16]As for Herod, when he learned about this he said, "This is John, the man I have had beheaded; he has been raised to life."

[17]In fact, this same Herod had had John arrested and kept him bound in prison, all on account of Herodias, the wife of his brother Philip, whom Herod himself had married. [18]For John had said to Herod, "It is not permissible that you should have your brother's wife." [19]As for Herodias, she, having a grudge against him, wanted to kill him, but she had no power of accomplishing this. [20]For Herod, who knew John to be an upright and holy man, stood in awe of him and so gave him his protection. Having heard John speak, he remained in a state of great perplexity, while on the other hand it gave him great pleasure to listen to him.

[21]Opportunity soon presented itself. On his birthday Herod gave a banquet for his notables, his chief commanders, and the leading men of Galilee. [22]Herodias's daughter came in and performed a dance, which charmed Herod as well as those reclining with him at table. So the king said to the girl, "Ask of me whatever you like and I will give it to you." [23]And he swore this oath to her: [l]**"I shall give you whatever you ask of me, up to half of my kingdom."** [24]She went out, saying to her mother, "What am I to ask for?" the mother's reply being, "Ask for the head of John the Baptist." [25]So the girl hastened back to the king at once, making her request and saying, "It is my wish that you should let me have without the least delay the head of John the Baptist, placed on a dish." [26]As for the king, he was greatly distressed at this, but bearing in mind the oath he had sworn, as well as those reclining with him at table, he had no mind to break faith with her. [27]And so the king sent one of his bodyguards, giving the order that he was to bring John's head. The man went off, beheaded John in the prison, [28]brought the head placed on a dish, and gave it to the girl, who in turn gave it to her mother. [29]When John's disciples

[l]Est 5:3.6; 7:2

heard of this, they came along, removed John's body, and laid it in a tomb.

30 The apostles returned to Jesus, reporting to him what they had done and what they had taught. 31 And this is what he said to them: "Be on your way to a solitary place so that you may be by yourselves, and rest awhile." He said this because so many were coming and going that the apostles did not even have time to eat their food. 32 So they went off in the boat to a solitary place to be by themselves. 33 However, many people saw them depart and recognized them, and so, emerging from all the towns, they hurried towards the place on foot and reached it before the apostles did. 34 When Jesus got out of the boat, he saw a large crowd and was moved by pity for the people because they were **m like sheep having no shepherd**; and he began to teach them many things. 35 When the day was already far advanced, his disciples approached him and said to him, "This is a solitary place, and the day is already far advanced. 36 Dismiss the people and give them the opportunity to go to the hamlets and villages round about so as to buy themselves something to eat." 37 But Jesus replied, "Give them something to eat yourselves." "Are we to go off," they said, "to spend two hundred pieces of silver on bread, just to be able to give them something to eat?" 38 "How many loaves do you have?" he asked them. "Go and look for yourselves." And they, having found out, said to him, "We have five loaves and two fish." 39 At that he gave them the order to get all the people to sit down in parties on the green grass. 40 And so they reclined in groups of a hundred or of fifty each. 41 Then he took the five loaves and the two fish into his hands, looked up towards heaven, pronounced a blessing, and, breaking the loaves into pieces, handed them to his disciples, that they might set them before the people. He likewise distributed the two fish among them all. 42 So they all ate, and they all had their fill. 43 In fact, when the pieces left over were removed, there was enough to fill twelve baskets, and there was also what was left of the fish. 44 As for the men who had eaten of the loaves, they numbered five thousand.

45 Immediately after this Jesus made the insistent demand that the disciples were to cross over to the other side ahead of him, going to Bethsaida, while he would engage in the task of sending the crowds away. 46 He bade them farewell and then went up the hillside to pray. 47 When evening came, there was the boat in the middle of the lake, while he was alone on land. 48 He perceived that, the wind being contrary, they had to labour hard at the oars, and so, at about the fourth watch of the night, there was Jesus, making his way towards them, walking on the water of the lake. He made every sign that he was

m Nm 27:17; Ezk 34:5

76

going to pass them by. [49]But they, believing that what they were seeing was an apparition, cried out. [50]They all saw him and they were dismayed. But he, speaking to them at once, said to them, "Be of good courage; it is I; cast off all fear." [51]He went up into the boat with them, and the wind ceased. They were dumbfounded beyond all measure, [52]and that was because the incident of the loaves had not helped them to understand anything, their minds being dull of comprehension.

[53]Completing the crossing, they came ashore at Gennesaret and moored there. [54]When they got out of the boat, people recognized them at once. [55]So they rushed all over the district and began to carry about on pallets those who were sufferers from ill health, taking them to wherever they had heard Jesus was. [56]And this is what they did in whatever place he came to, be it a village, a town, or a hamlet. They would lay down the sick in the market place, while appealing to him to grant them one wish only, that he would let them touch the fringe of his cloak. And all who touched it found themselves restored to health.

7 On one occasion the Pharisees and certain of the experts in the law came to him from Jerusalem and gathered round him. [2]They became aware that some of his disciples sat at table with defiled hands, that is, without having washed them. [3](In fact, the Pharisees, and indeed all Jews, do not sit at table without first washing their hands thoroughly. They hold fast to the tradition handed on by the men of old, [4]and when they return from the market place they will not eat without performing an ablution. Besides, they have had many other things handed on to them to observe, such as the cleansing of cups, jugs, and copper bowls.) [5]Now this is the question the Pharisees and the experts in the law asked him: "Why do your disciples fail to conduct themselves in conformity with the traditions handed down by the men of old? Is it not true that, instead of doing so, they sit at table with hands defiled?" [6]And this is the reply Jesus made them: "How aptly did Isaiah prophesy about you, dissemblers that you are! For these are the words that stand written: [n]**This people pays honour to me with their lips. But as for their hearts, they are far away from me.** [7]**Their worship of me is to no purpose; and the precepts found in the doctrines they teach have their source in mere men.'** [8]Letting God's commandment fall by the wayside, you hold fast to a tradition having its source in mere men."

[9]And he added these words: "How skilful you are in setting God's commandment aside, so as to be able to conform to that tradition of

[n]Is 29:13 LXX

yours! [10]What Moses said was, *°'Pay honour to your father and to your mother'*, and '**He who speaks evil of his father or of his mother shall be punished by death'.** [11]But this is what you say: 'If a man declares to his father or his mother, "Anything of mine from which you might have profited is Corban"', that is to say, an offering set apart for God, [12]'then he is no longer permitted to do anything for his father or his mother.' [13]Thus you have made God's word null and void for the sake of the tradition handed on to you. And there are many similar things which you do."

[14]After that he called the crowd together, and said to them, "Listen to me, all of you, and come to understand. [15]Nothing that enters a man from outside him can defile him. What defiles a man is what comes out of him."*

[17]When he had separated himself from the crowd and gone into the house, his disciples questioned him about the meaning of the figurative saying which he had employed. [18]And this is the answer he made them: "Are you, too, without any comprehension? Do you not understand that whatever enters a man from the outside is incapable of defiling him? [19]And that is so because it does not enter his heart but his stomach, and is then passed out into the place set up for drainage." (In this way, then, he declared all foods to be clean.) [20]And he added these words: "What comes out of a man is that which defiles him. [21]For from the inside of the hearts of men come malicious thoughts and things such as these: fornication, theft, murder, adultery, [22]greed, evil intent, guile, debauchery, envy, slander, arrogance, and folly. [23]All these evil things come out of a man and defile him."

[24]Jesus then left that place and set out for the district of Tyre. He went into a certain house, and his wish was that no one should know him. However, it was impossible for him to remain hidden, [25]for a woman whose daughter was possessed of a tarnished spirit, as soon as she heard about him, came to him, throwing herself at his feet. [26]This woman, who was a Gentile, Syrophoenician by descent, appealed to him to drive the demonic spirit out of her daughter. [27]And he made her this reply: "You must first of all allow the children to have their fill. It is not right to take the children's bread away from them, throwing it to the dogs." [28]"How true that is, sir," said the woman in response; "and yet even the dogs eat of the morsels of the children's food from under the table." [29]And this is what he said to her: "Be on your way; seeing that you have spoken the way you have, the demonic spirit has come out of your daughter." [30]The woman

---

°Ex 20:12; 21:17; Dt 5:16

* V. 16 is probably not part of the original text.

went home and found the child lying in bed, and the demonic spirit had come out of her.

31 Leaving the district of Tyre once more, Jesus went by way of Sidon to the Sea of Galilee, right through the region of the Decapolis. 32 They brought a man to him who was deaf and hardly able to speak, and they appealed to him to lay his hands on him. 33 And he took him aside, away from the crowd, where they could be alone, put his fingers in the man's ears, spat out, and touched his tongue. 34 Then, looking up towards heaven, he sighed. *"Ephphatha"* is what he said to him, the meaning of this being, 'Be opened'. 35 At that his ears were opened, and that which had bound his tongue was loosed in an instant, and he began to speak properly. 36 Jesus gave strict orders to the others not to tell anybody; but the more insistent his orders the more eagerly they proclaimed the news. 37 Moreover, they were amazed beyond all measure, and this is what they said: "Everything he has done, he has done well. Why, he makes the deaf hear and the dumb speak."

8 On another occasion at about this time a large crowd had gathered and there was nothing for them to eat. So Jesus called his disciples to his side and addressed them thus: 2 "I am moved by pity for this crowd, because they have already been with me for three days and they have nothing to eat. 3 If I send them away hungry to their homes, they will find themselves overcome by weakness on the way. Indeed, some of them have come from a great distance." 4 The disciples made him the following reply: "How could anyone in this solitary place provide himself with a sufficient number of loaves to feed all these people?" 5 "How many loaves do you have?" he asked. "Seven," was their reply. 6 So Jesus gave the order to the crowd that they were to sit down on the ground. He then took the seven loaves into his hands, gave thanks to God, broke the food into pieces, and handed it to his disciples to set before the people. And they did set it before the crowd. 7 They also had a few small fish; and Jesus, invoking a blessing, ordered the disciples to set these before the people as well. 8 They ate and they had their fill. Indeed, when the pieces left over were removed, there were seven basketfuls. 9 Now the people present numbered about four thousand. 10 Jesus dismissed them and at once got into a boat with his disciples, making for the district of Dalmanutha.

11 Then the Pharisees came forward and began to engage in discussion with him, demanding that he should let them have a sign from heaven. It was to put him to the test that they acted in this way. 12 And heaving a heavy sigh within himself, he exclaimed, "Why is it that this generation demands a sign? Indeed, I can give you solemn assurance

of this. This generation shall have no sign vouchsafed to it." [13]With that he left them and, embarking once again, went over to the other side.

[14]Now they had forgotten to take bread with them; they had but a single loaf with them in the boat. [15]Jesus, for his part, gave them strict warning in these words: "Look out and be on your guard against the leaven there is in the Pharisees, against the leaven there is in Herod." [16]And they reasoned with one another, saying, "It is our not having brought any bread that he has in mind." [17]Being well aware of this, he spoke to them thus: "Why are you reasoning with one another in this way, while imagining that what I had in mind was your not having brought any loaves of bread? Do you still not understand? Are you still without comprehension? Have you minds that are altogether dull? [18]Or is it that [p]**having eyes you do not see, and having ears you do not hear?** Do you fail to remember? [19]When I broke the five loaves for the five thousand how many basketfuls of pieces left over did you collect?" "Twelve," they replied. [20]"And when I broke the seven loaves for the four thousand, how many basketfuls of broken pieces did you collect?" "Seven," was their answer. [21]"Are you still without comprehension?" he said.

[22]They reached Bethsaida, and there some people brought to him a blind man and requested that he should touch his eyes. [23]He took the blind man by the hand, led him outside the village, and applied spittle to his eyes. Then, laying his hands on him, he asked, "Can you see anything?" [24]And he, beginning to recover his sight, said, "I can see men looking like trees but walking about." [25]At that, Jesus laid his hands on his eyes once again. Then the man, on opening his eyes wide, found himself restored and was able to see everything plainly. [26]As for Jesus, he sent him back to his own home with the words, "Do not so much as enter the village."

[27]At one time Jesus and his disciples were making their way towards the villages in the neighbourhood of Caesarea Philippi. As they went along, Jesus asked this question of his disciples: "Who do people say that the Son of Man is?" [28]"Some say," they replied, "that he is John the Baptist, some that he is Elijah, others that he is one of the prophets." [29]"But you yourselves," he asked, "who do you say that I am?" "You are God's anointed," was Peter's reply. [30]At that he gave them stern warning not to talk about him to anyone. [31]This was the time when Jesus began to teach them that the Son of Man was destined to undergo great sufferings, to be repudiated by the elders of the people, the chief priests as well as by the experts in the law, to be put to death, and then to rise up again after three days. [32]What he said, he said quite openly. But Peter, taking him aside, began to remonstrate

[p]Jr 5:21; Ezk 12:2

with him. [33] At that, Jesus turned round, and when his eyes fell on his disciples he remonstrated with Peter, saying, "Out of sight, Satan, get right behind me, because the thoughts you harbour are not those of God but those of men."

[34] It was after this that Jesus called the crowds to his side, and his disciples with them, and addressed them thus: "If anyone is desirous to walk in my steps, he must set his own self at nought, take up the burden of my cross,* and follow me. [35] In fact, anyone desirous to save his life will suffer the loss of it, while if there be someone losing his life, for my sake and that of the gospel, he will save it. [36] Indeed, what advantage will a man reap if he gains the whole world, yet suffers the loss of his true self? [37] Or what is there a man can offer in exchange for his self? [38] Truth to tell, if there be someone, amidst this disloyal and sinful generation, who is ashamed of me, as well as of the words I utter, the Son of Man will be ashamed of him at the time when, accompanied by his holy angels, he makes his appearance invested with his Father's glorious majesty." [9:1] And he said another thing to them: "Indeed, I can give you solemn assurance of this. Among those standing here are some who will not have tasted death before they have seen the kingdom of God making its appearance in all its power."

9 [2] Six days afterwards Jesus took Peter, James, and John with him and led them up a high mountain, where they might be all alone. There, before their very eyes, he was transformed. [3] His clothes turned brilliantly white, of a whiteness such as no fuller on earth would be able to achieve. [4] Then Elijah appeared to them, and Moses with him. And there they were engaged in conversation with Jesus. [5] Whereupon Peter addressed Jesus in these words: "Master, how good it is to be here. So let us set up three places of shelter, one for you, one for Moses, and one for Elijah." [6] (He was in fact at a loss what to do or say, for they were overcome by fear.) [7] Then a cloud appeared, casting its shadow over them, and there was a voice coming from the cloud calling out the words, "This is my [q]**Son, my dearly-loved one; lend your ear to him.**" [8] Then, all of a sudden, as they were looking round, they no longer saw anyone; no one was with them except Jesus only.

[9] As they were coming down the mountain, he warned them sternly not to tell anyone of what they had seen until after the Son of Man had risen from the dead. [10] So they kept to themselves what he had

[q] Ps 2:7; Gn 22:2; Dt 18:15

* [Lit. 'He must take up his cross'. See the note on Mt. 16:24.]

said, while at the same time discussing among themselves what this 'rising from the dead' could possibly mean. [11]Moreover, there is one thing they did ask him: "Why do the experts in the law maintain that it is preordained that Elijah must appear first of all?" [12]And this is what he said to them: "True, ʳ**Elijah** appears, first of all, and brings the **restoration** of everything. Yet, if this is so, how is it that the scriptures say of the Son of Man that he will have to undergo great suffering and be treated with contempt? [13]But what I am saying to you is this: Elijah has already appeared, and they dealt with him just as they chose, as it is written about him in scripture."

[14]On rejoining the other disciples, they saw that a large crowd was surrounding them, and that experts in the law were there engaged in discussion with them. [15]As soon as they saw him, the whole of the crowd was overcome with awe, and running towards him, they bade him welcome. [16]"What are you discussing with them?" asked Jesus; [17]and one of the crowd made him this answer: "Master, I brought my son to you. He is possessed of a spirit inducing dumbness. [18]It dashes him to the ground whenever it seizes him; then he foams at the mouth, gnashes his teeth, and goes rigid. I appealed to your disciples to cast the spirit out, but they lacked the power to do so." [19]And this is what Jesus said to them in reply: "Unbelieving generation that you are! How long shall I have to remain in your company? How long shall I have to bear with you? Bring him to me." [20]So they brought the boy to him. As for the spirit, no sooner did it see Jesus than it threw the boy into convulsions; and he fell to the ground and rolled about, foaming at the mouth. [21]At that, Jesus asked the boy's father, "How long has he been in this condition?" "From childhood," the father replied; [22]"and many a time the spirit has thrown him into fire or water to make an end of him. But if you are able, come to our aid, taking pity on us." [23]"As for your words, 'If you are able'," Jesus said to them, "he who has faith is able to do anything." [24]At that the father of the boy immediately cried out, "I have faith; be my helper where there is still a lack of faith in me." [25]On becoming aware that a crowd was running towards them from all sides, Jesus administered a rebuke to the tarnished spirit. And this is what he said: "You dumb and deaf spirit, I command you to come out of him and never enter him again." [26]The spirit, crying out and throwing him into violent convulsions, came out, while the boy looked so much like a corpse that many said that he had died. [27]However, Jesus took him by the hand, raised him up, and put him on his feet.

[28]On his having returned home, the disciples asked him, when they

ʳMal 4:5

were by themselves, "Why were we powerless to cast the spirit out?" 29 And this is the reply he made them: "There is no means but prayer of casting out this sort of spirit."

30 Then they left the place and journeyed through Galilee, as Jesus did not want anyone to know him. 31 For he was occupied with teaching his disciples, and this is what he said to them: "The Son of Man will be given into the power of men. They will put him to death, and after he has been put to death, he will rise up again after three days." 32 As for his disciples, they did not understand what was being said to them but they were afraid to ask.

33 They came to Capernaum, and there, on finding himself indoors, Jesus asked them the question, "What were you discussing while we were on the way?" 34 They said nothing because what they had been discussing among themselves was which of them was the greatest. 35 And he, sitting down, called the twelve disciples to his side and spoke to them thus: "If any of you wishes to come first, he must be last of all and servant of all." 36 At that he took a child to himself, placed it right in their midst, and, enfolding it in his arms, addressed these words to them: 37 "Whoever gives a welcome to one of these children, and does so for my name's sake, gives a welcome to me; and whoever gives a welcome to me gives a welcome not to me but to him who has sent me forth."

38 On one occasion John said to him, "Master, we have seen a certain man—not one of our company—casting out demonic spirits in your name. And because he is not of our company, we forbade him to do so." 39 "Cease hindering him," replied Jesus, "for no one performing a miracle in my name can then turn round quickly and speak evil of me. 40 Indeed, he who is not against us is on our side.

41 "If anyone gives you a cup of water to drink because of the name you bear, being followers of God's anointed, I can indeed give you solemn assurance of this: he will by no means suffer the loss of the reward due to him.

42 "And again, if anyone provides an occasion for sinning to one of those little ones who believe in me, it would be better for him that he should be thrown into the sea with a heavy millstone put round his neck.

43 "And then this: if your hand should provide you with an occasion for sinning, cut if off. It is better for you to find entry, crippled, into the place where true life is to be found than, having two hands, to make your way to hell, into the unquenchable fire.* 45 Again, if your foot leads you into sin, cut it off. It is better for you to find entry into the place where true life is to be found, even though you are lame,

* V. 44 is probably not part of the original text.

than, possessing two feet, to be thrown into hell.* [47] And again, if your eye leads you into sin, throw it away. It is better for you to find entry into the kingdom of God with only one eye than, possessing two eyes, to be thrown into hell, [48]where the *worm devouring **them does not die nor is the fire ever quenched.**

[49]"And indeed, fire will be everyone's seasoning.

[50]"Salt is indeed a useful thing. But if salt itself loses its saltiness, with what will you season it? You must have salt in yourselves and be at peace with one another."

10 On leaving those parts, Jesus came to the regions of Judaea and that on the far side of the Jordan. Crowds were once again flocking towards him and, as was his custom, he engaged in teaching them. [2]It was then that the Pharisees approached him, the point which they questioned him about being whether it was permissible for a man to send his wife away. It was with a view to putting him to the test that they did this. [3]And Jesus asked them this question in return: "What did Moses command you to do?" [4]"Moses," they said, "permitted a man to *t*write his wife **a writ of dismissal and** then **send her away."** [5]"It is because of the coldness of your hearts," was Jesus' reply, "that Moses wrote this commandment for you. [6]Yet this is how things stood from the very beginning of the world: 'He *u***made them male and female,** [7]and **for this reason a man will leave his father and mother and be joined to his wife,** [8]**the two of them becoming a single body'.** So it is that they are no longer two bodies but a single one. [9]Well then, let no man separate those whom God has joined together."

[10]When they were at home again, the disciples asked him a question about this matter. [11]And this is what he said to them in reply: "Any man who sends his wife away and marries another commits adultery against her; [12]and if a woman sends her husband away and marries another man, she commits adultery."

[13]People brought children into his presence that he might touch them with his hands. His disciples administered a rebuke to them. [14]Yet Jesus, on becoming aware of this, became indignant and spoke to them thus: "Let the children come to me, and do not prevent them. For it is to such as these that the kingdom of God belongs. [15]Indeed, I can give you solemn assurance of this. He who does not accept the kingdom of God in the way in which a child would, will never find

*s*Is 66:24   *t*Dt 24:1.3   *u*Gn 1:27; 2:24

* V. 46 is probably not part of the original text.

84

entry into it." [16] Then he enfolded the children in his arms and, speaking a blessing over them, he laid his hands on them.

[17] On one occasion when he was setting out on a journey, a certain man came up to him and asked him this question: "Good master, what do I have to do so as to secure for myself possession of everlasting life?" [18] "Why do you call me good?" Jesus said in reply. "There is only one that is good: God himself. [19] The commandments are known to you: [v] **Do not do murder; do not commit adultery; do not steal; do not give false testimony;** do not defraud anyone; **pay honour to your father and to your mother'**." [20] "Master," replied the other, "all these have I kept since I was but a child." [21] Jesus fixed his gaze upon him, and then, being filled with love for him, he said, "One thing you still lack. Sell everything that you have and give the proceeds to the poor. Then a treasure shall be yours, a treasure in heaven. After that come to my side and follow me." [22] At these words the man's face fell, and he went on his way full of sorrow, for he had great possessions.

[23] Jesus looked round at his disciples and then addressed these words to them: "With what great obstacles in their way will those who have money find entry into the kingdom of God!" [24] The disciples were amazed at what he said, but Jesus, resuming, spoke to them thus: "My children, how great is the obstacle placed in the way of those who seek entry into the kingdom of God! [25] Why, it is easier for a camel to slip through the eye of a needle than it is for a rich man to find entry into the kingdom of God." [26] At that the disciples were all the more astounded, and this is what they said to one another: "Who, then, is capable of obtaining salvation?" [27] And Jesus, fixing his gaze upon them, made this reply: "Such a thing is indeed impossible for men, but not so for God. [w] **Everything is possible for God.**"

[28] At that, Peter began to speak to him in this way: "Here we are, having given up everything we possessed and become your followers." [29] And Jesus said to him in reply, "Indeed, I can give you solemn assurance of this. There is no one who has given up his house, or his brothers, or his sisters, or his mother, or his father, or his children, or his field, having done so for my sake and that of the gospel, [30] who will not find himself repaid a hundred times over in this order of things—receiving houses, brothers, sisters, mother, children, fields, yes, and suffering persecution as well—while in the world to come having everlasting life bestowed upon him. [31] And indeed, many that took first place will be last; many that took last place will be first."

[32] They were on their way up to Jerusalem, and Jesus was walking at the head of them. Bewilderment filled their minds, and the people

[v] Ex 20:12-16; Dt 5:16-20   [w] Gn 18:14; Job 42:2; Zc 8:6 LXX

following on were apprehensive. So Jesus once more took the Twelve aside and began to tell them of the things which would happen to him. ³³ And this is what he said: "Here we are, on our way up to Jerusalem, and what will happen is that the Son of Man will be handed over to the chief priests and the experts in the law; they will pronounce a sentence of death on him, and they will hand him over to the Gentiles. ³⁴They will sneer at him, spit in his face, flog him, and put him to death. And after three days he will rise up again."

³⁵James and John, the two sons of Zebedee, came up to him and said, "Master, it is our wish that you should do for us whatever we ask of you." ³⁶"What do you wish that I should do for you?" he replied. ³⁷"Grant it to us," they said, "that when you are in your state of glory we are to sit beside you, one on the right side and the other on the left." ³⁸"You do not know what you are asking," was Jesus' reply to them. "Do you have the strength to drink the cup which I am drinking, or to undergo the baptism which I am undergoing?" "We do have it," was their answer. ³⁹And this is what Jesus said to them: "You shall indeed drink the cup that I am drinking and undergo the baptism I am undergoing. ⁴⁰Yet, as to having seats on my right hand or on my left, it is not for me to bestow this. It will be granted to those who have been destined for it beforehand."

⁴¹When the other ten disciples heard of this, they began to be filled with indignation against James and John. ⁴²And Jesus, calling them to himself, addressed them thus: "You know that those who are acknowledged as bearing rule over the Gentiles lord it over them, and that their great ones act in a tyrannical way. ⁴³This is not how things stand as regards yourselves. On the contrary, if anyone among you should wish to rank high, he must be your servant; ⁴⁴and if he wishes to come first, he must be everyone's slave. ⁴⁵Indeed, the Son of Man made his appearance not to be served but to serve, offering up his very life as a ransom paid on behalf of a multitude of men."

⁴⁶They arrived at Jericho; and as Jesus was coming out of the town with his disciples and a large crowd there was a blind beggar, Bartimaeus the son of Timaeus, sitting by the roadside. ⁴⁷When he heard that it was Jesus of Nazareth, he began to cry out and exclaim, "Jesus, son of David, take pity on me!" ⁴⁸And many there administered a rebuke to him, seeking to make him hold his peace. But he cried out all the louder, "Jesus, son of David, take pity on me!" ⁴⁹Jesus stopped and said, "Call him to my side." So they called the blind man, saying to him, "Courage; rise up; he is calling for you." ⁵⁰The beggar, throwing off his cloak, leapt to his feet and went up to Jesus. ⁵¹"What would you have me do for you?" Jesus asked him in response to this. "Make me see again, Master," was the blind man's reply. ⁵²So Jesus said to him, "Be on your way; it is by your faith that your health has been re-

stored." At this, he regained his sight in an instant and followed Jesus along the road.

11 As they were drawing near Jerusalem and reached Bethphage and Bethany at the Mount of Olives, Jesus sent two of his disciples on an errand, ²giving them these instructions: "Make your way to the village that lies opposite you. As soon as you enter it, you will find a tethered colt on which as yet no one has ever ridden. Untie it and bring it to me. ³If someone says to you, 'Why are you doing this?' let this be your answer: 'The master has need of it, and he will send it back to this place without delay'." ⁴So they went off and, finding a colt tethered close to a doorway in the open street, they untied it. ⁵Some of the men standing there asked them, "What are you about, untying that colt?" ⁶The disciples spoke to them as Jesus had told them they should, and the men let them have their way. ⁷So they brought the colt to Jesus and spread their cloaks over it. And he sat down on it. ⁸Moreover, many spread their cloaks on the road, while others spread leafy branches which had been cut from the fields. ⁹And both those who went on ahead and those who were following on behind cried out, ˣ**"Hosanna! A blessing rests on him who appears in the name of the Lord!** ¹⁰A blessing rests on the kingdom to come, that of David our forefather! **Hosanna** in the highest heaven!"

¹¹Jesus made his entry into Jerusalem and went into the temple. He looked round at everything that was there, but since it was already late in the day he went out to Bethany, accompanied by the twelve disciples.

¹²The next day, when they were on their way back from Bethany, he was feeling hungry. ¹³And when, from some distance away, his eyes fell upon a fig tree in leaf, he went towards it to see if he could find anything on it. However, when he got to it, he found nothing but leaves; for it was not the season for figs. ¹⁴And he reacted by addressing the tree in these words: "May no one ever again eat fruit from you." As for his disciples, they heard what he was saying.

¹⁵So they came to Jerusalem, and he, going into the temple, began to drive out of it those who were buying and selling their goods there. He overturned the tables of the money changers and likewise the seats of those selling pigeons. ¹⁶Moreover, he would not allow anyone to carry his wares through the temple. ¹⁷And he began to teach, addressing these words to them: "Does not scripture say, ʸ**My house shall be known as a house of prayer for all peoples'**; but you have turned it into ᶻ**a robbers' den**?" ¹⁸The chief priests and the experts in the law,

ˣPs 118:25f   ʸIs 56:7   ᶻJr 7:11

on hearing of this, looked out for means of making an end of him, frightened of him as they were, for the entire populace was carried away by the amazement they felt at his way of teaching. ¹⁹As for Jesus, when evening came he went out of the city.

²⁰The next morning, as they were passing by the fig tree, they saw that it had withered away to its roots, ²¹and so Peter, calling to mind what had happened, said to Jesus, "Look, Master, the fig tree which you cursed has withered away!" ²²And this is the reply Jesus made them: "Have faith in God. ²³Indeed, I can give you solemn assurance of this. If anyone says to this mountain here, 'Lift yourself up and throw yourself into the sea', and does so with no doubt in his heart, but confident that what he is saying will happen, he shall have it granted to him. ²⁴This is why I am saying to you, whatever you pray for, whatever request you make, be confident that you have obtained it, and you shall have it granted to you. ²⁵Moreover, whenever you stand up to give yourself to prayer, should you have anything to complain of against someone, forgive it, so that your Father may likewise forgive you your wrongs against him."*

²⁷They found themselves once again in Jerusalem. And as Jesus was walking about in the temple, the chief priests, the experts in the law, and the elders of the people came up to him. ²⁸And this is the question they put to him: "What kind of authority makes you act in this way, and from whom does the authority making you act in this way derive?" ²⁹And this is what Jesus said to them: "I, too, will ask you a question. Answer it properly and I, in turn, will tell you by whose authority I am acting in this manner. ³⁰Where did the baptism administered by John come from? Did it have its source in God or in men? Give me your answer." ³¹At that they set about reasoning the matter out with one another, their words being these: "If we say, 'In God', then he will ask us, 'Why, then, did you refuse to trust him?' ³²Are we to say, then, that it had its source in men?" But in fact they were afraid of the people. For they all held that John was a true prophet. ³³So the answer they made to Jesus was, "We do not know." And Jesus said to them, "Neither shall I tell you by whose authority I am acting in the way I do."

12 Then Jesus set out to address them by means of parables: "A certain man *ᵃplanted a vineyard, put a fence round it, dug out a trough for the winepress, and built a tower.* Then he hired it out to

ᵃIs 5:1f

* V. 26 is probably not part of the original text.

certain vinegrowers, and went off to another country. [2]Later, when the proper time for this had come, he sent out one of his servants to the vinegrowers for the purpose of collecting from them his share of the vineyard's produce. [3]The vinegrowers, however, caught hold of him, gave him a thrashing, and sent him away empty-handed. [4]And a second time the owner sent a servant to them. But him they struck on the head, treating him in a most humiliating manner. [5]He sent still another, and him they put to death. There were many others, and to some of them they gave a thrashing, and some of them they put to death. [6]He had only one left to send, his dearly-loved son. In the end he did send him, saying to himself, 'They will be moved by respect for my son'. [7]However, what these vinegrowers did was to say to one another, 'This man is the heir. Come on then, let us kill him, and the inheritance will be ours'. [8]So they got hold of him, put him to death, and threw the body out of the vineyard. [9]Now what do you think the owner of the vineyard will do? He will come himself and make an end of these vinegrowers, handing over the vineyard to others. [10]And indeed, have you never read this passage from scripture: [b]**The very stone which the builders rejected has become the cornerstone.** [11]**This was the Lord's doing, and how wonderful it is in our eyes.'?"**

[12]They sought for appropriate means of having Jesus seized by force, for they knew well enough that the parable was directed against them. However, they were afraid of the populace, so they left him alone and went on their way.

[13]They sent to him a number of Pharisees as well as certain adherents of Herod's party with the intention of catching him out in something he might say. [14]And this is what they said when they made their appearance: "Master, we know how sincere you are, and that you court no man's favour. Indeed, you show no undue preference for anyone, but teach the way of life required by God with complete honesty. Is it permissible, we would ask you, to pay tax to the Emperor? Are we to pay, or are we not to pay?" [15]But Jesus, well aware of their hypocrisy, said, "Why are you putting me to the test? Bring me a silver piece, that I may see for myself." [16]They brought one, and he said to them, "Whose head and whose inscription is this?" "The Emperor's," they replied. [17]"Pay the Emperor what is due to the Emperor," said Jesus, "and pay God what is due to God." And they were lost in amazement at him.

[18]A number of Sadducees came to him one day—the men who maintain that there is no such thing as a resurrection of the dead— and asked him a question. [19]"Master," they said, "Moses has laid down in writing the following commandment for us: [c]**If a man's**

[b]Ps 118:22f   [c]Dt 25:5f; Gn 38:8

brother dies and leaves a wife behind **but no children,** it is the **brother's** duty to **marry the widow, raising offspring on his brother's behalf.'** [20]Now there were seven brothers. The first married a woman and died without leaving offspring. [21]The second married her and died, not leaving offspring. It was the same with the third. [22]In fact, the seven left no offspring. Last of all, the woman likewise died. [23]Whose wife will the woman be at the resurrection, when they rise up again, seeing that she had been married to all seven?" [24]And Jesus made them this reply: "Is not this the reason why you are going astray, that you have no proper comprehension of either the scriptures or of the power of God? [25]Indeed, when they rise from the dead, men and women neither marry nor are joined together in marriage. Their nature is like that of the angels in heaven.

[26]"Moreover, as for the dead being raised to life, have you not read in the Book of Moses, in the passage about the bush, how God addressed these words to Moses: [d]**'I am the God of Abraham, the God of Isaac, and the God of Jacob'?** [27]Now God is God not of the dead, but of the living. You are greatly misguided."

[28]Now there was a certain expert in the law who had heard them dispute with one another and who realized how well Jesus had answered them. He went up to him and asked him this question: "Which of the commandments comes first of them all?" [29]"This," said Jesus in reply, "is the first commandment: [e]**'Listen, Israel, the Lord our God is the one and only Lord.** [30]**And you are to love the Lord your God with all your heart, with all your soul,** with all your mind, **and with all your strength'.** [31]And this is the commandment which comes second: [f]**'You are to love your neighbour as yourself'** . There is no other commandment greater than these." [32] At that the expert in the law said to him, "Well spoken, Master, what you have said is the very truth: He is [g]the one and only one, and there is no other besides him. [33]Moreover, **to love him with all one's heart, with all one's understanding, with all one's strength,** and, further, **to love one's neighbour as oneself**—that far surpasses in worth any [h]**holocaust* or sacrifice".** [34]When Jesus perceived how thoughtfully he had answered, he said to him, "You are not far from the kingdom of God." And after that no one had the courage to ask him any further questions.

[35]When engaged in teaching in the temple, Jesus took up a different point, and this is what he said: "How is it that the experts in the law maintain that God's anointed is a descendant of David's? [36]After

---

[d]Ex 3:2.6.15   [e]Dt 6:4f   [f]Lv 19:18   [g][Dt 4:35; 6:4; Is 45:21]   [h]1 Sm 15:22; Ps 40:6

* [I.e., whole burnt offerings.]

all, this is what David himself said under the impulse of the Holy Spirit, [i]**The Lord said to my Lord: "Take your seat at my right hand until I make your enemies a footstool for your feet"**'. [37]In other words, David himself calls him Lord. How then can he be a descendant of his?"

The large crowd that was listening to him did so gladly. [38]And this is something he said in the course of his teaching: "Beware of the experts in the law who take delight in strutting about in their flowing robes and in exchanging greetings in the market place, [39]in obtaining the best seats in the synagogues, and in securing the places of honour at banquets. [40]These are the men who swallow up the property of widowed women and who engage in lengthy prayers for the sake of appearances. The sentence they have to expect will be all the heavier for that."

[41]On one occasion he was sitting right opposite the receptacle set up for the contributions and watching how the crowd put their money into the receptacle. A good many rich people put in a great deal. [42]But then a poverty-stricken widow appeared who put in two tiny coins, the equivalent of a farthing. [43]At that he called the apostles to his side and addressed them thus: "Indeed, I can give you solemn assurance of this. That widow, poor as she is, has put in more than any of the others did. [44]For what they put in came in every case out of a superfluity of means, while what she put in came out of her insufficiency of means. In point of fact, she put in all she possessed, indeed everything she had to keep herself alive."

13 As he was leaving the temple, one of his disciples said to him, "Look, Master, what magnificent stones, what magnificent buildings these are!" [2]And this is what Jesus said to him: "You are gazing at these large buildings, are you not? Not a single stone will be left standing on another. It will all be thrown down."

[3]Later, when he was on the Mount of Olives, sitting opposite the temple, Peter, James, John, and Andrew asked him, in private, this question: [4]"Will you tell us when these things will happen and what will be the sign indicating that all things are about to be accomplished?" [5]And Jesus set out to speak to them in this way: "Take care that no one leads you astray. [6]Indeed, many will appear, making use of my name. They will say, 'It is I', and they will lead you astray. [7]If you are told of wars and of rumours of wars, make sure that you are not thrown into a panic. [j]**It is preordained that these things should happen,** while it is true at the same time that the end does not

[i]Ps 110:1   [j]Dn 2:28

come immediately after that. [8][k]**One nation will rise up in arms against another nation, and one kingdom against another kingdom.** There will be earthquakes, there will be famines, in place after place. This is how the birth pangs of the new age will begin.

[9]"Take care of yourselves. They will hand you over to their courts, they will have you flogged in their synagogues, and you will have to appear, on my behalf, before governors and kings to bear testimony before them. [10]Indeed, what is necessary first of all is that the gospel should be proclaimed to all nations. [11]Moreover, when they lead you away to hand you over, do not consider anxiously beforehand what you are to say. Use what words are given you when the time comes, because it will not be you yourselves but the Holy Spirit who will be doing the speaking. [12]Brother will betray brother to have him given over to death. The father will betray his child. [l]**Children will rise up against their parents** and put them to death. [13]As for yourselves, you will be hated by everybody because of your allegiance to the cause which bears my name. And yet, if a man remains steadfast to the last, salvation shall be his.

[14]"When you see the [m]**detestable thing of which the desolation comes,** taking up its stand in a place where it ought not to be—let him who reads this ponder it—those who find themselves in Judaea should flee into the mountains; [15]he who finds himself on the roof must not come down, entering his house to fetch his possessions from it; [16]and he who finds himself in the field must not turn back to collect his cloak. [17]Alas for women with child in those days, and for those who have infants at the breast! [18]Pray that it will not happen in wintertime. [19]For those days will bring [n]**such affliction as there has never been to the present day** since the beginning of the world which God created, nor ever shall be again. [20]In fact, but for the Lord's shortening these days no creature of flesh and blood would be able to survive. Yet the truth is that, on behalf of the elect whom he chose for himself, he has shortened the days.

[21]"If anyone says to you at that time, 'Look, here is God's anointed,' 'Look, there he is,' do not believe it. [22]False Christs and [o]**false prophets** will appear, **showing forth signs and portents** such as, were it possible, would have the power of misleading even the elect. [23]As for yourselves, be on your guard. I have given you warning of it all.

[24]"But this is what will happen after that time of affliction in those days: [p]**The sun will be darkened, and the moon will not send forth her light.** [25][q]**The stars will be falling from the sky, and the hosts which have their dwelling in the heavens** will be made to totter.

[k]Is 19:2; 2 Ch 15:6   [l]Mic 7:6   [m]Dn 9:27; 11:31; 12:1.11   [n]Dn 12:1; Jl 2:2   [o]Dt 13:2
[p]Is 13:10   [q]Is 34:4

26Then people will see ʳ**the Son of Man appearing in the clouds,** equipped with great power and majesty. 27It will be then that he will send forth the angels and ˢ**gather together** his chosen ones from the **four** corners from which the **winds** blow, **from the ends of the earth to the ends of heaven.**

28"Let the fig tree serve you as a simile teaching you a lesson. When its branches have become tender and it puts forth leaves, you know that summer is near. 29In the same way, when you see these things coming about, you may be certain that he is close to you, standing at the very doors. 30Indeed, I can give you solemn assurance that this generation will not have passed away before all this has taken place. 31Heaven and earth will pass away, but my words will not pass away.

32"As for the day or the hour when these things will be, no one knows about this, neither the angels in heaven nor the Son. Only the Father knows.

33"Be on the alert; be wakeful; you do not know when the time appointed for this will come. 34It is as though a man were away on a journey. He has left his house and put his servants in charge, assigning to each his proper task, and he has ordered his doorkeeper to keep awake. 35Keep awake, then. You do not know at what time the master of the house will return, whether it will be evening, midnight, cockcrow, or morning. 36See to it that he does not come home suddenly and find you asleep. 37And what I say to you I say to everyone: Keep awake."

14 It was now no more than two days till the Passover and the Feast of Unleavened Bread; and the chief priests and the experts in the law were looking out for means of catching hold of Jesus by way of trickery and putting him to death. 2And this is what they said: "It must not be during the festival, to make sure that there is no uproar among the people."

3On one occasion, when Jesus was at Bethany sitting at table in the house of Simon the leper, a woman made her appearance. She had with her a small flask containing ointment of nard unadulterated and of the most precious kind; and breaking open the flask, she poured the contents over his head. 4Now certain people were there who were full of indignation at this, and they said to one another, "Why this waste? 5It would have been possible to sell this ointment for more than three hundred pieces of silver, the proceeds being given to the poor." So they gave her a severe scolding. 6And this is what Jesus said to them: "Why are you causing trouble for her? She has done a noble work on my behalf. 7As for the poor, there never will be a time when

ʳDn 7:13   ˢZc 2:6; Dt 30:4

you will not have them with you, and you will be able to do good to them whenever you wish. But me you will not always have. 8She has done what lay in her power, anointing my body beforehand to prepare it for burial. 9Indeed, I can give you solemn assurance of this. Wherever in the whole world the gospel is proclaimed, her deed will be spoken of as a memorial offered to her."

10At that, Judas Iscariot, one of the twelve disciples, went off to make an approach to the chief priests, with the intention of handing Jesus over to them. 11When they learned of this, they were overjoyed and made the promise to give him money. So Judas began to look out for an opportunity of betraying him.

12On the first day of the Feast of Unleavened Bread—at the time of the slaughtering of the Passover lamb—his disciples asked him, "Where do you want us to go to make our preparations so that you are able to eat the Passover meal?" 13So he sent out two of his disciples, addressing these words to them: "Make your way into the city, where you will encounter a certain man carrying a water jar. 14Follow him, and then say to the owner of whatever house he enters, 'This is the message the Master is sending you: "Where is the guest room in which I may eat the Passover meal with my disciples?"' 15Then he himself will show you a large room in the upper part of the house, all set out and made ready. Prepare the meal for us there." 16So the disciples went on their way, came into the city, and found things just as he had told them. And they prepared the Passover meal.

17When evening came, Jesus arrived at the place in the company of the twelve disciples. 18While they were at table, having their food, Jesus said to them, "Indeed, I can give you solemn assurance of this. One of you will betray me, the one who is *t*eating in my company." 19Thereupon they began to feel grieved and said to him, one after the other, "Surely it is not I." 20"One of the Twelve it will be," he said to them in reply; "the man who dips his hand into the dish at the same time as I do. 21For this is how matters stand. The Son of Man, as has indeed been foretold about him in scripture, goes on his way. Still, woe upon that man by whom the Son of Man is betrayed. It would be better for that man if he had never been born."

22While they were partaking of their food, Jesus laid hold of some bread and, having spoken a blessing over it, he broke it into pieces, handed it to them, and said, "Take it; this is my body." 23Moreover, having seized a cup with his hands, he gave thanks to God. Then he handed it to them, and they all drank out of it. 24And this is what he said to them: "This is my *u*blood sealing the covenant, my blood which is being poured out on behalf of multitudes. 25Indeed, I can

*t*Ps 41:9   *u*Ex 24:8; Zc 9:11

give you solemn assurance of this. No longer shall I drink of the produce of the vine until the day comes when I drink it, as something altogether new, in the kingdom of God." 26Then, after the hymn-singing,* they made their way to the Mount of Olives.

27 And this is what Jesus said to them: "You will all take offence and fall away, for this is what stands written in scripture: *v***'I shall strike the shepherd, and the sheep shall be scattered far and wide'.** 28However, after I have been raised to life again, I shall make my way into Galilee ahead of you." 29 At that, Peter said to him, "Even though they should, one and all, take offence and fall away, I shall never do so." 30 And Jesus said to him, "Indeed, I can give you solemn assurance that this very night, before the cock crows twice, you will have disowned me three times." 31Peter, however, spoke all the more insistently and said, "Even if I had to suffer death by your side, I shall never disown you." And all the others spoke in the same way.

32 They reached a certain place called Gethsemane. "Stay here while I pray," he said to his disciples; 33but Peter, as well as James and John, he took with him. Then a feeling of bewilderment and desolation began to fill his mind, 34and so he addressed these words to them: "*w***My soul is sadly distressed;** it feels as though I were dying. Stay here in this place and be wakeful." 35Then he went some distance further, threw himself on the ground, and prayed that, if it were possible, this hour might pass him by. 36 "*Abba*, Father," he exclaimed, "take this cup of misery away from me. Still, make everything happen as you, not as I, would have it." 37 At that he went back to the others and found them asleep. And this is what he said to Peter: "Simon, are you asleep? Did you lack the strength to remain wakeful for one hour? 38Do remain wakeful, while uttering a prayer to be spared from having to undergo the final test. The spirit is indeed eager enough; it is the flesh that makes us weak." 39Then he went away once more and prayed again, using the very same words as before. 40When he returned to the others he found them asleep, for their eyes were heavy with drowsiness. So they were at a loss what to say for themselves.

41 On returning to them a third time, he addressed them in these words: "From now on *do* sleep and take your rest. But enough of this. The hour has come when the Son of Man is being delivered into the hands of men given over to sin. 42Rise to your feet and let us go. Here he is; my betrayer is drawing near."

43No sooner had he uttered these words than Judas, one of the twelve disciples, appeared. With him was a crowd, equipped with

*v*Zc 13:7   *w*Ps 42:6; 43:5

* [At the Passover meal, this would have been the *Hallel*, i.e., Pss. 115–118.]

swords and cudgels, men that had been sent out by the chief priests, the experts in the law, and the elders of the people. [44]Now his betrayer had made an arrangement with them on a signal to be given, and this is what he had said: 'Whomsoever I shall be greeting with a kiss: he is the man himself. Lay hold of him and take him safely off.' [45]So he went straight up to Jesus, calling out, "Rabbi." Then he kissed him. [46]At that the others laid their hands on Jesus and made him a prisoner.

[47]However, one of the bystanders drew his sword, struck the High Priest's servant, and cut off his ear. [48]And Jesus responded to this by addressing those assembled in these words: "It is with swords and cudgels in hand that you have come out to apprehend me. [49]Day after day I was in your company in the temple giving instruction, and you did not seize me. Be that as it may, it was necessary that the scriptures should be brought to fulfilment." [50]At this his followers all left him and took to flight. [51]However, a certain young man who was there followed him. He had nothing on except a linen cloth on his bare body. They seized him, [52]but he, letting the linen cloth go, fled away naked.

[53]They led Jesus off to the High Priest; and there gathered together in his house all the chief priests, the elders of the people, and the experts in the law. [54]As for Peter, he followed him at some distance right into the High Priest's courtyard; and there he sat by the side of the attendants, warming himself at the fire. [55]Now the chief priests and the whole of the High Council were looking for testimony against Jesus, so as to be in a position to put him to death. However, they did not find what they were looking for. [56]Indeed, a great many men bore false witness against Jesus, but the evidence provided by their testimony did not tally. [57]Still, certain men did rise to their feet and bore false testimony against him in these words: [58]"What we have heard him say is this: 'I shall destroy this present temple made by human hands, and within three days I shall build another temple not made by the hands of man.'" [59]However, even then the evidence provided by these men did not tally.

[60]At that the High Priest rose up, moved right into the centre of the assembly, and questioned Jesus in these words: "Is there no answer you have to make? Why are these men testifying against you?" [61]Jesus, however, kept silent and made him no reply. So the High Priest questioned him again, his words being these: "Are you God's anointed, the Son of the Blessed One?" [62]"I am," said Jesus; "and you will see [x]**the Son of Man sitting on the right side of the God of all power and coming down with the clouds of heaven**". [63]The High Priest [y]rent his robes when he heard this, and exclaimed, "What need of further witnesses do we have? [64]You have heard the blasphemy with your own

[x]Ps 110:1; Dn 7:13   [y][Lv 10:6; 21:10; 2 K 18:37]

ears. What is your view of the matter?" They all found against him, declaring that he deserved to die.

65 It was then that certain people began to spit at him, to cover his head, to strike him with their fists, and to shout at him, "Play the prophet!" Moreover, the attendants rained blows upon him.

66 Meanwhile Peter was sitting below in the courtyard. Now one of the High Priest's servant girls came up, 67 and when she saw Peter there warming himself, she fixed her gaze on him and exclaimed, "You, too, were in the company of Jesus, that man from Nazareth!" 68 But Peter denied it and said, "I do not know what you are talking about; I have no comprehension of it." Then he went outside into the gateway. 69 And when the servant girl saw him there, she once again said to the bystanders, "That man is one of their number." 70 He denied it once again. After a little while the bystanders in turn said to Peter, "In very truth, you are one of their number. Indeed, you are a native of Galilee". 71 At that, Peter began calling down curses on himself and swearing, "I do not know the man of whom you are talking". 72 Immediately upon this the cock crowed a second time. Then Peter called to mind how Jesus had spoken to him these words: 'Before the cock crows twice, you will have disowned me three times'. And as it came home to him he burst into tears.

15 As soon as morning came, the chief priests, the elders of the people, the experts in the law, as well as the whole of the High Council, made ready a plan. They put Jesus in fetters, led him away, and handed him over to Pilate. 2 "Are you the king of the Jews?" Pilate asked him. "It is you who say that I am," was Jesus' reply. 3 Now the chief priests were bringing a large number of accusations against him. 4 So Pilate questioned him again in these words: "Have you nothing whatever to say in reply? Note what grave charges these men are bringing against you." 5 Jesus, however, would not utter a word in reply, with the result that Pilate was greatly surprised.

6 It was Pilate's practice, every year as the festival came along, to pardon one prisoner, whichever they might ask for, as a favour to the people. 7 Now there was a man called Barabbas, who was kept in custody, along with the rebels who had committed murder during the uprising. 8 The crowds went up to where Pilate was and began to appeal to him that he should do for them what he customarily did. 9 And Pilate made his reply to them in these words: "Is it your wish that I should pardon the king of the Jews as a favour to you?" 10 In point of fact, he was perfectly well aware that it was out of spite that the chief priests had handed Jesus over. 11 But now the chief priests incited the crowd to ask for Barabbas instead to be pardoned as a favour to them. 12 So Pilate spoke to them again and addressed them in these words:

"What, then, am I to do with the man you call the king of the Jews?" [13] "Crucify him!" they shouted back. [14] At that, Pilate asked them, "Why, what crime has he committed?" But they cried out all the louder, "Crucify him!" [15] So it was that Pilate, who was desirous to satisfy them, pardoned Barabbas as a favour to them, while, as for Jesus, he had him scourged first of all, and then handed him over to be crucified.

[16] After that, the soldiers took him along with them into the inner part of the palace, that is, the Governor's place of residence, the whole of the cohort being called together. [17] They clothed him in purple and placed upon his head a crown which they had woven out of thorns. [18] Then they began to give their salutation to him, exclaiming, "Hail to you, you king of the Jews!" [19] Then they struck him on the head with a staff, spat at him, and, falling upon their knees, paid homage to him. [20] And then, when they had done with their sneering, they took the purple garment off him and put his own clothes on him.

And now they led him forth to crucify him. [21] They encountered a certain man on the way, one Simon, a native of Cyrene, the father of Alexander and Rufus. He was on the way home from the country; and it was he whom they pressed into service, making him carry the cross of Jesus. [22] So they took Jesus to the place called Golgotha, which, correctly translated, means 'The Place of a Skull'. [23] They offered him wine flavoured with myrrh, but he refused to take it. [24] They put him on the cross. Then [z]**they divided** his **clothes** among themselves, **casting lots over them** to decide what each should get.

[25] It was the third hour when they crucified him. [26] There was an inscription, naming the charge which had been made against him. It read: 'THE KING OF THE JEWS'. [27] Moreover, they crucified two men who were brigands with him, one on his right and one on his left.*

[29] Now those who passed by poured abuse on him. [a]**Shaking** their **heads,** they exclaimed, "Alas, for the destroyer of the temple, for the man who builds it up again in three days! [30] Deliver yourself by coming down from the cross!" [31] In the same way the chief priests and the experts in the law sneered in talking of the matter to one another, and this is what they said: "He came to the rescue of others, but has no power to rescue himself. [32] You, the anointed of God, the King of Israel, come down from the cross, so that, seeing it, we may come to believe." And those crucified with him reviled him as well.

[33] When the sixth hour arrived, darkness fell over the whole land until the ninth hour. [34] And at the ninth hour Jesus cried out in a loud

[z]Ps 22:18   [a]Ps 22:7; 109:25; Lm 2:15

* V. 28 is probably not part of the original text.

voice, *"Eloi, Eloi, lama sabachthani?"* which, correctly translated, means
[b]**My God, my God, why have you abandoned me?'** 35Certain of the
bystanders heard him and said, "Why, he is calling for Elijah." 36A
certain man ran off to get hold of a sponge. He soaked it in [c]**sour wine,**
fixed it on a reed, and **gave** it to Jesus **to drink,** saying, "Let us see if
Elijah will come to take him down."

37But Jesus gave a loud cry and breathed his last. 38And the curtain
in the temple was torn in two from top to bottom. 39When the centurion, who was standing there right opposite him, perceived that he
was breathing his last in this manner, he exclaimed, "In very truth this
man was a son of God!" 40Certain women were there as well, watching things from afar, among whom there was Mary of Magdala, Mary
the mother of James the younger and of Joseph, and Salome. 41They
had followed him when he was in Galilee and had been ministering
to his needs. And there were many other women as well who had
come up with him to Jerusalem.

42It was now already late in the day, and since this was Preparation
Day, that is, the day before the Sabbath, 43a certain man made his appearance. He was Joseph, a native of Arimathaea, a councillor of high
repute. He was one of those men who were in eager expectation of the
kingdom of God; and so he summoned up courage, went into Pilate's
presence, and asked him for the body of Jesus. 44Pilate, for his part, was
wondering whether Jesus could have died so soon. And so he summoned the centurion, enquiring of him whether Jesus was already
dead. 45Having ascertained from the centurion that this was so, he let
Joseph have the corpse. 46And he, having bought a linen cloth, took
the body down, wrapped it in the linen cloth, and deposited it in a tomb
which had been cut out of the rock. Then he rolled a stone against the
entrance of the tomb. 47Mary of Magdala and Mary the mother of
Joseph were watching and took note of where the body had been laid.

16 Sabbath being over, Mary of Magdala, Mary the mother of
James, and Salome set out to buy spices with which they might go to
anoint him. 2They reached the tomb very early in the morning, immediately after sunrise. 3And this is what they said to one another:
"Who will roll the stone away for us from the entrance of the tomb?"
4As they looked up, they perceived that the stone, which was indeed
a very large one, had been rolled away. 5And when they had entered
the tomb, they saw a youth sitting there on the righthand side, clad
in a white robe, and they were dismayed. 6But this is what he said to
them: "There is no need for dismay. You are looking for Jesus of

[b]Ps 22:1   [c]Ps 69:21

Nazareth, the one who has been crucified. He has been raised to life; he is no longer here. Look and let your eyes dwell upon the place where they laid him. [7]However, be on your way and give to his disciples—and to Peter particularly—this message: 'He is proceeding into Galilee ahead of you. There you will see him, as he told you that you would'." [8]At that the women went out of the tomb and fled away. For they were seized with trembling and frightened out of their wits. They said nothing to anybody, for they were afraid.

* * * * *

*[[9]Having risen to life, early on the first day of the week Jesus appeared, first of all, to Mary of Magdala, the woman from whom he had cast out seven demonic spirits. [10]And she, for her part, went on her way and gave the news to those who had been his companions, whom she found lamenting and weeping. [11]But these, when she told them that he was alive and had been seen by her, refused to believe her.

[12]Some time after this he appeared, in another form, to two of them as they were walking out into the country. [13]And they, too, went off and gave the news to the others. But they did not believe them either.

[14]Still later he appeared to the eleven disciples themselves as they were at table. He rebuked them for their lack of faith and their stubbornness of mind, seeing that they had refused to believe those who had seen him after he had been raised to life. [15]And this is what he said to them: "Go forth into every part of the world and proclaim the gospel to the whole of creation. [16]He who believes and receives baptism will find salvation, while he who refuses belief will incur a judgment of condemnation. [17]And these are the signs which will attend those who have come to believe. They will cast out demonic spirits at the invocation of my name. They will give utterance in tongues unheard of. [18]They will take up serpents with their hands; and if they swallow a deadly poison, it will do them no harm whatever. They will lay their hands on those beset by ill health and they will recover."

[19]After having spoken these words to the disciples, the Lord Jesus was [d]**taken up into heaven,** and there **he sat down at the right hand of God.** [20]And they, going forth, made proclamation everywhere, while the Lord stood by them in the accomplishment of their task, bringing confirmation of their message by the signs and wonders attending it.]

[d]2 K 2:11; Ps 110:1

* [The Longer Ending, vv. 9-20, is not part of the Gospel, but is found in most later manuscripts.]

THE GOSPEL STORY
AS TOLD BY LUKE

1 A large number of men have come forward and made the attempt to compose a narrative concerning the things which have been accomplished in our midst. [2] These men, in setting about their task, conformed to the tradition handed down to us by those who, from the first, were eyewitnesses of the unfolding of the word of God and gave themselves up to serving its cause. [3] And it is in consideration of all this, most noble Theophilus, that I decided, having investigated everything carefully from the beginning, that I was to address myself to you in writing, [4] my purpose being that you should obtain full and certain knowledge concerning matters in which you have already received instruction.

[5] During the reign of Herod, king of Judaea, there lived a certain priest called Zechariah, who belonged to the priestly division which takes its name after Abijah. His wife belonged to Aaron's family, and her name was Elizabeth. [6] Both of them were seekers after uprightness in God's sight, and they conducted their lives in conformity with all God's commandments and ordinances, being wholly free from reproach. [7] They were without child, Elizabeth being barren; moreover, by now they were, both of them, advanced in age.

[8] Now the day came when he was doing a priest's duty before God, since it was the turn of the division to which he belonged. [9] He was chosen by lot, as the custom is in the priestly office, to go into the sanctuary of the Lord and offer incense, [10] while the mass of the people stood praying outside. It was the hour of the incense offering. [11] Then an angel of the Lord appeared to him, taking up his position on the right of the altar of incense. [12] When Zechariah saw him, he found himself greatly troubled, and a feeling of dread came upon him. [13] However, the angel addressed him in these words: "[a]**Banish all fear,** Zechariah, for **your** prayer has been **received with favour** and your wife Elizabeth will bear a son. John shall be the name you will give

[a]Dt 10:12

101

him, [14]and your heart will be filled with joy and exultation. Moreover, there will be many rejoicing at his birth, [15]for he will be great in the eyes of the Lord. [b]**Wine and strong drink he will never touch,** but from his very birth he will be filled with the Holy Spirit. [16]He will cause many among Israel's sons to return to the Lord their God. [17]He will proceed in advance of the Lord, paving his way, and he will do so by virtue of the spirit and power of [c]**Elijah.** And this will be his purpose: **turning the hearts of fathers towards their children,** bringing back the rebellious to the frame of mind to be found in the upright, preparing for the Lord a people fully equipped for him."

[18][d]**"What are the means,"** was Zechariah's reply to the angel, **"which will enable me to know** for certain that it will be so? After all, I am an old man, and my wife likewise is advanced in age."

[19]"I am Gabriel," was the angel's rejoinder, "the one who stands in God's presence, serving attendance on him. I have been sent forth to speak to you and to bring this happy news to you. [20]Well then, you will lose the use of your tongue and be unable to speak until the day that these things are accomplished. And this will be so because you have put no trust in my words, the very words which will find fulfilment at the appointed time."

[21]Meanwhile the people were waiting for Zechariah, wondering why he should make so long a delay. [22]However, when he came out and was unable to speak, they realized that he had had a vision in the sanctuary. As for Zechariah himself, he persisted in addressing them in the language of signs and remained without the power of utterance. [23]However, when his time for offering divine service had come to an end, he returned to his home. [24]Some time later his wife Elizabeth conceived and kept herself hidden for five months. And she spoke these words: [25]"This is what the Lord has done for me during the days when he saw fit to take away from me the disgrace which I suffered at the hands of men."

[26]In the course of the sixth month, the angel Gabriel was sent by God to Nazareth, a town in Galilee, to visit [27]a certain young woman who was promised in marriage to a man called Joseph, who was of the house of David, the name of the young woman being Mary. [28]And the angel, on entering the house, addressed her in these words: "My welcome to you who have had all the graces bestowed upon you: [e]the Lord is on your side!" [29]Mary, for her part, was thrown into confusion by this mode of address and was pondering in her own mind what might be the meaning of a greeting such as this. [30]But the angel said to her, "Cast off all fear, Mary, for you have found favour with God. [31]You will—attend to my words—conceive in your womb and give

[b]Nm 6:3; Jg 13:4.14   [c]Mal 4:5f; 3:1   [d]Gn 15:8   [e][Jg 6:12; Rt 2:4]

birth to a son; and the name you will give him will be Jesus. [32]He will be great in renown, people giving him the title 'Son of the Most High', and the Lord will bestow upon him the *f*throne of his ancestor **David.** [33]*g***He will be king** over the house of Jacob **for ever and ever,** and his kingship will never come to an end." [34]"How can this be?" was Mary's reply to the angel, "seeing that I have not come together with any man?" [35]The angel spoke to her thus: "The Holy Spirit will come over you, and the power of the Most High will overshadow you: that is why this *h***holy** offspring will have the **name** 'Son of God' given to him. [36]And know this too: Elizabeth your kinswoman has conceived a son in her old age; and this is already the sixth month that she, to whom people used to refer as the barren one, has been with child. [37]And all this has come about by virtue of the fact that *i***nothing is impossible for God.**" [38]"Be it then," said Mary; "I am nothing more than the Lord's bondmaid; may everything happen to me in accordance with the words you have spoken." Upon this the angel left her presence.

[39]It was a few days after this that Mary made herself ready and set out in haste for a certain Judaean town situated in the hill country. [40]On arriving, she entered the house of Zechariah and gave her greeting to Elizabeth. [41]Now this is what happened when Elizabeth heard Mary's greeting. The coming child began to stir lustily in her womb, and Elizabeth herself, being filled with the Holy Spirit, [42]raised her voice and cried out loudly, *j*"You have, of all women, a special blessing resting upon you, and the fruit of your womb is likewise specially blessed. [43]How is it that I should be the one to have a visit paid to me by the mother of the Lord? [44]Why, no sooner had your greeting reached my ears than the coming child stirred exultantly in my womb. [45]Yes, blessedness is indeed in store for her who was ready to believe that the words spoken to her by the Lord would find their fulfilment."

[46]And Mary spoke thus:

"*k***My soul** gives itself up to extolling **the Lord** in his greatness; [47]and my spirit **exults in God my deliverer.** [48]For *l***his eye has fallen graciously upon** his **bondmaid, humbly placed** as she is. Indeed, from this time onwards, I shall be pronounced blessed by generation after generation, [49]because he who is mighty has done wonderful things for me. *m***His name is holy.** [50]*n***The compassion he shows towards those who stand in awe of him extends from generation to generation.** [51]He has displayed his power by what is his own right *o***arm.** Those who have a *p***high conceit** of themselves in their own

*f*Is 9:7   *g*Mic 4:7   *h*Ex 13:12   *i*Gn 18:14; Jr 32:27   *j*[Jg 5:24]   *k*1 Sm 2:1; Hab 3:18
*l*1 Sm 1:11   *m*Ps 111:9   *n*Ps 103:13.17   *o*Ps 89:10   *p*2 Sm 22:28

minds **he has scattered far and wide.** [52] *q***He has cast down the mighty ones** from their seats of power and **raised up those who were humbly placed.** [53] *r***Those that were hungry he has filled with good things, and the rich he has dismissed with nothing to call their own.** [54] *s***He has held out his helping hand to Israel his servant, mindful of the merciful way** in which, [55] true to the promise *t***made to our forefathers,** he was to deal with **Abraham** and his **posterity** for ever."

[56] Mary remained with Elizabeth for about three months and then returned to her own home.

[57] As for Elizabeth herself, when the time came for her to be delivered of child, she gave birth to a son. [58] Her neighbours and her kindred shared her joy when they learned what great compassion the Lord had displayed towards her. [59] Moreover, when the eighth day arrived, they presented themselves for the circumcision of the child and were about to have him named Zechariah after his father. [60] His mother, however, intervened and said, "Not so: his name shall be John." [61] "There is not one among your kindred," they replied, "who is called by that name." [62] They then proceeded to make signs to his father, with a view to ascertaining what he wished him to be called. [63] He, for his part, asked for a writing tablet and inscribed on it the words, 'His name is John.' They were, one and all, astounded at this. [64] All at once the power of speech returned to Zechariah's mouth, and his tongue was loosened. He began to speak, and his words were words in praise of God. [65] So it came about that all the inhabitants of these regions were gripped by a feeling of awe, and the whole story went from mouth to mouth throughout the hill country of Judaea. [66] Everybody that heard it laid it to heart, and this is what they said: "What do you suppose will become of that child?" And it did indeed turn out that God held his protecting hand over him.

[67] As for Zechariah his father, being filled with the Holy Spirit he burst forth into this prophetic utterance:

[68] "*u***Praise to the Lord, the God of Israel.** For he has visited us, *v***setting his people at liberty.** [69] *w***He has raised up** one wielding a **mighty weapon** to secure our salvation, a man coming of the house of **David** his servant. [70] All this he has done, just as he proclaimed it from ancient times, by the mouth of his holy prophets. [71] And this is what he promised, that he would bring us deliverance *x***from** our **enemies,** rescuing us **out of the hand** of all **those that hate us,** [72] that he would show *y***mercy towards our forefathers,** and **be mindful of his** holy **covenant.** [73] The oath which he *z***swore to Abraham** our forefather

*q*Job 12:19; 5:11; 1 Sm 2:7   *r*1 Sm 2:5; Ps 34:10 LXX; 107:9   *s*Is 41:8; Ps 98:3   *t*Mic 7:20; Gn 17:7; 18:8; 22:17   *u*Ps 41:13; 72:18; 106:48   *v*Ps 111:9   *w*1 Sm 2:10; Ps 132:17; 18:2   *x*Ps 106:10   *y*Ps 105:8; 106:45; Gn 17:7; Lv 26:42   *z*Gn 22:16f; Mic 7:20; Jr 11:5

made this proclamation, [74]that, having rescued us out of the hand of our enemies, he would grant it to us that we were to serve him with no fear in our hearts, [75]and that piety and uprightness in his sight were to be our guides all the days of our lives. [76]But you, my child, will rightly be called prophet of the Most High. For you will go forth, *[a]ahead of the Lord, to pave his way.* [77]You will bestow upon his people knowledge of the way in which they will obtain their deliverance: through having their sins forgiven them, [78]and this by the tender compassion of our God. It is in this manner that the rising sun from heaven will be visiting us, [79][b]**to shine upon those that dwell in darkness and in the shadowy realm of death,** to guide our feet into the way of peace."

[80]Meanwhile the child grew and his spirit gained in strength. Moreover, he spent his days in the wilderness until the time when he made his public appearance before Israel.

2   Now at this time an edict went forth from the emperor Augustus to the effect that a census covering the whole of the Empire was to be held. [2]This census—the first of its kind—took place when Quirinius was governor of Syria. [3]So everyone made his way to his own city, for the purpose of being registered. [4]Among them was Joseph, who set out for Judaea from the town of Nazareth in Galilee, his destination being one of David's cities called Bethlehem. He did so because he himself was of David's house and lineage, [5]and his purpose was to register there, along with Mary, the woman promised to him in marriage, who was with child. [6]The time for her to have her child arrived while they were there; [7]and so it happened that she brought forth a son, her firstborn, put his infant wrappings round him, and laid him in a manger. This she did because no room could be found for them at the inn.

[8]Now there were certain shepherds in this same district, men who lived in the open, keeping watch over their flock during the night. [9]And all of a sudden, one of the Lord's angels was standing by their side, and the Lord's light of glory shone round them. They were terror-struck; [10]but the angel spoke to them thus: "Cast off all fear and attend to my words. What I have to proclaim to you is most joyful news, and the joy it brings will be shared by all the people. [11]And this is what it is. This very day there has been born to you in David's city one who will accomplish your deliverance. It is he who is God's anointed, who is the Lord. [12]And here is something which may serve you by way of a sign. You will come upon a little child clothed in in-

[a]Mic 3:1   [b]Is 9:2

105

fant wrappings and placed in a manger." [13] At this the angel was, all of a sudden, joined by the entire heavenly host, singing God's praises and calling out, [14] "Glory to God in the highest heaven, and peace on earth to the men on whom his favour rests."

[15] After the angels had left the shepherds' presence, returning to heaven, the shepherds said to one another, "Let us go to Bethlehem to see for ourselves this thing which has happened, the thing which the Lord has made known to us." [16] So they went on their way, making haste, looking for Mary and Joseph. And here they were, with the little child lying in the manger. [17] On setting eyes upon the child, they made known to the others what they had been told about him. [18] All that heard it were amazed at what the shepherds said to them, [19] while Mary, for her part, treasured up all these things and pondered them in her heart. [20] As for the shepherds, they returned home and, as they did, gave glory and praise to God on account of everything they had seen and heard. It had all fallen out exactly as they had been told it would.

[21] When eight days had passed and the time had come to have the infant circumcised, he was called Jesus, the name the angel had given him before he was conceived in the womb.

[22] And when the [c]**days had come to an end** after which they had to submit to their **purification** as required by the law of Moses, they took Jesus up to Jerusalem, in order to present him to the Lord [23] (as prescribed by the law of the Lord: [d]**'Every firstborn male is to be thought of as sacred to the Lord'**) [24] and to offer sacrifice, in conformity with the law of the Lord: [e]**'A pair of turtledoves or two young pigeons'.**

[25] Now there was a certain man in Jerusalem at that time whose name was Simeon. He was a man of uprightness and devotion, who spent his days in expectation of the time when comfort would be brought to Israel. The Holy Spirit was upon him; [26] and it had been revealed to him by the Holy Spirit that he was not to meet his death until after he had seen the Lord's anointed. It was he who entered the temple impelled by the Spirit. [27] And when the child Jesus was brought in by his parents, that they might do for him what was required by the custom laid down in the law, [28] he took him into his arms, gave praise to God, and exclaimed, [29] "Lord and Master, this very day you are setting your servant free, and he can go on his way in peace, as indeed you have promised. [30] This must be so, for my eyes have [f]**seen** him who is to accomplish **your work of deliverance,** [31] which you have made ready **for all the nations to see.** [32][g]**A light** will appear, coming to the **Gentiles** by way of serving as a **revelation,** and it will be cause for **glory to** your people **Israel.**"

[c]Lv 12:6   [d]Ex 13:2.12.15   [e]Lv 12:8; 5:11   [f]Is 40:5; 52:10   [g]Is 42:6; 49:6; 25:7; 46:13

33 As for his father and his mother, they were astounded at what was being said about him, 34 while Simeon invoked a blessing upon them, and thereupon addressed the mother in the following words: "Why, he who is here present with us is destined to cause the downfall and the rise of many in Israel. He is indeed intended to serve as a sign, but it will be a sign that people will repudiate; 35 and so the designs of many a human heart will be brought into the open. As for yourself, the time will come when your very soul will be pierced by a sword."

36 There was also a prophetess called Anna, who was the daughter of Phanuel and a member of the tribe of Asher. She was greatly advanced in age, seeing that, her girlhood days being over, she had first lived with a husband for seven years 37 and had then lived in the state of widowhood until by now she was eighty-four years old. She never absented herself from the temple, and instead offered her worship night and day by fasting and by prayer. 38 It was she who, at that very moment, was drawing near, expressing her gratitude to God and speaking about the child to all those who were looking forward to the deliverance of Jerusalem with eager expectation.

39 When the parents had fulfilled all the requirements of the law, they set out on their return journey into Galilee, making their way to Nazareth, their own city.

40 And so the child grew, gained in strength, and was filled with wisdom, the favour of God resting upon him.

41 Now it was the practice of the parents to go to Jerusalem every year for the celebration of the Passover festival. 42 And when Jesus was twelve years old, they, going up in accordance with the custom prevailing at the festival, 43 and having remained for the whole time during which it was celebrated, were on their journey home, while the child Jesus had stayed behind in Jerusalem. The parents, however, did not know this, 44 but thought that he was among their travelling companions. And so it was that they had gone a whole day's journey before they enquired for him among their kinsfolk and acquaintances. 45 When they could not find him, they returned to Jerusalem to make further enquiries. 46 Three days went by, and then they did find him in the temple, sitting there in the midst of those who were engaged in teaching, listening to them and asking them questions. 47 All who heard him were astonished at the acuteness of his mind and the answers he made. 48 As for his parents, they were amazed when they saw him there, and his mother spoke to him thus: "My child, why have you done this to us? Here we are, your father and I, looking for you and suffering anguish of heart." 49 And he made them this reply: "What grounds did you have for looking for me? Did you really not know that it was my bounden duty to be occupied in my Father's con-

107

cerns?" [50]But they did not comprehend the meaning of his words. [51]As for Jesus, he went back with them to Nazareth, and there he continued to be subject to their authority, while his mother treasured in her heart everything that happened. [52]And so it was that Jesus ever [h]**advanced** in wisdom and in stature, and in the **favour** he enjoyed **with both God and men.**

3 During the fifteenth year of the reign of the emperor Tiberius, when Pontius Pilate was governor of Judaea, while Herod held the position of tetrarch over Galilee, his brother Philip over the lands of Ituraea and Trachonitis, and Lysanias over Abilene, [2]in the course of the high priesthood of Annas and Caiaphas, the word of the Lord came to John, son of Zechariah, while he was in the desert. [3]And so he moved from place to place all over the districts adjoining the Jordan, preaching a baptism which was to issue from repentance and result in people having their sins forgiven them. [4]All this is in accordance with the words set down in the writings of the prophet Isaiah:

[i]'**A voice of one crying aloud in the desert: Prepare a way for the Lord; straighten out the paths** which he is to tread. [5]**Wherever there is a valley, it shall be filled to the brim, wherever a mountain or a hill, they shall be levelled to the ground. What is bent shall be straightened, and the rough ways shall be made smooth.** [6]**And so every human creature will become witness of God's work of deliverance.**'

[7]And John addressed the crowds that came out to be baptized by him in the following words: "A brood of vipers that you are! Who has given you warning to take flight from the retribution which is to come? [8]What you must do is act in such a way that the fruit borne by what you do is in keeping with a state of repentance. And do not embark on harbouring thoughts such as these: 'We have Abraham as father.' For what I have to say to you is this: God has the power of creating children for Abraham out of these very stones. [9]Why, even now the axe lies poised at the root of the trees, and so every tree failing to yield good fruit will be cut down and cast into the fire."

[10]At this the crowds put him the question, "What, then, is it that we have to do?" And he made them this answer: [11]"The man who has two tunics must hand over one of them to the man who has none. And the man who has something to eat must go by the same rule." [12]Among those who came to him for the purpose of having themselves baptized were certain tax collectors saying to him, "What is it we ought to do?" [13]"In setting about your task," was his answer, "you

[h]1 Sm 2:26; Pr 3:4   [i]Is 40:3-5

must not go beyond your instructions." [14]Moreover, there was a number of men who were soldiers by profession. They asked him, "What is it we have to do?" He replied to them thus: "Do not intimidate anyone or make false accusations against anyone. Moreover, be content with what you are paid."

[15]By now the people were in a mood of expectancy. Everyone was wondering in his own mind about John, and they were all asking themselves whether he might not, after all, be God's anointed one. [16]And this is the reply which John made before them all: "I am baptizing you with water, but another is to come endowed with much greater power than I have. In fact, he will be such a man that, as regards myself, I shall not even be worthy to unfasten the straps of his shoes. The baptism he will administer to you will be one by the Holy Spirit and by fire. [17]He will be holding his winnowing shovel in his hand to clean out his threshing floor and to gather the wheat into his granary. The chaff, however, he will burn up in a fire never to be extinguished."

[18]In many other ways he exhorted the people and proclaimed the Good News to them. [19]Moreover, Herod the tetrarch, having been reprimanded by John on account of Herodias, his brother's wife, as well as on account of all the other misdeeds of which he had made himself guilty, [20]added yet another crime to the rest by having John shut up in prison.

[21]One day when general baptism was being administered to the people, Jesus likewise undergoing baptism and giving himself up to prayer, it happened that the heavens opened up [22]and that the Holy Spirit descended on him in bodily form, having the appearance of a dove. At the same time a voice came down from heaven, uttering these words: "You are my Son, my dearly-loved one; it is you on whom my favour rests."

[23]When Jesus set about his task, he had reached the age of about thirty. He was by general repute Joseph's son. And Joseph was son of Heli, [24]son of Matthat, son of Levi, son of Melchi, son of Jannai, son of Joseph, [25]son of Matthathias, son of Amos, son of Nahum, son of Esli, son of Naggai, [26]son of Maath, son of Mattathias, son of Semein, son of Josech, son of Joda, [27]son of Johanan, son of Rhesa, son of Zerubbabel, son of Shealtiel, son of Neri, [28]son of Melchi, son of Addi, son of Cosam, son of Elmadam, son of Er, [29]son of Joshua, son of Eliezer, son of Jorim, son of Matthat, son of Levi, [30]son of Symeon, son of Judah, son of Joseph, son of Jonam, son of Eliakim, [31]son of Melea, son of Menna, son of Mattatha, son of Nathan, son of David, [32]son of Jesse, son of Obed, son of Boaz, son of Salmon, son of Nahshon, [33]son of Amminadab, son of Admin, son of Arni, son of Hezron, son of Perez, son of Judah, [34]son of Jacob, son of Isaac, son of Abraham, son of Terah, son of Nahor, [35]son of Serug, son of Reu, son of Peleg, son

of Eber, son of Shelah, [36] son of Cainan, son of Arphaxad, son of Shem, son of Noah, son of Lamech, [37] son of Methuselah, son of Enoch, son of Jared, son of Mahalaleel, son of Cainan, [38] son of Enosh, son of Seth, son of Adam, son of God.

4 Now Jesus, filled with the Holy Spirit, turned away from the Jordan and let himself be led by the Spirit [2] in the desert for forty days. And there he was being put to the test by the devil. During those days he ate nothing, and when they had come to an end he was plagued by hunger. [3] And the devil spoke to him thus: "If it be true that you are the Son of God, then order this stone to turn into a loaf of bread." [4] "This is what is written in scripture," was Jesus' reply, [j] " **Man cannot live with bread as his only support'.**" [5] Moreover, the devil took him up to a high point, showing him, in a flash, all the kingdoms of the world. [6] And this is what he said to him: "I shall give you authority over all this domain, as well as over the splendour that goes with it. For it is to me that it has been committed and I am bestowing it upon whomsoever I choose. [7] So if you are ready to do homage to me, it shall be yours." [8] "This is what is written in scripture," was Jesus' reply, [k] " **You shall do homage to the Lord your God, and you shall worship** no one but **him.'**" [9] He then brought him to Jerusalem and placed him on the summit of the temple, saying to him, "If it be true that you are the Son of God, throw yourself down from here. [10] For as scripture says, [l] **He will give his angels this commission concerning you, that they are to keep you in safety'.** And again it says, [11] **They will bear you up on their hands, that there may be no risk of your striking your foot against a stone'.**" [12] Jesus made him this reply: [m] " **You must not put the Lord your God to the test'.** This is what we have been told." [13] So the devil, having exhausted every way of tempting him, parted company with him until a more opportune moment should arise.

[14] As for Jesus, he returned to Galilee, impelled by the power of the Spirit. The tale about him spread over the whole region. [15] The task he set himself was to give instruction in the synagogues, and he found himself highly praised by everyone.

[16] So he came to Nazareth, the place where he was reared, and, as was his custom, he entered the synagogue on the Sabbath day. He rose to perform the office of public reader, [17] and the scroll handed to him was that containing the writings of the prophet Isaiah. He opened it and looked until he came to the place where the following words are written:

[j]Dt 8:3   [k]Dt 6:13f   [l]Ps 91:11f   [m]Dt 6:16

[18][n]'The spirit of the Lord is upon me because it is he who has given me my anointing. I was to proclaim happy news to those that are poor. He has sent me forth to announce to the captives that they would be set free, to the blind that they would recover their sight, to the down-trodden that they would be set at liberty. [19]The task I was set was to make proclamation of the year of the Lord's favour.'

[20]Upon this he rolled up the scroll, returned it to the attendant, and took his seat, everyone having his gaze fixed upon him.

[21]He then began to address them. "Today," he said, "this passage from scripture has found its fulfilment in your very hearing." [22]He met with general approval, and they were all amazed at the graceful manner in which the words proceeded from his lips. On the other hand, they asked, "Is this man not the son of Joseph?" [23]So he replied, "No doubt you will quote to me the saying 'Physician, provide healing for yourself'. And another thing you will be telling me is this: 'We have heard of everything that happened at Capernaum; do the same things here in your home city'. [24]Believe me," he went on, "no prophet finds favour in his own country. [25]Why, I can assure you in very truth: there were many widows in Israel at the time of Elijah, when the skies never opened for three years and a half, and a dread famine raged throughout the land. [26]But Elijah was not sent to any of them. He was sent to a [o]widowed woman who lived at Zarephath, a settlement of Sidon. [27]Moreover, there were many lepers in Israel in the time of the prophet Elisha. But none of them was healed. Only Naaman the Syrian was."

[28]At this, all those who were listening to him in the synagogue became furious with indignation. [29]They rose to their feet, hustled him out of the city, and took him up to the brow of the hill on which it was built, intending to hurl him over the edge. [30]But he passed through the midst of them and went on his way.

[31]Coming down to Capernaum, a city in Galilee, he began to teach the people there on the Sabbath; [32]and they were astounded at his teaching, because what he said had a ring of authority. [33]Now there was a man in the synagogue who was possessed by a spirit, that of a tarnished demon. He cried out in a mighty voice, [34]"Ha! [p]What do you want with us, Jesus of Nazareth? Have you come to bring ruin upon us? I know well enough who you are. You are God's Holy One!" [35]As for Jesus, he administered a rebuke to him, exclaiming, "Be silent and come out of him!" At this the demon, after having thrown him into convulsions in front of them all, did come out of him, without doing him any injury. [36]Astonishment seized everybody present, and they talked about the matter in these words: "What are we to make of

[n]Is 61:1f; 58:6   [o]1 K 17:9   [p]Jg 11:12; 1 K 17:18

a speech so powerful as this? He gives his orders to the tarnished spirits, doing so with authority and strength, and they come out of their victims!" 37 And so it came about that the story of his doings spread all over the countryside.

38 On taking his departure from the synagogue, Jesus made his way to Simon's house. Now Simon's mother-in-law had been seized by a violent fever, so they solicited his aid for her. 39 He drew near, bent over her, and reprimanded the fever, which thereupon left her. And all at once she rose up and waited on them.

40 Sunset having come, all those who had friends afflicted by diseases of one kind or another brought them to him, he, for his part, laying his hands on each one and bringing them healing. 41 Moreover, many who had demons cast out of them cried out and exclaimed, 'You are the Son of God!' But he reprimanded them and would not let them continue speaking, because they were aware of the fact that he was God's Anointed One.

42 When daylight came, he left and made his way to a deserted place. As for the crowds, they were looking for him, and on reaching him they sought to prevent him from leaving their company. 43 But he spoke to them thus: "It is necessary that I should proclaim God's kingdom to the other cities as well, for this is the very purpose for which I have been sent forth." 44 And so he set out to proclaim his message in the synagogues of Judaea.

5   One day it happened that a crowd of people were pressing hard against Jesus to hear the word of God proclaimed to them, while he himself was standing by the Lake of Gennesaret. 2 There he saw two boats lying close inshore, the fishermen, who had stepped out of them, washing their nets. 3 So he went on board one of the boats—it was Simon's—and requested him to put out a little distance away from the land. He then sat down and began to teach the crowds from the boat. 4 When he had finished speaking he said to Simon, "Move on a little until you come to a place where the water is deep; then you must let down the nets for a catch." 5 "Master," was Simon's rejoinder, "we have been toiling all night and have caught nothing. Still, it is your word; and trusting it I shall let down the nets." 6 The men obeyed instructions, and it turned out that they had hauled in a huge quantity of fish. 7 The nets were beginning to break, and so they signalled to their comrades in the other boat to come over and help them. They came, and both boats were made full to the point of sinking. 8 When Simon saw it, he fell to the ground, catching hold of Jesus' knees, and exclaimed, "Take yourself away from me, Lord, for I am nothing more than a sinful man!" 9 He, as well as all his companions, had been seized

by astonishment because of the catch of fish they had made, [10]the same feeling arising in James and John, sons of Zebedee, who were partners to Simon. Then Jesus said to Simon, "Banish all fear; from this time onwards it will be men that you will be catching." [11]So, having brought their boats ashore, they followed him, abandoning everything they had.

[12]One day Jesus found himself in a certain city, when he came upon a man with leprosy all over him. The man, on seeing him, fell on his face, imploring Jesus in these words: "Lord, you have the power of cleansing me if only you wish to." [13]Thereupon Jesus stretched out his hand, touched him, and exclaimed, "Be cleansed; it is my wish that you should be." All at once the leprosy departed from him, [14]Jesus, for his part, giving him the order not to tell anybody about what had happened. "However, one thing you must do," he added. "Be on your way, [q]**show** yourself to the **priest,** and make the offering in token of your cleansing, in accordance with what has been laid down by Moses. This will suffice as evidence for them." [15]But still the effect of all this was that the tale of him spread even further, and large crowds would gather together, with a view to listening to his words and finding healing from their ailments. [16]But he reacted to this by adopting the practice of withdrawing to solitary places and giving himself up to prayer.

[17]One day when he was giving instruction, there sat at his feet Pharisees and teachers of the law who had come from villages all over Galilee, as well as from Judaea and Jerusalem. Jesus was guided by the power of the Lord to engage in works of healing. [18]At that moment certain people appeared carrying on a bed a man who was struck down by paralysis. Their intention was to bring him into the house and set him down in front of Jesus. [19]But as it proved impossible on account of the crowd to find a way of getting him in, they proceeded to climb onto the roof and to let him down through the tiling, placing him, bed and all, in the middle of the gathering, right in front of Jesus. [20]When Jesus perceived the faith which was in them, he said, "Your sins are forgiven you, friend."

[21]At that the experts in the law and the Pharisees began to argue with one another, and this is what they said: "Who is this fellow who utters blasphemies? Who except God alone has the power of forgiving sins?" [22]But Jesus, who was perfectly well aware of the nature of their reasonings, made them this rejoinder: "What reasonings do you harbour in your minds? [23]Which is more easily said, 'Your sins are forgiven you,' or 'Rise up and walk'? [24]Things turned out the way

[q]Lv 13:49; 14:2.32

they did in order that you should be made to realize that the Son of Man, while he is on earth, has the authority granted to him to forgive sins." He then turned to the paralyzed man. "I am telling you," he said, "to rise to your feet, to lift your bed, and to make your way home." ²⁵Without the least delay the man got up, in full view of them all, lifted up his bedding, and went home, praising God. ²⁶Everybody present was filled with amazement. They praised God, while at the same time a feeling of awe took possession of them. And this is what they said: "What we have been witnessing are things beyond all belief."

²⁷When, some time later, Jesus was leaving the house, his eyes fell on a collector of taxes by the name of Levi, who was occupying his place in the tax office. "Follow me," Jesus said to him; ²⁸and he rose up, left everything behind, and followed him.

²⁹Then Levi gave a large banquet in his house in honour of Jesus; and among the guests was a large number of tax collectors and other people of the same kind. ³⁰The Pharisees and the law experts in their service found fault with this and put their complaints before Jesus' disciples in these words: "Why is it that you eat and drink with tax collectors and other sinful people?"* ³¹"It is not those enjoying good health," replied Jesus, "who are in need of a physician; it is those who are in bad health. ³²And indeed, if I have appeared among men, this has been to hold out an invitation, not to people of virtue, but to invite sinners that they should repent."

³³On another occasion they said to him, "John's disciples keep frequent fasts and give themselves up to prayer; and the disciples of the Pharisees act in the same way. But your followers go on eating and drinking." ³⁴Jesus made them the following reply: "Is there a way of making those who are friends of the bridegroom's resort to fasting while the bridegroom is still with them? ³⁵However, the time will come when the bridegroom is taken away from them, and it is during those days that they will be fasting."

³⁶He added this illustration: "No one tears a piece off a new cloak to patch up an old one. Otherwise a tear will be made in the new cloak, and, further, the patch coming from the new cloak will not match the old one. ³⁷Moreover, no one pours new wine into old wineskins. Otherwise the new wine will cause the wineskins to burst, the wine being spilt and the skins being ruined. ³⁸No, new wine must be poured into fresh skins. ³⁹Besides, no one, having drunk old wine, expresses a desire to have new wine. What he says is this: 'It is the old wine that is good.'"

---

* [Usually understood as those who were less observant of the dietary and other Jewish laws, and who were treated as pariahs.]

6 One Sabbath day it happened that Jesus was making his way through fields of corn; and his disciples fell to plucking some for themselves, rubbing ears of corn together with their hands and beginning to eat. ²Upon this certain of the Pharisees enquired, "How is it that you are doing something forbidden on the Sabbath day?" ³Jesus made them this reply: "Can it be that you have never read about what David did when he and his companions were plagued by hunger; ⁴how he entered the house of God and ate the ʳ**Loaves of Presentation,** distributing what remained among those who were with them, these being the loaves which no one but the priests are permitted to eat?" ⁵And he added these words: "The Son of Man exercises his lordship even over the Sabbath."

⁶On another Sabbath he made his way into the synagogue for the purpose of teaching. There was a man whose right hand had withered away, ⁷and the experts in the law and the Pharisees put a close watch on him to ascertain whether he would engage in a work of healing on the Sabbath day, so that they might have something to accuse him of. ⁸As for Jesus himself, he knew what turn their reasoning was taking. "Rise up and come out into the middle," he said to the man with the withered hand. Whereupon the man did rise to his feet and took up his stand. ⁹Jesus then said to the others: "There is one question I have to put to you: which of these is permitted on the Sabbath—to do good or to do evil, to save life or to destroy it?" ¹⁰Then he looked round, fixing his gaze on them all, and said to the man, "Stretch out your hand." He did so, and his hand was restored to its former soundness. ¹¹As for the others, they were beside themselves with fury and began to discuss what was the best way of dealing with Jesus so as to render him harmless.

¹²It was at this time that, one day, Jesus went out into the hills to pray. Throughout the night he persevered in his prayer to God. ¹³Then, when daylight came, he called his disciples to his side, choosing twelve from among them whom he called his apostles. They bore the following names: ¹⁴Simon, to whom he gave the name of Peter, Andrew his brother, James, John, Philip, Bartholomew, ¹⁵Matthew, Thomas, as well as James son of Alphaeus, and Simon, surnamed the Zealot, ¹⁶Judas son of James, and Judas Iscariot, the one who turned traitor.

¹⁷Jesus came down the hill with them and took up his stand on a piece of level ground where a large number of his disciples had assembled, together with a crowd of people that came from every part of Judaea, from Jerusalem, and from the coastal region belonging to

---

ʳLv 24:5.9; Ex 40:23; 1 Sm 21:6

Tyre and Sidon. [18]They had come because they wished to hear him and to be healed of their ailments. Moreover, those troubled by tarnished spirits found themselves restored to health. [19]Throughout the crowd, people attempted to touch him because power went forth from him, and he brought healing to them all.

[20]As for Jesus himself, he lifted up his eyes, and, turning to his disciples, spoke to them as follows:

"A blessing rests on you who live in ⁵**poverty,** for the kingdom of God will be yours.

[21]"A blessing rests on you who now go hungry, because time will come when you shall have your fill.

"A blessing rests on you who are shedding tears now, because time will come when you shall be laughing.

[22]"A blessing rests on you when men feel hatred for you, when they outlaw you, when they revile you, when they denounce your very name as something infamous, all on account of the Son of Man. [23]When that time comes, you should be full of gladness, you should be dancing for very joy, for assuredly a rich reward awaits you in heaven. After all, the forefathers of these people treated the prophets in precisely the same way.

[24]"What misery, on the other hand, is in store for you who are rich, seeing that all the consolation due to you has already been paid in full.

[25]"What misery is in store for you who now have food in plenty, seeing that you will be going hungry.

"What misery is in store for you who are laughing now, seeing that you shall be mourning and shedding tears.

[26]"What misery is in store for you when everybody speaks well of you. After all, this is precisely the way in which the false prophets were treated by the forefathers of these people.

[27]"But this is what I have to say to you who are listening to me: Love your enemies; do good to those who feel hatred for you. [28]Return a blessing to those who call down curses on you. Pray for those who make you suffer cruel treatment. [29]If a man strikes you on the cheek, offer him the other cheek as well. Should someone take your cloak away from you, do not grudge him your tunic along with it. [30]Give to everyone who asks, and do not ask him who takes away what is yours to restore it. [31]Let the way in which you wish to be treated be your measure for treating others.

[32]"If you love none but those who love you, what credit is that to you? After all, even sinners love those who love them. [33]If you do good to none but to those who do good to you, what credit is that to you? After all, even those leading sinful lives do the very same thing.

⁵Is 57:15; 61:1

³⁴ And if you lend to none but to those from whom you expect repayment, what credit is that to you? After all, even sinners lend to other sinners, with a view to being repaid in full. ³⁵No, what you must do is love your enemies and do good to them; and you must lend without expecting anything in return. If you act in this way, you will reap a rich reward, being true sons of the Most High, because he himself is kind to the ungrateful and to the wicked. ³⁶Show yourselves compassionate, just as your Father is compassionate.

³⁷"Moreover, do not pass judgment on others, and then you will not have judgment passed on yourselves. Do not condemn others, and then you yourselves will not be condemned. Show forgiveness towards others, and then you yourselves will be shown forgiveness. ³⁸Give to others, and there will be gifts for you: a full measure, the contents pressed down, well shaken and overflowing being poured out into your lap. For whatever measure you deal out to others you will have dealt out to you in return."

³⁹He also offered them an argument as an illustration. "There is no way, is there, in which a blind man can act as guide to another blind man? Will they not both fall into the ditch? ⁴⁰It is impossible that a pupil should be his master's superior. Still, it remains true that a fully equipped pupil will be like his master.

⁴¹"How is it that you can observe the speck of dust in your brother's eye while yet you are not aware of the piece of wood in your own? ⁴²By what right can you say to your brother, 'Brother, give me leave to take the speck of dust out of your eye,' when you are incapable of observing the piece of wood in your own eye? Dissembler that you are, first take the piece of wood out of your own eye, and then you will see clearly enough to take the speck of dust out of your brother's eye.

⁴³"It is not possible that a good tree should bring forth worthless fruit; and again it is not possible that a decayed tree should bring forth good fruit. ⁴⁴For each tree is known by its fruit. Men do not gather figs from thistles, nor do they pick grapes from a thornbush. ⁴⁵A good man produces what is good out of the store of good which is in his heart, while an evil man produces out of the evil within him that which is evil. For what the mouth utters comes from what the heart is full of.

⁴⁶"How is it that you keep calling me, 'Lord, Lord', and do not do what I tell you? ⁴⁷Everyone that comes to me listening to my words and acting on them—I will make you see what he is like. ⁴⁸He is like a man who, in building a house, has dug, and has dug well, and has sunk the foundations into the rock. When the full flood came, the river burst upon that house. But it did not have the strength to shake it because it had been built so well. ⁴⁹But then there is the person who hears my words and fails to act on them. He is like a man who built

his house right on the soil, without any foundations. When the river burst forth upon it, the house collapsed at once. And the fall of that house was indeed a great one."

7 When he had come to the end of everything he had meant to say in the hearing of the people, he made his way to Capernaum. [2]In that place there lived a certain centurion who had a servant whom he valued highly. And that man was gravely ill. In fact, he was on the point of death. [3]His master, having heard the story of Jesus, sent a delegation of Jewish elders to him, requesting that he come and restore his servant to health. [4]So they presented themselves before Jesus and made an urgent appeal to him. "The man who has sent us," they said, "deserves to have this granted to him. [5]He is a lover of our nation, and indeed has built our synagogue for us." [6]At that, Jesus set out in their company. However, when he was but a short distance from the house, the centurion sent out certain friends of his with this message for him: "Cease troubling yourself, sir, because I do not deserve to have you entering my house. [7]That is why I did not consider it right to come to you. However, let the word of command be spoken, and let my servant find healing in that way. [8]For I know what it means to be placed under authority; and I myself have soldiers who are subject to me. I say to one of them, 'Go', and he goes; and to another, 'Come', and he comes. I tell my servant to do this or that, and he does it." [9]When Jesus heard the man speaking these words he was amazed, and turning to the crowd which was following him, he spoke to them thus: "Nowhere, I assure you, have I found faith such as this, not even in Israel." [10]As for the messengers who had been sent to him, they found, when they returned to the house, that the servant had been fully restored to health.

[11]Some time later Jesus was making his way into a town called Nain, his disciples and a large crowd accompanying him. [12]Just as he drew near the gate of the town, a dead man was being carried out of it for his burial. He was the only son of his mother, she being a widow, and a large number of the townspeople was with her. [13]When the Lord saw her, pity for her filled his heart. He told her to stop her tears. [14]He drew near and put his hand on the bier, those carrying it coming to a halt. And this is what he said: "Rise to your feet, young man. I am telling you to do so." [15]The man who had been dead sat up. And so it was that Jesus [†]**gave him back to his mother.** [16]Everybody present was filled with awe, and gave praise to God in words such as these: "A great prophet has made his appearance in our midst," or "God has

[†]1 K 17:23; 2 K 4:36

paid a visit to his people." [17]Moreover, this way of talking of him spread over every part of Judaea and through the entire region.

[18]As for John, he was told about all this by his disciples. So he called two of them to his side [19]and sent them to the Lord, instructing them to ask him this question: "Are you the one of whose coming we have been told, or are we to wait for some other man?" [20]When the men reached Jesus, they said, "John the Baptist has sent us to you with instructions to ask you, 'Are you the one of whose coming we have been told, or are we to wait for some other man?'" [21]It was at this very time that Jesus was occupied with bringing healing to large numbers of people, freeing them of their diseases, of scourges by which they were plagued, and of evil spirits which possessed them. Moreover, he bestowed upon those who were blind the gracious gift of eyesight. [22]So he made the messengers this reply: "Go on your way and report to John the things which you have seen and heard: how [u]**the blind recover their sight**, the lame can walk, the leprous are cleansed, the deaf can hear, the [v]**dead** are **raised to life**, and [w]**the poor are having good news proclaimed to them.** [23]And one more thing: a blessing rests on all those who take no offence at me."

[24]When John's envoys had gone, Jesus took the opportunity of talking about him to the crowds. "When you went out into the desert," he said, "what did you expect to encounter? One partaking of the character of a reed which the wind moves to and fro? [25]What kind of man, then, did you expect to meet when you went out? One clothed in soft, silky garments? Why, you must look in the palaces of kings if you want to find men who go about in splendid and luxurious apparel. [26]What, then, did you expect to encounter? A prophet? Yes, and indeed you can have my assurance that he is something much greater than a prophet. [27]In fact, it is he of whom it is written in scripture, [x]**'Take note of this: I am sending my herald ahead of you; and it is he who will make ready the way** for your **coming'.**

[28]"And one thing I must tell you: among the sons of women there is not one greater than John. Yet he who holds the lowest place of all in the kingdom of God is greater than he."

[29]All the common people that heard him, and the tax collectors as well, acknowledged the justice of God's ways by allowing themselves to be baptized with John's baptism; [30]while the Pharisees and the experts in the law, in refusing to be baptized by him, frustrated the purpose God had had for them.

[31]"To whom do I compare the men of this generation, and to whom do they bear a likeness? [32]They are like children sitting in the market place, calling out to one another and exclaiming, 'We have played the

[u]Is 35:5   [v]Is 26:19   [w]Is 61:1   [x]Mal 3:1

flute for you, and you would not dance; we have sung dirges to you, and there has been no weeping'. [33]For John the Baptist makes his appearance, not eating bread, not drinking wine, and you say, 'He is a man possessed of a demon'. [34]The Son of Man appears, eating and drinking like any other man, and you say, 'Look at this glutton ᵞ**gulping down wine**, this man who befriends tax collectors and sinners'. [35]Yet, for all that, wisdom found the rightness of her ways acknowledged by all those having a natural kinship with her."

[36]One of the Pharisees invited him for a meal, and Jesus, having entered the Pharisee's house, took his place at table. [37]Now there was a woman in the city who led a sinful life; and she, having learned that he would be dining in the Pharisee's house, had brought along with her oil of myrrh contained in a small flask. [38]She took her place behind him at his feet, weeping. Then, when her tears were making his feet wet, she fell to wiping them dry with her hair, kissed them, and anointed them with the myrrh. [39]When the Pharisee who had invited Jesus saw this, he began to think about the matter. "If this man were a prophet," he said to himself, "he would know what kind of woman is touching him: one that leads a sinful life." [40]Upon this, Jesus addressed these words to him: "Simon, I have something to tell you." "Have your say, Master," was the reply of the other. [41]"There was a creditor who had two debtors. One owed him five hundred pieces of silver, the other fifty. [42]Neither of them having anything to pay with, he cancelled the debt of both. Now which of them do you think will bear him greater love?" [43]And this is the reply Simon made: "I suppose it must be the one who had the larger debt cancelled." "You have judged rightly," Jesus said to him. [44]Then turning to the woman, he addressed the following words to Simon: "Do you see this woman? I came to your house. You gave me no water for my feet, while she made my feet wet with her tears and dried them with her hair. [45]You gave me no kiss of greeting, while she, ever since she came in, never ceased covering my feet with kisses. [46]You did not pour oil on my head, while she has anointed my feet with myrrh. [47]And so I will tell you this: her sins, her great sins, must have been forgiven her, seeing that she has shown such love. It is the person who has had but little forgiven him who shows little love." [48]And to the woman he said, "Your sins are forgiven." [49]At that his fellow guests were beginning to wonder. "Who is this," they asked themselves, "that he even has the power to grant forgiveness of sins?" [50]And Jesus made this further remark to the woman: "Your faith has brought you salvation. ᶻ**Go on your way in peace."**

ᵞPr 23:20　　ᶻ1 Sm 1:17

8   After this came a time when he journeyed from one village to another, preaching and spreading the happy news of God's kingdom. He was accompanied by the twelve apostles [2]as well as by certain women whom he had healed, setting them free from evil spirits, or from bodily infirmities. And this is who they were: Mary, known as the woman from Magdala, the one from whom seven demonic spirits had come forth; [3]Joanna wife of Chuza, Herod's steward; Susanna; and many others. It was these who provided for the men's upkeep out of their own resources.

[4]At one time, a large crowd having gathered together and the inhabitants of city after city flocking towards Jesus, he addressed them by way of a parable: [5]"A man whose business it was to sow seed went on his way for that purpose. Now while he was engaged in this task of sowing, some of the seed fell by the roadside, where it was trodden underfoot, the birds coming from the sky and eating it up. [6]Some seed fell on rock; on coming up, it withered away from lack of moisture. [7]Some fell right in the midst of thistles, and when the thistles grew at the same time as the seed did, they were choked by it. [8]Other seed, again, fell into good soil. When it came up, it brought forth fruit, and the yield was a hundredfold." As Jesus said this, he cried out loud, "He who has ears to hear with, let him listen."

[9]The disciples asked him what the parable meant, and this is what he said to them: [10]"As regards yourselves, you have been granted the privilege of knowing the very secrets of God's kingdom, while the rest have to be spoken to by way of parables. And the point of it all is that, while [a]**looking, they should yet see nothing, and** while **listening, they should yet understand nothing.**

[11]"And this is what the parable means: The seed is the word of God. [12]Those who are being compared to that which falls by the roadside are the people who listen to it, but then the devil comes and plucks it from their hearts, so that they should not come to believe and thus find salvation. [13]Those who are being compared to the seed that falls upon the rock are the people who, when they first hear the word, give it a joyful welcome. But afterwards, since they are without roots, they keep to the faith only for a while, and when the time of testing comes they fall away. [14]Those who are being compared to the seed that falls among the thistles are the people who give the word a hearing, but then, as they go on their way, they find themselves stifled by anxieties, by riches, as well as by the pleasure life has to offer; so they fail ever to reach maturity. [15]The seed that falls on good soil, on the other hand, signifies those who bring a noble and generous heart to the hearing

[a]Is 6:9f

of the word, who hold fast to it, who, by virtue of their power of endurance, yield a rich harvest.

16 "No one, having lit a lamp, then covers it with a vessel or puts it under the bed. On the contrary, it is placed on a lampstand, so that anyone coming in may see light. 17 And indeed, there is nothing hidden which will not be brought into the open, nothing kept secret which will not become known and be brought to light. 18 Take care, then, how you use your power of hearing. Whoever has something already, gifts will be made to him; and whoever is without means, will have taken away from him even that which he believes to be his."

19 On one occasion his mother and his brothers paid him a visit. But on account of the crowd, they were unable to reach him. 20 So he was given the message, "Your mother and your brothers are standing outside, wishing to see you." 21 And this is the reply he made to the people who told him this: "Those who listen to the word of God and act in accordance with it: it is they who are my mother and my brothers."

22 One day, on boarding a boat with his disciples, he said to them, "Let us cross over to the other side of the lake." They set sail, 23 and while they were on their way he fell asleep. But then a wind of great fierceness struck down upon the lake, and the boat being swamped by water, they found themselves in great danger. 24 They went to the place where Jesus was, to waken him from his sleep, and exclaimed, "Master, O Master, we are perishing!" Whereat he, being roused from sleep, administered a rebuke to the wind as well as to the turbulent water. Upon this they subsided, and a great stillness arose. 25 "What has become of that faith of yours?" he said to them. But they, filled with awe and amazement, said to one another, "What kind of man, then, is this? He gives his orders to the winds and to the waves, and they obey him."

26 They sailed on until they came to the country of the Gerasenes, which is situated opposite Galilee. 27 As Jesus was stepping ashore, he encountered a man from the city. This man was possessed by demonic spirits and had gone about with no clothes for a considerable time. Moreover, he refused to stay in a house; instead he lived among tombs. 28 When he saw Jesus, a shout broke forth from him, and falling at Jesus' feet he cried out in a powerful voice, "[b]**What do you want with me,** Jesus, you Son of God Most High? Do not torture me, I implore you!"

29 He acted in this way because Jesus was already engaged in the task of bidding the tarnished spirit to come out of the man. As for that spirit, on many an occasion it had seized the man with great violence, people then binding him with chains and fetters so as to make him

[b]1 K 17:18

safe. However, he would always break his bonds, and then the demonic spirit would drive him into the wilds.

30 Jesus asked him what his name was, the man replying, "It is Legion." He bore this name because of the large number of demon spirits that had taken possession of him. 31 And these appealed to Jesus not to order them back to the abyss.

32 Now a herd of swine was nearby, grazing there on the hillside. The spirits asked leave of Jesus to let them go into the swine. So he gave them leave, 33 with the result that the demon spirits came out of the man and went into the swine, and the herd, rushing headlong down the slope of the hill, sank in the water and was drowned.

34 When the men in charge of the swine saw what had happened, they took to flight, spreading the story in the city and the country round about. 35 The people went out to see for themselves what had happened; and when they reached Jesus they found there the man from whom the demonic spirits had been expelled, properly clad, in his right mind, and sitting at Jesus' feet. And they were terrified. 36 Those who had witnessed the scene reported to them the manner in which the man possessed by the demon spirits had had his health restored to him. 37 And so it was that all the inhabitants of the Gerasene district made the urgent request to Jesus that he was to depart from them. This they did because they were in the grip of a great fear. So Jesus got into the boat to make his return journey. 38 The man from whom the demon spirits had been expelled asked for leave that he might accompany him. But Jesus would have none of it and said to him, 39 "Return to your home and tell the people there about everything God has done for you." So the man went on his way and spread all over the city the news of all the things Jesus had done for him.

40 On his return Jesus received a warm welcome from the crowd, since they had all been waiting for him. 41 Just then a certain man made his appearance. His name was Jairus, and he was the president of the synagogue. Throwing himself at Jesus' feet, he implored him to come to his house. 42 He acted in this way because he had an only daughter, a girl about twelve years old; and she was on her deathbed. While Jesus was on his way, the crowd was pressing closely against him. 43 Now a woman was there who had been suffering from continual bleeding for twelve years, while no one had the power to heal her. 44 Coming up from behind him, she touched the fringe of Jesus' cloak, and, all of a sudden, the flow of blood came to a halt. 45 Upon this Jesus asked, "Who was it that touched me?" Everybody denied that they had, and Peter said, "It is the crowds that hem you in and are pressing against you." 46 "Someone *did* touch me," replied Jesus, "for I became clearly aware that power had gone out from me." 47 When the woman realized that the matter had come into the open, a trembling

seized her and, falling down at Jesus' feet, she declared in front of all the people what had been the reason for her touching him, and how she had found instant healing. [48] "My daughter," Jesus said to her, "it is by your faith that your health has been restored. Go on your way in peace."

[49] While these words were still being spoken, someone came from the house of the president with this message: "Your daughter is dead; cease troubling the Master." [50] Jesus, on hearing the words, made this rejoinder: "Banish all fear. All you need is to have faith, and then her health shall be restored." [51] On arriving at the house, he would let no one enter except Peter, John, and James, as well as the father and the mother of the child. [52] Everybody was in tears and mourning over her, while Jesus spoke to them thus: "Dry your tears; she is not dead, only resting in sleep." [53] They, for their part, only laughed at him since they knew perfectly well that she had died. [54] But he, taking her by the hand, called out, "My child, rise up!" [55] At that she rose to her feet at once, Jesus giving the order that she was to be given some nourishment. [56] Her parents were astounded; but Jesus instructed them that they were on no account to tell anybody about what had happened.

9

The day came when he called the twelve apostles together and furnished them with power and authority to hold sway over demonic spirits of every sort, while enabling them at the same time to heal diseases. [2] On sending them forth to proclaim the kingdom of God and to engage in works of healing, [3] he spoke to them thus: "You must not take anything with you for your journey, be it a staff, a knapsack, bread, or money. Neither is anyone to take a second coat with him. [4] Moreover, when you enter a house, make it the place where you settle, as well as the place from which you set out on your way. [5] As for those who decline to bid you welcome, you must, on leaving their city, shake the dust from off your feet by way of a testimony against them." [6] So they went forth and travelled from one village to another, proclaiming the good news and engaging in works of healing everywhere.

[7] Now Herod the tetrarch, on hearing about all these happenings, was greatly at a loss what to think of it all. Some people told him that John had risen from the dead, [8] others that Elijah had reappeared, and others again that one of the prophets of old had returned to life. [9] And this is what Herod said to himself: "John I have had beheaded. Who then is this man of whom I am hearing things such as these?" And he was most eager to see him.

[10] When the apostles returned from their journey they reported to Jesus about everything they had been doing, and he, taking them with

him, withdrew to a certain place called Bethsaida, where they could be by themselves. 11But the crowds, on hearing about this, followed him, he, for his part, bidding them welcome and speaking to them about the kingdom of God. Moreover, he engaged in healing those who stood in need of treatment. 12But now the day was drawing to its close, and so the twelve apostles approached him, addressing him in these words: "Dismiss the crowd so that they can go to the villages and hamlets round about, and find places to lodge in and obtain food. For we are in a solitary place here." 13"Give them something to eat yourselves," was his response. But they said, "Five loaves of bread and two fish is all we have, and nothing more. Or do you have in mind that we ourselves are to go and buy provisions for the whole of this huge crowd here?" 14In fact, those assembled were about five thousand in number. And this was Jesus' reply to the apostles: "Get them to sit down in clusters of about fifty each." 15They did what he had told them to do and got them all seated. 16Then he took the five loaves and two fish and, looking up towards heaven, he invoked a blessing upon them. Next he broke the food into pieces, handing it to the disciples so that they might set it before the crowd. 17And the people did eat, everybody having his fill. In fact, when the pieces left over were gathered, it was found that there was enough to fill twelve large baskets.

18One day Jesus was devoting himself to prayer in the company of his disciples, having withdrawn from everybody else. It was on that occasion that he put to them the question, "Who do the crowds say that I am?" 19"Some," they replied, "say that you are John the Baptist, others Elijah, others again that you are one of the prophets of old who has risen to life." 20Upon this he enquired of them, "But you yourselves, who do you say that I am?" "That you are the one whom God has anointed," was Peter's reply. 21But Jesus gave them the order, by way of administering a rebuke to them, not to make this known to anyone. 22And he added this: "The Son of Man is destined to undergo great suffering, to be repudiated by the elders of the people, by the priests, as well as by the experts in the law, to be put to death, and then to rise to life again on the third day."

23And these are remarks which he addressed to everybody alike: "If anyone is desirous to walk in my steps, he must set his own self at nought, take up the burden of my cross* day in and day out, and thus follow me. 24In fact, anyone desirous to save his life will suffer the loss of it, while if there be someone losing his life, and that for my sake, he is the very person who will save it. 25Indeed, should someone gain

---

* [Lit. 'He must take up his cross'. See note on Mt. 16:24.]

the whole world, yet suffer the loss of his true self, surrendering it as his forfeit, what advantage will he reap from that? 26 Truth to tell, if there be someone who is ashamed of me, as well as of the words I utter, the Son of Man will be ashamed of him at the time when he makes his appearance in his state of glory, which is likewise the glory of the Father and of the holy angels. 27 And one more thing I can assure you of in very truth. Among those standing here are some who will not have tasted death before they have seen the kingdom of God."

28 About eight days after Jesus had spoken these words, he took Peter, John, and James with him and went up the hillside to devote himself to prayer. 29 And as he was praying, it came about that the appearance of his face changed its nature, while his clothing turned a brilliant white, gleaming forth like lightning. 30 Moreover, all of a sudden two men were found holding converse with him, and these men were Moses and Elijah. 31 They, having made their appearance in their state of glory, spoke to him of his departure from life and of the destiny he was to fulfil in Jerusalem. 32 As for Peter and his companions, they were sunk in deep sleep. However, when they awoke they saw him in his state of glory and the two men standing by his side. 33 Furthermore, as the time came for them to be parting company with him, Peter said to Jesus, "Master, how good it is to be here; let us build three places of shelter, one for Moses, one for Elijah, and one for you." (He did not know what he was saying.) 34 While he was speaking, a cloud appeared, throwing its shadow over them. They were greatly frightened on entering the cloud. 35 Then a voice sounded forth out of the cloud, uttering these words: "He is ᶜmy Son; he is the one **whom I have chosen: lend your ear to him.**" 36 And while the voice was still speaking, Jesus found himself alone. As for the others, they kept their peace, and at that time told no one anything about what they had seen.

37 The next day, when they were coming down the hillside, they encountered a large crowd. 38 And then a certain man from the crowd came forth, shouting, "Master, I implore you to show a loving concern for my son, for he is my only child. 39 Now what happens is this: all of a sudden, a spirit gets hold of him. Then he screams, as the spirit throws him into convulsions, and he foams at the mouth. It is but rarely that it can be made to withdraw from him, and when it does, the boy gets exhausted in the process. 40 I appealed to your disciples to expel it; but they lacked the power to do so." 41 "What an unbelieving and perverted generation you are!" Jesus replied. "How long shall I have to remain in your company and bear with you? Bring forward your son." 42 Now even as the boy was drawing near, the demon spirit

ᶜPs 2:7; Is 42:1; Dt 18:15.19

rent him and threw him into convulsions. But Jesus administered a rebuke to the tarnished spirit, brought healing to the boy, and gave him back to his father, 43everybody being awestruck by the majesty of God.

At a time when everyone was full of wonder at all the things which Jesus was accomplishing, he addressed his disciples thus: 44"There are certain words of mine which you must keep in your minds once and for all: 'The Son of Man is destined to be betrayed and to be given up into the power of men.'" 45They did not, however, comprehend what they were told; indeed, it was being kept hidden from them, so that they should fail to grasp its meaning. On the other hand, they were afraid to ask him any questions about the words which had just been addressed to them.

46An argument developed between them on the question which of them was to be considered the greatest. 47As for Jesus, he knew well enough what were the thoughts occupying their minds. So he took a child by the hand, placing him by his side. 48Then he spoke these words to them: "Whoever gives a welcome to this child, and does so for my name's sake, gives a welcome to me; and whoever gives a welcome to me gives a welcome to him who has sent me forth. And indeed, the truth is that he who finds himself in the lowest place of all is the one that is truly great."

49At that, John spoke up and said, "Master, we have seen a certain man casting out demonic spirits, invoking your name. However, since he is none of our company, we forbade him to do so." 50"Cease hindering him," replied Jesus; "he who is not against you is on your side."

51As the period during which he was to be taken away from the earth was approaching, he became resolutely determined to make his way to Jerusalem. 52And so he sent messengers ahead of him. When these reached a certain Samaritan village, they entered it, so as to make the necessary preparations for him. 53However, the inhabitants declined to welcome him because of his determination to make for Jerusalem. 54On witnessing this, the apostles James and John asked him, "Lord, would you have us ^d**call down fire from heaven to consume** them?" 55Upon this he turned round and reprimanded them. 56And so they went on to another village.

57While they were on their way, someone said to him, "I shall follow you no matter where you are going." 58Jesus made him this reply: "Foxes have their holes to go to, and the birds of the air have their nesting places. Yet the Son of Man has no place where to rest his head." 59Another to whom he said, 'Follow me', made this reply: "Before I do, give me leave first of all to go and bury my father." 60"Let

^d2 K 1:10.12

those who are dead," was Jesus' reply, "go and bury the dead who belong to them. To be on your way and proclaim the kingdom of God far and wide, that is where your duty lies." 61 Yet another said to him, "I shall follow you, Lord; but give me permission in the first place to take leave of my people at home." 62 And Jesus spoke to him thus: "No one who has once set his hand to the plough and then glances backward is suited to have a place in the kingdom of God."

10 After this the Lord appointed another set of men, seventy-two in number. These he would send out in advance of himself whenever he intended to visit a town or some other place, *e*making them go in pairs. 2 And this is what he said to them: "The harvest is indeed plentiful, but of labourers there are few. Well then, turn to the man who is the owner of the harvest, requesting him to send out labourers to bring in his harvest. 3 Go forth, then, and remember this: in being sent out by me, you will find yourselves in the position of lambs thrown right into the midst of wolves. 4 You must take nothing with you, be it a purse or knapsack, and you must travel barefoot. *f*Do not exchange greetings with anyone you meet on the road. 5 Whenever you are about to enter a house, let your first words be, 'Peace to this house'. 6 And if the man who lives in the house has a natural kinship with peace, then the peace for which you have been expressing a wish will come to rest on him. But if it be otherwise, your wishes will be coming back to you the way they went. 7 Remain in the same house, and accept whatever its occupants have to offer you in the way of food and drink. The labourer has a right to his maintenance. Let there be no moving from one house to another. 8 Whenever you go into a city and you are made welcome, partake of any nourishment which is put before you. 9 At the same time, you must bring healing to those in it who are ill, addressing them in these words: 'The kingdom of God has drawn near you to make its home with you'. 10 And this is what you must do when you come into a city and they refuse to make you welcome. Go forth into the streets of that city and call out, 11 'The very dust of your city, which is clinging to our feet, we are wiping off from ourselves. Still, one thing you may be sure of: the kingdom of God has drawn near'. 12 And to you who are present here I say, 'What will befall Sodom, when the Great Day comes, will be more bearable than what that city will have to endure.'

13 "How pitiful is your condition, Chorazin; how pitiful is your condition, Bethsaida! For, truth to tell, if miracles such as have been performed in your midst had taken place in Tyre or in Sidon, the people

e[Ec 4:9] *f*[2 K 4:29]

there would have given themselves up to repentance long since, sitting on the ground in sackcloth and ashes. [14]Still, even as things are, what will befall Tyre and Sidon when the Judgment comes will turn out to be more bearable than what will befall you. [15]As for you, Capernaum, is it to be supposed that *g***you will be lifted up as high as heaven?** Far from it: **you will have to make the descent to Hades* itself.**

[16]"Whoever lends his ear to you lends his ear to me. Whoever sets you at nought sets me at nought. And whoever sets me at nought sets at nought likewise him who sent me forth."

[17]The seventy-two returned full of rejoicing. "Lord," they said, "even the demonic spirits submit themselves to us at the invocation of your name." And this is the reply Jesus made them: [18]"I saw Satan falling down from heaven after the manner of a flash of lightning. [19]And remember this: I have given you the power to *h***tread underfoot snakes** and scorpions and to exercise control over the enemy in all his strength. In fact, nothing will be able to injure you in any way. [20]Yet, in spite of it all, what you should rejoice over is not that the spirits submit themselves to you but that your names are recorded in the heavenly regions."

[21]At that very instant Jesus burst forth in exultation, impelled by the Holy Spirit, and this is what he said: "Father, Lord over heaven and over earth, here I am giving praise to you for concealing these things from those possessing wisdom and cleverness, while revealing them to the childlike. Yes, Father, that was the very thing which it was your good pleasure to accomplish. [22]My Father has committed everything into my hands. Moreover, no one but the Father knows who the Son is, and no one knows who the Father is but the Son, as well as all those to whom the Son chooses to reveal him."

[23]Then he turned to the disciples and said to them in private, "A blessing rests on the eyes which see what you are seeing. [24]Indeed, what I am telling you is that many prophets have been longing to see what you see and never seeing it, to hear what you hear and never hearing it."

[25]On one occasion a certain lawyer suddenly rose to his feet and, with the intention of putting Jesus to the test, asked him, "Master, what do I have to do to obtain a share in everlasting life?" [26]And this was Jesus' rejoinder: "What is written in the law? What is your reading of it?" [27]The lawyer replied to him thus: *i***"You are to love the Lord your God with all your heart, with all your soul, with all your strength,**

---

*g*Is 14:13.15   *h*Ps 91:13   *i*Dt 6:5

* [Heb. = *Sheol*; 'the pit' or 'world below'.]

129

and with all your mind, and ^{j}**your neighbour as you love yourself"**. ^{28}"You have answered aright," said Jesus. ^{k}**"Do this, and life is yours"**.

^{29}But the lawyer, wishing to put himself in the right, asked Jesus, "And who is my neighbour?" ^{30}while Jesus spoke to him thus in reply: "A man who was on his way down to Jericho from Jerusalem fell into the hands of robbers. They stripped him, gave him a beating, and then went off, leaving him half dead. ^{31}Now it so happened that a priest was going down the same road, and when he saw him he passed him by, moving to the other side. ^{32}Likewise there was a Levite, coming to that spot, who, on seeing him, passed him by, moving to the other side. ^{33}Yet another man, a native of Samaria, was making the same journey. He came upon him and, when he saw him, was filled with compassion. ^{34}So he drew near him and bound up his wounds, pouring wine and oil on them. He then put him on his own pack animal, brought him to an inn, and took care of him there. ^{35}The following day he produced two silver pieces, gave them to the innkeeper, and said, 'Take care of him. And should you incur any further expense, I shall pay you back when I am on my journey home'. ^{36}Now which of these three do you suppose proved himself to be neighbour to the man who had fallen into the hands of robbers?" ^{37}"He who showed compassion towards him," remarked the other. And this is what Jesus said to him: "Be on your way and act in the same manner as he did."

^{38}One day, when they were journeying, they reached a certain village in which a woman called Martha lived. She welcomed him into her house. ^{39}This woman had a sister by the name of Mary, who sat at Jesus' feet listening to his words. ^{40}Martha, however, felt herself overburdened by having so much to prepare. So she drew near and said, "Lord, are you not concerned that my sister has left me to do the serving all by myself? Tell her, I beg of you, to come and lend me a hand." ^{41}But the Lord replied to her thus: "Martha, Martha, so many things make you feel anxious and distracted. ^{42}Yet only one thing is necessary.* It is the best part which Mary has chosen, that which no one will ever take away from her."

11 One day Jesus found himself in a certain place giving himself up to prayer. When he had finished, one of his disciples said to him, "Lord, teach us to pray, just as John did with his disciples." ^{2}And this is what Jesus said to them: "Let these be your words when you are at prayer:

^{j}Lv 19:18 ^{k}Lv 18:5

* Or, 'Yet so few things are necessary, in fact, only one.'

*l*Father, may your very name be treated as holy.
May your kingdom appear.
*m3*Give us, day by day, the bread which is needful to us.
*n4*Forgive us the sins which we have committed.
For we, too, owe forgiveness to all who have done us an injury.
And do not bring us to the point of being put to the final test.'"

5 Then he spoke to them as follows: "Suppose one of you has a friend to whom he goes at dead of night and says to him, 'My friend, lend me three loaves of bread, 6 for a friend of mine, interrupting his journey, has made his appearance in my house, and I have nothing I can put before him'. 7 Suppose further that the other makes this reply from the inside of the house: 'Do not put me to an inconvenience such as this. Why, the door is locked. Moreover, my children and I are already in bed. It is out of the question that I should give you what you are asking for.' 8 Now what I have to say to you about this is that, even though he will indeed refuse to bestir himself for friendship's sake, giving him what he wants, yet shameless asking will have the effect of making him rise and give the other everything he stands in need of. 9 And so I must tell you this: Ask for something, and you will be given it; look for something, and you will find it; knock, and the door will be opened to you. 10 And indeed, everyone that asks receives; everyone that looks finds; he who knocks will have the door opened to him.

11 "If one of you who is a father is asked by his son to give him a fish, will he offer him a snake in the place of the fish; 12 or if he is asked for an egg, will he offer him a scorpion? 13 Well then, if you who are evil know how to make good gifts to your children, how much readier will the heavenly Father be to make a gift of the Holy Spirit to those who ask him for it?"

14 On one occasion Jesus was engaged in driving out a demonic spirit, one of those that cannot speak. Now what happened was that, no sooner had the demon spirit come out of the dumb man than he found speech. The crowds were amazed at this. 15 Still, some of them were saying, "It is with the help of Beelzebub, the prince of demonic spirits, that he is casting the demonic spirits out," 16 while others, in order to put him to the test, asked him for a sign from heaven. 17 As for Jesus, he knew well enough what was in their minds, and so he spoke to them thus: "Every kingdom in which there are internal divisions is doomed to fall into a state of desolation, one house after another suffering a collapse. 18 So, in the event of Satan being internally divided, how do you suppose that his kingdom could stand firm? I am saying this because of your contention that it is with Beelzebub's

l[Ezk 36:22f]   *m*[Pr 30:8]   *n*[Lv 4:26ff; Ec'us 28:2ff] help that I am casting out demons. [19] Moreover, if it is with the help of Beelzebub that I cast out demons, what of those who are of your turn of mind? With whose help do they cast demons out? Why, if that is the view you take, they themselves will play the part of judges condemning you. [20] But if it is in reliance upon the finger of God that I cast out the demons, then there is only one safe conclusion: the kingdom of God has already made its appearance in your midst.

[21] "When a strong man, fully armed, keeps guard over his own palace, his possessions are left in peace. [22] But when a man still stronger than he makes his appearance and gains the mastery over him, then he will take away from him all the armour in which he had placed so much confidence, and divide among others the spoils which he has won.

[23] "He who is not on my side opposes me, and he who gathers in his store without having me by his side scatters his goods.

[24] "This is what a tarnished spirit does when it comes out of a man. It roams through waterless tracts, looking for a place where it may find rest; and when it cannot find one, it says, 'I shall return to the house I came from.' [25] When it gets there, it finds the house swept clean and neatly kept in order. [26] Then it goes off and brings along with it seven other spirits worse than itself. They enter and settle down; and so the man's condition is in the end worse than it was at first."

[27] While Jesus was speaking in this way, it happened that a woman from the crowd raised her voice and exclaimed, "How great was the blessing which rested on the womb that carried you, on the breasts you sucked!" [28] "By no means," was his rejoinder; "A blessing rests on those who hear the word of God and act on it."

[29] Larger and larger crowds were gathering together, and so he set out to address them. "This generation," he said, "is an evil generation. It insists on having a sign vouchsafed to it, but it shall have none except such a sign as Jonah was. [30] Indeed, just as Jonah was a sign for the people of Nineveh, so the Son of Man will become one for this generation. [31] The queen of the South will come forward at the time of the Judgment, the men of this generation being brought face to face with her, and she will show them up as deserving of condemnation. For time was when she came from the farthermost ends of the earth to listen to Solomon's wisdom. And what is here now is one greater than Solomon. [32] The people of Nineveh will make their appearance at the time of the Judgment, this generation being brought face to face with them, and they will show it up as deserving of condemnation. For when Jonah preached to them, they were not led to repentance. And what is here now is one greater than Jonah.

[33] "No one, having lit a lamp, then takes it to an out-of-the-way place, nor does he put it underneath a grain measure. On the contrary,

he puts it on a lampstand, so that anyone coming in may see the light. 34The body has the eye for its lamp. And indeed, when your eye is sound, your whole body will be full of light, while when it is in poor condition, your body will be shrouded in darkness. 35See to it, then, that that which brings you light is true light, not darkness. 36Then, if the body is all in light, no part of it being in darkness, it will become light all over, after the fashion of a lamp illumining you with its brilliant rays."

37When Jesus finished speaking, a certain Pharisee invited him for a meal. When he had entered the house and sat down at table, 38his host was greatly surprised that he refrained from performing any ablutions before his meal. 39And the Lord spoke to him thus: "The outsides of your cups and plates you do indeed keep clean, you Pharisees, but as for your inward nature, it is brimful with rapacity and wickedness. 40Foolish men that you are! Did not he who made the outward part make the inward part as well? 41So then, give alms out of what you have, and then everything will be clean to you.

42"Woe upon you, you Pharisees, you pay tithes for mint, for rue, and for all garden herbs you will. But as for God's justice and love, you let them fall by the wayside. The truth is that you ought to do the one thing, and not leave the other undone.

43"Woe upon you, you Pharisees, because of your fondness for taking the seats of honour in the synagogues and for exchanging greetings in the market place.

44"Woe upon you, seeing that you are like graves left unmarked, men walking over them without knowing it."

45One of the lawyers addressed him in this way: "Master, by speaking like this you are insulting us as well." 46And this is the answer Jesus gave him: "Woe upon you also, you lawyers; you are heaping burdens upon men so heavy that they can carry them only with the greatest difficulty; but you yourselves will not move one finger to touch these burdens.

47"Woe upon you, seeing that you are the builders of the tombs of the prophets, your forefathers being the men that put them to death. 48In this way, then, you bear testimony in their favour, expressing your approval of your forefathers' deeds. They did the killing; you do the building. 49And so it is that the wisdom of God warns you in these words: 'I will send out my prophets and my apostles, and some of these they will persecute and murder'. 50Thus this generation may be held answerable for the blood shed from the foundation of the world —51from when Abel's blood was shed until the time when Zechariah perished between the altar and the sanctuary. And indeed, I assure you, this generation will be held answerable for it all.

52"Woe upon you, lawyers, you have taken away the key of knowledge. You did not yourselves enter, and you prevented those who wanted to enter from doing so."

53When Jesus had left the house, the experts in the law and the Pharisees took up an attitude of fierce hostility towards him, plying him with a host of questions 54and laying traps for him, so as to catch him out in something he might say.

12 It was in the circumstances just described that there gathered together a crowd of many thousands, a crowd so dense that they were treading on one another. Jesus addressed himself first of all to his disciples. "Be on your guard," he said, "against hypocrisy, that seed of corruption which permeates the souls of the Pharisees. 2Indeed, there is nothing, however carefully hidden away it may be, that will not be revealed, nothing kept concealed that will not be made known. 3The very things which used to be said in darkness will be heard in broad daylight; that which you used to whisper into each other's ears in secret places will be proclaimed aloud from the housetops.

4"And there is one more thing I have to say to you who are my friends: Do not be afraid of those who put the body to death and after that can do nothing further. 5No, I shall give you warning of whom you ought to be afraid. Be afraid of him who, having killed, has the power to cast you into hell. Him, I assure you, you should indeed fear. 6Do not two copper coins buy five sparrows? Yet not one of them escapes God's notice. 7Why, the very hairs on your head have been counted, one and all. Cease feeling anxious; there is more in you than in many sparrows. 8Moreover, one thing I can assure you of: Everyone who acknowledges me before men I will acknowledge before the angels of God; 9and anyone who repudiates me before men I will repudiate before the angels of God. 10Moreover, anyone who speaks against the Son of Man can find forgiveness, while he who slanders the Holy Spirit will not be forgiven.

11"When they bring you before their synagogues, their state authorities, and their magistrates, do not be anxious as to how to conduct your defence or what words to use 12because, when the time comes, the Holy Spirit will immediately proceed to instruct you what you must say."

13There was someone in the crowd who said to him, "Master, tell my brother that he must divide our inheritance with me." 14"My dear man," was Jesus' reply, "who has appointed me to play the part of judge or arbitrator between the two of you?" 15On one occasion he said to the people, "Mark my words, and be on your guard against greediness of every kind. True life is not secured by having a super-fluity of possessions." [16] And he told them this parable: "There was a rich man whose land bore fruit in abundance. [17] 'What am I to do?' he asked himself. 'I have not the space to collect the harvest. [18] This is what I shall do,' he then exclaimed. 'I shall pull down my storehouses, building larger ones, and into them I shall collect my corn and my other goods! [19] And then I shall be saying to myself, "My good man, you have many good things laid by for many a year to come. Take your rest now; eat, drink, enjoy yourself."' [20] Yet God spoke to him thus: 'Foolish man that you are! This very night your life will be demanded of you. Well then, the things which you have made ready—to whom will they belong?' [21] Indeed, this is how matters stand with the man who stores up riches for himself but has none in the sight of God.

[22] "I would entreat you, therefore," he said, turning to his disciples, "not to bestow anxious care upon the food by which you sustain your life or upon the clothes with which you cover your bodies. [23] Life means more than nourishment, the body more than clothing. [24] Consider the way in which the ravens live. They neither sow nor harvest; they are without storehouses or barns. And yet God nourishes them. How much more will he nourish you who are worth so much more than feathered creatures! [25] Which of you can, by being anxious, add a single cubit to his stature? [26] Well then, if you cannot even do such a little thing, why be anxious about the rest?

[27] "Consider the lives of the lilies; how they neither spin nor weave. Yet this I can assure you of: even Solomon in all his splendour was not arrayed as one of these. [28] But if God clothes the grass, which grows in the field today and is thrown into the furnace tomorrow, how much more will he be ready to clothe you, you men that have but little faith. [29] As for yourselves, do not set your hearts on things to eat or to drink, nor must you let yourselves worry. [30] These are the things which all the Gentiles in the world strive for. But you have a Father who knows that you stand in need of these things. [31] Still, it is his kingdom that you must be in pursuit of; then these other things will be given to you as well.

[32] "Have no fear, my little flock, for it has been your Father's pleasure to give you the kingdom. [33] You must sell your possessions and employ yourselves in acts of mercy. Make yourselves purses, but such as will never wear out. Heap up a treasure for yourselves, a never failing one, with its home in heaven, where no thief can reach nor moth do its work of destruction. [34] For where your treasure is, there also will your heart be.

[35] "With your belts fastened round you, with lamps kept burning, [36] you must conduct yourselves like men expecting their master,

wondering at what time he will return from the feast, so that they can let him in as soon as he arrives and knocks at the door.

37 "Those of his servants whom the master finds remaining wakeful for him are indeed most fortunate. I give you my solemn word that he will put his belt round himself, make them sit down at table, and minister to their needs. 38 Whether he comes during the second watch of the night or during the third, these servants, if he finds them thus wakeful for him, are fortunate indeed. 39 And this you must also know: had the master of the house known at what time the burglar would be coming, he would not have permitted his house to be broken into. 40 So you, for your part, must likewise stand ready; for the Son of Man will be coming at a time when you least expect him."

41 Thereupon Peter asked him, "Lord, is it ourselves whom you are addressing, or is this parable meant for everyone?" 42 And this is the rejoinder the Lord made him: "Who then is the steward, reliable and prudent, whom the master will put in charge of his servants to give them their allowance of food at the proper time? 43 As for that servant, how fortunate he is if the master finds him occupied with this task. 44 He will, I assure you, put him in charge of all his possessions. 45 Yet should the servant say to himself, 'My master is taking a long time in coming home,' and then proceed to beat the menservants and the maids and give himself over to eating, drinking, and getting drunk, 46 then when the master of that servant returns on a day when the servant least expects him and at a time which he does not know, the master will cut him in pieces and apportion the place which has been assigned to him, that by the side of the faithless.

47 "The servant who knew his master's wishes, yet made no preparations for them or did not carry them out, will receive a severe beating with the lash. 48 But the servant who did not know them, and yet has done things deserving of harsh treatment, will receive but few strokes. If a man has had much given to him, much will be demanded of him; and if he has a great deal handed over to him on trust, more than that will be expected of him in return.

49 "I have come to bring fire to the earth, and how I wish that it were ablaze already! 50 There is a baptism I must still be baptized with; and what vexation I must endure until it is accomplished! 51 Do not suppose that I have come to bring peace to the earth. By no means, I assure you—not peace, but rather dissension. 52 Indeed, from now on five members of one household will be at variance with one another, two with three and three with two. 53 Father will be at variance with son and °**son with father,** mother with daughter and **daughter with**

°Mic 7:6

mother, mother-in-law with daughter-in-law and **daughter-in-law** with **mother-in-law."**

54 And this further thing he said to the crowd: "When you see a cloud coming up in the west, you say at once, 'There is rain coming'; and so it is. 55 And when you perceive that the wind is coming from the south, you say, 'There is scorching heat on the way'; and so it is. 56 Dissemblers that you are! To interpret the appearance of the earth and the sky is something you *do* understand. How is it that you are incapable of interpreting this decisive hour?

57 "And why is it that you have no power of deciding for yourselves what is the right thing to do? 58 If you are being taken before a magistrate with your opponent at your side, make a strenuous effort, while you are still on the way, to get quit of his claim. Otherwise he will drag you into the presence of the judge, and the judge will hand you over to the bailiff, and the bailiff will have you thrown into prison. 59 Believe me, you will not come out of there until you have paid the very last penny."

13 It was at the same time that some people arrived, bringing Jesus news about the Galileans whose blood Pilate had spilled, mingling it with that of the animals which they were offering in sacrifice. 2 And this is how Jesus responded: "Do you suppose that these Galileans were more sinful than all other Galileans, seeing that they suffered such a fate? 3 By no means, I assure you. Still, unless you repent, you will, one and all, perish as they did. 4 Or what of those eighteen men who were killed when the tower of Siloam fell on them? Do you suppose that these were chargeable with a greater guilt than all the other inhabitants of Jerusalem? 5 By no means, I assure you. Still, unless you repent, you will all perish after the same fashion."

6 Jesus also told them this parable: "There was a man who had a fig tree planted in his vineyard. He came along to see whether there was any fruit on it, but found none. 7 So he said to the man in charge of his vineyard, 'Look here, for these three years I have been coming to look for fruit on this fig tree without finding one. Cut it down. Why let it go on wasting good soil?' 8 The other, however, made him this reply: 'Let it remain one more year, sir, so as to give me time to dig round it and put down dung. 9 If it bears fruit in the future, well and good; if it turns out otherwise, that will be the time for you to cut it down.' "

10 On one occasion Jesus was teaching in one of the synagogues on the Sabbath day. 11 There he came upon a woman who for eighteen years had been beset by a spirit which threw her into a state of feebleness. Moreover, she was bent double and quite unable to keep herself upright. 12 When Jesus saw her, he called out to her, "You have been

set free of your enfeebling state, my dear woman." [13]Then he laid his hands on her, and all at once she straightened herself up and gave glory to God.

[14]But the president of the synagogue, being full of indignation with Jesus for undertaking a work of healing on the Sabbath day, sought to counter him by saying to the crowd, "There are six days during which work is to be done. So then, come along on one of these days to be healed, and not on the Sabbath." [15]And Jesus made him this reply: "Hypocrites that you are! Does not each of you untie his ox or his donkey from the manger on the Sabbath day, taking it out for watering? [16]And here is this woman, one of Abraham's daughters, kept in bonds by Satan for these eighteen years. Was it not right, I ask, that she should be set free of her bonds?" [17]When he said this, all his opponents felt humiliated. As for the people, they greatly rejoiced at all the glorious works which he was performing.

[18]And this is what he went on to say: "What bears a likeness to the kingdom of God; and what am I to compare the kingdom with? [19]It is like the seed of a mustard plant which a man took and put down in his garden. There it increased, growing up into a tree, with **[p]the birds of the air nesting in its branches**".

[20]Yet again he said, "What am I to compare the kingdom of God with? [21]It is like a quantity of yeast which a woman brought along and buried away in three measures of flour until the whole batch was leavened all through."

[22]Continuing his journey from town to town and from village to village, Jesus engaged in teaching as he made his way to Jerusalem. [23]"Lord," someone asked him, "are only a few marked out for salvation?" In answer to this, he addressed these words to his companions: [24]"Strain every nerve to find entry by the narrow door. Many, I assure you, will attempt to find entry without having the power to do so." [25]Ever since the master of the house rose from where he was sitting and locked the door, you have been standing outside, knocking at the door and calling out, 'Lord, open the door to us.' And this is the reply he will make you: 'I do not know where you come from'. [26]Then you will find yourselves saying, 'We have eaten and drunk in your company, and you have taught in our streets.' [27]And he will answer you, 'I do not know where you come from. **[q]Out of my sight, you perpetrators of evil deeds.**'

[28]"Weeping there will be and gnashing of teeth at the time when you see Abraham, Isaac, and Jacob, as well as all the prophets, within God's kingdom, and you yourselves are expelled from it. [29]People will be coming **[r]from the east and the west,** from the north and the

[p]Dn 4:12.21; Ezk 17:23; 31:6   [q]Ps 6:8   [r]Mal 1:11; Is 59:19; Ps 107:3

south, to take their places at the feast in the kingdom of God. [30]Yes, and some who are now last will be first, and some who are now first will be last."

[31]It happened at the same time that a number of Pharisees approached Jesus and said, "You ought to leave this place and be on your way, because Herod is out for your life." [32]"Go to this fox," he replied, "and give him this message: 'Mark my words: my task today and tomorrow is to expel demonic spirits and to accomplish works of healing, and on the third day I will reach my goal.' [33]Still, as for today and tomorrow, and the third day, too, I must needs continue on my way. It is unthinkable that a prophet should meet his death anywhere except in Jerusalem.

[34]"Jerusalem, O Jerusalem, the city that puts the prophets to death and stones the messengers who have been sent out to her. How often have I longed to gather together your children, as a hen gathers her brood under her wings; but you would not have it! [35]Look out: God [s]**is abandoning your house** of worship, **leaving it to you.** Moreover, I tell you this: you shall not see me again until the time comes when you say, [t]**A blessing rests on him who appears in the name of the Lord.'"**

14   One Sabbath day he had gone into the house of one of the leading men who was a Pharisee, to partake of a meal; and he was being closely watched by the people present. [2]There, right in front of him, was a man suffering from dropsy. [3]Jesus' way of responding to this was to put this question to the experts in the law and the Pharisees: "Is it permissible to perform a work of healing on the Sabbath or not?" [4]They said nothing. So he took the man by the hand, healed him, and sent him away. [5]Whereupon, turning to the others, he said to them, "Is there one among you who, when his son, or even his ox, has fallen into a well, will not at once pull him out, even though it be the Sabbath day?" [6]And to this they could find no effective reply.

[7]Moreover, on observing how the invited guests were showing a preference for the places of honour, he told them this parable: [8u]"When anyone has invited you to a marriage feast, do not take your seat in the place of honour. For there is a risk that the host may have invited someone more distinguished than yourself, [9]with the result that he who has invited both of you will come up to you and tell you to make room for the other. Then, as you are making your move to occupy the lowest place of all, you will feel disgraced. [10]No, when you are invited as a guest, make your way to the lowest place and take

[s]Jr 22:5; 12:7; Ps 69:25; 1 K 9:7f   [t]Ps 118:26   [u][Pr 25:6f]

your seat there, so that your host, as he comes up to you, may say, 'My friend, move up higher'. And honour shall be yours in the sight of all those who are reclining with you at table. [11]For everyone who exalts himself shall be humbled, and everyone who humbles himself shall be exalted."

[12]And this is what he said to the man who had given him the invitation: "When you hold an entertainment, a midday meal, or a dinner, [v]do not invite your friends, your brothers, your other relatives, or your rich neighbours, for fear that they might send you invitations in return, and you may thus find yourselves repaid. [13]No, when you play the host, ask the poor, the crippled, the lame, and the blind. [14]Then a blessing will be resting upon you, because they do not have the means to repay you; but as for yourself, repayment will be made to you on the day when the upright are raised to life."

[15]When one of those who were with him at table heard this, he said to Jesus, "A blessing rests on the man who is to partake of the feast in the kingdom of God." [16]And this is what Jesus said to him in reply: "There was a man who was giving a banquet and he had sent out many invitations. [17]When the hour for the banquet arrived, he sent out his servant to those invited with this message: 'Come along; everything is now ready.' [18]However, all of them without exception set about making excuses. The first said to him, 'I have bought a piece of land, and it is essential that I should go and look over it. Count me excused, I beg of you.' [19]Another said, 'I have bought five yoke of oxen, and I am on my way to examine them. Count me excused, I beg of you.' [20]And still another said, 'I have just got married, and that is why I am unable to come.' [21]When the servant returned to his master, he reported all this to him. At that the head of the house flew into a rage and called out to his servant: 'Make haste, go out into the streets and lanes of the town, bringing in here the poor, the crippled, the blind, and the lame.' [22]And when the servant said to him, 'Sir, your command has been carried out, but there is still room,' [23]the master spoke to him thus: 'Go out into the highways and the hedgerows and compel them to come in here, to make sure that my house is properly filled. [24]For I can assure you: not one of those men who were invited will have a taste of my banquet'."

[25]Once when large crowds were accompanying Jesus on his way, he turned to them and addressed them as follows: [26]"Anyone who joins me and does not hate his father, his mother, his wife, his children, his brothers, his sisters, yes, and his own life, too, cannot be one of my disciples. [27]Further, if a man will not carry his cross, [w]following in my footsteps, he cannot be a disciple of mine.

[v][Dt 14:29; Pr 22:9]   [w][Dt 13:4]

²⁸ "Is there a man among you, I ask, who, intending to build a tower, would not first sit down to calculate the expense, making sure that he has enough to complete the task? ²⁹He wishes to avoid the risk that, in the event of his having laid the foundation, and then finding himself unable to finish the work, all the onlookers would set about jeering at him ³⁰and exclaim, 'That is the man who started to build and then was unable to finish!' ³¹Or again, what king, marching against another king to engage him in battle, would not first sit down to calculate whether with his ten thousand men he has the power to stand up against the one who is advancing against him with twenty thousand? ³²And should he find that he did not have the power, then, while the other was still a long way off, he would send envoys to him to ask for conditions of peace. ³³You are all in the same position. Not one of you can be a disciple of mine unless you renounce everything that you possess.

³⁴ "Salt is indeed a useful thing. But if the salt itself becomes insipid, with what can it be seasoned? ³⁵It is of no use for either the soil or the dunghill. People throw it away altogether. Let him who has ears to hear with, listen."

15   The tax collectors and those leading sinful lives were all flocking to listen to his words. ²However, the Pharisees and the experts in the law complained loudly about this, saying, "This fellow tenders a welcome to those given over to sin and has his meals with them." ³So he told them the following parable by way of a reply: ⁴"Is there a man among you who, if he owns a hundred sheep yet loses one of them, would not leave the ninety-nine in the open grassland and go after the lost one till he had found it? ⁵Moreover, when he has found it, he lifts it on to his shoulders, full of joy. ⁶Then, on reaching home, he calls together his friends and his neighbours, saying to them, 'Share my joy: I have found my sheep that had been lost.' ⁷And what I am saying is this: in the same way more joy will be felt in the heavenly realms over one sinful person who repents than over ninety-nine upright ones who have no call to be repentant of anything.

⁸ "Or again, what woman is there who, having ten silver coins yet losing one of them, does not then light a lamp and sweep the house, searching most carefully until she has found it? ⁹And when she has, she calls together her friends and her neighbours, saying, 'Share my joy: I have found the silver coin which I had lost.' ¹⁰And so I tell you this: in the same way ˣthere is rejoicing among God's angels over one sinner who is led to repentance."

ˣ[Ezk 18:23; 33:11]

[11]Moreover, he told them the following tale: "There was a man who had two sons, [12]and the younger of them said to his father, 'Father, let me have the portion of the property which falls to me.' So the father divided the estate between them. [13]Not long after this, the younger son gathered all his belongings together and went off to a distant country. [y]There he frittered away what he had on a life of dissipation. [14]After he had spent everything, a dire famine fell upon that country, and he began to find himself in want. [15]So he went and attached himself to one of the citizens of that country, who put him on his farm to feed the swine. [16]He was longing to fill his belly with the pods the swine were feeding on, but nobody gave him anything. [17]And so, coming to his senses, he exclaimed, 'How many paid servants of my father's have more food than they can eat! Yet, as for myself, here I am dying of hunger! [18]I shall set out and go to my father, and this is what I shall say to him: 'Father, I have sinned against the God of heaven and against you. [19]I no longer deserve to be spoken of as your son. Assign to me the position of a paid servant of yours.' [20]At that he rose up, setting out for his father's house. However, when he was still a far distance away, the father saw him and was filled with compassion for him. So he ran to meet him, threw his arms round his neck, and kissed him tenderly. [21]'Father,' the son said to him, 'I have sinned against the God of heaven and against you. I no longer deserve to be spoken of as your son.' [22]But the father turned to his servants, saying, 'Go in haste and bring out the best robe that I have. Clothe him with it. Put a ring on his finger and sandals on his feet. [23]Moreover, let the calf which we have been fattening be fetched and killed, so that we can have our fill and give ourselves over to rejoicing. [24]For this son of mine was dead and has come back to life; he was lost and has been found again.' And they began to celebrate a joyous feast.

[25]"Meanwhile the elder son was out in the fields. When he was approaching the house, on his way home, he could hear music and dancing. [26]So he called one of the servants to him to enquire what the meaning of this could possibly be. [27]'Your brother,' the man replied, 'has come back; and your father has killed the calf we have been fattening because he has been restored to him safe and sound.' [28]As for the brother, he got furiously angry at this and refused to go in. The father came out to seek to win him over, [29]but he made him this reply: 'Look, all these years have I been slaving for you, and there was not one command you gave me I ever disobeyed. Yet at no time did you let me have as much as a goat's kid so that I might be able to give myself over to rejoicing in the company of my friends. [30]Yet when that son of yours turned up, he who has swallowed up his patrimony in

[y][Pr 29:3]

the company of harlots, you kill for him the calf which had been fattened up by us.' 31'Dear child,' replied the father, 'you are always with
me, and everything that I have is yours. 32I was bound to rejoice and
to be full of gladness. For this brother of yours was dead and has come
back to life; he was lost and has been found again.'"

16 Another time Jesus addressed his disciples as follows: "There
was a certain rich man who had a steward; and a denunciation was
laid before him to the effect that the steward was squandering the
property. 2So the master summoned the steward and said, 'What is
this I am hearing about you? Draw up an account of your stewardship
for me. It is out of the question that you should remain my steward
any longer.' 3At that the steward said to himself, 'What am I to do,
now that the master is taking the stewardship away from me? Am I
to take to digging with a spade? I do not have the strength for it. Am
I to go begging? I should feel disgraced. 4Ah, I know what I must do
to make sure that, when I am discharged from my position, some will
welcome me into their houses.' 5He then proceeded to summon his
master's debtors, one by one, saying to the first, 'How much do you
owe my master?' 6'One hundred measures of oil,' was the reply. And
the steward said to him, 'Take this bill you have written out, sit down
with all speed, and make it fifty.' 7Then he enquired of another, 'And
you, how much do you owe?' 'One hundred measures of wheat,' was
the reply, the steward saying, 'Take this bill you have written out and
make it eighty.'

8"Now the master commended the knavish steward for the
shrewdness he had shown in what he had done. For the truth is that
the worldly are more prudent in the way they deal with their own
kind than are those who, in the conduct of their lives, aim at following the light.

9"And my counsel to you is this: let money, that base thing, yet
serve you to win friends for yourselves, so that, in the event of its
giving out, they may bid you welcome into the tents of eternity.

10"Whoever can be trusted in little things can also be trusted in
great; and whoever is dishonest in little things is also dishonest in
great. 11If, then, you have been found untrustworthy with money, that
base thing, who will entrust to you that which is of true worth? 12And
if you have been found untrustworthy with what belongs to another,
who will let you have what is truly yours?

13"No servant can be slave of two masters. If he is, he will either
love the one and hate the other, or treat the one with respect and the
other with contempt. You cannot be servants of both God and
money."

¹⁴The Pharisees, who were great lovers of money, heard him say all this and scoffed at him. ¹⁵And Jesus said to them, "You are the ones who are always attempting to pass yourselves off as upright in people's sight. Yet God knows the value of that which is in your hearts. Small wonder, for the very same thing that is considered great among men is in God's sight a thing to be detested.

¹⁶"Up to the time when John appeared it was the law and the prophets that were all in all. Since then it is the kingdom of God that is being proclaimed, everyone seeking by any and every means to find entry into it.

¹⁷"Yet it is easier for heaven and earth to vanish away than that the most trifling point found in the law should cease to be valid.

¹⁸"Anyone divorcing his wife and marrying another woman is an adulterer, and so anyone marrying a woman divorced from her husband is an adulterer.

¹⁹"There was once a rich man, clothed in purple and the finest linen, who feasted in the most sumptuous manner day in and day out. ²⁰At his gate there lay stretched out a poor man by the name of Lazarus, a man covered with sores ²¹and longing to have his fill of the scraps which fell from the rich man's table. Far from it: instead, things became so bad for him that even the dogs came to vex him by licking his wounds.

²²"In due course the poor man died and was carried away by the angels to Abraham's bosom. In turn the rich man also died and was buried.

²³"When he found himself in Hades, being in great torment, he looked up and saw Abraham, a long way off, with Lazarus leaning on his bosom. ²⁴So he cried out, 'Father Abraham, have pity on me and send Lazarus over here, so that, dipping the tip of his finger in water, he may bring refreshment to my tongue. For I am suffering agonies here in this flame.' ²⁵'My son,' replied Abraham, 'be mindful that during your lifetime the good things came your way, just as bad things came the way of Lazarus. And so it is that he is being comforted here, while you are suffering agonies. ²⁶What is more, a great gulf is fixed between you and us, so that those wishing to pass from our side to yours cannot do so; neither do any cross over from your side to ours.'

²⁷"'I beg of you, father,' was the rich man's answer, 'to send him to my father's house. ²⁸I have five brothers, and he is to give them warning, so that they may not, in their turn, have to come to this place of torment.' ²⁹'They have Moses and the prophets,' was Abraham's answer; 'let them listen to them.' ³⁰'Ah no, father Abraham,' said the other, 'if they have somebody coming to them from the realm of the dead, they will be made to feel repentant.' ³¹'If they do not listen to

Moses and the prophets,' said Abraham to him, 'neither will they allow themselves to be convinced, even though someone should rise from the dead.'"

17 One day Jesus addressed these words to his disciples: "That occasions for sinning should arise is indeed wholly inevitable. Still, what wretchedness is in store for the person providing such an occasion. ²It would be better for him to be thrown into the sea with a millstone put round his neck than that he should be the cause of one of these little ones' being led astray. ³Keep a check on yourselves.

"If your fellow man does you a wrong, administer a rebuke to him; and if he repents, forgive him. ⁴And if he wrongs you seven times in one day, and seven times comes back to you saying, 'I feel repentant', you are to forgive him."

⁵"Make our faith increase," the apostles said to the Lord. ⁶And this is what the Lord said in reply: "If you had faith, even though it were no more than the size of a mustard seed, you might say to this sycamore tree,* 'Be uprooted and replanted in the sea,' and it would obey you.

⁷"Suppose one of you had a servant whom he employed for ploughing or for tending the sheep, would he say to him on his returning from the fields, 'Come here immediately and sit down to eat'? ⁸Would he not rather say, 'Get my meal ready, put your belt round you, and then, while I eat and drink, wait on me. You can do your own eating and drinking afterwards'? ⁹Moreover, when the servant has carried out the order he has been given, there is no question of the master's being grateful to him. ¹⁰You are in the very same position. After you have done everything you have been ordered to do, this is what you must say to yourselves: 'We are merely servants, not deserving of any credit whatever. We have done nothing except what we were obliged to do.'"

¹¹At one time when, in the course of his journey to Jerusalem, he was travelling along the border between Samaria and Galilee ¹²and was entering a certain village, he encountered ten men who were lepers. They took up their stand at a considerable distance and, ¹³raising their voices, exclaimed, "Jesus! Master! Have pity on us!" ¹⁴When his eyes fell on them, he addressed them with the words, "Go off and ᶻ**present** yourselves **to the priests.**" And while they were on their

ᶻLv 13:49; 14:2f

* Or mulberry tree.

way, they were cleansed. [15] One among them, on realizing that he was healed, turned back, giving praise to God at the top of his voice, [16] and threw himself at Jesus' feet to express his gratitude to him. And the man was a Samaritan. [17] In response to this Jesus exclaimed, "How is this? Were not ten men cleansed? Where are the other nine? [18] Was not even one of them found turning back to give thanks to God? Not one among them did, except this man of alien descent." [19] Then he turned to the man and said, "Rise up and be on your way. It is your faith that has given you back your health."

[20] On one occasion Jesus was asked by the Pharisees at what time the kingdom of God would be coming. And this is the reply he made them: "The kingdom of God does not come by being watched out for. [21] People will not be saying, 'Look, here it is!' or 'Look, there it is!' In point of fact, the kingdom of God is right among you."

[22] Moreover, he spoke to his disciples as follows: "Time will come when you will be longing to witness but a single day of the era when the Son of Man will bear rule, and shall not witness one such day. [23] They will be saying to you, 'Look, there it is!', 'Look, here it is!' Do not move away from the spot where you are; do not go off in pursuit. [24] For as lightning flashes forth, illuminating one part of the sky and then another, so will the nature of the Son of Man be when his day arrives. [25] However, it is laid down that, before this can happen, he will have to undergo great sufferings and be repudiated by this generation.

[26] "Moreover, just as things were in the time of Noah, so they will be when the days of the Son of Man appear. [27] People ate, they drank, they married, they were joined together in marriage, up to the very day [a] **when Noah entered the ark.** Then the deluge came and destroyed them all. [28] Things will happen in the same way as they did in the time of Lot. People ate, they drank, they bought, they sold, they planted, they built houses. [29] However, the day Lot came out of Sodom [b] **a rain of fire and sulphur descended from the sky** and destroyed them all. [30] Things will proceed after the same fashion when the day comes for the Son of Man to stand revealed.

[31] "On that day he who finds himself on the roof, with his belongings inside the house, must not come down to collect them. And he who finds himself in the field must not [c] **turn back.** [32] Remind yourselves of Lot's wife. [33] The truth is that the man whose aim is to preserve his own life is the one that will lose it. It is he who loses it who will keep it safe, and live. [34] And this I have to tell you: during the night, if two men are in the same bed, one will be taken, the other left. [35] If two women are grinding corn in the same place, one will be

[a] Gn 7:7.23   [b] Gn 19:24   [c] Gn 19:26

taken, the other left."* [37] At that they enquired of him, "Where is it to be, Lord?" And this is the reply he made: "Where the corpse is, that is the place in which the vultures gather together."

18
One day he told them a parable with a view to showing them that it was their duty to devote themselves to constant prayer, never allowing themselves to be discouraged. [2] "In a certain town," he said, "there lived a judge, a man who had no fear of God and was without any regard for man. [3] And there was a widow in the same town who kept coming to him, saying, 'See to it that I obtain justice against my foe.' [4] For a long time he flatly refused. But then he said to himself, 'True enough, I have no fear of God and I am without any regard for man. [5] Still, seeing that this widow is troubling me so, I shall obtain justice for her, lest her coming should in the end wear me out completely.' [6] You hear," the Lord added, "the words of the unjust judge. [7] Will not God obtain justice for his chosen ones who cry out to him night and day? Will he make long delay in coming to their aid? [8] I am telling you: he will obtain justice for them with all speed. Still, will the Son of Man, when he appears, find any faith upon the earth?"

[9] And this is a parable he addressed to certain people who were convinced in their own minds that they were upright, pouring contempt on everybody else. [10] "Two men went up to the temple to pray, one a Pharisee and the other a tax collector. [11] The Pharisee took up his stand and proceeded to say this prayer to himself: 'My thanks to you, O God, seeing that I am not like the rest of them, rapacious, unjust, given over to adultery, or, for that matter, like this tax collector. [12] I fast twice a week; I pay tithes on all the goods that I obtain.'

[13] "As for the tax collector, on the other hand, standing a long way off he did not even have the courage to lift up his eyes towards heaven. He merely kept beating his breast, exclaiming, 'O God, have mercy on me, sinful man that I am!' [14] What I am saying to you is this: it was he, rather than the other, who returned to his home, a man again at rights with God. The truth is that he who exalts himself will find himself humbled, while he who humbles himself will find himself exalted."

[15] People even went so far as to carry small infants into his presence that he might touch them with his hands. The disciples, on seeing this, rebuked them. [16] But he, calling the little ones to his side, spoke these words: "Let the children come to me, and do not prevent them. For it is to such as these that the kingdom of God belongs. [17] And I am telling you this in solemn truth: he who does not accept the kingdom of God in the way in which a child would, will never find entry into it."

* V. 36 is probably not part of the original text.

¹⁸On one occasion a man who occupied a position of influence put this question to him: "Good Master, what must I do to obtain possession of eternal life?" ¹⁹"Why call me good?" Jesus said in reply. "There is only one that is good: God himself. ²⁰The commandments are known to you: ^d**do not commit adultery, do not do murder, do not steal, do not give false testimony, pay honour to your father and to your mother**". ²¹"All this," was the man's reply, "have I kept since I was but a child." ²²When Jesus heard this, he said to him, "One thing you still lack. Sell everything you have and divide the proceeds among the poor. Then a treasure shall be yours, a treasure in heaven. And after that, come to my side and follow me." ²³When the man heard this, he began to feel very dejected, for he had great wealth.

²⁴And Jesus, for his part, fixing his eyes upon him, said, "What obstacles are placed in the way of those having money when it comes to making their way into the kingdom of God! ²⁵Truth to tell, it is easier for a camel to slip through the eye of a needle than it is for a rich man to make his entry into the kingdom of God." ²⁶When the others heard this, they asked him, "Who then is there capable of obtaining salvation?" ²⁷"Things that are impossible for men," he replied, "are possible for God."

²⁸Upon this, Peter addressed these words to him: "Here we are, having given up everything we possessed to become your followers." ²⁹Jesus made him this reply: "I am telling you in solemn truth: there is no one who has given up his house, his wife, his brothers, his parents, or his children, for the sake of the kingdom of God, ³⁰who will not find himself repaid many times over in this order of things, while in the world to come having eternal life bestowed upon him."

³¹One day he took the twelve disciples aside, and this is what he said to them: "Here we are, going up to Jerusalem, and all the things the prophets have written about the Son of Man will find their fulfilment. ³²He will be handed over to the Gentiles, sneered at, have insults poured on him, and he will be spat upon. ³³Having flogged him, they will put him to death, but on the third day he will rise again." ³⁴However, as far as the disciples were concerned, they were incapable of comprehending any of this. The matter remained completely hidden from them, Jesus' words being entirely beyond their grasp.

³⁵Now as they were approaching Jericho, it happened that a blind man was sitting on the side of the road begging for alms. ³⁶And that man, hearing the crowd going past him, enquired, being at a loss, what it could possibly mean. ³⁷They told him that Jesus of Nazareth was passing by. ³⁸Upon this he shouted out the words, "Jesus, Son of

^dDt 5:16-20; Ex 20:12-16

David, have pity on me!" [39]The people in front rebuked him sharply, telling him to hold his peace. But he cried out all the louder, "Son of David, have pity on me!" [40]At that, Jesus stopped and gave the order for the man to be brought to him. And as he was drawing near, Jesus enquired of him, [41]"What would you have me do for you?" "Make me regain my sight, Lord," replied the man. [42]Jesus exclaimed, "Regain your sight; your faith has restored you!" [43]Immediately the man, regaining his sight, followed Jesus and glorified God. And all the people, on witnessing this, spoke out in praise of God.

19
After Jesus had entered Jericho, and while he was passing through it, [2]a man called Zacchaeus came upon the scene. He was the head of the tax collectors and a man of great wealth. [3]Although full of eagerness to set eyes on Jesus to find out what kind of man he was, he was prevented by the crowd from doing so, because he was a man of small stature. [4]So he ran some distance ahead and climbed a sycamore tree to catch a glimpse of Jesus, who was to pass that way. [5]When Jesus reached the spot, he looked up and said to him, "Make haste, Zacchaeus, and come down, for today is the day when I must come and stay at your house." [6]He came down with all possible speed and joyfully bade Jesus welcome. [7]At that there was a general murmur of disapprobation among those witnessing the scene, people exclaiming, "He has entered the house of one leading a sinful life, to stay with him!" [8]As for Zacchaeus, he was standing there, and this is what he said to the Lord: "Here and now, Lord, I am making over half of what I have to the poor; and if I have extorted anything from anyone, I am ready to make a fourfold return." [9]Jesus replied to him thus: "Today salvation has come to this house, for the truth is that this man, too, is one of Abraham's sons. [10]And indeed, if the Son of Man has made his appearance, it was so that he should be able to [e]**seek out** and save **that which had been lost.**"

[11]The people's attention was still fixed on this when Jesus proceeded to tell them a parable. And this he did because, since he had now drawn close to Jerusalem, the people were under the impression that God's kingdom was to be shown forth in the immediate future. [12]"There was once," he told them, "a man of noble birth who was setting out on a journey to a distant country, there to obtain a royal title for himself, and then to return home. [13]But first of all he summoned ten of his servants, giving them a pound each, and addressing them in these words: 'Trade with this while I am away.' [14]As for his compatriots, they did in fact hold him in detestation, and so

[e]Ezk 34:16

they sent a delegation, right on his heels, with this message: 'We will not have this man as our king.' 15However, back he came, having obtained his kingship, and gave the order that the servants to whom he handed over the money were to come into his presence, so that he might be in a position to ascertain what profit each one had made from his trading. 16The first made his appearance, saying, 'Sir, your pound has made ten more pounds.' 17'Well done, excellent servant that you are,' he replied. 'Seeing that you have shown yourself to be deserving of trust even in so insignificant a matter, you shall be given authority over ten cities.' 18After that the second came, saying, 'Your pound, sir, has made a profit of five pounds.' 19And to him he spoke in the same way, saying, 'You, too, shall be a ruler, with authority over five cities.' 20Along came the third, saying, 'Look, sir, here is your pound. I put it away safely wrapped in a handkerchief. 21This was because of the fear I had of you. After all, you are a very harsh man, one claiming as his own that which he never ventured on, one harvesting that which he never sowed.' 22And this was the master's reply: 'I am condemning you out of your own mouth, worthless servant that you are! You knew that I was a very harsh man, claiming as my own that which I never ventured on and harvesting that which I never sowed. 23Why then did you not put my money into the bank, so that on my return I could have collected it, along with the interest that had accrued?' 24And this is what he said to those who were present at the scene: 'Take the pound from him and give it to the man with the ten pounds.' 25'But sir,' they replied, 'he has ten pounds already.' 26'I am telling you,' he answered, 'everyone who has something will have more given to him, while he who has nothing will have taken away from him even the little that he has. 27And as for these enemies of mine who did not want me for their king, bring them here and make havoc of them before my very eyes.' "

28Having told this story, Jesus went on with his journey, going up to Jerusalem. 29As he was approaching Bethany and Bethphage, two places lying close to the hill called the Mount of Olives, he sent two of his disciples on an errand, giving them these instructions: 30"Go on to the village that lies right opposite us. There, as you enter, you will find a colt tethered, on which as yet no one has ever ridden. Untie it and bring it here. 31And if anyone should ask you, 'Why are you untying the colt?' this must be your answer: 'The master has need of it.' 32The messengers went off and found everything just as he had told them. 33And as they untied the colt its owners asked them, "Why are you untying the colt?" 34"The master has need of it," they said. 35So they brought it to Jesus. Then they threw their cloaks over the colt, for Jesus to mount it; 36and as he moved forward, they proceeded, as they went along, to carpet the road with their garments. 37And now when he was reaching the downward slope of the Mount of Olives, the whole company of the disciples was filled with great joy and began to burst forth in praise of God on account of all the wondrous things they had been witnessing. 38 And they exclaimed, "*f*Blessings on the king, on him **who makes his appearance in the name of the Lord!** Peace be in heaven, and glory in the highest heavens!"

39 Upon this some of the Pharisees in the crowd said to him, "Master, reprimand your disciples." 40 "One thing I can assure you of," he said in reply, "even though these were to hold their peace, the very *g*stones would be **crying out.**"

41 And as he was approaching the city, and saw it lying before him, he shed tears over it, 42 exclaiming, "If only you in your turn had understood, this very day, the things which make for your peace! Yet, as it is, they are hidden from your sight. 43 Indeed, the time is coming when your enemies will be *h*setting up siege works all round you, when they will encircle you, when they will hem you in on every side. 44 *i***They will dash you to the ground,** you yourself as well as **your children** that live within your walls. Moreover, they will not leave you one stone standing on another. And all this because, when the moment came for you to receive a gracious visit, you failed to recognize it."

45 Then he went into the temple and began to drive out those who were selling their goods there, 46 saying to them, "This is what stands written in scripture, *j*'**My house shall be a house of prayer'**; but you have turned it into a *k***robbers' den.**"

47 Day by day he taught in the temple. The chief priests and the experts in the law, with the support of those holding positions of influence among the people, were bent on making an end of him. 48 However, they were incapable of discovering means suitable for achieving their purpose, by reason of the fact that all the people were hanging on his words.

20 One day Jesus was giving instruction to the people in the temple, proclaiming the gospel, when the chief priests and the experts in the law, along with the elders, came up to him in protest and asked him, 2 "Will you be good enough to tell us what kind of authority makes you act in this manner, and from whom that authority derives?" 3 "I, too, will ask you a question," he retorted, "and you must give me the proper answer. 4 Did the baptism administered by John have its source in God or in men?" 5 Upon this they set about debating the matter with one another. "If we say, 'In God'," they argued,

*f*Ps 118:26   *g*Hab 2:11   *h*Is 29:3   *i*Ps 137:9   *j*Is 56:7   *k*Jr 7:11

"then he will ask us, 'Why, then, did you refuse to trust him?' 6 And if we say, 'In men', then the people will, one and all, join in stoning us, because they are convinced that John was a prophet." 7So they replied that they did not know what source it had. 8"Neither shall I tell you," retorted Jesus, "by whose authority I am acting the way I do."

9 And he went on to tell the people this parable: "A certain man *l*plantęd a vineyard, hired it out to vinegrowers, then went away to spend a long time in a foreign country. 10Later, when the proper time had come, he sent out one of his servants to the vinegrowers to collect his share of the vineyard's produce. Yet what the vinegrowers did was to give the servant a thrashing and to send him away empty-handed. 11The owner did not give up, however, and proceeded to send another servant. Him, too, they thrashed, and having treated him in a most humiliating manner, they sent him away empty-handed. 12The owner still would not give up, and sent a third servant. But they, for their part, wounded him badly and threw him out. 13So the owner of the vineyard asked himself, 'What am I to do? I know; I shall send my own dear son to them. It may be that they will be moved by respect for him.' 14However, the vinegrowers, when they saw him, set about arguing the matter out with one another, and this is what they said: 'This man is the heir. Let us kill him, so that the inheritance may pass into our hands.' 15And so, throwing him out of the vineyard, they did away with him.

"Now what do you think the owner of the vineyard will do to these men? 16He will come himself and make an end of these vinegrowers, handing over the vineyard to others." On hearing this his audience exclaimed, "God forbid that that should happen." 17But he, fixing his gaze on them, called out, "What then, is to be made of these words in scripture, *m*'**The very stone which the builders rejected has become the cornerstone**'? 18Indeed, if a man falls on that stone, he will be dashed to pieces, while if the stone falls on him, it will grind him to powder."

19The experts in the law and the Pharisees, who were perfectly well aware that this parable was directed against them, dearly wished that they could lay their hands on him there and then, but they were afraid of the people. 20And so, being on the lookout for their opportunity, they despatched certain men who pretended to be seekers after uprightness but were in fact paid agents. Their reason for acting this way was that they desired to catch Jesus out in something he might say, so that they might be in a position to hand him over to the jurisdiction and authority of the Governor. 21The emissaries put this ques-

*l*Is 5:1   *m*Ps 118:22

tion to him. "Master," they said, "we are aware that everything you say and teach is perfectly straightforward, that you do not allow yourself to have favourites but teach the way of life required by God with complete honesty. 22Well then, is it permissible or is it not to pay taxes to the Emperor?" 23Jesus said to them, seeing through their trickery easily enough, 24"Show me a piece of silver. Whose head and inscription do you find on it?" "The Emperor's," they replied. 25"Well and good," he said. "Pay the Emperor what is due to the Emperor, and pay God what is due to God." 26Because of these words of his their attempt to catch him out in something he might say came to grief; and, being taken aback by his reply, they kept their peace.

27Then certain Sadducees approached him—this being the group which denies that there is any such thing as a resurrection. They proceeded to interrogate him. 28"Master," they said, "Moses has laid down in writing the following command for us: *n***If a man's brother dies, married but childless, the one left must marry the widow to raise up offspring on his brother's behalf**. 29Well then, there were seven brothers. The first took a wife and died childless. 30The second and then the third married the widow. 31In fact, things fell out in the same way with all seven. They died leaving no children. 32Finally, the woman also died. 33Now our question is this: whose wife will she be at the resurrection, seeing that she had been married to all seven?"

34Jesus replied to them thus: "Those who have their home in this world of ours marry and are joined to another in marriage. 35But those who are held worthy of the other world and of having a share in the resurrection from the dead neither marry nor are joined together in marriage, 36because they are no longer subject to death. Their nature is like that of the angels. In fact, they are God's sons, having become so by being partakers of the resurrection. 37As for the fact that the dead are raised to life again, this is indicated by Moses in the passage about the burning bush, in the place where he calls the Lord *o***the God of Abraham, the God of Isaac**, and **the God of Jacob**. 38Now God is the God not of the dead, but of the living. All are alive through having him for their God."

39The response made to this by the experts in the law was that they said, "Master, you have indeed spoken well." 40In point of fact, they did not have the courage to ask him any further questions.

41Jesus then asked them, "What do people mean by asserting that God's anointed is a descendant of David's? 42Why, David himself says in the Book of Psalms, *p***The Lord said to him who is my Lord,** 43**"Take your seat at my right hand until I make your enemies a**

*n*Gn 38:8; Dt 25:5f   *o*Ex 3:2.6   *p*Ps 110:1

footstool for your feet."' ⁴⁴Now, seeing that David calls him Lord, how can he be a descendant of his?"

⁴⁵In the hearing of all the people Jesus addressed these words to the disciples: ⁴⁶"Be on your guard against the experts in the law. They take a delight in strutting about in their flowing robes and have a fondness for exchanging greetings in the market place, for obtaining the best seats in the synagogues, and for securing the places of honour at banquets. ⁴⁷These are the men who swallow up the property of widowed women and who engage in lengthy prayers for the sake of appearances. The sentence they have to expect will be all the heavier for that."

21

He looked up, and his eyes fell on the rich people putting their offerings into the receptacle set up for the contributions. ²Then he noticed a poverty-stricken widow putting in two tiny coins. ³"I assure you in very truth," he said, "that this widow, poor as she is, has put in more than all the rest of them. ⁴For these, without exception, made their offerings out of a superfluity of means, while she made hers out of an insufficiency of means. In point of fact, she gave everything she had to keep herself alive."

⁵When certain people talked about the temple, remarking how beautifully adorned it was with stonework and votive offerings, he said, ⁶"As regards that which you are seeing before you, time will come when not a single stone will be left on another." ⁷So they asked him this question: "Master, when will that be, and what will be the sign indicating that it is about to happen?" ⁸"Take care," he retorted, "not to allow yourselves to be led astray. Indeed, many will appear and make use of my name, saying, 'It is I', or 'The time is close at hand.' You must on no account go after them. ⁹And again, when you hear of wars and insurrections, you must not allow yourselves to be overcome by terror. ⁋**It is preordained that these things should happen,** while it is true at the same time that the end does not come immediately after this." ¹⁰Then he resumed and said to them, "ʳ**One nation will rise up in arms against another nation, and one kingdom against another kingdom.** ¹¹Violent earthquakes there will be, and there will be pestilence and famine in place after place. Moreover, there will be awesome signs and sinister portents from heaven.

¹²"However, before any of this happens, people will lay their hands on you and persecute you. They will hand you over to the synagogues and drag you into prison, all on account of your defending the cause that bears my name. You will be haled before kings and before gover-

⁋Dn 2:28   ʳIs 19:2; 2 Ch 15:6

nors by reason of your speaking in my name. [13]This will serve you as an opportunity for bearing testimony. [14]And so there is one more thing that you should keep carefully in mind: you must not consider beforehand the manner in which your defence is to be made, [15]for I shall bestow upon you such eloquence and such wisdom that none of your adversaries shall be able to offer effective resistance to it or confute it. [16]You will be betrayed by parents, by brothers, by your kindred, and by your friends. Some of you they will put to death, [17]and you will be hated by everyone because of your allegiance to the cause that bears my name. [18]Still, you may be sure of this: you will not suffer the loss of one hair on your head. [19]It is by holding out that you will secure possession of your souls.

[20]"When you see Jerusalem encompassed by a mass of troops, then you may be certain that the time of her devastation is at hand. [21]Then let those who find themselves in Judaea take flight, seeking for shelter in the hills. Moreover, those who are inside the city must depart from it, while those who are in the open country must not make their entry into it. [22]For these are [s]**the days of retribution,** the days during which all that stands written in scripture is to find its fulfilment. [23]Alas for women with child in those days and for those who have infants at the breast! For bitter distress will be upon the land, and anger will rage against this people. [24]They will perish by the edge of the sword, be carried captive into all the lands of the Gentiles, and [t]**Jerusalem will be trampled on by the Gentiles** until the time allotted to the Gentiles has run its course.

[25]"Moreover, portents will be appearing in the sun, in the moon, and in the stars. Upon earth nations will be dismayed, finding themselves in anxious perplexity by reason of the [u]**roaring of the sea** and the violent **motion** of its waves. [26]Men will be fainting with terror because of their expectation of what will befall the inhabited world. Indeed, the [v]**celestial hosts** themselves will be made to **totter.** [27]And then they will see the [w]**Son of Man appearing in a cloud,** equipped with great power and majesty. [28]When these things begin to take shape, then hold yourselves erect, lifting up your heads, because your liberation is close at hand."

[29]And he gave them an illustration in the form of a parable: "Consider the fig tree," he said, "or for that matter, any other tree. [30]Once they have put out their leaves, you know by yourselves, on looking at them, that summer is now near. [31]In the same way, when you see these things happening, be sure that the kingdom of God is close at hand. [32]And I am telling you this in solemn truth: this generation will

[s]Dt 32:35; Hos 9:7; Jr 5:29   [t]Dn 8:13; Is 63:18; [Tb 14:5-7]   [u]Ps 65:7   [v]Is 34:4   [w]Dn 7:13

not have passed away before all this has taken place. ³³Heaven and earth will pass away, but my words will not pass away.

³⁴"Take care of yourselves to make certain that your minds are not dulled by a life of dissipation and drunkenness or by your being taken up with anxieties about everyday matters, with the result that this great day is sprung on you, all of a sudden, ³⁵like a ^x**trap.** For it will indeed come down **upon** every person **living** on the face of the **earth.** ³⁶Be on the alert, praying at all times to be given the strength to escape from all these things which are destined to happen, and to be able to stand erect in the presence of the Son of Man."

³⁷The daytime he would devote to giving instruction in the temple, but at night he left it, spending his time on the Mount of Olives. ³⁸And from early morning onward all the people gathered round him in the temple to listen to his words.

22 The time for the Feast of Unleavened Bread, known as the Passover, was now drawing near. ²The chief priests and the experts in the law, while afraid of the people, were still debating about how they could do away with him.

³And it was then that Satan entered the heart of Judas, surnamed Iscariot, he being one of the twelve disciples. ⁴So he went off to discuss with the chief priests and the officers of the temple the most suitable means of handing Jesus over to them. ⁵They were overjoyed and came to an agreement with him that they were to give him money. ⁶Judas gave his consent and began to look out for a favourable opportunity of handing him over without causing a public disturbance.

⁷The day of unleavened bread, on which the Passover lamb was to be slaughtered, arrived; ⁸and Jesus sent out Peter and John, saying to them, "Go and make the necessary preparations which will enable us to eat the Passover meal." ⁹"Where do you want us to prepare it?" they asked. ¹⁰"Listen carefully," he replied; "on entering the city you will encounter a man carrying a water jar. Follow him into the house where he is going, and say to the owner of the house, ¹¹'This is the message the Master is sending you: "Where is the guest room in which I may eat the Passover meal with my disciples?"' ¹²Upon this the man will show you a large room in the upper part of the house, all set out. There you are to make your preparations." ¹³They went on their way, finding things just as he had told them, and prepared the Passover meal.

¹⁴When the time came, Jesus took his place at table, and his apostles

^xIs 24:17

were with him. And this is what he said to them: [15]"How great has been my longing to eat this Passover meal in your company before having to undergo my sufferings. [16]And indeed, I must tell you: I shall not eat it again until the time when it finds its fulfilment in the kingdom of God."

[17]Then he seized a cup with his hands, and having first of all given thanks, he spoke to them thus: "Take this and share it among yourselves. [18]And indeed, I have to tell you this: never again, from this time on, shall I drink of the produce of the vine until the kingdom of God has made its appearance." [19]Thereupon he laid hold of some bread, and, having given thanks, he broke it into pieces, handed it to them, then said, "This is my body, offered up for your sake. Do this by way of a memorial of me." [20]The meal having been completed, he did the same with the cup, saying, "This cup is the New Covenant sealed with my ʸblood, which is to be poured out for your sake.

[21]"But mark this: the hand of the man who is to betray me is lying here on this table by the side of mine. [22]So the Son of Man is setting out on his road, in accordance with what has been decreed. And yet, woe upon the man by whom he is being betrayed!" [23]At this they fell to debating among themselves which of them could conceivably be the one who would do such a deed.

[24]There also arose a controversy among them about which of them was to rank highest. And this is what Jesus said to them: [25]"Those who bear kingly rule over the Gentile nations lord it over them, while at the same time they refer to those having authority over them as their benefactors. [26]It is not to be so with you. On the contrary, let him who occupies the highest position bear himself as if he were the youngest, him who is leader as though he were performing the part of the servant. [27]Well then, which is the greater: the man who sits at table or the man who serves him? Surely the man who sits at table. Yet here I am in your midst, acting the part of the servant.

[28]"You are the men who have stood firmly by me throughout my trials. [29]And now I am vesting in you the kingship which my Father vested in me. [30]You are to eat and drink at my table in my kingdom. Moreover, you are to take your seats on thrones, acting as judges over the twelve tribes of Israel.

[31]"Simon, O Simon, attend to my words. Satan has demanded that you should all be given over to him, so that you may be subjected to sifting as grain is sifted. [32]And as for yourself, I have prayed on your behalf that your faith should not fail you. And you, once you are restored, must play your part in giving strength to your brothers." [33]"Lord," was Peter's reply, "with you at my side I should be ready

ʸEx 24:8; Zc 9:11

to go anywhere, even though it were to prison or to my death." [34] And Jesus made him this answer: "I am telling you, Peter, before cockcrow today you will three times have denied all knowledge of me."

[35] Then he spoke to them thus: "After my sending you forth barefoot, without either purses or knapsack, were you ever short of anything?" "We were not," they replied. [36] "Yet now," he said to them, "things are different. Everyone having a purse or a knapsack may take them with him. Whoever does not have a sword, let him sell his cloak and buy one. [37] For what I am telling you is that there are words in scripture which had to find their fulfilment in me, and they are these: [z]'**He was counted among the outlaws**'. Indeed, whatever in the scripture has reference to me is even now finding its fulfilment." [38] "Master, there are two swords here," was their rejoinder. "That will do," he said to them.

[39] Upon this he took his departure and, as was his custom, made his way to the Mount of Olives. His disciples did the same, following in his footsteps. [40] On reaching the place, this is what he said to them: "Pray that you do not have to go the way which leads to the hour of trial." [41] Then he withdrew himself from their presence, moving about a stone's throw away, fell on his knees, and prayed thus: [42] "If this be your will, Father, take this chalice away from me. However, your will is to be accomplished, not mine." [43] And an angel coming from God made his appearance before him to give him strength. [44] A great struggle ensued, one which made him pray all the more fervently. He broke out in a sweat, one that resembled clots of blood falling on the ground.

[45] On rising from his prayer, he went back to his disciples, whom he found to have fallen asleep by reason of their grief. [46] "Why is it that you are sleeping?" he said to them. "Rise up and pray that you do not have to go the way which leads to the hour of trial."

[47] While these words were still being uttered, a crowd appeared all of a sudden, and at the head of it the man called Judas, one of the twelve disciples. He went up to Jesus to kiss him, at which Jesus exclaimed, [48] "Is it with a kiss, Judas, that you are betraying the Son of Man?"

[49] When his companions saw what was about to happen, they asked, "Lord, shall we strike out with our swords?" [50] One of them actually did strike out, cutting off the right ear of one of the High Priest's servants. [51] But Jesus called out, "Leave off; no more of this." Then he touched the man's ear and healed him.

[52] Then Jesus turned to those who had come out to take action against him: the chief priests, the captains of the temple guard, and the elders. And this is what he said: "It is with swords and with cudgels in hand that you have set out, as though you had to deal with

[z]Is 53:12

a brigand. [53]Why, when I was day after day in your company in the temple, you did not stretch out your hands against me. But let it be: this is the hour which belongs to you; this is the reign of darkness."

[54]So they seized him, took him away, and brought him to the house of the High Priest. As for Peter, he followed, some distance away. [55]They lit a fire in the centre of the courtyard, proceeding to sit down round it. And there was Peter, sitting right among them. [56]Now a certain servant girl was present. On seeing him seated there by the blaze, she fixed her gaze on him and exclaimed, "That man, too, was in his company!" [57]But Peter called out, by way of a disclaimer, "Woman, I have no knowledge of him!" [58]A short time after that someone else saw him and said, "You, too, are one of their number", Peter's retort being, "I am nothing of the sort, man!" [59]About an hour had passed when yet another firmly asserted, "Of a truth, he also was one of his companions. Indeed, he is a native of Galilee." [60]"Man, I do not know what you are saying!" was Peter's reply. At this very instant, while he was still uttering these words, a cock was heard to crow; [61]and the Lord, turning round, looked Peter straight in the face. And Peter called to mind the words which the Lord had spoken to him: 'Before the crowing of the cock today you will have denied me three times'. [62]And going outside, he burst into bitter tears.

[63]Meanwhile the men guarding Jesus sneered at him and gave him a beating. [64]Moreover, they blindfolded him and kept flinging questions at him. "Well now," they said, "play the prophet. Who is it that has struck you?" [65]They spoke many other words against him, covering him with insults.

[66]When daylight came, the elders of the people, the chief priests, and the experts in the law gathered together, led him away, and brought him before their Council. [67]And this is what they said to him: "If you are the one anointed by God, tell us." [68]"If I tell you that I am," was Jesus' reply to them, "you will never believe me; and if I question you, you will never make me an answer. [69]Be that as it may, from this very moment [a]**the Son of Man will be seated at the right hand** of the majesty **of God**." [70]"Are you the Son of God, then?" they all asked. "It is you who say that I am," was his reply to them. [71]"What need of further testimony do we have?" was their rejoinder; "Why, we have heard it ourselves from his own lips." **23**[1]Upon this the whole assembly rose, and they brought him before Pilate.

23 [2]They began to bring accusations against Jesus such as these: "We have found this man subverting our people, seeking to prevent

[a]Dn 7:13; Ps 110:1

men from paying taxes to the Emperor, while at the same time making the claim to be God's anointed and a king." [3] At that Pilate asked him, "Are you the king of the Jews?" "It is you who say that I am," was Jesus' reply. [4] So Pilate said to the chief priests and to the crowds, "I can find no guilt in this man." [5] They were insistent, however, calling out, "He is inciting the people. He started out from Galilee, then he went on teaching all over Judaea, until finally he reached this place."

[6] Thereupon Pilate enquired whether the man came from Galilee. [7] Having ascertained that he belonged to the province ruled over by Herod, he had him despatched to Herod, who was also in Jerusalem at that time. [8] Herod, for his part, was delighted to see Jesus because, having heard of him, he had long been hoping to set eyes on him. Moreover, he was hoping to witness some miracle performed by him. [9] So Herod questioned Jesus at length, but without receiving any reply. [10] And there they were, the chief priests and the experts in the law, taking up their stand and accusing him with great vehemence. [11] As for Herod with his body of troops, they treated him with contempt and made him the object of their mockery. Then, after he had been clothed in a robe of great splendour, he was sent back to Pilate. [12] Herod and Pilate, who up to that time had been hostile to one another, became friends the very same day.

[13] Pilate then called together the chief priests, the men in leading positions, as well as the people, [14] and addressed them thus: "You have brought this man before me, contending that he was inciting the people to rebellion. Yet here I am, having myself investigated the matter, and that in your presence, without my discovering anything in this man which could make him guilty of the charges you have brought against him. [15] Indeed, Herod, too, was unable to discover anything, as is evident from the fact that he has sent him back to us. Well then, it can be seen clearly enough that he has in fact done nothing that would deserve to be punished by death. [16] Am I to have him flogged and grant him a pardon after that?"* [18] At that they all burst into a shout, exclaiming, "Away with him! Pardon Barabbas as a favour to us!" [19] Now Barabbas had been thrown into prison for causing a riot in the city and committing murder. [20] Pilate, in his eagerness to set Jesus free, addressed them again. [21] But they shouted back, "Crucify him! Crucify him!" [22] And he spoke to them a third time. "Why, what crime has he committed? I was unable to discover anything in him to merit death. I shall have him flogged and then set him free." [23] But they raised their voices powerfully, demanding with the greatest urgency that he was to be crucified. And it was these voices of theirs which prevailed. [24] Pilate resolved to accede to their demand.

* V. 17 is probably not part of the original text.

25 He released the man for whom they were asking, the one who had been thrown into prison for causing a riot and committing murder. And as for Jesus, he abandoned him to what they desired.

26 As they were leading him off, they laid hold of a certain man called Simon, a native of Cyrene, who was on his way home from the country, and laid the cross upon his shoulders, making him carry it behind Jesus. 27 A large crowd of people followed him, including certain women, beating their breasts and mourning over him. 28 But Jesus, turning his face towards them, called out, "Do not weep for me, daughters of Jerusalem, but for yourselves *do* weep, and also for your children. 29 For the time is coming—of this you may be sure—when people will say, 'How fortunate are the women who are barren, how fortunate the wombs that never bore children and the breasts that never gave milk!' 30 Then people will *b*call out to the mountains, 'Fall upon us', and to the hills, 'Hide us from sight'. 31 And indeed, if that is how they act when the tree is full of sap, what will they do when it is already dried up?"

32 There were two others—men who were malefactors—who were being taken off with him to be executed. 33 They reached a place, known as the Skull, and there it was that they crucified him, and the malefactors with him, one on his right and the other on his left. 34 "Father," he exclaimed, "forgive them; they do not know what they are doing." Meanwhile, *c*they divided his clothes among themselves by way of casting lots over them. 35 And there the people stood *d*looking on, while their leaders poured scorn on him, saying, "He came to the rescue of others; let him rescue himself if it be true that he is God's anointed, his chosen one." 36 The soldiers also took part in the mocking of him and drew near, offering him of their sour wine. 37 And this is what they said: "If you are the king of the Jews, deliver yourself." 38 (There was, in fact, an inscription above his head reading, 'THIS IS THE KING OF THE JEWS'.)

39 Moreover, one of the malefactors who was hanging there began to pour abuse on him, saying, "Are you not God's anointed? Well then, deliver yourself and deliver us." 40 Upon this the other reprimanded him, saying, "Has all fear of God deserted you because you are under the same condemnation as he is? 41 But then we have been treated justly; for the punishment we received was simply what we deserved for what we had done. Yet this man has committed no wrong at all." 42 Then he added, "Jesus, remember me when you come into your kingdom." 43 "I can assure you of this," was Jesus' reply; "this very day you shall be with me in paradise."

44 By now it was already about midday; and for three hours, the sun

*b*Hos 10:8   *c*Ps 22:18   *d*Ps 22:7

withdrawing its rays, darkness fell over the whole land. [45]Moreover, the curtain in the temple was torn right down the middle. [46]And Jesus, with a mighty voice, exclaimed, "Father, [e]**I am entrusting my spirit to the care of your hands!**" And having said this, he breathed his last. [47]When the centurion saw what had taken place, he spoke words redounding to the glory of God, saying, "Of a certainty, that was a man wholly free from guilt." [48]And all the people who had gathered there for the spectacle, when they saw what had happened, went home beating their breasts. [49]Moreover, all his [f]**intimate friends stood** there, watching things **from afar,** and with them, seeing it all, were the women who had accompanied him from Galilee.

[50]Then there appeared on the scene a man by the name of Joseph, who was a member of the Council. He was a man good and true, [51]who had not found himself in agreement with the Council and its doings. Moreover, he was a native of the Jewish city of Arimathaea, who spent his days in expectation of the kingdom of God. [52]It was he who approached Pilate and asked him for the body of Jesus. [53]He then took it down from the cross, wrapped it in a linen cloth, and placed it in a tomb hewn in the rock, one in which no one had ever been buried. [54]It was the Day of Preparation, and the Sabbath was about to dawn. [55]The women who had been his companions on his journey from Galilee took note of the place where the tomb was and observed how his body was being laid to rest. [56]They then went home to prepare spices and ointment. And on the Sabbath day they did nothing, as the law prescribes.

24 But at very early dawn, on the first day of the week, the women went to the tomb, bringing with them the spices which they had prepared. [2]And what they found was that the stone had been rolled away from the tomb. [3]So they went in, but were unable to find the body anywhere. [4]While they were still wholly at a loss about this, it happened all of a sudden that two men, clothed in gleaming apparel, were by their side. [5]The women were greatly alarmed and were standing with their faces cast down to the ground when the men addressed them in the following words: "Why are you looking among the dead for one who is alive? [6]Remind yourselves of what he told you when he was still in Galilee: [7]that the Son of Man was destined to be given into the hands of sinful men, that he was to be crucified, and that on the third day he was to rise to life again." [8]At that they recalled his words; [9]and when they had returned from the tomb, they reported everything to the eleven disciples and to all the others. [10]The women were Mary of Magdala, Joanna, and Mary the mother of James. The

[e]Ps 31:5   [f]Ps 88:8; 38:11

other women in their company likewise told the apostles the story.
¹¹But to them their words seemed to have every appearance of being
nothing more than empty chatter, and they refused to believe them.

*¹³Moreover, it happened that on the same day two of their com-
pany were walking to a certain village called Emmaus, about seven
miles distant from Jerusalem. ¹⁴They were conversing with one
another about everything that had occurred. ¹⁵And while they were
still holding converse and debating things with one another, there
was Jesus himself, drawing near and walking by their side. ¹⁶However, as far as they were concerned, something was restraining their
vision, so that they did not recognize him. ¹⁷And he spoke to them
thus: "What is it that concerns you in this conversation you are holding as you walk along?" So they stopped, with a sullen look on their
faces. ¹⁸Then one of them—his name was Cleopas—replied to him in
these words: "Why, are you a man who lives in Jerusalem so much
apart from others that you have heard nothing of the things which
have been happening there during the last few days?" ¹⁹"What kind
of things?" he enquired of them. "Things concerning Jesus of
Nazareth," was their reply, "a prophet powerful in both action and
speech, in the sight of God and of all the people: ²⁰how the chief priests
and our rulers handed him over to be sentenced to death and have
him crucified. ²¹As for ourselves, our hope was that he was the man
who would set Israel free. Moreover, to crown it all, three days have
already passed since all this happened. ²²On the other hand, there are
certain women in our company who have caused us great astonishment. They went to the tomb very early in the morning, ²³not finding the body, and, on returning home, they maintained that they had
had a vision of angels, these assuring them that Jesus was alive. ²⁴So
some of our number went off to the tomb and found that things were
exactly as the women had told them. But him they did not see."

²⁵At that Jesus exclaimed, "Men without sense that you are, and
too dull-witted to believe fully in the message proclaimed by the
prophets! ²⁶Was it not preordained that God's anointed should undergo these sufferings, and that this was to be the way in which he
was to enter his state of glory?" ²⁷And taking Moses for his text first
of all, and then all the prophets, he expounded to them all the scripture passages referring to himself.

²⁸By this time they were close to the village for which they were
making, Jesus, for his part, acting as if he wanted to go on further.
²⁹But they urged him strongly to remain with them, saying, "It is already towards evening, and the day is far advanced." So he went into
the house to stay with them. ³⁰When he sat down with them at table,

* V. 12 is probably not part of the original text.

he took some bread into his hands, said a blessing over it, broke it in pieces, and handed it to them. [31] And then it was that their eyes were opened, and they recognized him. With that he vanished from their sight, [32] leaving them saying to one another, "Were not our hearts burning within ourselves as he spoke to us on the road and expounded the scriptures to us?"

[33] Having spoken these words, they rose instantly and made their way back to Jerusalem. They found the eleven disciples gathered there with their companions; [34] and this is what they were told by them: "In very truth the Lord has risen and has appeared to Simon." [35] Then the two described to them what had occurred on the road, and how they had recognized Jesus in the breaking of the bread.

[36] While they were still telling their story, there he was in their midst. [37] They were greatly startled and became thoroughly frightened, because they were under the impression that they were seeing a ghost. [38] But he addressed to them the following words: "Why are you so troubled, and how do such doubts arise in your minds? [39] Look at my hands and my feet to assure yourselves that it is I myself. Touch me as well as look at me. After all, a ghost does not have flesh or bones, as you can perceive that I have."* [41] They were still incredulous because of the joy they were feeling, and full of astonishment. So he asked them, "Have you anything to eat here?" [42] They handed him a piece of broiled fish. [43] And he took it into his hands, eating it before their eyes.

[44] Then he spoke to them thus: "This is what I meant when, while still in your company, I told you that everything written about me in the law of Moses, the prophets, and in the psalms was bound to find its fulfilment." [45] He then went on to open up their minds so as to make them grasp the meaning of the scriptures. [46] "This," he said, "is how it stands written, that the Lord's anointed would suffer death, would rise up on the third day, [47] and that proclamation would be made in his name, addressed to all the nations, calling for repentance, so that people might have their sins forgiven them. As for yourselves, you are [48] to bear witness to all this, beginning from Jerusalem. [49] Moreover, be sure of this: I shall be sending forth to you, for you to receive, the gift promised by my Father. And you must stay on in the city until you have been clothed with the power coming to you from High Heaven."

[50] He led them forth as far as Bethany, raised up his hands, and invoked a blessing upon them. [51] And then, while he was still bestowing his blessing, he separated himself from them and was taken up into heaven. [52] The others then did homage to him and returned, full of joy, to Jerusalem, [53] where they spent their time continually in the temple giving praise to God.

* V. 40 is probably not part of the original text.

THE GOSPEL STORY
AS TOLD BY JOHN

1 It was the Word that was at the very beginning; and the Word was by the side of God, and the Word was the very same as God. [2]It was he who at the very beginning was by the side of God. [3]All things came into being through him, and there was nothing that came into being apart from him. [4]In him there was life, that life which was ever the light of men, [5]the light which shines on in the darkness, and the darkness failing to gain mastery over it.

[6]There was a man that made his appearance, a man sent forth by God; and his name was John. [7]He came to bear witness: he was to be witness of the light, so that everyone might learn to believe through him. [8]It was not that man who was the light; to be a witness of the light was the task appointed to him. [9]Meanwhile, the true light which sheds its light on every man was ever coming into the world. [10]He was in the world, and it was through him that the world came into being. Yet the world did not acknowledge him. [11]He came into a realm that was his, and those who were his very own would not accept him. [12]Yet to those who would receive him, to those placing their trust in his very name, he granted the right to become God's children, [13]they being the ones whose birth was not owing to their bodily descent, not to the promptings of fleshly desire, nor to the promptings of man, but who took birth from God himself. [14]So the Word became a creature of flesh and blood and made his stay in our midst. And we saw his glory, the glory which is his as the Father's only Son, coming forth from the Father, full of grace and truth.

[15]John bears him witness, crying aloud, "He it is concerning whom I spoke the words, 'He who comes after me has taken precedence over me, because he was before I was.'" [16]Out of his fullness we have, all of us, received grace upon grace. [17]For while the law was given through Moses, truth and grace have come through Jesus Christ. [18]No one has ever seen God. It is his only Son, who rests on the breast of the Father, who has made him known.

[19]And this is the testimony borne by John when the Jews sent priests

and Levites from Jerusalem to ask him who he was. [20]He admitted the truth. He denied nothing but admitted that he was not the Christ. [21]"How is it then," they enquired; "are you Elijah?" He replied, "I am not." "Are you the prophet, then, that is expected?" He answered, "No." [22]"Who are you, then?" they asked. "We must take back an answer to those who have sent us. What have you to say about yourself?" [23]And this is what he replied: "I am, as the prophet Isaiah has foretold, the [a]**voice of one crying out in the desert: Make the Lord's highway straight.**" [24]Now these men, who had been sent out by the Pharisees, [25]asked of him this further question: "How is it that you are baptizing if you are neither the Christ nor Elijah nor the prophet that is expected?" [26]John replied to them in these words: "I baptize with water. Yet standing in your midst is one whom you do not know. [27]He is the one who is to make his appearance after me: the very man the straps of whose shoes I am not worthy to unfasten." [28]These things took place at Bethany beyond the Jordan, where John was baptizing.

[29]The next day John saw Jesus coming towards him and said, "Look, there is the Lamb of God, who takes the world's sin away! [30]He is the man about whom I said, 'He who comes after me has taken precedence over me, because he was before I was'. [31]I myself did not know him. Yet, if I came forth baptizing with water, it was so that he might be revealed to Israel." [32]John testified further, saying, "I saw the Spirit coming down from heaven like a dove and resting upon him. [33]I did not know him. Yet he who sent me out to baptize with water had said to me, 'If there be someone on whom you see the Spirit coming down and resting upon him, that is the man who will baptize with the Holy Spirit.' [34]And I myself have seen it, and bear testimony that it is he who is the Son of God."

[35]The following day John was once again standing there with two of his disciples. [36]And when Jesus was passing, John fixed his gaze on him and said, "Look, there is the Lamb of God!" [37]The two disciples, hearing him say this, followed Jesus. [38]And when Jesus, on turning round, saw them following him, he asked them, "What is it you want?" They said to him, "Rabbi" (which, correctly translated, means 'Teacher'), "where are you staying?" [39]He answered them, "Come and see for yourselves." So they went and saw where he was staying and spent the rest of the day with him. It was then about four o'clock in the afternoon. [40]Now one of the two who had heard what John had said and had followed Jesus was Andrew, Simon Peter's brother. [41]The first thing he did was to seek out his brother Simon; and when he came upon him, he said to him, "We have found the Messiah" (which, correctly translated, means 'Christ'). [42]He took him

[a]Is 40:3

to Jesus, who, fixing his gaze upon him, said, "You are Simon, son of John. Your name shall be Cephas" (the proper rendering of this being 'Peter', that is to say, 'Rock').

[43] The next day Jesus, having resolved to set out for Galilee, came upon Philip and said to him, "Follow me." [44] Now the place from which Philip came was Bethsaida, the town to which Andrew and Peter belonged. [45] Philip went to look for Nathanael and, on finding him, said to him, "We have found the man of whom Moses wrote in the law and of whom the prophets have written: he is Jesus, son of Joseph, from Nazareth." [46] "Can anything good come out of Nazareth?" Nathanael asked him, Philip replying, "Come and see for yourself." [47] Now this is what Jesus said about Nathanael when he saw him coming towards him: "Here is an Israelite worthy of that name, a man with no guile in him." [48] "How is it that you know me?" Nathanael asked him. "Before Philip came to you with his summons," was Jesus' reply, "I saw you when you were underneath the fig tree." [49] "Rabbi," said Nathanael, "you are the Son of God; you are the king of Israel." [50] "Is this the ground of your faith," was Jesus' rejoinder, "that I said I saw you when you were underneath the fig tree? You shall see greater things than that." [51] And he added, "I am telling you in solemn truth. You shall see heaven opening wide, with the angels of God ascending and descending over the Son of Man."

2   Three days afterwards a wedding took place at Cana in Galilee. Jesus' mother was there, [2] and Jesus and his disciples had likewise been invited to the wedding. [3] The wine ran out, and Jesus' mother said to him, "They have no wine left." [4] "Good woman," was Jesus' reply, "[b]**how** can **you and I** have a **common concern** about this? The hour appointed for me has not as yet arrived." [5] His mother said to the servants, [c]**"Do whatever he tells you"**. [6] Now there were in that place six water jars made of stone, each with a capacity of twenty or thirty gallons, laid up there for the ablution such as is customary among the Jews. [7] Jesus said to the attendants, "Fill the water jars with water"; and they filled them to the brim. [8] Then he told them to draw some off and take it to the man supervising the feast. And they took it there. [9] But when the man who supervised the feast tasted the water which had now turned into wine—he did not know where it came from; only those who had drawn the water knew—he called the bridegroom to his side [10] and said to him, "Everyone serves the best wine first, and only after his guests have drunk freely does he serve wine of the poorer sort. But you have kept the best wine until now."

[b]1 K 17:18   [c]Gn 41:55

¹¹This sign at Cana in Galilee was the first of those shown forth by Jesus. Thus he made his glory known, and his disciples learned to believe in him.

¹²Some time after this he went down to Capernaum, he, his mother, his brothers, and his disciples; and they stayed there but for a short time. ¹³Then, the time of the Jewish Passover being near, Jesus went up to Jerusalem. ¹⁴Here, in the temple, he came upon the traders in cattle, sheep, and pigeons, and likewise upon the money changers who were sitting there. ¹⁵So he made a whip out of cords of rushes, and drove them, one and all, out of the temple with their sheep and their cattle. He scattered the coins of the money changers, overturning their tables, ¹⁶and said to those selling pigeons, "Take these things away from here; do not turn my Father's house into a place of barter." ¹⁷Then his disciples recalled that these words stand written in scripture, *d'*My zeal on behalf of your house shall consume me'. ¹⁸The Jews, however, challenged him and said, "What sign can you bring before us as your warrant for doing these things?" ¹⁹Jesus gave his reply to them in these words: "Destroy this temple, and in three days I shall raise it up again." ²⁰"It has taken forty-six years to build this temple," the Jews retorted, "and you will raise it up again in three days?" ²¹However, it was his own body he had in mind in speaking of the temple. ²²So it came about that, after he had been raised from the dead, the disciples recalled that he had said this, and learned to believe in the scripture and in the words which Jesus had spoken.

²³Now when Jesus was in Jerusalem for the feast of the Passover, there were many who came to believe in his name and what it stood for, by reason of their seeing the signs which he showed forth. ²⁴But Jesus, for his part, would not trust himself to them, on the ground that human beings were, one and all, known to him, ²⁵and that he never needed any evidence from others about anyone. For he knew of himself what a man had in him.

3   There was a man, Nicodemus by name, a Pharisee and one of the Jewish leaders, ²who came to Jesus one night and addressed him in these words: "Rabbi, we know that you have made your appearance as a teacher sent out by God; for no one could show forth the signs which you are showing forth unless he had God on his side." ³Jesus made him this answer: "I am telling you in solemn truth: unless a man be born afresh, he cannot see the kingdom of God." ⁴"How is it possible," Nicodemus enquired of him, "for someone already old to be born? Is he to enter his mother's womb a second time, and so come to

*d*Ps 69:9

birth?" 5"I am telling you in solemn truth," replied Jesus, "that a man cannot enter the kingdom of God unless he be born through water and through the Spirit. 6That which takes its birth from the flesh is no more than a thing which is of the flesh, while that which takes its birth from the Spirit is a thing which is of the Spirit. 7Let it not be a matter of surprise to you if I said that what is required of you all is that you should be born afresh. 8The wind blows wherever it pleases. You can hear its sound, but you do not know where it comes from or where it is going. So it is with anyone whose birth comes of the Spirit." 9"How can this possibly be?" was Nicodemus's rejoinder. 10"Do you not understand these things," was Jesus' reply, "you who are one of those that teach in Israel? 11I am telling you in solemn truth: We speak of that which we know, and we testify to that which we have seen with our own eyes. Yet you do not accept our testimony. 12If I tell you of things which pertain to this earth and you do not believe, how will you believe when I tell you of the things of heaven? 13No one has ever gone up into heaven except he who came down from heaven, the Son of Man whose home is in heaven. 14And just as Moses lifted up the serpent in the desert, so the Son of Man must be lifted up, 15so that anyone believing in him may, through union with him, obtain eternal life."

16Yes, God had such love for the world that he gave up his only Son, so that anyone believing in him might not perish but lay hold of eternal life. 17For God did not send his Son into the world that he might pronounce judgment on the world, but that the world might be saved by him. 18He who believes in him does not come under condemnation, while he who does not believe in him already stands condemned, because he has refused to repose his belief in God's only Son and what his very name stands for. 19And the judgment of condemnation lies in this, that the light has come into the world, and that men preferred darkness to the light because their doings were evil. 20And indeed, anyone who does what is bad hates the light and refuses to approach it, for fear that his deeds might be exposed to view. 21But he who does what truth demands comes out into the light, that his deeds might be seen for what they are, deeds done in oneness with God.

22Some time after this, Jesus and his disciples went into Judaea, and there he remained with them, administering baptism. 23John likewise was baptizing, and he did so at Aenon near Salim, because an abundance of water was to be found in that place. And people came to him to be baptized. 24(John had not as yet been thrown into prison.) 25Now it came about that a dispute over purification arose between a Jew and some of John's disciples. 26So they went to John saying, "Rabbi, what of him who was in your company on the other side of the Jordan, the man to whom you have borne witness? There he is engaged in baptizing, and people are all flocking to him." 27The reply John made to them was this: "There is nothing a man can receive except what has been granted to him by heaven. 28You yourselves can bear witness that I said, 'I am not the Christ. I am the one sent forth ahead of him.' 29It is the bridegroom who has the bride as his own, while the bridegroom's friend, who stands by listening to the bridegroom, rejoices greatly at hearing his voice. That is the joy which is mine, and it has reached its fullness. 30He cannot but increase more and more, while I must diminish."

31The one who comes from the realm above is set over all things, while he who comes of the earth belongs to the earthly realm, and the things that he speaks of are things earthly. He who has come from heaven is set over all things. 32He bears witness to the things he has seen and heard. Yet there is no one to accept his witness. 33To accept the witness which he bears is to set one's seal to the fact that God speaks true; 34for it is God's very words that are spoken by him whom God has sent forth—so boundless is the gift he makes of his Spirit. 35The Father loves the Son and has committed everything into his hands. 36He who believes in the Son lays hold of eternal life, while he who refuses to put his faith in the Son will never have a glimpse of that life. On the contrary, he will have God's anger resting upon him.

4 Now a report had reached the ears of the Pharisees that Jesus was making a greater number of disciples than John and was baptizing them, 2although, as a matter of fact, it was not Jesus himself who baptized, but his disciples. 3And when Jesus got to know about this, he left Judaea and once again set out for Galilee. 4To reach it, he had to go by way of Samaria; 5and so he came to a Samaritan city called Sychar, 6close by the piece of land which Jacob bestowed upon his son Joseph as a gift. Now Jacob's well was in that place, and so it happened that Jesus, being tired out by the journey, sat down by the well. The time was about noon. 7And when a Samaritan woman came there to draw water from the well, Jesus said to her, "Give me something to drink." 8(His disciples had gone off into the city for the purpose of buying food.) 9"How is it," the Samaritan woman said to him, "that you, who are a Jew, ask for a drink from me, a woman of Samaria?" (The reason for her saying this was that Jews and Samaritans have no dealings with one another.) 10Jesus answered her thus: "If only you knew the gift which God offers, and who it is that is saying to you, 'Give me something to drink', it would have been you that had done the asking, and he, for his part, would have made you a gift of living water." 11"Sir," replied the woman, "you have nothing to draw water with and the well is deep. How, then, is it that you have living water to bestow?

¹²Are you greater than our forefather Jacob, who made us a gift of this well and who drank from it, he himself, his sons, and his cattle?" ¹³"Anyone who drinks of this well," replied Jesus, "will again be thirsty. ¹⁴But he who drinks of the water that I shall give him will never again suffer thirst. No, what will happen is that the water which I shall give him will, within him, become a spring of water which wells up and brings eternal life with it." ¹⁵"Sir," the woman said to him, "make me a gift of this water, so that I shall feel thirsty no more, nor have to come here again to draw water." ¹⁶"Be on your way," he said to her, "and, after having called your husband, come back here." ¹⁷"I have no husband," was the woman's reply. "You have spoken aright," remarked Jesus, "in saying that you have no husband, ¹⁸seeing that you have had five husbands, and that the man you are with now is not your husband. You have told the truth about this." ¹⁹"I can see, sir, that you are a prophet," the woman said to him. ²⁰"Our forefathers worshipped on this mountain, while you Jews maintain that Jerusalem is the place where men should offer worship." ²¹"Believe me, my good woman," said Jesus, "the time is coming when you will worship the Father neither on this mountain nor in Jerusalem. ²²You worship not knowing what you worship, while we worship that which we know; for it is from the Jews that salvation comes. ²³Yet the time is approaching, indeed it is already here, when the true worshippers will worship the Father in a spiritual manner and in accordance with the truth. Indeed, what the Father requires is worshippers such as these. ²⁴God is spirit, and those worshipping him must worship in a spiritual manner and in accordance with the truth." ²⁵"I know," the woman said to him, "that Messiah is to come, the one whom they call the Christ, and that, when he comes, his message will make everything plain to us." ²⁶"I am he," Jesus said to her; "I, the man who is talking to you."

²⁷At this point the disciples returned. They were surprised that he was talking to a woman; yet none of them asked, "What is it you want with her?" or "Why are you talking to her?" ²⁸As for the woman, she left her water jar behind and went away to the city, saying to the people there, ²⁹"Come with me and you will see a man who told me everything I ever did. Can it be that it is he who is the Christ?" ³⁰And so the people went out of the city, making their way towards him.

³¹In the meantime the disciples urged him, saying, "Rabbi, take something to eat." ³²But this is what he told them: "I have food to eat of which you know nothing." ³³"Can it be," the disciples said to one another, "that someone has brought him some food to eat?" ³⁴Jesus made his reply to them in these words: "This is the food which is mine, that I should carry out the will of him who has sent me forth and bring his work to completion. ³⁵Is there not a saying current among you, 'There are still four months to go until harvest comes'? But these are

the words which I am addressing to you: mark them well. 'Lift up your eyes and survey the fields, how white they are, already ripe for the harvest.' [36]He who reaps the harvest receives his wage and gathers fruit which leads him to eternal life, so that sower and harvester may rejoice together. [37]Indeed, this confirms the truth of the saying, 'One man sows, another gathers the harvest.' [38]I have sent you out to harvest that for which you have not laboured. Others have laboured for it, and what has come out of their labour has become yours."

[39]Many Samaritans of that city came to believe in him on account of the woman's testimony, "He told me everything I ever did." [40]And so the Samaritans who came to him urged him to stay with them; and he stayed on there for two days. [41]There were many more who learned to believe because of the words which he addressed to them, [42]while they said to the woman, "It is no longer because of what you told us that we believe. We have heard him ourselves, and we know that this man is in very truth the Saviour of the world."

[43]After the two days had passed, Jesus set out from there and went on to Galilee, [44]since he had himself declared that a prophet goes unhonoured in his own country. [45]And when he arrived in Galilee, the Galileans gave him a warm welcome, having seen everything that he had done in Jerusalem at the time of the festival; for they themselves had also been present at the festival.

[46]So he came once again to Cana in Galilee, where he had turned the water into wine. Now there was a certain member of the royal court at that place whose son was lying sick at Capernaum. [47]When he heard that Jesus had come from Judaea into Galilee, he went after him and urged him to go down to Capernaum and heal his son, who was on the point of death. [48]"Unless you see signs and portents happen," Jesus told him, "none of you will believe." [49]"Sir, come down before my son dies," the royal courtier retorted. [50]"Go back to your home," was Jesus' reply; "your son will live." The man believed the word which Jesus had spoken and went on his way. [51]While he was still on his homeward journey, his servants came to meet him and said to him, "Your son will live." [52]So he enquired of them at what time he had taken a turn for the better. "It was yesterday," they told him, "at one o'clock in the afternoon, that the fever left him." [53]Now the father knew it was at that very hour that Jesus had said to him, 'Your son will live'; and he became a believer, he and his whole household. [54]This was the second sign which Jesus showed forth after departing from Judaea and coming into Galilee.

5 Some time after this there was a Jewish festival for which Jesus went up to Jerusalem. [2]Now there is a pool in Jerusalem, close to the

Sheep Gate, a place consisting of five porticos, whose Hebrew name is Bethesda. ³Under these porticos there used to lie a crowd of sick people, who were blind, or lame, or who had withered limbs. *[What they did was wait for the water to be disturbed. ⁴For from time to time an angel went into the pool and stirred up the water. And he who stepped in first, after the water had been stirred up, regained his health, no matter what ailment may have been troubling him.] ⁵Now a certain man was present there who had an illness which had been troubling him for thirty-eight years. ⁶When Jesus saw him lying there, and knowing at the same time how long his condition had lasted, he asked him, "Do you want to regain your health?" ⁷"I have no one, sir," the sick man replied, "to put me into the pool after the water has been disturbed, and while I am still on my way someone else steps in before me." ⁸"Rise up," Jesus said to him, "taking up your stretcher, and walk on your own feet." ⁹In an instant the man regained his health, took up his stretcher, and began to walk.

¹⁰Now the day on which this happened was a Sabbath, and so the Jews said to the one who had been healed, "This is the Sabbath day; you are not permitted to carry your stretcher." ¹¹His reply was this: "The one who made me well—that very man—said to me, 'Take up your stretcher and walk.' " ¹²So they asked him, "Who is the man that told you to take it up and walk?" ¹³In fact, the one who had been made well did not know who it was, and, as for Jesus, he had slipped away because a large crowd was gathered in that place. ¹⁴Some time later Jesus came upon him in the temple and said to him, "You have recovered your health. Let your mind dwell on this, and cease from sinning for fear that something worse might befall you." ¹⁵As for the man, he went on his way and told the Jews that it was Jesus who had given him back his health.

¹⁶For this reason the Jews began to persecute Jesus: what provoked them was that he did things such as these on the Sabbath day. ¹⁷But Jesus made his answer to them in these words: "My Father has been working to this very hour, and so I, too, must be at work." ¹⁸Because of this, the Jews became all the more eager to do away with him, not only for the reason that he was breaking the Sabbath, but that, in speaking of God as his own Father, he made himself out to be God's equal.

¹⁹Now Jesus made his answer to them in these words: "I am telling you in solemn truth: the Son can do nothing by himself. He can do only what he sees the Father doing. Indeed, it is the very things the Father does which the Son does in like manner. ²⁰For the Father loves the Son and discloses to him all that he does. In fact, the Father will

---

* Vv. 3b-4 added in some manuscripts.

disclose to him even greater things than these: works which will cause you to be filled with astonishment. [21] And just as the Father raises the dead, giving them life, so the Son gives life to anyone whom he chooses. [22] Again, the Father passes judgment upon no one. He has entrusted all judgment to the Son, [23] so that everyone may honour the Son as they honour the Father. He who refuses to honour the Son refuses at the same time to honour the Father who has sent him forth. [24] I am telling you in solemn truth: he who lends his ear to my message, and believes in him who has sent me forth, has laid hold of eternal life. He does not come under judgment. On the contrary, he has already passed from death to life. [25] I am telling you in solemn truth: the time is coming, indeed it is already here, when the dead shall hear the voice of the Son of God and will live. [26] For just as the Father has the gift of life within him, so he has granted it to the Son that he likewise should have the gift of life within him; [27] while, since he is the Son of Man, he has at the same time granted to him the authority to act as judge. [28] Do not be astonished at this, seeing that the time is already coming when all those who are in their graves will hear the Son's voice [29] and will come forth, those who have done what is good rising to new life, while those whose deeds have been evil will be rising up to meet their sentence. [30] By myself I can indeed do nothing, and, in pronouncing judgment, I do as I am bidden; and if my judgment is a just one, that is because what I aim at is not to do my own will but the will of him who has sent me forth.

[31] "Were I to testify on my own behalf, my testimony would have no truth in it. [32] But there is another who testifies on my behalf, and I know that the testimony he bears on my behalf is a truthful one. [33] You have sent messengers to John, and he has borne his testimony to the truth. [34] Yet, as for myself, it is not any man's testimony on which I take my stand, and if I speak the way I am doing, the reason is my desire that you should obtain your salvation. [35] John was a lamp burning and shining brightly, and for a time you were ready to exult in the light that he shed. [36] But I rely on a testimony weightier than any which John could supply. The works which my Father has entrusted to me, so that I might accomplish them—the very works which I am performing—these bear me testimony that it is the Father who has sent me on my errand. [37] And the Father who has sent me forth: it is he who has borne testimony on my behalf. You have never heard his voice nor seen the way in which he is fashioned; [38] and as for his word, no abiding place is to be found for it within you, since you refuse to believe in him whom he has sent out on his errand. [39] You scrutinize the scriptures, believing that through them you can lay hold of eternal life; and indeed it is these very scriptures which bear testimony on my behalf. [40] Yet you refuse to turn to me so that you might lay

hold of life. ⁴¹I repudiate any honour which men may bestow upon me, ⁴²while I have come to know about you yourselves, that no love of God is to be found in your hearts. ⁴³I have come in my Father's name, and you will not accept me. Should another come in his own name, you will give him a welcome. ⁴⁴Receiving honour from one another as you do, while having no concern for that honour which has its source in him who alone is God, what way is there of making you learn to believe? ⁴⁵Do not suppose that it is I who will be your accuser before the Father. It is ᵉMoses who will be accusing you, he on whom you have been setting your hopes. ⁴⁶And indeed, did you believe in Moses, you would believe in me, seeing that it is of me that he wrote. ⁴⁷But if you do not believe in what he has set down in writing, how can you believe in the words which I am saying to you?"

6 Some time after this, Jesus went over to the other side of the Sea of Galilee (also called the Sea of Tiberias), ²and a large crowd followed him because they had seen the signs which he had shown forth in healing the sick. ³Then Jesus went up the hillside and sat down there with his disciples. ⁴Now this was shortly before the Jewish festival of the Passover, ⁵and Jesus, on looking up and seeing a great crowd coming towards him, said to Philip, "Where are we to buy bread to feed these people?" ⁶He said this to him to put him to the test, for he himself knew what he intended to do. ⁷Philip answered him thus: "Two hundred pieces of silver would not buy a sufficient quantity of bread for them, not even to give but a small amount to each." ⁸One of his disciples—it was Andrew, Simon Peter's brother—said to him, ⁹"There is a boy here who has five barley loaves and two fish with him. But of what avail is that for so large a number?" ¹⁰"Tell the people to sit down," was Jesus' reply. There was plenty of grass where they were; so the people sat down, about five thousand of them. ¹¹Thereupon Jesus seized the loaves with his hands, and, after having given thanks, he shared them among those who were sitting there. He did the same with the fish, giving the people as much as they wanted. ¹²And when they had had their fill, he said to his disciples, "Gather the pieces which have been left over, so that nothing may be wasted." ¹³So they gathered them, filling twelve baskets with the pieces left over by those who had partaken of the five barley loaves.

¹⁴When the people who were present saw the sign which he had shown forth, they said, "In very truth, this must be the prophet of whom we have been told that he was to come into the world." ¹⁵But Jesus, who was well aware that they intended to come to him, carry-

ᵉ[Dt 31:26]

ing him off to proclaim him king, withdrew once again into the hills, all by himself.

16 As for the disciples, they went down to the lake at nightfall, 17 got into the boat, and began to cross the lake, making for Capernaum. Darkness had already set in, and Jesus had not as yet joined them. 18 Meanwhile, as a strong wind was blowing, the lake was getting turbulent. 19 When they had rowed for a distance of about three or four miles, they saw Jesus walking on the water of the lake and coming close to the boat. They were terrified, 20 but he said to them, "It is I; cast off all fear." 21 They meant to take him aboard, but in an instant the boat reached the land for which they were making.

22 On the following day a crowd was still standing on the other side of the lake. They had seen that only one boat had been there and were likewise aware that Jesus had not gone on board with his disciples but that they had sailed away alone. 23 However, boats from Tiberias came ashore near the place where the people had eaten the bread over which the Lord had given thanks. 24 When the crowd realized that neither Jesus nor his disciples were any longer there, they went aboard these boats and made for Capernaum in search of Jesus. 25 When they found him on the other side of the lake, they asked him, "Rabbi, when did you make your way here?" 26 And this is the answer Jesus made them: "I am telling you in solemn truth, you are not seeking me out because you have seen signs, but because you have eaten of the loaves and have had your fill. 27 However, it is not perishable food you must work for, but for food which endures and which leads to eternal life. The Son of Man will be the one that gives you that food; for it is he upon whom God the Father has set his seal." 28 They asked him, "What are we to do to perform such works as God would have us do?" 29 "This is the work which God requires," was Jesus' reply, "that you should believe in him whom he has sent." 30 "What is the sign which you show forth," they said to him, "so that, seeing it, we may come to believe you? What is the work that you do? 31 Our forefathers had manna to eat in the desert. As scripture has it, *f***He gave them food from heaven to eat.'** 32 "I am telling you in solemn truth," was Jesus' rejoinder, "it is not Moses who gave you bread from heaven; it is my Father who is giving you bread from heaven, the true bread. 33 And what is the bread bestowed by God? It is he who has come down from heaven, giving life to the world." 34 "Sir," they said to him, "make us a gift of this bread now and at all times." 35 "I am the life-giving bread," was Jesus' reply. "He who turns to me will never go hungry, and he who believes in me will never suffer thirst. 36 Yet as I have told you before, even though you have seen you refuse to believe. 37 All who

*f*Ps 78:24; Ex 16:4.15

are given to me as my own by the Father shall turn towards me, and, as for myself, I shall by no means drive away anyone who turns to me, [38] seeing that I have come down from heaven not to do my own will but to do the will of him who has sent me forth. [39] And indeed, the will of him who has sent me forth is this, that I should lose none of those whom he has given me as my own and that I should raise them up on the last day. [40] In truth, my Father's will is that he who sees the Son and believes in him should lay hold of eternal life, while it will be I who will be raising him up on the last day."

[41] Meanwhile, there were murmurs of disapproval about Jesus on the part of the Jews because he had said, 'I am the bread that has come down from heaven'; [42] and they asked, "Is this not Jesus, the son of Joseph, who is known to us and whose father and mother are known to us? How then is it that he says, 'I have come down from heaven'?" [43] "Cease murmuring among yourselves," was Jesus' reply. [44] "No one can turn towards me unless he be drawn by the Father who has sent me forth. And it is I who shall be raising him up on the last day. [45] This is what stands written in the book of the prophets, *8*'**They shall, one and all, have God for their teacher.**' Anyone that lends his ear to the Father, learning from him, turns towards me.

[46] "Not that anyone has seen the Father. It is he who has come forth from God, it is he alone, who has seen the Father. [47] I am telling you in solemn truth, the person who believes has laid hold of eternal life. [48] I am the life-giving bread. [49] Your forefathers ate the manna in the desert but died none the less. [50] But the nature of the bread which comes from heaven is just this, that anyone eating of it shall never die. [51] I am the bread which has life within it, I, the one who has come down from heaven. If anyone eats of this bread, he shall live for ever. Besides, my own flesh is the bread that I shall have to offer, and I shall offer it on behalf of the life of the world."

[52] Upon this the Jews fell to disputing with one another and asked, "How can this man give us his flesh to eat?" [53] But Jesus said to them, "I am telling you in solemn truth, unless you eat of the flesh of the Son of Man and drink of his blood, you can have no life in you. [54] Whoever eats of my flesh and drinks of my blood has laid hold of eternal life, and I shall raise him up on the last day. [55] For it is my flesh that is food in very truth, and my blood that is drink in very truth. [56] Whoever eats of my flesh and drinks of my blood has his dwelling within me, and I have my dwelling within him. [57] As the Father who has life within him has sent me forth, so do I have life through the Father, while whoever eats me will have life through me. [58] This is how things are with the bread which has come down from heaven, quite unlike what they were

_8_Is 54:13; [Jr 31:33f]

with our forefathers, who ate of the food but died none the less. Whoever eats of the bread of which I am speaking will live for ever."

59 He said all this while engaged in teaching at the synagogue at Capernaum. 60 Now many among his disciples, when they heard these words, said, "This is language not to be borne. Who can give his assent to it?" 61 But Jesus, inwardly aware that his disciples were muttering about this, put this question to them: "Does this offend you? 62 How then will it be with you when you see the Son of Man ascending to the place where he was before? 63 It is the spirit that gives life; what is but flesh and blood avails nothing. And the words which I have spoken are spirit and they are life. 64 Yet there are some among you who refuse to believe." (And indeed, Jesus knew from the first which were those who did not believe, and he knew at the same time who was the man who was to betray him.) 65 And so he went on: "That is what I meant when I told you that no one could turn towards me unless the power to do so had been granted to him by the Father."

66 From that time onwards many of his disciples withdrew themselves and no longer went about with him. 67 So Jesus enquired of the Twelve, "Can it be that you, too, desire to make your departure?" 68 "Lord," was Simon Peter's reply, "to whom are we to go? What you speak are words which carry eternal life with them. 69 As for ourselves, we have come to believe, and indeed have come to know for certain, that you are the Holy One of God." 70 "Is it not I that have chosen you, all twelve of you?" was Jesus' reply to them. "And yet one of you is a devil." 71 He meant Judas, the son of Simon Iscariot, for this was the man—one of the Twelve—who was to betray him.

7 After this Jesus went about from place to place in Galilee. He was no longer prepared to do so in Judaea because of the Jews there who had designs on his life. 2 However, as the Jewish festival of Tabernacles was approaching, 3 his brothers said to him, "Depart from here and make your way into Judaea, so that the works which you perform may be seen by the disciples whom you have there. 4 Surely a man who desires to be in the public eye will not do anything in secret. If then the works you do are of this kind, you must show yourself to the world." 5 (The fact was that, even among his brothers, there was a lack of faith in him.) 6 "The time right for me has not as yet come," was Jesus' reply, "while the time right for you is always at hand. 7 As for yourselves, it is impossible that the world should hate you. But it does hate me because of the testimony I bear concerning it, that the deeds which it does are evil ones. 8 Go up for the festival yourselves. I myself am not going up for the festival because the time appointed to me as the right time has not arrived as yet." 9 Having said this, he stayed be-

hind in Galilee. [10]Yet after his brothers had gone up for the festival, the time came when he, too, went up, not publicly however, but as though he would keep himself hidden. [11]The Jews, for their part, were looking for him during the festival, asking, "Where can that man be?" [12]At the same time, there was a good deal of whispering about him among the crowds, some saying, "There is goodness in that man," while others said, "By no means: he is leading the multitude astray." [13]On the other hand, there was no one who would speak about him openly, because they were all afraid of the Jewish authorities.

[14]When the festival was already half over, Jesus went up to the temple and began to teach. [15]The Jews were astonished at him and asked, "How is it that there is so much learning in this man who has never studied?" [16]Jesus made them this answer: "It is not my own teaching which I propound; it is the teaching of him who has sent me forth. [17]If there be a man who desires to act in accordance with his will, he will know for himself whether the teaching I give comes of God, or whether what I say is of my own devising. [18]He who says what is of his own devising seeks to gain honour for himself, whereas he who seeks honour for him who has sent him forth is telling the truth and is free from any kind of wrongdoing.

[19]"Was not the law given to you by Moses? Yet not one among you keeps the law. Why are you seeking my life?" [20]"You are out of your mind," the crowd replied; "Who is seeking your life?" [21]Jesus replied to them thus: "There is but one work that I have performed, and you are all perplexed at it. [22]Yet Moses made circumcision incumbent upon you. (Not that it derives from Moses; it derives from the patriarchs.) And this provides you with a reason for having your males circumcised even on the Sabbath day. [23]So then, if your males are circumcised on the Sabbath day, in order that the law of Moses should not be broken, how is it that you are indignant with me for restoring the whole of a man's body to health on the Sabbath? [24]Do not judge things by their appearances, but let your judgment of them be one that accords with what is right."

[25]At this point some of the people of Jerusalem began to make remarks such as these: "Is not this the man whose life they seek? [26]Yet here he is speaking publicly, and they have not a word to say to him. Can it be that the ruling authorities have in fact come to acknowledge that this man is the Christ? [27]But then we know well enough where this man comes from, while, when the Christ appears, no one—so we are told—is to know where *he* comes from."

[28]And so it came about that Jesus cried out loud, as he taught in the temple, his words being these: "No doubt you know me, and you know where I come from. Yet it is not of my own accord that I have come. No, there is one who truly *is*. It is he who has sent me forth, and

him you do not know. 29But I know him because it is from him that I came forth, and because it is he who sent me on my errand."

30At that they sought to apprehend him, but no one laid a hand upon him, because the time appointed for him had not as yet run its course. 31However, many among the crowd came to believe in him, saying, "Can the Christ, when he appears, show forth greater signs than this man has shown forth?" 32The Pharisees came to know that the crowd was whispering such things about him, so the chief priests and the Pharisees despatched officers of the law for the purpose of having him apprehended. 33Upon this Jesus spoke thus: "It is but a little time longer that I shall be staying with you. Then I shall go back to him who has sent me forth. 34You will be looking for me, but you will not find me. You do not have the means of reaching the place where I am." 35At that the Jews said to one another, "To what place does that man propose to go, that we shall be unable to find him? Does he propose to go to those who are scattered among the Greeks and engage in teaching the Greeks? 36What can be the meaning of the words he has spoken, 'You will be looking for me, but you will not find me', and 'You do not have the means of reaching the place where I am'?"

37On the last and greatest day of the festival Jesus took up his stand and cried aloud, "If anyone be thirsty, let him turn to me and let him drink. 38Yes, as the scripture has foretold, if there be one believing in me, *h*streams of living water will pour forth from within him". 39It is the Spirit he had in mind when he said this, the Spirit those believing in him were to receive. For the Spirit had not so far been bestowed, because Jesus had not as yet been raised to glory. 40Some of the crowd, on hearing these words, said, "Surely there can be no doubt that this is the prophet we have been told to expect?" 41Others said, "This man is the Christ"; while others again remarked, "It is impossible that the Christ should come from Galilee. 42Does not the scripture say that he must be of the *i*stock of David, and that he is to come from Bethlehem, David's village?" 43And so contention arose among the crowd. 44Some, indeed, were in favour of having him apprehended. Yet in fact there was no one who would lay a hand upon him.

45In the meantime the officers of the law had come back to the chief priests and the Pharisees, who asked them, "Why have you not brought him here?" 46And this is what the officers replied: "Nobody has ever spoken as this man speaks." 47"Have you, too, been deluded?" the Pharisees retorted. 48"Has any among the ruling authorities or among the Pharisees come to believe in him? 49As for this rabble, on the other hand, they have no knowledge of the law, a

h[Is 43:20; 44:3; 55:1; 58:11; Ezk 47:1-12; Jl 4:18; Zc 14:8]   *i*2 Sm 7:12; Mic 5:2; Ps 89:3f curse rests upon them." [50] At that, Nicodemus, who was one of their number (the man who had come to see Jesus at an earlier time), said to them, [51] "Is it the way of our law to condemn a man without first giving him a hearing and ascertaining what he is about?" [52] "Are you, too, a Galilean?" was their rejoinder. "Go into the matter, and you will see for yourself that no prophet ever comes out of Galilee."

---

*[[53] And they went away, each to his own home. 8[1] As for Jesus, he betook himself to the Mount of Olives.]

8 [[2] However, at the break of day he once again made his way into the temple; and, as all the people gathered round him there, he took his seat and began to teach them. [3] Now the experts in the law and the Pharisees brought with them a woman who had been caught in the act of committing adultery. They made her stand up in the centre of the court [4] and addressed Jesus in these words: "Master, this woman here was caught in the very act of committing adultery. [5] [j] Now Moses has laid it down for us in the law that women such as she are to be stoned to death. What, then, is the view which you yourself take of the matter?" [6] They said this to put him to the test, that they might have some charge to bring against him. But Jesus, bending down, began to write on the ground with his finger. [7] And as they persisted in questioning him, he sat up straight and addressed them in these words: "If there be a man among you who is free from sin, let him be the one to throw the first stone." [8] At that he bent down once again, writing on the ground. [9] When the men heard the words he spoke, they went away one after the other, beginning with the eldest, until Jesus was left alone with the woman standing there in the centre of the court. [10] And sitting up he addressed her in these words: "Where are they, my dear woman? Is there no one who has condemned you?" [11] "No one, sir," she replied. "Neither do I condemn you," said Jesus. "Be on your way and cease from sinning from this time on."]†

---

[12] Jesus spoke to the people at yet another time, and this is what he said: "I am the light of the world. Whoever follows me shall by no

j[Lv 20:10; Dt 22:22]

* 7:53–8:11 are misplaced; they are either not part of the true text or belong somewhere else.
† End of misplaced passage.

means be walking in darkness. No, he shall have the life-giving light guiding him." [13]The Pharisees said to him, "You bear testimony on your own behalf: there is no truth in your testimony." [14]And this is the answer Jesus gave to them. "Even though I were to bear testimony on my own behalf, my testimony is one that conforms to the truth, since I know where I have come from and where I am going. But as regards yourselves, you do not know where I have come from or where I am going. [15]You pass judgment, taking outward things for your standard, while I pass judgment on no one. [16]And yet, even though I were to pass judgment, my judgment is one guided by the truth, since it is not I alone that do the judging but I and, by my side, the Father who has sent me forth. [17]Besides, it is set down in your law that when [k]two men come forward, their testimony is to be taken as true. [18]And here I am, bearing testimony on my own behalf; yet there is another bearing testimony on my behalf, the Father who has sent me forth." [19]"Where," they asked, "is this father of yours?" "You do not know me," was Jesus' reply; "neither do you know my Father. Indeed, if you knew me you would know my Father as well." [20]He spoke these words in the Treasury, while teaching in the temple. Yet there was no one to have him seized by force because the time appointed for him had not as yet arrived.

[21]On another occasion he spoke to them thus: "I am going away, and you will be looking for me. Yet you will have to die with your load of sin upon you, while unable to reach the place where I am going." [22]At that the Jews asked, "Is he about to kill himself, seeing that he says, 'You are unable to reach the place where I am going'?" [23]He next addressed these words to them: "You are from the realm that is below; I am from the realm that is above. You belong to this world, while I do not belong to this world. [24]I have told you already that you will die with your load of sin upon you. Indeed, it is in refusing to believe that I am the one who truly is, that you will die with your load of sin upon you." [25]So they asked him, "Who are you?" And Jesus made them this reply: "Why am I speaking to you at all? [26]I have much to say about you and much to condemn. Yet he who has sent me forth ever speaks the truth; and it is the very things I have heard from him that I am proclaiming to the world."

[27]They did not understand that he was speaking to them about the Father. [28]So Jesus said to them, "When you shall have lifted up the Son of Man, it is then that you will know that I am the one who truly is, that there is nothing I do of myself, and that it is the very things which the Father has taught me that I proclaim. [29]Besides, he who has sent me forth is by my side. He has not left me all alone. And he has

[k][Dt 19:15]

acted in this way because at all times I do what is pleasing to him." [30]As he was saying this, many came to believe in him.

[31]Now these are the words which Jesus addressed to the Jews who had come to have faith in him: "If you hold fast to what I have spoken to you, then you will in very truth be disciples of mine, [32]and you will know the truth, and the truth will set you free." [33]"We are Abraham's descendants," they replied, "and have never been anybody's slave. What then do you mean by saying, 'You will become free'?" [34]Jesus answered them thus: "I am telling you in solemn truth, anyone who commits sin is enslaved to sin. [35]Besides, the standing in a household appertaining to a slave does not endure for ever, while the Son's standing does endure for ever. [36]If, then, it is the Son who makes you free, you will be free in very truth. [37]I know well enough that you are descendants of Abraham. Yet none the less you are bent on putting me to death because my message finds no room in your hearts. [38]I proclaim what I have seen when I was at the Father's side, while your actions are the outcome of what you have learned from your father." [39]"Abraham is our father," they retorted. "If you were Abraham's children," was Jesus' reply, "you would be doing deeds such as Abraham did. [40]As it is, however, you are bent on putting me to death, a man who has told you the truth as he learned it from God. That is not how Abraham acted. [41]And as for the deeds which you perform, it is your father upon whom you model yourselves." "We are no bastard children," they replied; "God, and only he, is our Father." [42]"If God were your Father," was Jesus' rejoinder, "you would love me. For it is from God that I have come forth; and here I am. Moreover, if I have come, that is not of my own doing; it is because he has sent me forth. [43]Why is it that my language is beyond your grasp? It is because you are devoid of the power of listening to the message I am bringing to you. [44]It is the devil who is your father, and what you are determined to do is to carry out your father's desires. He was a manslayer from the very beginning, and as for truth, he did not take his stand on it, because truth does not find any room in his heart. Indeed, it is when he is speaking falsehood that he draws on what is his very own, because he is a liar, and because all falsehood takes its birth from him. [45]Yet, as for myself, if you refuse to believe me, the reason is that I am speaking the truth. [46]Can any of you convict me of sin? Well then, why is it that, when I tell you the truth, you refuse to believe me? [47]He who is a child of God listens to God's words. If you do not listen, the reason is just this, that you are no children of God." [48]"Are we not right in saying," the Jews replied, "that you are a Samaritan and that you are possessed of a demon?" [49]"I am not possessed of a demon," was Jesus' rejoinder. "No, what I am about is to honour my Father, while, as for yourselves, you seek to dishonour me. [50]Not that I am

intent on my own glory. But there is one who is intent on it, and it is he who acts as judge. [51]I am telling you in solemn truth: anyone holding fast to my message shall never, to all eternity, look upon death." [52]"Now we know," the Jews said to him, "that you are possessed of a demon. Abraham died and the prophets died. Yet you say, 'If anyone holds fast to my message, he shall never, to all eternity, know the taste of death.' [53]Are you greater than our father Abraham who died, just as the prophets have died? What do you make yourself out to be?" [54]Jesus answered them thus: "If I bestowed glory upon myself, my glory would amount to nothing at all. It is the Father who bestows glory upon me, he of whom you say that he is your God. [55]Yet you have no knowledge of him, while I *do* know him. Were I to say that I did not know him, I should be a liar like you. Yet I *do* know him and hold fast to his message. [56]Abraham your father rejoiced at the thought of seeing the day of my coming, and he saw it and was gladdened." [57]"You are not as yet fifty years old," the Jews retorted. "How is it that you have seen Abraham?" [58]"I am telling you in solemn truth," was Jesus' reply; "before Abraham ever came into being, I am the one who is." [59]At this they lifted up stones to throw at him, but Jesus went out of the temple and hid himself.

9 As Jesus went on his way he saw a man who had been blind from birth. [2]His disciples asked him, "Rabbi, who is it that has sinned, for him to have been born blind—the man himself or his parents?" [3]"It was not that he sinned or that his parents did," was Jesus' reply. "What was to come about was that the deeds of God should find themselves manifested in his person. [4]The task laid upon ourselves is that, so long as daylight lasts, I should perform deeds such as have their source in him who has sent me forth. Yet there comes the time of night when no work can be done by anyone. [5]So long as I am in the world, I am the light of the world." [6]Having said this, he spat on the ground, made a paste with the spittle, and spread it on the man's eyes, [7]saying to him, "Be on your way and wash in the pool of Siloam." (The name means 'sent'.) He went off, washed himself, and on coming back, he was able to see. [8]Now his neighbours and those who had previously known him as a man who begged for alms asked, "Is not this the man who used to sit and beg for alms?" [9]Some said, "Yes, this is the man." Others again said, "No, but it is somebody who resembles him." The man himself said, "I am he." [10]So they asked him, "How then has it come about that your eyes were opened?" [11]And this is what he replied: "The man called Jesus made a paste and spread it on my eyes and said to me, 'Be on your way, go to Siloam, and wash.' So I went off, washed myself, and, having done so, there I was: endowed with

the power of sight." 12"Where is he?" they asked him. "I do not know," was his reply.

13They took him along to stand before the Pharisees, this man who had once been blind. 14Now the day on which Jesus had made the paste and opened the man's eyes was a Sabbath. 15And so the Pharisees asked him how he had come to be endowed with the power of sight. And he said to them, "He put a paste on my eyes, and then I washed, and now I can see." 16At that some of the Pharisees said, "This man cannot be a messenger from God, seeing that he does not keep the Sabbath." But others asked, "How could he be a sinful man while showing forth signs such as this?" Thus dissension arose among them. 17They turned once again to the sightless man, asking him, "What account do you yourself have to give, seeing that it was your eyes he opened?" "He must be a prophet," was his reply.

18Now the Jews would not believe that the man, having been blind, had been endowed with the power of sight until they summoned the parents of the man on whom the power of sight had been bestowed, 19asking them this question: "As regards that son of yours of whom you say that he was born blind, how is it that he is now able to see?" 20The parents replied, "We know that this is our son and that he was born blind. 21But how it is that he is now able to see we do not know. Neither do we know who it was that opened his eyes. Address your questions to him. He is of age and will be able to speak for himself." 22His parents spoke in this way because they were afraid of the Jews; for the Jewish authorities had already agreed among themselves that anyone declaring Jesus to be the Christ should be expelled from the synagogue. 23It was for this reason that his parents said, 'He is of age; address your questions to him'.

24For a second time the others summoned the man who had once been blind, saying to him, "Let God be the one whom you glorify. We know well enough that this fellow is a sinful man." 25"Whether he is a sinful man," he replied, "I do not know. But one thing I *do* know, that I was once blind and am now able to see." 26They asked him, "What did he do to you; and how did he open your eyes?" 27"I have told you already," was his answer. "Why do you want to hear it all over again? Do you, too, intend to become disciples of his?" 28Upon this they began to hurl abuse at him, saying, "Are you one of that fellow's disciples? We are Moses' disciples. 29We know that God spoke to Moses; yet as for him, we do not know where he comes from." 30"Now this is the astonishing thing," was the man's reply, "that there is one of whom you do not know where he comes from, and yet he has opened my eyes. 31We all know that God does not lend his ear to sinful men. He lends his ear to those who are God-fearing and do his will. 32That anyone should open the eyes of a man born blind is unheard of since the world began. ³³Unless that man came from God, he could do nothing at all." ³⁴"Are we to take lessons from you," was their reply, "a sinner through and through from your very birth?" At that they thrust him outside.

³⁵Jesus had heard that they had driven him away, and, on encountering him, he addressed him thus: "Do you believe in the Son of Man?"* ³⁶And this is the reply which the man made: "Tell me who he is, sir, that I might learn to believe in him." ³⁷"You have seen him," said Jesus; "indeed, it is he who is talking to you." ³⁸"Lord, I believe," said the man, and threw himself at his feet to worship him.

³⁹"It is for judgment," said Jesus, "that I have come into this world, so that those without sight may see and those having sight turn blind." ⁴⁰Certain of the Pharisees who were in his company heard this and said to him, "Surely it is not we that are blind." ⁴¹"If you were blind," Jesus said to them, "there would be no guilt in you. But you claim that you can see, and so your guilt remains.

10

"I am telling you in solemn truth: the man who enters the sheepfold not by way of the gate but climbs up into it some other way, that person is nothing but a thief and a robber. ²The shepherd who tends the sheep enters by way of the gate. ³It is he to whom the keeper of the gate gives admittance, and, as for the sheep, they are attentive to his voice. He calls the sheep, which are his very own, each by its name and leads them out; ⁴and when he has brought them all out— they that are his very own—he proceeds on his way, walking at the head of them. And they follow him because his voice is known to them. ⁵As for the stranger, they will by no means follow him. On the contrary, they will take flight because they do not know the voices of those who are strange to them." ⁶It was this figure of speech Jesus used in talking to them, but they did not understand the meaning of what he said to them.

⁷So Jesus spoke to them again, his words being these: "I am telling you in solemn truth: I am the gate leading to where the sheep are. ⁸All the others that have made their appearance before I did have been nothing more than thieves and robbers; and, as for the sheep, they took no heed of them. ⁹It is I that am the gate. Anyone who makes his entry through me will be kept safe. He will come in and go out at will and be sure of finding pasture. ¹⁰But as for the thief, when he comes, he comes only that he may steal, kill, and bring destruction. I have come that they may lay hold of life in all its fullness. ¹¹I am the good shepherd. The good shepherd lays down his life for the sheep. ¹²But

* *Var. lect.* 'Son of God'.

the hired man—he who is not a shepherd and has no sheep of his own —deserts the sheep when he sees a wolf coming towards them, and takes to flight; and the wolf carries them off and scatters them. ¹³This is because he is no more than a hired man and because he has no care for the sheep. ¹⁴I am the good shepherd. I know those that are mine, and those that are mine know me; ¹⁵just as the Father knows me, and I know the Father—and I am laying down my life for the sheep. ¹⁶Besides, there are other sheep that are mine, sheep which do not belong to this fold. These, too, I must lead forth; and so there will be one flock and one shepherd. ¹⁷As for the Father, he does indeed love me, and this because I am laying down my life, doing so that I might take it up again afterwards. ¹⁸No one takes it away from me. I am laying it down of my own free will. I have been given the right to lay it down, and I have been given the right to take it up again afterwards. This is the charge which I have received from my Father."

¹⁹Dissension arose once again among the Jews by reason of his uttering these words. ²⁰Many of them said, "He is possessed of a demon and has gone out of his mind. Why is it that you take heed of him?" ²¹Others said, "These are not the words of one possessed of a demon. Could anyone acting under the influence of a demon open blind men's eyes?"

²²The festival of the Dedication was being celebrated in Jerusalem, the time being winter. ²³As for Jesus, he was in the temple, walking to and fro in the portico of Solomon. ²⁴So the Jews gathered round him and said to him, "How long will you go on keeping us in suspense? If you are the Christ, tell us so plainly." ²⁵"I have told you before," was Jesus' reply, "but you refuse to believe. The deeds which I perform in my Father's name bear witness on my behalf. ²⁶Yet you will not believe because you do not belong to those who are sheep of mine. ²⁷Those who are sheep of mine listen to my voice, and I know them, and they follow me. ²⁸It is everlasting life that I bestow upon them. To all eternity they shall not perish, and no one shall ever be able to tear them from my grasp. ²⁹That which my Father has committed to me is of greater worth than anything else; and there is no one who has the power to tear it from my Father's grasp. ³⁰I and the Father are one."

³¹Once again the Jews took up stones from the ground, that they might stone him to death. Upon this Jesus spoke to them thus: ³²"I have shown forth many good deeds in your sight, deeds which have their source in the Father. For which of these deeds would you stone me?" ³³"It is not for any good deed," the Jews replied, "that we are bent on stoning you. It is for your blasphemy; it is because you who are nothing more than a man make yourself out to be God." ³⁴Jesus made this answer to them: "Are not these words set down in your

own law: [l]**I declare to you that you are gods'?** [35]Now if those to whom God addressed these words are referred to as gods (and scripture can never be set aside), [36]what is one to make of the way in which you speak of him whom the Father has hallowed and whom he has sent into the world? How can you say of me, 'You are a blasphemer', because of my telling you that I am the Son of God? [37]If it is not deeds wrought by my Father that I perform, then refuse to believe me. [38]But if I do perform them, then, even though you should not believe me, base your belief on the deeds I perform, so that you may learn and come to believe that the Father dwells in me, and I dwell in the Father." [39]At that the desire once again arose in them to seize him by force, but he escaped their hands.

[40]After this Jesus withdrew again across the Jordan to the place where John used to be when he was first baptizing. There he remained, [41]while there were many who came out to see him. And this is what they said to one another: "John never showed forth any sign, but everything he said about this man has turned out to be true." [42]And so it came about that there were many in that place who learned to believe in him.

11 There was a certain man, Lazarus by name, whose home was at Bethany, the village to which Mary and her sister Martha belonged; and that man was lying sick. [2](Mary, whose brother Lazarus was lying sick, was the woman who had anointed the Lord with a perfume and wiped his feet dry with her hair.) [3]Now the sisters sent a message to Jesus, saying, "Master, the man whom you love is lying sick." [4]When Jesus heard this, he said, "This sickness is not one that is to end in death. It has come in furtherance of God's glory, that the Son of God might be glorified by means of it." [6a]And so it came about [5]that Jesus, who loved Martha, loved her sister, and loved Lazarus, [6b]on hearing that Lazarus was lying sick, remained in the place where he was for two more days. [7]These having passed, he said to his disciples, "Let us go into Judaea again." [8]"Rabbi," his disciples said to him, "but a short while ago the Jews were bent on stoning you to death, and you wish to go to that place once again?" [9]Jesus answered them thus: "Are there not twelve hours of daylight? Anyone that walks in daylight can do so without stumbling because he has that which gives light to this world to see by. [10]But if a man walks at night-time he stumbles, because then he has no light to guide him." [11]He said this, and then he added, "Our friend Lazarus is resting, but I shall go and wake him up." [12]"If he is resting, Master," his disciples said to him, "he will

[l]Ps 82:6

recover." [13]Jesus, however, had been talking of his death, while they imagined that what he had in mind was the rest which comes with sleep. [14]So Jesus told them plainly, "Lazarus has died. [15]And if I am glad I was not there, this is for your sake, that you may learn to believe. Let us be on our way, then, and go to him." [16]Thereupon Thomas— the one called 'The Twin'—said to his fellow disciples, "Let us go, too, that we may die with him."

[17]On arriving, Jesus found that Lazarus had already been in the tomb for four days. [18]Bethany was close to Jerusalem, only about two miles distant from it; [19]and many of the Jews had come from there to Martha and Mary, that they might console them on the death of their brother. [20]On hearing that Jesus had come, Martha went out to meet him, while Mary stayed behind, sitting in the house. [21]And so it was that Martha said to Jesus, "Master, if you had been here, my brother would not have died. [22]Yet, even as things are, I know that, whatever you ask of God, he will grant it to you." [23]Jesus said to her, "Your brother will rise again." [24]"I know," Martha replied to him, "that he will rise again at the resurrection, when the last day comes." [25]"I am the resurrection and I am life," was Jesus' rejoinder. "Whoever believes in me will lay hold of life, even though he die, [26]and no one laying hold of life and believing in me will ever die, to all eternity. Do you believe this?" [27]"Yes, Lord," she said to him, "I have learned to believe that you are the Christ, the Son of God: he who was to come into this world." [28]Having said this, she went away to call her sister Mary, and taking her aside said to her, "The Master is here and asking for you." [29]On hearing this, Mary rose up quickly to go to him. [30]As for Jesus, he had not as yet come as far as the village but was still at the place where Martha had met him. [31]When the Jews who had been in the house with Mary to console her saw that she had risen quickly and gone away, they followed her in the belief that she was on her way to the tomb to weep there. [32]But Mary, on reaching the place where Jesus was, fell at his feet when she saw him, and said, "Master, had you been here my brother would not have died." [33]As for Jesus, he was deeply stirred in spirit and greatly shaken at the sight of her tears and the tears of the Jews who had come with her. [34]"Where have you buried him?" he asked. "Sir," they replied, "come and see for yourself." [35]And Jesus burst into tears. [36]"See what love he bore him," said the Jews, [37]while some of their number remarked, "Could not he who opened the blind man's eyes have prevented this man from dying?" [38]Jesus, for his part, found that he was once more deeply stirred within himself when he reached the tomb. (The tomb was a cave with a stone placed against the opening.) [39]"Take the stone away," said Jesus. "Master," Martha, the dead man's sister, said to him, "the smell of death must be about him by this time, for it is al-

ready four days since he died." [40]"Have I not told you," Jesus said to her, "that if you will but believe, you will see God glorified before your eyes." [41]So they took the stone away. Then Jesus raised up his eyes and exclaimed, "Father, how thankful I am to you for listening to me. [42]As for myself, I knew well that you listen to me at all times. Yet I spoke as I did for the sake of the crowd which is standing round me, so that they might learn to believe that it was you who have sent me forth." [43]And on having spoken these words, he cried out in a loud voice, "Lazarus, come forth; here to my side!" [44]The dead man came out, having his hands and his feet swathed in bandages and his face wrapped up in a kerchief. "Untie him," Jesus said to the other, "and let him go his way."

[45]Many of the Jews who had visited Mary and had seen what Jesus had done came to believe in him, [46]while there were some of them who went off to the Pharisees to report what had been done by Jesus.

[47]Upon this, the chief priests and the Pharisees summoned a meeting of the supreme council, and this is what was said: "What are we achieving? Here there is this man showing forth many a sign. [48]If we let him go on in this way, then everybody will believe in him, and the Romans will come destroying both our place of worship and our nation." [49]But one among them, Caiaphas, who held the high priesthood that year, spoke to them thus: "You are wholly devoid of understanding. [50]You even fail to grasp that it is better for you that one man should die for the people than that the whole nation should perish." [51]This pronouncement of his was not of his own making. On the contrary, what really happened was that, since he held the high priesthood that year, he was to be the one to give utterance to the prophecy that Jesus was destined to die on behalf of the nation— [52]and indeed, not only for the nation's sake but also that he might gather together in unity God's children scattered far and wide. [53]From that day onwards, then, they plotted to put him to death.

[54]So Jesus no longer went about openly among the people of Judaea but left the district for a town called Ephraim, which lay in the country bordering on the desert. And there he stayed with his disciples.

[m][55]The Jewish Passover was at hand, and many from the country went up to Jerusalem to purify themselves in preparation for the Passover. [56]They looked out for Jesus and, as they were standing about in the temple, said to one another, "What is your opinion? It is scarcely possible that he should be coming to the festival." [57]By that time the chief priests and the Pharisees had given their orders: Anyone knowing where he was should report the matter, so that they might be in a position to have him apprehended.

[m][Nm 9:11ff]

12 Six days before the Passover, Jesus went to Bethany, the home of Lazarus, whom he had raised from the dead. ²So they prepared a meal for him there in his honour at which Martha did the serving, while Lazarus was one of those at table with Jesus. ³Then Mary came in, bringing with her a pound of very costly perfume made up of pure nard. With it she anointed Jesus' feet, and then she wiped them dry with her hair, while the house was being filled with the fragrance given forth by the perfume. ⁴Upon this, Judas Iscariot —one of the disciples, the man who was to betray him—remarked, ⁵"Why was this perfume not sold? Three hundred pieces of silver could have been obtained for it and the money given to the poor." ⁶It was not out of any concern for the poor that he said this but because he was a thief. The common purse was under his care, and it was his practice to help himself to what had been put into it. ⁷"Leave her alone," said Jesus, "that she may keep what she has for the day when my body will be prepared for burial. ⁸There never will be a time when you will not have the poor with you, but me you will not always have." ⁹Meanwhile a large number of the Jews had heard that he was in that place, and they went there not merely on Jesus' account but also that they might see Lazarus, whom he had raised from the dead. ¹⁰The chief priests, on the other hand, had come to the decision that they must do away with Lazarus as well, ¹¹because it was on his account that a good many among the Jews fell away and learned to believe in Jesus.

¹²The next day the large crowd which had come to attend the festival, on hearing that Jesus was on his way to Jerusalem, ¹³took palm branches into their hands and went forth to meet him, crying out, "ⁿHosanna! A blessing rests on him who is coming in the name of the Lord, on the king of Israel!" ¹⁴As for Jesus, he mounted a donkey which had come his way, this being the very thing written about in scripture: ¹⁵ᵒ**'Cast off all fear, Zion's daughter. ᵖLook, it is your king who is coming, seated on a donkey's colt.'**

¹⁶Jesus' disciples failed to understand this at the time. But when he attained to his state of glory, then they called to mind that it was about him that these words had been written, and that it was in accordance with them that they had been dealing with him the way they did. ¹⁷Large numbers were bearing him witness, those who had been with him when he summoned Lazarus out of the tomb and raised him from the dead. ¹⁸Indeed, this was the reason why the crowd went out to meet him, that they had heard of his showing forth that sign. ¹⁹And so the Pharisees said to one another, "You can see for yourselves that

ⁿPs 118:25f   ᵒIs 40:9   ᵖZc 9:9

nothing you can do is of any avail. Why, all the world has gone after him."

20 Among those who had gone up for the festival to worship there were certain Greeks. 21 They approached Philip—the man who came from Bethsaida in Galilee—and laid this request before him: "Sir, it is our desire to see Jesus." 22 Philip went to tell Andrew, and Andrew and Philip went to tell Jesus. 23 And this is the answer which Jesus made them:

"The hour has come for the Son of Man to be invested with glory. 24 I am telling you in solemn truth: a grain of wheat remains but a solitary grain unless it first falls into the ground and dies. Yet if it die, it brings forth a rich harvest. 25 He who loves his life is losing it, while he who makes an enemy of his own life in this world will preserve it, eternal life being the outcome. 26 Anyone who is a servant of mine must follow me on my way; and where I am, there, too, will my servant be. Whosoever does a service to me will be honoured by my Father.

27 "Yet, as things are, my soul finds itself in a state of turmoil. What then shall I say? 'Father, rescue me from this hour of trial'? By no means. For if this hour has come to me, it has been my very purpose that I should come to it. 28 Father, show forth the glory of your name."

At that a voice came forth from heaven uttering these words: "I have shown it forth to be glorious, and shall yet do so again." 29 On hearing the voice, the crowd which was standing by asserted that there had been a clap of thunder, while others were saying, "An angel has spoken to him." 30 Jesus made them this answer: "If this voice has come forth, that has not been for my sake but for yours. 31 Now is the time that sentence is being passed upon this world; now is the time that he who rules this world is to be cast out. 32 As for myself, once I have been lifted up from the earth I shall draw all men to myself." 33 He said this to signify the kind of death by which he was destined to die. 34 And the crowd replied to him thus: "We have learned from our law that the Christ will remain for ever. What then do you mean by saying that it is decreed that the Son of Man is to be lifted up? Who is this Son of Man?" 35 Upon this, Jesus addressed these words to them: "It is for but a little while longer that you will have the light in your midst. Go on your way while you have the light, so that the darkness may not overtake you. He who makes his way in the dark does not know where he is going. 36 Believe in the light while you still have the light, so that it may be the light whose offspring you become." Having spoken these words, Jesus went on his way and hid himself from them.

37 Yet even though he had shown forth so many signs in their sight, they would not believe in him. 38 And that happened so that these

words spoken by Isaiah the prophet might be brought to fulfilment: *q***'Lord, is there anyone who has believed what he has heard from us, anyone who has had revealed to him the strength of the Lord's arm?'** ³⁹Indeed, if it was impossible for them to believe, the reason is to be found in words spoken by Isaiah in another place: ⁴⁰ *r***"He has blinded their eyes and dulled their minds, to make sure that they would see nothing with their eyes and understand nothing with their minds, that they would not turn back, I, God, becoming their healer.'** ⁴¹Isaiah said these things because he had a vision of Jesus in his state of glory, and it was of him that he spoke.

⁴²Yet, for all that, there were many, even among those in authority, who came to believe in him. However, they would not profess it openly on account of the Pharisees, for fear of being expelled from the synagogue. ⁴³For honour such as men bestow was dearer to them than the honour which comes of God.

⁴⁴As for Jesus, he cried out and spoke thus: "If a man believes in me, it is not I in whom he believes; he believes in him who has sent me forth. ⁴⁵Moreover, to see me is to see him who has sent me forth. ⁴⁶I have come into the world as light, so that no one believing in me should remain in darkness. ⁴⁷Besides, if anyone who has heard my words were not to keep true to them, it is not I that pronounce judgment on him. For if I have made my appearance, it was not that I might pronounce judgment on the world, but that I might bring salvation to it. ⁴⁸Still, there is a judge at hand for him who sets me aside and does not accept my words. It is the message delivered in what I have spoken which will be his judge on the last day. ⁴⁹And indeed, nothing spoken by me has come of myself. The Father who has sent me forth: it is he who has commanded me what I was to say and how I was to speak. ⁵⁰Moreover, I know what the meaning of his commandment is: it means eternal life. Whatever I say, therefore, I speak as my Father has bidden me."

13 The time was now just before the festival of the Passover, and Jesus knew that the hour had arrived for him to depart from this world and go to the Father. He had always loved those in the world who were his, and now he was to show forth the very depth of his love. ²They were at supper, and the devil had already put it into the mind of Judas, the son of Simon Iscariot, that he was to betray him. ³Jesus himself knew that the Father had committed everything into his hands, that he had come forth from God, and that he was returning to God. ⁴And now he rose up from his place at supper, laid his outer

q Is 53:1   *r* Is 6:9f

garments aside, and, taking a towel, tied it round his waist. 5Then he poured water into a basin and began to wash the disciples' feet, wiping them dry with the towel which he had been tying round himself. 6When Simon Peter's turn came, Peter asked him, "Is it for you, Lord, to wash my feet?" 7Jesus replied, "What I am doing you cannot grasp at present, but later you will understand." 8"Never, so long as I live," exclaimed Peter, "shall you wash my feet!" "Unless I wash you, you have no fellowship with me," was Jesus' reply. 9"If that is so, Lord," Simon Peter said to him, "then do not wash my feet merely; wash also my hands and my head!" 10"The man who has bathed," Jesus replied to him, "does not need any washing except for the stains on his feet; he is clean all over. And you are clean, though not every one of you is clean." 11He knew well enough who was going to betray him. That is why he added the words, 'though not every one of you is clean'.

12Then, having washed their feet, he replaced his garments and returned to his seat, saying to them, "Do you understand what I have done for you? 13You call me 'Master' and you call me 'Lord', and rightly so; for that is what I am. 14Well then, if I who am your Lord and your Master have washed your feet, you in your turn are required to wash one another's feet. 15What I have done is set you an example, so that what I did you may do likewise. 16I am telling you in solemn truth: no slave can be greater than his master, no messenger greater than the one who has sent him forth. 17If you know all this, a blessing rests on you, so long as you act on what you know. 18In what I am saying, it is not all of you that I have in mind; and I do indeed know what manner of men are those I have chosen. But a passage from scripture remains to be fulfilled, and it is this: *'**The man who ate of my bread has lifted up his heel, turning against me.**' 19I am telling you this now, before it has happened, so that when it happens you may come to believe that I am the one who truly *is*. 20I am telling you in solemn truth, whoever welcomes any messenger of mine gives a welcome to me, and whoever welcomes me welcomes him who sent me forth."

21Having spoken these words, Jesus was greatly troubled in his spirit, and he gave evidence of this by exclaiming, "I am telling you in solemn truth: one of you will betray me." 22As for the disciples, they looked at each other, being at a loss which of them he had in mind. 23There was one of the disciples at table—and it was a man whom Jesus held dear—who was reclining with his head on Jesus' breast. 24So Simon Peter made a sign to him and said, "Tell us which of us he means." 25And he—the one who was reclining on Jesus'

*Ps 41:9

breast—leaned back and asked, "Lord, who is it?" 26Jesus answered him thus: "It is he to whom I shall give the piece of bread which I shall be dipping in the dish." Upon this, he dipped the piece of bread in the dish, took it into his hands, and gave it to Judas, the son of Simon Iscariot. 27And no sooner had the piece of bread been given him than Satan took possession of him. As for Jesus, he said to him, "That which you are about to do, do it as quickly as you can." 28None of the others reclining at table understood why he was speaking to him like this. 29Some of them supposed that, since Judas had the money box under his care, Jesus was saying to him, 'Buy what we need for the festival', or that he was ordering him to make some gift to the poor. 30As for Judas, on receiving the piece of bread he went forth at once.

And now night had fallen.

31After he had gone out, Jesus spoke these words: "Now it is that the Son of Man is glorified, and that God is glorified in him. 32And if God is glorified in him, God in his turn will glorify him in himself, and will glorify him forthwith. 33Dear children of mine, it is for but a little while longer that I shall be remaining with you. You will be looking for me. Yet I am now telling you what I said to the Jews, 'You cannot reach the place where I am going'. 34I have a new commandment to give you, that you are to love one another. As I have loved you, so you are bidden to love one another. 35If you bear love to one another, this shall be the token by which all will know that you are my disciples."

36"Lord," Simon Peter asked him, "where is the place to which you are going?" "You cannot follow me now to the place where I am going," was Jesus' reply, "but you will follow me later." 37"Lord," Peter enquired, "why is it that I cannot follow you now? I will lay down my life for you." 38"Will you indeed lay down your life for me?" was Jesus' reply. "I am telling you in solemn truth: before the cock crows, you will have disowned me three times.

14 "Set your troubled minds at rest. Believe in God, and believe in me likewise. 2There is many a resting place in my Father's house. Were it not so I would have told you, because it is to prepare a place for you that I am going there. 3And having gone there, preparing a place for you, I shall return and take you to myself, so that where I am you may be too. 4As for the way which leads to the place where I am going, it is known to you." 5"Lord," asked Thomas, "We do not know the place to which you are going. How then can we know the way?" 6"I am the way," was Jesus' reply; "I am truth; and I am life. Except through me, no one can come into the presence of the Father. 7If you knew me, the Father would likewise be known to you. In fact, from

this time onwards you *do* know him, and indeed have seen him." [8]"Lord," Philip said to him, "let us see the Father and we shall rest content." [9]"Have I been with you all this time, Philip," Jesus said to him, "and you still do not know me? He who has seen me has seen the Father. How then can you say, 'Let us see the Father'? [10]Do you not believe that I am in the Father, and that the Father is in me? The words I am speaking do not come of myself. No, what is happening is that the Father who dwells within me is accomplishing his own works. [11]Believe me when I say that I am in the Father, and that the Father is in me; or if you cannot, let the works themselves serve you as a ground for believing. [12]I am telling you in solemn truth: whoever believes in me will perform the very same works as I do myself. In fact, he will perform even greater works, and the reason for this is that I am going to the Father. [13]Besides, whatever you shall ask for in my name, I shall bring it about, so that the Father may be glorified in the Son. [14]If you ask for anything in my name, I shall bring it about.

[15]"If you love me, you must obey the commandments which I give you. [16]And then I shall entreat the Father, and he will appoint another for you to stand by your side, one who is to remain with you for ever: [17]the Spirit who leads to the truth. It is impossible for the world to give the Spirit a welcome since it does not either see him or know him. But you know him because he stands close to you and dwells within you. [18]I shall not leave you bereft. I am ever coming to you. [19]It will be but a short while now and the world shall see me no longer, but you will see me. Besides, because I live on, you too shall have life. [20]When that time comes, you will know that I have my being in the Father, and you have your being in me, and I have my being in you. [21]If there be anyone who has received my commandments and keeps true to them, this is the very one who loves me. Moreover, whoever loves me shall be loved by my Father; and I shall love him and reveal myself to him."

[22]"Lord," asked Judas (the other Judas, not Iscariot), "how has it come about that you intend to reveal yourself only to us and not to the world?" [23]Jesus answered him thus: "Whoever loves me will keep true to my message, and then my Father will love him, and we shall go forth to him and make our home with him. [24]He who does not love me fails to keep true to the words which I utter. Moreover, the message you are hearing does not come of myself. It comes of the Father who has sent me forth.

[25]"These things I have said to you while I am still remaining with you. [26]However, there is one who will stand by your side, the Holy Spirit whom the Father will send forth in my name. He will teach you everything, and you will call to mind all that I have told you. [27]Peace is my bequest to you; the peace which is my very own is what I am

bestowing upon you. It is not after the manner in which the world bestows its gifts that I am making my gift to you. Set your troubled hearts
at rest, and banish all anxiety from them. [28]You have heard me say, 'I
am going away and I am coming back to you'. Did you truly love me,
you would rejoice that I am on my way to the Father; for the Father is
greater than I am. [29]As it is, I have told you now, before it has come
about, so that, after it has come about, you may learn to believe. [30]I
shall be telling you but a few more things while I am still in your midst;
for he who bears rule over the world is on his way. He will indeed
find nothing in me to enable him to gain power over me. [31]Still, what
has to be accomplished is this, that the world is to come to know that
I love the Father, and that the commandment laid down for me by the
Father is the very thing I do. Well then, rise up and let us depart from
here.

15 "I am the vine, the true vine, and my Father is the one who
tends it. [2]Any branch found in me which does not bear fruit he
removes, and any branch which does bear fruit he cleanses so that it
may bear still more fruit. [3]As for yourselves, you have already had
your cleansing through the message which I have been delivering to
you. [4]Have your dwelling place within me, as I have mine within you.
As a branch cannot bear fruit by itself but must remain one with the
vine, no more can you bear fruit unless you remain one with me. [5]I
am the vine, and you are the branches. He who has his dwelling place
within me, while I have mine within him, is the one who bears much
fruit; for apart from me you can do nothing at all. [6]If there be anyone
who does not have his dwelling place within me, he is cast off, as a
branch is cast off, and withers away: branches which men gather up,
throwing them into the fire and burning them. [7]If you dwell within
me and my words dwell within you, you may ask for whatever you
will, and it shall be granted to you. [8]Moreover, if you bear much fruit,
becoming disciples of mine, that is the very thing which redounds to
the Father's glory. [9]As the Father has loved me, so have I loved you.
Let my love be the place where you dwell. [10]It is through keeping true
to my commandments that my love shall be the place where you
dwell, just as I have kept true to my Father's commandments and have
my dwelling place in his love. [11]I have said these things so that the
joy which is mine may be found in you and be yours in full measure.
[12]As for the commandment laid down by me, this is what it is, that
you should love one another as I have loved you. [13]The greatest love
that a man can show is that he should lay down his life for his friends;
[14]and you, if you do what I command you to do, *are* my friends. [15]I
no longer speak of you as servants because a servant has no com-

prehension of what his master is about. And if I have called you friends, that is because I have made known to you everything which I have learned from my Father. ¹⁶Moreover, it was not you who chose me. I have chosen you, the task appointed for you being this, that you should go forth and bear fruit—fruit which will endure—so that the Father may grant to you whatever you shall be asking in my name.

¹⁷"That you should love one another is the commandment I am laying down for you. ¹⁸If the world hates you, you know well enough that it hated me first before it learned to hate you. ¹⁹Were the world the place to which you belong, you would be at one with it and the world would love you. Yet the world is not your home because I have chosen you, taking you out of the world. And so it is that the world hates you. ²⁰Call to mind the words I have spoken to you, 'No servant can be greater than his master'. If they have persecuted me, they will persecute you likewise. If they have kept true to my message, then they shall keep true to yours.* ²¹Yet, in fact, they will bring all this upon you because you serve the cause which bears my name. For the truth is that they have no knowledge of the one who has sent me forth.

²²"Had I not made my appearance and spoken to them, no sin would be found attaching to them, but as things stand, there is no excuse they can offer for their sin. ²³Anyone who hates me hates my Father. ²⁴Had I not performed works in their midst such as no other man has ever performed, no sin would be found attaching to them; but as things stand, they have seen and have hated both me and my Father. ²⁵Still, it had to be, so that these words written down in their law might be brought to fulfilment, ᵗ'**They have hated me for no reason at all.**'

²⁶"However, when he who will stand by your side makes his appearance, he whom I shall be sending forth from the Father, the Spirit leading to the truth who proceeds from the Father: it will be he who will bear witness on my behalf. ²⁷And you, too, will be bearing witness, and that because you are the men who have been with me from the very beginning.

16

"My purpose in saying these things to you has been to make certain that you should not be shaken in your faith. ²They will expel you from the synagogues. Indeed, the time will come when everyone who seeks to kill you will suppose that he is performing a service for God. ³And they will act in this way because they have failed to come

---

ᵗPs 35:19; 69:4

* [The translator supplied this optional translation: 'Had they kept true to my message, they would be keeping true to yours.']

to know either the Father or me. [4]Moreover, if I have told you these things, this was the reason, that when the time arrives for them to happen, you should call to mind what I have said and that I have given you warning. On the other hand, I did not tell you about them from the beginning because of my still being in your midst. [5]Now, however, I am going to him who has sent me forth; yet none among you is asking me, 'Where are you going?' [6]On the other hand, sorrow has taken possession of your hearts because of my having talked to you in this manner. [7]Yet I tell you the truth, and it is this. It is for your own good that I shall be going away from you. For were I not to go away, the one who is to stand by your side would not be coming to you; but when I have made my way there, I shall send him to you. [8]And what he will do when he comes is to convict the world of wrong in what it has thought of sin, of righteousness, and of judgment. [9]He will show that sin is to be found in their refusal to believe in me, [10]righteousness in my going back to the Father, you being unable to see me any longer, [11]and judgment in the fact that judgment has already been passed on him who is the ruler of this world.

[12]"I have many more things to tell you, but you are not as yet able to bear with them. [13]However, when the truth-giving Spirit makes his appearance, it will be he who will be guiding you to the whole of the truth. For what he will say he will not say of his own accord; rather, he will say only that which he has heard. Besides, he will proclaim the things which are yet to come. [14]And it will be I whom he will show forth to be glorious, because that which he will proclaim to you he will be drawing forth from what is my very own. [15]Everything that belongs to the Father belongs to me. That is why I said, 'That which he will proclaim he will be drawing forth from what is my very own'.

[16]"It will be but a short while now, and you shall see me no longer; and again a short while, and you shall see me." [17]At that, some of his disciples asked one another, "What does he mean by saying, 'It will be but a short while, and you shall see me no longer; and again a short while, and you shall see me'? And what do his words, 'Because I am going to the Father', mean? [18]What is this 'short while' that he speaks of? We do not understand what he is talking about." [19]As for Jesus, he knew that they wished to question him, and so he said to them, "The point you are disputing with one another is my saying, 'It will be but a short while, and you shall see me no longer; and again a short while, and you shall see me.' [20]I am telling you in solemn truth: You will weep and lament, and the world shall rejoice. You will indeed feel anguish, yet your anguish shall turn into joy. [21]A woman, while giving birth to a child, feels anguish, but when the child has been born she no longer feels her distress, on account of the joy she feels because a human being has been born into the world. [22]As for yourselves, you,

too, are feeling anguish now. Yet I shall see you again, and then your hearts will rejoice, and no one will be able to take that joy from you. ²³When that day comes, you will not ask me any questions. I am telling you in solemn truth: whatever you shall be asking of the Father in my name, he will grant it to you. ²⁴So far you have asked nothing in my name. Ask, and you will receive, so that joy in all its fullness may be yours.

²⁵"In what I have said I have spoken to you in the figures of speech. Yet the time will come when I shall no longer resort to figures in my speech, but shall proclaim to you in plain words what I have to proclaim to you about the Father. ²⁶When that day arrives, you will make your requests in my name. In saying this, I do not mean that I shall appeal to the Father on your behalf. ²⁷For the Father himself holds you dear because of your holding me dear, and because you have learned to believe that I have come forth from the Father's presence. ²⁸I have come forth from the Father and have entered the world. And now in turn I am leaving the world and am on my way to the Father."

²⁹His disciples said, "Why, this is indeed the language of plain words, and there is no figure of speech in what you are saying. ³⁰Now we are certain that everything is known to you and that there is no need for anyone to subject you to questioning. And so it is that we believe that you have come forth from God." ³¹"Is this how things stand," was Jesus' reply to them, "that you now have faith? ³²Why, the time is coming, indeed has already come, when you ^uwill be scattered, each going to his own home, and leaving me alone. Yet I am not alone because I have the Father by my side. ³³I have told you all this so that you may find your peace in me. In the world you cannot but suffer distress. But be of good courage. I have vanquished the world."

17

These are the words Jesus spoke, and then, lifting up his eyes towards heaven, he exclaimed,

"Father, the time has arrived. Show forth the glory of your Son, so that your Son might, in his turn, show forth your glory, ²he being the one to whom you have entrusted power over the whole of mankind, in order that he might bestow eternal life upon all whom you have committed to his hands. ³And this is what eternal life is, that they should know you who alone are truly God, and know Jesus Christ whom you have sent forth. ⁴I have shown forth your glory upon earth by accomplishing the work you have given me to do. ⁵And now,

^u[Zc 13:7]

Father, glorify me, in your very sight, with that glory which, in your very sight, belonged to me before the world ever began. 6I have made known your name to the men whom you have entrusted to me, taking them out of the world. They were yours, and you have entrusted them to me, while they, for their part, have kept true to your word. 7Now they do indeed know that it was from you that there came all the things which you have entrusted to me. 8For I have handed on to them the words of teaching which you have handed on to me, and they have given them a welcome, recognizing truly that it is from you that I have come forth, and learning to believe that you are the one who has sent me forth. 9It is on their behalf that I am making entreaty. I do not make entreaty on the world's behalf but on behalf of those whom you have entrusted to me, acting in this way because it is to you that they belong. 10All that is mine is yours, and all that is yours is mine, while it is in these men that my glory is shown forth. 11Besides, there is this: I am no longer in the world—being on my way to you— whereas these are still in the world. Father, Holy One, be their protector by virtue of the power of your name, that name which I bear as a gift from you, so that they may become one, as we are one. 12While being in their midst, I have kept them safe in virtue of the power of your name, that name which I bear as a gift from you. I protected them; and there was not one of them who perished except the man who was destined for perdition: the words set out in scripture had to find their fulfilment. 13But now I am on my way to you, saying these things while still in the world, so that there may be in them, in all its fullness, the joy which is mine. 14I have handed on your message to them, and the world came to hate them because they do not belong to the world, just as I do not belong to the world. 15The entreaty I am making is not that you should remove them from the world, but that you should keep them safe from the evil one. 16They do not belong to the world, just as I do not belong to the world. 17Hallow them by the truth; it is your message that is truth. 18As you have sent me into the world, so do I send them into the world. 19It is for their sake that I hallow myself, so that they, too, should be hallowed by the truth.

20"Yet it is not for them only that I am making entreaty but also for those who will believe in me in the future, being ready to do so because of the message which these men will deliver, 21so that all may be one, as you, Father, are in me, and I in you, so that they, for their part, may be in us, the world coming to believe that it was you who have sent me forth. 22Moreover, the glory which you have bestowed upon me I have bestowed upon them, so that they might be one, as we are one, 23I in them, and you in me, that they might find perfection in oneness. And what is to be accomplished by all this is that the world is to come to know that you have sent me forth, and that you have bestowed your love upon them as you have bestowed it upon me. 24Father, it is my wish that those men who are your gift to me should be by my side in the place where I shall be, and that they should be beholders of my glory, which I have had bestowed upon me by you, because you gave me your love from before the foundation of the world. 25Father, righteous one, here was the world not knowing you, but I knew you; and as for these men, they have come to know that it was you who have sent me forth. 26I have made your name known to them, and shall ever make it known, so that the love you have borne me may be in them, and I may be in them."

18 Having spoken these words, Jesus took his departure, in the company of his disciples, and went on his way across the Kidron valley, until they arrived at a place where there was a garden. Here he, and his disciples with him, entered. 2Now this place was likewise known to Judas, his betrayer, because many a time Jesus and his disciples had forgathered there. 3And so it happened that Judas, bringing with him a detachment of soldiers as well as officers of the law provided by the chief priests and the Pharisees, presented himself there, the men being equipped with lanterns, with torches, and with weapons. 4As for Jesus, who knew well enough everything that was to befall him, he went out to them, saying, "Who are you looking for?" 5"Jesus of Nazareth," was their reply. "I am he," Jesus told them. And there stood Judas, his betrayer, in their midst. 6Now when Jesus said to them, "I am he," they retreated and threw themselves on the ground. 7So Jesus asked them once again, "Who are you looking for?" their reply being, "Jesus of Nazareth." 8"I have told you that I am he," said Jesus. "If then it is I that you are looking for, let these others go free." 9(He said this so that these words spoken by him before might find their fulfilment: 'I have not lost one among those whom you have given me as my own'.) 10Upon this, Simon Peter drew the sword which he was carrying and struck the High Priest's servant, cutting off his right ear. (The servant's name was Malchus.) 11But Jesus called to him saying, "Put your sword back into its sheath. Shall I not drink the cup which has been given into my hands by the Father?"

12And so it was that Jesus was apprehended and put in fetters by the detachment of soldiers with its commanding officer, and by the Jewish officers of the law. 13They took him first to Annas because he was the father-in-law of Caiaphas, who held the position of High Priest that year. 14(Now Caiaphas was the man who had given his advice to the Jews by pointing out that it was a far better thing for them that one man should die on behalf of the people.)

15Simon Peter was following Jesus, and so was another disciple. This disciple, who was known to the High Priest, went with Jesus into the courtyard of the High Priest's official residence, [16]while Peter was waiting outside, standing close to the door. The other disciple—the one known to the High Priest—then came out, spoke to the doorkeeper, and brought Peter inside. [17]And so the maidservant who was keeping the door asked Peter this question, "Can it be that you are another of that man's disciples?" "I am not," was Peter's reply. [18]It was cold, and a charcoal fire had been lit by the servants as well as by the officers of the law who were standing there warming themselves. As for Peter, he, too, stood there with them and warmed himself.

[19]Now the High Priest questioned Jesus about his disciples and his doctrine. [20]"I have spoken openly to all the world," was Jesus' reply. "I have taught at all times in synagogue and in the temple, where all the Jews forgather. [v]Not a word have I spoken in secret. [21]Why are you questioning me? Ask those who have heard me what I have told them; they know what I have said." [22]At these words one of the officers of the law, who was standing by, struck Jesus in the face and exclaimed, "Is that the way to answer the High Priest?" [23]"If I have spoken amiss," was Jesus' reply, "produce evidence of the evil I have done. But if I am in the right in what I have said, why is it that you strike me a blow?" [24]Then Annas sent him, still in fetters, to Caiaphas the High Priest.

[25]Simon Peter, for his part, remained standing there and warming himself. And so it came about that the others asked him, "Can it be that you are another of his disciples?" But Peter denied it, saying, "I am not." [26]And there was one of the servants of the High Priest—a kinsman of the man whose ear Peter had cut off—asking him, "Did I not see you in his company in the garden?" [27]Yet Peter once again made a denial. Immediately upon this there was a cock crowing.

[28]What happened then was that Jesus was led from Caiaphas' house into the Governor's place of residence. It was early in the morning. The men did not themselves enter the place, that they might avoid defilement and be able to eat the Passover meal. [29]So Pilate went out to them, asking, "What accusation do you bring forward against this man?" [30]Their reply was this: "Were he not a malefactor, we should not be delivering him into your hands." [31]"Take him yourselves," Pilate said to them, "and pronounce judgment upon him in accordance with your law." "We have no power," was the Jews' reply, "to put any man to death." [32](This took place so that the words spoken by Jesus might find their fulfilment, those signifying by what kind of death he was to die.)

[33]As for Pilate, he went back into his place of residence, summoned

[v][Is 45:19; 48:16]

Jesus, and asked him, "Are you the king of the Jews?" 34 "Are you asking this of your own accord," was Jesus' reply, "or is this the way in which others have spoken of me?" 35 "Am I a Jew?" was Pilate's rejoinder. "Your own people and their chief priests have delivered you into my hands. What is the offence you have committed?" 36 Jesus made him this reply: "My kingdom does not belong to this world. Did my kingdom belong to this world, those who serve me would be fighting on my behalf, to prevent my being delivered into the hands of the Jews. Yet as things are, it is not from here that my kingdom takes its origin." 37 "Are you a king then?" Pilate asked him. "It is you," replied Jesus, "who are saying that I am a king. This has been the task which has been assigned to me from my birth, and it is for this that I have come into the world, that I should bear witness on behalf of the truth. Anyone who is on the side of the truth is attentive to my voice." 38 "What is truth?" Pilate asked him; and having spoken these words, he once again went out to the Jews, saying to them, "There is nothing I can find him guilty of. 39 Now there is a custom among you that, as a favour done to you, I should grant a pardon to one man at the Passover. Would you have me grant a pardon to the king of the Jews?" 40 At that they made a fresh outcry and exclaimed, "Not him but Barabbas!" (Now Barabbas was a brigand.)

19   After this, Pilate ordered Jesus to be taken away and had him flogged, 2 while the soldiers put a crown on his head, which they had woven out of thorns, and dressed him in a purple robe. 3 They persisted in coming up to him and exclaiming, "Greetings to you, king of the Jews!" And they struck him in the face.

4 As for Pilate, he once again came out of his place of residence, saying to them, "Here he is; I am bringing him out to you so that you might come to know that there is nothing I can find him guilty of." 5 At that, Jesus came forth wearing the crown of thorns and the purple robe, while Pilate said to them, "Here is the man; look at him." 6 Now when the chief priests and the officers of the law saw him, they cried out and exclaimed, "Crucify him! Crucify him!" Pilate said to them, "Take him away yourselves and crucify him; for there is nothing that I can find him guilty of." 7 "We have a law," the Jews replied to him, "and according to that law he ought to suffer the penalty of death because he made himself out to be God's son." 8 When Pilate heard these words, he became more frightened than ever, 9 went back into his place of residence, and asked Jesus, "Where have you come from?" But Jesus made him no answer. 10 So Pilate said to him, "Do you refuse to speak to me? Do you not know that I have the power to set you free and the power to crucify you?" 11 "You would have no power

whatever over me," replied Jesus, "unless it had been granted to you by him who is above all; and that is why the guilt of the man who has delivered me into your hands is all the greater." [12]From that time onwards Pilate made every effort to set him free. The Jews, however, made an outcry and exclaimed, "If you set that man free, you are no friend of the Emperor's! Anyone who claims that he is a king sets the Emperor at defiance!" [13]On hearing these words, Pilate had Jesus brought out, and he himself took his seat on the judicial bench, at a place known as 'The Pavement', or in Hebrew 'Gabbatha'.* [14]The time was the eve of the Passover, about midday. "Here he is, your king," said Pilate to the Jews. [15]Whereupon the Jews cried out, exclaiming, "Away with him; away with him; crucify him!" "Am I to crucify your king?" Pilate asked them. "The Emperor is the only king we have," was the chief priests' reply. [16]Thereupon Pilate let them have their way with him and resolved that he was to be crucified.

They then led Jesus away, and he, [17]carrying his own cross, made his way to the place bearing the name 'Place of a Skull', or 'Golgotha' as it is called in Hebrew.* [18]And it was there that they crucified him, and with him two other men on either side of him, Jesus being in the middle. [19]As for Pilate, he wrote out an inscription and had it put on the cross. And what it said was, JESUS OF NAZARETH, KING OF THE JEWS. [20]Now many among the Jews read the inscription, because the place where Jesus was crucified was near the city. Moreover, the inscription was written in three languages, in Hebrew,† in Latin, and in Greek. [21]And so the chief priests of the Jews said to Pilate, "'King of the Jews' is not what you ought to be writing. You ought to write, 'That man said: "I am king of the Jews"'." [22]"What I have written I have written," was the reply Pilate made to them.

[23]The soldiers, after they had nailed Jesus to the cross, took possession of his garments and divided them into four parts, one part for each soldier. And they took his tunic as well. Now this tunic had no seam, being woven from the top in one piece. [24]That is why the soldiers said to one another, "We must not tear it, but instead let us cast lots over it to decide to whom it is to belong." Things happened in this way in order that the following passage from scripture might be brought to fulfilment: *w*'**They have divided my garments among themselves, and have drawn lots over my clothing.'**

That is what the soldiers did. [25]Meanwhile, close to the cross on

*w*Ps 22:18

* [The Greek is 'in Hebrew'. The last syllable in 'Gabbatha' and 'Golgotha', however, indicates a clear Aramaic construction and is never found in Hebrew.]

† [Almost certainly, a formal indictment for which a prisoner was convicted and executed would have been written in Hebrew.]

which Jesus was hanging were standing his mother, his mother's sister, Mary wife of Clopas, and Mary of Magdala. 26 Now when Jesus saw his mother and the disciple whom he held dear standing by her side, he said to his mother, "Look, good woman; here he is: your son". 27 Then he said to the disciple, "Look, here she is: your mother." And from that very hour the disciple received her into his home.

28 After this, Jesus, knowing that everything had now come to its appointed end, said, "I am ˣthirsty", speaking in this way so that what is said in scripture should be brought to fulfilment. 29 A jar filled with sour wine was standing there. So they soaked a sponge in the wine, wound it round a stalk of hyssop, and held it up to his lips. 30 As for Jesus, he took the wine, and after that he exclaimed, "It is accomplished!" And bowing his head he breathed his last.

31 Meanwhile the Jews, since it was the eve of the Passover, being anxious that the bodies should not remain on the cross during the Sabbath (that Sabbath being a day of great solemnity), requested Pilate that the legs of the bodies should be broken and that the bodies should be removed. 32 And so soldiers appeared and broke the legs of the first man who had been crucified with Jesus, and then of the other one. 33 But when they came to Jesus, they found that he was already dead; and so, instead of breaking his legs, 34 one of the soldiers pierced his side with a lance, and immediately there came forth a flow of blood and water. 35 This is borne witness to by a man who saw it with his own eyes, and his witness is trustworthy. He knows that he is telling the truth, and he speaks out so that you, too, might learn to believe. 36 Indeed, things happened in this way so that these words from scripture might be brought to fulfilment: ʸ'Not a bone of him shall be broken.' 37 And another place in scripture says: ᶻ'They shall fix their gaze on him whom they have pierced through.'

38 Some time after this, Pilate was asked by Joseph of Arimathaea, who was one of Jesus' disciples (but was so only in secret because he was afraid of the Jews), that he might be given permission to take away Jesus' body; and this Pilate granted him. So he came and took Jesus' body away, 39 and with him came Nicodemus, the man who on a former occasion had paid Jesus a visit by night; and he brought with him a mixture of myrrh and aloes weighing about a hundred pounds. 40 They took the body of Jesus and wrapped it, along with the spices, in linen cloths, obeying the Jewish custom of burying the dead. 41 Now there was a garden in the place where Jesus had been crucified, and in that garden was a new tomb, where no one had ever been laid to rest. 42 And it was there that they laid the body of Jesus,

ˣPs 22:15; 69:21   ʸEx 12:46; Nm 9:12; Ps 34:20   ᶻZc 12:10

because it was the eve of the Sabbath and because the tomb was near at hand.

20 Early on the first day of the week, while it was still dark, Mary of Magdala went to the tomb, and when she came to it, she saw that the stone had been removed from the opening of the tomb. ²So she came away, running to Peter and to the other disciple—the one whom Jesus held dear—and said to them, "They have carried the Lord away from the tomb, and we cannot tell where they have taken him." ³At that, Peter, and the other disciple with him, set out to make their way to the tomb. ⁴To begin with, they ran at the same pace; but then the other disciple, running faster than Peter, overtook him, and so it was that he arrived first at the tomb. ⁵He stooped down, and when he did, he saw the linen cloths lying on the ground, but he did not go in. ⁶Simon Peter, who was following, now came up; he *did* go into the tomb, and saw the linen cloths lying on the ground. ⁷And apart from this, he perceived that the kerchief which had been put over Jesus' head was not with the linen cloths but was lying rolled up in a place by itself. ⁸Then the other disciple—the one who had arrived at the tomb first—likewise went in, saw, and learned to believe. ⁹This happened the way it did because up to this very time they had not understood what is said of him in scripture, that he was destined to rise from the dead.

¹⁰So the disciples went home again, ¹¹but Mary took up her stand close by the tomb, outside of it, and she was weeping. And as she wept, she stooped down to glance at the tomb; ¹²and her eyes fell on two angels, clothed in white, seated in the place where Jesus' body had lain, one angel at the head and the other at the feet. ¹³"Why are you weeping, dear woman?" they asked her. "Because," she replied, "they have carried away my Lord, and I cannot tell where they have taken him." ¹⁴With these words she turned round and saw Jesus standing before her. Yet she did not know that it was Jesus. ¹⁵"Why are you weeping, my dear woman," asked Jesus, "and who is it that you are looking for?" "Sir," she replied, while supposing him to be the man who tended the garden, "if it was you who carried him off, tell me where you have taken him, and I shall move him to another place." ¹⁶Jesus said, "Mary." And she, turning towards him, exclaimed, "Rabboni!" (which is the Hebrew* for 'My Master'). ¹⁷"Do not cling to me thus," Jesus said to her, "for I have not as yet gone upwards to the Father; but instead take this message to my brothers, that I am about to go upwards to him who is my Father and your Father, and my God and your God." ¹⁸So

---

* [Mary's exclamation would almost certainly have been in the vernacular, i.e., Aramaic.]

Mary of Magdala went on her way and announced to the disciples that she had seen the Lord and that he had said these things to her.

¹⁹ And now it was the evening of the same day, the first day of the week. The disciples, because they were afraid of the Jews, had locked the doors of the place where they were assembled. Yet there was Jesus having come to them, and standing in their midst. "May peace rest upon you," he said to them. ²⁰ And having spoken these words, he showed them his hands and his side, the disciples being overjoyed at seeing the Lord. ²¹ "May peace rest upon you," he said to them once more. "I have been sent by my Father, and now in turn I am sending you forth." ²² Having spoken these words, he breathed upon them and said, "Receive the Holy Spirit. ²³ If there be any whose sins you forgive, their sins shall be forgiven them; and if there be any whom you declare to be bound to their sins, bound to them they shall be."

²⁴ Now there was one of the twelve disciples called Thomas, the meaning of this name being 'The Twin', who was not present with the rest when Jesus made his appearance. ²⁵ So the others told him that they had seen the Lord. And this is what he said to them: "Until I have seen the marks made by the nails on his hands, until I have put my finger into the marks made by the nails, and, moreover, have put my hand into his side, I shall never believe it." ²⁶ Eight days later the disciples were once again inside the house, and Thomas was with them. Yet, although the doors were locked, Jesus entered, stood in their midst, and said, "May peace rest upon you." ²⁷ Then he said to Thomas, "Put your finger here; and look, here are my hands. Stretch out your hand and put it into my side. And be unbelieving no longer, but believe." ²⁸ Thomas replied to him, exclaiming, "My Lord and my God!" ²⁹ while Jesus said to Thomas, "It is because you have seen me that you have come to believe. What a blessing rests on those who have not seen and have learned to believe."

³⁰ Jesus showed forth many other signs, not written down in this book, in the sight of his disciples. ³¹ Those which are written here have been set forth, so that you should believe that Jesus is the Christ, the Son of God, and that, in believing this, you may lay hold of eternal life by virtue of giving your allegiance to the cause which bears his name.

21 Some time after this, Jesus once again let himself be seen by his disciples. It happened close to the Sea of Tiberias; and this is the way in which he let himself be seen. ² Simon Peter, the man called Thomas, that is to say, 'The Twin', Nathanael who hailed from Cana in Galilee, the sons of Zebedee, and with them two more of Jesus' disciples were together in one place. ³ Simon Peter said to them, "I am going out to

fish," their reply being, "We, too, shall be going with you." So they set out and went aboard the boat. However, they caught nothing that night. 4Now when morning light was already dawning, there was Jesus, standing on the shore, while they, for their part, did not know that it was Jesus. 5Jesus asked them, "Do you have any fish with you, my dear friends?" their reply being, "We have not." 6"Throw your net over the right side of the boat," Jesus told them, "and a catch shall be yours." So they did throw it, and what happened was that so great was the number of fish caught that it was no longer within their power to haul in the net. 7At that, one of the disciples—the one whom Jesus held dear—said to Peter, "It is the Lord!" And Simon Peter, on hearing him say that it was the Lord, wrapped his coat round himself (for he was wearing nothing but his undergarments) and threw himself into the lake, 8while the other disciples came on in the boat (for they were only a short distance from the land, about a hundred yards away), towing the net, which was full of fish. 9When they came ashore, they saw a charcoal fire piled up there, with fish and bread laid upon it. 10"Bring me some of the fish you have just caught," Jesus said to them. 11So Simon Peter went aboard, dragging to the shore the net, which was filled with large fish: a hundred and fifty-three of them. Yet, although there were so many, the net did not break. 12"Go to it," said Jesus, "and have your breakfast." None of the disciples had the courage to ask him who he was. (As a matter of fact, they knew full well it was the Lord.) 13As for Jesus, he came up to them, took the bread, and handed it to them; and he did the same with the fish. 14This was already the third time that Jesus, after having been raised from the dead, let himself be seen by the disciples.

15Breakfast being over, Jesus said to Simon Peter, "Simon, son of John, do you love me more than these others do?" "Indeed I do, Lord," he answered him, "you know that you are dear to me." "Put my lambs out to pasture," was Jesus' reply to him. 16And he asked him a second time, "Simon son of John, do you love me?" "Indeed I do, Lord," he answered him. "You know that you are dear to me." "Lead forth my sheep that they may graze," was Jesus' reply. 17And he asked him a third time, "Simon son of John, am I dear to you?" Peter, being distressed at his asking him a third time whether he was dear to him, answered him in these words: "Lord, nothing is unknown to you; you know well enough that you are dear to me." "Put my little sheep out to pasture," said Jesus. 18"And besides, there is this I have to tell you in solemn truth: when you were a young man you would fasten your girdle round you and go wherever you chose. But when you have grown old, you will stretch out your hands, and it shall be a stranger who will be girding you up and carrying you off to a place where you have no wish to go." 19He spoke these words to signify what manner of death it would be through which Peter was to show forth God's glory. And having said this, he added, "Follow me."

20 As for Peter, he saw, on turning round, that they were being followed by the disciple whom Jesus held dear, the one who had been resting his head on Jesus' breast during the supper and had asked him, 'Who is to be your betrayer?' 21 When Peter caught sight of him, he enquired of Jesus, "What is to happen to him, Lord?" 22 Jesus replied to him thus: "If it is my wish that he should stay behind till I come, what concern is that of yours? What is required of you is that you should follow me."

23 It was as the result of this incident that the story spread among the brothers that this disciple was not to die. Yet Jesus had not said to Peter that this disciple was not to die. No, this is what he said: 'If it is my wish that he should stay behind till I come, what concern is that of yours?'

24 It is this very disciple who bears witness concerning these things and has set them down in writing. And we do indeed know that his testimony is in conformity with the truth.

25 There are many other things Jesus did which, if they were set down one by one, would, I am inclined to believe, require so many books to be written that the whole world would be unable to contain them.

THE APOSTLES
AND THEIR DEEDS

1 The first treatise which I composed, my dear Theophilus, concerned itself with everything Jesus set out to do and teach ²until the day that he was taken up into heaven, having given his orders, by means of the Holy Spirit, to the apostles whom he had chosen. ³It was likewise to them that, after his passion, he presented himself as alive, and gave many a proof of this, appearing to them throughout the course of forty days, and speaking to them about the things which pertain to the kingdom of God. ⁴And while being in their midst,* he gave them the order not to take their departure from Jerusalem, but to stay there, waiting for the fulfilment of the Father's promise: "You have heard from my own lips what it is. ⁵John, I told you, baptized with water. Yet there is a baptism, by means of the Holy Spirit, which you shall have administered to you not many days from now." ⁶So they asked him, one day when they were in his company, "Lord, is this the time when you are bringing to Israel the restoration of its kingdom?" ⁷"It is not for you," he replied, "to know about the times and the occasions which the Father has determined on by virtue of his own authority. ⁸However, power shall be yours at the time when the Holy Spirit will descend upon you; and you shall be my witnesses in Jerusalem, all over Judaea and Samaria, and indeed to the ends of the earth." ⁹After he had spoken these words he was lifted up from the ground as they were looking on, and a cloud took him out of their sight. ¹⁰And while they fixed their gaze on the sky, as he was making his way, two men clad in white garments were all at once by their side, ¹¹addressing these words to them: "Men of Galilee, why do you stand here looking up into the sky? This Jesus who has been separated from you and taken up into heaven will return in the same manner as you have seen him making his way into heaven."

¹²At that they returned to Jerusalem, leaving Mount Olivet, as it is called, a place which lies close to Jerusalem, about a Sabbath day's

---

* Or 'eating in their company'.

211

journey distant. ¹³And when they arrived there, they went to the room upstairs where they were staying. And this is who they were: Peter, as well as John and James, Andrew, Philip and Thomas, Bartholomew as well as Matthew, James son of Alphaeus, Simon the Zealot, and Judas son of James. ¹⁴All these gave themselves up with one accord to constant prayer; and with them were certain women, Mary, Jesus' mother, among them, and so were the brothers of Jesus.

¹⁵It was at that time that Peter rose up one day in front of the assembled brotherhood. (The number of persons who had come together was about one hundred and twenty, all told.) And this is what he said to them: ¹⁶"There is, my brothers, a prophecy in scripture which had to find its fulfilment, the one which the Holy Spirit uttered by the lips of David, and it concerns the fate of Judas, the man who offered himself as a guide to the men who arrested Jesus. ¹⁷For this is how the matter stands. He was counted as one of our number and was allotted a share in this ministry of ours. ¹⁸It was he who acquired a certain piece of land, with the purchase price provided by what he had received as recompense for his infamous deed. Yet what happened was that he fell over headlong and burst open in the middle, all his bowels gushing forth. ¹⁹This became known to all the inhabitants of Jerusalem, with the result that the piece of land came to be called 'Akeldama', as they put it in their own language, that is to say, 'Field of Blood'. ²⁰The passage I have in mind is to be found in the Book of Psalms, in the place where these words stand written: ᵃ'**Let his homestead become desolate, and may there be no one dwelling in it.**' And again, ᵇ'**As for the office which he held, let another man take his place.**' ²¹Now this is what we have to do. There are the men who were in our company all the time that the Lord Jesus went in and out amongst us, ²²beginning from the time when John was administering baptism until the day when Jesus was taken upwards and separated from us. What has to be done, I say, is this: one of these men is, along with us, to become witness of the resurrection." ²³Upon this, two men were put forward: Joseph, who went by the name of Barsabbas and who was also called Justus; and Matthias. ²⁴Then they offered prayer and spoke these words: "O Lord, to whom all hearts are known, reveal to us which of these you have chosen, ²⁵that he might receive the office which belongs to this ministry and apostolate, the one which Judas abandoned, making his way to the place marked out for him." ²⁶So they gave them lots, and the lot fell on Matthias, who then took rank with the eleven apostles.

ᵃPs 69:25   ᵇPs 109:8

2   When the day of Pentecost had come, they were all together in the same place. ²All of a sudden, there came a sound from the sky which was like the rush of a powerful wind and which filled the whole house where they were sitting. ³Moreover, there appeared to them tongues, like flames of fire, tongues which parted themselves and took their resting place upon each one of them. ⁴Those present were, one and all, filled with the Holy Spirit and began to speak in tongues other than their own, according as the Spirit granted them power of utterance.

⁵Now there were certain Jews in Jerusalem who resided there, devout men drawn from every land under heaven. ⁶And when this sound came, they thronged together and were astounded when each heard these men talking in his own language. ⁷They were perplexed and astonished, and so they said, "Are not all these men Galileans? ⁸How then is it that we hear each of them speaking in our language in which we were reared? ⁹There are among us Parthians, Medes and Elamites, there are those who live in Mesopotamia, in Judaea, in Cappadocia, in Pontus, and in the province of Asia. ¹⁰There are those who come from Phrygia, and from Pamphylia, from Egypt, and from those regions of Libya which lie in the neighbourhood of Cyrene, and there are those who have come as visitors from Rome. Some of us are Jews, some proselytes. ¹¹Some come from Crete and some from Arabia. Yet what we hear them doing is proclaiming the wondrous deeds of God in our own languages." ¹²They were astounded and greatly at a loss, one saying to the other, "What can be the meaning of this?" ¹³But there were others who mocked and said, "They are full to the brim with sweet wine."

¹⁴Peter, however, who was standing there with the Eleven, raised his voice and addressed the following words to them: "Men of Judaea and all of you who live in Jerusalem, this is what I have to make known to you. Pay close attention to my words. ¹⁵These men are not drunk, as you suppose. After all, the time is only nine o'clock in the morning. ¹⁶No, what this signifies has been foretold by the prophet Joel in these words: ¹⁷ᶜ'It will come about,' God says, 'in the last days, that I shall take of my Spirit and pour it out upon everyone. Your sons and your daughters shall prophesy, your young men shall see visions, and the men among you that are old shall dream dreams. ¹⁸Indeed, in those days I shall pour out a portion of my spirit even upon those belonging to me who are slaves, both men and women, and they shall prophesy. ¹⁹And I shall show forth portents in the sky above and signs on the earth below: blood and fire and smoky

ᶜJl 2:28-32

213

vapour. [20]The sun will be turned into darkness and the moon into blood before the day of the Lord comes, that great and glorious day. [21]And then it shall happen that everyone invoking the name of the Lord will find salvation'.

[22]"Men of Israel, listen to these words of mine. Jesus of Nazareth, a man shown forth to you by God as what he truly was, through the wondrous deeds, the portents, and the signs which God wrought through him in your midst, as you well know; [23]this Jesus, when he was delivered up to you—and that happened through God's fixed design and his foreknowledge—you have nailed to the cross by the hands of men outside the law, and have put him to death. [24]But God raised him up again, bringing the pangs of death to an end, because it was impossible that death should gain the mastery over him. [25]Indeed, it was he whom David had in mind when he spoke thus: [d]'I have had the Lord at all times before my eyes. For he is standing at my right hand, so that I should not be shaken in my purpose. [26]This is why my heart has rejoiced and my tongue has been full of exultation. Yes, and my body, too, will have its hope in which it can rest. [27]For you will not leave my soul in the world below, nor will you allow him who has been consecrated to you to suffer decay. [28]You have shown forth to me the ways which lead to life. You will, by your presence, fill me with gladness'.

[29]"My brothers, what I have every right to say to you quite openly about the patriarch David is this: that he died, that he was buried, and that his grave is in our midst to this very day. [30]Now since he was a prophet, and since he knew that God [e]had promised him on oath that one of his descendants would sit on his throne, [31]he spoke, looking into the future, of the resurrection of God's anointed, saying this about him, that [f]he was not to be left in the world below, and that his body was not to suffer corruption. [32]Jesus is the man of whom we are speaking, and it was he who was raised to life, an event to which we can bear witness. [33]Now having been exalted by God's right hand and having received from the Father that which had been promised, the Holy Spirit, you are witnessing by both eye and ear the outpouring of that Holy Spirit. [34]For it was not David who went up to heaven, his own words being the following: [g]'The Lord said to him who is my Lord, "Take your seat at my right hand [35]until I make your enemies a footstool for your feet"'. [36]Let it be known, then, to the whole house of Israel for a certainty, that the man whom God has made Lord and his anointed is the very Jesus whom you have crucified."

[37]When they heard these words, they were stabbed to the heart,

[d]Ps 16:8-11   [e]Ps 132:11   [f]Ps 16:10   [g]Ps 110:1

and what they asked Peter and the other apostles was this: "What are we to do, dear friends?" [38]Peter replied, "Repent what you have done; and let each one of you be baptized in the name of Jesus Christ, so that your sins may be forgiven you. And then you will receive the Holy Spirit as a gift bestowed upon you. [39]For the promise which has been given is meant for you and your children, and indeed for all those, however [h]**far away, whom the Lord** our God **shall call to himself**."

[40]There were many more words which he spoke by way of bearing testimony in support of his case, and he exhorted them thus: "Rescue yourselves from the doom awaiting this crooked generation." [41]As for his listeners, those who accepted what he said were baptized, some three thousand additional persons being won over on that day.

[42]These devoted themselves continually to the teaching of the apostles, to the shared life, to the breaking of the bread, and to offering prayer. [43]A feeling of awe was upon them all, and many wondrous deeds and many miracles were performed by the apostles. [44]All those whose faith had drawn them together shared everything in common. [45]They sold their property and their possessions, and distributed the proceeds among them all, according to each one's need. [46]They persevered with one accord in visiting the temple day by day, and as they broke bread, in this house or that, they took their share of food, being filled with exultation and in simplicity of heart. [47]As they offered praise to God, they found favour with all the people, while the Lord day by day increased the number of those to be saved, and to become one with the fellowship.

3   One day Peter and John went up to the temple at three o'clock in the afternoon, the hour of prayer. [2]Now there was a certain man who, being lame from birth, had to be carried by others. This man was put down at the gate of the temple called 'Beautiful Gate', so that he might beg for alms from people as they went in. [3]When he saw Peter and John on the point of entering the temple, he asked them for alms. [4]But Peter fixed his gaze on him—and so did John—and said, "Look us in the face," [5]the man being all attention because he was expecting to receive something from them. [6]Peter, however, spoke to him thus: "Silver and gold I do not possess. But what I do possess I am giving to you. In the name of Jesus Christ of Nazareth, walk on your feet." [7]And taking him by his right hand, he lifted him up. All at once strength came to the man's feet and ankles. [8]He leapt up, stood upright, and proceeded to walk. So he went with them into the temple, walking and leaping and giving praise to God. [9]All the people saw

[h]Is 57:19; Jl 2:32

him walk and give praise to God. [10]Moreover, they recognized him as the man whose wont it was to sit at the 'Beautiful Gate' of the temple begging for alms; and they were filled with wonder and bewilderment at what had happened to him. [11]Now, as he would not let go of Peter and John, the whole crowd, in a state of utter amazement, ran towards them in what is called 'Solomon's Porch'. [12]And Peter, on seeing them, addressed these words to the people: "Men of Israel, why are you so surprised at this? Or why do you fix your gaze on us, as though it were our own power and piety which had enabled this man to walk? [13][i]**The God of Abraham, of Isaac, and of Jacob, the God of our forefathers, has bestowed glory upon** Jesus **his servant,** whom you have handed over, disowning him before Pilate, when his judgment was that he was to be released. [14]Him, who is holy, who is righteous, you have disowned, demanding that a man who was a murderer should be pardoned as a favour to you. [15]As against this, you have put to death him who leads men to life, him whom God has raised up from the dead, a circumstance of which we are witnesses. [16]It is because of his having faith in Jesus' name that the man whom you are seeing here, and whom you know, has been given strength, by virtue of that name; his faith, rooted in Jesus' name as it is, restoring him to full strength in the sight of you all. [17]But now, friends, I know that what you and your leaders have done has been done in ignorance. [18]In point of fact, what has occurred is that God has brought to fulfilment in this way what he had foretold by the mouth of all the prophets: that it was to be the lot of his Anointed One to suffer. [19]Repent, then, and turn back to God, that your sins may be wiped out, that the times of giving you rest may come to you through the Lord's activity, [20]and that he may send forth to you him whom he has appointed beforehand, Jesus Christ, [21]who must have his dwelling place in heaven until the times come for the restoration of all things, the times of which God has for ages past spoken by the mouth of his holy prophets. [22]And indeed, these are the words which Moses has spoken:[j]**'The Lord will raise up for you a prophet like myself, taken from among your own brothers. Attend to him, and hold fast to everything he tells** you. [23][k]**Moreover, this is how things shall be, that, whoever refuses to listen to the voice of that prophet shall be rooted out and severed from his people.'** [24]Furthermore, all the prophets who have ever spoken, from Samuel onwards, have forecast these days. [25]As for yourselves, you are the inheritors of the prophets and of the covenant which God has concluded with your forefathers, speaking these words to Abraham: [l]**'It is in your descendants that all the nations upon earth shall find blessing.'** [26]And indeed, it was for

[i]Ex 3:6.15; Is 52:13; 53:11   [j]Dt 18:15.18f   [k]Lv 23:29   [l]Gn 22:18; 26:4

your sake in the first place that God raised up his servant, and that he sent him forth, bestowing his blessing upon you, so that through him you would, one and all, be made to turn away from your wicked ways."

4 While these words were being addressed to the people, there suddenly came upon them a number of priests, the officer in charge of the temple, as well as certain Sadducees [2]who were vexed because the apostles were giving instruction to the people, and because—taking Jesus as the basis of their argument—they were proclaiming the resurrection of the dead. [3]They seized the apostles and placed them in custody. Their purpose was to deal with them on the following day, for evening had already come. [4]However, many among those who had been listening to what had been said came to embrace the faith, and the number of these men amounted to about five thousand.

[5]On the next day there was called together in Jerusalem a gathering which included the leaders of the people, the elders, and the experts in the law; [6]and there were likewise present Annas the High Priest, Caiaphas, Jonathan, Alexander, and in fact all those who were of high-priestly descent. [7]They made the apostles stand before them and put to them this question: "By what power, and in whose name, have you done this thing?" [8]At that, Peter, filled with the Holy Spirit, addressed them in these words: "Leaders of the people and you elders, [9]if the matter about which we are being scrutinized concerns an act of mercy done for the sake of a sick man, and we are being asked by what means his health has been restored to him, [10]be it known to you all and to the whole people of Israel that this has been accomplished by virtue of the name of Jesus Christ of Nazareth, the man whom you have nailed to a cross but whom God raised up again from the dead. It is on his account that this man is standing here before you fit and well. [11]It is Jesus who is [m]**the stone thrown away with contempt** by you, **the builders, and which has yet become the very cornerstone.** [12]And indeed, salvation is to be found in no one else. Neither is there any other name under heaven vouchsafed to men which has the power of obtaining salvation for us."

[13]When the others observed how boldly Peter and John spoke, while aware at the same time that they were without learning and quite untrained, they were greatly surprised. On the other hand, they recognized them as former companions of Jesus. [14]As for the man who had been healed, they were unable, as they saw him standing by their side, to say anything by way of contradiction. [15]However, they con-

[m]Ps 118:22

ferred with one another, having ordered the apostles to leave the council chamber. [16]"What are we to do with these men?" they asked. "For that a remarkable miracle has been performed by their means is manifest to all the inhabitants of Jerusalem; and there is no way of denying it. [17]Still, to prevent the news from spreading yet further, let us threaten them and warn them never again to speak to anybody in this man's name." [18]So they called them back and gave them strict orders neither to speak nor to teach in the name of Jesus. [19]And this is what Peter and John said in reply to them: "Whether it is right in God's eyes that we should listen to you rather than to God, you can judge for yourselves. [20]Yet, as far as we are concerned, it is impossible that we should not speak of what we have seen and heard." [21]The others uttered further threats. Yet they let them go since they were unable, because of the people who were all glorifying God on account of what had happened, to devise any other means of punishing them, [22]seeing that the man on whom the miracle of healing had been performed was over forty years old.

[23]The apostles, having been dismissed by the court, went home to their friends and reported what the chief priests and the elders had said to them. [24]And on hearing this, they raised their voices to God in unison: "Ruler of all," they exclaimed, "[n]**Maker of heaven and earth, and of the sea, and of everything they contain!** [25]These are the words you have spoken through your Holy Spirit by the mouth of your servant David, our forefather. [o]**Why is it that the Gentiles have given vent to their rage, that the peoples have come to hatch plots which are futile? [26]The kings of the earth have taken up their stand, and those who are leaders have assembled themselves in one place, to turn against the Lord and against him whom he has anointed.'** [27]And indeed, [p]**they have assembled themselves** in this very city to defy Jesus your holy servant, **whom you have anointed.** There were Herod and Pontius Pilate, and with them the [q]**Gentiles** and Israel's **peoples,** [28]ready to do the very things which you, by virtue of your strength and your wise counsel, had preordained should happen. [29]And now, Lord, look upon their threats, and grant that your servants may proclaim your message with complete fearlessness, [30]empowered to do so by your stretching out your hand for the healing of men and by your causing signs and wonders to be shown forth through invocation of the name of your holy servant Jesus." [31]While they were thus offering prayer, the place where they were assembled was shaken. They were all filled with the Holy Spirit, proclaiming God's message with no fear in their hearts.

[32]The whole body of those who had come to be believers were

[n]Ex 20:11; Ps 146:6; Neh 9:6   [o]Ps 2:1-2   [p]Is 61:1   [q]Ps 2:1f

united in heart and soul. There was not one among them who claimed anything he possessed as his own property. On the contrary, everything was held in common. 33 The apostles of the Lord Jesus bore their witness to the resurrection with great power, and a rich store of grace was resting upon them all. 34 There was not one among them who suffered want. For those who owned pieces of land or a house, sold what they had, brought along what the sale had fetched, 35 and laid it at the feet of the apostles. Then there was a distribution for each according to what his need might be. 36 To take an example, there was a certain Levite of Cypriot descent who went by the name of Joseph but to whom the apostles gave another name, Barnabas, which, correctly translated, means 'Man of Encouragement'. 37 He was the owner of a field which he then sold, taking the money along and laying it at the feet of the apostles.

5 Yet there was another man by the name of Ananias, with his wife Sapphira, who sold a piece of land but, 2 with the full knowledge of his wife, laid some of the purchase money aside for himself. He took a portion of the money with him and laid it at the feet of the apostles. 3 But Peter addressed him in these words: "How is it, Ananias, that Satan has taken possession of your mind so that you came to tell the Holy Spirit a falsehood and to lay aside for yourself some of the money which you had received for the piece of land? 4 Was it not yours so long as it was left untouched, and was it not at your disposal even after it had been sold? How could you have conceived in your mind such a deed as this? It is not men to whom you have told your lie: it is God." 5 When Ananias heard these words, he fell down on the ground, breathing his last; and a feeling of great awe came upon those who heard what had happened. 6 The younger men rose up, wrapped up the body, carried it away, and buried it.

7 About three hours passed, and then the wife, not knowing what had happened, made her entry. 8 "Tell me," said Peter, challenging her, "was such and such a price paid by you for the piece of land?" "Yes," she said, "that was the price." 9 And Peter spoke to her thus: "How is it that you came to agree between yourselves to put the Spirit of the Lord to the test? Listen! The footsteps of the men who have buried your husband are at the door, and these men shall carry you away." 10 At that she fell down at Peter's feet, in an instant, and breathed her last. When the young men entered they found her dead, and, carrying her away, they buried her by the side of her husband. 11 And a feeling of great awe came upon the whole church and upon all who heard the story.

12 There was many a sign and many a wonderful thing shown forth

among the people at the hands of the apostles. The portico of Solomon was the place where they all met, by common consent, [13] while no one outside their number had the courage to join them. Still, the people gave them high praise [14] and, what is more, a large number of men and women were added to them as believers in the Lord; [15] so much so that the people carried their sick out into the street, putting them on beds or pallets, in the hope that, when Peter passed, at least his shadow might fall upon one person or another. [16] Moreover, crowds of people from the towns round Jerusalem gathered together, carrying their sick and those harassed by tarnished spirits; and all of them were healed.

[17] This provoked the High Priest into action, him and all those associated with him, the men commonly referred to as the Sadducean party. They were filled with envy, [18] and so it was that they seized the apostles and had them put in the common jail. [19] However, during the night one of the Lord's angels opened the prison doors, led them out, and said to them, [20] "Go forth, take your stand in the temple, and proclaim to the people everything which concerns this new way of life." [21] On hearing this, they went into the temple at daybreak and began to teach.

When the High Priest and his associates made their appearance, they summoned the Sanhedrin, that is to say, the full complement of elders among the Jewish people, and then sent men to the prison to have the prisoners brought out. [22] However, when the officers of the law arrived in the place they did not find the apostles, and when they returned they reported the matter in these words: [23] "We found the prison locked up with the greatest care, and there were guards standing at the gates. Yet when we opened the gates and went in, we found no one." [24] When the officer in charge of the temple and the chief priests heard these words, they were wholly at a loss as to what this could possibly mean. [25] However, another man arrived with this message for them: "As for the men whom you have put in prison, let this be known to you, that they have taken up their stand in the temple and are giving instruction to the people." [26] At that the officer in charge went off with his men and fetched them, using no force because of their fear of the people, there being a risk that they might be stoned. [27] After they had brought the apostles in, they made them stand on their feet to face the Council, and the High Priest began his questioning with these words: [28] "We have given you the strictest orders to desist from teaching in that man's name, and here you are filling Jerusalem with your doctrine, determined to lay that man's death at our door." [29] But Peter made this reply in his own name and that of the apostles: "Our duty requires that we should render obedience to God rather than to men. [30] It was the God of our forefathers who raised up Jesus, the man whom you have put to death ʳby **hanging him on a gibbet.** ³¹He it is whom God has exalted by his own right hand to be Leader and Saviour, so that he might bestow upon Israel the gift of repentance and the remission of their sins. ³²As for ourselves, we bear witness to these things, and so does the Holy Spirit whom God has granted to all who render obedience to him."

³³On hearing these words they were filled with fury, and there arose in them the desire to put them to death. ³⁴At this, a certain member of the Council rose to his feet, a man by the name of Gamaliel, who belonged to the Pharisaic party and who was a teacher of the law, being held in high honour by all the people. He proposed that the men be taken outside for a while, ³⁵and then addressed the assembly in the following words: "Men of Israel, be circumspect as to what is to be done about these men. ³⁶There was Theudas who made his appearance some time ago, claiming that he was someone to be reckoned with; and a number of men, about four hundred in all, attached themselves to his cause. He was put to death, and all his followers were dispersed and vanished into nothing. ³⁷After him Judas the Galilean made his appearance, at the time of the census, and drew a crowd after him to follow him as their leader. Yet he, too, perished, and all those accepting his authority were scattered. ³⁸And what I have to say to you now is this: Keep your hands off these men and let them go. For if their scheme and the way they are carrying it out are of human devising, a collapse will follow. ³⁹But if God is the source of it all, you will never succeed in bringing destruction upon them; and besides, you will be running the risk of finding yourselves making war against God." ⁴⁰They took his advice and sent for the apostles. And after having them flogged, they ordered them that on no account were they to speak in defence of Jesus' cause. Then they let them go. ⁴¹The apostles, for their part, left the presence of the Council full of joy that they had been found worthy to suffer indignity on behalf of the cause which bears Jesus' name. ⁴²And day by day they never ceased teaching, both in the temple and in private houses, proclaiming the good news that Jesus was the Anointed One of God.

6 At that time, as the number of disciples were increasing, a complaint was made by those who spoke Greek against those who were Hebrew-speaking,* the complaint being that the widows in their group

ʳDt 21:22

* [Although Aramaic was the common language of the Jews in Palestine at that time, serious argument would often be carried out in Hebrew by learned native Judaeans.]

were being overlooked in the daily distribution. ²So the Twelve called together the full number of the disciples and addressed them in these words: "It is far from desirable that we should forsake the preaching of God's message and devote our attention to ministrations at table. ³What you have to do, therefore, friends, is this: Look out from among your number for seven men of good reputation, men who are filled with the Holy Spirit and with wisdom; and we shall appoint them to perform this office. ⁴As for ourselves, we shall devote ourselves wholly to prayer and to the ministry of the Word." ⁵What he said found favour with all the assembled, and the election fell upon the following: Stephen, a man full of faith and of the Holy Spirit, Philip, Prochorus, Nicanor, Timon, Parmenas, and lastly, Nicolaus, a proselyte who came from Antioch. ⁶They presented these men to the apostles, who, having offered prayer, laid their hands upon them in blessing.

⁷And so God's message spread, the number of disciples in Jerusalem increasing greatly. And in particular, there was a large number of priests who embraced the faith.

⁸As for Stephen, who was full of grace and of power, he began to show forth many a miracle and many a sign among the people. ⁹At that, certain men came forward who belonged to the synagogue which bore the name 'Synagogue of Freedmen', comprising Cyrenaeans and Alexandrians, and people from Cilicia and Asia. What they meant to do was to engage in argument. ¹⁰However, they were unable to hold their own against Stephen's wisdom and the spirit which gave him utterance. ¹¹And so they proceeded to suborn a number of men, prompting them to say things such as these: "We have heard him utter words of defamation against Moses and against God." ¹²Having thus stirred up the feelings of the people, the elders, and the experts in the law, they set upon him, dragged him away, and brought him before the Council. ¹³Moreover, they put forward lying witnesses who declared, "This man never ceases uttering insults against the holy place and against the law. ¹⁴Indeed, we have heard him say that Jesus, that man from Nazareth, would destroy this holy place and alter the customs handed down to us by Moses." ¹⁵All who were seated there in the council chamber fixed their gaze on Stephen, and they saw that his face had the appearance of an angel.

7¹The High Priest asked Stephen whether these things were true. ²ᵃAnd Stephen answered as follows:

7   ²ᵇ"You who are my brothers, who are the nation's fathers, attend to me. ˢ**God, the all-glorious one,** appeared to Abraham when he was

ˢPs 29:3

222

still in Mesopotamia, before he settled at Haran, [3]and spoke to him thus: [t]'Move away from the country where you live and from your kinsfolk, and go forth to a country to which I shall show you the way'. [4]So Abraham went out of the country of the Chaldeans and settled at Haran. From there, after the death of his father, God removed him to this country where you now live. [5]However, nothing in the country was [u]given him as his own property, not even a foot of ground, but God made him the promise that [v]he and his descendants would receive it from him as their possession. And he made that promise notwithstanding the fact that Abraham at that time had no child. [6]What God actually told him was that [w]his descendants would live in a foreign country as aliens, and that people would make slaves of them and treat them cruelly for four hundred years. [7]'But I shall pass judgment upon the nation making them slaves,' said God, [x]'and after that they shall go forth from there, and worship me in this place'. [8]Then he made a [y]covenant with them, a covenant ordaining circumcision. And so it was that Abraham, having become Isaac's father, had him [z]circumcised on the eighth day after he was born. Isaac did the same for Jacob, and Jacob for the twelve patriarchs.

[9]"The patriarchs [a]sold Joseph into slavery in Egypt, being moved by jealousy of him. But God was on his side [10]and delivered him from all his miseries, by [b]making him win favour and a name for wisdom in the eyes of Pharaoh, king of Egypt, who set him up to be ruler of Egypt and of the entire royal household. [11c]However, a famine came upon all Egypt and upon Canaan, and great misery prevailed when our forefathers could find nothing to eat. [12d]So Jacob, on hearing that grain was to be had in Egypt, sent our forefathers out on their first visit. [13]It was during their second visit that [e]Joseph made himself known to his brothers, and so it happened that Pharaoh came to be informed about Joseph's kindred. [14]Joseph then sent out messengers to call to himself his father Jacob and his whole family, [f]seventy-five persons all told; [15]and Jacob [g]went down into Egypt. [h]There he ended his days, and so did our forefathers. [16i]Their bodies were later removed to Shechem, and there they were buried in the tomb which Abraham bought at Shechem from the sons of Emmor for a sum of money paid in silver. [17]As the time drew near for the fulfilment of the promise which God had made to Abraham, the people [j]increased and grew in number in Egypt [18]until a [k]new king, who knew nothing of Joseph, ascended the throne of Egypt. [19]He [l]used

---

[t]Gn 12:1; 48:4   [u]Dt 2:5   [v]Gn 12:7; 13:15; 17:8; 48:4   [w]Gn 15:13f   [x]Ex 3:12   [y]Gn 17:10   [z]Gn 21:4   [a]Gn 37:11.28; 45:4; 39:1.2.21   [b]Gn 41:38-45; Ps 105:21   [c]Gn 41:54; 42:2.5   [d]Gn 42:2   [e]Gn 45:1.3   [f]Gn 46:27; Ex 1:5; Dt 10:22   [g]Gn 46:6   [h]Gn 49:33   [i]Gn 23:16f; 33:19; 50:13; Jos 24:32   [j]Ex 1:7   [k]Ex 1:8   [l]Ex 1:10f

craft against our people and dealt cruelly with our forefathers, making them expose their children, so that they should not be *m*preserved alive. 20 It was at this time that Moses was born, a *n*lovely child and pleasing in the sight of God. During the first three months he was reared in his father's house; 21 and then, when he had been exposed, *o*Pharaoh's daughter declared him to be hers and brought him up as her own son. 22 And so it came about that Moses received instruction in every branch of Egyptian learning, becoming a man of great power in both word and deed.

23 "When he attained the age of forty, it came to his mind that he was to pay a visit to the men who were *p*his kindred, the descendants of Israel. 24 And so it happened that when one day he saw one of them being ill-treated, he came to the rescue, and *q*by slaying the Egyptian avenged the one who had suffered cruel treatment. 25 He acted thus in the conviction that his kinsfolk would understand that he was God's instrument for bringing them deliverance. In fact, however, they failed to grasp this.

26 *r*"On the following day he came in sight of two of them who were engaged in a fight, and seeking to reconcile them and talk them into making peace, he said, 'Friends, you are brothers. Why do you inflict injury on each other?' 27 At that the man who had been first to *s*make his fellow countryman suffer wrong thrust him aside with the following words, *t*'Who has set you over us as our ruler and judge? 28 Do you propose to kill me as you killed the Egyptian yesterday?' 29 On hearing this, Moses fled the country, and settled as a stranger in the land of Midian, where he became the father of two sons.

30 "After forty years had gone by, *u*he had a vision. When he was in the desert close to Mount Sinai, there appeared to him a bush which was ablaze, and in the midst of the flames there stood an angel. 31 Moses was amazed at the spectacle, but when he sought to draw near for a closer look, the voice of the Lord was heard uttering these words: 32 *v*'I am the God of your forefathers, the God of Abraham, of Isaac, and of Jacob'. A trembling came upon Moses when he heard this, and he did not dare to look any more. 33 *w*And the Lord spoke to him thus: 'Take your shoes off your feet, for the ground upon which you are standing is holy ground. 34 In truth, I have seen the oppression suffered by my people in Egypt, and I have heard their sighing. And so it is that I have come down to bring them deliverance. Well then, to my side; I am sending you forth into Egypt'.

35 "The man to whom this was said was the Moses whom they had

*m*Ex 1:22   *n*Ex 2:2   *o*Ex 2:5.10   *p*Ex 2:11   *q*Ex 2:12   *r*[Ex 2:13]   *s*Ex 2:13   *t*Ex 2:14f   *u*Ex 3:1-2   *v*Ex 3:6   *w*Ex 3:5.7.8.10; 2:24

repudiated with the words, *x*'**Who has set you over us as our ruler and judge?'**. It was he whom God sent forth to be their ruler and deliverer, with the aid of the angel who had appeared to him in the bush. [36]It was he who led the people out, performing many a *y***wondrous deed** and many a **sign** in Egypt, as well as at the Red Sea and in the desert, over a period of *z***forty years.** [37]It was this same Moses who said to the Israelites, *a*'**God will raise up a prophet for you, a man from among your number, just as I was raised'.** [38]It was he who, at the time when the congregation was in the desert, encountered the angel who had spoken to him on Mount Sinai, the angel who also held converse with our forefathers. It was Moses who received God's life-giving utterance to be handed on to us.

[39]"However, our forefathers refused to render obedience to him. On the contrary, thrusting him aside *b***they turned** their thoughts **towards Egypt,** [40]**while saying to Aaron, 'Make us gods to go ahead of us on our march. As for that Moses who has led us out of Egypt, we do not know what has become of him'.** [41]It was at that time that *c***they made the calf and offered sacrifice** to the idol, being gladdened by the things which their own hands had fashioned. [42]But God turned away from them and gave them over to worshipping *d***the host of heaven,** just as it stands written somewhere in the prophetic books: *e*'**Did you present me with offerings and sacrifices those forty years in the desert, you house of Israel?** [43]**No; you carried aloft the shrine of Moloch and the star of your god Rephan, the images which you yourselves had made** as objects for your adoration. **And I will banish you afar, to a place** beyond Babylon.'

[44]"When our forefathers were in the desert, they had with them the *f***tent of witness,** fashioned according to the direction given by him who had *g***told Moses to make it after the pattern which he had seen.** [45]After that, our forefathers, having had the tent handed over to them, took it with them when they were with Joshua as they were entering the land at the time of the *h***dispossession** of the Gentiles, whom God was driving out from before our forefathers. And so it continued until the time of David, who, [46]finding favour with God, asked that he might be given leave to *i***search out a dwelling place for the God of Jacob.** [47]In the end, however, it was *j***Solomon who built him the house.**

[48]"Yet the fact remains that the Most High does not dwell in any building made by human hands. As the prophet says, [49]*k*'**Heaven is my throne, and the earth is my footstool. What kind of house do you**

*x*Ex 2:14   *y*Ex 7:3   *z*Nm 14:33   *a*Dt 18:15.18   *b*Ex 32:1.23   *c*Ex 32:4.6   *d*Jr 7:18 LXX; 19:13   *e*Am 5:25-27   *f*Ex 27:21   *g*Ex 25:40; [Jos 3:14; 18:1]   *h*Gn 17:8; 48:4; Dt 32:49   *i*2 Sm 7:2; Ps 132:5   *j*1 K 6:1   *k*Is 66:1f

mean to build for me, says the Lord, **or what can be the place in which I am to find my rest?** [50] **Was it** not **my own hand which made all this?'**

[51] [l]**"You stiffnecked men, with no circumcision of either heart or ear: the onslaughts** which you make **upon** the **holy spirit** are never-ending. You are the very same as your forefathers were. [52] Is there one among the prophets whom your forefathers did not persecute? Moreover, they put to death those who foretold the coming of the one who is truly righteous; and now you have become his betrayers and his murderers. [53] You are the men who received the law, as it was delivered at the hand of God's angels. And you have not kept it."

[54] When they heard these words, they were cut to the heart and gnashed their teeth at him. [55] But he, filled with the Holy Spirit, fixed his gaze on heaven; and what he saw was God's glory, and Jesus standing at God's right hand. [56] And he spoke thus: "Look, I see heaven opening, and the Son of Man standing at the right hand of God." [57] At that they gave a mighty cry, stopped their ears, and, with one accord, rushed towards him. [58] And thrusting him out of the city, they made ready to stone him. As for the witnesses, they cast off their outer clothing and laid it at the feet of a young man called Saul.

[59] So they stoned Stephen, and as they did so, he called out in prayer, "Lord Jesus, receive my spirit into your hands." [60] Then he fell upon his knees and made this outcry in a powerful voice: "Lord, do not hold them guilty of this sin." And having said this, he went to his rest. [8:1a] As for Saul, he gave his hearty consent to his murder.

8 [1b] It was at this time that a fierce persecution of the church in Jerusalem set in, all its members, with the sole exception of the apostles, being scattered all over the country districts of Judaea and Samaria. [2] Stephen was buried by certain God-fearing men, who made great lamentation over him. [3] As for Saul, his aim was to bring ruin upon the church, and so he went from house to house, dragging away both men and women and casting them into prison.

[4] Those who had been scattered moved from place to place proclaiming God's message. [5] Philip, on reaching the principal city of Samaria, proclaimed Christ to the people there, [6] each member of the crowd paying the closest attention to what Philip was saying to them, both because of what they heard and because of their witnessing the miracles which he performed. [7] Many who were possessed of tarnished spirits were in that place, and these spirits, crying out in a loud

[l]Ex 32:9; 33:3; Lv 26:41; Jr 9:26; Is 63:10

voice, came out of them. Besides, large numbers of people in the city who were paralyzed or crippled in some way were finding themselves healed of their infirmity. [8]And so it came about that the city was full of rejoicing.

[9]Now in that city there lived a certain man called Simon, a man who had been there for some time practising magic and being a source of astonishment to the people of Samaria, claiming that he was someone great. [10]Everyone, high and low, paid attention to him and declared, "This man is what is called the Great Power of God." [11]And if they did thus attend to him, this was because for some considerable time he had astonished them by his magical arts. [12]However, when they began to believe Philip, as he was delivering to them the message concerning the kingdom of God and telling them about the significance of the name of Jesus Christ, they submitted themselves to baptism, both men and women. [13]In the end, even Simon himself became a believer and, after his baptism, attached himself with great persistence to Philip, because of his amazement at the great signs and wonders which he saw happening.

[14]When the apostles in Jerusalem heard that God's message had been given a welcome in Samaria, they sent out Peter and John to visit the people there. [15]When they arrived, they prayed on behalf of the people, asking that they might receive the Holy Spirit. [16]For as yet the Spirit had not descended upon any of them. All that had so far occurred was that they had been baptized in the name of the Lord Jesus. [17]And this being so, the apostles laid their hands upon them in blessing. And they received the Holy Spirit.

[18]Now when Simon became aware that the Holy Spirit was granted through the imposition of the apostles' hands, he brought along a certain sum of money to offer to the apostles, [19]saying, "Let me, too, have this power, so that anyone upon whom I lay my hands may receive the Holy Spirit." [20]Peter replied to him thus: "Take your silver and yourself to perdition, because you have come to suppose that God's bounty can be bought for money. [21]You have neither part nor share in this matter. And indeed, in the eyes of God you have an altogether [m]**crooked heart.** [22]Well then, repent of this wickedness of yours and beseech the Lord that, if possible, the intent of your heart may be forgiven you. [23]I can see plainly that a [n]**bitter poison** has taken hold of you, and **unrighteousness holds you in its grip.**" Thereupon, Simon made this response: [24]"Pray to the Lord on my behalf, so that none of the things of which you have spoken may befall me."

[25]As for the apostles, they returned to Jerusalem, having borne

[m]Ps 78:37   [n]Dt 29:18 LXX; Jr 4:18; Is 58:6

their witness and made proclamation of God's message, and carried the Good News into many a Samaritan village.

²⁶Meanwhile one of God's angels addressed Philip in these words: "Rise up and make your way towards the south until you reach the road which leads from Jerusalem to Gaza—it is the little frequented road which I have in mind." ²⁷So he rose up, went on his way, and when he reached his destination, he caught sight of an Ethiopian. This man, who was a eunuch, was a high official at the court of the Kandake, that is, the Queen of Ethiopia. In fact, he was in charge of all her wealth, and he had gone to Jerusalem to worship there. ²⁸He was now on his way home, and, seated in his chariot, was engaged in reading the prophet Isaiah. ²⁹As this was happening, the Spirit addressed the following words to Philip: "Go up there, and keep close to the chariot." ³⁰Philip ran up towards it, and what he heard was that the man was reading the prophet Isaiah to himself. So he asked him, "Do you understand what you are reading?" ³¹"How can I," was the reply, "unless there be someone to show me the way?" And he invited Philip to come up and sit beside him.

³²Now it was the following passage from scripture which he was reading: ⁰**'He was taken off like a sheep to be slaughtered, and like a lamb which remains dumb before those who shear it, he never opened his mouth. ³³Suffering humiliation, he was deprived of every means of obtaining justice. Who will be able to recount the story of his posterity, seeing that his life is being taken away from this earth?'**

³⁴"Now be good enough," said the eunuch to Philip, "to tell me whom the prophet has in mind in speaking like this. Is he speaking of himself or of somebody else?" ³⁵When he heard this, Philip opened his mouth and, taking this scripture passage as his starting point, expounded to him the Good News about Jesus. ³⁶Now as they were travelling along the road, they reached a place where there was water; and the eunuch said, "Look, there is water here. Is there anything to prevent my being baptized?"*³⁸And he gave the order that the chariot was to be stopped. Then they both went down into the water, Philip and the eunuch, and Philip baptized him. ³⁹But when they came up out of the water, Philip was carried off by the Spirit of the Lord; and the eunuch, no longer seeing him, went on his way, being full of joy. ⁴⁰As for Philip, the next thing which happened to him was that he found himself at Azotus, and setting out from there, he proclaimed

---

⁰Is 57:7f LXX

* V. 37 is probably not part of the original text.

the Good News in every city through which he passed, until he finally reached Caesarea.

9 Meanwhile, there was Saul still breathing out murderous threats
against the disciples of the Lord. And so it came about that he approached the High Priest, ²asking him to equip him with letters to be
taken to Damascus, and intended for the synagogues there, the pur-
port of these letters being that, should he find anyone, man or woman,
who professed to be a follower of the New Way, he was to be given
leave to have them shackled and to bring them back with him to
Jerusalem. ³However, as he was on his way, being but a little distance
from Damascus, he found himself all at once surrounded by the flashing of a light that had come down from heaven. ⁴Falling to the ground,
he heard a voice addressing him in these words: "Saul, Saul, why are
you persecuting me?" ⁵"Who are you, Lord?" he asked; and this was
the reply made to him by the voice: "I am Jesus; I am the one whom
you are persecuting. ⁶No matter: rise up and make your way into the
city; there you will be told what you have to do." ⁷Meanwhile the men
who were his travelling companions stood speechless, hearing the
voice as they did but seeing no one. ⁸As for Saul, he rose up from the
ground. However, it was found that, although his eyes were open, he
was unable to see anything. So they took him by the hand, leading
him into Damascus. ⁹Here he remained without sight for three days,
and neither ate nor drank anything.

¹⁰Now there was a certain disciple at Damascus whose name was
Ananias. He had a vision during which he heard the Lord calling out
to him, "Ananias!" "Here I am, Lord," he answered. ¹¹And these were
the words the Lord addressed to him: "Rise up and make your way
towards the street called 'Straight Street', and enquire there in the
house of Judas for a man from Tarsus called Saul. For there he will be
engaged in prayer, ¹²having had a vision of a man called Ananias
coming to him and laying his hands upon him, so that he may regain
his sight." ¹³"Lord," was Ananias's reply, "there are many who have
told me about that man and what great harm he has done in Jerusalem
to those consecrated to your service. ¹⁴And here he is, in reliance upon
authority received from the chief priests, casting into prison all those
who invoke your name." ¹⁵"Be on your way," was the Lord's reply,
"seeing that this man is the very instrument which I have chosen to
carry my name before the Gentiles and their kings and before those
who are descendants of Israel. ¹⁶And indeed, I myself shall let him
know what great sufferings he will have to endure for the sake of the
cause which bears my name." ¹⁷So Ananias set out, and having
entered the house and laid his hands upon Saul, he said to him,

"Brother Saul, I have been sent to you by the Lord Jesus, by him who appeared to you on your way here. And my purpose in coming here has been that you should regain your sight and be filled with the Holy Spirit." 18 Immediately upon this, something which did not look unlike scales fell from Saul's eyes, and he regained his sight. So he rose up, received his baptism, 19 and after he had partaken of some food, his strength returned to him.

After this, Saul remained for some days with the disciples at Damascus, 20 and began, without delay, to proclaim Jesus in the synagogues, declaring, "It is he who is the Son of God." 21 All those who heard of it were amazed, and this is what they said: "Is this not the very same man who, when he was in Jerusalem, sought to make havoc of those invoking that name? And has he not come to this place for the express purpose of having such people put in fetters, and bringing them before the chief priests?" 22 As for Saul, he increased all the more in power on account of this, and he set out to confute the Jews who lived in Damascus by demonstrating that it was this very Jesus who was God's anointed.

23 After a good many days had gone by, the Jews consulted together, with a view to putting him to death; 24 but their plot became known to Saul. Night and day they kept watch at the city gates, looking for an opportunity of doing away with him. 25 However, one night the disciples contrived to haul him over the city wall, lowering him down in a basket.

26 On arriving in Jerusalem, he made the attempt to attach himself to the disciples. But everybody was afraid of him, since they did not really believe that he was a disciple. 27 Because of this, Barnabas one day took him by the hand, brought him to the apostles, and recounted to them how, while he was on his way, he had seen the Lord and had held converse with him; and how, when he was at Damascus, he had spoken out fearlessly in defence of the cause bearing Jesus' name. 28 And so he remained in the disciples' company, going in and out among them at Jerusalem 29 and speaking fearlessly in defence of the Lord's name. He also addressed himself to the Greek-speaking Jews, engaging them in argument. But they, for their part, were seeking to have him put to death. 30 When this came to the disciples' ears, they conducted him down to Caesarea, and then sent him off to Tarsus.

31 Meanwhile, the Church throughout Judaea, Galilee, and Samaria enjoyed a period of peace. It built itself up in the faith, ruled its life by the reverence it had for the Lord, and, finding itself consoled by the Holy Spirit, it greatly increased in the number of its followers.

32 Peter, for his part, was moving about from place to place, going everywhere; and so it came about that, one day, he visited those consecrated to God who had their home at Lydda. 33 There he found a

man, Aeneas by name, who, being paralyzed, had been lying helpless on his bed for eight years. ³⁴And this is what Peter said to him: "Aeneas, Jesus Christ is bringing you health; rise up and make your bed." At that, Aeneas immediately rose to his feet. ³⁵The inhabitants of Lydda and Sharon all saw him, and their hearts turned to the Lord.

³⁶Now there was a woman disciple at Joppa called Tabitha (which correctly translated into Greek means 'Dorcas', that is to say, a gazelle). She filled her days with good works and with acts of mercy. ³⁷It so happened that she fell ill and died at that time. So they washed the body and laid it out in an upstairs room. ³⁸Now Lydda is near Joppa; and when the disciples heard that Peter was in that place, they sent two men out to him with this urgent message: "Do not hesitate to come over to us." ³⁹So Peter rose up and went with them, and when they arrived, they took him to an upstairs room where all the widows who were present clustered round him, shedding tears and showing him the shirts and cloaks which Dorcas had made when she was still among them. ⁴⁰At that, Peter insisted that everybody was to go out of the room, knelt down, and offered prayer. Then, turning towards the body, he exclaimed, "Tabitha, rise up!" ⁴¹He gave her his hand, helping her to her feet. Then he called for the members of the brotherhood and for the widows, and showed her to them safe and sound. ⁴²This became known all over Joppa, and so it happened that many came to believe in the Lord. ⁴³As for Peter, he remained at Joppa for some time, staying with a certain Simon, who was a tanner.

10   There was at Caesarea a man whose name was Cornelius, a centurion who belonged to what is called the Italian cohort. ²He was a devout man who, with his whole household, revered the true God, performed many a compassionate deed on behalf of the Jewish people, and was constantly offering prayer to God. ³Now there came the day when he had a vision—it was about three o'clock in the afternoon—and what he perceived quite clearly in this vision was one of God's angels approaching him and saying, "Cornelius". ⁴Fixing his gaze on him, he asked, being in a state of terror, "What is it, my Lord?" And this is the reply the angel made him: "Your prayers and your deeds of compassion have gone up to heaven to serve as a memorial offering in God's very presence. ⁵Well then, send a number of men to Joppa, that they might fetch for you a certain Simon, who is also called Peter. ⁶He lodges with another Simon, a tanner, who owns a house by the seashore." ⁷When the angel who had been speaking to him had left, Cornelius summoned two of his servants and one God-fearing soldier who was in attendance on him, ⁸and, after explaining everything to them, sent them off to Joppa.

⁹The following day, about midday, while these men were still on their way and were drawing near to the city, Peter went up to the roof of the house where he was staying, to engage in prayer. ¹⁰However, he began to feel extreme hunger, and there arose in him a longing for food. But while the food was being prepared, he fell into a trance. ¹¹What he saw was that the sky was opening up and that some object which looked like a large linen cloth was descending to the ground, and that it was being let down to the earth by its four corners. ¹²It contained every kind of four-footed animal or reptile existing on earth, and the birds of the air were likewise to be found in it. ¹³And then a voice reached his ears, addressing these words to him: "Rise up, Peter; kill and eat." ¹⁴"By no means," was Peter's reply, "for never at any time have I eaten any unclean and impure food." ¹⁵And the voice spoke to him a second time: "Do not declare unclean that which God has cleansed." ¹⁶This happened three times over, and then the object was immediately taken up again into the sky.

¹⁷While Peter was still trying to puzzle out in his mind what the vision he had had could possibly mean, there appeared the men sent by Cornelius, who had been asking the way to Simon's house. They were standing in the gateway, ¹⁸raising their voices to enquire whether a certain Simon, also known by the name of Peter, was lodging there. ¹⁹As for Peter, who was still pondering over the vision, he found himself addressed by the Spirit in these words: "There are three men here looking for you. ²⁰Well then, rise to your feet, go down to them, and accompany them without hesitation; for it is I who have sent them." ²¹So Peter went down to the men and said, "Here I am, the man for whom you are looking. What is the reason for your being here?" ²²And they replied, "We have come from the centurion Cornelius, an upright man who worships the true God and is highly regarded by all the Jewish nation. He has been given an order divinely inspired at the hand of one of God's holy angels, to ask you to his house and to listen to what you have to say." ²³So Peter invited them into the house and received them as his guests. And on the following day he made himself ready and set out with them, accompanied by a number of fellow believers who were members of the congregation at Joppa.

²⁴The day after that, he arrived at Caesarea, where Cornelius was expecting them, having called together his relatives and his intimate friends. ²⁵When the time had come for Peter to enter the city, Cornelius went to meet him, and, falling down at Peter's feet, proceeded to do homage to him. ²⁶Peter, however, raised him up, saying, "Rise up from the ground; for I, like yourself, am nothing more than a man." ²⁷While he was still holding converse with him, he entered the house,

finding that a large number of men had been gathering there. 28 And
he said to them: "You know full well how strictly it is forbidden for a
Jew to associate with Gentiles or to visit them in their houses. God,
however, has made it clear to me that I am not to look on anyone as
profane or unclean. 29 And that is why, when I was being sent for, I
came without raising any objection. So then, I should like to know
what purpose you had in mind when you sent for me."

30 Cornelius replied, "Four days ago I was in my house offering
prayer, at about this time of day, when, all of a sudden, a man clad in
shining garments stood before me, 31 saying, 'Cornelius, the prayer
which you offered and the compassionate deeds which you performed have won remembrance in the sight of God. 32 Well then,
despatch messengers to Joppa to summon a certain Simon, who also
bears the name of Peter. He is lodging in the house of Simon the tanner, near the seashore.' 33 So I sent for you without delay; and it has
been very good of you to come. Moreover, we are all gathered here
now so that we might be told about everything the Lord has commanded you to do."

34 Thereupon Peter opened his mouth, saying, "In truth, there is one
thing I now comprehend, that [p]favouritism is not God's way of dealing with men. 35 On the contrary, he gives a welcome to all, no matter
what nation they belong to, so long as they treat him with reverence
and are in pursuit of uprightness in whatever they do. 36 True enough,
it was to [q]**Israel**'s sons that he **sent forth his message,** and it was to
them that, at the hands of Jesus Christ, the **Good News of peace was
brought.** It is this Jesus Christ who is Lord of all. 37 As for yourselves,
you know well enough of the events which have lately occurred
throughout Judaea, events which took their rise in Galilee, after the
baptism proclaimed by John. 38 You know of Jesus of Nazareth, and
how God [r]**anointed him** with his **Holy Spirit** and bestowed upon him
the power which flows from this; how Jesus went from place to place,
doing kindnesses to men and women, and bringing healing to all
those who had fallen into the power of the devil's tyranny. And he
was able to do all this because he had God by his side. 39 As for ourselves, we can bear witness to everything he did throughout the
Judaean countryside and in Jerusalem. In the end they put him to
death, [s]**hanging him on a gibbet.** 40 However, it is this very man
whom God raised up again on the third day after he had died.
Moreover, it was also granted to him that he should become visible,
41 not to the people at large, but to the eyes of certain witnesses whom
God had chosen beforehand. And we are witnesses, we who ate and
drank in his company. 42 And the commission he gave us was this,

[p][Dt 10:17] [q]Is 52:7; Ps 107:20; Ps 147:18 LXX [r]Is 61:1 [s]Dt 21:22

that we were to proclaim to the people and testify that he was the one chosen by God to be judge over both the living and the dead. 43 It is to him that all the prophets bear witness, declaring that every one who puts trust in him will be granted forgiveness of sins by virtue of his very name."

44 While Peter was still speaking, the Holy Spirit descended upon all who were listening to his message. 45 And all the believers of Jewish descent who had come with Peter were astounded that the gift of the Holy Spirit had been poured out upon the Gentiles as well; 46 for what they heard was that they gave utterance in tongues of ecstasy, extolling the greatness of God. And Peter's reply to their questionings was this: 47 "Is there anyone who would presume to withhold the water of baptism from those people who have received the Holy Spirit in the same way as we have?" 48 So he gave the order that they were to be baptized in Jesus Christ's name. And this having been done, they asked him to stay on with them for a few days.

11 Now the apostles and the rest of the brotherhood in various parts of Judaea got word that the Gentiles, too, had lent a willing ear to God's message. 2 So when Peter went up to Jerusalem, those brothers who held to the tradition of circumcision took issue with him on this point, 3 their words being these: "You have gone into the houses of uncircumcised men and have sat at table with them." 4 At that, Peter began to explain the facts to them point by point. And this is what he said:

5 "I was in the city of Joppa engaged in prayer, and, a trance coming upon me, I had a vision. An object which looked like a large linen cloth was being let down from the sky by its four corners until it reached the place where I was. 6 Upon this object I fixed my gaze, wondering what it might be; and in it I saw four-footed creatures of the earth as well as wild beasts, and there were also reptiles and birds of the air. 7 Moreover, I heard a voice saying to me, 'Rise up, Peter, kill and eat'. 8 'By no means,' I replied, 'for never at any time has any unclean or impure food entered my mouth.' 9 Upon this, the voice from heaven came a second time, saying, 'Do not declare to be unclean that which God has cleansed.' 10 This happened three times over, and then everything was pulled up again into the sky. 11 At that very moment three men who had been sent to me from Caesarea arrived at the house where we were. 12 The Spirit bade me go with them without hesitation. And so I went, and with me were these six fellow believers. On entering the man's house, 13 he told us how he had seen one of God's angels taking up his stand in his house, and saying to him, 'Send out messengers to Joppa, that they might fetch you a certain

Simon, who is also called Peter. [14]He will have a message for you of such a kind that it will bring salvation to you and to all your household.' [15]Hardly had I begun speaking when the Holy Spirit descended upon them, just as it did upon us at the first. [16]And so I came to recall these words of the Lord, 'John's baptism was one with water, but there is a baptism by means of the Holy Spirit which you shall receive.' [17]Well then, if God made them the very same gift as he made us when we came to believe in the Lord Jesus Christ, who was I, and what power did I have, to stand in God's way?"

[18]When they heard this, they kept their peace, extolling God in these words: "This is how it is, then: the Gentiles, too, have received from God the gift of life-giving repentance."

[19]Meanwhile the disciples who had been scattered as a result of the dire oppression which arose over the issue of Stephen made their way as far as Phoenicia, Cyprus, and Antioch. They were proclaiming God's message, but, in so doing, addressed themselves only to Jews. [20]However, there were among them a number of men, natives of Cyprus and Cyrene, who, when they reached Antioch, spoke with Gentiles as well, bringing them the Good News of the Lord Jesus. [21]God's strong arm was on their side, and a large number of persons came to believe, and turned to the Lord.

[22]Rumours of what they were doing reached the ears of the Jerusalem church, and so they despatched Barnabas to Antioch. [23]And when, on arriving there, he became witness of the gracious gift bestowed by God, he was full of joy, urging everybody to hold fast to the Lord with resolute hearts. [24]He acted in this way because, being the good man he was, he was filled with the Holy Spirit and with faith. So it came about that those adhering to the Lord were greatly increased in number.

[25]Barnabas then went off to Tarsus to look for Saul; [26]and when he found him, he brought him to Antioch. As things turned out, they were to live there together for a full year, joining in the worship of the church and giving instruction to large numbers of people. Moreover, it was at Antioch that the disciples first came to be called Christians.

[27]During this period certain prophets came from Jerusalem to Antioch. [28]One of these, Agabus by name, one day rose to his feet and, prompted by the Spirit, foretold that a grievous famine would spread all over the world (a famine which occurred during the reign of Claudius). [29]And so it happened that the disciples resolved to send relief to those of their fellow believers who lived in Judaea, each contributing as much as his means would allow. [30]They carried out what they had decided and had the money sent to the Judaean elders, with Barnabas and Saul in charge of the enterprise.

12 It was at this time that Herod the king resorted to a policy of violence, his aim being to subject certain members of the church to cruel treatment. ²And so he had James the brother of John executed by the sword. ³Moreover, when he discovered that this was pleasing to the Jews, he went on, proceeding to take Peter into custody. This happened at the time of the Feast of Unleavened Bread. ⁴After having had him apprehended, he threw him into prison. There Peter was committed to four squads of soldiers, each of four men, to keep him under military guard, Herod's intention being that, once Passover was out of the way, he would produce him in public.

⁵So Peter was kept under watch in the prison, while the church was offering up constant prayer to God on his behalf. ⁶Now the day came when Herod meant to have him brought before the court; and on the night before that day, Peter was sleeping between two of the soldiers, fettered with two chains. Moreover, there were guards at the gates, watching the prison. ⁷However, all of a sudden one of the Lord's angels appeared and stood over him, while a light shone forth in his place of confinement. Upon this, the angel gave Peter a nudge in the ribs, and, having wakened him, said, "Rise up with greatest speed!" As for Peter's fetters, they fell off his hands, ⁸while the angel addressed these further words to him: "Now gird up your loins and put your sandals on your feet." Peter did so, the angel saying to him, "Now wrap your cloak round you and follow me." ⁹So Peter left the place and followed him. He did not know, however, that the things done by the angel were real happenings. On the contrary, he supposed that what he saw was all part of a vision.

¹⁰Having passed first one man who was doing guard duty, and then another, they reached the iron gate which leads out into the city, this gate opening before them of its own accord. So they came out, and after they had walked the length of one street, the angel suddenly withdrew himself from Peter's presence. ¹¹And Peter, coming to himself, spoke the following words: "Now I do indeed know that the Lord has sent his angel to me and has rescued me from Herod's power and from all the misfortunes which the Jewish people expected would befall me."

¹²Then, when he had fully realized how things stood, he made his way to the house of Mary the mother of John Mark, where a large company had assembled and was engaged in prayer. ¹³When Peter knocked at the door leading to the gateway, a slave girl called Rhoda came to answer the call. ¹⁴And she, when she recognized that the voice was Peter's, was so overcome with joy that, instead of opening the door leading to the gateway, she ran back into the house and announced that Peter was standing outside in the gateway. ¹⁵At that they told her

that she had gone out of her mind, while she insisted most strongly that she had been telling them the truth, their rejoinder being, "It must be his angelic counterpart."

16Meanwhile Peter went on knocking, and when they opened the door and saw him, they were amazed. 17Peter raised his hand as a signal to them to hold their peace; then he told them the story of how the Lord had led him out of prison; and he ended up as follows: "Report this matter to James and to the other fellow believers." And having said this, he left the house and went somewhere else.

18When daylight came, there was great consternation among the soldiers, who were wondering what could have become of Peter. 19As for Herod, he instituted a thorough search for him; and when he could not be found he interrogated the guards. Then he gave the order that they were to be led away to be executed.

After that, Herod departed from Judaea and for a time took up residence at Caesarea. 20He had for some time been in a state of furious anger with the inhabitants of Tyre and Sidon; and their representatives came, by common consent, into his presence, having managed to enlist the support of Blastus, the royal chamberlain. What they meant to ask of the king was that he should grant them peace; and they had to proceed in this manner, because their country was dependent for its supplies on the king's country. 21On the appointed day, having put on royal apparel and having taken his seat on the rostrum, Herod was haranguing them. 22The people reacted by crying out, "This is a god's voice, not a man's!" 23However, at that very moment the king was struck down by one of the Lord's angels, because he had failed to render due honour to God; and so, *t*eaten up by worms, he expired.

24Meanwhile the Lord's message continued to prosper, and those accepting it increased in number.

25Barnabas and Saul returned to Jerusalem after they had completed their mission, bringing with them John, whose other name was Mark.

13 There were certain prophets and teachers active at Antioch, in the church which was centred there, their names being the following: Barnabas, Simeon, who was also known as Niger, Lucius of Cyrene, Manaen who had been brought up with Herod the tetrarch, and Saul. 2Now one day when these men were *u*ministering to the Lord and keeping a fast, the Holy Spirit addressed these words to them: "I must have Barnabas and Saul set apart, that they may perform for me the

t[2 M 9:5-9]   *u*[2 Ch 13:10; 35:3; Ezk 40:46; 44:16; 45:4] task for which I have appointed them." ³Thereupon, after further fasting and prayer, the others laid their hands upon Barnabas and Saul in blessing and let them go on their way.

⁴Now these men, who had been sent out by the Holy Spirit, first went down to Seleucia, and from there they set sail for Cyprus. ⁵On arrival at Salamis, they proclaimed God's message in the Jewish synagogue, having John Mark with them as their assistant. ⁶And after they had made their way through the whole length of the island as far as P·phos, they came upon a man who was Jewish, a magician who made the false claim that he was a prophet. His name was Bar-Jesus, ⁷and he belonged to the retinue of Sergius Paulus, a proconsul, the latter being a man equipped with sound good sense. He called Saul and Barnabas to his side because he had a strong desire to be informed about God's message. ⁸However, the magician Elymas (which is the man's name in Greek) made every effort to resist them, his intention being that the proconsul should on no account come to embrace the faith. ⁹But Saul—also known as Paul—being filled with the Holy Spirit, fixed his gaze on him and spoke to him thus: ¹⁰"You who are versed in every kind of trickery and cunning, child of the devil that you are and an enemy to all uprightness, will you never cease making crooked *v*the straight ways of the Lord? ¹¹Well then, look out; the hand of the Lord is being raised up against you. You will lose your sight, and for some time you will be unable to see the light of the sun." These words having been spoken, a dark mist fell upon Elymas in an instant, and when he wished to move, he had to ask for a guide to take him by the hand. ¹²At that the proconsul, who had been witnessing what had happened, was filled with awe at what he had learned about the Lord's teaching; and as a result he became a believer.

¹³The next thing Paul and his companions did was that, putting out to sea from Paphos, they sailed to Perga in Pamphylia. John, on the other hand, separated himself from them and returned to Jerusalem. ¹⁴As for the rest, they went on from Perga until they reached the Pisidian town of Antioch. Here, when Sabbath had come, they made their way to the synagogue and took up their places. ¹⁵Later, when passages from the books of the law and the prophetic writings had been read out, the leaders of the synagogue sent them this message: "My friends, if you have any words of exhortation to offer to the people, please speak out."

¹⁶At this, Paul rose from his seat. And having made a gesture with his hand to ensure silence, he spoke thus: "Men of Israel and you others who reverence the true God, give me your attention. ¹⁷The God

*v*Hos 14:9

who is the ruler of this nation, the God of Israel, chose our forefathers to be his very own. He made our nation great at the time when they were living as strangers in Egypt, and *w*with his outstretched arm he led them out of there. [18]Later *x*he bore up patiently with their conduct in the desert for a period of forty years. [19]*y*And when they were in the land of Canaan he overthrew seven nations and gave their land to his people as their inheritance. This lasted for about four hundred and fifty years. [20]Then he appointed judges to be their rulers up to the time of the prophet Samuel.

[21]"They then asked for a king, and God gave them Saul the son of Kish to govern them for forty years; [22]and after having deposed him, God raised up David in his stead, giving him his approval in these words: *z*'I have found David son of Jesse *a*to be a man after my own heart, a man who *b*will carry out all my designs'. [23]At a later time God raised up, in conformity with his promise, one of David's descendants to be the deliverer of Israel. And that man was Jesus, [24]John proclaiming to the whole people, in anticipation of Jesus' coming, a baptism which was to flow from repentance. [25]Moreover, when John was nearing the end of his course, he said, 'I am not what you suppose me to be. No, you must look for another coming after me, a man so great that I am not worthy to unfasten the shoes he wears on his feet.'

[26]"My brothers, both you who come of the stock of Abraham and those who do not, but nevertheless revere the true God, it is to us that this *c*message of salvation has been sent out. [27]As for the inhabitants of Jerusalem and their rulers, they remained wholly uncomprehending of Jesus as well as of the utterances of the prophets, even though they are read out Sabbath after Sabbath. Nevertheless they brought them to fulfilment, which they did through their condemnation of Jesus. [28]Being unable to find any valid grounds that would warrant a death sentence, they still urged Pilate to have him executed. [29]And when they had done everything the scriptures had predicted they would do, they took Jesus down from the cross and laid him in a tomb. [30]But God raised him up from the dead, [31]and after that he appeared over the space of many days to the men who had been accompanying him on his journey from Galilee to Jerusalem.

"It is these very men who are now bearing witness to him before the people[32]—and this is the Good News which we are proclaiming: There was a promise which God made to our forefathers. [33]And this promise he has redeemed to their descendants through raising Jesus from the dead. As indeed it stands written in the second psalm, *d*'You

---

*w*Ex 6:1.6; 14:8   *x*Ex 16:35; Nm 14:34; Dt 1:31   *y*Dt 7:1; Jos 14:2   *z*Ps 89:20   *a*1 Sm 13:14   *b*Is 44:28   *c*Ps 107:20   *d*Ps 2:7

are my son; this very day I have become your Father.' [34] Again, as for God's raising Jesus to life, and the assertion that he was never to return to the realm of those who have **suffered decay,** that is alluded to in the following words: *e'***I will grant you the sure decrees of God relating to David.'** [35] This is also why it is said in another place, *f'***You will not allow it that he who has been consecrated to you should suffer decay.'**

[36] "Now as for *g***David, he went to his death and was gathered to his forefathers,** after he had, in furtherance of God's purpose, done service on behalf of his own generation. David, then, did suffer decay. [37] But the man whom God raised from the dead has not suffered decay. [38] So, my brothers, let this truth be known to you, that the release from your sins which is being proclaimed to you is offered to you through him. [39] There is many a sin for which no acquittal could be found under the law of Moses; but everyone who believes in Jesus does find acquittal through him. [40] Be on your guard, then, lest there should come upon you the fate spoken of in the prophetic books, [41]*h'***Cast your eyes around you, you scoffers, be amazed, be made to vanish, for I am accomplishing a deed in your lifetime,** a deed which **you will by no means believe in, even though someone should recount it to you in every detail.'"**

[42] As Paul and his companions were leaving, certain members of the congregation requested them to return on the following Sabbath so that they might address them on the same topic. [43] When the meeting of the synagogue had broken up, a large number of the Jews and worshippers of Gentile extraction who were converts to Judaism followed Paul and Barnabas, who, for their part, spoke to them, urging them to remain steadfast in their attitude towards God's gracious gift.

[44] On the following Sabbath almost the whole of the city was gathered to hear God's message proclaimed. [45] However, when the Jews saw the crowds, their minds were filled with jealous zeal in opposition to everything Paul said, so they had recourse to blasphemy. [46] Paul and Barnabas spoke out boldly, replying to them thus: "It was necessary that God's message should be proclaimed to you first. But since you see fit to repudiate it, signifying by this that you consider yourselves unworthy of eternal life, so be it. We will turn to the Gentiles. [47] For this is what the Lord has commanded us to do when he uttered the words, *i'***I have appointed you to be a light for the Gentiles, and a means of salvation extending to the very ends of the earth.'"**

[48] When the Gentiles heard this, they were gladdened and gave praise to God's message, while those who were destined for the enjoyment of eternal life came to embrace the faith. [49] And so it happened

*e*Is 55:3 LXX   *f*Ps 16:10 LXX   *g*1 K 2:10; [Jg 2:10]   *h*Hab 1:5 LXX   *i*Is 49:6

that God's message spread all over the land. ⁵⁰But the Jews stirred up hostility among the women of high standing as well as among the leading men of the city, thus setting in train a persecution against Paul and Barnabas and causing them to be driven out of the district. ⁵¹And they, for their part, shook the dust from their feet as a protest against them, and went off to Iconium. ⁵²But as for their converts, they were filled with joy, and in them was that state of grace which comes of the Holy Spirit.

14 At Iconium they adopted the same procedure as before. They made their way to the Jewish synagogue. *And* there they spoke with such power that a large number of both Gentiles and Jews came to embrace the faith. ²However, there were Jews who would not give their assent to anything Paul said; and these succeeded in stirring up the minds of the Gentiles and in exciting animosity against the members of the Christian brotherhood. ³Still, Paul and Barnabas remained in the place for a considerable time, and, in reliance upon the Lord, spoke out fearlessly in support of their cause, the Lord, for his part, adding his own testimony in vindication of the gracious message they were proclaiming, through bringing many a sign and many a wondrous deed into being by their means. ⁴As for the population of the city, they were divided, some siding with the Jews and others with the apostles. ⁵Still, when both Gentiles and Jews, with the connivance of the city authorities, made a move to subjecting the apostles to cruel treatment and having them stoned, ⁶the apostles, sensing what was happening, took to flight and went off to the Lycaonian towns of Lystra and Derbe and the surrounding countryside. ⁷And it was there that they set about proclaiming the Good News.

⁸Now at Lystra they came upon a man who was sitting helpless on the ground, unable to make use of his feet because he had been lame from birth and had never been able to walk. ⁹He was listening to Paul's preaching. Paul, for his part, fixed his gaze on him and, on perceiving that his faith was strong enough to make it possible for him to be healed of his infirmity, ¹⁰cried out in a loud voice, "*ʲ***Stand upright on your feet!**" At that the man leapt up and began to walk. ¹¹When the crowd saw what Paul had accomplished, they raised their voices and exclaimed, in their native Lycaonian, "The gods, having taken on human shape, have come down to us!" ¹²Moreover, they addressed Barnabas as Zeus, and since Paul was the principal speaker they called him Hermes. ¹³And the priest of Zeus, whose temple was in the immediate neighbourhood of the city, being eager for the crowd

ʲEzk 2:1

to join him in offering sacrifice, brought out to the gates bulls as well as garlands of flowers with which to adorn the apostles.

[14] Paul and Barnabas, on perceiving how matters stood, rent their clothes, leapt into the crowd, and exclaimed in loud voices, [15] "Friends, why are you acting in this manner? We are no more than men, of the same nature as yourselves; and this is the message we are bringing you: Give up your idols, futile as they are, and turn to the living God. *k***It is he who is the creator of heaven, of the earth, of the sea, and of all the creatures in them.** [16] In past ages he allowed all the nations to go their own ways. [17]*l*Yet even then he did not leave them without supplying evidence of his nature. He conferred benefits upon them, sending them rain from the sky and crops in their season, granting them nourishment, and filling their hearts with gladness."

[18] Yet, although the apostles were speaking in this way, it was only with great difficulty that they succeeded in preventing the crowd from offering sacrifice to them.

[19] At this stage certain Jews from Antioch and Iconium came upon the scene. They won over the crowds, proceeded to throw stones at Paul, and, in the belief that he had been killed, they dragged him out of the city. [20] At that some of the disciples formed a ring about him, and he, rising to his feet, made his way back into the city. The next day he and Barnabas left the place for Derbe, [21] where they proclaimed the Good News; and having made a large number of converts, they returned to Lystra, then to Iconium, and finally to Antioch. [22] Everywhere they sought to strengthen the hearts of their converts, admonishing them to keep true to the faith and addressing them in such words as these: "If we are to enter the kingdom of God, we can do so only through undergoing a great deal of suffering." [23] Moreover, the apostles appointed elders for them, church by church; they prayed and fasted with them, and committed them to the Lord in whom they had put their trust. [24] They then traversed Pisidia and, on reaching Pamphylia, [25] preached God's message at Perga. Having done this, they went down to Attalia, and from there set sail for Antioch, [26] the place from which they had gone out on their journey, having been commended to God's grace, that it might equip them for the task which they had now completed. [27] When they arrived there, they reported—the church having been called together—what great things God had accomplished, with them as his instruments, and that he had opened up a door for the Gentiles, giving them admission to the faith. [28] After that they remained for quite a long time at Antioch with the disciples who were resident there.

*k*Ex 20:11   *l*[Ps 147:20]

15 At this stage certain men came down from Judaea propounding the following to the brotherhood: Unless a man be ready to submit to circumcision, in conformity with the tradition deriving from Moses, there is no way of his obtaining salvation. [2]This gave rise to bitter strife, and a fierce debate arose between these men, on the one hand, and Paul and Barnabas, on the other. The latter party argued in opposition to the former; and so it was decided that Paul and Barnabas, together with some other members of the group, were to go up to the apostles and elders in Jerusalem to consult with them on this controversial question. [3]These men, after they had been given their send-off by the church, passed through both Phoenicia and Samaria, where they reported the conversion of the Gentiles, this news causing great rejoicing among all the congregations. [4]On arriving in Jerusalem they received a warm welcome from the church, from apostles as well as from elders, and so they gave an account of everything that God had done to aid them. [5]However, certain men who had come to embrace the faith (even though they belonged to the party of the Pharisees) stood up and insisted that the Gentile converts were obliged to submit to circumcision and were to be ordered to keep the law of Moses.

[6]When the apostles and the elders assembled to look into the matter, [7]a fierce dispute arose, until Peter stood up and addressed the following words to the assembly: "My friends, you know that, from the very earliest days, it has been God's choice that the Gentiles should hear the gospel message from me, and so learn to believe. [8]Furthermore, God, to whom the human heart is fully known, has borne testimony of his favour by the bestowal of the Holy Spirit upon them, just as he has done upon us, [9]making no distinction between us and them, and removing, in virtue of their faith, all uncleanness from their hearts. [10]Well then, why are you now setting out to provoke God by putting a yoke upon the necks of these converts, a yoke which neither we nor our forefathers were able to bear? [11]But the truth is that we are convinced that we shall obtain our salvation in precisely the same way as they will: through the gracious favour bestowed by the Lord Jesus."

[12]At that the whole company held their peace and listened to Barnabas and Paul giving an account of all the signs and wondrous deeds which God had, by their means, shown forth among the Gentiles.

[13]When Paul and Barnabas had finished speaking, James made his reply in these words: "Dear friends, listen to what I have to say. [14]Simeon has given us an account of the first occasion on which God looked upon the Gentiles, his concern being with choosing from among them a people dedicated to his name. [15]And this is something with which the words of the prophets are in full agreement. As scrip-

ture has it, [16m]'In days to come I shall return and build up again David's dwelling place which has fallen to the ground. I shall build up the ruins again, [17]so that the rest of mankind may come to seek after the Lord: all the nations which I have called to myself to be bearers of my name. [18n]Those are the words of the Lord who has accomplished all this, and has made these things known from of old.' [19]Well then, in view of all this, I am of the opinion that we ought not to put any obstacles in the way of those Gentiles who are turning to God. [20]What we should do instead is send them a letter, instructing them to abstain from meat polluted by idol worship, from engaging in unlawful sexual activities, from the flesh of animals killed by strangling, and from flesh which still has the blood in it. [21]From the earliest times Moses has had spokesmen proclaiming his message in every city, his words being read out aloud in the synagogues Sabbath after Sabbath."

[22]These words having been spoken, a resolution was passed by the apostles and the elders, the whole church giving its assent, to the effect that certain men were to be chosen out of their number, and that these were to be sent to Antioch with Paul and Barnabas. The election fell upon Judas, also known as Barsabbas, and upon Silas, who occupied a leading position in the brotherhood. [23]They sent them with a letter, its contents being as follows: 'The apostles and the members of the brotherhood who occupy the position of elders send their greetings to those brothers resident in Antioch, Syria, and Cilicia who are of Gentile descent. [24]We have learned that certain men who have gone out from our midst have disquieted you by their words and have thrown your minds into confusion, although they did not have any mandate from us. [25]This being so, we have resolved unanimously to elect certain persons and send them to you in the company of Barnabas and Paul, [26]those dearly-loved men who have dedicated their lives to defending the cause which bears the name of our Lord Jesus Christ. [27]Accordingly, we are sending out Judas and Silas to you, and they will convey to you by word of mouth the very same message as is contained in this letter. [28]It has been decided by the Holy Spirit and by ourselves that no burden is to be imposed upon you beyond these essentials: [29]You are to abstain from meat which has been used in sacrifice to an idol, from flesh which still has the blood in it, from the flesh of animals killed by strangling, and from engaging in unlawful sexual activities. If you keep yourselves from these things, you will be doing what is right. Farewell.'

[30]The envoys went on their journey to Antioch, and having called an assembly of the church together, they delivered the letter. [31]The

[m]Am 9:11f LXX; Jr 12:15   [n]Is 45:21

congregation, on reading it, rejoiced at these words of encouragement, [32] while Judas and Silas, who were themselves prophets, said much to encourage the brotherhood and strengthen its members in their faith. [33] These two stayed on for a while. Then, the brotherhood having given them their send-off in a spirit of peace, they returned to those who had sent them out.* [35] Paul and Barnabas remained at Antioch, and there, together with many others, they made proclamation of the Lord's message.

[36] Some time after that, Paul said to Barnabas, "Let us return and pay a visit to those of our brothers, wherever they may be, who are resident in all the cities where we proclaimed the Lord's message, to find out how they are faring." [37] As for Barnabas, his wish was that they should take John Mark with them. [38] Paul, however, was of the opinion that they ought not to take with them the men who had deserted them in Pamphylia and who had failed to support them in their task. [39] And so it happened that a disagreement of the most violent nature arose between the two men, the result of this being that they parted company, Barnabas taking Mark with him and setting sail for Cyprus, [40] while Paul, who chose Silas as his companion, went on with his journey, having been commended to the grace of the Lord by the members of the brotherhood. [41] And he made his way all through Syria and Cilicia, strengthening the churches in the faith.

16 So Paul eventually reached Derbe, and then Lystra; and here he came upon a convert, Timothy by name, who was the son of a Greek father, and of a Jewish mother who had been converted to the faith. [2] Timothy was well spoken of by the brotherhoods at Lystra and Iconium. [3] As for Paul, his wish was to have him as his companion when he left the place. So he got hold of him and had him circumcised, acting in this manner so as to conciliate the Jews who were living in those parts; for everyone knew that his father was a Greek.

[4] As they made their way from one city to another, they passed on the decrees which had been decided on by the apostles and the presbyters in Jerusalem, with instructions to observe them. [5] In this way the churches found themselves strengthened, and those belonging to them increased in number.

[6] Thus they passed through Phrygia and the Galatian region, having been warned by the Holy Spirit that they must not preach God's message in the province of Asia. [7] Then, when they reached the Mysian border, their intention was to make their way into Bithynia, but the Spirit of Jesus did not permit them to do so. [8] So they traversed Mysia and

* V. 34 is probably not part of the original text.

went down to the sea at Troas. [9] And there it happened that Paul had a vision during the night. What he saw was a man from Macedonia standing before him and entreating him in these words: "Come over to Macedonia and help us." [10] This vision having appeared to Paul, we lost no time in arranging a passage to Macedonia. For we concluded that God had sent out a call to us to proclaim his message there.

[11] And so we set sail from Troas, had a straight run to Samothrace, and arrived at Neapolis the following day. [12] From there we went to Philippi, the most important city in that particular district of Macedonia and a Roman colony. We remained in that city for a few days, [13] and then, on the Sabbath day, we went outside the city gate to a spot by the river where, we conjectured, there was a place customarily used for prayer. We sat down, engaging in conversation with the women who had gathered there. [14] One of these was called Lydia. She was a trader in purple dyes, a native of the city of Thyatira, and a worshipper of the true God. She was listening attentively, the Lord opening her heart to make her a ready listener to what Paul said. [15] This woman, after she and her whole household had received baptism, made an urgent appeal to us. "If," she said, "you consider me to be a true believer in the Lord, come to my house and stay there for a while." And her insistence was so great that we had to give way to her.

[16] One day when we were on our way to the place of prayer, we came upon a slave girl who was possessed of a spirit enabling her to engage in divination and who, by her foretelling of the future, brought in a very considerable profit to those who were her masters. [17] It was this woman who kept running after Paul and us, crying out, "These people are servants of God Most High; it is they who are proclaiming to us the way of salvation." [18] She went on with this for several days. Finally, Paul, greatly annoyed, turned round and addressed the spirit in the following words: "I command you, in the name of Jesus Christ, to come out of her." And it did come out of her, there and then.

[19] When her masters became aware that all hope of making a profit out of her had gone, they got hold of Paul and Silas and dragged them off to the market place, to be brought before the city authorities. [20] And indicting them before the magistrates, they spoke thus: "These men, Jews as they are, are throwing our city into confusion [21] by recommending us to adopt certain customs which, as Roman citizens, we cannot possibly either accept or put into practice." [22] Upon this, the mob joined the attack, while the magistrates had the apostles' clothes torn off their backs, at the same time giving the order that they were to be flogged. [23] After they had inflicted many a blow upon them, they threw them into prison, instructing the jailer to keep them under close guard. [24] And he, thus instructed, had them taken to the inner part of the prison and had their feet secured in the stocks.

25 At about midnight, when Paul and Silas were engaged in prayer and offering praise to God, while the other prisoners were listening, 26an earthquake of such violence broke forth, all of a sudden, that the foundations of the prison were shaken, all the doors bursting open and every prisoner's shackles falling off. 27 As for the jailer, when he woke up and saw that the prison doors had been thrown wide open, he drew his sword, intending to make away with himself. And he acted in this manner because he supposed that the prisoners had made good their escape. 28But Paul cried out in a powerful voice, "Do not do yourself an injury; for we are all here!" 29 At that the jailer called for lights, rushed in, 30and then, seized by a violent trembling, threw himself down at the feet of Paul and Silas and led them out of the prison. "What must I do, honoured gentlemen, to be saved?" he said. 31 "Put your faith in the Lord Jesus," the apostles replied; "it is there that salvation lies for yourself and for your whole household." 32Then they expounded God's message to him as well as to all those who belonged to his household. 33 And so it came about that, at this late hour of the night, they were made welcome, and that, the wounds which the apostles had received from the flogging having been washed, the jailer and his entire household immediately received their baptism. 34He then led them up to his house and set a meal before them, the hearts of all his household overflowing with joy by reason of his new-found faith in God. 35When daylight came, the magistrates sent out their sergeants with the message that the men were to be given their freedom. 36The jailer reported to Paul the message which he had received in these words: "The magistrates have sent word to me that you are to be set free. Well then, go forth and °**proceed** on your way **in peace.**" 37But Paul made the following reply to the messengers: "They have had us flogged in public and have condemned us without a proper trial. After that, notwithstanding that we are Roman citizens, we have been thrown into prison. And what they mean to do now is to push us out on the quiet. This must not be. Let them come in person and lead us out." 38The sergeants reported these words to the magistrates, who, when they heard that the men were Roman citizens, became greatly frightened. 39They came, doing their best to conciliate the apostles, and, leading them out, requested them to leave the city. 40And the apostles, after leaving the prison, went to Lydia's house, where they met the members of the brotherhood; and having spoken words of encouragement to them, they went on their way.

17 Having made their way through Amphipolis and Apollonia, they reached Thessalonica, where there was a Jewish synagogue.

°Jg 18:6

2Paul, according to his custom, attached himself to those who were meeting there, and for three Sabbaths in succession he engaged in argument with them, taking the scriptures as the basis of his reasoning. 3The task he was setting himself was to make it clear to them what was the meaning to be attached to various passages from scripture, his thesis being, first, that the sufferings of God's anointed and his rising to life again were events which had been preordained; and secondly, his contention was this: "Jesus, the man whose message I am proclaiming to you, is in fact God's anointed." 4The result of his efforts was that there were some who allowed themselves to be convinced and who, as a result of this, threw in their lot with Paul and Silas. These included a large number of Greeks who were worshippers of the true God. Moreover, the same course was adopted by not a few of the women who were of high standing.

5The Jews, on the other hand, were filled with jealousy at all this, and so they got hold of certain low fellows from the dregs of the population to form a mob and throw the city into confusion. They took up their station in front of Jason's house, intending to bring Paul and Silas face to face with the popular assembly. 6But, failing to find them, they dragged Jason himself and some other members of the Christian brotherhood before the city magistrates, shouting out, "These men who have stirred up trouble all over the world have now made their appearance here, 7Jason receiving them into his house. All of them do things which are contrary to the decrees of the Emperor, and assert that there is another king, one called Jesus." 8On hearing these words, the crowd was thrown into confusion, and so were the magistrates. 9And because of that, they would not let Jason and the others go, but demanded that they first of all deposit a considerable sum as bail.

10Darkness having fallen, the members of the brotherhood immediately sent Paul and Silas off to Beroea. And they, for their part, made their way to the Jewish synagogue as soon as they arrived. 11The Jews who belonged to the place were of a much more generous turn of mind than those at Thessalonica; and so it was that they gave a welcome to God's message, with the utmost good will, scrutinizing the scriptures day in and day out in the hope of discovering whether things were really what they had been told they were. 12This had the result that large numbers of them came to embrace the faith—including many Greek women of noble birth and not a few of the men as well. 13However, when the Jews in Thessalonica learned that Paul was now proclaiming God's message at Beroea, they went there intent on causing a disturbance among the crowds and throwing them into confusion. 14This being so, the members of the brotherhood, without the least delay, sent Paul off to the coast, while Silas and Timothy stayed behind. [15]Those who were escorting Paul brought him as far as Athens, and came away with instructions for Silas and Timothy to rejoin Paul as soon as possible.

[16]Now while Paul was waiting for them in Athens, he was stirred up to great indignation in his heart because he perceived that the city was altogether given over to idolatry. [17]So he engaged in discussions in the synagogue both with men born as Jews and with worshippers of Gentile descent. But not only this: he addressed himself every day to those he encountered in the market place. [18]As a matter of fact, there were a few among the Epicurean and Stoic philosophers who engaged in conversation with him, some of them remarking, "Is there any way of discovering what this idle prattler is getting at?" Others said, "The deities whose advocate he is would seem to be outlandish indeed." (They would speak in such a way on the ground that he was preaching about Jesus and the resurrection.) [19]And so it came about that they got hold of him and led him up to the Areopagus. And there they spoke to him thus:

"Is there any way of coming to know what is the meaning of this new teaching which you are propounding? [20]For the notions you are putting before us sound strange indeed to our ears, and that is why we are desirous of finding out what their bearing could possibly be." [21](In point of fact, all Athenian citizens—and this applies likewise to those on a visit to the city—used to spend their time in nothing else than in saying something novel or in hearing it said.)

[22]Paul, then, standing in the centre of the Areopagus, spoke as follows: "Men of Athens, I have seen for myself how very scrupulous you are in all matters which concern religion. [23]And indeed, while I was strolling through your city and looking carefully at the objects of your worship, I came, among other things, upon an altar bearing the inscription, 'TO THE UNKNOWN GOD'. Now what you worship, not having any proper knowledge of it, is the very thing which I am proclaiming to you. [24]*p***The God who created** the world **and** everything **contained in it,** he who is the Lord **of heaven and of earth,** does not live in temples made by human hands; [25]nor is it because of his lacking anything that he allows men to serve him. It is he who, for all of us, is the *q***giver** of life and of **breath** and bestows upon us everything that is ours. [26]He has created of one single stock the whole human race, so that it should occupy the entire earth; and he has fixed for each nation how long it should flourish and what were to be the limits of its territory. [27]And the purpose of it all was that they should seek after God, in the hope that they might grope their way towards him and perhaps find him. Yet in fact he is not far

*p*Is 42:5; 1 K 8:27   *q*Is 42:5

from any of us. 28And indeed, it is in him that we live and move and
have our being, some of your own poets having expressed this in the
words, 'We also are descended from him.' 29Since, then, we are descended from him, we must not imagine that the divine nature bears
any resemblance to gold, silver, or stones carved by human skill and
ingenuity. 30Yet as regards the period when people were ignorant of
God, he deals with it as though it had never been; and what he now
proclaims to people everywhere is that they must all repent their
deeds, 31in consideration of the fact that he has appointed a day on
which he will ʳhave the world justly judged by a man of his own
choosing. Moreover, God has given sure proof of this through
making faith available to everyone, and that by way of raising that
man from the dead."

32When Paul's audience heard him speak of the resurrection of the
dead, some of them jeered while others made this observation: "You
must tell us more about this matter on some other occasion." 33And
so Paul parted company with them. 34Still, there were a few who attached themselves to him and became believers, among them
Dionysius, a member of the Council of the Areopagus, also a woman
called Damaris, and some others besides.

18 After this, Paul took his departure from Athens and went to
Corinth. 2There he came upon a certain Jew, Aquila by name, a native
of Pontus who, with his wife called Priscilla, had recently arrived from
Rome, the reason for this being that Claudius had issued an edict that
all Jews were to be expelled from Rome. Paul approached them, 3and
on finding that they were tentmakers, of the same trade as himself, he
made his home with them, and they did their work together. 4Every
Sabbath he engaged in argument in the synagogue, his purpose being
to carry conviction with both Jews and Gentiles.

5It was at the time when Silas and Timothy had arrived from
Macedonia that Paul was wholly absorbed in preaching, bearing
solemn witness to the Jews that Jesus was God's anointed one. 6But
when they set their faces against him and had recourse to blasphemy,
he ˢshook out his clothes, speaking to them thus: "Your blood be on
your heads. I am guiltless, and from this time onwards I shall go to
the Gentiles." 7So he left the place and went on to the house of one
Titius Justus, a worshipper of the true God, who had a house adjoining the synagogue. 8Crispus, the president of the synagogue, now became a believer in the Lord, and so did his whole household.
Moreover, a large number of Corinthians, on hearing Paul, embraced

ʳPs 9:8; 96:13; 98:9   ˢ[Neh 5:13]

the faith and submitted themselves to baptism. [9]One night the Lord said to Paul in a vision, "[t]**Shake off all fear** and speak out instead, not allowing yourself to be silenced. [10][u]**For I am on your side.** And there shall be no one who will set on you so as to harm you, because there are many here in this city who are people of mine." [11]After this, Paul settled in the place for eighteen months and instructed the people there, proclaiming God's message to them.

[12]However, at the time when Gallio was proconsul in the province of Achaia, the Jews made a concerted attack on Paul and dragged him before the judicial bench. [13]"This fellow," they said, "is seeking to persuade men to worship God in a manner which is contrary to the law." [14]Paul was just about to open his mouth when Gallio addressed the Jews in the following words: "Jews, if this were a matter of a wrongful deed or of a piece of fraud, it would indeed be no more than reasonable that I should give you a patient hearing. [15]But if all this is nothing but questions about words, names, and the law which is in force among you, you must deal with it yourselves. I have no mind to play the judge in matters such as these." [16]And he drove them away from the judicial bench. [17]At that, a general onslaught was made on Sosthenes, the president of the synagogue, and they all gave him a beating in the immediate neighbourhood of the judicial bench. As for Gallio, he did not care in the least about any of this.

[18]After these events Paul stayed on some time longer; and then, having taken his leave of the brotherhood, he set sail for Syria, taking Priscilla and Aquila with him. At Cenchreae he had his head shaved because he had bound himself to a vow. [19]When they reached Ephesus, he left the others behind and made his way by himself to the synagogue to engage in discussion with the Jews. [20]But when they asked him to stay on for some time, he would not consent, [21]though, before taking his leave of them, he addressed them in these words: "If it be the will of God, I shall be returning to you at some later time." After that he departed from Ephesus by sea. [22]On landing at Caesarea, he went up from there to pay his respects to the church. Then he went down again, making his way to Antioch. [23]And having stayed there for some time, he left, visiting one place after another in Galatia and Phrygia, and bringing strength and encouragement to all those who had been converted to the faith.

[24]Now a certain Jew arrived at Ephesus whose name was Apollos. He was a native of Alexandria, and, moreover, a cultured man, with a special gift for interpreting the scriptures. [25]Having received instruction regarding the Way of the Lord and being filled with a spirit of burning zeal, he preached and taught accurately enough about

[t]Jr 1:8   [u]Ex 3:12; Jos 1:5.9; Is 41:10; 43:5

what Jesus had accomplished, although he knew of no baptism but John's. 26 And so he set out to speak boldly in the synagogue, while Priscilla and Aquila, after hearing him, took him aside and explained God's way to him in greater detail. 27 However, when the brotherhood found that he had set his mind on crossing over into the province of Achaia, they gave him their support, and wrote a letter to the converts there asking them to give him a cordial welcome. And after he arrived, he was of great assistance to those who, through God's grace, had come to embrace the faith. 28 For he stood up in public and refuted the Jews with the greatest vigour, demonstrating, by taking the scriptures for his text, that it was Jesus who was God's anointed.

19 At the time when Apollos was at Corinth, it so happened that Paul was travelling through the inland districts until he reached Ephesus. There he came upon a number of converts 2 whom he asked, "Did you receive the Holy Spirit when you came to believe?" "We have not even heard that there is such a thing as the Holy Spirit," was their reply. 3 "If that is so," Paul asked, "what kind of baptism did you receive?" "John's baptism," was their answer, 4 while Paul said, "John's baptism was one issuing from repentance, while at the same time John told the people that they were to believe in one coming after him, that is to say, in Jesus." 5 As soon as they had been told this, baptism in the name of the Lord Jesus was administered to them. 6 And when Paul laid his hands upon them, they received the Holy Spirit, spoke in inspired tongues, and uttered prophecies. 7 The number of these men was about twelve, all in all.

8 During the next three months Paul attended the synagogue and spoke up with great boldness, engaging in controversy and seeking to carry conviction about the kingdom of God. 9 However, when a number of people hardened their hearts and, refusing to accept what they had been told, set out to vilify the New Way in the hearing of the whole congregation, Paul left and withdrew his converts, at the same time continuing to discuss things day by day in a certain school which belonged to a man called Tyrannus. 10 This went on for a period of two years, with the result that all the inhabitants of the province of Asia, both Jews and Gentiles, came to hear of the message sent forth by the Lord. 11 Moreover, God performed, at the hands of Paul, many miracles of a most remarkable nature, 12 so much so that, when handkerchiefs or scarves which had been in contact with his skin were taken to the sick, people were freed from their diseases, and the evil spirits by which they were possessed departed from them.

13 However, there were certain itinerant Jewish exorcists who embarked on invoking the Lord Jesus' name over those possessed of evil

spirits, exclaiming, "I adjure you in the name of Jesus, the one whom Paul proclaims!" [14] Now there were the seven sons of a certain Sceva, a Jewish chief priest, who were employing this practice. [15] And this was the rejoinder made by the evil spirit: "I know of Jesus and I am acquainted with Paul, but you yourselves, who are you?" [16] At that the man with the evil spirit in him leapt up flying at them, over-powered them all, and gained the mastery over them, with the result that they ran out of the house stripped and covered with wounds. [17] This became known to every inhabitant of Ephesus, to Jews as well as to the Gentiles. They were all filled with a feeling of awe, and the name of the Lord Jesus came to be glorified. [18] Now many among those who had become believers came forward, confessing their practices and making them public. [19] Moreover, a large number of those who had been occupying themselves with the magical arts collected their books in one place, in the sight of all, and burned them; and on their calculating the value of these books, it was found that they were worth fifty thousand pieces of silver. [20] It was in ways such as these, then, that the message sent forth by the Lord increased mightily in both scope and strength.

[21] These things having taken their course, Paul formed in his mind the resolution to go to Jerusalem, and to do so by way of Macedonia and Achaia. "And after that," he exclaimed, "I must see Rome!" [22] So he sent two of his assistants, Timothy and Erastus, to Macedonia, while he himself remained in the province of Asia for some time longer.

[23] It was about this time that those teaching the New Way became the cause of a disturbance which was by no means inconsiderable. [24] There was a certain silversmith, Demetrius by name, who was making silver shrines of the goddess Artemis, providing in this way a great deal of employment for his craftsmen. [25] He called together a meeting of these and of the workmen occupied with such things, and said to them, "My friends, you know well enough that all our prosperity derives from this trade of ours. [26] Now you can both see and hear for yourselves that, not only here at Ephesus but over near-ly the whole of Asia, this Paul sets out to mislead the people, and that he has succeeded in winning over large numbers of them to his opinion that gods made by human hands are not gods at all. [27] But not only that: he has exposed us to the danger that our line of business might fall into disrepute and, over and above that, to the risk that the temple of the great Artemis should come to be looked upon as being of no value, and that she herself, who is worshipped in Asia and in-deed all over the world, should suffer the loss of her magnificence."

[28] When they heard this, they were roused to fury and cried out, "Great is Artemis, goddess of the Ephesian people!" [29] The city was in a state of utter confusion, and everybody rushed into the am-

phitheatre, dragging with them Gaius and Aristarchus, men from Macedonia who were Paul's travelling companions. 30 Paul's own wish was to appear before the assembly. The converts, however, would not let him do this, 31 and even some of the delegates of the province of Asia, who were favourably disposed towards him, sent a message imploring him not to venture by himself into the amphitheatre.

32 Meanwhile, the assembly was in complete disorder, some shouting one thing and some another, most people being in fact ignorant of what they had come for. 33 Certain members of the crowd explained the position to Alexander, whom the Jews had put forward. But when Alexander, who wished to offer his defence before the popular assembly, made a motion with his hand to enforce silence, 34 and they recognized that he was a Jew, there was a general outcry for about two hours, and they shouted, "Great is Artemis, goddess of the Ephesian people!"

35 The town clerk, however, succeeded in restraining the crowd with the following words: "Men of Ephesus, is there anyone in the world who does not know that the city of Ephesus is the guardian of the temple of the great Artemis, and of her image which fell from heaven? 36 Now since these facts are beyond contradiction, it is essential that you should keep calm and refrain from doing anything hasty. 37 After all, the men whom you have brought here are not charged with robbing temples or with uttering blasphemy against our goddess. 38 And if Demetrius and his fellow craftsmen have anything of which to accuse them, why, we have days when the courts are in session, and besides, there are proconsuls to appeal to. Let the parties bring their charges and counter-charges. 39 If, on the other hand, there are other matters which you wish to have enquired into further, let them be settled in the lawful assembly. 40 The fact is that we do indeed run the risk of being charged with riot for today's work, there being no satisfactory explanation we can offer, and if the matter be brought forward, it will be impossible for us to account for this commotion in a way which will carry conviction." 41 Having spoken these words, he dismissed the assembly.

20 The disturbance being over, Paul summoned the disciples, and having spoken words of encouragement to them, bade them farewell and set out on his journey to Macedonia. 2 On traversing the intervening districts, he encouraged the Christians there with great eloquence, and so made his way into Greece, 3 where we spent three months. When he was just about to set sail for Syria, a plot was laid against him by the Jews, and so he decided to make his return journey by way

of Macedonia. ⁴He was accompanied by Sopater son of Pyrrhus, a citizen of Beroea, as well as by Aristarchus and Secundus, who came from Thessalonica, by Gaius, a native of Derbe, by Timothy, and, moreover, by Tychicus and Trophimus, both of whom belonged to the province of Asia. ⁵These set out ahead of us, and it was arranged that they were to wait for us at Troas. ⁶We ourselves set sail from Philippi, after the days of the Feast of Unleavened Bread, and in five days we reached them at Troas, where we stayed for a week.

⁷On the first day of the week, when we were gathered to break bread together, Paul addressed those who had assembled, on the eve of his departure, and extended his speech until midnight. ⁸There were a good many lamps in the upstairs room of our meeting place; ⁹and a certain youth called Eutychus, who was sitting on the window sill, grew more and more drowsy as Paul went on talking, until, wholly overcome by sleep, he fell all the way from the third storey to the ground; and when he was lifted up from the ground, it was found that he was dead. ¹⁰As for Paul, he went downstairs, threw himself upon him, put his arms round his neck, and exclaimed, "Do not distress yourselves on his account! For the truth is that there is still life in him!" ¹¹Then he went upstairs again, broke bread, and partook of it. And then, after he had talked on for a considerable time, in fact until daybreak, he went on his way. ¹²As for the boy, he was alive when they brought him home, and they found themselves greatly comforted.

¹³As for ourselves, we went down to the ship and set sail for Assos, where we were to take Paul on board. Paul had ordered it so because he himself intended to travel by road. ¹⁴And so we took him on board, when he met us at Assos, and went on to Mitylene. ¹⁵The next day we sailed away from there and arrived opposite Chios. The following day we crossed over to Samos, and on the day after that we reached Miletus. ¹⁶For Paul had decided to pass Ephesus by, to avoid spending an unduly long time in the province of Asia. He meant to make haste because he was anxious to be in Jerusalem by the time of Pentecost, if that were possible.

¹⁷However, he sent messengers from Miletus to Ephesus, to summon the elders of the church. ¹⁸And when these arrived, he addressed them in the following words: "You know what my conduct has been during the whole of the time when I was in your midst, from the first day when I set foot on Asian soil, ¹⁹how I served the Lord in all humility, though I shed many a tear, and had to undergo many a trial because of the plots devised against me by the Jews. ²⁰You are aware that I never shrank from disclosing anything to you from which you might benefit. I never ceased unfolding the truth to you, and I gave you instruction both publicly and in your own homes. ²¹And this is

the cause in support of which I gave my testimony: I addressed myself
to both Jews and Gentiles, telling them that they ought to repent, turning to God and reposing their confidence in the Lord Jesus. 22 And now,
as you see, I am on my way to Jerusalem, impelled by the Spirit. I know
nothing of what may befall me there, 23 except this, that the Holy Spirit
gives me his assurance that, in city after city, bondage and affliction
are what I have to expect. 24 Still, as far as my life is concerned, I do not
consider it of any account, except that my purpose is to finish the race
and to discharge in full the task which the Lord Jesus has assigned to
me, the task, that is, of bearing testimony on behalf of the Good News
which proclaims the gracious favour bestowed by God.

25 "And there is one more thing. I know full well that none of you
will see my face again, you the people among whom I have gone about
heralding the kingdom. 26 That being so, I assure you solemnly this
very day that my conscience is clear and that no man's blood is upon
my hands. 27 For I have withheld nothing from you, unfolding to you
the whole of God's purpose. 28 Be on your guard for your own sakes
and for the sake of the whole flock of which the Holy Spirit has made
you overseers, so that you should watch over the church *v*of God,
which he has won for himself through the sacrifice of his own blood.
29 I know only too well that, when I am gone, savage wolves will come
among you which will deal mercilessly with the flock, 30 and that, out
of your midst, men will be coming forward who will give utterance
to perverted opinions, with a view to drawing the disciples after them
and making them come over to their side. 31 Be on the alert, therefore,
and remind yourselves how for three whole years I never ceased,
night or day, giving counsel to each one of you, and that frequently
amidst tears.

32 "And now I am commending you to the Lord and to the gracious
message which he has sent forth, to the message which has the power
of building you up in the faith and of giving you your *w***heritage**
among all those **who have been consecrated** to God. 33 I have never
asked anyone for silver, for gold, or for clothing. 34 You yourselves
know well enough that it has been these hands of mine which have
done service for my needs and for those of my companions. 35 On any
and every occasion I have explained to you that it is our duty to toil
in this manner and to hold out a helping hand to those in want, mindful of the words which the Lord Jesus himself spoke: *x*'The greatest
happiness is not to receive a gift: it is to bestow one.'"

36 As he finished speaking, he fell upon his knees, offering prayer
together with the whole company. 37 At this they all burst into copious
tears, threw their arms round Paul's neck, and kissed him. 38 What

*v*Ps 74:2   *w*Dt 33:3-4   *x*[Ec'us 4:31]

grieved them most was the word which he had spoken, that they would never see his face again. It was in this manner, then, that he was given his send-off to the ship.

21 When the time came for us to tear ourselves away from them and put to sea again, we set a straight course for Cos. The next day we reached Rhodes, and from there we went to Patara. ²Here we found a ship bound for Phoenicia; so we went on board and sailed in her. ³When we sighted Cyprus, we left it behind us on our left and sailed on to Syria, putting in at Tyre because it was there that the ship was to unload her cargo. ⁴Seeking out the converts who were resident there, we remained in the place for seven days, while the people told Paul—and that under the guidance of the Holy Spirit—not to embark for Jerusalem. ⁵When the time was up, we left them and continued on our journey, while all the converts, together with their wives and children, escorted us till we were out of the city. On reaching the beach, we fell upon our knees and prayed. ⁶Then, when farewells had been exchanged, we went on board ship, while the others returned to their own homes.

⁷We ourselves, completing the journey from Tyre, arrived at Ptolemais, where we saluted the Christian brothers there and remained with them for one day. ⁸The following day we left, and, on arriving at Caesarea, went to the house of Philip the evangelist, one of the seven deacons, and stayed with him. ⁹He had four unmarried daughters who were endowed with the gift of prophecy. ¹⁰We made a stay of several days there, and during that time a prophet called Agabus came down from Judaea to the place. ¹¹He walked towards us, took Paul's belt from him, and then, binding his own feet and hands, exclaimed, "These are the words of the Holy Spirit: 'The man to whom this belt belongs will be fettered, just like this, by the Jews in Jerusalem, and they will hand him over to the Gentiles.'" ¹²When we heard this, we, as well as the local residents, implored Paul not to go up to Jerusalem. ¹³On hearing this, Paul made them this rejoinder: "What are you about, weeping and breaking my heart? I, for my part, stand ready not merely to suffer bondage but to suffer death in defence of the name of the Lord Jesus." ¹⁴As for ourselves, we held our peace when we found that he would not be persuaded, exclaiming, "May the Lord's will be done!"

¹⁵The days of our visit having come to an end, we made our preparations for the journey and then set out for Jerusalem, ¹⁶accompanied by some of the disciples from Caesarea. These escorted us as far as the house where we were to take up our lodging. It belonged to a man called Mnason, a native of Cyprus and a disciple from the ear-

liest days. [17]When we arrived in Jerusalem, the Christian brothers gave us a hearty welcome.

[18]The following day Paul took us with him to pay a visit to James, all the elders being assembled in the place. [19]Greetings being over, Paul gave them a detailed account of all that God had done among the Gentiles through the instrumentality of his ministry. [20]When the men heard this, they offered praise to God and said to Paul, "Brother, you are no doubt aware how many thousand Jews there are among those who have become believers. All of them are staunch upholders of the law. [21]At the same time they have been informed about you that you teach the Jews who live among the Gentiles that they are, one and all, to abandon Moses, telling them to cease circumcising their children and not to conform to the customs handed down to them. [22]How, then, do matters stand? Assuredly, they are bound to hear of your arrival, [23]and, in view of this, you must do as we tell you. We have with us here four men who have bound themselves by a vow. [24]You are to take them with you, join in their purification, and defray all the expenses incurred to enable them to have their heads shaved. Then everybody will know that the information they have received about you is baseless and that you live according to the law. [25]But as for those who have come to the faith as Gentiles, to these we have sent out a letter containing the decision we have come to—that they are to abstain from meat which has been offered in sacrifice to an idol, from eating blood from the flesh of animals killed by strangling, and from committing fornication." [26]At that Paul, after having had himself purified along with the men in question, went into the temple on the following day, giving notice that when [y]**the days of purification would end,** an offering would be presented on behalf of each of them.

[27]However, when the seven days were about to end, the Jews who belonged to the province of Asia, on seeing Paul in the temple, proceeded to throw the whole crowd into confusion. And laying their hands on him, [28]this is what they cried out: "Men of Israel, to the rescue! Here is the man who teaches everyone all over the world in a manner which is hostile to our people, to the law, as well as to this place of worship. And what is more, he has brought Gentiles into the temple and has defiled this holy place." [29]They said this because, on an earlier occasion, they had seen Trophimus the Ephesian with him in the city, thus imagining that it was he whom Paul had introduced into the temple.

[30]The whole city was in an uproar because of this, people coming running from every direction. They got hold of Paul and dragged him out of the temple, the doors being closed immediately after that hap-

[y]Nm 6:9-20

pened. [31] While they did their best to kill him, a report reached the tribune in charge of the Roman cohort to the effect that all Jerusalem was in a tumult. [32] The tribune, acting immediately, took a detachment of soldiers and their centurions with him, and raced towards them. When the people saw the tribune with the soldiers, they desisted from beating Paul. [33] At that the tribune drew near, got hold of Paul, and gave the order that he was to be bound with two chains. He also enquired who he was and what he had done. [34] However, some in the crowd shouted one thing, some another, and since the tribune found it impossible to obtain any reliable information on account of the noise, he gave the order that Paul was to be taken away to the soldiers' quarters. [35] When Paul reached the steps, it fell out that he had to be carried by the soldiers because of the violence of the crowd; [36] for the mob of people followed on closely, shouting, "Put him to death!"

[37] But Paul, just as he was about to be taken into the soldiers' quarters, enquired of the tribune, "May I have a word with you?" the tribune replying, "Do you know Greek? [38] Are you not the Egyptian who, some time ago, raised a revolt and led a force of four thousand cut-throats into the desert?" [39] Paul made him this answer: "I am a Jew, a native of Tarsus in Cilicia, a city by no means insignificant. Permit me to address the people." [40] Permission being given, Paul, standing at the top of the steps, made a motion with his hands to the people. And when all was completely still, he addressed them, in Aramaic,* as follows:

22 "My friends, you who are the fathers of this people, attend to what I am about to say to you now by way of offering my defence." [2] When they heard that he was speaking to them in Aramaic, they became even quieter than they had been before, and he addressed them in these words:

[3] "I am a Jew, born at Tarsus in Cilicia, but trained in this city with the greatest strictness at the feet of Gamaliel, in conformity with the law which has come down to us from our forefathers. I have ever been an enthusiast for God, as you all are to this day. [4] As for this New Way, I turned against it with a deadly persecution, putting both men and women in fetters and throwing them into prison. [5] Indeed, the High Priest and the whole council of elders may serve as my witnesses in this matter, seeing that, while I was on my way to Damascus, I had on me letters from them addressed to our Jewish brothers in that place. Their purpose was to empower me to bring any Christians

---

* [Gk. literally 'in the Hebrew language', but it is likely that Paul addressed them in Aramaic, the language commonly spoken by the Jews in Palestine at that time.]

whom I found there back to Jerusalem in fetters, so that they might
receive their punishment.

⁶"However, this is what happened. I was on that journey, and had
nearly reached Damascus, when suddenly, about midday, a powerful light coming from the sky flashed round me. ⁷I fell to the ground,
and then I heard a voice addressing me in these words: 'Saul, Saul,
why are you persecuting me?' ⁸'Tell me, Lord, who are you?' I replied;
and this is what he said to me: 'I am Jesus of Nazareth, the man whom
you are persecuting.' ⁹(My travelling companions saw the light but
they heard no voice speaking.) ¹⁰'What must I do, Lord?' I asked. And
the Lord replied to me thus: 'Rise up and proceed on your way to
Damascus, and there you will be told of all the tasks which you have
been appointed to perform.' ¹¹However, so great had been the bril-
liance of the light that I was unable to see anything, and so it was that
I had to be taken by the hand of my companions. It was in this way,
then, that I made my way to Damascus.

¹²"Now there was a certain man by the name of Ananias who was
a careful observer of the law and was well spoken of by all the Jewish
inhabitants of Damascus. ¹³He came to me, stood by my side, and said,
'Brother Saul, recover your sight.' I recovered my sight in an instant
and saw him before me. ¹⁴And these are the words which he addressed
to me: 'The God of our forefathers has chosen you for himself, with the
intention that you may know his will, setting your eyes on the
Righteous One and hearing his very voice, ¹⁵because you are to be his
witness before all mankind, testifying to what you have seen and
heard. ¹⁶Why, then, do you hesitate? Rise to your feet, receive your
baptism, and wash yourself clean of your sins, invoking his name.'

¹⁷"At a later time, after my return to Jerusalem, a remarkable thing
happened to me when I was in the temple offering prayer. I fell into
a trance, ¹⁸and then I saw Jesus and heard him address the following words to me: 'Depart from Jerusalem, and do so in haste, seeing
that the people who are there will refuse to accept the testimony you
bear on my behalf.' ¹⁹'Lord,' was my reply, 'these are the very men
who know that I am the one who used to imprison those putting their
faith in you and who had them beaten up in the synagogues.
²⁰Moreover, when they were shedding the blood of Stephen, of the
man who was bearing testimony on your behalf, there I was, standing by and giving my approval, while keeping an eye on the clothes
belonging to those who were putting him to death.' ²¹And this is the
answer he made me: 'Be on your way, because I am sending you far
away, to the Gentiles.'"

²²Until he spoke these words his hearers had been willing to listen
to him. But now they raised their voices and exclaimed, "Rid the earth
of a man like this! He does not deserve to be alive!" ²³However, while

they were screaming like this, throwing down their garments and flinging dust into the air, 24the tribune gave the order that he was to be taken back into the soldiers' quarters. He commanded that Paul was to be made subject to examination by way of having the lash applied to him, so that it might be discovered on what grounds they were thus reviling him. 25However, when they were strapping him down for the lashing, Paul said to the centurion who was standing by watching, "Have you any right to condemn a Roman citizen without a proper trial, and subject him to flogging?" 26The centurion, hearing this, went to the tribune and reported to him in these words: "What are you about? This man is a Roman citizen." 27At that the tribune came along and asked Paul this question: "Is it true that you are a Roman citizen?" "Yes, I am," was Paul's reply. 28"It cost me the outlay of a large sum of money to acquire that citizenship," was the tribune's rejoinder. "I, on the other hand, was born to it," said Paul. 29Upon this, those who were about to subject him to examination withdrew hastily; and the tribune himself was greatly alarmed that this was a Roman citizen, and that he had put him in fetters.

30The next day, since the tribune wanted to know the precise nature of the charge which the Jews were laying against Paul, he had him freed of his fetters and gave the order that the chief priests and the entire council were to assemble. After that he had Paul brought down to them and made him stand up in front of them.

23 And Paul, fixing his gaze upon the Council, said, "Friends and brothers, as regards myself, I have led my life to this very day with a conscience free from guilt, ever having God before my eyes." 2At that the High Priest Ananias gave his attendants the order to strike him on the mouth, 3while Paul retorted with these words: z"God will strike you in return, you, the very image of a wall daubed over to deceive! You are sitting here, supposed to pronounce judgment in conformity with the law, and what you are really doing is breaking the law by ordering your people to strike me!" 4Thereupon the High Priest's attendants exclaimed, "The man whom you are insulting is God's High Priest!" 5Paul's response being this: "I did not know, my brothers, that he was the High Priest. If I had, I should have refrained, for it stands written in scripture, a**Speak no evil of the leader of your people.**'"

6Now Paul knew that one section of those assembled was Sadducees and the other Pharisees, and that is why he raised his voice, crying out in the council chamber, "My friends, my brothers, I myself am a Pharisee and a descendant of Pharisees. The matter concerning

z[Dt 28:22; Ezk 13:10.15]   aEx 22:28

which I am being brought to judgment before the court is the hope I entertain that there will be a resurrection of the dead." ⁷At these words a dispute arose between the Pharisees and the Sadducees, and the assembly became wholly divided. ⁸And that was because the Sadducees will not have it that there is any such thing as a resurrection of the dead, or that angels exist, or that spirits do, whereas the Pharisees accept all these tenets. ⁹So it came about that a great uproar arose between the two parties, some learned doctors of the Pharisaic persuasion defending their position in a truculent manner and saying, "We can find no fault with this man. Suppose he has had a message from a spirit or an angel?" ¹⁰And so when a violent dissension arose between them, the tribune began to fear that Paul might be torn to pieces by them. And that is why he gave the order that the troops were to go down to them, snatch Paul out of their midst, and bring him back to the barracks.

¹¹The following night the Lord appeared by Paul's side, saying, "Pluck up your courage! As you have borne witness in support of my cause in Jerusalem, so you must be my witness in Rome."

¹²When daylight came, some of the Jews entered into a conspiracy, this being accompanied by their invoking a curse upon themselves that, until they had put Paul to death, they would neither eat nor drink. ¹³Those implicated in this plot numbered more than forty. ¹⁴So they went to the chief priests and the elders, saying to them, "We have invoked a solemn oath upon ourselves and have agreed that we are to take no food until we have put Paul to death. ¹⁵Well then, let an application be made to the tribune both by ourselves and the Council, to the effect that he is to bring Paul down to you. And let this serve as your pretext, that you desire to be more accurately informed about his affairs. We, for our part, stand ready to have him put to death before he reaches his destination." ¹⁶However, the son of Paul's sister, on hearing of the ambush which they were laying, went to the place where the barracks were situated, entered it, and reported the matter to Paul. ¹⁷And he, for his part, called one of the centurions to his side, saying, "Take this youth to the tribune, for there is something he has to report to him." ¹⁸At that the centurion took the man and brought him to the tribune, addressing him in these words: "The prisoner Paul called me to his side and requested me to take this young man to you because there is something he has to tell you." ¹⁹Thereupon the tribune took the young man by the hand, drew him aside, and asked him, "What is it you have to tell me?" ²⁰"The Jews," was the youth's reply, "have devised a scheme that they were to put before you the request to bring Paul before the Council, on the pretext that they mean to enquire more accurately into his case. ²¹Do not allow yourself to be persuaded by them; for the truth is that more than forty of them are

lying in wait for him. And these have invoked a curse upon themselves that they would neither eat nor drink again until they had destroyed him. And now they stand ready, waiting only for your promise to fall in with their scheme." [22] At that the tribune dismissed the young man, with the order that he was on no account to tell anyone that he had given him this information.

[23] Next he summoned two of his centurions, saying to them, "Hold two hundred soldiers in readiness to set out for Caesarea by nine o'clock tonight, together with seventy cavalry and two hundred light troops. [24] Moreover, provide horses so that Paul may be mounted and taken safely to Felix the Governor." [25] He also wrote a letter to Felix in these terms: [26] 'Claudius Lysias sends his greetings to His Excellency, Governor Felix. [27] This man was seized by the Jews and was on the point of being murdered by them when I with my troops intervened and got him away, having learned that he was a Roman citizen. [28] Moreover, since I desired to ascertain on what grounds they were accusing him, I took him down to the place where the Council was meeting. [29] However, I found that the accusation was concerned with disputed points of their law, and that he was not charged with any crime punishable by death or imprisonment. [30] Moreover, I received information that a conspiracy against the man was afoot; that is why I immediately proceeded to send him to you, at the same time instructing his accusers to bring their charges against him in your presence.'

[31] The soldiers took Paul, in conformity with the orders which they had been given, and escorted him by night to Antipatris. [32] The next day they took leave of the horsemen who were to go with him, and they themselves returned to quarters. [33] When they arrived at Caesarea, the horsemen handed the letter over to the Governor, at the same time presenting Paul to him. [34] The Governor, having read the letter, enquired what province Paul came from. And on hearing that it was Cilicia, he said, [35] "I shall hear your case as soon as your accusers have arrived." He then gave the order that he was to be kept in custody at Herod's palace.

24 Five days later the High Priest Ananias came down, accompanied by some of the elders and a certain orator called Tertullus; and it was these men who made a deposition against Paul before the governor. [2] When Paul was called in, Tertullus opened the case for the prosecution in these words: "A state of profound peace having become ours to enjoy under your rule, through the reforms which your foresight has brought to this people, [3] we have, most noble Felix, come to acknowledge all this in every way, and wherever we may be, with hearts truly grateful. [4] Nothing could be further from my purpose than

to detain you for an unduly long time. Still, I would beg of you to listen to us with your customary graciousness as we are briefly stating our case. [5]We have found this man a most pestilential fellow. It is he who has sown discord among the Jews all over the world, being as he is the ringleader of the sect of the Nazarenes. [6]Besides, he made the attempt to desecrate the temple, and it was in these circumstances that we arrested him,* [8]while, as regards yourself, you will be in a position, simply by questioning him, to ascertain from him the truth of all the charges we are making against him." [9]The Jews gave their full support to the indictment, insisting that the facts were as stated.

[10]And now, in response to a signal from the Governor, Paul made his reply in the following terms: "Knowing as I do that for many a year you have been performing the function of a judge on behalf of this people, my defence concerning my affairs is being offered with a confident heart. [11]The facts of the case are easily ascertained. It was no more than twelve days ago that I went up to Jerusalem to worship. [12]Yet no one found me engaged in conversation with others when I was in the temple; nor was I discovered in an attempt to stir up a crowd, my conduct in the synagogue and in the city being in no way different from this. [13]Thus my accusers are not in a position to make good the charges which they are now bringing against me. [14]But this I freely admit to you, that in worshipping the God of our forefathers I am a follower of the New Way (they refer to it as a sect). At the same time I retain my belief in whatever is laid down by the law and in everything that is set down in the prophetic books, [15]while entertaining a hope with regard to God—a hope shared by these men—that there is to be a resurrection from the dead for good and bad alike. [16]And it is in consideration of all this that I myself am ever doing my best to have at all times a conscience free from guilt before God and before men.

[17]"After an interval of several years I returned to bring charitable gifts to my nation and to offer sacrifices; [18]and I was engaged in this task of offering sacrifices in the temple, having purified myself ceremonially, when they came upon me. There was no crowd, neither was there any uproar; only certain Jews from Asia were with me. [19]These are the men who ought to be present here before you if they have anything to charge me with. [20]Since they are not here, let those who are declare what offence they found me guilty of when I was confronting the Council—[21]except this, that when I was in their midst I burst out exclaiming, 'If this day I am being brought to judgment before you, that is because of the view I take of the resurrection of the dead.'"

---

* Vv. 6b-8 are probably not part of the original text.

²²Upon this, Felix, who had a fair knowledge of the New Way, adjourned the hearing, after having made this remark: "As soon as Lysias, the military tribune, has come down here, I shall pronounce my decision in your case." ²³He then gave the centurion the order that Paul was to be kept in custody, but that he should enjoy freedom from restrictions, and that none of his friends should be prevented from looking after his needs.

²⁴A few days later Felix came, along with his wife Drusilla, who was a Jewess, and, sending for Paul, listened to what he had to say on the subject of faith in Christ Jesus. ²⁵However, when the discourse turned to questions of upright conduct, of self-control, and of the judgment to come, Felix became alarmed and said, "Leave my company for the time being. I shall send for you again when opportunity arises." ²⁶He was at the same time entertaining the hope that Paul would give him money, this being the reason why he frequently summoned him and engaged in conversation with him. ²⁷So two years passed, and after that Felix was succeeded by Porcius Festus; and Felix, who wished to curry favour with the Jews, left Paul behind as a prisoner.

25 When Festus set foot in the province, he let three days pass, and then went up from Caesarea to Jerusalem, ²where the chief priests and the Jewish leaders brought formal charges against Paul. Moreover, they made the request ³(contrary to the interests of Paul but as a special favour for them) that they should summon Paul to Jerusalem, their scheme being to lay an ambush and have Paul put to death on the way. ⁴Festus, however, replied, "Paul is being kept in custody at Caesarea and I myself shall be leaving Jerusalem in the near future. ⁵So let those among you who occupy a leading position come down with me to Caesarea; and if it be found that there is something untoward about the man, they can prefer their charges there." ⁶After staying with them for a week, or ten days at the most, he went down to Caesarea; and the next day he took his seat on the judicial bench, giving the order that Paul was to be brought in.

⁷As soon as Paul appeared, the Jews from Jerusalem formed a ring round him and brought many serious charges against him. However, they were unable to substantiate these, ⁸Paul making his defence in the following terms: "I have not committed any offence either against the Jewish law, or against the temple, or against the Emperor." ⁹Festus, however, wishing to ingratiate himself with the Jews, turned to Paul and asked, "Are you prepared to go up to Jerusalem, standing your trial there in my presence on these charges which are being brought against you?" ¹⁰But Paul made this reply to him: "I am stand-

ing before the Emperor's judgment-seat, and this is the place where I must be tried. Against the Jews I have committed no offence at all, as you yourself know well enough. [11]If, on the other hand, I am guilty of any capital offence, I do not ask to escape the death penalty. But as there is no substance whatever in any of these accusations brought against me, it is impossible that anyone should have the right to surrender me as a favour to my adversaries. I appeal to the Emperor!" [12]Upon this, Festus conferred with his advisers, and then made Paul the following reply: "You have appealed to the Emperor, and to the Emperor you shall go!"

[13]After a few days' interval, King Agrippa and Bernice made their appearance at Caesarea to pay a courtesy visit to Festus. [14]They spent several days in the place, and so it came about that Festus embarked on giving an account of Paul's case to the king. "There is a certain man here," he said, "a prisoner left behind by Felix, [15]and when I was in Jerusalem the chief priests and those among the Jews who held the position of elders asked for a sentence of condemnation against him. [16]I made them this reply: 'Romans are not in the habit of surrendering any man until the defendant has been brought face to face with his accusers and has had the opportunity of clearing himself of the charge which has been preferred against him.' [17]So, at a later stage, when his opponents joined me here, I acted without the least delay. I took my place on the judicial bench the very next morning, giving the order that the man was to be brought before the court. [18]However, when his accusers rose up to state their case, they did not charge him with any misdemeanour, as I had expected they would; [19]instead of this, they argued with him about a number of controversial issues relating to their peculiar religion and about a certain dead man called Jesus, whom Paul declared to be alive. [20]Since I myself was completely at a loss how matters such as these were to be investigated, I asked Paul whether he was willing to go to Jerusalem, to stand trial there on these issues. [21]Paul, however, resorted to bringing forward an appeal, to the effect that he was to be kept in custody and that his case was to be reserved for His August Majesty's decision. And in consideration of this, I gave the order that he was to be detained until I could send him to the Emperor." [22]At that Agrippa said to Festus, "I should like to hear the man myself." "Tomorrow you shall," was Festus' reply.

[23]And so it came about that on the following day Agrippa and Bernice made their appearance with great pomp, entering the auditorium attended by the tribunes and the city notables. Then, on Festus' giving the order, Paul was brought in. [24]Thereupon Festus spoke these words: "King Agrippa, and all of you who are here present with us, you see before you the man concerning whom the whole Jewish community approached me, both in Jerusalem and here, crying out that

he no longer had the right to live. ²⁵Yet my own impression was that he had committed no offence deserving the death penalty; and, seeing that he himself had made an appeal to His August Majesty, I decided to send him off to Rome. ²⁶On the other hand, I have nothing I can write to our sovereign about him. And this is why I have brought him before you all, and more particularly before you, King Agrippa, so that, a preliminary hearing having taken place, I may have something to report. ²⁷For it seems to me wholly unreasonable that, when sending a prisoner, one should do so without any indication of the charge to be brought against him."

26 "You are permitted," Agrippa said to Paul, "to speak on your own behalf." Upon this, Paul stretched out his hand and began his defence:

²"As I set out, King Agrippa, to make my answer to all the charges brought against me by the Jews, I consider myself most fortunate that the man in whose presence I am about to make my defence today should be yourself, ³particularly since you are an expert in all matters Jewish, both our customs and our controversies. I therefore beg you to be patient and hear me out.

⁴"My manner of life from my youth up, the life which from the very beginning I led among my own people in Jerusalem, is common knowledge among the Jews. ⁵They, having known me for a long time, could easily testify, if they only would, that I lived in conformity with what is laid down by the strictest sect of our religion. In other words, I lived as a Pharisee. ⁶Moreover, if I am here on trial, it is by reason of the hope which I entertain that God will make good the promise he made to our forefathers, ⁷the very promise our twelve tribes hope to see fulfilled, as they are offering their service to God, with the greatest fervour, by day and by night. The matter stands like this then, your gracious majesty, that it is because of my entertaining the hope of which I have spoken that I am being called to account by the Jews. ⁸Why should that be so? Do you really consider it a thing past belief that God should raise the dead to life?

⁹"As for myself, there was a time when I became convinced in my own mind that it was my bounden duty to do many things in opposition to the very name of Jesus of Nazareth. ¹⁰And this is how I acted during my stay in Jerusalem. Many of those dedicated to God were thrown into prison by me—this being done on the authority of the chief priests—and when the question was whether they were to be sentenced to death, I cast my vote against them. ¹¹Moreover, in synagogue after synagogue I took frequent occasion to subject them to punishment and to force them into uttering blasphemies. And so

great was my fury against them that I even pursued them into foreign cities.

12 "On one such occasion I was travelling to Damascus, authorized and commissioned by the chief priests, 13 when, your gracious majesty, in the middle of the day, as I was proceeding on my way, a light more brilliant than the light of the sun made its appearance from the sky. And that light shone all around me and my travelling companions. 14 We all fell to the ground and then I heard a voice saying to me in the Hebrew language, 'Saul, Saul, why are you persecuting me? It is hard for you, kicking against the goad like this.' 15 'Who are you, Lord?' I asked; and the Lord said, 'I am Jesus, the man whom you are persecuting. 16 Enough of this: *b*rise up and stand on your feet.** For if I have appeared to you, that was for the purpose of appointing you as my servant and my witness, that you might testify to what you have seen of me and to what you shall yet see in the future. 17 *c*I shall bring you deliverance** from this people and **from the Gentiles to whom I am sending you,** 18 that you may *d*open their eyes,** and make them turn **from darkness to light,** from the dominion of Satan to God, so that, because of their trust in me, they may be granted forgiveness of their sins and receive a place by the side of those whose lives have been consecrated to God.'

19 "In view of all this, King Agrippa, I had to be obedient to what I had been told by the vision from heaven which I had seen. 20 I addressed myself first of all to the people of Damascus, and later to the inhabitants of Jerusalem, and indeed, to all those living in the Judaean countryside, making proclamation to them as well as to the Gentiles that they were to repent, that they were to turn to God, and that their deeds were to be such as to be in keeping with a state of repentance. 21 This is why the Jews apprehended me in the temple and sought to make an end of me. 22 However, I have God by my side to succour me, and so it is that, to this day, I stand upright, testifying to great and small alike. At the same time my assertions do not in any way go beyond what the prophets and Moses had foretold, 23 namely, that God's anointed one was bound to undergo suffering, and that he, being the first to rise from the dead, was destined to proclaim a light-bringing message to both the Jewish people and to the Gentiles."

24 When Paul had come to this point in making his defence, Festus cried out in a loud voice, "Paul, you are mad; that great learning of yours is driving you into madness!" 25 "I am by no means mad, most noble Festus," said Paul. "On the contrary, I am speaking nothing but the sober truth. 26 The king understands about these things, and that is why I am addressing myself to him, speaking out boldly. Indeed, I

*b*Ezk 2:1   *c*Jr 1:7   *d*Is 35:5; 42:7.16

am convinced that the king cannot but be aware of these things, since it is not in some remote corner that they have been done. ²⁷Do you have faith in the prophets, King Agrippa? I know that you have." ²⁸"But a short time will pass," was Agrippa's reply to Paul, "and you will be setting yourself the task of persuading me to turn Christian." ²⁹"Be it short, be it long," replied Paul, "my prayer to God is that not only you but also all those who have been listening to me today should become what I am—with the sole exception of these chains."

³⁰The king then rose, and the Governor with him, as well as Bernice and the rest of the company. ³¹After they had left the auditorium they spoke these words, on having discussed the matter with one another: "This man has done nothing deserving of death or of a prison sentence." ³²As for Agrippa, the words he addressed to Festus were these: "It would be permissible to set this man free but for the fact that he has appealed to the Emperor."

27 Once the decision had been made that we were to go to Italy by sea, Paul, with a few other prisoners, was handed over to a centurion called Julius, who belonged to the Augustan cohort. ²We boarded a vessel from Adramyttium which was about to sail for certain places on the coast of the province of Asia, and put out to sea, one of our party being Aristarchus, a Macedonian from Thessalonica. ³The next day we put in at Sidon, Julius treating Paul with great kindness and giving him permission to see his friends and let them take care of him. ⁴When we left Sidon and set sail again, we were forced by contrary winds to coast under the lee of Cyprus. ⁵After that we made a straight course across the open sea which lies off the coast of Cilicia and Pamphylia until we arrived at Myra in Lycia.

⁶There the centurion found a ship hailing from Alexandria which was bound for Italy, and he put us aboard her. ⁷For a good many days we made but little headway, and it was with considerable difficulty that we made Cnidus; and then, with the wind not letting us proceed any further, we sailed under the lee of Crete, off Cape Salmone. ⁸We then struggled along the coast until we reached a place called Fair Havens, which lies near the city of Lasea.

⁹But now, a great deal of time having already gone by, and navigation being hazardous because it was well after the time of the fast, Paul gave them this warning: ¹⁰"Friends, I foresee that our voyage will meet with disaster and that we run the risk of losing not only the cargo and the vessel but our lives as well." ¹¹The centurion, however, paid more attention to the steersman and the captain of the ship than to the advice which Paul had given. ¹²The harbour was unsuitable for wintering, and the majority were in favour of putting out to sea from

there, in the hope of succeeding in wintering at Phoenix, a Cretan harbour facing northeast and southeast. 13So, when a gentle southerly wind sprang up, they thought their purpose as good as accomplished, and coasted along Crete, hugging the land. 14However, before long, a hurricane, the 'Northeaster' as they call it, burst upon them from across the island. 15The ship was caught in it, and since we found it impossible to turn her head-on to the wind, we had to give way and let ourselves be driven. 16We ran under the lee of a small island called Clauda, and managed, with considerable difficulty, to get the ship's boat under control. 17They hoisted it aboard, made use of tackle, and undergirded the ship. After that, because they were afraid they would be driven on to the shallows of Syrtis, they lowered the sea anchor and let themselves drift. 18The next day, as we were making very heavy weather, they began to jettison the cargo; 19and on the third day they threw the ship's gear overboard with their own hands. 20Since both the sun and the stars remained invisible for days on end and the storm raged unabated, all the hope we had had that we might be saved was finally abandoned.

21Then, when they had gone without food for a long time, Paul, standing up among them, addressed them as follows: "My good friends, you ought to have followed my advice and not to have sailed from Crete, thus sparing yourselves such a disaster and incurring so heavy a loss. 22Still, even as things are, my suggestion to you is to keep up your courage. For there is not one of you who will lose his life; the only loss you will suffer is that of the ship. 23I know that this will be so. For last night I saw an angel standing by my side, sent by the God to whom I belong and whose servant I am. 24And this is what he said to me: 'Have no fear, Paul; you are destined to stand in the Emperor's presence. Moreover—attend to my words—God has made certain (as a gracious favour to you) of the safety of all your fellow voyagers.' 25Be of good courage, then, my friends. I have full confidence in God, and I am convinced that things will turn out as I was told they would. 26What is bound to happen is that we shall be cast ashore on some island."

27The fourteenth night came, and we were still drifting helplessly in the Sea of Adria. However, about midnight the sailors began to suspect that they were approaching land. 28So they took soundings and made it twenty fathoms; and after a brief interval they took soundings again and made it fifteen fathoms. 29Afraid, therefore, that we might run aground on some rocky spot or other, the sailors dropped four anchors from the stern, while being filled with a longing that daylight might come. 30The next thing they did was try to abandon ship. They had already lowered the ship's boat into the sea, under the pretext of meaning to lay out anchors from the bows, 31when Paul said to the centurion and to the soldiers, "Unless these men stay on board there is no possibility of your being saved." [32] At that the soldiers cut the ropes which secured the boat and let it drop down.

[33] Just when day was about to dawn, Paul urged them all to partake of some food. "This is the fourteenth day," he said, "that you have been under severe strain, while at the same time going hungry. In fact, you have taken no food whatsoever. [34] So I would beg of you to take some nourishment, for this is essential to your safety. And keep this in mind, that not one of you will be losing a hair of his head." [35] Having spoken these words, he took some bread into his hands, gave thanks to God in front of them all, then broke the bread and began to eat. [36] Upon this, they all found themselves encouraged, and partook of nourishment. [37] (There were two hundred and seventy-six of us, all told, on board ship.) [38] When they had had their fill, they lightened the ship by throwing the corn overboard into the sea.

[39] When daylight came and they could see land, they did not recognize it. However, they were in a position to make out that there was a kind of bay there with a sandy beach; and their plan was, if possible, to run the ship on that beach. [40] So they cut the anchors free, leaving them in the sea. At the same time they loosened the ropes which secured the steering rudders, and setting the foresail to the wind, they headed for the beach. [41] However, they found themselves caught between cross-currents, and so came upon a spot that had water on both sides. It was there that they let the ship run aground, the forepart becoming fixed and immovable, while the stern began to break up with the pounding of the waves. [42] Upon this, the soldiers came to the decision that the prisoners were to be killed, fearing that they might swim ashore and make good their escape. [43] The centurion, however, who was determined to bring Paul safely through, frustrated their plan, giving the order that those who could swim should jump overboard first and so reach the shore, [44] while the rest should follow, making use of planks or other pieces from the ship. In this way, then, it came about that they all reached the land safe and sound.

28 Having thus been brought back to safety, we subsequently learned that the name of the island was Malta. [2] Its inhabitants, uncultured as they were, showed a concern and care for us which was quite out of the ordinary. To take an instance, because heavy rain had begun to fall and on account of the cold, they kindled a huge fire and made us all welcome to it. [3] As for Paul, he had collected a large number of sticks which were dry and was engaged in placing them on the fire when a snake, brought out by the heat, fastened on his hand. [4] The natives, on seeing the creature hanging from his hand, exclaimed, "As-

suredly, this man is a murderer. He has been rescued from the sea, but the goddess of justice would not let him live."

⁵Paul, however, shook the creature off into the fire, there being no sign that he had suffered any harm. ⁶The others still expected that he would swell up, or else drop dead suddenly, but after waiting for a long time without anything out-of-the-way happening to him, they came to a different opinion and now declared that he must be a god.

⁷Among the estates in the neighbourhood of this spot was one which belonged to the leading citizen of the island. His name was Publius. He took us into his house for three days and treated us in the kindest manner possible.

⁸Now it so happened that Publius' father had to take to his bed because he was suffering from feverish attacks and dysentery. Paul visited him and said a prayer over him. Having laid his hands upon the man, he brought him healing; ⁹whereupon the other people who were victims of disease approached Paul, and he brought them healing as well. ¹⁰It was these men who heaped honours upon us and who, when we were leaving, furnished us with everything we needed.

¹¹Three months having gone by, we put out to sea again. The vessel we used was one from Alexandria which had been wintering in the island and which had the Heavenly Twins for its figurehead. ¹²We put in at Syracuse, spending three days there; ¹³and when we left, we made a circuit, finally arriving at Rhegium. A south wind springing up on the second day out, we made Puteoli ¹⁴where we came upon a number of fellow believers, who invited us to stay with them for a week. This is the story of our journey to Rome. ¹⁵But before we actually arrived, the fellow believers from Rome, who had heard about us and our affairs, came out as far as the Forum of Appius and the Three Taverns to bid us welcome. When Paul saw them, he expressed his gratitude to God and found himself greatly encouraged.

¹⁶When we entered Rome, Paul was given permission to stay in lodgings of his own, together with the soldier who guarded him. ¹⁷After three days he called a meeting of the leading Jews of Rome; and when they had assembled, he addressed them in the following terms: "My friends and my brothers, I have at no time done anything which was in any way hostile to our nation or to the customs passed on to us by our forefathers. Nevertheless, here I am, a prisoner from Jerusalem who was arrested there and handed over to the Romans. ¹⁸They, for their part, were ready to release me, after they had examined the matter, because there was no offence in my case which would justify a sentence of death. ¹⁹But the Jews opposed this course, and so I was compelled to appeal to the Emperor. However, it is not as though I had any accusation to bring against my own people. ²⁰And this is the reason why I have called you together and why I desired

the opportunity of seeing you and talking to you. For the truth is that, if I am wearing this chain, that is precisely on account of my sharing the hope which is entertained by the nation of Israel."

21 They answered thus: "We have had no communication from Judaea; nor has any countryman of ours arrived here with a direct report or a rumour which might bring discredit on you. 22 Still, we should like to have your own account of the opinions you hold. For as regards the sect in question, all that we know about it is that it is decried everywhere."

23 They arranged the time for a meeting, and on the day in question the greater number of the Jews came to see him in his lodging. He expounded to them the significance of the kingdom of God, bearing witness on its behalf. Moreover, he sought to carry conviction about Jesus, basing his arguments on what is said in the law of Moses and on the utterance of the prophets. All this went on from morning to nightfall, 24 with the result that some of them were won over by what they were told, while others refused to give their assent. 25 And so, being at variance with one another, they took their leave, but not before Paul had addressed them in these words:

"How aptly did the Holy Spirit speak when, through the prophet Isaiah, he made this utterance to your forefathers: 26 *e'***Go to these people and say to them, "You will hear with your ears, but understand you never will. You will look and look, but never will you see anything. 27 For the minds of these people have become gross, their ears are hard of hearing, and their eyes they have closed. And all this they have done to make sure that they would see nothing with their eyes, and understand nothing with their minds, and that they might not return to me, and I become their healer."'** 28 Be it known to you, therefore, that this message of *f***salvation** has been sent by **God to the Gentiles.** It is they who will listen to it."*

30 Paul remained where he was for two full years, doing so in his own rented lodgings. And, giving a welcome to anyone who would come to him, 31 he taught the truth about the Lord Jesus Christ with complete openness, without let or hindrance.

---

*e*Is 6:9f   *f*Ps 67:2; 98:3

* V. 29 is probably not part of the original text.

The Letters of St. Paul

PAUL'S LETTER TO
THE CHURCH IN ROME

1 Paul, a servant of Christ Jesus, called to be an apostle, set apart to proclaim God's gospel, ²which was promised by God beforehand in the sacred scriptures through the mouth of his prophets, ³the gospel concerning his Son, descended, in respect of his human birth, from the line of David, ⁴yet, in virtue of the holiness of spirit which was his, shown forth to be—and that in a powerful manner—the Son of God by his resurrection from the dead: Jesus Christ our Lord. ⁵It is through him that the office of the apostleship has been graciously bestowed upon me, in order that everywhere among the Gentiles people might be won over to render obedience to the faith to the honour of his name. ⁶And you are among these, you who have received the call to belong to Jesus Christ. ⁷To all God's beloved who are in Rome, to the consecrated ones to whom the call has come: Grace be yours and peace from God our Father and the Lord Jesus Christ.

⁸First of all, I offer, through Jesus Christ, thanks to my God for all of you, because your faith is renowned all over the world. ⁹Indeed, God is my witness—he to whom I render spiritual service by preaching the gospel of his Son—that I make mention of you unceasingly, ¹⁰never failing to entreat him in my prayers that somehow I may, by God's will, be granted the opportunity of visiting you. ¹¹For I am longing to see you, so as to impart to you some spiritual gift, that you may find yourselves strengthened; ¹²in other words, that when I am with you we may receive mutual encouragement by one another's faith, yours and mine. ¹³Moreover, my brothers, I want you to know that I have often intended to visit you (although hitherto I have always been prevented), so that I might gather some harvest among you also, as I have already done among the rest of the Gentiles. ¹⁴I have the same duty to all, Greek or barbarian, learned or untutored. ¹⁵And so there is every readiness, as far as I am concerned, to preach the gospel also to you who are in Rome. ¹⁶And indeed, I am not ashamed of the gospel: it is the power displayed by God for the salvation of everyone

who has faith, Jew first and then Greek. [17] And in this gospel there is revealed the righteousness which has God for its source, the righteousness that springs from faith and leads to faith. As it stands written in scripture, [a]**'The righteous man shall gain life by his faith.'**

[18] For this is how things stand. God's anger is being revealed from heaven against every kind of impiety and iniquity found in the men who, abiding by their iniquity, hold the truth in check. [19] Indeed, what can be known about God lies plainly before their eyes, God himself having made it plain to them. [20] Ever since the foundation of the world his invisible attributes, his eternal power and divine nature, have been perfectly evident from the things he has created, as we let our thoughts dwell on them. And so it is that these men are without excuse, [21] since, although they had come to know God, they did not honour him as God or give thanks to him, but instead became futile in their reasonings, their senseless minds being filled with darkness. [22] Claiming to be wise, they turned fools [23] and [b]**exchanged the glory** of the imperishable God **for images** made in the likeness of mortal men, birds, quadrupeds, and reptiles.

[24] That is why God gave them over to viciousness, in accordance with the lustful cravings of their hearts, to the dishonouring of their bodies among themselves. [25] They were the men who had exchanged God's truth for a lie, and who had come to reverence and worship the creature in preference to the Creator—he who is blessed for ever, Amen. [26] And so it was that God gave them over to passions by which they brought dishonour upon themselves. Their women exchanged natural intercourse for unnatural; [27] and the men, for their part, giving up natural intercourse with women, were consumed by desire for one another, men committing vileness with men, and receiving in their own person the recompense which they deserved for their perverted ways. [28] And just as they scorned to hold on to the knowledge of God, God gave them over to a mind worthy of all scorn, so that they did the things which are wholly contrary to what is right. [29] They were filled with all manner of wickedness, with mischief, greed, and malice. They were full of envy, murderous designs, strife, guile, and spite. They were backbiters [30] and slanderers; haters of God, insolent, haughty, and boastful; inventive in wickedness, disobedient to parents; [31] without sense, without loyalty, without affection, without pity. [32] These are the men who, although knowing full well God's decree that those practising such things deserve to die, not only do them but express their hearty approval of those who practise them.

[a]Hab 2:4   [b]Ps 106:20; Jr 2:11

2 You are without excuse, therefore, whoever you are, you the man who sits in judgment. For in passing judgment on another you condemn yourself, seeing that you, who pass judgment, do the very same things. ²Now we do indeed know that God's judgment falls unerringly on those who do such things. ³Is what you are counting on, then, that you will escape God's judgment, you the man who passes judgment on those who do such things, while doing them himself? ⁴Or is it that you think slightingly of God's abundant kindness, forbearance and patience, and are unaware that God's kindness is meant to lead you to repentance? ⁵The truth is that by your callousness and your impenitent heart you are storing up for yourself anger on the day of anger, when the righteousness of God's judgment will stand revealed. **⁶ᶜHe will repay each man according to what he deserves for what he has done.** ⁷To those who by perseverance in well-doing strive to obtain glory, honour, and immortality, he will award eternal life, ⁸while it is anger and indignation which will be dealt out to those who are given to factiousness, who are disobedient to the truth and who take wrong for their guide. ⁹Tribulation and distress will come upon every human soul that does evil, upon the Jew first, and then upon the Greek; ¹⁰whereas there will be glory, honour, and peace for everyone who does what is good, for the Jew in the first instance, and then for the Greek. ¹¹There are no human preferences with God.

¹²For this is how things stand: all who have sinned, and who are not within the compass of the law, will perish outside its orbit; whereas all who have sinned, with the law to guide them, will be judged by the law. ¹³It is not those who merely listen to what the law says who are righteous in God's sight. It is those who are doers of what the law enjoins who will be accepted as righteous by him. ¹⁴The truth is that, when the Gentiles, who have no law, do by nature what the law requires, they are, even though they have no law, in themselves a source of law. ¹⁵And what they give proof of is that the kind of conduct demanded by the law is something inscribed on their hearts, and this is borne witness to by their conscience as well as by the reasonings to which they have recourse in their dealings with one another, with a view either to condemning or else to maintaining innocence. ¹⁶And this will be the issue on the day on which, as declared by the gospel which I preach, God will, through Christ Jesus, pass judgment on the hidden thoughts of men.

¹⁷But if you bear the name of a Jew, and rely on the law, and make your boast in God, ¹⁸and know his will, and can discern the things which really matter, being instructed by the law; ¹⁹if you are confi-

ᶜPs 62:12; Pr 24:12

dent that you are a guide to the blind, a light to those who are in darkness, [20]a corrector of the foolish, a teacher of the untutored, because in the law you have the embodiment of knowledge and of truth— [21]you, then, who teach others, do you not teach yourself? You who preach against stealing, do you steal? [22]You who say there is to be no adultery, do you commit adultery? You who abhor idols, do you rob temples? [23]You who make your boast in the law, do you dishonour God by breaking the law? [24]And indeed, what is set down in scripture comes here to mind: [d]'**The name of God is blasphemed among the Gentiles because of you.**'

[25]Circumcision, to be sure, is of value if you practise what the law prescribes; but if you break the law, then your circumcision is as if it had never been. [26]In the same way, then, if a man who is not circumcised keeps the ordinances of the law, will he not be counted as circumcised, though in fact he is not; [27]and will not the man who is not physically circumcised, but who nevertheless carries out what the law demands, bring condemnation upon you who, with your written code and your circumcision, are yet a lawbreaker? [28]To be a Jew is not to be a Jew outwardly; to be circumcised is not to be circumcised outwardly, with a mark made in the flesh. [29]He is a Jew who is one inwardly. And true [e]**circumcision** is a matter **of the heart**—spiritual, not literal. And the praise such a one receives does not come from men; it comes from God.

3   What, then, is the privilege the Jew has? And what advantage is there in circumcision? [2]It is great in every way. There is first of all the fact that the Jews have had God's revelation entrusted to them. [3]And what if some among them proved unfaithful? Shall their unfaithfulness bring God's faithfulness to nought? [4]Far be the thought! Let God be seen to be true even though [f]**every man** should prove **false**. As it stands written in scripture, [g]'**that you may be shown to be in the right in everything you say and that, if any charge be brought against you, you may win a verdict wholly in your favour.**'

[5]But what shall we say if it be found that our failure to deal justly exhibits God's justice the more clearly? That God is unjust when he inflicts punishment? (I put the matter in human terms.) [6]Far be the thought! For in that case how is God to be judge of the world?

[7]Or again, if my falsehood has had the effect of showing forth God's truthfulness in all its abundance, thus bringing him further glory, why is it that I am still being condemned as a sinner? [8]And why should not our watchword be—and so they slanderously mis-

[d]Is 52:5; Ezk 36:20   [e]Dt 30:6; Jr 4:4   [f]Ps 116:11   [g]Ps 51:4

represent us, and there are certain people who maintain that we actually *do* say this—'Let us do evil that good may come'? The condemnation of those who argue thus is only what they deserve.

⁹How then do matters stand? Are we Jews any better off? No, not at all! Indeed, we have already charged everyone, Jews and Gentiles alike, with being in the bondage of sin. ¹⁰As it stands written in scripture,

> *ʰ*'**None is righteous: not one.**
> ¹¹ **No one understands; no one searches for God.**
> ¹² **All have turned aside; all have become unprofitable. There is no one who does what is good—no, not so much as one.**
> ¹³ *ⁱ***Their throat is an open grave;**
> **with their tongues they have wrought deceit.**
> *ʲ***The venom of vipers is on their lips.**
> ¹⁴ *ᵏ***Their mouths are full of cursing and bitter words.**
> ¹⁵ *ˡ***They are swift on their feet to shed blood.**
> ¹⁶ *ᵐ***Ruin and misery mark their paths,**
> ¹⁷ **and the way of peace they do not know.**
> ¹⁸ *ⁿ***Reverence for God is something to which they shut their eyes.**'

¹⁹Now we know that all the words of the law are addressed to those who are the law's immediate subjects, so that everyone should be deprived of the power of opening his mouth by way of justifying himself, and that the whole world may own itself liable to God's judgment. ²⁰For the truth is that *ᵒ***no** human being **will be accepted as righteous in God's sight** by virtue of works performed in obedience to the law. What the law does is give us clear knowledge of sin.

²¹But now there has been shown forth the righteousness which has its source in God, the righteousness which stands apart from the law, while both the law and the prophets bear witness to it— ²²God's righteousness which comes through faith in Jesus Christ and extends, without exception, to all who have faith. No distinctions are made, ²³seeing that all have sinned and have fallen short of what was demanded of them by God in his glory. ²⁴And if they are accepted as righteous, that is by virtue of his grace bestowed as a free gift, through the redemption to be found in Christ Jesus. ²⁵It was he whom God put forward as being, by virtue of his sacrificial death, a means of expiation, faith being the instrument for accomplishing this. God's righteousness was to be shown forth, seeing that there had been, in virtue of the divine forbearance, a passing over of the sins previously com-

---

*ʰ*Ps 14:1-3; 53:2-4   *ⁱ*Ps 5:9   *ʲ*Ps 140:3   *ᵏ*Ps 10:7   *ˡ*Pr 1:16   *ᵐ*Is 59:7f   *ⁿ*Ps 36:1
*ᵒ*Ps 143:2

mitted. 26 And it was to be shown forth likewise at the present time, so that it might be seen that he himself is righteous and the giver of righteousness to those who take their stand on faith in Jesus.

27 What room, then, is there left for any boasting? It is shut out once and for all. On what principle? On one basing itself on works performed? No, on the principle of faith. 28 For our contention is that it is by reason of faith that a human being is accepted as righteous, apart from works done in obedience to law. 29 Besides, is God the God of the Jews only? Is he not the God of the Gentiles too? Of the Gentiles, too, assuredly. 30 Indeed, there is only one God, who will accept as righteous the circumcised man on the ground of faith and the one who is not circumcised by reason of the same faith. 31 Is it, then, that through this faith we do away with the law? Far be the thought! On the contrary, we give the law a surer footing.

4   What then shall we say about Abraham, our forefather by natural descent? 2 If it was by reason of works which Abraham performed that he was accepted as righteous, then, it is true, he has something to boast of. But he has no such ground before God; 3 for what does scripture say? *P'Abraham put his faith in God, and this was reckoned to him as righteousness.'* 4 Now the reward given to one who works to earn it is not reckoned as a favour but as his due; 5 while when a man, instead of taking his stand on works which he has performed, puts his faith in him who accepts sinners as righteous, he has his faith reckoned to him as righteousness. 6 So also David pronounces his blessing upon the man who has righteousness reckoned to him by God, apart from any works he has performed. 7 *q'A blessing rests on those whose iniquities have been forgiven and whose sins have been covered over; 8a blessing rests on the man against whom the Lord will not reckon his sin.'* 9 Is this blessing pronounced upon the circumcised only, or also upon the uncircumcised? It was *r'*faith—so we affirm—**which was reckoned to Abraham as righteousness.** 10 In what circumstances, then, was it so reckoned? Was it after he had been circumcised, or before? It was not after he had been circumcised, but before he was. 11 *s***Circumcision** he received as a token, **as a sign** of that righteousness grounded in faith which was his when he was still **uncircumcised.** He was to be the father of all those who, although uncircumcised, yet have faith, so as to have righteousness reckoned to them. 12 And he was to be the father of the circumcised, those, that is, who are not circumcised merely but also walk in the footsteps of that faith which our father Abraham had when he was as yet uncircumcised.

*P*Gn 15:6   *q*Ps 32:1f   *r*Gn 15:6   *s*Gn 17:10f

13The promise to Abraham and his descendants that they would inherit the world did not come through law, but by virtue of his righteousness grounded in his faith. 14If the heirs are those who place reliance upon the law, then faith has been made void and the promise has been set aside. 15The effect of the law is only that it brings God's anger upon us, while, where there is no law, there is no transgression. 16This, then, is the reason why the inheritance was made to rest on faith, that it might come by virtue of grace, the promise being made sure to the whole of Abraham's posterity, not only to those who hold by the law but also to those who take their stand on Abraham's faith: it is he who is the father of us all. 17As scripture says, *t*'**I have made you the father of many nations.**' And indeed, he is our father in the eyes of God in whom he put his trust, who can raise the dead to life and sends out his call to that which has no being as though it already were. 18In circumstances defying all hope he believed, taking his stand on hope, so that he might become the *u***father of many nations,** in agreement with the words which had been said to him, *v***Like these shall your posterity be**'. 19There was no weakening of his faith when he considered his own body, which was as good as dead—he was about a hundred years old—and the deadness of Sarah's womb. 20As for God's promise, no lack of faith made him waver. On the contrary, he became mighty in faith and proceeded to glorify God, 21being fully convinced that he had the power to perform what he had promised. 22This, then, was the reason why *w***it was reckoned to him as righteousness.** 23Yet the words '**it was reckoned to him**' were not written for his sake alone, 24but also for ours: we were to have righteousness reckoned to us, we who believe in him who raised from the dead the Lord Jesus, 25who was handed over to death for our sins and raised to life again for our justification.

5　Therefore, being justified by faith, let us enjoy peace with God through our Lord Jesus Christ: 2it is through him that we have obtained access to the state of gracious favour in which we are now securely placed. Moreover, we rejoice by reason of the hope we have of sharing God's glory. 3And not only that: we also rejoice in our sufferings, knowing as we do that suffering produces fortitude, 4fortitude a character which has stood the test, while a character that has stood the test produces hope. 5And this *x***hope** is something that can **never** bring any **disappointment,** seeing that God's love has been poured into our hearts through the Holy Spirit which has been given to us. 6While we were still helpless, Christ died for the ungodly, doing

*t*Gn 17:5　　*u*Gn 17:5　　*v*Gn 15:5　　*w*Gn 15:6　　*x*Ps 22:5; 25:3

so at the time appointed for it. [7]Now it is hard enough to find anyone who will die for a just man,* though here and there someone may be found who has the courage to lay down his life for a really good man. [8]Yet it was while we were still sinners that Christ died on our behalf, this being the proof supplied by God himself of the love he bears us. [9]All the more surely, then, shall we, now that we have found justification through Christ's sacrificial death, be saved, through him, from God's anger. [10]For if, at the time when we were God's enemies, we were reconciled to him through the death of his Son, there is greater certainty still that, now that we have been reconciled, we shall obtain salvation through his Son's life. [11]And not only that, but we also exult in God through our Lord Jesus Christ, through whom we have obtained the reconciliation.

[12]It was through one man that sin came into the world, and death through sin, death thus spreading to all men because they were all sinners. [13]Sin was indeed in the world before the law came; only, where there is no law, it is not entered into the account against us. [14]None the less death reigned from Adam to Moses, holding its sway even over those who had not been sinning in the same way as Adam had, he who was the type prefiguring the one who was to come.

[15]Still, the fact remains that the gracious favour is out of all proportion to the trespass. For if a whole multitude died through the trespass of the one individual, it was in a much greater measure that there came to a whole multitude the grace of God in all its abundance, that there came the free gift graciously bestowed through the one man, Jesus Christ. [16]And again, it was not with the gift as it was with the effect of one man's sinning. The sentence following on one man's action resulted in condemnation, whereas the gracious favour following on many trespasses results in acquittal. [17]Indeed, if because of one man's trespass death reigned through that one man, all the more shall those who receive in abundance the grace and gift of righteousness, enter upon a truly life-giving reign as kings through the one man, Jesus Christ.

[18]It follows, then, that, just as a single transgression resulted in a condemnation extending to all men, so one acquittal results in a life-giving justification extending to all men. [19]For just as by one man's disobedience a whole multitude came to be ranked as being sinners, so by one man's obedience a whole multitude will come to be ranked as being righteous. [20]Law made its entry so that transgression might increase, while, where sin increased, grace made its appearance in an abundance exceeding all measure, [21]in order that, as sin exercised its kingly rule by bringing death, so grace in turn might exercise its king-

---

* Or 'a man who is fair-minded'; but *not* a 'righteous man'.

ly rule by means of a righteousness bringing with it eternal life through Jesus Christ our Lord.

6 What conclusion, then, are we to draw from this? Are we to persist in sinning so that there may be all the more scope for grace? ²Far be the thought! How can we who have died to sin continue to live within its orbit? ³Or is it that you do not know that all of us who were baptized into union with Christ Jesus were baptized into his death? ⁴Well then, by virtue of undergoing baptism into death we were buried with him, in order that, as Christ was raised from the dead by the Father's glorious power, we, too, might live and move in a new kind of existence.

⁵And indeed, if through a death after the likeness of his death we have become one with him, a resurrection after the likeness of his resurrection will likewise be ours. ⁶And this we *do* know, that our old self has been crucified with him, in order that the body, as an instrument of sin, may be done away with altogether, so that we should no longer be the slaves of sin. ⁷For if a man has undergone death, he is quit of any claim which sin may make. ⁸But if we have thus undergone death with Christ, we believe that we shall also live with him, ⁹while we are clearly aware at the same time that Christ, having been raised from the dead, cannot die any more. Death has no more power over him. ¹⁰The death which he died, he died to sin once and for all; the life which he lives is a life that looks towards God. ¹¹And you, too, must think of yourselves as dead to sin and alive with a life which looks towards God in Christ Jesus.

¹²Let not sin, therefore, reign over this perishable body of yours to make you subject to its appetites. ¹³And do not put your bodily powers at the disposal of sin as instruments of unrighteousness. On the contrary, put yourselves at God's disposal, being men who have been dead and come to life again; and as for your bodily powers, use them as instruments of righteousness in the service of God. ¹⁴For sin will no longer have any power over you, since it is not the law to which you are subject now but grace.

¹⁵How then does the matter stand? Are we to sin because it is not the law but grace to which we are subject now? Far be the thought! ¹⁶Do you not know that in putting yourselves as slaves at someone's disposal, to render obedience to him, you are enslaved to whatever you render obedience to, either slaves of sin, with death as the result, or slaves of such obedience as results in righteousness? ¹⁷But thanks be to God that, though you were once slaves of sin, you have now come to render obedience from the heart to the pattern of teaching which was handed on to you. ¹⁸Having been set free from sin, you

have become the slaves of righteousness. [19](It is because of my bearing in mind the weakness of your natural faculties that I am putting the matter in the language of common life.) And just as you once put your bodily powers at the service of a life of impurity and ever-increasing lawlessness, so you must now put your bodily powers at the service of righteousness, as being its slaves, till all is holiness. [20]When you were slaves of sin, you were free from the claims made by righteousness. [21]But then, what harvest were you reaping from the things of which you are now ashamed? Why, these things lead only to one end: death itself! [22]Now, however, that you have been set free from sin and have become the slaves of God, there is a harvest for you, your sanctification, the end of it all being eternal life. [23]For death is the wage paid out by sin, while God's free gift is eternal life in union with Christ Jesus our Lord.

7 You must surely be aware, my brothers—for I am addressing myself to people who are conversant with the law—that the law has claims on a person only so long as he is alive. [2]A married woman, for instance, is bound by the law to her husband while he lives, but if her husband dies, she is quit of the claim the law made on her concerning her husband. [3]Thus, if she gives herself to another man during her husband's lifetime, she will be called an adulteress, while if her husband is dead, she is free from the claim which the law made, so as not to be an adulteress should she give herself to another. [4]So you, too, my brothers, have, through becoming one with Christ's body, undergone death as far as the law is concerned, so that you now belong to another, to him who has been raised from the dead, the purpose of all this being that we should yield a harvest for God. [5]And indeed, at the time when it was our lower nature which determined what we did, our sinful passions—and it was the law which evoked them—were ever active in the various parts of our bodies, with the result that the harvest which we yielded was one leading to death. [6]But now we have been set free from the law, having died to that which once held us captive; and so it is that we render service in a new manner, according to the spirit, not according to the letter as of old.

[7]What are we to say then? That law and sin are one and the same thing? Far be the thought! Still, had it not been for the law I should have had no knowledge of sin. For instance, but for the law having said, *y*'**You shall not covet**', I should not have had any knowledge of what covetousness was. [8]And sin, making use of its opportunity, stirred up within me all kinds of covetousness, the commandment

*y*Ex 20:17; Dt 5:21

being the instrument which it used for this. For in the absence of law sin is a dead thing. 9There was a time when, having no law over me, I was indeed alive; but when the commandment came, sin sprang into life and I died. 10As it turned out, the very commandment which was to bring me life brought me death. 11For sin, the commandment serving as its opportunity, led me astray altogether and killed me through the instrumentality of the commandment.

12Are we to say, then, seeing that the law is something holy, and that the commandment is likewise holy and right and good, 13that what happened was that a thing which is good was found to bring me death? Far be the thought! No, it was sin which, so as to be seen in its true light as sin, produced death in me through that which is good, in order that, the commandment being the means of achieving this, sin might show itself as sinful beyond all measure.

14The law, as we know, is something spiritual. As against this, I myself am unspiritual, having been sold to sin to act as its slave. 15The truth of the matter is that my way of acting is something beyond my comprehension, seeing that I do not do what I desire to do, but instead do the very thing I detest. 16But then, if I do what I have no desire to do, this implies that I acknowledge the excellence of the law, 17my action meanwhile being no longer accomplished by myself but by the sin which dwells within me. 18Of this I am certain, that nothing good dwells in me, that is to say, in my unspiritual self, since the desire to do right is ready at hand, while at the same time I have no power of carrying it into effect. 19It is not the good thing which I desire to do that I do, but the evil thing which I do not desire. 20But then, if I do that which I have no desire to do, it follows that it is no longer I that accomplish it. It is accomplished by the sin which has its dwelling within me. 21And so I find that this law holds good for me, that, when I desire to do what is good, evil lies close at hand. 22In my inmost self I delight in the law of God. 23Yet I discover in my bodily powers* another law that is at war with that law of which my understanding approves, and which enslaves me to the law operative in the various parts of my body, the law of sin. 24Wretched man that I am! Who will deliver me from a body doomed to a death such as this? 25Thanks be to God, through Jesus Christ our Lord! So then, I—my true self—am in servitude to the law of God, while as regards my lower self† I am in servitude to the law of sin.

* [Lit. 'members'.]
† [Lit. 'flesh'.]

8 Well then, no sentence of condemnation stands against those who are in union with Christ Jesus. [2]For the law of the Spirit which issues in life has set me free, in Christ Jesus, from the law issuing in sin and death. [3]There was one thing which the law was unable to achieve, because our lower nature had deprived it of all its power. And this God has effected. Sending his Son in a form like that borne by our own sinful nature, and doing so for the purpose of dealing with sin, he passed a judgment of condemnation on sin right within its own field of operation, [4]so that the just requirement of the law might be fully met in us, who rule our lives not in accordance with our lower nature but in accordance with the dictates of the Spirit. [5]For those whose lives are ruled by what their lower nature bids them do have their minds set on the things pertaining to that nature, while those whose lives are ruled by the Spirit have their minds set on the things of the Spirit. [6]And to set the mind on what our lower nature would have us do means death, while to set the mind on the Spirit means life and peace. [7]That is because the mind which is set on what are the requirements of our lower nature is in a state of enmity towards God; it does not submit to God's law, indeed it cannot. [8]It is impossible that those whose lives are ruled by their lower nature should please God.

[9]But your lives are not such as to be ruled by your lower nature. They are ruled by the Spirit, if indeed it be true that the Spirit of God dwells within you. One cannot belong to Christ unless one has the Spirit of Christ. [10]But if Christ is within you, then, although the body be a thing which must die by virtue of sin, yet the spirit is a thing which truly lives by reason of your having received your justification. [11]Moreover, if the Spirit of him who raised Jesus from the dead dwells within you, then he who has raised Christ Jesus from the dead will give life to your perishable bodies, doing so on behalf of the Spirit, whom you have dwelling within you.

[12]Therefore, my brothers, it is no longer our lower nature which has claims on us, so that we should live according to the dictates of that nature, [13]the truth being that, if it is your lower nature which rules your lives, you are marked out for death, while if through the Spirit you put to death the vile deeds which the body gives rise to, you shall have life. [14]Indeed, all those who let themselves be led by the Spirit of God are sons of God. [15]After all, it is not the spirit of slavery which you have received, so as to fall back into a state of anxious dread. No, what you have received is the spirit of sonship which makes us cry out, 'Abba! Father!' [16]Besides, along with our own spirit, the Spirit himself testifies to the fact that we are God's children. [17]But if we are his children, then we are his heirs too: heirs of God and fellow heirs

of Christ; only we must share his sufferings if we are to be made sharers of his glory.

¹⁸Not that I consider the sufferings of this present time worthy of being compared with the glory which is to be manifested in us. ¹⁹For if all creation is full of eager expectancy, that is because it is waiting for the sons of God to be manifested. ²⁰Creation was subjected to futility (not by its own choice but by the will of him who so subjected it); yet with a hope to look forward to, ²¹namely, that creation itself would be set free from the thraldom of decay, and obtain that liberty which is bound up with the glory which belongs to the children of God. ²²The whole creation, as we know, has been groaning in a common travail until this very hour. ²³And more than that, we ourselves who are in possession of the firstfruits of the Spirit groan in our hearts as we are waiting to become God's sons by adoption, this having the result that our bodies will be set free from their enslavement. ²⁴We have indeed obtained our salvation, but only in the sense of our reposing our hope in it. But then, an object of hope is such no longer when it is present to view; for if we can see a thing, how can we be said to hope for it? ²⁵On the other hand, what is implied in our hoping for something which as yet we do not see is this, that we should be waiting for it with patience.

²⁶In the same way, the Spirit comes to the aid of our weakness; when we do not know what prayer to offer, to pray as we ought, the Spirit himself intercedes for us with groans too deep for words. ²⁷And the ᶻ**searcher of hearts** knows what the Spirit's intent is, that it is in God's own way that he intercedes on behalf of those consecrated to God. ²⁸Moreover, we ourselves know that for those who love God all things work together to secure their good—for those, I mean, whom he has called in fulfilment of his design. ²⁹For this is how matters stand. Those whom he foreknew he also predestined to be conformed to the likeness of his Son, in order that his Son might be the firstborn among many brothers. ³⁰And those whom he predestined he also called; and those whom he called he also accepted as righteous; and those whom he accepted as righteous he also glorified.

³¹What, then, are we to say in view of these things? If God is on our side, who is there to prevail against us? ³²He who did not spare even his own Son, but gave him up on behalf of us all, will he not also, along with this gift of his, make us a gift of all else? ³³Who will come forward to accuse God's elect? It is God who ᵃ**accepts them as righteous. ³⁴Who, then, is there to condemn them?** It is Christ Jesus who died, or rather was raised from the dead, he who is present at God's side, and indeed is interceding on our behalf. ³⁵Who will separate us from

ᶻ1 K 8:39; Ps 7:9; 139:1.23; 1 Sm 16:7; 1 Ch 28:9; Jr 17:10   ᵃIs 50:8

Christ's love? Will affliction, or distress, or being persecuted, or going hungry, or being in want of clothing, or being beset by danger, or the sword threatening us? [36]*b*'**For your sake**,' says the scripture, '**we are all day long exposed to death, reckoned no better than sheep marked out for slaughter.**' [37]Yet in all this we are winning a most glorious victory through him who granted us his love. [38]And indeed, I am fully convinced of this, that nothing in either death or life, that no angels, no rulers in the world of spirits, nothing present or future, none of the forces governing the universe, [39]that there is nothing, whether it be found high above us or deep down below, in fact, that there is not anything in all creation which shall have the power of separating us from the love of God which comes to us in Christ Jesus our Lord.

9 I am speaking the truth as a man who has his being in Christ; I am not telling any falsehood—my conscience, indwelt as it is by the Holy Spirit, at the same time adding its testimony— [2]when I assure you that there is a great sorrow, an unceasing anguish in my heart. [3]Indeed, I could wish that I myself was accursed and cut off from Christ for the sake of my brothers, my kinsmen by natural descent. [4]This indeed is the very thing the Israelites are, the men to whom there belongs the adoption as sons of God, as well as the glorious presence, the covenants, the giving of the law, the temple service, and the promises. [5]To them the patriarchs belong, and theirs is the human stock from which Christ came, he who rules as God over all things. May he be blessed for ever. Amen.

[6]However, there is no question of God's word having failed of its purpose, the truth of the matter being this. Not all who are descended from Israel belong to Israel; [7]not all the posterity of Abraham's children. On the contrary, as scripture asserts, *c*'**it is through the line of Isaac that you are to have your descendants.**' [8]And that means that it is not the children by natural descent who are the children of God. No, it is only those children, made such as the result of the promise, who are reckoned as Abraham's descendants. [9]And these are the words uttered when the promise was made: *d*'**I shall come again at the time appointed for this, and Sarah shall have a son.**'

[10]Nor is that all; there was Rebecca, too, bearing two sons to the same husband, our forefather Isaac. [11]They had not as yet been born; they had done nothing either good or evil. Yet, in order that God's elective purpose might be seen to stand firm, [12]based as it was not on their actions but on the will of him who sent out the call, it was said

*b*Ps 44:22.11   *c*Gn 21:12   *d*Gn 18:10.14

287

to her, *e*'**The elder shall be the servant of the younger.'** [13]As it stands written in scripture, *f*'**Jacob I have loved, but Esau I have hated.'**

[14]What, then, is our conclusion to be? That God acts unjustly? Far be the thought! [15]After all, this is what he said to Moses, *g*'**I will show mercy to whom I would be merciful, and have pity for him whom I would pity.'** [16]Everything, then, turns not on human will or exertion, but on God's having mercy. [17]And indeed, this is what is said to Pharaoh in scripture, *h*'**I have raised you up for this very purpose, that in you I might show forth my power, and that my name may be proclaimed all over the earth.'** [18]The position, then, is this: he shows mercy where it is his will, and where it is his will he *i***hardens** people's hearts.

[19]Now you will wish to ask me, 'If that is how things stand, why does God still find fault? After all, who is there who can resist his will?' [20]Who are you, my friend, I would say in reply, to bandy words with God? *j***Shall the thing moulded say to him who moulded it, 'Why have you made me in this way?'** [21]Or is it that you wish to deny that *k***the potter** has the right to do with **the clay** whatever he likes, to make out of the same lump one vessel for noble use and another for ignoble use? [22]And what if God, while ready to display his anger and make known his power, has yet *l***borne** most patiently with those **vessels** which were the very objects of his **anger,** fit for nothing but **destruction;** [23]and that he has acted in this way in order to make known his glory, in all its abundance, bestowing it upon the vessels singled out for mercy, those, I mean, that had been prepared by him from the very first, so that glory might be theirs?

[24]And it is we ourselves who are these vessels of mercy, we whom he has called to himself not from among the Jews only but also from among the Gentiles. [25]As indeed it is said in the Book of Hosea, *m*'**I will call "my people" those who were not my people, and I will call "my beloved" her who was not my beloved.** [26]**And indeed, what will come about is this, that in the very place where it was said to them, "You are not my people", they will be called "sons of the living God".'** [27]Moreover, there is Isaiah crying out concerning Israel, *n*'**Though the number of Israel's sons was to be like the grains of sand on the seashore, it is but a remnant of them that will be saved;** [28]**for the Lord will make a reckoning upon the earth, accomplishing it and cutting it short.'** [29]Then there are the words uttered by Isaiah in an earlier place: *o*'**Unless descendants had been left to us by the Lord of hosts, we should have become as Sodom and have gone a way like that of Gomorrah.'**

*e*Gn 25:23   *f*Mal 1:2f   *g*Ex 33:19   *h*Ex 9:16   *i*Ex 4:21; 7:3; 9:12; 14:4.17   *j*Is 29:16; 45:9   *k*Jr 18:6   *l*Is 13:5; 54:16; Jr 50:25   *m*Hos 2:23; 1:10   *n*Is 10:22f   *o*Is 1:9

288

30 What then is our conclusion to be? It is this, that the Gentiles who were not in pursuit of righteousness have attained to righteousness—a righteousness, however, which comes through faith; 31 whereas the people of Israel, being in pursuit of a law which would impart righteousness, have failed to arrive at such a law. 32 Why has that happened? Because they have not pursued it as something resulting from faith, but have dealt with it as something that was to be the result of works performed. They have stumbled against the *p*stumbling stone 33 which is written about in scripture in these words: 'Look, how I am laying down in Zion a stone which causes men to stumble, a rock which will make them fall. Yet he who reposes his faith in it will not find himself disappointed.'

10 My brothers, the people of Israel have all the good will of my heart; they have the prayers which I offer to God on their behalf that they may obtain their salvation. 2 And indeed, I bear witness to them that they have a zeal for God, but it is one that does not accord with true knowledge. 3 In fact, being ignorant of the righteousness which comes from God, and seeking to establish a righteousness deriving from themselves, they have not submitted themselves to the righteousness which has God for its source. 4 But then, the truth of the matter is that Christ has brought the law to an end, bringing righteousness to everyone who will believe.

5 Moses, for his part, writes this concerning righteousness grounded in law: *q*'The man who practices it shall gain life by it.' 6 The righteousness, however, which is grounded in faith speaks thus: *r*'Do not say in your heart, "Who will ascend into heaven?"' (that is, to bring Christ down), 7 or *s*"Who will descend into the abyss?"' (that is, to bring Christ up from the dead). 8 But now, what does this righteousness declare? It is this. *t*'The word is near you, in your mouth and in your heart.' (It is the very word of faith which we proclaim that is signified here.) 9 And indeed, if with your mouth you confess Jesus as Lord, and believe in your heart that God raised him from the dead, you will be saved. 10 And so it is. It is with the heart that one believes and obtains righteousness; and it is with the mouth that one makes confession and obtains salvation.

11 *u*'None of those who repose their faith in him will find themselves disappointed', says the scripture. 12 And this is indeed but the truth, no distinction being made here between Jew and Gentile, since it is the same Lord who is Lord over all and who lavishes his riches upon everyone who calls on him. 13 And so it says in another place,

*p*Is 28:16 LXX; 8:14   *q*Lv 18:5   *r*Dt 9:4   *s*Ps 107:26   *t*Dt 30:12-14; 9:4   *u*Is 28:16

v'Everyone who calls on the name of the Lord shall be saved.' [14]But then, how are they to call on one in whom they have never learned to believe? How can they believe in one of whom they have never heard? How are they to hear unless there be someone preaching to them? [15]And how are men to preach unless they have been sent out to do so? And so it stands written in scripture, *w*'What a welcome there is for the bringers of joyful tidings!'

[16]But not all of them have paid heed to the gospel. True enough. And so Isaiah says, *x*'Lord, who has believed what he has heard from us?' [17]Faith, then, comes through what is heard, and what is heard has its source in its having been spoken by Christ.

[18]Yet, I ask, is it perhaps that they have not heard? Of course they have, as is indeed expressed in these words: *y*'Their voice has gone out to all the earth, and their words to the end of the world.' [19]Again, I ask, is it possible that Israel did not understand? Why, in the first place, there is Moses saying, *z*'I will make you jealous of a nation which is no nation at all; I will make you angry with a nation which is devoid of understanding.' [20]And there is Isaiah speaking out boldly, *a*'I have been found by those who were not seeking for me; I have become manifest to those who never enquired after me.' [21]But to Israel he speaks thus: *b*'All day long have I stretched out my hands to a people that refuses to obey and rebels against me.'

11 Let me put a further question then. *c*Has God disowned his people? Far be the thought! Why, I myself am an Israelite, a descendant of Abraham, a member of the tribe of Benjamin. [2]*d*God has not disowned his people, whom in times long past he acknowledged as his own. Surely, you know what the scripture says in the place where it tells us of Elijah—the complaint, I mean, which he makes before God against Israel, [3]'Lord, *e*they have killed your prophets, they have demolished your altars, and I alone am left, and they are seeking to put me to death.' [4]But what is the reply God makes to him? *f*'There are seven thousand men whom I have kept for myself, those that have not bowed down to Baal.' [5]So, too, at the present time there has come to be a remnant, a remnant chosen by grace. [6]But if it is due to grace, then it is no longer the result of works performed. Otherwise grace would be grace no longer.

[7]How then does the matter stand? That Israel has failed to attain what it is seeking. The chosen have attained it, while the rest have had

---

*v*Jl 2:32   *w*Is 52:7; Nah 1:5   *x*Is 53:1   *y*Ps 19:4   *z*Dt 32:21   *a*Is 65:1   *b*Is 65:2 LXX
*c*Ps 94:14; Jr 31:37   *d*1 Sm 12:22   *e*1 K 19:10.14   *f*1 K 19:18

290

their hearts made callous. [8]As it stands written, *8'***God has bestowed upon them a spirit of stupefaction, eyes that they should not see and ears that they should not hear. And so it is to this very day.'** [9]And we find David speaking thus: *h'***Let their very food become to them a snare, a trap, a pitfall, and a means of retribution;** [10]let their eyes be darkened, so that they may be unable to see; keep their backs bowed down continually.'

[11]In view of all this, I would wish to raise this question: Have they come to grief in the sense of having suffered a complete downfall? Far be the thought! The truth is that by their false step salvation has come to the Gentiles, in order that this might rouse the Jews to *i*emulation. [12]But now, if their false step means riches for the world, and their overthrow riches for the Gentiles, surely their full inclusion will mean much more even than that.

[13]But as regards you Gentiles, this is what I have to say to you. Inasmuch as I am an apostle sent to the Gentiles, I do indeed take great pride in my ministry, [14]provided only that I succeed in stirring up to emulation those who are of my own flesh and blood, and in this way lead at least some of them to salvation. [15]And indeed, if their rejection has meant a world reconciled to God, what can their being accepted again mean but life risen from the dead? [16]When that which is being *j*offered as firstfruits is consecrated, the whole batch is consecrated along with it. If the root is consecrated, so are the branches. [17]But what if some of the branches have been broken off, while you, a shoot coming from a wild olive, have been grafted in right in the place where they were and have thus become a sharer in the rich sap of the olive tree? [18]Be on your guard not to boast of your superiority over those branches. And if you cannot but boast, remember that it is not you who uphold the root. The root upholds you.

[19]'Branches have been broken off,' you will tell me, 'so that I might be grafted in.' [20]True enough, but it was for want of faith that they were broken off; and it is only faith which keeps you where you are. Do not be arrogant, then; rather, stand in awe. [21]For if God did not spare the branches which belonged to the tree by nature, neither will he spare you. [22]Take note, then, of the kindness and the severity of God: his severity towards those who suffered a fall, and his kindness towards you, provided, that is, that you remain within the scope of that kindness; otherwise you, too, will be cut off. [23]As for these others, if they do not hold on to their unbelief, they also will be grafted in; for God has the power to graft them in again. [24]And indeed, if you were cut off from what is by nature a wild olive tree and, contrary to nature, were grafted into an olive tree which is truly so, how much more

*8*Dt 29:4; Is 29:10   *h*Ps 69:22f   *i*Dt 32:21   *j*[Nm 15:19-21]

certainly will those natural branches be grafted back into the olive tree native to them.

²⁵There is a profound truth concealed here, my brothers, of which I do not wish you to lose sight, lest you become unduly self-satisfied. And it is this. A state of callous insensibility has indeed come upon Israel. Yet it is no more than temporary, lasting till the full number of Gentiles has been brought in. ²⁶And so all Israel shall obtain their salvation. As it is written, ᵏ'**The deliverer will come from Zion.** ˡ**He will remove all ungodliness from Jacob,** ²⁷**this being the fulfilment of my covenant with them, at the time when I shall be taking their sins away from them.'**

²⁸In the preaching of the gospel they are looked upon as the enemies of God, and that for your sake, while, as regards God's elective purpose, they are dearly-loved by him for the sake of their forefathers. ²⁹There is no such thing as God's coming to regret the gracious gifts which he bestows or the calls which he sends out. ³⁰And just as you at one time were disobedient to God but have now received mercy by virtue of their disobedience, ³¹so they have now become disobedient, but only in order that, by virtue of the mercy shown to you, they in their turn might receive mercy. ³²For this is the truth of the matter, that God has confined everyone to the prisonhouse of disobedience, so that he might have mercy upon all alike.

³³What inexhaustible depth there is in the riches which God calls his own, in his wisdom, and in his knowledge! How unsearchable are his judgments, how inscrutable his ways! ³⁴And so we read, ᵐ'**Who has known the mind of the Lord, or who has become his counsellor?** ³⁵**Who has ever been the first to make him a gift, to receive from him a gift in return?'** ³⁶And indeed, all things are from him, through him, and he is the goal of them all. To him be glory for ever. Amen.

12 In view of all this, my brothers, I would make an appeal to you, doing so by the very compassion of God. Offer up your bodies as a living sacrifice, one that has been consecrated, one that finds glad acceptance from God, this being the service which is due from you as rational creatures. ²And do not allow yourselves to conform to the fashion of this present world, but let there be a renewal of your minds by which you are transformed so as to discern the will of God, thus coming to know that which is good, that which finds acceptance, that which is perfect.

³And so, in virtue of the gracious favour which I have had bestowed upon me, I would ask each one among you not to be haughty

ᵏIs 59:20f ˡIs 27:9; Jr 31:33f ᵐIs 40:13 LXX; Job 15:8; Jr 23:18; Job 41:11

in mind, thinking of yourselves more highly than you ought, but to be intent on becoming sober-minded, according to the measure of faith which God has allotted to each. [4]Just as in a single human body there are many parts, these parts all performing functions which differ from one another, [5]so we, though many, form one body in Christ, while we belong to one another as parts of that body. [6]And, finding ourselves in possession of gifts which vary according to the special grace which has been allotted to each of us, let us make use of them. If it be prophecy, let us prophesy in conformity with the faith which is in us. [7]If we have the gift of service, let us use it in serving; one who teaches should be active in teaching; [8]he who exhorts in exhortation; he who gives alms should do so with single-mindedness; he who exercises authority should perform his task with zeal; he who has an errand of mercy should carry it out cheerfully.

[9]Your love must be a sincere love. Hold in abomination that which is evil; cling to that which is good. [10]Let the love you bear to the brotherhood be the means of your being affectionately drawn to one another, eager to give one another precedence. [11]As for zeal, I would have you unwearied, aglow with the Spirit, serving the Lord. [12]Let the hope in your hearts fill you with joy; be steadfast in the midst of tribulation; be constant in prayer. [13]Contribute to the needs of those who have consecrated themselves to God; make it your aim to exercise hospitality. [14]Bestow a blessing upon those who persecute you, a blessing, not a curse. [15]Rejoice with those who rejoice; mourn with those who mourn. [16]Let it be the spirit of harmony which rules you in your dealings with one another. Do not give your minds to high things, but let yourselves be drawn to humble pursuits. [n]**Do not become self-satisfied, being wise in your own eyes.**

[17]Repay no one evil for evil, but [o]**take thought** to do only such things as will appear **good in the sight of everyone.** [18]If it be possible, so far as it rests with you, live at peace with everyone. [19]My dearly-loved ones, do not seek your own revenge, but instead let God's anger take its course. So we read in scripture, [p]**'Vengeance is mine, I will repay'**, says the Lord. [20]Rather, take these words for your model, [q]**'If your enemy is hungry, feed him; if he is thirsty, give him something to drink. For by so doing you will heap burning coals upon his head.'** [21]Do not be overcome by evil, but overcome evil with good.

13 Every person, without exception, is under obligation to submit himself to the authorities which are set above him. This must be so, for all authority derives from God, and the authorities which exist are

[n]Pr 3:7; [11:20; 15:9]; Is 5:21   [o]Pr 3:4 LXX   [p]Dt 32:35   [q]Pr 25:21f

of God's ordinance. [2]Anyone who opposes authority, therefore, is offering resistance to what has been ordained by God; and those who thus offer resistance will bring punishment upon themselves. [3]It is bad conduct, not good, which inspires fear of those who rule. Is it your wish that you should not have to fear the man in authority? Then do what is good, and you will have his approbation; [4]for he is God's servant working for your good. But if you do what is wrong, then be afraid. It is not for nothing that he is the bearer of the sword. He is God's servant, bringing upon the evildoer the anger which God feels against him. [5]It is necessary, therefore, that we should submit ourselves—not only on account of the anger threatening us but also on grounds of conscience. [6]If you pay taxes, that is for the same reason: the authorities are in the service of God and are earnestly engaged in the task which has been committed to them. [7]Pay to all what is due to them: taxes to whom taxes are due, customs to whom customs are due, respect to whom respect is due, honour to whom honour is due.

[8]You must owe no debt to anyone except the debt of loving one another. And indeed, he who loves his neighbour has met the demands of the law in full. [9]For all the commandments, *r***'You shall not commit adultery; you shall not do murder; you shall not steal; you shall not covet'**, as well as the rest of them, are summed up in this one precept, *s***'You shall love your neighbour as yourself.'** [10]Where there is love, no wrong is done to a neighbour; and this is why, if there be love, all the demands of the law have been fulfilled.

[11]And then this. You know how decisive is this present time, and so you cannot but be aware that it is high time that you should rouse yourselves from your sleep, salvation being closer to us now than it was when we first learned to believe. [12]The night is far on its course; day draws near. Let us, then, put away from ourselves the deeds that are done in the darkness and put on the armour of light. [13]Let us conduct ourselves becomingly, as by the light of day, not engaging in revelling and drunkenness, in lust and debauchery, in quarrels and rivalries. [14]No, let the Lord Jesus Christ be your garment, and do not be intent on making provision for your carnal nature, to arouse its appetites.

14   Give a warm welcome to one whose faith shows a lack of vigour—without, however, entering into a debate on mere matters of opinion. [2]One man is convinced that he has the right to eat anything he fancies, while a less vigorous one confines himself to eating nothing but vegetables. [3]Let not him who eats look down on him who

*r*Ex 20:13-17; Dt 5:17-21   *s*Lv 19:18

abstains, and let not him who abstains from eating pass judgment on the one who eats. After all, God has made him welcome. ⁴And who are you that you should sit in judgment on the servant of another? Whether he stands or falls is his own master's affair. And stand he will. The Master has the power to make him stand.

⁵Again, one man esteems one day more highly than another; another esteems all days alike. Let it be each man's own mind which causes him to reach a clear conviction. ⁶He who observes particular days does so in honour of the Lord, just as he who is ready to eat meat acts the way he does in honour of the Lord. After all, it is God to whom he gives thanks. As for him who will not eat meat, it is in the Lord's honour that he abstains. He, too, gives thanks to God.

⁷This indeed is how matters stand. None of us lives to be his own master, and none of us dies to be his own master. ⁸When we live we live serving the Lord, and when we die we die serving the Lord. Whether we live, then, or whether we die, we belong to the Lord. ⁹It was for this that Christ died and lived again, that he might be Lord both of the dead and of the living. ¹⁰Why, then, is it, my friend, that you pass judgment on your brother? Or why do you, the other man, treat your brother with contempt? One day we shall—all of us— stand before God's judgment seat. ¹¹So we find it written in scripture, ᵗ'As I live, says the Lord, to me every knee shall bow, and every tongue shall give praise to God.' ¹²And so each one of us will have to give an account of himself before God.

¹³Let us cease, therefore, passing judgment on one another; rather, let this be the judgment at which you arrive, that you must never put a stumbling block in the way of a brother, or do anything else which might entangle him. ¹⁴I am aware, indeed I am fully convinced—as a man united to the Lord Jesus—that there is nothing unclean in itself; it is only when someone thinks of a thing as unclean that, to him, it is unclean. ¹⁵But if your brother has his feelings hurt on account of the food you are eating, it is no longer love that rules your conduct. You must not, through food, bring ruin on the man for whose sake Christ died. ¹⁶Take care, then, that what is a good thing for you yourself should not become the occasion for slanderous talk. ¹⁷The kingdom of God is not a matter of eating one thing or drinking another. It means doing what is right; it means finding peace and joy in the Holy Spirit. ¹⁸And he who thus shows himself to be a servant of Christ finds glad acceptance from God, while at the same time he is esteemed among men.

¹⁹Let us pursue, then, what makes for peace and for building up one another in the faith. ²⁰You ought on no account to destroy the

ᵗIs 49:18; 45:23

work of God over a question of food. Nothing, it is true, is unclean. Yet it goes ill with the man who eats his food in such a way as to prove a stumbling block to another. ²¹It is a fine thing indeed if you do not eat meat, or drink wine, or do anything that makes your brother stumble. ²²As for the conviction which you hold, look on that as a matter which concerns only you yourself in the sight of God. Happy is the man who sees no reason why he should pass judgment against himself concerning what he has come to approve of. ²³Yet the man who entertains doubts and who eats none the less stands self-condemned, because his action does not come of a settled conviction. But then, the truth is that any action not proceeding from a settled conviction partakes of the nature of sin.

15 We who are endowed with strength ought to bear with the weaknesses of those who are lacking in strength, and ought not to seek to please ourselves. ²Let each one of us do what pleases his neighbour for his good, to build him up in the faith. ³Christ, after all, did not please himself. On the contrary, these words set down in scripture apply to him: ᵘ'**The insults of those who offered insults to you have fallen on me.**' ⁴Indeed, whatever was written down in days of old was written for our instruction, so that hope may be ours through the message of steadfastness and encouragement which the scriptures bring us. ⁵And may God, the giver of steadfastness and encouragement, grant it to you to be of one mind, conforming yourselves to Christ Jesus, ⁶so that, having but one heart and one voice, you may glorify the God and Father of our Lord Jesus Christ.

⁷In view of all this, you ought to give a welcome to one another, as Christ has given a welcome to you, one redounding to the glory of God. ⁸What I mean to say is this, that Christ became a servant to the Jewish people on behalf of God's truthfulness: he was to make good the promises made to the patriarchs. ⁹The Gentiles, on the other hand, were to ascribe glory to God for his mercy. So we find these words in scripture, ᵛ'**Therefore, I will laud you among the Gentiles and sing praises to your name.**' ¹⁰And somewhere else it is said, ʷ'**Rejoice, you Gentiles, with his people.**' ¹¹And besides, ˣ'**Praise the Lord, you Gentiles, one and all, and let all the nations extol him.**' ¹²And again there is Isaiah saying, ʸ'**There shall be the scion sprung from Jesse, he who will rise up to bear rule over the Gentiles. The Gentiles will repose their hope in him.**' ¹³Now may God, the bringer of hope, fill you with all joy and peace, through your faith in him, so that you may have hope in abundance through the power of the Holy Spirit.

ᵘPs 69:9 ᵛPs 18:49; 2 Sm 22:50 ʷDt 32:43 ˣPs 117:1 ʸIs 11:10.1

[14]My brothers, I have indeed not the least doubt in my mind that you are full of goodness, endowed with knowledge of every kind, and well able to tender advice to one another. [15]Yet if I have written to you here and there somewhat boldly, that was by way of refreshing your memory, by virtue of the office graciously entrusted to me by God. [16]My task was to be a minister of Christ Jesus sent to the Gentiles, with God's gospel for my priestly charge, so that the Gentiles might become an offering gladly accepted by God, one consecrated by the Holy Spirit. [17]And so it is that, as a man united to Christ Jesus, I have some reason to boast concerning work done in the service of God. [18]On the other hand, the only cases I shall venture to speak of are those in which it was I, myself, who was Christ's instrument in bringing the Gentiles into his allegiance, by word and by deed, [19]by the power of signs and wonders, by the power of the Holy Spirit. And so it fell out that, beginning at Jerusalem and making a wide sweep as far as Illyricum, I have brought to completion the preaching of Christ's gospel. [20]On the other hand, it has been a point of honour with me that I should not preach the gospel in any place where Christ's name was already known. I would not run the risk of building on another man's foundation. [21]And instead of that, I took these words from scripture for my model: [z]'**He shall be seen by those who have had no tidings of him; he shall be understood by those who had never heard of him.**'

[22]These are the reasons why I have been prevented, time and again, from coming to see you. [23]But now that I have no further scope in these regions, while having, for many years, had a longing to see you, [24]you shall have a visit from me as soon as I can set out on my journey to Spain. Indeed, what I am hoping is that I shall see you on my way, and that I shall be helped forward on my journey there, having first enjoyed, for some time, the comfort of your society to the full. [25]At present, however, I am going to Jerusalem, to be of service to those in the city who are consecrated to God. [26]For this is what has happened. The congregations in Macedonia and Achaia have been pleased to offer a certain contribution for the benefit of the poor among those in Jerusalem who are consecrated to God. [27]They have been pleased to do so, and indeed the poor are in their debt. For if the Gentiles have come to have a share in their spiritual treasures, they in turn are under obligation to be of service to them in respect of their temporal needs. [28]When this duty is discharged, and I have set my seal upon this bounty as duly theirs, I shall proceed on my journey to Spain by way of you. [29]And this I do indeed know, that, when I come to you, I shall do so with Christ's blessing resting upon me in all its fullness.

[z]Is 52:15

[30]Only I would make this appeal to you, by our Lord Jesus Christ and the love of the Spirit. Lend succour to me in the fight in which I am engaged, during the prayers you offer to God on my behalf, [31]asking that I may be kept safe from those in Judaea who oppose themselves to the faith, and that the contribution which I shall be offering for the benefit of the congregation in Jerusalem will be well received by those consecrated to God, [32]so that when, God willing, I come to see you, I shall do so with a glad heart, enjoying a time of rest and refreshment in your company. [33]And may God, the giver of peace, be with you all. Amen.

16 I commend to you Phoebe, our sister in the faith, who is a deacon* of the congregation at Cenchreae. [2]Make her welcome in the Lord's fellowship in a manner worthy of those who have consecrated themselves to God. Moreover, stand by her in any matter where she may need your help, for she has shown herself a kind helper to many, myself included.

[3]Greet Prisca and Aquila, my fellow workers in the service of Christ Jesus. [4]They have risked their necks to save my life, and it is not only I, but all the Gentile congregations as well, who are filled with gratitude towards them. [5]I send my greetings also to the congregation which assembles at their house. Greet Epaenetus, who is dear to me, the first man in Asia to offer himself for the service of Christ's cause. [6]Greet Mary, who has toiled much on your behalf, [7]and greet also Andronicus and Junias, fellow countrymen of mine who share my imprisonment.† They occupy a prominent place among the apostles, and, moreover, they joined themselves to Christ's cause before I did. [8]Greet Ampliatus, that dear comrade of mine in support of the Lord's cause. [9]Greet Urbanus, my fellow worker in Christ's service, and Stachys, a man dear to me. [10]Greet Apelles, a man of approved worth in the service of Christ. Greet those who belong to the household of Aristobulus [11]as well as Herodion, who is a fellow countryman. Greet those members of Narcissus' household who belong to the Lord's fellowship. [12]Greet Tryphaena and Tryphosa, who labour in the Lord's service, as well as Persis, the much-loved one. She, too, has toiled hard for the Lord. [13]Greet Rufus, a chosen servant of the Lord, and also his mother, who has been a mother to me. [14]Greet Asyncritus, Phlegon, Hermes, Patrobas, Hermas, as well as the other brothers who are of their company. [15]Greet Philologus, Julia, Nereus and his sister, and Olympas. And give my greetings as well

---

* [The New Testament does not distinguish between male and female deacons.]
† Or '. . . Andronicus and Junia, my fellow Jews and fellow prisoners.'

to those among God's consecrated people who are associated with these.

¹⁶Greet one another with the kiss of peace. All Christ's congregations send you their greetings.

¹⁷I appeal to you, my brothers, to be on your guard against those who cause dissensions and put obstacles in other people's way, acting in opposition to the doctrine which you have been taught. Avoid their company. ¹⁸Men such as these are no servants of Christ our Lord. They are enslaved by their own appetites, and by their fair speaking and flattering words they lead astray the minds of those lacking in guile. ¹⁹As for yourselves, the report of your loyal obedience has spread everywhere, and so it is that I rejoice over you. Still, what I would wish is that you should show yourselves to be men endowed with shrewd wisdom, wherever a good purpose is to be served, while being mere innocents as regards the accomplishment of anything evil. ²⁰And before long, God, the giver of peace, will crush Satan underneath your feet. The grace of our Lord Jesus be with you.

²¹Timothy, my fellow worker, sends his greetings to you. So do Lucius, Jason, and Sosipater, my fellow countrymen. ²²(I, Tertius, who have taken this letter down, send my greetings to you as one who is united to the Lord.) ²³Gaius, my host and that of the whole congregation, greets you. Erastus the city treasurer and our brother Quartus send their greetings.*

²⁵There is one who is able to endow you with strength, making you conformable to the gospel which I preach, to the message about Jesus Christ which I proclaim, and that by virtue of the unfolding of a truth kept hidden for countless ages, ²⁶but now brought fully to light and made known, through the instrumentality of the prophetic writings, to all the nations, at the eternal God's command, to secure their obedience to the message of faith. ²⁷To him, to God who alone is wise, may glory be ascribed, through Jesus Christ, for ever and ever. Amen.

* V. 24 is probably not part of the original text.

PAUL'S FIRST LETTER
TO THE CHURCH AT CORINTH

1 Paul, by the will of God, called to be an apostle of Christ Jesus, and with him Sosthenes, your brother in the faith, ²send their greetings to the church gathered at Corinth, to those sanctified by virtue of their union with Christ Jesus, to those who have received God's call to consecrate themselves to him. These greetings are addressed at the same time to all those who call upon the name of our Lord Jesus Christ, their Lord and ours, in whatever place they may find themselves. ³Grace be yours and peace from God our Father and the Lord Jesus Christ.

⁴I render thanks to God at all times on your behalf for the grace bestowed upon you through your union with Christ Jesus. ⁵It is by him that you have been made rich in every way, being endowed with the highest degree of eloquence and knowledge; ⁶so firmly has the testimony borne to Christ established itself among you. ⁷Thus there is no gift in which you are still lacking as you wait for our Lord Jesus Christ to reveal himself, ⁸who will keep you steadfast to the very end, so that no charge will lie against you on the day when our Lord Jesus makes his appearance. ⁹And indeed, the God by whom you have been called into the fellowship of his Son Jesus Christ is true to his word.

¹⁰Only I appeal to you, brothers, in the name of our Lord Jesus Christ, that you are all to speak with one voice. There should be no dissensions among you. On the contrary, you must see to it that you find yourselves fully equipped, having the same mind and the same judgment. ¹¹I am speaking in this way, my brothers, because I have had a report concerning you from Chloe's people, to the effect that contention is rife among you. ¹²Each of you, I mean, has a slogan of his own, saying, 'I belong to Paul', or 'I belong to Apollos', or 'I belong to Cephas', or 'I belong to Christ'. ¹³What, has Christ been divided up? Was it Paul that was crucified for you? Or was it in Paul's name that you were baptized? ¹⁴I am thankful indeed that I did not baptize any of you except Crispus and Gaius, ¹⁵so that no one can say that it was in my name that you were baptized. ¹⁶Yes, I did baptize the household

of Stephanas. Yet, as for the rest, I do not know that I baptized anyone else. [17]The truth is that Christ did not send me forth to baptize but to proclaim the gospel. Moreover, it was not to be a wisdom relying on mere words that I was to employ in so doing, as I wanted to avert all danger that Christ's cross might be emptied of its true meaning.

[18]For this is how matters stand. The message of the cross is foolishness to those who are on the way to perdition, while to us who are in the way of salvation it is the power of God. As it stands written, [19][a]**'I will destroy the wisdom of the wise, and I will bring to nought the discernment of the discerning.'** [20][b]**What has become** of **the wise** man whose allegiance is to this present age of ours? **What has become of the expert in the law? What has become of the** subtle debater? Has not God [c]**shown the wisdom** of this world to be a **foolish thing?** [21]For this is what has happened. Since, as God ordained in his wisdom, the world failed to come to know God through its own wisdom, God chose to bring salvation to those who have faith, and that by the very foolishness of the message proclaimed. [22]Here are the Jews demanding signs; here are the Greeks in search of wisdom. [23]Yet, as for ourselves, we proclaim Christ crucified, an offence to the Jews and folly to the Gentiles, [24]but to those to whom the call has been sent forth, be they Jews or Greeks, Christ the power of God and the wisdom of God. [25]And so it is. Divine folly is wiser than any human wisdom, and divine weakness is stronger than any human strength.

[26]Consider, my brothers, how you were placed when the call came to you. Not many of you were wise by human standards, not many powerful, not many well-born. [27]On the contrary, God has chosen what the world thinks foolish, to put the wise to shame. God has chosen what the world thinks weak, to put the strong to shame. [28]God has chosen what the world thinks ignoble and contemptible. Indeed, he has chosen that which the world thinks of as being nothing, so as to bring to nothing that which is. [29]No human creature was to have any ground for boasting in the presence of God. [30]It is his doing that your life is one in union with Christ Jesus, he who has become wisdom to us—God willed it to be so—he who is the source of our righteousness, of our sanctification, of our redemption, [31]in order that it may be as scripture says, [d]**'He who boasts, let him make his boast in the Lord.'**

2   When I came to see you, my brothers, it was not with any high pretensions to eloquence or wisdom that I gave you my message, bearing testimony concerning God and his nature. [2]In fact, the resolution I came to was that, while I was in your midst, everything else was

---

[a]Is 29:14   [b]Is 19:12   [c]Job 12:17; Ps 33:10; Is 33:18   [d]Jr 9:23f

to be forgotten, and that I was to concern myself solely with Jesus Christ, and with him nailed on a cross. ³When I came among you, I found myself in a state of weakness, of timidity, of great anxiety. ⁴And my speech and the message I proclaimed did not rely on plausible words of wisdom but on giving a demonstration of the Spirit in all his power, ⁵so that your faith might have for its foundation not the wisdom of man but the power of God.

⁶Yet, when we are among those who have reached their full stature, we give utterance to what indeed deserves the name of wisdom. True enough, it is not the wisdom relied on by this present age or by those who play the part of rulers in this present age, men who are destined to be done away with. ⁷No, it is God's wisdom to which we give utterance —his secret purpose hidden until now—which God foreordained from before all time, so that glory might be ours. ⁸None of the men who bear rule in this present age knew of that wisdom. Had they done so, they would not have nailed to a cross the one in whom all glory resides. ⁹The truth of the matter, however, is expressed in these words from scripture: 'Those things which *ᵉno eye has ever seen, no ear has ever heard, which have never ʲentered the mind* of any man: **all the things which God** has prepared **for those who love him!**' ¹⁰And it is these very things which God has revealed to us through the Spirit.

Now, the Spirit has the power to search out everything, even the very depths of God's nature. ¹¹Who, indeed, is there among men that knows what is in a man except his own spirit within him? In the same way, there is no one that knows who God is except the Spirit of God. ¹²As for ourselves, the spirit we have received is not that of the world but the Spirit that comes from God, and we have received it in order that we might come to comprehend the things which God has graciously bestowed upon us. ¹³And it is these things we give utterance to, in words taught not by human wisdom but in words taught by the Spirit, treating of spiritual matters in a spiritual way. ¹⁴The man who is bound to nature rejects the things which are of the Spirit of God. Indeed, they are folly to him, and he is unable to grasp them because they demand a scrutiny which is spiritual. ¹⁵The spiritual man, on the other hand, has the power to scrutinize anything and everything, while himself not being subject to anyone's scrutiny. ¹⁶ᵍ'**Who,**' says the scripture, '**has** ever **known the mind of the Lord? Who, then, can instruct him** in anything?' We, however, possess the mind of Christ.

3   For my part, however, I found it impossible, my brothers, to address myself to you as men endowed with the Spirit. I had to deal with

ᵉIs 64:4   ʲJr 3:16   ᵍIs 40:13; [Wis 9:13]

you as men remaining on the level of mere nature, as but infants in the life of Christ. [2]It is milk, not solid food, I provided you with. You were not as yet strong enough to be given solid food. In fact, you still lack that strength, [3]seeing that even now you are not spiritually-minded. Indeed, when there is jealousy and strife among you, does that not go to show that you are unspiritual and that your conduct is guided by merely human standards? [4]When one man says, 'I belong to Paul', another 'I belong to Apollos', is it not plain that your attitude is that of men of the common run? [5]After all, what is Apollos, what is Paul? Surely, nothing more than servants who became the means of your coming to have faith, in the measure which the Lord granted to each. [6]I did the planting, Apollos did the watering, but it was God who made it grow. [7]And so it is that neither he who plants nor he who waters is anything: God who makes it grow is everything. [8]This one plants, that one waters. It all comes to the same thing. Yet each will receive his reward in proportion to his labour. [9]As for us, we are fellow workers with God, and you yourselves are a field of God's tilling, a building of God's design.

[10]In reliance on the gracious favour which God has bestowed upon me, I, like a skilled master-builder, have laid the foundation: it is left to someone else to build upon it. Only let each man take care how he builds upon it. [11]For no foundation can anybody lay other than the one that has been laid: Jesus Christ. [12]Now if anyone builds on this foundation, whether in gold, or silver, or precious stones, or wood, or hay, or straw, [13]the workmanship of each will be made manifest. It is the Day of the Lord that will disclose it, since that day will reveal itself in a blaze of fire. And the fire will test what kind of work each man has done. [14]If that which a man has built upon the foundation stands firm, he will receive a reward. [15]If anyone's work is burned up, he will be the loser. And yet he himself will be saved, but only as someone making his escape by passing through fire is saved. [16]Surely, you know what you are, that you are God's temple, and that God's Spirit dwells within you. [17]If anyone ruins the temple of God, God will bring ruin upon him. It is a holy thing, this temple of God. And you yourselves are that temple of God.

[18]Let no one deceive himself. Should anyone suppose that he stands out among you as a wise man—wise, I mean, by the standards of this present age—let him first of all become a fool, that he may become wise. [19]For this world's wisdom is but folly in the sight of God. As we find written in scripture, [h]'**He entraps the wise in their own cunning.**' [20]And again, [i]'**The Lord knows the reasonings** of wise men, **and how futile they are.**' [21]So let there be no one making a boast

[h]Job 5:12f   [i]Ps 94:11

of men. For everything is yours, 22be it Paul, or Apollos, or Cephas, or the world, or life, or death, or the present, or the future. It all belongs to you. 23And you belong to Christ, and Christ belongs to God.

4 This is the view which men should take of us, that we are Christ's servants, and stewards of the secret purposes of God. 2Now as for stewards, I would wish to add this, that the requirement to be met with in their case is that a man should prove himself worthy of trust. 3Yet, as for myself, it is in fact of the smallest possible concern to me that I should be made the object of your scrutiny or, for that matter, the object of any audit-day of human devising. The truth is that I do not even scrutinize my own conduct, 4for there is nothing against myself of which I am conscious. However, this does not imply that, for that reason, I stand acquitted. It is the Lord's scrutiny which I must undergo. 5So then, things being what they are, it is your duty not to pass judgment before the proper time has arrived, before the coming of the Lord, who will bring to light what is hidden in darkness and will lay bare the springs of action by which the minds of men have been guided. And then the praise due to each man will come to him from God.

6I have made the things I have said apply to the special case of myself and Apollos, and this I have done for your sake, so that, taking us for an example, you may be taught the truth of the words, 'Nothing beyond what is written', and may be prevented at the same time from becoming full of arrogance, favouring one man to the disparagement of another. 7Why, what is it that singles you out among men? Or what powers do you possess which you did not receive as a gift? And if you did receive them as a gift, why boast of them as if no gift were in question?

8You already call your own everything that heart can desire. Riches have already become yours. Already—without us—you have come into your kingdom. How I wish that you had indeed come into your kingdom, so that we, too, might become kings along with you! 9As it is, it seems to me as if God has exhibited us apostles as occupying the lowest place of all, like men under the sentence of death. Such a spectacle have we been made of to the whole of creation, to men and angels alike. 10We are fools for Christ's sake; your life as men in union with Christ is that of reasonable men. We are weak; you are strong. You are held in honour, we in disrepute. 11To this very hour, we suffer hunger and thirst; we are ill-clad; we are being maltreated; we have no home to settle in. 12We toil hard, working with our own hands. Men revile us and we answer with a blessing; they persecute us, and we bear it patiently; 13they speak ill of us, and we seek to conciliate them. We have become and are, to this very hour, as the refuse of the world, as the scum of all things.

[14]It is not to make you ashamed that I am writing to you like this, but to bring you to a better mind, as my children whom I dearly love. [15]Indeed, even though you were to have ten thousand instructors guiding your lives as followers of Christ, you have not more than one father. I brought you into union with Christ Jesus, through delivering the gospel to you, and it was thus that I became your father. [16]That is why I would urge you to take me for your model, [17]and why I have sent Timothy to you, who is my son, dearly loved and greatly to be trusted, in pursuit of the Lord's cause. He will remind you of the path which I tread in my life for Christ—of the manner in which I teach everywhere, in all the churches alike.

[18]There are, it is true, certain people who, having conceived the notion that I would not come to see you, have grown full of arrogance. [19]In fact, however, I shall be coming to see you soon, if the Lord so pleases. And what I shall then take cognizance of, as regards these people so full of arrogance, will not be their fine words but the power which they can show. [20]For it is power, not words, which builds up the kingdom of God. [21]Make your choice, then; am I to come to you, stick in hand, or lovingly, in a spirit of gentleness?

5 Why, there are reports of sexual misdemeanour among you of a kind which is not practised even by pagans: a man taking to himself a woman married to his father. [2]You, however, have taken up an attitude of self-complacency in this matter, when you ought rather to have felt grievously hurt, to the extent of removing the perpetrator of the deed from your midst. [3]As for myself, although absent in body, I am present with you in spirit; and I have already, as though I were present, passed judgment on the man who has so acted. [4]When you and my spirit are gathered together, attended with all the power of our Lord Jesus, [5]you should, in the name of the Lord Jesus, hand over to Satan such a man as this for the destruction of the corrupt part of his nature, so that his spirit might find salvation on the Day of the Lord.

[6]There is nothing good about this, which you make the ground for boasting. Surely, you know that even a little leaven causes the whole of the lump of dough to ferment. [7]Cleanse out the old leaven, that you may be a new lump of dough—even as you really are free from leaven. Has not Christ *j*been offered up in sacrifice, our Passover lamb? [8]Let us celebrate the feast, then, not with the leaven of old, that

*j*Ex 12:21

305

of malice and wickedness, but with unleavened bread, the bread of sincerity and truth.

⁹In the letter I wrote to you I told you that you were to keep yourselves from those committing fornication, ¹⁰not meaning by this, of course, every fornicator on earth, or those filled with greed, or extortioners, or idolaters. If that were your rule of conduct, you would be compelled to go out of the world altogether. ¹¹No, what my letter meant was that you were to keep yourselves aloof, should anyone known as one of the brothers be engaged in fornication, or be filled with greed, or be an idolater, a slanderer, a drunkard, or an extortioner. With a man of this sort you ought not even to sit at table. ¹²Why, indeed, should I make it my business to pronounce judgment on outsiders? And is it not those inside the church on whom you pronounce judgment? ¹³As for those outside, it is God who will be their judge. ᵏ**Remove the evildoer from your midst.**

6 If one of your number has a dispute with another, has he the audacity to go to law before a pagan court instead of bringing the matter before those who are consecrated to God? ²Surely, you know that it is those consecrated to God who will be passing judgment on the world. And if the world is to be judged at your bar, are you unworthy to serve on tribunals of the most trifling import? ³Surely, you know well enough that we shall be sitting in judgment over angels. Is it to be supposed, then, that we are not competent to deal with everyday matters? ⁴And if, as is indeed the case, there have to be tribunals dealing with everyday matters, how is it that you entrust jurisdiction to men who, from the point of view of those in the church, are held to be of no account? ⁵I say this to put you to shame. Has it come to this, that there is not a single man with sufficient skill to act as arbiter between one of his brothers and another, ⁶but brother goes to law with brother, and that at the bar of unbelievers? ⁷To be having lawsuits at all already amounts to your having suffered a defeat. How is it that you do not prefer to suffer wrong, to suffer loss? ⁸Instead of that, you yourselves inflict wrong, inflict loss, and that at a brother's expense. ⁹Surely, you know that wrongdoers will obtain no share in the kingdom of God. Do not allow yourselves to be deluded. It is not those engaging in fornication, the idolaters, the adulterers, those acting as partners in unnatural vice, the sodomites, ¹⁰the thieves, the greedy, the drunkards, the slanderers, the extortioners, who will obtain a share in the kingdom of God. ¹¹And such some of you once were. But you washed yourselves clean, you have been made holy,

ᵏDt 13:5; 17:7; 19:19; 22:21.22.24

306

you have been accepted as righteous in the name of the Lord Jesus Christ and by the Spirit of our God.

¹²'I am free to do as I will'. Yes, but not everything can be done without harm. 'I am free to do as I will'. But there is nothing that I will allow to gain the mastery over me. ¹³Food is meant for the stomach, and the stomach is meant for food. But then, God will bring to nought both the one and the other; while, as regards the body, it is not meant for fornication but for the Lord, and the Lord for the body. ¹⁴And God, just as he raised the Lord to life, will, by his power, raise us up too. ¹⁵Do you not know that your bodies are but parts of the body of Christ? Shall I take away, then, from Christ what forms part of his body, and make it over to a harlot? Far be the thought! ¹⁶Surely, you know that he who joins himself to a harlot becomes one with her in body. *'**The two,**' says scripture, '**shall become a single body.**' ¹⁷But the man who joins himself to the Lord becomes one with him, spiritually speaking. ¹⁸Keep clear, then, from fornication. Any other sin which a man may commit is taking place outside his body, but he who engages in fornication commits a sin against his own body. ¹⁹Or is it that you do not know that your body is a sanctuary of the Holy Spirit within you—the Spirit being a gift which God has bestowed upon you—and that you are not your own masters? ²⁰A great price was paid to redeem you. So let your bodies serve to glorify God.

7 I now turn to the questions raised in your letter. A man indeed does well if he abstains from all contact with women. ²However, because of the danger of fornication, let the position be this, that each man has his own wife, and each woman her own husband. ³Let the husband give his wife what is her due, and let the wife behave in the same way towards her husband. ⁴The wife has no right over her own body; it belongs to the husband. Equally, the husband has no right over his body; it belongs to the wife. ⁵Do not refuse one another, unless perhaps by mutual consent you do so for a time, to have more leisure to give yourselves to prayer; and then come together again, lest, through your lack of self-control, Satan should succeed in tempting you. ⁶What I have been saying has been said by way of making a concession, not by way of issuing a command. ⁷My own wish is that everybody should be as I am myself. However, each of us has his own gift graciously bestowed upon him by God, one to live in this way, another in that.

⁸To the unmarried and the widows I would say that they will do well to remain in the same state as I am myself. ⁹However, if they lack

*Gn 2:24

307

the gift of continence, let them marry. Better to marry than to be aflame with passion. [10] To those already married my instructions—or rather, the Lord's, not mine—are that a wife is not to separate from her husband [11] (should she have done so, she must remain unmarried, or else be reconciled to her husband), and that a husband is not to put away his wife. [12] As for the remaining cases, my directions—not the Lord's —are the following. If one of the brothers has a wife who is an unbeliever, and she consents to live with him, he is not to send her away. [13] And a woman who has a husband who is an unbeliever, he consenting to live with her, is not to send her husband away. [14] The unbelieving husband has shared in his wife's consecration, and the unbelieving wife has shared in the consecration of one who is a member of the brotherhood. Were it otherwise, your children would be tainted by a stain, whereas in fact they are consecrated throughout. [15] On the other hand, if the case be that the partner who is not a believer is for separating, let there be a separation. Under such circumstances the man or woman who belongs to the brotherhood is under no compulsion. It is in a spirit of peace that God's call has come to us. [16] And, after all, how can a woman know for certain that she will be the means of bringing salvation to her husband, or a man that he will be the means of bringing salvation to his wife?

[17] Be that as it may, let each man's life be in accordance with the part God has assigned to him, and with the condition in which he found himself when God's call came to him. That is the rule which I am laying down in all the churches. [18] Was anyone already circumcised when the call came to him? Let him do nothing to efface the circumcision. Was anyone uncircumcised when the call came to him? Let him not undergo circumcision. [19] Neither circumcision nor the want of it is of any consequence; it is keeping the commandments of God that matters. [20] Each should remain in the condition in which he was when the call came to him. [21] Were you a slave when the call came to you? Let not that weigh on your mind; on the other hand, should you be in a position to gain your freedom, you had better avail yourself of your opportunity. [22] The man who was a slave when he received the call to give his allegiance to the Lord's cause is the Lord's freedman, while, in a way corresponding to this, the man who received the call as a free man is the slave of Christ. [23] A great price was paid to redeem you; do not enslave yourselves to human masters. [24] So, my brothers, in whatever state each was called, there, before God, let each remain.

[25] In the case of women who are unmarried, I have no command to give you from the Lord, but I am offering you my opinion, which is that of a man who, having obtained mercy from the Lord, is worthy to be trusted. [26] This, then, is what I think. In view of the times of

stress which are upon us, it is well for a man to remain as he is. [27] Are you bound to a wife? Do not seek to free yourself. Are you free from wedlock? Do not seek a wife. [28] On the other hand, should you marry, you have committed no sin; nor has the unmarried woman committed a sin if she marries. It is only that people such as these will have trouble coming upon them in respect of their outward condition, whereas my wish is that you may be spared. [29] However, my brothers, I would wish to make this observation. The time of the end has drawn very close to us, so that henceforth even those who have wives should be as though they had none, [30] those who mourn as though they were not mourning, those who rejoice as though they were not rejoicing, those who buy as though they were not entering into full ownership; [31] and those who take advantage of what the world offers as though they were not taking full advantage of it. The world as it is fashioned now is passing away. [32] And I would wish you to be free from anxious care. When a man is unmarried, it is the Lord's concern that he cares about, and what interests him is how he can please the Lord. [33] When a man is married, he cares about worldly concerns, and what interests him is how he can please his wife. [34] The married and the unmarried woman differ from one another in the same way. The unmarried woman cares about the Lord's concerns, her aim being that she may be a woman consecrated in both body and spirit, while, once a woman is married, she cares about worldly concerns, being interested in how she can please her husband. [35] In making these observations, I have your own advantage in mind, and my aim is by no means to bind you in any way but to help you towards that which is seemly, making it possible for you to attend on the Lord without distraction.

[36] If anyone considers that he is acting unbecomingly towards the girl in his charge—she being past the bloom of her youth—and there is no way of avoiding it, he should do as he wishes. There is nothing sinful in it. Let the marriage take place. [37] But if a man is fixed in his resolution, being free from external constraint and master over his own choice, the course he has decided upon being that the girl in his charge is to remain unwed, such a man does well. [38] It comes to this, then, that he who gives the girl in his charge in marriage does well, while he who does not give her in marriage will do still better. [39] As for a wife, she is bound to her husband while he is alive. Should her husband be dead, she is free to marry anyone she will, so long as the union is within the Lord's fellowship. [40] Yet, in my judgment, she has a greater blessing resting on her if she remains as she is. And I, too—I would venture to suppose—am a man who has the Spirit of God dwelling within him.

8 I now turn to the question of food used in idolatrous worship. Now, we are fully aware that we are all endowed with knowledge. But then, what knowledge does to one is that it breeds self-conceit; it is love that builds one up. 2Indeed, if someone supposes that he has acquired knowledge of something, he may be sure that he does not yet possess as much knowledge of it as he ought to have. 3No, it is he who loves God who is acknowledged by God.

4As for eating food, then, which has been used in idolatrous worship, we are well aware that, wherever in the world an object of idol worship may be found, that object has no real existence—and moreover, that there is no God but one. 5Even granted that there are so-called gods, whether in heaven or on earth (as indeed, there are many 'gods' and many 'lords'), 6yet for us there is only one God, the Father, who is the source of all things and the goal of our very existence; only one Lord, Jesus Christ, through whom all things were made and through whom we are what we are.

7The truth, however, is that the knowledge in question is not to be found in all men. Instead, there are some who, through the force of habit still clinging to them concerning the idol, eat such food as though it had actually been offered to an idol, and their conscience, being that of men lacking in vigour, suffers defilement. 8But then, it is not the food we eat which gives us our standing with God. We are no worse off if we do not eat, and no better if we do. 9One thing, however, you must make sure of: this liberty of yours should not prove a stumbling block to those who are deficient in vigour. 10Indeed, were someone to see you—the man who possesses knowledge —at table in an idol's temple, will not the other man, who is supposed to have his conscience built up, be led instead to eat his food in such a way as to imply offering idolatrous worship—seeing that he is a man who lacks strength? 11And so it comes about that, as the result of your knowledge, ruin is being brought on him who lacks vigour, on the brother for whose sake Christ died. 12Why, by thus sinning against your brothers, by inflicting a blow on their conscience in its weakness, you sin against Christ. 13And that is why, if what I eat is an occasion of sin to my brother, I shall for evermore refrain from touching meat, so as not to be the occasion of my brother's sin.

9 Am I not my own master? Am I not an apostle? Have I not seen Jesus our Lord? If you are in the Lord's service, is it not I who have made you what you are? 2While to others I may not be an apostle, yet assuredly I am one to you. Why, you are, in your own persons, the

very seal attesting the apostolate which I undertook with the Lord by my side.

3 To those seeking to make me the object of their scrutiny I would answer thus in my defence. 4 Do we not have the right to eat and drink? 5 Do we not have the right to take a sister in the faith on our journeys as our wife, as the other apostles do, as do the Lord's brothers and Cephas? 6 Is it only I and Barnabas who are to be deprived of the right to refrain from working for our living? 7 Why, what soldier ever fought at his own expense? Who plants a vineyard and does not eat of the fruit it yields? Who tends a flock without having his share of the milk which the flock produces? 8 Am I considering the matter merely from a human point of view? Is it not true rather that the law says the very same? Indeed it does, 9 for what stands written in the law of Moses is this: *m*'**You shall not muzzle an ox when it is treading out the corn.**' Now are we to suppose that it is oxen God is concerned about? 10 Is it not clear rather that, when he speaks as he does, this is assuredly for our sakes? And indeed, those words were written for our sakes, to show that the ploughman should plough in hope, and the thresher thresh in the hope of obtaining his share.

11 If we have sown a spiritual harvest for your benefit, is it too much to ask that we should reap a temporal harvest from you? 12 If others partake of such a right, do we ourselves not have a still better claim? And yet we have not availed ourselves of that right. On the contrary, we bear every hardship sooner than prove in any way an obstacle to the preaching of Christ's gospel. 13 You know, surely, that those who perform the temple service get their living out of the temple's revenues, that those who are serving at the altar claim their share of the sacrifice. 14 In the same way the Lord has directed that those who proclaim the gospel are to get their livelihood from doing so. 15 Yet, as regards myself, I have not availed myself of any of these rights, nor am I writing as I do in order to claim any such provision. Indeed, I would rather die than allow anyone to render null and void my ground for boasting. 16 For when I preach the gospel, that gives me no ground for boasting. It is simply a necessity which is laid upon me. It would go hard with me indeed were I not to preach the gospel. 17 Suppose I were to do this of my own choice, then a reward would be due to me. But if it is not of my own choice, that simply amounts to my having been entrusted with a stewardship. 18 What, then, is my claim to a reward? Why, that in preaching the gospel I should do so free of charge, not making use to the full of the rights to which gospel-preaching entitles me.

*m*Dt 25:4

[19]Thus, although there was nobody to take my freedom away from me, I have made myself everybody's slave, so that I might win over all the more souls. [20]To the Jews I became as a Jew, that I might win over the Jews. To those subject to the law I became as one subject to the law—though not being myself subject to the law—that I might win over those subject to the law. [21]To those outside the scope of the law I became as one outside the law (although I am, indeed, not outside God's law, being, on the contrary, bound to the law of Christ), so that I might win over those who are outside the law. [22]To those with no vigour in their faith I became as a man lacking vigour, so that I might win over those who are without vigour. I have been everything by turns to everybody, so that in each one of these ways I might bring salvation to some. [23]And I do it all for the sake of the gospel, that I might become one of those sharing in its blessings.

[24]You know that, when men run in a race, the race is for all, but only one man wins the prize. Run, therefore, that you may secure it. [25]Now all those entering an athletic contest practise self-control in every respect. And they do it for the sake of a crown that perishes, while our aim is to win one that is imperishable. [26]As regards myself, then, I do not run my course as a man in doubt of his goal; I do not fight as a boxer who wastes his blows beating the air. [27]No, I buffet my body, making it my slave, lest, having preached to others, I myself should be rejected as worthless.

10

My brothers, there are certain matters of which you ought to remind yourselves. Our forefathers all found shelter under the pillar of cloud; all of them passed safely through the sea. [2]All alike were, by virtue of the cloud and the sea, baptized into the fellowship of Moses. [3]They all ate the same spiritual food [4]and they all drank the same spiritual drink. For it was from a supernatural rock following them in their path that they were accustomed to have their drink. And the rock was Christ. [5]But for all that, God was ill-pleased with most of them. As scripture has it, [n]'they were laid low in the desert.'

[6]Now these things came about as pointers to the future, to serve as warning examples. We were not to [o]set our hearts, as they set their hearts, on things which are evil. [7]And do not turn into idolaters, as some of them did. As it stands written in scripture: [p]'The people sat down to eat and drink, and rose up to make merry.' [8]Neither must we commit fornication, as some of them did; and twenty-three thousand fell in a single day. [9]Neither must we put the Lord to the test, as some of them put the Lord to the test, and were destroyed by

[n]Nm 14:16.23.30   [o]Nm 11:34.4   [p]Ex 32:6

the serpents. [10]Neither must we grumble, as some of them gave way to grumbling, and perished at the hand of the destroying angel.

[11]Now these things kept happening to them as a pointer to the future, by way of serving as a warning. And they were put on record to be an admonition to us, upon whom the end of the ages has come. [12]So then, let him who thinks that he stands firm take care lest he should fall. [13]No temptation has ever held you in its grip but such as is the common lot of man. No, God is true to his word, and so he will not allow you to be tempted beyond what you are able to endure. Instead, he will provide, along with the temptation, the way of escape, that you may be able to bear up under it.

[14]And so, my dear brothers, in consideration of all this, it is your duty to keep far away from the worship of idols. [15]I am addressing myself to you as men of good sense; bring your own judgment to bear on my words. [16]The cup of blessing which we bless, is it not a sharing in the blood of Christ? The loaf of bread which we break, is it not a sharing in the body of Christ, [17]seeing that we, many as we are, are but one loaf, one body, all of us partaking of the same loaf?

[18]Or consider the case of Israel, in the natural sense of that word. Are not those who eat the sacrifices sharers in the altar? [19]What, then, do I mean to assert? That a thing sacrificed to an idol is anything, or that an idol is anything? [20]No, but that, when the pagans offer sacrifice, they are offering it, not to God ⁋**but to demons.** And I would not have you become partners with demons. [21]You cannot drink the cup of the Lord and the cup of demons; you cannot partake of the Lord's table and the table of demons. [22]Or do we mean to ʳ**provoke the Lord to jealousy?** Have we greater powers than he has?

[23]'I am free to do as I will'. Yes, but not everything can be done without harm. 'I am free to do as I will'. Yes, but not everything serves to build one up in the faith. [24]Let no one be concerned about his own well-being, but each about the well-being of the other.

[25]When things are sold in the open market, you may eat them, whatever they are, without raising any questions on grounds of conscience. [26]ˢ**The earth is the Lord's, and all that is in it.** [27]If some unbeliever invites you to his table, and you care to go, you may eat whatever is put before you without raising any questions on grounds of conscience. [28]But should someone say to you, 'This has been offered in sacrifice', then refuse to eat it, out of consideration for your informant and for conscience' sake—[29]his own conscience, I mean, not yours.

'What,' you say, 'is my freedom of action to be called in question by another's conscience? [30]If it is with thanksgiving that I partake of

⁋Lv 17:7; Dt 32:17; Ps 106:37   ʳDt 32:21; 4:24   ˢPs 24:1

such food, why should I incur reproach over that for which I give thanks?' Well and good. Take this, then, for your guide. [31]Whether you are eating or drinking, or whatever else you are doing, do it for the glory of God. [32]And give no offence to Jew, or to Greek, or to God's Church, [33]just as I, for my part, am ready to make myself acceptable to everyone in every respect, not aiming at my own advantage but at that of the many, so that they might obtain their salvation. 11[1]Model yourselves on me, as I model myself on Christ.

11

[2]I praise you for keeping me in remembrance in every way and for upholding the traditions, just as I handed them on to you. [3]But this I would have you know. Every man has Christ as his head over him, while a woman's head is her husband, and Christ's head is God. [4]And there is this. A man who keeps his head covered when he is praying or uttering prophecy brings shame on his head, [5]whereas a woman brings shame on her head if she unveils it when she is praying or uttering prophecy. In point of fact, there is no difference between her and one who has her head shaved. [6]And indeed, a woman who will not wear a veil may just as well go to the length of having her hair cut off. Well then, since it is a disgraceful thing for a woman to be shorn or shaven, let her go veiled. [7]As for a man, on the other hand, he ought indeed not to have his head covered: he is [t]**God's image** shining forth to his glory, while a wife shines forth to the glory of her husband. [8]For the truth is that man does not take his origin from woman, but woman takes hers from man; [9]and moreover, it was not man who was created for woman's sake, but woman for man's. [10]That is why a woman, if only for fear of offending the angels, ought to have on her head something signifying her subjection to authority. [11]Not that woman is anything apart from man, or man anything apart from woman, as regards our life in fellowship with the Lord. [12]If it be true that woman takes her origin from man, it is true also that it is through woman that man now comes into existence. And it is God who is the source of it all.

[13]Bring your judgment to bear on the question whether it is fitting that a woman should offer prayer to God unveiled. [14]Does not nature herself teach you that, whereas it is a disgrace for a man to wear his hair long, [15]when a woman wears her hair long, this is something she may glory in? That is so because her hair has been given her to serve as a covering. [16]Besides, if anyone is disposed to be contentious about this, suffice it to say that no such custom is found among us or, for that matter, in any of God's churches.

[17]But, while giving you these instructions, I may mention that

[t]Gn 1:27; 5:1

there is one thing I can give you no praise for; when you meet together, you do so in a way that does harm rather than good. [18]To begin with, I am informed—and I am inclined to believe that there is some truth in this—that when you meet in assembly, divisions are apt to be formed among you. [19]Now I admit that there is no way of avoiding faction, if only so that those of approved worth should stand out from the rest. [20]However, this is how matters really stand: when you assemble, no eating of the Lord's Supper does in fact take place, [21]since what happens when one eats is that each goes ahead with his own supper, one going hungry, while another has drunk deep. [22]What, have you no houses to eat and drink in? Or is it that you hold God's Church in contempt, at the same time being intent on humiliating the poor? What am I to say to you? Am I to give you praise? There is no room for praise here.

[23]Now this is the message which I myself received at the hand of the Lord, and which I, in turn, handed on to you. On the night when he was being delivered up, the Lord Jesus took into his hands a loaf of bread, [24]and when he had given thanks, he broke it into pieces, saying, 'This is my body. It is for you. Do this by way of a memorial of me.' [25]And so with the cup when supper was ended. 'This cup,' he said, 'is the new [u]**covenant** sealed by my **blood.** Do this, whenever you drink of it, by way of a memorial of me.' [26]Thus it is the Lord's death which you are heralding whenever, until the day of his coming again, you eat this bread and drink of the cup. [27]And therefore, if anyone eats the bread or drinks of the cup of the Lord unworthily, he will be called to account for profaning the body and the blood of the Lord. [28]A man ought to examine himself first, and then eat of that bread and drink of that cup. [29]And indeed, he who eats and drinks will, if he fails to judge the Lord's body aright, be eating and drinking judgment on himself. [30]That is why so many of your number are wanting in strength and health, and not a few have died. [31]On the other hand, did we judge ourselves aright, there would be no such thing as our being judged. [32]As it is, we are, in being judged, chastised by the Lord, so that we might not, along with the world, incur a judgment of condemnation. [33]So, my brothers, when you meet together for your meal, wait for one another. [34]If anyone be hungry, let him take his food at home, lest your meeting together might lead to your having judgment pronounced against you. As for the other questions, I shall give my directions at whatever time I may be coming to see you.

[u][Jr 31:31;] Ex 24:8; Zc 9:11

12 And now, my brothers, I turn to spiritual gifts, about which I do not wish you to remain in ignorance. ²You know full well that when you were still pagans, you allowed yourselves to be led off, wherever you happened to be led, to worship false gods that gave no utterance. ³That is why I would have you understand this, that, just as no one can be speaking through God's Spirit if he says 'Jesus is accursed', so it is only through the Holy Spirit that anyone can say, 'Jesus is Lord'.

⁴As for gifts, they are, it is true, variously distributed, while yet it is one and the same Spirit who bestows them; ⁵just as different kinds of service are variously distributed, while yet it is one and the same Lord to whom they are to be rendered; ⁶and different kinds of power are variously distributed, while it is one and the same God by whom all things in all men are wrought. ⁷Now that which shows forth the Spirit is given to each, with the intention that it should serve a beneficent end. ⁸To one, utterance of wisdom is given through the Spirit; to another, utterance of knowledge by the leading of the same Spirit. ⁹Still another has faith given to him by means of the same Spirit, another gifts of healing by means of the one Spirit, ¹⁰another the power of working miracles, another prophetic utterance, another the ability to distinguish true spirits from false; still another the gift of speaking in tongues of inspiration of this or that sort, another that of interpreting such tongues. ¹¹And all this is wrought by one and the same Spirit, distributing severally to each, in accordance with his will.

¹²And indeed, just as the human body is one, while it has many organs, and all these organs, many as they are, go to form but one body, so it is with Christ. ¹³For we were, all of us, baptized, and that by virtue of the one Spirit, to form a single body, Jews and Greeks, slaves and free men, alike. We have all been given to drink at a single source, the one Spirit. ¹⁴As for this body of ours, it does not consist of one organ but of many. ¹⁵If the foot were to say, 'I am not a hand, and therefore I do not belong to the body', it does not on that account belong any less to the body. ¹⁶And if the ear were to say, 'I am not an eye, and therefore I do not belong to the body', it does not on that account belong any less to the body. ¹⁷Where would the power of hearing be if the body were all eye? Where the power of smell if it were all ear? ¹⁸As it is, God assigned to the organs, to each one of them, its place in the body. ¹⁹If the whole were a single organ, where would the body be? ²⁰The truth, however, is this, that we have many organs and one body. ²¹The eye cannot say to the hand, 'I have no need of you', nor again, the head to the feet, 'I have no need of you'. ²²On the contrary, it is much nearer the truth to say that it is the organs which appear to be somewhat feeble which are the indispensable ones.

23Moreover, the parts of the body which we regard as less honourable are precisely those which we clothe with all the more abundant honour; and so it is that our uncomely parts are having comeliness bestowed upon them all the more abundantly, 24no such need arising in the case of the comely ones. The truth, however, is that it was God who thus blended the body together, bestowing upon that which was placed in an inferior position an honour all the more abundant. 25There was to be no discord in the body. On the contrary, its members were to make each other's welfare their common care. 26Thus, when one member suffers, all the members suffer with it; when one member has honour bestowed upon it, all the members share its joy.

27And as for yourselves, you are the body of Christ, and, looked upon individually, you are members of that body. 28God has assigned to us different positions in the Church—first, apostles, secondly, prophets, thirdly, teachers. Then come miraculous powers, then gifts of healing, works of mercy, management of affairs, the gift of speaking in inspired tongues of this or that sort. 29Are all of us apostles, all prophets, all teachers? Do all have miraculous powers? 30Do all have gifts of healing? Do all speak in inspired tongues? Do all have the gift of interpreting them? 31However, you should persist in striving after those gifts which are of the greatest value.

And meanwhile, I will show you a way that surpasses all else in excellence.

13 Were I to open my mouth in inspired tongues, such as men, such as angels, give utterance to, while at the same time I was a man with no love in his heart, I have become no better than brass echoing forth sound, than a cymbal giving out its clashing noise. 2And if I have powers of prophecy, if I can unravel all secret truths, am endowed with perfect knowledge, if I have a faith so unshakable as to be able to move mountains, yet there is no love in my heart, I am nothing. 3And if I give away to others all that I possess, if I surrender my body to be burned, but there is no love in my heart, it avails me nothing. 4Love is patient and kind; love knows of no envy, is no braggart, not swollen with pride. 5It never acts indecorously, does not claim its rights, cannot be provoked; it bears no resentment of an injury. 6It never rejoices over an injustice, and it is in the truth that it finds all its joy. 7It bears up patiently to the last; it trusts to the last, it hopes to the last, it endures to the last.

8Love will never come to an end. As for prophecies, they will be swept out of the way; as for tongues of inspiration, they will cease; as for knowledge, it will be swept out of the way. 9For this is how matters stand. It is but part of the truth which we lay hold of in our knowledge, in our prophesyings. [10] And when the time comes for the completeness of things to show itself, that which yields us but partial glimpses of them will be swept out of the way. [11] When I was a child, I talked like a child, I thought like a child, I reasoned like a child, while, since I became a man, I have put away from myself the ways of childhood. [12] At present our sight of things is one through a mirror which throws them into bewildering confusion, but there will be a time when we shall see them [v]face to face. At present my knowledge is one yielding but partial glimpses, but there will be a time when I shall know completely, even as God, from the first, completely knew me. [13] Meanwhile, faith, hope, and love endure, these three; but the greatest of them all is love.

14 May love be that of which you are in pursuit. And make the spiritual gifts the object of your strivings, your concern being mainly with being able to prophesy. [2] He who speaks in an inspired tongue is not speaking to men but to God. He is not understood by anyone, for what he does is that in his spirit he gives expression to truths hidden in darkness. [3] It is otherwise with him who is engaged in prophesying. He is addressing himself to his fellow men to build them up in the faith, to encourage them, to comfort them. [4] He who speaks in an inspired tongue is having his own faith built up, while it is the faith of the assembled church which is built up by the man who prophesies. [5] I would gladly have you all speaking in inspired tongues, but what I should like even better is to have you prophesy. And, in fact, the prophet ranks higher than the man speaking in inspired tongues, unless, that is, the latter has the ability to provide an interpretation of his words, so that the church may receive something which may contribute to her upbuilding. [6] But as things are, my brothers, how could I benefit you in any way were I to come among you speaking in an inspired tongue, without imparting a revealed truth or a piece of knowledge by way of prophecy or instruction? [7] There are lifeless things capable of producing sound, a flute, for example, or a harp; but even with these, unless there be clear distinctions between the sounds they produce, how are we to recognize what tune is being played on the flute or the harp? [8] If the bugle—to take another example—gives out an indistinct sound, what man will make himself ready for battle? [9] So it is with you. If no precise meaning attaches to that 'tongue' of yours, how is anyone to know what is being said? Why, your words will be falling on empty air. [10] There are, I dare say, all sorts of languages in the world, none of them incapable of con-

[v][Nm 12:8]

veying meaning. [11] Well then, if I am ignorant of what is signified by a language I am being addressed in, the result will be this: I shall be the barbarian from the point of view of the one who is doing the talking, while he will be a barbarian from mine. [12] So it is with you. Since you are in such eager pursuit of the spiritual gifts, let it be with a view to contributing to the upbuilding of the church that you strive to possess them in abundant measure.

[13] That is why anyone endowed with the gift of speaking in an inspired tongue should pray to be given the power of interpreting. [14] And indeed, what happens when my prayer is one uttering itself by way of an inspired tongue is this: even though my spirit is engaged in prayer, my understanding fails to be fruitful in any way. [15] What then is the proper way of proceeding? It is that I shall use understanding as well as spirit when I offer prayer, use understanding as well as spirit when I give praise. [16] Otherwise, if you bless God in this spiritual fashion, how can anyone who finds himself in the position of the man who lacks the gift, say 'Amen' at the close of your thanksgiving? After all, he is ignorant of what you are saying. [17] True enough; but while you are duly giving thanks, there is nothing here to build up the other man's faith. [18] As for myself, I am indeed thankful to God for possessing the gift of speaking in inspired tongues to a higher degree than any of you. [19] Yet in church I would rather speak five words having their source in my understanding, so as to be able to play my part also in instructing others, than ten thousand of them in an inspired tongue.

[20] My brothers, do not prove yourselves to be children in your thinking. No, while being very babes in respect of malicious intent, prove yourselves in your thinking men fully mature. [21] We read in the law, *w*'**By men of strange tongues, by the lips of strangers, will I speak to this people, and even** so **they will not listen** to me.' [22] This goes to show that 'tongues' serve as a sign, not for believers but for unbelievers, whereas prophecy is meant not for unbelievers but for believers. [23] Now what will be the outcome if the whole church is met together, everybody speaking in inspired tongues, and there come in ordinary men without the gift, or else men who are unbelievers? Will they not say that you have lost your reason? [24] If, on the other hand, everybody is prophesying, and there comes in someone who is an unbeliever, or an ordinary man without the gift, everybody will be bringing guilt home to him, everybody will be scrutinizing him. [25] The secrets of his heart will be brought to light, and so, falling on his face, *x***he will pay homage** to God, proclaiming that **God is, in very truth, in your midst.**

*w*Dt 28:49; Is 28:11f   *x*Is 45:14; Dn 2:47; Zc 8:23

26 How then, my brothers, does the matter stand? Whenever you meet together, each of you has something to offer: one man makes himself ready to sing a song of praise, another to make known a revealed truth, another to speak in an inspired tongue, another to perform the task of interpreting. Now you must make sure that all this is done, so that it may result in building up the soul. 27 And if there should be any speaking in an inspired tongue, only two are to speak, or three at the most, and that one at a time, while, as for interpreting, let one man suffice to perform that task. 28 But if no interpreter be present, let the man with the gift keep silence, when the congregation is assembled, holding converse with himself and with God. 29 As for the prophets, let two or three of them speak, while the rest sit in judgment on what is being said. 30 But if some revelation be vouchsafed to another who is sitting by, let the first man hold his peace. 31 There is nothing to make it impossible that you should all prophesy, so that the whole company may receive instruction and encouragement, 32 the truth being that the prophets' spirits are under the prophets' control. 33 God is the author of peace, not of disorder. All the assemblies of those consecrated to God give proof of it.

34 As for women, they should keep silent when the congregations are assembled. Utterance is not permitted to them. No, it is their duty to submit themselves, as the law also says. 35 And if there be any question on which they wish to be informed, let them ask their husbands at home. It is a disgraceful thing that a woman should make her voice heard in a meeting of the congregation. 36 If you have doubts on this, is it perhaps that you suppose that God's word came forth from you yourselves, that you are the only people it has reached?

37 If anyone considers himself to be a prophet or a man endowed with spiritual gifts, let him acknowledge that what I am writing to you are words of command from the Lord. 38 And should someone be in ignorance of that, let him remain in his ignorance. 39 To sum up, then, my brothers: make prophesying the object of your strivings, and as for speaking in inspired tongues, do nothing to forbid it. 40 Only see to it that everything is done decently and in an orderly fashion.

15 And now, my brothers, I would bring before your mind the gospel which I proclaimed to you, the very gospel which you accepted and on which you have taken your stand. 2 Moreover, it is this gospel which is the means of your obtaining your salvation, so long, that is, as you hold fast to what I proclaimed to you, preserving the very tenor of my preaching. Otherwise, if you fail to do this, it would have to be concluded that, when you came to embrace the faith, it was all quite superficial. 3 Well then, first and foremost I passed on to you what I,

for my part, had handed on to me. And it was this: that Christ died for our sins, as the scriptures had foretold, [4]that he was buried, and then, as the scriptures had foretold, was raised to life again on the third day, [5]and that he appeared to Cephas and then to the Twelve. [6]Afterwards he appeared to five hundred and more of our brothers on the same occasion, most of these surviving to this day, while some of them have gone to their rest. [7]Still later he appeared to James, and then to all the apostles. [8]And last of all he appeared to me also, this having to be looked upon as being, as it were, the fruit not of a proper birth but of an untimely one. [9]For I am the least of all the apostles; indeed, I am not fit to be called an apostle, seeing that I was a man who had been persecuting the church of God. [10]However, by the grace of God I am what I am; and the grace he has shown me did indeed not prove fruitless. No, I took on greater toils than any of the rest. Or rather, it was not I but the grace of God by my side. [11]That is our preaching, mine or theirs, as you will; that is the faith which has become yours.

[12]Now if the message proclaimed about Christ is this, that he has been raised from the dead, how is it that there are some among you who assert that there is no such thing as a resurrection of the dead? [13]Surely, if it be true that there is no resurrection of the dead, it follows that Christ himself was not raised to life. [14]And it follows further that, if Christ was not raised to life, then that proclamation of ours is a vain and empty thing, and so is your faith a vain and empty thing. [15]Worse still, we are found guilty of having given false testimony about God; we bore God witness that he raised Christ to life, while in fact he did not raise him, if it be true that the dead are not raised to life. [16]If the dead, I say, are not raised, then Christ has not been raised either; [17]and if Christ has not been raised, then your faith is futile— you are still in your old state of sinfulness. [18]Moreover, there is another thing which follows: those who have gone to their rest, as persons committed to Christ, have in fact perished. [19]And indeed, if it be true that any hope we may have come to repose in Christ is for this life only, then in fact we are of all men the most pitiable.

[20]The truth, however, is that Christ has been raised from the dead, being the firstfruits of those who have entered their rest. [21]For this is how the matter stands. It was through a man that death was brought to us, and so it was a man who brought the resurrection of the dead. [22]And indeed, just as all die in virtue of being one with Adam, so it is in virtue of being one with Christ that all will have life bestowed upon them. [23]But each in his own order: Christ the firstfruits, and then, at his coming, those who belong to Christ. [24]And after that there will come the End, when he will be surrendering the kingship to him who is his God and Father, having first brought to nought every other sort

of rule, authority, and power. [25]As for his kingship, it is destined to continue until the time when God *y*will have put all his enemies under his feet. [26]The last enemy to be brought to nought is death. [27]This must needs happen, since, as scripture says, 'God has *z*put all things in subjection under his feet.' But when it is said that all things have been made subject to him, it is plain enough that that excludes the one who subjected all things to him. [28]And indeed, what will happen when all things have been made subject to him is that the Son himself will be made subject to him who made all things subject to him, so that God may be all in all.

[29]Another point. If what we have been saying is not true, what will be the position of those who undergo baptism on behalf of the dead? If it is not true at all that the dead are raised to life, why in the wide world should they undergo baptism on their behalf? [30]And why, for that matter, should we ourselves face peril hour after hour? [31]I swear to you, my brothers, by the pride I take in you, as a man who has united himself to Christ Jesus our Lord, that death is upon me day in and day out. [32]If it was, while looking at the matter from a purely worldly point of view, that I engaged in a fight against 'wild beasts' at Ephesus, what use was it? If the dead are not raised to life, then, as scripture says, *a*'let us eat and drink, for tomorrow we die.'

[33]Do not allow yourselves to be led astray. 'Bad company,' as the saying goes, 'can corrupt the character of one naturally good.' [34]Come back to your senses, like right-minded men, and sin no longer. There are certain people who are devoid of all knowledge of God. I say this to put you to shame.

[35]But perhaps someone will ask, 'How can the dead be raised up? Why, with what kind of body will they be coming forth?' [36]Foolish men that you are! The seed you sow in the ground has no life given to it unless it first dies. [37]And what you sow is not the body which is one day to be, but just a bare grain—say, one of wheat or one of some other sort. [38]God, however, bestows a body upon it in accordance with his choice: upon each kind of seed a body of its own. [39]Flesh is not all of the same kind. No, men have one kind of flesh, cattle another, birds another, the fish another. [40]So, too, there are bodies that belong to heaven and bodies that belong to the earth, while the splendour of the heavenly bodies is one thing, and the splendour of the earthly bodies another. [41]The sun has its own splendour, the moon hers, the stars theirs, one star differing from another in splendour. [42]So it is with the resurrection of the dead. What is sown corruptible is raised incorruptible; [43]what is sown unhonoured is raised a thing of splendour; what is sown as something weak is raised a thing of might; [44]what is sown

*y*Ps 110:1   *z*Ps 8:6   *a*Is 22:13

as a natural body is raised as a spiritual body. If, on the one hand, there is a natural body, on the other there is a spiritual one. [45]The first *b***man,** Adam, scripture tells us, **became a living creature,** while the 'last Adam' has become a life-giving spirit. [46]Observe further that it is not what is spiritual which comes first, but what is natural; what is spiritual comes afterwards. [47]*c***The man** who came first **is of the earth,** made **of dust;** the man who came second is from heaven. [48]The nature of the earthly man is shared by those who are of the earth, while the nature of the man from heaven is shared by those who belong to heaven. [49]And just as we have worn the likeness of the earthly man, so also shall we wear the likeness of the man from heaven.

[50]What I mean to tell you, my brothers, is this. It is impossible that a share in the kingdom of God should be obtained by what is but flesh and blood; nor does that which is corruptible obtain a share in what is incorruptible. [51]And here I am unfolding to you—mark it well—a truth kept hidden hitherto. Not all of us will be sleeping in death, but we shall all be changed. [52]It will happen in an instant, at the flicker of an eyelid, when the time comes for the last trumpet to sound forth. And it will sound forth. The dead will be raised to life freed from corruption, and we shall find ourselves changed. [53]For so it must be: this corruptible nature of ours is destined to clothe itself with incorruptible life, this mortal nature with immortality. [54]Then, when this corruptible nature has put on its incorruptible garment, this mortal nature its immortality, what is said in scripture will find its fulfilment: *d***'Death has been swallowed up; victory has come';** and, [55]*e***'Death, where is your victory? Death, where is your sting?'** [56]It is sin which gives death its sting; it is the law which gives sin its power. [57]But thanks be to God, who is giving us the victory through our Lord Jesus Christ.

[58]Therefore, my brothers, my dearly-loved ones, show yourselves to be steadfast, immovable in your resolve, taking at all times your share, and more than your share, in the work the Lord has assigned to you, while knowing full well that your toil in the Lord's service will not fail to bear fruit.

16 And now about the collection for the benefit of those consecrated to God. In this matter I have given my directions to the congregations in Galatia; and you, too, are to act in conformity with these. [2]On the first day of the week, each one of you should put a certain sum aside, this sum bearing a proportion to whatever profit a man may have made, so that no collecting should be going on at the time of my visit. [3]And this is how I shall proceed when I have arrived in

*b*Gn 2:7   *c*Gn 2:7   *d*Is 25:8   *e*Hos 13:14

your midst: I shall send out whatever men you may have judged fit for the task, equipped with letters accrediting them; and it is these that are to convey your gracious gift to Jerusalem. 4If, however, it should turn out that it is worth my while to make the journey myself, these men will be travelling as my companions.

5It is after passing through Macedonia—for my plan is to travel by way of Macedonia—that I shall be paying you my visit. 6And it is then that I shall perhaps remain with you for a time, or even spend the whole of the winter in your company, so that you will be the ones who put me on the way to my next stage, whatever that may be. 7And indeed, I have no intention of seeing you just in passing, my hope being that I shall be by your side for some considerable time, if the Lord will let me. 8Until Pentecost, however, I shall be staying on at Ephesus; 9for a great opportunity which calls for much effort lies before me, and there is many a foe to be fought.

10When Timothy arrives, make sure that in his dealings with you all anxiety is taken away from him; he is doing work in the Lord's service, just as I am. 11Let no one, therefore, treat him as being of no account. Send him on his way happily to join me. I am expecting him here, and so are the brothers who are with me.

12As for our brother Apollos, I have repeatedly urged him to accompany the brothers who are on their way to you. But no, he was determined that he would not on any account pay you a visit at the present time. However, he will be coming to see you, whenever an opportune moment shall present itself.

13Be on the alert, stand firm in the faith, acquit yourselves like men, be strong in resolve. 14Let everything you do be done in a spirit of love. 15And here, my brothers, I would make an appeal to you. You know the household of Stephanas, how they were the very first of the harvest which Achaia has yielded, and how they appointed themselves to the task of rendering service for those who are consecrated to God. 16I would urge you, then, to show deference to men such as these, and indeed, to every fellow worker, to everyone who toils. 17I rejoice that I have Stephanas, Fortunatus, and Achaicus here by my side. They have made up for your absence, 18refreshing my spirit, and indeed, yours as well. See to it, then, that you give due recognition to men such as these.

19Greetings from the congregations in Asia. Aquila and Prisca send you their greetings, given in the name of the Lord, and so does the congregation that meets at their house. 20All the brothers here send you their greetings. Greet one another with the kiss of peace.

21This greeting is in my own hand—PAUL. 22If there be anyone who has no love for the Lord, let him be held accursed. '*Marana tha*'— 'Come, O Lord'. 23The grace of the Lord Jesus be with you. 24My love, given in Christ Jesus' name, to each and every one among you.

PAUL'S SECOND LETTER
TO THE CHURCH AT CORINTH

1 Paul, by the will of God an apostle of Christ Jesus, and with him Timothy, your brother in the faith, send their greetings to the church gathered at Corinth, these greetings being addressed at the same time to those in Achaia who are consecrated to God, wherever they may be. ²Grace be yours and peace from God our Father and the Lord Jesus Christ.

³Praise be to the God and Father of our Lord Jesus Christ, the Father who shows compassion at all times, the God who is ever giving comfort. ⁴It is he who, whenever we suffer affliction, comforts us, so that we may be able to comfort those who are in any affliction, our means of bringing comfort being the same as the comforting which we ourselves have had bestowed upon us by God. ⁵For this is how matters stand. Just as we have had an abundant share in Christ's sufferings, so we have, through Christ, an abundant share of comfort. ⁶Are we afflicted? It makes for your having comfort, for your having salvation, brought to you. Are we comforted? It makes for your receiving that comfort which is brought to fruition by your patient endurance of the same sufferings as we also endure. ⁷And it is a sure hope which we have concerning you, knowing as we do that, as you are sharers in the sufferings, so you are sharers in the comfort.

⁸Now, brothers, what we have in mind in addressing you in this manner is our desire that you should not remain in ignorance of the nature of the afflictions which came upon us in Asia, that they were weighing us down excessively and were quite beyond our strength, so much so that we came to despair of life itself. ⁹Why, looking into ourselves, we could find but one answer: that death must come. However, the purpose of it all was that we should place our confidence not in ourselves but in God, who raises the dead to life. ¹⁰He delivered us—and will deliver us—from so deadly a peril. It is on him that we have set our hope that he will deliver us yet again, ¹¹while you, for your part, lend us your aid by praying on our behalf, so that the outcome may be that thanksgiving will be offered up on our be-

half by the mouth of a multitude of persons for the gracious favour shown us.*

[12] For this is our boast, this is the testimony borne by our conscience, that we have trodden our path in this world—and especially in our relations with you—guided by that holiness and purity which have their source in God, guided not by the wisdom of the worldly but by God's grace. [13] And so nothing is to be found in the letters we write to you other than what shows itself to you on reading them, indeed, nothing but what you recognize as the truth, and will, I trust, so recognize to the end, [14] just as you have come to recognize—to some extent, at any rate—that it is we who will provide you with your ground for boasting, even as you will provide us with ours, on the day when the Lord Jesus comes.

[15] And it was in reliance on this confidence of mine that my original intention was to pay you a visit in such a way that a twofold joy might be yours, [16] going to Macedonia by way of you, and returning to you from Macedonia, you being the ones to give me my send-off for my journey to Judaea. [17] Well, was it levity of mind which I displayed in having this intention? Or is it that, when I make a plan, my planning is like that of the worldly ones, so that with me it is, first, 'Yes, yes', and then, 'No, no'? [18] The faithful God warrants it that our message to you is no such thing as 'Yes' first, and then 'No'. [19] And indeed it was not 'Yes' and 'No' which were found in the Son of God, Jesus Christ, in him who was proclaimed among you by us—by myself, by Silvanus, and by Timothy. On the contrary, what was found in him was 'Yes', [20] all God's promises having their fulfilling 'Yes' in him. And so it is that, when the Amen is said by us, to the glory of God, it is through Christ that this is done. [21] But he who causes us—yes, and you as well—to be securely established in your union with Christ, he who has given us our anointing, is God himself. [22] It is he who has set his seal upon us, and has put into our hearts his Spirit, the pledge of what is to be.

[23] As for myself, I call God to witness, with my life as forfeit, that it was out of consideration for you that I did not, after all, come to see you again at Corinth. [24] Not that we wish to lord it over your faith. No, we are fellow workers with you, your joy being what we aim at. As for faith, it is a thing in which you are firmly grounded.

2   However, I became determined in my own mind that, when I came to see you, it was not to be a visit of sorrow. [2] Indeed, were I to

---

* Or '. . . for the gracious favour shown to us, thanksgiving will, through the mouth of a multitude of persons, be offered up by many on our behalf'—extracted from the 'Categories'. The Greek here is notoriously overloaded.

be the one to make you sorrowful, who would there be to gladden my heart but the very people who through me are being made sorrowful? [3]In point of fact, what I said in the letter which I wrote to you was just this, that I was not, when I came, to have sorrow brought upon me by those who ought to be bringing me joy, confident as I am at the same time with regard to every one of you, that when I rejoice, you all rejoice with me. [4]As for the letter which I wrote to you, it was as one sorely afflicted that I wrote it, as one having anguish in his heart and shedding many a tear. As for yourselves, my purpose was not that you should be made sorrowful. No, what I desired was that you should come to know my love, the love I bear you so abundantly.

[5]Now if, as is actually the case, there is a man who has been causing sorrow, it is not so much to me that he has done it as, in some measure—I have no wish to press my point unduly—to all of you. [6]And as for such a man, it is sufficient that this punishment should have been inflicted upon him by the greater number of you, [7]so that now you ought rather to take the opposite course, forgiving him and encouraging him. Otherwise a man so placed might be overwhelmed by the abundance of his sorrow—[8]and this is why I would urge you to reinstate him in your love. [9]What I had in mind when I wrote you that letter was to bring you to the test, so that I might come to know if you were ready to be obedient in every respect. [10]On the other hand, when you forgive anyone an offence, I, too, forgive it. And as regards what I have forgiven, if I have forgiven anything, it has been done for your sake—in the sight of Christ—[11]to prevent Satan from overreaching us. For we know only too well how wily he is in his devices.

[12]Now this is what happened when I came to Troas, meaning to preach the gospel which tells us of Christ. There did indeed open up before me the most promising prospect of labouring for the Lord's cause. [13]Still, failing as I did in my efforts to find my brother Titus, there was no resting for my spirit, and thus I did, after all, take leave of the men there and went to Macedonia. [14]But thanks be to God, who, making us one with Christ, is ever carrying us away captive in his triumphal procession, and who, through us, is making manifest, all over the world, what sweet savour there is in having knowledge of God. [15]For we are—Christ made us such—a fragrance offered up to God. That is what we are both to those who are in the way of salvation and to those who are on the way to perdition, [16]being to the latter a savour arising from death and leading to death, and to the former a savour arising from life and leading to life. And who is worthy of such a calling? Who indeed? [17]Still, as for ourselves, at least we do not, as so many others do, deal with the word of God like hawkers offering their wares. No, we proclaim it with complete sincerity; we proclaim it as

it has come to us from God. All enveloped in Christ, we proclaim it in the very sight of God.

3 Are we once again setting out to speak in our own commendation? Is not the truth rather that we are in no need, as certain people are, of commendatory letters either to you or from you? [2]Why, it is you yourselves who are the letter which we have upon us, one written on our very hearts, known to, and read by, people everywhere. [3]Indeed, what is becoming manifest about you is that you are a letter which has Christ for its author, and that we are the ones to whose care it has been committed; a letter not [a]**written** with ink but with the Spirit of the living God, not on **tablets of stone** but on **hearts of flesh** and blood serving as **tablets**. [4]A confidence as great as this—one which comes from Christ and looks to God—we do indeed have. [5]However, it is not that we are of ourselves competent to look upon anything as coming of ourselves. No; such competence as we have comes to us from God, [6]he being the one who has made us competent to do service on behalf of a New Covenant—not a written code but a thing of the Spirit. For the written code brings death; it is the Spirit which imparts life. [7]Now if the dispensation resulting in death, which was a matter of letters being set down, of letters being engraved upon stones, brought in its trail such splendour that the sons of Israel were unable to look [b]**Moses** steadfastly **in the face** for the **splendour it radiated**, fading as that splendour was, [8]how could the dispensation which has its source in the Spirit fail to be attended with a splendour still more glorious? [9]Surely, if splendour was bestowed upon the dispensation resulting in a judgment of condemnation, the dispensation issuing in an acquittal* has a much greater abundance of splendour about it. [10]In fact, [c]**that which has splendour bestowed upon it** is, in a sense, a thing having no **splendour** at all, on account of the splendour which wholly outshines it. [11]And indeed, if the thing whose nature it was that it should fade away was attended with splendour, how much greater must be the splendour of that which endures?

[12]With such a hope as this, then, we speak out in all boldness, [13]quite unlike [d]**Moses,** who would **put a veil over his face** to prevent the sons of Israel from fixing their gaze upon the fading splendour until it had vanished altogether. [14]Yet what has happened is that dullness has crept over the minds of the Israelites. And indeed, to this very

[a]Ex 24:12; 31:18; 34:1; Pr 3:3; 7:3; Ezk 11:19; 36:26; Jr 31:33   [b]Ex 34:30   [c]Ex 34:29f
[d]Ex 34:33.35

* Or 'dispensation offering righteousness'—extracted from the 'Categories'.

day, whenever the words from the Old Covenant are read out, that same veil remains unlifted. (It is only when a man unites himself to Christ that it is done away with.) [15]To this day, I say, a veil is spread over their minds whenever the law of Moses is being read out, [16]while, in the words of scripture, [e]**the veil is taken away when a man turns to the Lord.** [17]Now what is signified by 'Lord' here is the Spirit; and where the Lord's Spirit is, there is freedom. [18]And we—all of us— fixing our gaze with faces unveiled upon [f]**the glory of the Lord,** are being transfigured into his likeness from one degree of glory to another—and that fittingly enough, seeing that everything is wrought by the Lord, is wrought by none other than the Spirit.

4   Seeing, then, that we have been entrusted with a ministry such as this, and that it is entirely due to the mercy which we have received from God that it has become ours, our courage never deserts us. [2]No, we have put away from ourselves those things which men hide from sight for the shamefulness of them. We do not tread our path in craftiness. We do not falsify the word of God. On the contrary, we show forth the truth with openness so as to make ourselves acceptable— and that in the sight of God—to every man's conscience. [3]As for the gospel which we preach, it may, it is true, be looked upon as a thing hidden in darkness. Yet it is that only when it is brought before those who are on their way to perdition, [4]before those who, devoid of faith, have had their minds blinded by the god whom the world worships, to prevent them from beholding the light shed by the gospel which tells of Christ's glory, which tells of him who is the very image of God. [5]After all, it is not ourselves that we proclaim. We proclaim Christ Jesus as Lord, and ourselves as your servants for Jesus' sake. [6]And indeed, it is the God who said, [g]'Let light shine out of darkness', who has shone into our hearts for the spreading abroad of the light sent forth by the revelation of God's glory, even as it is seen upon the face of Christ.

[7]Such a treasure is indeed ours, but it is carried by us in what are but vessels of clay to show that the power exceeding all else is God's and does not belong to ourselves. [8]Hard pressed we are in every way, but never in a plight from which there is no escape. We find ourselves in desperate perplexity, yet we are never driven to despair. [9]We are made the victims of persecution, but never do we find ourselves forsaken. Struck down we are, but never destroyed. [10]We are ever carrying about with us in our body the putting to death of Jesus, in order that Jesus' life might likewise be manifested in this body of ours. [11]We

[e]Ex 34:34   [f]Ex 16:7.10; 24:17   [g][Gn 1:3f]

—the ones who are alive—are at all times being handed over to death for Jesus' sake, in order that the life of Jesus might likewise be manifested in this mortal flesh of ours. [12] And so it is that death is at work in us, but life in you.

[13] However, since the spirit imbuing our faith is the very same as was found in him of whom it is written in scripture, [h]**'I believed, and so I spoke out,'** we, too, believe and so speak out, [14] knowing as we do that he who raised the Lord Jesus to life will, with Jesus, raise us up also, bringing us—and you with us—into his presence. [15] And indeed, whatever we do we do for your sake, so that grace having widened its scope by embracing a greater and ever greater number of souls, the result may be this, that thanksgiving will abound more and more to the glory of God.

[16] And so it is that we do not lose courage. That part of us which makes up the outward man is indeed rotting away. Yet there is a making anew day by day of the inward part of our nature. [17] And as for the affliction we suffer, it is, after all, a thing which lasts but for a moment, which sits but lightly on us; and what it accomplishes is this, that we are having heaped upon us—and that to a degree immeasurable, to a degree exceeding all bounds—a load of eternal glory. [18] We know this to be the truth, we who fix our gaze not upon the things which are seen, but upon the things which are not seen. For the things which can be seen come and vanish again. It is the things which are unseen that endure for ever.

5 Moreover, being what we are, we know this for certain, that, when the time shall come for the dwelling which is ours upon earth— mere tent as it is—to be falling to pieces, there stands ready for us a habitation which has God for its maker, a dwelling not made by human hands but one lasting eternally, with its site in the heavens. [2] And indeed, we utter groans while we are here, longing as we do to be clothed with our heavenly habitation, [3] and justly so, seeing that having clothed ourselves with it, we shall indeed not find ourselves bare of shelter. [4] Yes, we the ones to whom this tent serves as their dwelling place utter groans and are heavy-hearted, not for a wish to divest ourselves of what clothes us but for a wish to clothe ourselves further, so that the mortal part of us may become absorbed into life. [5] And it is God who has fitted us out for this very purpose, bestowing the Spirit upon us, the pledge of what is to be. [6] And so it is that we are ever full of courage, while at the same time we are clearly aware that, so long as the body is our home, we are away from the Lord,

[h]Ps 116:10

[7] faith being that which guides our steps, not sight. [8] We are full of courage, I say. Still, what we would much rather have is that we should be away from the body and make our home with the Lord. [9] And this being so, our earnest endeavour is that—whether still in the body or away from it—we should be found acceptable in Christ's sight. [10] For it is decreed that all of us are to appear before his judgment-seat, everything being brought to light, so that each may reap his due recompense for the things he has done by the agency of the body, according to what his conduct has been, good or evil.

[11] And so it is that we who have this fear of the Lord before our eyes, while resorting to persuasion to win men's approval, have always had God truly knowing us. And my hope is that, the matter having been brought before your consciences, you, too, have come to know us truly. [12] It is not that we are once again addressing you by way of speaking in our own commendation. Our desire is to provide you with the means of boasting on our behalf, so that you may have your answer ready for those who, in their boasting, have only outward things to point to, not anything found in their hearts. [13] We are the ones who took leave of their senses: it was because of our zeal for God. We are once again sober-minded: it is because of our being zealous for your welfare. [14] For with us it is Christ's love that governs everything; and this is the conviction which has become ours: one man having gone to his death on behalf of all, they all became dead men. [15] And he went to his death on behalf of all, so that, being alive, they should no longer live for themselves but for him who went to his death on their behalf and was raised to life again. [16] From this time on, therefore, we do not look upon anyone as what he is from a merely human point of view; even though there was a time when we looked upon Christ from a merely human point of view, we do so no longer. [17] And it follows further that, if anyone is united to Christ, he has in fact been created anew. The old state of things has passed away: a new one has taken its place. [18] And all this is God's doing; it is he who, through Christ, has reconciled us to himself, and has entrusted us with the ministry of reconciliation. [19] Yes, God—Christ being the means of accomplishing this—has wrought reconciliation between himself and the world by not charging men's transgressions to their account, while he has appointed us to the task of proclaiming that reconciliation.

[20] We are ambassadors, then, on Christ's behalf, while it is God who is sending out his appeal through us. We implore you in Christ's name: Become reconciled to God. [21] For our sake he made him who was a stranger to sin become one with human sinfulness, so that, united to him, the very righteousness of God might become ours.

6 We who are fellow workers with God would make this appeal to you, that you must not receive God's gracious gift in a manner tending to make it profitless. [2]After all, these are God's own words, [i]'**At a time appointed for bidding you welcome have I lent you my ear; on a day marked out for deliverance have I come to your aid.**' Well then, now is **the time of the glad welcome;** now is the **day of deliverance.**

[3]As for ourselves, we are intent on giving no offence in anything we do, lest we should be bringing discredit upon the ministry. [4]On the contrary, as befits those who are God's servants, we make ourselves acceptable in every way: by unflinching courage, in afflictions, in vexations, in calamities; [5]under the lash, in prison, in the midst of tumult, wearied by toil, having to go without sleep, having to go without food; [6]by purity of life, by discernment, by long-suffering, by kindness, by being imbued with the Holy Spirit, by love unfeigned, [7]by proclaiming the truth, by showing forth a power which is of God; with the weapons of righteousness in right hand and left; [8]now honoured, now slighted, now slandered, now spoken of well. They call us impostors, and we love the truth; [9]they call us men not known to anyone, and everybody knows us. They call us [j]**dying men,** and see, **we live; chastised,** yes, **but not put to death;** [10]sad men who are ever joyful; beggars who bring riches to many; men who have nothing, and the world is ours.

[11]Our lips are unsealed to you, men of Corinth. We have thrown our [k]**hearts wide open** to you. [12]This constraint which has come between us is not of our making; your own affections are at fault. [13]Pay us back in the same coin (I am speaking to you as my own children); open your hearts wide too.

[14]Take care that you do not become unevenly matched with those who do not share your faith. Why, what kinship is there between righteousness and lawlessness? What partnership between light and darkness? [15]What concord between Christ and Belial? What is there to be shared by a believer and an unbeliever? [16]How can God's temple have any commerce with idols? And we are the temple of the living God. As God has said, 'I [l]**will live in their midst and move among them, and I will be their God, and they shall be my people.**' [17]Therefore, as we also find in scripture, [m]'**Come out from among them, separating yourselves,** says the Lord, and **touch nothing unclean.** [n]**Then I will make you welcome.** [18][o]**I will be a father** to you, and you shall be **sons** and **daughters to me, says the Lord, the ruler of all.**' 7[1]And so, dearly-loved ones, such promises having been made to us,

---

[i]Is 49:8   [j]Ps 118:18   [k]Ps 119:32 LXX   [l]Lv 26:12; Ezk 37:27   [m]Jr 51:45; Is 52:11
[n]Ezk 20:34   [o]2 Sm 7:14.8; Is 43:6; [Hos 1:10]

let us cleanse ourselves of everything that may defile either flesh or spirit and, taking our reverence for God as our guide, let us do everything in our power to attain to perfect holiness.

7 ²Make room for us in your hearts. We have wronged no one; we have brought ruin upon no one; we have taken advantage of no one. ³In saying this, I have no intention of putting any blame on you. For as I have told you before now, we hold you so close to our hearts as to be one with you always, in death or in life. ⁴I am addressing myself to you with perfect frankness. Great is the pride which I take in you. I am filled with comfort. My heart is overflowing with joy for all the affliction we have to bear.

⁵For even after we had reached Macedonia, no relief was to be had anywhere for this frail frame of ours. On the contrary, we found ourselves afflicted at every turn: foes to be fought from without, fears from within. ⁶But God—he who is ever a bringer of comfort to those who are cast down—comforted us by the coming of Titus; ⁷and not by his coming only but by the comfort with which he found himself comforted on your account, as he was reporting to us about your longing to see us, about your lamenting the past, about your zeal for me. And so it was that I came to rejoice still more.

⁸Yes, even though I did make you sorrowful by the letter which I wrote to you, that is to me no cause for regret. There was a time when I did regret it. (I am aware that I brought sorrow upon you, though it was one that lasted but for a short while.) ⁹Yet now I rejoice, not because of your having had sorrow brought upon you, but because it was brought upon you in such a way as to lead to repentance. And indeed, it was in God's way that you had sorrow brought upon you: you were not in any respect to be losers through what we had done. ¹⁰For sorrow, when it is suffered in God's way, carries with it a repentance leading to salvation, a repentance which can never be the cause of any regret, whereas it is death itself that is wrought by those who suffer sorrow in the way the worldly ones do. ¹¹Mark well, then, the effect of this very thing, your having come to feel sorrow in God's way: what earnestness it has called forth in you, what eagerness to clear yourselves, what indignation, what alarm, what longing affection, what zeal, what meting out of punishment! At every point you have proved yourselves to be free from all blemish in this matter. ¹²And so it turns out that, while I did indeed write to you the way I did, it was, after all, not on account of the man who did the wrong, nor on account of the man who suffered the wrong: it was so that your earnest concern for us might be made manifest to yourselves in the sight of God. ¹³That is what brought such comfort to us; and be-

sides this comfort there was one thing which made us rejoice still more abundantly, the joy which Titus feels, now that his spirit has been refreshed, thanks to all of you. [14]For if in anything I had been boasting to him on your behalf, I have indeed not been put to shame. On the contrary, just as everything we said to you was spoken in truth, so the boast we made before Titus has turned out to be nothing more than the truth. [15]And so it is that his heart goes out to you, with his affection towards you deepened still more, as he calls to mind the ready obedience of you all, and how you received him in dread and anxiety. [16]I am rejoicing that I can place such full confidence in you.

8 And now, my brothers, we would tell you how God's grace has been shown forth in the churches of Macedonia; [2]how it was that, while they found themselves beset by affliction testing them in every way, their abundant joy, and a poverty reaching to the very depths, have flowered into the riches of their generosity. [3]And indeed, I myself bear witness to them how they offered—and that of their own accord—that they would do all they were able to do, in truth more than they were able to do; [4]how they appealed to us most urgently that they should be permitted, as a favour to them, to be sharers in the task of bringing relief to those consecrated to God. [5]It was not by any means, then, that things went merely in accordance with what we had been expecting. Why, these men surrendered their very selves—it was God's will that they should—to the Lord first and foremost, and then to us. [6]In view of all this, I urged Titus that, as he had been the one to make a beginning with this gracious work among you, so he was to be the one who completed it. [7]Well then, as you have everything in abundance: faith, eloquence, knowledge, the utmost zeal, as well as the loving concern you have for us, see to it that this gracious service should likewise be yours in abundance.

[8]I do not say this by way of issuing an order. I say it by way of making the zeal of others serve also as a means for testing whatever genuine love there may be in you. [9]And indeed, you know how matters stood with the generosity to be found in our Lord Jesus Christ, how, being rich, he impoverished himself for your sake, so that through his poverty you might become rich.

[10]As regards the matter at hand, then, I am simply offering an opinion, that being the proper course to take with people like you who led the way—and that as long ago as last year—not only in acting but in proposing to act. [11]And now see to it that the acting is also accomplished, in order that, as readiness of desire is found, so may be accomplishment, as your means will allow. [12]For if readiness to give

is forthcoming, favourable acceptance of what is given will depend on things being proportionate to whatever means may be at a person's disposal—not on their being proportionate to means he does not have. [13]It is not that I want others to be relieved at a price of your suffering distress, [14]but that, as a matter of equality, I want your abundance to serve at the present time to supply their want, their abundance in turn serving to supply your want, so that there may be equality. [15]As scripture has it, [P]'**He who gathered much had nothing over, and he who gathered little did not go short.**'

[16]But thanks be to God, who ever fills Titus's heart with the same eager desire for your welfare as is cherished by us. [17]For he has not only lent a ready ear to the appeal made to him, but, being the eager man he is, he is going out to you of his own unprompted choice. [18]Moreover, we are sending with him the brother, whose praise for the service he has given in spreading the gospel sounds forth throughout all the churches. [19]But not only that: he has been appointed by the churches to be our fellow traveller when we shall be engaged in this work of grace which we are administering in furtherance of God's glory and in token of our own resolve. [20]We are determined that no one should be able to put any blame on us in connection with this benefaction. [21]For what we [q]**aim at** is that the things which we do should be approved of as **right,** not only in **the Lord's sight** but also in the sight of **men.** [22]We are also sending another member of our brotherhood to accompany the others, a man who has often shown himself eager to serve, and who is all the more eager now by reason of the great confidence which he places in you. [23]Be it Titus, then, that is in question: he is a man united to me in fellowship, sharing my labours on your behalf. Be it these brothers of ours: they are delegates of the churches who perform their service in honour of Christ. [24]You must see to it, then, that you show forth— as though standing in the presence of the churches—clear proof of the love that is in you, as well as of the good grounds we have for boasting to these men on your behalf.

9 Now, about the undertaking to be set in motion for the benefit of those consecrated to God, I do indeed go beyond what is needful in writing to you about this matter. [2]After all, I am fully aware of that eager preparedness of yours and I am ever boasting about it to the Macedonians, saying that Achaia has been ready for as long as a year. And it is your zeal which has stirred up a goodly number of them. [3]Still, I am sending the brothers out to you, with the intention that this

[P]Ex 16:18   [q]Pr 3:4 LXX

boast of ours on your behalf should not be brought to nought in this particular, that you might be ready as I always said you were. [4]Otherwise, if there are Macedonians with us when we come to see you, and they find that you are not ready, it is to be feared that we—not to say yourselves—shall be put to shame for showing such confidence. [5]That is why I thought it necessary to urge these brothers to go to you ahead of me, making things straight well in advance with regard to this bounty already promised, that it may be at hand, and at hand as a bounty, not as a thing grudgingly bestowed.

[6]And remember this. He who sows meanly will have a mean harvest coming to him; and he who sows by a rule of bountifulness will have his harvest coming to him by a rule of bountifulness. [7]Each one must carry out the purpose he has formed in his mind, without regret, without constraint. It is a [r]**cheerful giver** that **God** loves. [8]And it is God who has the power to bestow upon you every gracious favour in abundance, so that, having sufficiency in all things and at all times, you may have means in abundance for every work of mercy. [9]As it stands written, [s]**'He has dispersed of his own, he has given to the needy; his beneficence will live on for ever.'** [10]And he who supplies [t]**seed to the sower and bread for food** will have a seed for you also, supplying you with it and multiplying it, and he will cause [u]**the harvest of your beneficence** to flourish. [11]You will be enriched in every way, and a generosity lacking in nothing will be yours, such as calls forth—with us taking the lead—the offering up of a thanksgiving to God. [12]For what the ministration of this devoted service accomplishes is not merely that relief is brought to supply the needs of those consecrated to God. It has its overflow in the offering up of many a thanksgiving to God. [13]With this ministration as proof, men will be glorifying God for your humble submission to anything which may be required of you as men professing the gospel of Christ, and for your generous way of entering into fellowship with them and with all others. [14]And they will offer up prayer on your behalf; they will be longing for you, on account of your having God's grace resting upon you in a degree above all measure. [15]Thanks be to God for his ineffable gift!

10 And now here am I—here is Paul—making an appeal to you by the gentleness and great-heartedness of Christ, I, the man supposed to be a groveller when he is face to face with you, while showing great courage in his dealings with you when he is at a distance. [2]Now what I would beg of you is this, that I may not, when I come to

[r]Pr 22:8 LXX; 1 Ch 29:17   [s]Ps 112:9   [t]Is 55:10   [u]Hos 10:12

you, be obliged to show courage by virtue of that sure confidence wherewith I reckon to summon up boldness against certain people by whose reckoning it is the principles of this world which govern our actions. [3] No doubt that it is this world we live and act in, but it is not on worldly principles that we fight our battles. [4] The weapons which we employ in our warfare are indeed not of the world. No, they are full of might, wielded in the sight of God, ready to overthrow strongholds. It is vain human sophistries that we are overthrowing, [5] yes, and every high and mighty thing which sets itself up in opposition to the true knowledge of God. And we take captive every human device to secure its submission to Christ, [6] while at the same time holding ourselves in readiness to visit condign punishment on all who have refused to submit themselves, when once your submission has been fully accomplished.

[7] Look at what lies before your very eyes. If any man be confident in his mind that he belongs to Christ, let him consider the matter once again, assuring himself that, as he belongs to Christ, so do we. [8] Even though I were to boast somewhat extravagantly about this authority of ours, which has been conferred on us by the Lord for building you up, not for bringing ruin upon you, I shall by no means find myself disappointed. [9] And let it not be supposed that I am trying to overawe you by my letters. [10] I know the sort of thing which is being said: "His letters are weighty and full of vigour, but when he appears in person he is seen to be but a feeble man, and his power of speech amounts to nothing at all." [11] As for those who talk in this way, they had better reckon with this: what we are in word, when we are absent and writing letters, we likewise are in deed when we are in your presence.

[12] No doubt we lack the courage to class ourselves or compare ourselves with those who are distinguished for their self-commendation, men who lack judgment altogether, accustomed as they are to measure themselves by one another and to compare themselves with one another. [13] We, on the other hand, shall not exceed due limits in our boasting, but shall keep ourselves within the limit of that sphere which God has apportioned to us as our limit: one which was to reach even as far as your place of habitation. [14] For we do not trespass beyond our domain, as we should be doing if we had never reached you. And we have indeed, in proclaiming Christ's gospel, come all the way to your region. [15] We do not exceed due limits in our boasting by taking credit for the labours of other men. At the same time, our hope is that, as your faith increases, we shall, while still keeping within our sphere, find our position among you to be greatly strengthened. [16] And so it will happen that we shall be enabled to carry the gospel into lands which lie beyond you, not being the ones to boast in the

sphere of another man about work already done by him. [17]No, let him who [v]**boasts** make **the Lord** the object of his **boast**. [18]It is not he who commends himself who finds acceptance, but the man whom the Lord commends.

11 Bear with me, I beg of you, if I indulge myself in a little foolishness! Well and good then; you *do* bear with me. [2]After all, if I am jealous over you, it is with the very jealousy of God. To one man, and one man only, did I espouse you: a spotless virgin was to be presented to Christ. [3]But my fear is that, just as the [w]**serpent beguiled** Eve in his craftiness, so it might somehow come about that your thoughts should be corrupted and you might be led away from your single-minded devotion to Christ. [4]And indeed, if there be a man coming along who proclaims another Jesus, not the one whom we proclaimed; or if it is a different spirit you are receiving, not the Spirit you received before; or a different gospel, not the one that you accepted before, there is something truly wonderful about your way of bearing up with this! [5]Why, I reckon that I am not a whit behind these superlatively great apostles. [6]Granted that I lack skill as an orator. Yet, as for knowledge, there is no lack of it. And that is a fact which we have made evident in every way among men, wherever they may be, through what we are in our relations with you.

[7]Or is the sin which I committed perhaps that, in seeking to raise you up, I lowered myself, seeing that I proclaimed God's gospel without making any charge? [8]Why, to be able to be of service to you, I robbed other churches, accepting maintenance from them. [9]And when I was staying with you and found myself in want, there was no one I crippled with expenses. No, it was the brothers who came from Macedonia who fully supplied my needs. Indeed, I did keep myself, and shall keep myself, from being burdensome to you in any way. [10]This boast of mine—and it is Christ's truth which is speaking in me when I say this—shall not be put to silence in all the country of Achaia. [11]Why is that? Because I have no love for you? God knows that I have. [12]And what I am doing I shall continue to do, so as to take away their opportunity from those who are desirous of an opportunity that, in the field where they exercise their boastfulness, they should be found to be working on the same terms as we are. [13]And indeed, people such as these are sham apostles, men whose work is nothing but fraud, while they disguise themselves as Christ's apostles. [14]And no wonder: Satan himself disguises himself as an angel of light. [15]No great thing, then, if his servants, too, put on a disguise, passing themselves off as

[v]Jr 9:23f   [w]Gn 3:4.13

men in the service of righteousness. But their end will be what their deeds have deserved.

16 I repeat, let no one regard me as a fool. Or if you cannot but regard me as one, accept me as a fool, so that I, too, may indulge in a little boasting. 17 It is not an injunction of the Lord which makes me say these things; I am saying them as one who, being in a state of folly, goes in for such bold-faced boastfulness. 18 Seeing that there are so many that boast, viewing things in a worldly light, I, too, will boast. 19 After all, it is with pleasure that you bear with fools, being so wise yourselves. 20 Indeed, you bear it if a man enslaves you, if a man preys upon you, if a man takes advantage of you, if a man gives himself airs, if a man strikes you in the face. 21 As for ourselves, I confess it to my shame, we did not have enough strength of mind for conduct such as this. Yet, if there be anybody making bold claims, no matter in what respect—remember that it is in a state of folly that I am saying this—I, too, am one to make bold claims. 22 Are they Hebrews? So am I. Are they Israelites? So am I. Are they descendants of Abraham? So am I. 23 Are they servants of Christ? (I am speaking as a man who has gone out of his mind.) I am more so than they are: surpassing them in the labours I undertook, surpassing them in the imprisonments I suffered, being subjected to countless beatings, being at death's door many a time. 24 Five times have I received, at the hands of the Jews, the forty lashes less one. 25 Three times have I been beaten with rods; once I was stoned. Three times have I been shipwrecked; for a night and a day I was adrift on the open sea. 26 On frequent journeys; amidst dangers from rivers, dangers from robbers, dangers from my own people, dangers from the Gentiles; dangers in the city, dangers in the desert, dangers at sea, dangers from so-called brothers playing me false. 27 In labour and toil, through many a sleepless night, in hunger and thirst, often denying myself food, suffering cold, being in want of clothing. 28 And apart from other things which I will pass over, there is that which presses upon me daily, my anxiety for all the churches. 29 Who is there suffering a weakening of his faith, and I am not by his side in his weakness? Who is enticed into sin, and I am not in a furnace of distress? 30 If I must needs boast, it will be of the things displaying my weakness. 31 The God and Father of the Lord Jesus, he who is blessed forever, knows that I am speaking the truth. 32 When I was at Damascus, the governor under King Aretas was having guard kept over the city of the Damascenes, intent on having me arrested. 33 But I was let down in a basket through an opening in the wall, and so escaped his hands.

12 There is no escape from this boasting. It is, it is true, an employment serving no useful purpose. Still, I will go on and tell you about

visions and revelations granted by the Lord. [2]I know a certain man, one united to Christ, who, fourteen years ago, was carried out of himself (whether remaining within his body, I do not know; or taken away from it, I do not know: it is God who knows), and he—this man of whom I am speaking—found himself caught up all the way to the third heaven. [3]And I also know, with regard to this man, that he was (whether remaining within his body or separated from it, I do not know: it is God who knows) [4]carried up into paradise, and there heard utterances unutterable, such as no human being is permitted to repeat. [5]On behalf of a man like that I am indeed ready to boast, but on my own behalf I will not boast, except when it is my weaknesses that are in question. [6]If indeed I chose to boast, I should not be a fool for so doing, as I should only be telling the truth. Yet I forbear. I have no mind that anyone called upon to form a true estimate of me should have to go beyond what his own eyes will let him see, what his own ears will let him hear. [7]Then there is the matchless grandeur of these revelations. And this is why, lest I should become over-elated, I have had an infliction imparted to me, something like a thorn to make its home in my body, a messenger of Satan to be my tormentor, lest I should become over-elated. [8]Three times have I made supplication to the Lord concerning him, asking that he was to depart from me. [9]And this is what the Lord's reply has been: "My grace is enough, and more than enough, for you. And indeed, it is in the very presence of weakness that power finds its consummation." It is with greatest joy, then, that my weaknesses rather than anything else will serve as grounds for boasting, so that the power of Christ may come and enshrine itself in me. [10]And because of this, I am well content with weaknesses, with insults, with hardships, with persecutions, with calamities, endured for Christ. Why, it is when I am weak that I am strongest of all.

[11]I have been making a proper fool of myself, and it was you that drove me to it. I ought to have been the one to have your commendation, seeing that in no respect have I fallen short of these superlatively great apostles, true though it be that I amount to nothing at all. [12]Why, the signs which are the mark of the true apostle were brought forth in your midst. There was an endurance that never failed; there were signs and wonders and mighty works. [13]In what way, then, were you placed in a position inferior to that of the other churches, except that I was the one who would not cripple you with expenses? Forgive me if I wronged you there.

[14]Here I am standing ready for the third time to pay you a visit. And there will be no crippling you with expenses. What I am desirous of is your very selves, not your possessions. After all, it is not the children's duty to make provision for their parents, but the parents' to do so for their children. [15]And for my own part, most gladly will I spend

all, indeed I am ready to be utterly spent myself, for the benefit of your souls. Does the case stand like this, then, that the more dearly I love you the less I am to be loved? [16] "Ah!" you say, "that is all very well. I myself refrained from becoming a burden to you, but, being the cunning knave that I am, I got the better of you by roundabout means." [17] What, was it through any of the men whom I sent out to you that I took advantage of you? [18] I urged Titus to go, and there was the brother whom I sent with him. Did Titus take advantage of you? Was it not one and the same spirit which guided our conduct? Was it not one and the same path that we trod?

[19] You have, I presume, been supposing all this time that what we are about is to make our defence before you. Far from it. It is as men standing in God's very presence, as men who are in union with Christ, that we speak as we do. And yet, dearly-loved ones, it is all done with the intention of building you up in the faith. [20] For this is what I dread, that when I come, I may somehow not find you to be what I desire, and you may find me to be what you do not desire, that somehow there may be strife, jealousy, angry tempers, party spirit, backbiting, gossip, self-conceit, and disorder; [21] that my God will, when I come again, have humiliation in store for me respecting you, and that I shall have to mourn over many of your number, sinners of long standing, and still unrepentant of the uncleanness, fornication, and licentiousness which they have practised.

13

This is the third time I am coming to visit you. [x]'Every issue,' so we read, 'shall be settled by the voice of two or three witnesses.' [2] Well then, I have forewarned those sinners of old, and indeed all the rest, and I am forewarning them again (as I acted when present on my second visit, so I act now when I am absent), that I will show no leniency next time I come. [3] After all, you wish to have proof that it is Christ who is speaking in me. And there is indeed no weakness about the way in which he deals with you; on the contrary, it is power which he shows forth in your midst. [4] For true though it be that he died on the cross in weakness, yet the life he has is one which has its source in the power of God. And as for ourselves, though we do indeed share his weakness, through being united to him, yet a life by his side will be ours, a life that has its source in the power of God, one enabling us to be of service to you.

[5] It is your own selves that you ought to be examining to make sure that you are true to the faith; it is your own selves that you ought to be testing. Surely, it cannot be that you yourselves do not know for

[x]Dt 19:15

certain that Jesus Christ dwells within you, unless what has happened is that you are failing your test. [6] At any rate, I am hoping you will come to recognize that we are not failing ours. [7] Yet when we pray to God that you may do no wrong, our purpose is not that we should be seen to be passing the test, but that you should do what is right, even though somehow we might seem to have failed. [8] For whatever powers we are endowed with, they are all in support of the truth, not in opposition to it. [9] Indeed, we are only too glad whenever our position is one of weakness, while you are the powerful ones—our prayer which we offer being this: that you should grow towards perfection. [10] As for my reason for writing to you like this, it is that I should not, when present, have to deal with you severely, in the exercise of that authority which the Lord has conferred on me, to build you up, not to tear you down.

[11] And now, my brothers, farewell. Perfect your lives, heed our appeal, be of one mind, live in peace. And God, the bringer of peace and love, will be by your side. [12] Greet one another with the kiss of peace. [13] All God's consecrated ones who are here send you their greetings.

[14] And may these be by the side of each and every one of you: the grace of the Lord Jesus Christ, the love of God, and the Holy Spirit communicating himself to you.

PAUL'S LETTER
TO THE CHURCH IN GALATIA

1 From Paul the apostle, who holds his commission not in virtue of any human authority, nor through the power of any man, but through Jesus Christ and God the Father, who raised him up from the dead. [2]Greetings to the churches in Galatia from myself and from all our brothers in the faith who are present with me here. [3]May grace and peace rest upon you, bestowed by God our Father and by the Lord Jesus Christ, [4]who surrendered his life for our sakes to free us from our sins, that he might come to our rescue and deliver us from this present wicked age. This he did in obedience to the will of him who is our God and Father, [5]to whom glory be ascribed for ever and ever. Amen.

[6]I am amazed at you for turning away so swiftly from him who has called you to himself, sending out his summons by virtue of Christ's grace, and for your readiness to go over to a different gospel. [7]Not that there is such a thing as another gospel. What has happened is simply that there are certain people who, intent on distorting Christ's gospel, have succeeded in throwing your minds into confusion. [8]Yet, were I myself, were an angel from heaven, to come to proclaim a gospel at variance with the one we proclaimed to you, let him be held accursed: [9]As we have told you before, so I am telling you once again: if there be anyone who proclaims to you a gospel at variance with the one which you have received, let him be held accursed.

[10]As for myself, is it to be supposed that at this juncture I am still striving to win men's approval rather than God's, that it is men that I am seeking to please? Surely, if it were still men I sought to please, I should not be what I am, the slave of Christ.

[11]And indeed, my brothers, there is one thing I would wish you to be clearly aware of. The gospel which I proclaimed to you is not of any man's devising. [12]I myself neither received it from any man, nor was I taught it by any: it came to me by a revelation at the hands of Jesus Christ.

[13]You have heard of my former manner of life during my Jewish

days, how I persecuted God's Church beyond measure and sought to make havoc of it. [14]In fact, in my attachment to the Jewish way of life I surpassed many of my contemporaries among my fellow countrymen, being far more zealous on behalf of the traditions handed down by my forefathers. [15]However, the time came when he who [a]**set me apart from my very birth,** he who, by virtue of his grace, **sent out his call,** [16]saw fit to reveal his Son to me and through me, so that I might proclaim him among the Gentiles. And what I did then was to resolve immediately not to hold consultation with any human creature. [17]I refrained even from going up to Jerusalem to see those who had been apostles before me, but went off to Arabia, and when I came back it was to Damascus.

[18]Then, after an interval of three years, I did go up to Jerusalem to pay a visit to Cephas, and remained with him for two full weeks. [19]But I saw none of the other apostles except James, the Lord's brother. [20]What I am writing to you—keep it well in mind—is the simple truth spoken in God's very presence; I am telling no falsehood. [21]Afterwards I visited the districts of Syria and Cilicia. [22]On the other hand, as for the churches in Judaea devoted to the service of Christ, I was not even known to them by sight. [23]Only that they learned this by way of hearsay: he who used to be our persecutor is now proclaiming the faith of which he once sought to make havoc. [24]And they gave glory to God for what he had wrought in me.

2 Then, fourteen years having gone by, I again went up to Jerusalem with Barnabas, taking Titus along with me as well. [2]I did so in obedience to a revelation, and I laid before the men there the gospel which it is my practice to proclaim to the Gentiles. I did this in private, putting the matter before the men thought to be of repute. Was there a risk perhaps that the course which I was taking, and had taken, might somehow fail of its purpose? [3]On the other hand, no attempt was made to enforce circumcision, not even in the case of my companion Titus, who was a Greek. [4]Still, certain people secretly smuggled in had to be taken into account, brothers in the faith, falsely so-called, the very men who had sneaked in to act as spies on the freedom which is ours in Christ Jesus, their intention being to reduce us to a state of slavery. [5]And as for these, we did not give ground to them even for a moment by submitting ourselves to their claims. The truth of the gospel was to remain continually in your possession.

[6]Now as regards what came from those who were reputed to be of importance—it makes no difference to me who or what they were;

[a]Jr 1:5; Is 49:1

after all, it is not *b***God**'s nature **to show partiality** in his treatment of men. As regards these men of repute, I say, they had no new suggestions to make to me. [7]On the contrary, they realized that I had been entrusted with preaching the gospel to the Gentiles, just as Peter had with preaching it to the Jews. [8](For he who was at work for Peter, making him competent for the apostleship to the Jews, was at work also for me, enabling me to become the apostle to serve the Gentiles.) [9]And so, recognizing as they did the grace which had been bestowed upon me, the men reputed to be the very pillars of our society— James, Cephas, and John—stretched out their right hands to me and to Barnabas in token of fellowship: we were to go to the Gentiles and they themselves to the Jews. [10]Only we should keep those suffering poverty in mind, which indeed was the very thing I myself had resolved to do.

[11]However, at the time when Cephas came to Antioch, I withstood him to his face: he stood self-condemned. [12]For this is what had happened. Until the arrival of certain men coming from James, he would sit at table with Gentiles, but after their arrival he drew back and held himself aloof, for fear of the advocates of circumcision; [13]and along with him the rest of the Jews played the hypocrite, with the result that even Barnabas was carried away by their hypocrisy. [14]But when I realized that they were not straightforward in holding on to the truth proclaimed by the gospel, I said to Cephas in front of them all, "If you, who are a Jew, live like a Gentile, how is it that you seek to compel the Gentiles to live in a Jewish manner?" [15]We are, as regards our natural condition, Jews, not Gentile sinners. [16]Yet having come to see that it is not by works done in obedience to law but by faith in Jesus Christ that a man is accepted as righteous, we, too, have learned to believe in Christ Jesus, so that we might be accepted as righteous because of our faith in Christ, not because of works done in obedience to law. As scripture says, *c***no one will be accepted as righteous** by works done in obedience to law.'

[17]Now if our seeking to be accepted as righteous, through our union with Christ, has resulted in our being found to be sinners like the rest of mankind, does that mean that Christ aids and abets sin? Far be the thought! [18]No, it is precisely by building up once again what I had previously demolished that I prove myself a transgressor. [19]And indeed, it was the law's own doing that I died away from it, so that I should live for God. [20]I have been crucified with Christ. And the life which I live now is no longer my own life. It is the life which Christ lives in me. My present life is a bodily one. Yet I live it by faith in the Son of God, who loved me and surrendered himself for my sake. [21]I

*b*Dt 10:17   *c*Ps 143:2

do not set the grace of God at nought. And indeed, this is the truth of the matter: if the law is able to lead men to righteousness, then Christ died to no purpose.

3 Surely, you have taken leave of your senses, you men of Galatia! Who has cast this spell over you, before whose very eyes Jesus Christ has been exposed to view as nailed on a cross? [2]Let me be content in asking you this one question: if you had the Spirit bestowed upon you, was that as the result of works done in obedience to law, or was it the result of a message which called for faith? [3]Are you so far gone in senselessness that, having set upon your course under the guidance of the Spirit, you now propose to reach your goal by placing reliance on merely outward matters? [4]All these things which happened to you: did you experience them to no purpose—if indeed it has been to no purpose? [5]Does he who supplies you with the Spirit and works miracles among you do so by virtue of works performed in obedience to law, or through a message calling for faith? [6]Consider the case of [d]**Abraham,** and how **he put his faith in God, and this was reckoned to him as righteousness.** [7]You will then perceive that it is those taking their stand upon faith who are Abraham's true sons. [8]And scripture, foreseeing that it was by virtue of their faith that God would accept the Gentiles as righteous, proclaimed the good news beforehand to Abraham, saying [e]'**In you shall all the nations find their blessing.'** [9]So it is those who take their stand upon faith who have a blessing bestowed upon them along with Abraham, the man of faith. [10]Indeed, those who take their stand upon works performed in obedience to law are under a curse. As scripture says, [f]'**Cursed be everyone who does not adhere to all the things set down in the book of the law, and practise them.'** [11]And indeed, that no one is accepted as righteous by virtue of obeying the law is plain from these words in scripture, [g]'**The righteous man shall gain life by his faith.'** [12]Now the law does not take its stand upon faith. No, this is what it says: [h]'**He who practises these things shall gain life by them.'** [13]Now Christ has delivered us from this curse invoked by the law, and this he has done by becoming for our sakes an accursed thing. For so it stands written, [i]'**A curse lies upon everyone who hangs on a gibbet.'** [14]And the purpose of it all was that Abraham's blessing should come to rest upon the Gentiles by virtue of their union with Christ Jesus, so that through faith we might receive the promised gift of the Spirit.

[15]My brothers, let me illustrate what I mean by an argument taken from common life. Even in the case of a legal disposition made by an

[d]Gn 15:6 [e]Gn 18:18; 12:3 [f]Dt 27:26 [g]Hab 2:4 [h]Lv 18:5 [i]Dt 21:23

ordinary human being no one ever declares it to be void, or adds fresh clauses to it, once it has been ratified. [16]Now the promises were made to Abraham *j*and his **descendant.** It does not say 'descendants', as though referring to a number of people, but as referring to one, **'and to your descendant'**—and it is Christ who is being signified here. [17]Now what I am contending is this. The law, which came four hundred and thirty years afterwards, does not invalidate the covenant previously ratified by God, so as to render the promise null and void. [18]And indeed, if the inheritance came by the law, then it would no longer be obtained as the consequence of a promise made; while yet it was in fulfilment of a promise made that God graciously bestowed it upon Abraham. [19]As regards the law, then, what role did it play? It was brought in in addition, with a view that transgressions should make their appearance, till the descendant should come to whom the promise had been made. It was promulgated by angels, and at the same time there was an intermediary. [20]Now there can be no such thing as an intermediary if there is only one party; and God is one.

[21]Is the law, then, something contrary to the promises? Far be the thought! In point of fact, had a law been given such as was capable of imparting life, then, indeed, righteousness would have come from keeping the law. [22]However, this is what happened instead. The scripture declared the whole world to be in bondage to sin: it was to be in virtue of their faith in Jesus Christ that the thing promised was to be bestowed upon those in which such faith is to be found.

[23]Before the said faith made its appearance we were held in custody and kept prisoners under the law, until the time when faith should be revealed. [24]And so it came about that the law became our tutor leading us to Christ: it was to be in virtue of faith that we were to be accepted as righteous. [25]But now that faith has come we are no longer under a tutor. [26]Indeed, you are, one and all, sons of God through your faith in Christ Jesus. [27]And this is the truth of the matter. As many of you as were baptized into union with Christ have clothed yourselves with Christ as your garment. [28]No more Jew or Gentile, no more slave or free man, no more male or female. United to Christ Jesus, all are one person. [29]And if you belong to Christ, then indeed you are Abraham's offspring and have been made heirs in fulfilment of a promise.

4   What I mean to say is this. If someone becomes an heir while still a child, he finds himself all the time in a position which in no way differs from that of a slave, even though he is the owner of everything.

*j*Gn 12:7; 13:15; 17:7; 22:18; 24:7

²He remains under the control of guardians and trustees until the time for his coming of age fixed by his father. ³So it is with us: During the time of our childish dependence we found ourselves in bondage to the world's rudimentary teachings. ⁴But when the time appointed for this had fully run its course, God sent forth his Son, born of a woman, born subject to the law, ⁵so that he might set free those subject to the law, so that he might receive us as his adopted sons. ⁶And because you are sons, God has sent forth the Spirit of his Son into your hearts, making you cry out, "Abba! Father!" ⁷And so it is that you are no longer a slave but a son; and if so, then an heir—all this by the will of God.

⁸There was a time when you had no knowledge of God, being in bondage to what were, by virtue of their very nature, no gods at all, ⁹while now you have come to recognize God, or rather have come to be recognized by him. How, then, is it that you are once again turning back to rudimentary teachings, so feeble, so beggarly, wishing to be enslaved to them once again? ¹⁰You scrupulously observe special days and months and seasons and years. ¹¹I am full of dread on your behalf. Can it be that all the labour I have bestowed upon you has somehow been to no purpose?

¹²My brothers, make common cause with me, I beg of you, as I have made common cause with you. Not that you have treated me amiss in any way. ¹³Why, you yourselves know well enough that, when I preached the gospel to you the first time, that came about as the result of my suffering from a bodily ailment. ¹⁴And as for the state I found myself in, you were far from looking upon it—trial as it was for you—with contempt or loathing. On the contrary, you received me as you might receive one of God's angels, as you might receive Christ Jesus himself. ¹⁵What, then, has become of this state of mind which made you count yourselves blessed? Why, I can give you my solemn word that there was a time when, had it been possible, you would have plucked out your very eyes and have given them to me. ¹⁶Can it be, then, that I have become your enemy by telling you the truth?

¹⁷As for the persons I have referred to, they pay court to you, but it is not for a good purpose. On the contrary, what they are after is to exclude you, so that you may pay court to them. ¹⁸To be paid court to in a good cause is a good and acceptable thing at all times. I wish it did not happen only when you have me present with you, ¹⁹my dear children over whom I am in travail once again, until the time that Christ is fully formed in you. ²⁰I wish I could be at your side now and speak to you in a different tone. As it is, I find myself in a state of bewilderment about you.

²¹Tell me, you who are so eager to have the law for your master, will you not listen to the law? ²²You will find it written there that

Abraham had two sons, one by the slave girl and one by the free woman. 23 Yet, while the birth of the son of the slave girl followed the ordinary course of nature, the birth of the son of the free woman came about in fulfilment of a promise which had been given. 24 All this is to be understood as an allegory, the women standing for two covenants. One comes from Mount Sinai, giving birth to offspring destined for slavery. This is Hagar, 25 Sinai being a mountain in Arabia. She answers to Jerusalem as she is now, she together with her children being in a state of bondage. 26 As against this, the heavenly Jerusalem is free, and it is she who is our mother. 27 And so we find written in scripture, *k*'**Rejoice, you barren woman, who never gave birth to a child; break forth and shout, you who are a stranger to the pangs of women in labour. For there are more children of the forsaken woman than of her who has her husband by her side.'**

28 As for you, my brothers, you are, like Isaac, children born in fulfilment of a promise. 29 Yet, just as he whose birth was one according to nature persecuted him whose birth was brought about under the Spirit's guidance, so it is now. 30 But what does the scripture say? *l*'**Drive out the slave girl and her son. For the son of the slave girl shall by no means share the inheritance with the son** of the free woman.' 31 And so it is, my brothers: we are children, not of the slave girl but of the free woman. 5 1 Christ has set us free so that we should put our freedom to its proper use. Stand firm, then, and do not let yourselves be caught once again in the yoke of slavery.

5   2 Well, here I am, here is Paul, assuring you that, if you submit to being circumcised, Christ will no longer be of any avail to you. 3 You can have my solemn word once again that any man who submits to circumcision is under obligation to fulfil the law in its entirety. 4 You have made yourselves strangers to Christ, you who, in your efforts to attain to righteousness, would place reliance upon the law. Grace has been lost to you. 5 As for ourselves, we take the Spirit for our guide, we take our stand upon faith as we are patiently waiting to attain to the righteousness for which we hope. 6 And indeed, neither circumcision nor the want of it has any meaning for those who have united themselves to Christ Jesus. There is only one thing which counts: faith finding its expression in love.

7 Till now you had been shaping your course so well. Who, then, has come between you and your loyalty to the truth? 8 Whatever means of persuasion he may have used, you may be certain that it does not have its source in God, who has sent out his call to you. 9 Even

k Is 54:1   *l* Gn 21:10

a little leaven', so they say, 'causes the whole of the lump of dough to ferment'. [10]For my own part, as a man united to you in the Lord, I have full confidence in you that you will come to take the same view of the matter as I do. But as for the man who is unsettling your minds, whoever he may be, he will have to bear the punishment which he deserves. [11]As for my own case, my brothers, if it be true that I am still an advocate of circumcision, how is it that I am still being persecuted? Why, if that were so, the very thing which causes offence in the preaching of the cross has been done away with. [12]I could wish that these disturbers of your peace would go to the length of making eunuchs of themselves.

[13]My brothers, if God's call has gone out to you, it was so that freedom should be yours. Only you must see to it that you do not let the possession of that freedom serve you as an opportunity for yielding to the promptings of your lower nature. On the contrary, be servants of one another in a spirit of love. [14]And indeed, the demands of the law are met in full by obedience to this one precept, [m]**'You shall love your neighbour as yourself.'** [15]But if you are always at one another's throats, if you are always tearing each other to pieces, it is to be feared that, in the end, you will bring complete destruction upon one another.

[16]What I mean to tell you is this: let your lives be guided by the Spirit, and then you will indeed be far from giving rein to the desires which have their source in our lower selves. [17]For any desire arising from our lower nature is at war with the Spirit, while the Spirit is at war with our lower nature. The two are in every way opposed to one another, with the result that a man finds himself deprived of the power of doing that of which his will approves. [18]But if you will let yourself be led by the Spirit, then you are no longer under the yoke of the law.

[19]And as for the doings which have their origin in our lower nature, they are plain to see: fornication, uncleanness, licentiousness, [20]idolatry, magic arts, hostility, quarrelsomeness, jealousy, outbursts of anger, selfish ambition, dissension, sectarianism, [21]intrigues, drunken bouts, revelling, and the like. And with regard to these I am forewarning you now, as I have forewarned you in the past, that those who practise them will obtain no share in the kingdom of God.

[22]But the harvest yielded by the Spirit is to be found in the following: love, joy, peace, patience, kindness, goodness, faithfulness, [23]gentleness, self-restraint. And there is indeed no law to pronounce against these. [24]Now those who belong to Christ Jesus have nailed that lower nature, with its passions and appetites, to a cross. [25]If it be through the Spirit that we have our life, let it be the Spirit that guides

[m]Lv 19:18

our steps. [26]Let us have no self-conceit, no provoking of one another, no envying one another.

6 My brothers, should a man be detected in the act of committing a wrong, it is for you, the spiritually minded, to set such a man to rights; but you must do so in a spirit of gentleness. At the same time let each look to himself, lest he, too, might be falling into temptation. [2]Bear the burden of each other's failings. It is by so doing that you will be satisfying the claims made by the law of Christ. [3]A man is only led away by his fancies if, being in fact nothing, he supposes himself to amount to something. [4]Instead, let each man scrutinize what he himself has accomplished. And then, should he boast, his reason for doing so will be something found in himself, not something due to his comparing himself to another man. [5]And each one, then, will have his own load to carry.

[6]Those who are receiving instruction in the word of God are to let their teacher have a share in all temporal blessings. [7]Do not allow yourselves to be deluded. God will not let himself be treated with contempt. As a man sows, so shall he reap. [8]He who makes his lower nature the field where he scatters his seed shall reap from it a harvest of corruption, while he who makes the Spirit the field where he scatters his seed shall, from the Spirit, reap a harvest of eternal life. [9]And let us not get weary of doing right, for if we do not slacken, we shall have our harvest coming to us at the appointed time. [10]So, as we have opportunity, let us do good to everyone, and above all to those who are fellow members in the community of the faith.

[11]Here is some bold lettering for you, written with my own hand. [12]There are those who are desirous that you should make a good showing in outward matters; and it is these very men who seek to compel you to submit to circumcision. But that is only in order to escape being persecuted for their advocacy of the cross of Christ. [13]In point of fact, even those who have themselves circumcised do not observe the law. No, if they want you to be circumcised, it is merely so that there should be something in your outward condition of which they can make their boast. [14]Yet, as for myself, far be it from me that I should make my boast in anything except the cross of our Lord Jesus Christ, by which the world stands crucified to me, and I to the world.

[15]As for circumcision or the want of it, they count for nothing. What counts is that a new creature should have been born. [16]And as for those who will follow this rule, may [n]**peace,** may mercy, rest upon them all, upon those who are the **Israel** of God.

[n]Ps 125:5; 128:6

¹⁷From this time onward let there be nobody who will be a cause of trouble to me; for I bear the marks of Jesus imprinted on my very body.

¹⁸My brothers, may the grace of our Lord Jesus Christ hold its protecting hand over your spirits. Amen.

PAUL'S LETTER
TO THE CHURCH AT EPHESUS

1 Paul, by the will of God an apostle of Christ Jesus, sends his greetings to those at Ephesus who are consecrated to God, to those who have come to repose their faith in Christ Jesus. [2]May grace and peace be yours, coming to you from God our Father and the Lord Jesus Christ.

[3]All praise be given to the God and Father of our Lord Jesus Christ, who has blessed us by way of imparting to us, in virtue of our union with Christ, every spiritual blessing to be found in the heavenly realms. [4]Before the world was created he chose us, that we should become merged in Christ, that we should be holy and without blemish. Giving us his love, [5]he predestined us to become, through Jesus Christ, his sons by adoption, to become his very own. All this was in pursuance of the good pleasure arising from his will, [6]while we, for our part, were to give ourselves up to the extolling of his grace, which he has so lavishly bestowed upon us in the person of his Beloved, [7]through whom we have been set free from our bondage, receiving pardon, in virtue of the blood shed by him, for the offences we had committed. It is here that God's grace is to be found in all its richness, the grace [8]which he made overflow to us in a full stream of wisdom and discernment. [9]And so it came about that he made known to us the mystery of his will—the result of his good pleasure which he purposed within himself—his hidden plan, [10]to be carried into effect when the time appointed for it would have run its full course, his plan to gather up all things in Christ, things in heaven and things on earth.

[11]And indeed, it is through Christ that we have obtained our share in the inheritance, being predestined for this in conformity with the design formed by him who, in pursuance of the counsel of his will, is the source of power for the whole of creation. [12]We were to devote ourselves to the extolling of his glorious majesty, we who were the first to rest our hope in Christ. [13]And you, too, having given a hearing to the message of truth, to the gospel proclaiming your salvation, have united yourselves to Christ. And so it has come about that,

having learned to believe in Christ, you have been sealed with the promised gift of the Holy Spirit, [14]the pledge of the inheritance which is to be ours: there will be a setting free of our souls, making us God's very own; there will be praise extolling his glorious majesty.

[15]This being so, I, for my part, having heard of your faith in the Lord Jesus and of the love you bear to all who are consecrated to the service of God, [16]never cease giving thanks on your behalf, as I bring you to remembrance in the prayers which I offer. And this is what I pray for. [17]May the God of our Lord Jesus Christ, the Father who is the source of everything glorious, bestow upon you a spirit of wisdom and illumination, in the knowledge which you have of him, [18]the eyes of your mind having light shed upon them, so as to make you comprehend what is the hope held out by his call, what is the wealth of glory coming of the [a]**inheritance** which he grants to those **consecrated** to him, [19]what is the immeasurable greatness of the power which he wields towards us who have faith, the power which is proportionate to the great work [20]which he wrought in honouring Christ, a work displaying his mighty strength. And this is what he accomplished. Having raised him from the dead, he [b]**bade him sit down at his right hand,** [21]high above any other source of rule, of authority, of power or dominion, high above any other title of sovereignty which can be named, not only in this age but in the age to come. [22][c]**He has put all things in subjection under his feet,** while at the same time appointing him to be head of the Church, to be sovereign ruler over all, of the Church [23]which is his body, the full expression of him who, for his part, ever fills the whole creation with himself.

2 As for yourselves, you lay dead by reason of your offences and of your sins, [2]these being what once ruled your conduct when you followed the evil ways of this world, when you rendered obedience to the prince whose domain is in the lower air, the spirit which is at work even now among those who are rebels against God. [3]And we, too—all of us—conducted ourselves in this manner, ruled by the passions which our lower nature stirred up in us. We did what our lower nature and our own calculations would have us do, being an offspring deserving of God's anger like the rest of mankind. [4]But God, rich as he is in compassion, out of the great love he bore us—[5]the very men who were lying dead by reason of their offences—made us alive together with Christ. (It is by grace that you have been saved.) [6]He raised us up with him, enthroning us, in union with Christ Jesus, in the heavenly realms, [7]so that in the ages to come he might display the

[a]Dt 33:3f   [b]Ps 110:1   [c]Ps 8:6

immeasurable wealth of his grace shown forth by his kindness to us in making us one with Christ Jesus. [8]And indeed, it is by grace that you have been saved, with faith as its instrument. It was not anything coming from ourselves; it was God's gift. [9]And it was not the result of works performed by us, so that there should be no reason for boasting on anyone's part. [10]For we are God's handiwork, created as men who have their being in Christ Jesus, in order that we should give ourselves up to the performance of good works which God has prepared beforehand, so that we might enjoy our lives in the doing of them.

[11]Call to mind, then, what you formerly were, you the Gentiles by all outward reckoning, you who were spoken of as "the uncircumcised" by those who spoke of themselves as "the circumcised"—not a true circumcision, however, but merely an outward one, one brought about by human hands. [12]Call to mind, I say, that at that time you were without Christ, excluded from the commonwealth of Israel, strangers to the covenants and the promise which goes with them, having no hope, with the world all round you, and no God. [13]But now, by virtue of being united to Christ Jesus, you who were once so [d]**far away** have now been brought near by the shedding of Christ's blood. [14]For it is he who is the maker of **peace** between us, he who has made us both one, tearing down as he did the barrier formed by the dividing wall which separated us, [15]and wiping out in his own mortal nature that which wrought hostility, the law with its commandments—consisting as they did in precise enactments—so that he might re-create in himself the two, as one new man, thus making peace, [16]and might reconcile both to God in one body by means of the cross, in this way putting an end to the hostility.

[17]So he came, and the [e]**happy message** he brought was one of **peace** for those who were so **far away,** of **peace** for those who were near. [18]For through him we all, both Jew and Gentile alike, have access to the Father by the one Spirit. [19]The status you hold is no longer that of aliens or of people making a temporary stay. No, you are fellow citizens of God's consecrated ones; you are members of his household. [20]Apostles and [f]prophets are the foundation on which you have been built, the cornerstone being Christ Jesus himself, [21]in whom the whole fabric, being fitly framed together, grows into a holy temple, finding its unity in the Lord, [22]you likewise being built in with the rest, the whole to become, under the Spirit's guidance, a place where God has his dwelling.

3   With all this in mind, I Paul, the man who is being held prisoner for his allegiance to Christ Jesus, am laying these things before you,

[d]Is 57:19   [e]Zc 9:10; Is 52:7; 57:19   [f][Is 28:16]

Gentiles, on whose behalf I am rendering this service of mine. ²You have doubtless heard of the stewardship, on behalf of God's gracious design, with which I have been entrusted for your benefit; ³and how, by means of a revelation, there was made known to me—as indeed I have been setting out briefly here—that which had been kept a secret hitherto. ⁴And as you read, you will, judging by what I have said, be able to comprehend my insight into the secret of Christ, ⁵which in other ages had never been made known to any human creature, but which has now been revealed through the Spirit, to God's holy apostles and prophets. ⁶And it is this: that the Gentiles are to win the same inheritance, that they are members of the same body, and that, being united to Christ Jesus, they share the same promise—all this being proclaimed by the gospel ⁷of which I was made a minister, by virtue of the gift of God's grace which he bestowed upon me in all the effectiveness of his power. ⁸Upon me, upon the man who holds the lowest place of all among those consecrated to God, there has been bestowed this gracious favour, that I was to preach to the Gentiles the unfathomable riches to be found in Christ, ⁹and that I was to bring to light the scheme which was at work in the mysterious design, kept hidden in the mind of God, the creator of everything there is, from the very beginning of time. ¹⁰This scheme was kept hidden to the intent that God's multifarious wisdom might now, through the Church, be made known to those rulers and authorities whose field of operation is in the heavenly realms. ¹¹All this is in accordance with the design he formed from before time ever began, the design finding its fulfilment in Christ Jesus our Lord, ¹²he being the source of this boldness of ours, he being the one who secures for us our access to God which we are expecting in all confidence, by reason of the faith which we repose in Christ. ¹³I beg of you, then, not to lose heart on account of the afflictions I am enduring on your behalf; it is all done in your honour.

¹⁴With all this before my mind, then, *8*I bow my knees before the Father, ¹⁵"father" being a title borrowed by every family of beings, earthly or heavenly. ¹⁶And this is my prayer to him, that, in accordance with the wealth of his glorious majesty, he may grant it to you to be mightily strengthened by his Spirit in your inmost being, ¹⁷that Christ may indwell your hearts through your faith, that, being rooted and grounded in love, you may, ¹⁸along with all those who are dedicated to God, have the power to fathom the breadth, the length, the height, the depth of whatever there is, ¹⁹and to come to know that which surpasses all knowledge, the love of Christ, so as to be filled with all the fullness of God.

²⁰Now to him who in what he does goes beyond every expectation,

8[1 Ch 29:20 LXX; Is 45:23]

who in what he accomplishes for us immeasurably surpasses anything that we are able to ask for, anything that we are able to conceive of, bringing about all this by virtue of the very power which, through him, is also at work within ourselves: 21may glory be ascribed to him, glory residing in the Church, glory residing in Christ Jesus, from generation to generation, for ever and ever. Amen.

4 I implore you then, I, the man who is being held captive for serving the Lord's cause, to lead a life worthy of the call which has gone out to you. 2Be humble and gentle in everything you do, be patient, show forbearance towards one another, as love bids you. 3And do your utmost to preserve the unity which the Spirit imparts, being held fast to one another by virtue of the bond in which all concord has its source. 4There is one body, one Spirit, just as there is one hope held out by the call through which you have been summoned; 5one Lord, one faith, one baptism, 6one God and Father of all, who rules all, who pervades all, who dwells in all. 7And each one of us has had grace bestowed upon him, Christ measuring out the gift apportioned to each. 8That is why we are told in scripture, *h*'**He has ascended into the heights; he has led captive a host of captives; he has brought gifts to men.**' 9(Now this "ascended"—what does it mean but that he first descended into the lower regions of the earth? 10And he who descended is the very same as he who has ascended far above all the heavens, that he might fill all things.) 11And these were the gifts bestowed by him, that some should be apostles, some prophets, some evangelists, some pastors and teachers, 12to equip God's consecrated ones for the work of serving him, to equip them for the building up of the body of Christ, 13until we all attain to oneness in faith, to oneness in the knowledge we have of the Son of God, to mature manhood, measured by nothing less than the stature of Christ himself in all its fullness. 14We are to be children no longer, no longer are we to be tossed to and fro and carried here and there by every gust of doctrine blown about by the trickery of men, by their craftiness which makes them have recourse to deceitful scheming. 15No, this is what we must do. Holding on to the truth, as love would bid us, we must in every way grow up into union with him who is set as head over us, into union with Christ, 16through whom the whole body, being fitted together and held together by every joint serving for its support, in virtue of a power proportionate to each individual part, is supplied with the means of having its natural growth, the purpose of it all being that it should build itself up, love leading the way.

*h*Ps 68:18

¹⁷All this being so, I appeal to you, I declare to you solemnly, as one who has his being in the Lord, that you must no longer live as the Gentiles do, with their minds fixed on futile things, ¹⁸with their understanding darkened, being estranged from the life of God by reason of the ignorance which fills their minds, by reason of the dullness of their hearts. ¹⁹And indeed, these are the very men who, having become all callousness, have given themselves up to debauchery for the practice of all kinds of uncleanness, in virtue of the greediness of their nature. ²⁰Yet, as for yourselves, this is not the lesson you have learned in making Christ your study ²¹—that is, provided it is he in whom you have had your schooling, as the truth is indeed to be found in Jesus. ²²There must be a laying aside of that which conforms to your former manner of life, a laying aside of the old nature which is bound for ruin, conforming as it is to lusts wrought by deceit. ²³You must become renewed in respect of the spirit imbuing your minds, ²⁴and you must clothe yourselves with the new nature which has been created after God's likeness, and which expresses itself in righteousness and devotion to God founded upon the truth.

²⁵Therefore, laying aside all falsehood, let ⁱ**each one** of you **speak the truth to his neighbour,** for we are bound to one another as parts of the one body. ²⁶If there be ʲ**anger** in your heart, **do not let it lead you into sin.** See to it that the sunset does not find you still filled with anger.

²⁷Do not allow the devil to have any chance of success with you. ²⁸The man who was a thief must be a thief no longer. Let him labour instead, doing honest work with his own hands, so that he may have something of which he can let the needy have their share.

²⁹No base talk must cross your lips; only good words such as will be helpful in the building up of the faith, as need may arise, the aim being that they should impart a blessing to the listeners. ³⁰And do not give pain to God's Holy Spirit, whose seal you have had set upon you, so as to mark you out for the Day of Redemption. ³¹Put away from yourselves all bitterness, rage, anger, clamour, and evil-speaking; and all malice as well. ³²Instead, you must show yourselves kindly disposed towards one another, compassionate, and granting forgiveness to one another, just as you yourselves, as men united to Christ, have received the forgiveness of God.

5 Let it be God, then, upon whom you model yourselves, as his beloved children; ²and let it be love which rules your lives, just as Christ loved you and gave his life on your behalf, an ᵏ**offering and**

ⁱZc 8:16   ʲPs 4:4   ᵏEx 29:18; Ps 40:6; Ezk 20:41

sacrifice made to God giving forth a **savour** which was **sweetness** itself.

³Yet, as for fornication or any kind of unclean or greedy conduct, may they not be so much as mentioned among you, this being the proper course to take for those who have consecrated themselves to God. ⁴Neither let there be any obscene talk, ribaldry, coarse jesting, unseemly things such as these; instead, devote yourselves to giving thanks to God. ⁵For there is one thing you know well enough, that no share in the kingdom of Christ and of God is obtained by any man who gives himself up to fornication or any other kind of impure conduct, or by one who yields to covetousness—which amounts simply to being an idol-worshipper. ⁶Do not allow anyone to lead you astray with empty words. It is the very things I have mentioned by which God's anger is brought down upon those who are in rebellion against him. ⁷See to it, then, that you should not be throwing in your lot with these. ⁸And indeed, as regards yourselves, while there was a time when you were all darkness, you are all light now that you are in union with the Lord. Rule your lives, then, as men native to the light —⁹the harvest yielded by the light is to be found in all that is goodness, that is righteousness, that is truth—¹⁰while endeavouring to learn what are the things which find the Lord's acceptance. ¹¹And have no fellowship with the unprofitable deeds which have their home in the darkness. On the contrary, make it your business to uncover them. ¹²True enough, the things which are done by these men in secret are such that it is disgraceful even to mention them by name. ¹³On the other hand, all things uncovered by the light are made visible, while everything made visible does itself come to partake of the nature of light.

¹⁴That is the meaning of the words:

'Rouse yourself, you who are lying asleep.
Arise from the dead.
And Christ will let his light shine upon you.'

¹⁵Take the utmost care, then, about the manner in which you lead your lives, not as fools but as wise men, ¹⁶making the most of the time granted to you, for these are evil days. ¹⁷And that being so, do not allow yourselves to lose your good sense, but come to understand instead what is the will of the Lord. ¹⁸Besides, ᵗ**do not become intoxicated with wine.** It is in this way that dissoluteness gets you into its grip. No, let it be the Spirit with whom you are filled, ¹⁹holding converse with one another in psalms, hymns, and spiritual songs, singing and chanting in your hearts in honour of the Lord, ²⁰giving thanks

ᵗPr 23:21.31 LXX

at all times and for all things to God the Father in the name of our Lord Jesus Christ. 21 And standing in awe of Christ, submit yourselves to one another.

22 You who are wives must submit yourselves to your husbands, just as though you were rendering submission to the Lord. 23 The husband is the head set over his wife, just as Christ is head over the Church: it is he who brings salvation to his body. 24 And indeed, as the Church submits herself to Christ, so you who are wives must submit yourselves to your husbands in everything. 25 You who are husbands, love your wives, just as Christ loved the Church, surrendering himself on her behalf, 26 that he might sanctify her, cleansing her by the washing in the water, with the word being spoken; 27 that he might set the Church before himself and make her all-glorious, having no spot or wrinkle or any such thing; that she might be holy and without blemish. 28 And this is how husbands should love their wives: as they love their own bodies. He who loves his wife loves himself. 29 And never yet has any man felt hatred for his own flesh. On the contrary, he nourishes it and cherishes it, as Christ does the Church, 30 for we are the living parts of Christ's body. 31 Thus it says in the words of scripture, *m'For this reason a man will leave father and mother and be joined to his wife, the two of them becoming a single body.'* 32 There is a great truth hidden in these words, as I am applying them here to Christ and the Church. 33 Meanwhile, let each one of you love his wife as he loves himself, and let the wife see to it that she pays reverence to her husband.

6   You who are children, be obedient to your parents. It is right that you should. As scripture says, 2 *n'Pay honour to your father and to your mother'* (and this is the first commandment with a promise attaching to it, namely), 3 *'that it may go well with you, and you may have a long life on earth.'* 4 You who are fathers, do not arouse resentment in your children. No, *o*discipline them and admonish them, as the Lord would have you do.

5 You who are slaves, be obedient to those who are your earthly masters, in anxious dread and with single-mindedness, as though your obedience were being rendered to Christ, 6 not in the way of a mere show of service, as is the custom of those who seek to please men, but as Christ's servants, doing the will of God from the heart. 7 Your service must be that of a devoted mind, a service you render to the Lord and not to men, 8 knowing as you do that whatever good a man does, be he slave or free, he will have his recompense from the

*m*Gn 2:24   *n*Ex 20:12; Dt 5:16   *o*[Pr 2:2 LXX.5]

Lord. [9] As for you who are masters, you must do the same by your slaves and desist from uttering threats, being aware that he who is your master and theirs dwells in heaven, and that with him no distinction is made between one person and another.

[10] What remains to be said is this. Draw your strength from the Lord, from the mighty power which is his. [11] Clothe yourselves with all the armour which God provides, so that you may be able to stand firm against the wily schemes of the devil. [12] For what we have to deal with in our struggle is not creatures of flesh and blood. It is rulers and authorities reigning in a place above the earth, those who have mastery over this world in these days of darkness; it is the spirit-hosts of wickedness domiciled in the heavens. [13] Well then, take up all the armour with which God provides you, that you may have the power to stand your ground when the evil day comes, that, having accomplished all, you may still be found upon your feet. [14] Take up your stand, therefore, [p]**having girded** your **loins with the truth,** [q]**having clothed yourselves with the breastplate of righteousness,** [15] with your [r]**feet** shod, **in readiness to proclaim the gospel of peace.** [16] And with all this, take up the shield of faith, which will give you the power to quench all the flaming arrows of the evil one; [17] and receive as your own the [s]**helmet of salvation** and the **sword of the Spirit,** which is the **word of God.** [18] Let there be prayer and supplication unceasing, and pray at all times, under the impulsion of the Spirit, keeping ever watchful of your goal, with unflagging steadfastness, with supplication on behalf of all who are consecrated to God; [19] and on my behalf, too, that utterance may be granted to me, that I may open my mouth in fearlessness to make known the truth of the gospel hitherto kept hidden, [20] for which I am an ambassador in chains, that I may fearlessly declare it, speaking as I ought.

[21] Now in order that you may also know the condition in which I find myself, and how I am faring, everything will be told you by Tychicus, the much-loved brother and faithful servant of the cause of the Lord, [22] whom I have sent to you with this very end in view, that you may come to know my circumstances and that he may bring comfort to your hearts.

[23] May peace be granted to the brothers, and love joined with faith, from God the Father and the Lord Jesus Christ. [24] May grace be by the side of all who love the Lord Jesus Christ with a love undying.

---

[p] Is 11:5　　[q] Is 59:17　　[r] Is 52:7; Nah 1:15　　[s] Is 59:17; Is 11:4; [51:16]; Hos 6:5

PAUL'S LETTER
TO THE CHURCH AT PHILIPPI

1 Paul and Timothy, servants of Christ Jesus, send their greetings to all those at Philippi who have consecrated themselves to Christ Jesus, their leaders* and deacons being included in this salutation. [2]May grace be yours, coming to you from God our Father and from the Lord Jesus Christ.

[3]I give thanks to my God at every remembrance of you, [4]always in every prayer on behalf of you all—and it is with joy that I offer such prayer—[5]on account of your having made common cause with the gospel, from the day when it first reached you up to this present hour. [6]At the same time I am fully convinced of this, that he who began in you so noble a work will have brought it to completion by the time that the Day of Christ Jesus makes its appearance. [7]For it is no more than right that I should be entertaining such thoughts about you all, seeing that I am holding you in my heart, you who are, one and all—whether at the time of my imprisonment, or whether the question be one of defending the gospel and establishing its truth—sharers in the same divine favour as has been bestowed upon me. [8]And indeed, God is my witness that I am longing for you with the very tenderness of Christ Jesus, [9]the prayer which I offer being this: May your love grow richer and richer still, bringing with it full knowledge and the very depth of perception, [10]so that you may become men who approve of what has real excellence, men of perfect sincerity and free from all blemish, ready for the Day when Christ will come again, [11]and yielding to the full that harvest of righteousness which comes through Jesus Christ, to the glory and praise of God.

[12]Now I would have you know, my brothers, that the circumstances in which I find myself have tended to make the gospel advance still further, [13]inasmuch as their result has been that, throughout the praetorian guard and indeed all over the world, it has become evident

* Or 'chief pastors'.

that my imprisonment is being suffered for Christ. [14]And so it has come about that the majority of our brothers, gaining, with the help of the Lord, fresh courage from my imprisonment, have become all the bolder to preach the word of God in complete fearlessness. [15]There are, it is true, certain people who, in proclaiming Christ, do so in a spirit of envy and contentiousness, while others are moved by nothing but good will. [16]These latter are prompted by love, while they know full well that it is because of my acting in defence of the gospel that I am where I am. [17]Still, there are others who make themselves Christ's heralds for reasons of partisanship and without sincerity, in the expectation that they will make my imprisonment vexatious to me. [18]What does it matter, so long as either way, whether with false motives or in honest truth, it is Christ that is being heralded? And this is something over which I rejoice, yes, and shall ever do so. [19]After all, I know full well that, through your prayers and through the aid I shall be receiving from the Spirit of Jesus Christ, all [a]**this will result in my** finding **salvation,** [20]eagerly expectant as I am, and full of hope as I am, that I shall never be put to the blush in anything, and that, while I shall be speaking with complete openness, Christ's greatness will be exhibited in my very person, be it in life or in death. [21] And indeed, to me life is Christ, and as for death, it means gain for me. [22]But then, if to live on in this mortal flesh should mean that my labour would bear fruit, I am at a loss which to choose. [23]I am torn between the two. I am longing to depart and to be by Christ's side, a better thing, a far, far better thing. [24]Yet there is a greater need, for your sake, that I should be staying on in this mortal flesh. [25] And being convinced of this, I know full well that I shall remain, and continue to remain, with you all, for the furtherance of your faith and your joy in it, [26]so that, Christ Jesus bidding you to do so, you may take greater pride in me than ever before when I come to see you again.

[27]Only see to it that you lead your lives in a manner worthy of the gospel of Christ, so that, whether I come to see you, or only hear about you at a distance, I may learn that you are standing fast in a common unity of spirit, and that, in complete single-mindedness, you are struggling side by side on behalf of the faith proclaimed by the gospel. [28] And do not allow yourselves to be intimidated in any way by your adversaries, your steadfastness being a sure sign—and one coming from God—of their impending doom and your salvation. [29]For the grace you have had granted to you on behalf of Christ is not merely that you should believe in him but that you should suffer for his sake. [30] And as for the struggle in which you are engaged, it is the same as you once saw and now hear to be mine.

[a]Job 13:16 LXX

2 If anything, then, be meant by finding encouragement in Christ, if there be any solace afforded by love, if there be any common sharing of the Spirit, if there be any feeling of tenderness and compassion, [2]fill up my cup of happiness by being of the same mind, bearing the same love, united in spirit, with your minds set on but one thing. [3]Do nothing in a spirit of factiousness or empty conceit, but let each one, in humility, look upon the rest as being of greater account than himself. [4]And may each of you study not merely his own welfare but that of others as well. [5]Your frame of mind ought to be the same as was found in Christ Jesus, who, [6]even though his nature was from the first one embodying divinity, did not look upon his equality with God as something to be held in his grasp. [7]No, he emptied himself, divesting himself of what was his, and took on the nature of a slave. And coming to be fashioned in the likeness of human beings, [8]and being found, in the form which he bore, the same as any other man, he humbled himself and rendered an obedience which remained his till his death: death upon a cross. [9]That is why God raised him to the loftiest height, conferring on him that name which is above all other names, [10]so that [b]everything, whether in heaven, on earth, or below the earth, should, at the name Jesus, **bend the knee,** [11]and that **every tongue should confess** "Jesus is Lord", to the glory of God the Father.

[12]Well then, my dearly-loved ones, as you have always shown yourselves obedient, work out your own salvation, and that in a spirit of anxious dread, not looking upon this as a thing to be done merely when I am present, but to be done even more strenuously now that I am absent. [13]And indeed, it is God himself who is at work within you, as regards both will and deed, in pursuit of his gracious design. [14]Do everything you have to do without complaining or engaging in futile arguments, [15]so as to become wholly free from blame, wholly free from blemish: [c]**God's children without reproach** in the midst of a **crooked and perverse generation,** in the midst of men among whom you shine out, as beacons to the world, [16]holding fast to the message which proclaims where life is to be found, so that I may make the boast, when the day of Christ comes, that I have not run my course in vain, that [d]**I have** not **undertaken** my **labour in vain.** [17]And indeed, even though my blood is to be poured out as a libation upon the sacrificial offering of your faith, I rejoice and share my joy with you all. [18]And you, for your part, must rejoice and share your joy with me.

[19]It is my hope—one grounded in the Lord Jesus—that I shall be sending Timothy to you before long, so that, having news of you, I may find myself cheered in heart. [20]I have no one else with a mind

[b]Is 45:23; [1 K 19:18]   [c]Dt 32:5   [d]Is 49:4; 65:23

like his, no one who will be as truly anxious for your welfare. [21] They all look after their own interests, not those of Christ Jesus. [22] Yet, as for Timothy, you know his well-tried worth and how, like a son helping his father, he has served by my side in spreading the gospel. [23] So it is he whom I am hoping to send, as soon as I can see how things go with me. [24] At the same time I have full confidence, placing my trust in the Lord, that I shall likewise be coming to you before long.

[25] Meanwhile, I consider it necessary to send out to you Epaphroditus, my brother, my companion both in labour and in battle, and your delegate who has been ministering to my needs. [26] Indeed, he has been longing for all of you, and is distressed that you should have heard about his illness. [27] And ill he certainly was, so seriously as to be brought near to death. Yet God took pity on him, and not on him only but on me, too, so that I might be spared from having sorrow upon sorrow. [28] I am sending him all the more readily, so that, seeing him again, you should be joyful once more, and my anxiety on your behalf should be lessened. [29] Give him a welcome, then, one that has its source in the Lord, and receive him with the greatest joy. You should hold in high esteem men such as he. [30] For indeed, if he came so close to death, it was on account of work done on Christ's behalf, hazarding as he did his very life, so that he might, by his service to me, make up as much as was in his power for that which was still lacking: your presence by my side. [31a] And now, my brothers, farewell. Find your joy in the Lord.

3 [1b] One more thing. To be writing to you the same things as before is not irksome to me, while it is a safe course as far as you are concerned. [2] Be on your guard against these impure dogs, against these workers of evil, against those who make incision in their own bodies. [3] As for 'circumcision', truly so-called, it is we ourselves who practise it, we who offer our worship under the guidance of God's Spirit, we who make our boast in Christ Jesus, placing no confidence in outward matters—[4] although, so far as I am concerned, I am the very man to have confidence also about outward matters. If there be anyone who supposes that he is entitled to feel confident about outward matters, I can do so with better reason. [5] I was circumcised on the eighth day; I come from the stock of Israel, from the tribe of Benjamin; I am a Hebrew sprung from Hebrews. As for the view which I took of the law, it was that of a Pharisee; [6] as for the zeal which I displayed, I was a persecutor of the Church; as for righteousness, inasmuch as it rests on law, I showed myself irreproachable. [7] Yet, whatever was once gain to me, I have, for Christ's sake, come to count as loss. [8] In fact, I count everything as loss because of the surpassing worth of knowing Christ Jesus my Lord. It is for his sake that I have suffered the loss of all things. In truth, however, I am counting them as mere refuse, my aim being that I should gain Christ, [9]and be found to have my being in him, not having any righteousness I could call my own, a righteousness based on law, but taking my place by the righteousness which has God for its source and which comes to us through faith in Christ and on condition of there being such faith. [10]So my concern is this, that I may come to know Christ and the power which is in his resurrection, and what it means to share his sufferings, being conformed to the pattern of his death, [11]in the hope that somehow I may succeed in being given a place among those who rise from the dead. [12]Not that I have already reached my goal, not that I have already attained perfection. Yet I press on to lay hold of it, this being the very thing for the sake of which Christ Jesus laid hold of me. [13]Brothers, I am convinced that so far I have not laid hold of it. But this at least I do. Forgetting what is behind me, and straining towards what lies before me, [14]I press on towards the goal of God's heavenward summons, eager for the prize which awaits those who are in union with Christ Jesus. [15]All of us who are fully grounded in the faith must be of this way of thinking. And if in any respect you think differently, time will come when God will reveal the truth to you. [16]Meanwhile, whatever point we have reached, let us continue in the same course.

[17]Join with one another, my brothers, in taking me for your model; and mark well those who live in such a way as to conform to the example which you are having set before you by us. [18]On the other hand, there are many—I have often told you of them, and now I am telling you again amidst tears—whose lives are such as to make them enemies of the cross of Christ. [19]Doom is the fate which awaits them; the god they pay homage to is their own stomach. It is their own shameful doings in which they find their pride—they, the men who have their minds set upon earthly things. [20]As for ourselves, however, the commonwealth of which we are part is one in heaven. And it is from there that we are eagerly awaiting a saviour, the Lord Jesus Christ, [21]who will change the fashion of this humbled body of ours, making it conformable to the body which is his in his glorified state, and who will accomplish this by exerting the very power which he has to make all things subject to himself. [4:1]Well then, my brothers, whom I love and for whom I long, you who are my delight and the crown of my achievements, stand firm, united to the Lord. This is what I bid you do, you dearly-loved ones.

4   [2]I call on Euodia, and I call on Syntyche, to make peace with one another in the Lord's name. [3]Yes, and I am urging you, loyal comrade

of mine, to come to the aid of these women who have fought side by side with me in spreading the gospel, along with Clement and the rest of my fellow workers whose names are recorded *e***in the book of life.**

[4] Find your joy in the Lord at all times. I will say it again: find your joy in him. [5] May your forbearing spirit become known to everyone. The Lord is at hand. [6] Do not be anxious about anything, but instead let your requests be laid before God in every way, by prayer and supplication; yes, and let there be giving of thanks as well. [7] And the peace of God, which far surpasses anything we can comprehend, will protect your hearts and your minds, with Christ Jesus keeping guard over them.

[8] And now, my brothers, all that is founded in truth, all that commands respect, all that makes for righteousness, all that is innocent, all that is lovable, all that is gracious in the telling; if there be any excellence, anything worthy of praise, let these be the things which you have your minds dwelling on. [9] Moreover, whatever you have learned, whatever you have come to accept, what you have heard or seen of my way of living, let these be the things by which you rule your conduct. And you will have God, the giver of peace, by your side.

[10] It has been a great joy to me—one having its source in the Lord— that now at length you should have let your concern for me blossom forth once again. You did indeed have a concern for my welfare; it was only that you lacked the opportunity to express it. [11] In mentioning this matter, I am not thinking of my own want; for, as far as I am concerned, I have learned to be content in whatever state I find myself. [12] I know how to deal with things when I am brought low. I know how to deal with them when I have abundant means. I have been initiated into all the secrets—of having my fill and of going hungry, of having abundant means and of being in want. [13] There is nothing beyond my strength, thanks to him who bestows his power upon me. [14] Still, as far as you are concerned, you did well to stand by me in my distress. [15] Indeed, men and women of Philippi, you are as well aware as I am myself that when the gospel was first preached, after I had left Macedonia, there was no church except you yourselves which made me its partner when it came to giving and receiving. [16] Yes, even when I was still at Thessalonica, you sent me help more than once to supply my needs. [17] It is not that I set store by the gift, but there is one thing I do set store by: the rich increase which is being credited to your account. [18] As for myself, I have received full payment and have more than enough. I am fully endowed, having received from Epaphroditus what you have sent me: an offering giving forth a *f***savour** which

is **sweetness** itself, a sacrifice which finds glad acceptance, truly pleasing to God. [19] And my God—so great are his riches—will supply every need of yours by placing you in glory united to Christ Jesus. [20] To him who is our God and Father let glory be ascribed for ever and ever. Amen.

[21] Give my greetings, in the name of Christ Jesus, to each and every one of those who are consecrated to God. All the brothers who are with me here send their greetings. [22] All who are consecrated to God send their greetings to you, and in particular those who belong to the Emperor's household.

[23] May the grace of the Lord Jesus Christ hold its protecting hand over your spirits.

PAUL'S LETTER
TO THE CHURCH AT COLOSSAE

1 Paul, by the will of God an apostle of Christ Jesus, and Timothy your brother, [2] send greetings to those at Colossae who are consecrated to God, to the brothers who have come to repose their faith in Christ. May grace and peace be yours, sent out to you by God who is our Father.

[3] We continually give thanks to God, the Father of our Lord Jesus Christ, in the prayers we offer on your behalf, [4] having heard of your faith in Christ Jesus and of the love which you bear to all who are consecrated to God, [5] all this being due to the hope you have come to embrace, the hope which is treasured up for you in heaven. Of the object of this hope you have heard before now through the message heralding the truth of the gospel [6] which has come to you, as it has to the whole world, bearing fruit there and increasing, just as it has done among you ever since the day when you learned of God's gracious favour and truly recognized it for what it is, [7] as you were taught it by Epaphras, that dearly-loved fellow bondsman of ours. He renders faithful service to Christ on your behalf, [8] and it is he who has brought us the news of the love you bear under the impulsion of the Spirit.

[9] And so it is that we, for our part, from the day when we first heard of it, have never ceased praying for you, asking that you may be filled with knowledge of God's will, such as brings with it spiritual wisdom and discernment of every kind, [10] to lead a life worthy of the Lord and wholly pleasing to him, a life which yields a harvest of good works of any and every kind, and makes you advance further and further in the knowledge which you have of God. [11] May you be endowed with all strength such as derives from the glory which belongs to God in his majesty, so as to be led to be steadfast and patient in every way, being filled with joy, [12] and giving thanks to the Father, who has provided us with the sufficiency to obtain a share in the inheritance intended for those who have consecrated themselves to him, dwellers in a realm of light. [13] It is he who has rescued us from the dominion where darkness reigns, and has moved us into the kingdom of his dearly-loved Son, [14] through whom we are being set free from our

bondage, obtaining pardon for the sins we had committed. [15] He is the visible representation of the invisible God. He it is who takes precedence over everything created, [16] since it is in him that all created things took their being, things in heaven and things upon earth, not only visible ones but invisible orders as well, such as thrones, dominions, rulers, and authorities. All things were created through him and for him. [17] He has the primacy of them all, and in him all subsist. [18] Furthermore, he is the head set over what is his body: the Church. It is in him that she has her origin. He was the firstborn from the dead, in order that he might take first place in everything, [19] since it was God's pleasure that divinity in all its fullness was to reside in him, [20] and that it was to be through him that he would reconcile all things to himself—things on earth and things in heaven—peace being established by virtue of Christ's blood shed on the cross.

[21] As for yourselves, time was when you were estranged from God, when, because of the very bent of your minds, you were hostile to him, being occupied with deeds which were evil. [22] But now Christ has, in his human body, reconciled you to God by his death, so as to bring you into God's presence, holy, without reproach, and free from all blame, [23] provided, that is, that you remain true to the faith, being grounded in it, being streadfast in it, never shifting from the hope held out by the gospel to which you have lent your ear—the gospel which has been preached to the whole creation under heaven and of which I, Paul, have been made a minister.

[24] And so it is that I rejoice in the sufferings I am undergoing on your behalf, as I fill up, in this frail frame of mine, whatever may still be lacking in respect of Christ's afflictions as yet to be endured for the sake of his body, the Church. [25] It was of her that I was made a minister to discharge the divine office entrusted to me for your benefit. I was to make known the word of God to the full, [26] unfolding the great truth which had been hidden from all the ages and generations of the past, but which has now been revealed to those who are consecrated to God. [27] And indeed, it was God's will to reveal to these what wealth of glory there was to be found for the Gentiles in the truth hitherto kept hidden. Christ is in your very midst: he who holds out the hope of a glory to come. [28] It is he whose heralds we are, admonishing everyone and instructing everyone, with all the wisdom at our disposal, so that we may be able to present every one as fully mature, in virtue of his union with Christ. [29] It is with this end in view that I toil and struggle, in reliance on the very energy of Christ which is powerfully at work within me.

2   And indeed, I would have you know in how great a struggle I am engaged for you, for those at Laodicea, in fact for all those who have

never seen me face to face, my wish for them all being this: [2]May they find themselves comforted in their hearts, as they are being knit together in love, as they have brought to them all the riches of an assured conviction, such as true discernment carries with it, and as they are obtaining knowledge of God's great secret, which is Christ, [3]in whom there is stored up, all *hidden from sight*, the whole **treasury** of God's **wisdom** and knowledge. [4]My aim in assuring you of this is to prevent anyone from having the power to delude you by resorting to plausible arguments which have no truth in them. [5]As for myself, though I am absent from you in body I am with you in spirit, full of joy, witnessing as I am your orderly array and the solid front presented by your faith in Christ.

[6]You have come to accept the proclamation of Christ Jesus as Lord. Well then, let it be he by whom you order your lives, [7]being rooted and grounded in him, being established in the faith as you were taught it, and offering thanksgiving in abundance. [8]Be on your guard not to let anyone succeed in robbing you of your treasure by his philosophizing, by concocting what is but an empty fraud which accords with a merely man-made tradition and with rudimentary teachings such as this world has to offer but does not accord with Christ. [9]And this is the truth about him, that in him there resides embodied all the fullness of God, [10]while, as for yourselves, you come to fullness in Christ, who has been set as head over every power and authority to be found anywhere. [11]Besides, it is through him that you have undergone a circumcision, not the work of any human hand but one consisting in your being divested of your bodies, inasmuch as they are the source of carnal appetites. That is the nature of the circumcision which has Christ for its author, while it is true at the same time [12]that you were buried together with Christ through your baptism, and it is in virtue of this very baptism that you have also been raised up to life together with him, and that because of the faith you reposed in the operation of God, who raised him from the dead. [13]Indeed, there you were lying dead by reason of the offences you had committed, by reason of that carnal nature of yours, uncircumcised as it was. But God made you alive together with Christ, granting us his pardon for whatever offences we had committed, [14]and by cancelling the writ which stood against us, consisting as it did in precise enactments which the law laid down. Christ made away with that writ altogether, nailing it to the cross, [15]while, as for the supramundane rulers and authorities hanging about him, he stripped them off himself, making a bold public display of them, and leading them captive in his triumphal procession, a conqueror by virtue of the cross.

[16]Therefore, let no one take you to task over what you eat and drink,

---

*Pr 2:3f; Is 45:3

or in the matter of observing a festival, a new moon, or a sabbath, [17]these things being no more than a pale foreshadowing of what was to come, the proper reality to be found nowhere but in Christ. [18]Do not allow yourselves to be robbed of your prize by people who take a delight in self-abasement or in the worship which they offer to angels, and who take their stand on visions they claim to have received. A person of this sort is ruled by the groundless conceit he has of himself, by thoughts which have their source in his own worldly mind, [19]a person who fails to hold fast to him who is the Head, through whom the whole body, supported and held together by its joints and ligaments, increases with a growth which it receives from God.

[20]If in dying with Christ you have parted company with rudimentary teachings such as this world provides, how is it that you submit yourselves to rules and regulations as though you still had your life in this world? [21]'Do not handle,' 'Do not taste,' 'Do not touch' [22](referring, every one of them, to things which are intended for destruction by being consumed), all this being laid down in obedience to [b]**injunctions and teachings** which have their source in mere **men**. [23]And indeed, true though it be that such things have an air of wisdom about them in the eyes of those who go in for self-imposed devotions, for a sham humility, and for an unsparing treatment of the body, they are of no value whatever in checking the indulgences which spring from the carnal side of our nature.

3   If, then, you have been raised up together with Christ, you must lift up your thoughts above, where Christ [c]**is seated at God's right hand.** [2]Set your minds on things belonging to this higher realm, not on things upon earth. [3]For you have undergone death, and the life which you have is hidden away with Christ in God. [4]And when Christ shall be manifested—he who is our life—then you, too, shall be made manifest, and all in a blaze of glory.

[5]Put to death, therefore, whatever in your nature belongs to the earth, such things as fornication or any other impure conduct, unbridled passion, evil desire, yes, and covetousness, too, which in fact is nothing but idolatry. [6]It is these very things which are bringing down God's wrath upon men; [7]and such was your conduct, too, at the time when you let your lives be ruled by them. [8]Yet now it is your turn to put them all away from you: anger, rage, evil speaking, slander, foul talk proceeding from your mouths. [9]And do not tell lies at one another's expense, for you have stripped off the old nature with the habits that went with it, [10]and have clothed yourselves with the

[b]Is 29:13   [c]Ps 110:1

new nature which is ever being renewed *d*in the image of him who created it, so that you may have deeper and still deeper knowledge of God. [11]And where lives such as these are led, no distinctions are made: there is neither Gentile nor Jew, neither circumcised nor uncircumcised; no one is barbarian or Scythian; no one a slave or a free man. No, Christ is all, and in all.

[12]Clothe yourselves, then, as God's chosen ones—consecrated to him and dearly loved by him—with a compassionate heart, with kindness, humility, gentleness, and patience, [13]bearing with one another, should anyone have a complaint against someone else. As the Lord has granted you his forgiveness, so you must forgive. [14]And over and above all that I have mentioned, clothe yourselves with love, love being that by which all things are bound together in a perfect unity. [15]And may the peace which has its source in Christ be what bears rule in your hearts, in you who, as members of the one body, have received God's summons, so that you might pursue that peace, being ever thankful. [16]May Christ's message dwell in you in all its richness, endowing you with the highest wisdom as you are instructing and admonishing one another, holding converse with one another in psalms, hymns, and spiritual songs, chanting in your hearts, under grace, in praise of God. [17]And whatever you are about, in word or in action, let all things be done in the name of the Lord Jesus, he being the one through whom you render thanks to the Father.

[18]You who are wives, submit yourselves to your husbands, as befits those who are in the Lord's service. [19]You who are husbands, love your wives and do not behave harshly towards them. [20]You who are children, be obedient to your parents in every way. That is a thing which finds glad acceptance with those who follow the Lord. [21]You who are fathers, do not embitter your children, so that they may not lose heart. [22]You who are slaves, be obedient to your earthly masters in every way, not in the way of a mere show of service, as is the custom of those who seek to please men, but with single-mindedness, standing in awe of the Lord. [23]Whatever your task, let your heart be in your work, and look upon it as a service rendered to the Lord and not to men. [24]You know that being made heirs of God is what you will receive as your recompense from the Lord. The Lord Christ is the master whose servants you are. [25]He who commits a wrong will have his wrongdoing paid back to him, no distinction being made between one person and another. 4[1]You who are masters, give your slaves just and equitable treatment. You know full well that you, too, have a master—a Master in heaven.

*d*Gn 1:27

4 [2]Devote yourselves steadfastly to prayer, with your minds wide awake and your hearts filled with gratitude. [3]Pray for us, too, that God may afford us an opening for preaching his message, for unfolding the secret of Christ—my doing so being the very cause of my imprisonment— [4]that I may declare it openly, speaking as I ought.

[5]Conduct yourselves with prudence toward those who are not of your company, making the most of your opportunities. [6]Your manner of speaking must always be gracious, never having anything insipid about it; you must do your best to discover how to give each questioner a fitting answer.

[7]You will learn all about the circumstances in which I find myself from Tychicus, that much-loved brother and faithful helper, that fellow bondsman in the Lord's service. [8]I have sent him for this very purpose, that you may learn how things are going for me, and that he may bring comfort to your hearts. [9]And with him I have sent Onesimus, the faithful and well-loved brother who is one of yourselves. They will tell you of everything that is happening here.

[10]Greetings to you from Aristarchus, who shares my imprisonment, and from Mark, the cousin of Barnabas. (You have received instructions concerning him; make him welcome when he comes to you.) [11]From Jesus, too, whom they call Justus. These are Jewish converts, and the only ones of that kind who have worked hand in hand with me for the furtherance of God's kingdom. [12]Greetings from Epaphras, who is one of yourselves, a servant of Christ Jesus. He is ever wrestling on your behalf when he is offering prayer, asking that you may stand firm as men who are fully mature and who have reached clear assurance with regard to everything which the will of God demands of us. [13]I can vouch for him as a man who is toiling hard for you as well as for those at Laodicea and Hierapolis. [14]Greetings from Luke, that healer of men, so dear to my heart, and from Demas. [15]Greetings to the brothers at Laodicea and Hierapolis and to Nymphas, as well as to the congregation which meets at his house. [16]Moreover, see to it that, when this letter has been read out to you, it is read out also to the congregation at Laodicea, and that you, for your part, have read out to you the one reaching you from Laodicea. [17]And give this message to Archippus. Keep your mind on the task which you have had entrusted to you as a servant of the Lord and make sure that you fully discharge it.

[18]The salutation is in my own hand—PAUL. Be mindful of my imprisonment. Grace be by your side.

PAUL'S FIRST LETTER TO THE CHURCH AT THESSALONICA

1 Paul, Silvanus, and Timothy send their greetings to the church of the Thessalonians, which has her very being in God the Father and the Lord Jesus Christ. May grace and peace be by your side.

²We give thanks to God at all times on behalf of you all, making mention of you unceasingly in our prayers, ³as we call to mind—and that in the very sight of God the Father—your deeds which spring from your faith, your toil springing from your love, and your steadfastness springing from the hope which you have come to repose in our Lord Jesus Christ. ⁴And indeed, my brothers, so dearly loved by God, you know well enough the circumstances in which you were chosen by God, ⁵how, when we brought the gospel to you, that was by no means a matter of mere words. No, what showed itself was the power we displayed, and how we were filled with the Holy Spirit and with a conviction that nothing could shake. Moreover, you know just as well what conduct towards you we adopted when we were in your midst, so as to be able to be of service to you. ⁶And you, for your part, proceeded to take us for your model, to take the Lord for your model, by the welcome you gave to our message, accepting it with such joy as has its source in the Holy Spirit, and doing so in spite of the many afflictions besetting you. ⁷It was in this way, then, that you became an example for all the believers in Macedonia and Achaia. ⁸And indeed, it was yourselves, men of Thessalonica, who were the cause of God's message sounding forth, and that not only in Macedonia and Achaia. No, it has become known all over the world how you came to repose your faith in God. There is no need, then, to say anything of this matter, ⁹seeing that people, when they speak of us, tell of their own accord the story of the glad welcome you gave us, how you turned away from your idols to become the servants of the living God, of him who is really God, ¹⁰and how you are awaiting expectantly the appearing from heaven of his Son, whom he raised from the dead, the appearing of Jesus, our deliverer from God's angry judgment which is to come upon the world.

2 And then, brothers, you do not need us to tell you that there was nothing purposeless about the visit we paid you. [2]On the contrary, even though we had already met with suffering and cruel treatment at Philippi, we were emboldened, with the help of our God, to proclaim to you the divine gospel with complete openness, and that in face of great opposition. [3]Indeed, the appeal we send out is not based on any delusive notions; it does not arise from impure motives, nor is there any guile about it. [4]On the contrary, just as we have been held worthy by God to be entrusted with the gospel, so we speak out, being intent not on pleasing men but on pleasing God, who ever [a]**scrutinizes** our **hearts.** [5]At no time were we found employed in words of flattery, as you yourselves well know, nor did we have recourse—God is our witness for that—to any make-believe, such as men out for gain might avail themselves of. [6]Neither did we seek for human praise—yours or another's—even though, as Christ's apostles, we might well have insisted on making our weight felt. [7]On the contrary, when we came among you, we were found to be gentle after the fashion of a nurse taking care of her children. [8]Indeed, so affectionately were we drawn towards you as to be ready not merely to let you have your share of God's gospel but to give our very lives for you; so tenderly had we learned to love you. [9]After all, brothers, you remember how we laboured and toiled, how we worked night and day, all the time we were preaching God's gospel to you, so that we might not be a burden to any of you.

[10]You are witness—and God is witness—how devout, how upright, how free from all blame we were found to be in the conduct we adopted towards you who had come to embrace the faith, [11]just as you are aware that we treated every one of you as a father treats his own children, admonishing you, encouraging you, and [12]appealing to you to lead a life worthy of God, who is sending out his summons to you, so that you might obtain a share in his kingdom and the glory which goes with it.

[13]Moreover, in consideration of all this, we give unceasing thanks to God also for this reason, that when you received the word of divine preaching which goes out from us, you accepted it not as a word coming from men but as what it really is, the word of God, the very word which displays its activity within you who have become believers. [14]And indeed, brothers, what has happened to you is the very counterpart of what happened to God's churches in Judaea dedicated to the service of Christ Jesus. You suffered at the hands of your fellow countrymen the very same things as they suffered at the hands of the

[a]Jr 11:20

Jews. [15]Of the Jews, I say: of the men who put the Lord Jesus and the
prophets to death, who are persecuting us cruelly, who incur the dis-
pleasure of God, and who show themselves to be the enemies of all
mankind, [16]seeking to hinder us, as they do, from preaching to the
Gentiles, that they might obtain their salvation. And so it is that they
must ever be *b*filling up the measure of their **sins**. Still, the judgment
expressing God's *c***anger** has now overtaken them *d*for good and all.

[17]Yes, as for you, brothers, when we found ourselves bereft of you,
even for a short while—though only in person, not in heart—we were
all the more eager to see you face to face; so great was our longing for
you. [18]And so it was that we resolved to pay you a visit—I, Paul, did
so more than once, but Satan put hindrances in our way. [19]Indeed,
what hope and joy do we have, what crown of achievement to pride
ourselves on, unless it be you yourselves in the sight of our Lord Jesus
at his coming? [20]Yes, you are that in which we glory, in which we find
our joy.

3 And so, when we could bear it no longer, we were content to be
left behind in Athens alone, [2]while we sent our brother Timothy,
God's fellow worker in spreading the gospel of Christ, that he might
give you strength and bring you encouragement for the furtherance
of your faith. [3]There must be no wavering on anyone's part, notwithstanding all the affliction by which we are beset. You know well
enough that such is our appointed lot, [4]since we told you beforehand,
when we were still in your midst, that we were destined to suffer affliction. So it has turned out, and you are well aware of it. [5]And in
view of all this, I, for my part, when I could bear it no longer, sent
Timothy out to you to make sure of the steadfastness of your faith.
Was there a risk perhaps that the tempter of souls might have put
temptations in your way, all my toil turning out to have been to no
purpose? [6]But now Timothy has just arrived back from his visit to
you, bringing us the happy news of your faith and your love, and how
you are ever holding us in kind remembrance, longing to see us as we
long to see you. [7]Thus, notwithstanding all the calamities and affliction with which we have to contend, we are comforted on your account, by reason of your holding on to the faith. [8]For the truth is that
fresh life is brought to us if only you stand firm in your loyalty to the
Lord. [9]And indeed, what thanksgiving can we put before God on your
behalf, as a proper return for the joy with which we are filled on your
account— and that in the very sight of our God— [10]when we are offering prayer night and day, with the greatest earnestness at our dis-

*b*Gn 15:16; [2 M 6:14]   *c*2 Ch 36:16; Ps 95:11   *d*[1 Ch 28:9; Ps 77:7f; Lm 3:31] posal, asking for an opportunity of seeing you face to face, and making good whatever shortcomings there may still be found in your faith? [11] Now may he who is our God and Father be himself our guide on our way to you, with our Lord Jesus beside him. [12] And as for yourselves, may the Lord cause you to increase and abound in the love you bear to one another and to all men, after the fashion of the love we bear you, [13] with the intent of giving strength to your hearts, so that you may stand, unreproved and imbued with holiness, in the very sight of him who is our God and Father, on the day when our Lord Jesus makes his appearance, accompanied by all those who are consecrated to him.

4 And now, brothers, we would exhort you, we would make this appeal to you in the name of the Lord Jesus. You have received instructions from us about how you are to live so as to find God's approval. And although you do in fact conduct your lives in this way, there remains this to be said, that it is your duty to make greater and ever greater progress in this matter. [2] You do indeed know well enough the nature of the commandments which we handed on to you by the authority of the Lord Jesus. [3] What God asks of you is that you should do all you can to become holy. Fornication is to be something you abstain from altogether, [4] and each of you is to learn how to gain mastery over his own body, as a thing to be held holy, to be held in honour. [5] You must not give way to passions aroused by lust, as do [e]**the Gentiles who have no knowledge of God.** [6] There must be no transgressing, no taking advantage of a brother in this matter,* seeing that all such wrongdoing carries with it the [f]**Lord's punishment,** as we have told you before now, as we have solemnly declared to you. [7] The life to which God has called us is not one of uncleanness; it is a life of holiness. [8] Thus, whoever acts in disregard of this, disregards not men but God himself, who [g]**bestows his** Holy **Spirit upon us.**

[9] As for the question of love for our brotherhood, there is no need that anyone should be writing to you about this, seeing that it is at God's prompting, and not at that of anyone else, that you have learned that you are to love one another. [10] And indeed, that is precisely what you practice towards all the brothers throughout Macedonia. Still, we would urge you, brothers, to make greater and ever greater progress in this, [11] and at the same time you should make it your aim to lead a quiet life, to mind your own affairs, and to work with your own hands,

---

[e]Jr 10:25; Ps 79:6   [f]Ps 94:2   [g]Ezk 36:27; 37:14

* Or 'not taking advantage of a brother in the matter being considered'.

as we bade you do, [12]so that your conduct may be such as to win commendation from the world around you, and that you may stand in no need of depending on others.

[13]And now, brothers, we do not wish you to be left in ignorance about those who have gone to their rest, in order that you may not grieve as the rest of the world does, with no hope to go by. [14]After all, we believe that Jesus went to his death and rose again. And just so will God bring back, with Jesus by his side, those who were in communion with him when they went to their rest. [15]Indeed, what we can declare to you, as a message from the Lord himself, is this, that we who are alive, who are left until the coming of the Lord, shall by no means reach the goal in advance of those who have gone to their rest. [16]No, the Lord himself will come down from heaven, with a cry of command, with an archangel raising his voice, and God's trumpet sounding. And those who have died united to Christ will rise first. [17]Only after that shall we who are alive be caught up together with them in the clouds to meet the Lord in the air. And so we shall be with the Lord for ever. [18]Let these words, then, enable you to bring comfort to one another.

5   Yet, brothers of ours, as to the question of when this is to be, or what is the precise moment appointed for it, you have no need to have anything written to you about that. [2]For you know perfectly well that the Day of the Lord will appear like a thief in the night. [3]It is just when people are saying, 'There is peace,' 'There is safety,' that sudden destruction shall fall upon them, like the birth pangs that come upon a woman when she is with child. And there shall be no escape. [4]Yet, as for yourselves, brothers, you are not living in the darkness for that day to take you by surprise, as one is taken by surprise by a thief. [5]No, you are, one and all, an offspring of the light, an offspring of the day. We do not belong to either night or darkness. [6]Well, then, let us not sleep, like the rest of mankind, but let us keep wakeful, let us keep sober. [7]It is at night that the sleepers sleep, it is at night that the drunkards get drunk. [8]Yet the realm where we have our home is one of daylight. Let us keep sober, then, [h]**clothing ourselves with the breastplate** of faith and love, and with the hope of salvation serving us as our **helmet.** [9]For God has not destined us to be objects of his anger but to obtain salvation through our Lord Jesus Christ, [10]who died for our sake, so that, whether we are still wakeful in life or sleeping the sleep of death, we might find a life which we share with him. [11]Therefore, encourage one another and build up one another in the faith, this being, in fact, the very thing that you do.

[h]Is 59:17

¹²Now, brothers, we ask you to give proper recognition to those who labour among you, who are set over you in the Lord's service and whose business it is to admonish you. ¹³Hold them in the highest possible esteem—and that in a spirit of love—on account of the work they are doing. Be at peace among yourselves. ¹⁴And then, brothers, we would make this appeal to you: admonish the idle; bring comfort to those who are discouraged; sustain the weak; adopt a patient attitude towards all. ¹⁵See to it that no one repays evil for evil. Your aim must always be to do the best you can for one another and for everyone. ¹⁶Be joyful at all times. ¹⁷Offer prayer continually. ¹⁸Give thanks in all circumstances. It is God's will—a will at one with that of Christ Jesus—that you should act in this way. ¹⁹Do not stifle the manifestations of the Spirit. ²⁰Do not hold prophetic utterances in low esteem. ²¹Put all things to the test, holding on to that which is good. ²²*ᶦ***Keep yourselves from evil** in **all** its forms.

²³May God himself, the bringer of peace, make you holy through and through, so as to be found preserved completely sound, and free from all blame in spirit, soul, and body on the day of the coming of our Lord Jesus Christ. ²⁴He who sends out his call to you is true to his word. And he will accomplish it.

²⁵Brothers, offer prayer on our behalf.

²⁶Greet one another with the kiss of peace.

²⁷I adjure you, in the Lord's name, to have this letter read out to all the brothers.

²⁸The grace of our Lord Jesus Christ be by your side.

ᶦJob 1:1.8; 2:3

PAUL'S SECOND LETTER TO THE CHURCH AT THESSALONICA

1 Paul, Silvanus, and Timothy send their greetings to the church of the Thessalonians, which has her very being in God our Father and in the Lord Jesus Christ. ²May grace and peace be yours, coming to you from God the Father and the Lord Jesus Christ.

³It is our bounden duty to give unceasing thanks to God on your behalf. And indeed, that we should be doing so is no more than fitting, seeing that there is such a mighty increase of your faith and so great an abundance, in each and every one of you, of the love you bear to one another. ⁴Moreover, this has resulted in our coming to boast about you before the churches of God, on account of your steadfastness and of the faith you have shown, notwithstanding all the persecutions you have to endure. ⁵All this is clear evidence of how just God's judgments are, for they signify that you are being held worthy of a share in God's kingdom, on behalf of which you are undergoing these sufferings.

⁶Moreover, God's justice, and what he understands by it, will be made evident in a way corresponding to this when he comes to recompense with affliction those who afflict you, ⁷while recompensing you who are afflicted—yes, and us as well—by granting relief on the day when the Lord Jesus will be revealed from heaven, with his mighty angels attending him. ⁸That will be the time when, *ᵃ*with fire flaming about him, he will be meting out punishment to those who do not acknowledge God, who refuse to submit themselves to the gospel which proclaims Jesus our Lord. ⁹It is these very people who will have to suffer punishment of eternal ruin, *ᵇ*being excluded from the presence of the Lord and the mighty glory which is his, ¹⁰on that great day when he shall appear to be glorified in those consecrated to him, and to be marvelled at by all who have learned to believe in him. (And the testimony which we put before you did indeed find belief.) ¹¹It is with all this in view that we are ever praying on your

---

*ᵃ*Is 66:15.4; Jr 10:25; Ps 79:6   *ᵇ*Is 2:10.19.21; Ps 89:7; Is 49:3; 2:11.17

behalf, asking that our God may count you worthy of the call he has sent out to you, and that he may mightily bring to fulfilment all the delight you have in well-doing, all the activity called forth by your faith, [12]^c**so that the name** of our Lord Jesus **may be glorified in you,** and you may be glorified in him, by virtue of the gracious favour bestowed by our God and the Lord Jesus Christ.

2 And then, brothers, as for the coming of the Lord Jesus Christ and our being gathered to be brought into his presence, we earnestly beg of you [2]not to allow yourselves to be rashly driven out of your sober judgment or become unsettled in your minds by any spiritual utterance, any message, or any letter purporting to come from us, to the effect that the Day of the Lord is already with us. [3]Do not allow anyone to lead you astray in any way. For there is no possibility that that day should come until the final rebellion against God has taken place and the man embodying wickedness stands revealed, the one destined to be brought to ruin, [4]the enemy of God ^d**who exalts himself above every** so-called **god,** above every object of worship, so that it ends in his ^e**taking his seat** in **God's** temple and in his proclaiming that he himself is **God.**

[5]Do you not remember my telling you all this when I was still with you? [6]Well then, if that is so, you must be aware also of the power restraining him, that he might not be revealed until the time appointed for him. [7]Meanwhile, lawlessness is already at work, as something hidden from sight, hidden, however, only until the time comes for the one who exercises the restraining influence to be swept out of the way. [8]And then the ^f**lawless one** will stand revealed, whom the Lord Jesus **will slay by the breath of his mouth,** whom he will overwhelm by the very radiance of his coming. [9]As for the nature of that man's coming, it will be accomplished in obedience to Satan's way of operation. It will be attended with the exercise of all sorts of power, with counterfeit signs and wonders, [10]with every kind of deception such as wickedness devises, falling upon those who are destined to ruin because of their refusal to give a welcome to the truth and so be saved. [11]And that is why God sends forth a mighty delusion to them which makes them give credit to what is false, [12]so that a judgment of condemnation may come upon all who did not believe the truth but took their delight in unrighteousness.

[13]Yet as for ourselves, brothers so dearly ^g**loved by the Lord,** it is our bounden duty to give thanks to God unceasingly, because he chose you from the first that you might obtain your salvation, in virtue of the

^cIs 66:5 LXX   ^dDn 11:36   ^eEzk 28:2   ^fIs 11:4; Ps 33:6; Job 4:9   ^gDt 33:12

Spirit's sanctifying influence and of your belief in the truth. [14]It is to this that he has called you by the gospel which we preach, so that you might obtain your share of the glory which is to be found in our Lord Jesus Christ. [15]Stand firm, then, brothers, and hold fast to the traditions which you have been taught by us, whether by word of mouth or by letter. [16]And may our Lord Jesus Christ himself, may God our Father who has shown such love for us, bestowing upon us, by virtue of his grace, inexhaustible consolation and a firmly grounded hope, [17]encourage your hearts and give you such strength as will make you give yourselves up to good deeds and words of every kind.

3 And now, brothers, we would urge you to pray for us, that the word of God may spread speedily, being received as a thing of glory, as it was when it reached you, [2]and that we may be delivered out of the hands of wicked and perverse men. For it is not everybody who has faith. [3]Yet the Lord is faithful; he will give you strength and guard you from the evil one. [4]Besides, we are fully confident—resting our confidence upon the Lord—that you are acting, and will act, in obedience to our injunctions. [5]And may the Lord be the one who guides your hearts, directing you to where God's love, where Christ's steadfastness, is to be found.

[6]Only, brothers, we charge you, in the name of the Lord Jesus Christ, to keep yourselves aloof from every member of the brotherhood who leads a disorderly life, contrary to the tradition you have had handed on to you by us. [7]Indeed, you are well aware of the way in which you ought to be modelling yourselves on us. After all, we did not behave in a disorderly manner when we were among you. [8]Neither did we let other people feed us without paying for what we had. On the contrary, we laboured and toiled night and day so as not to become a burden to any of you. [9]It is not that we had no special privilege to claim in this matter. However, our aim was to set you an example, so that you in turn might come to model yourselves on us. [10]For when we were still in your midst, we charged you that anyone who refused to work was to be left to go hungry. [11]And now we are told that there are certain people who lead disorderly lives, doing no work and being mere busybodies. [12]We charge all such, we admonish them, as the Lord Jesus Christ would have us do, that they are to do their work quietly, eating food they have earned for themselves. [13]As for yourselves, my brothers, you must never grow weary of doing good. [14]And if there be anyone refusing to take heed of the instructions set down in this letter, mark that man and avoid his company, so that he may become ashamed of what he has done. [15]Yet do not look upon him as an enemy, but admonish him as one admonishes a

brother. ¹⁶And may the Lord himself, the giver of peace, bestow peace upon you at all times and in every way. May the Lord be by the side of each and every one of you.

¹⁷The salutation is in my own hand—PAUL. This is the mark of genuineness in every letter of mine. This is the way I write. ¹⁸May the grace of our Lord Jesus Christ be by the side of each and every one of you.

PAUL'S FIRST LETTER
TO TIMOTHY

1 Paul, an apostle of Christ Jesus, at the command of God our Saviour and of Christ Jesus who is our hope, [2]sends his greetings to Timothy, his true son in his fight for the faith. May grace, mercy, and peace be by your side, brought to you by God the Father and our Lord Jesus Christ.

[3]When I was setting out for Macedonia, I charged you to stay behind at Ephesus so that you might give warning to certain people to desist from propounding strange doctrine, [4]paying no attention to mere legends or to endless genealogical researches, a procedure which tends to lead to idle speculations rather than be of any help to us in the effective performance of our office as God's stewards, something which depends on faith. [5]The aim and the object of the charge we gave you is that men are to be told that what they must work for is the possession of a love coming from a pure heart, of a conscience free from guilt, and of a faith free from all insincerity. [6]And these indeed are the very things which certain people have missed altogether, wandering away as they did to occupy themselves with fruitless speculations. [7]What they are desirous of is to be teachers of the law, while in fact they neither understand the meaning of what they themselves are saying nor do they have any grasp of the nature of the things about which they make such confident assertions.

[8]But as for ourselves, we know that the law is an excellent thing, so long as it is dealt with in a manner appropriate to it. [9]And what is to be kept in mind here is this, that the law is laid down not for those in pursuit of righteousness, but for the lawless and the rebellious, for the ungodly and sinful, for those who lay violent hand on father or mother, for murderers, [10]for those who engage in fornication, for men given up to unnatural vice; the slave dealers, the liars, the perjurers, or any others whose activities are contrary to what is enjoined by wholesome teaching, [11]the teaching, that is, which conforms to the gospel which tells of the glory of God in his eternal felicity, the gospel which has been entrusted to me to proclaim.

¹²I give my thanks to him who is the source of my strength, to our Lord Jesus Christ, because he has judged me faithful, appointing me to do service for him, ¹³even though I was at that time a blasphemer, a persecutor, a man full of insolence. However, mercy was shown me because it was in the ignorance of unbelief that I did what I did. ¹⁴And the grace of our Lord came upon me in its full flood, carrying with it that faith and that love which have their root in Christ Jesus. ¹⁵How faithful to the truth, how deserving of our fullest acceptance, are the words, 'Christ Jesus has come into this world to bring salvation to sinners.' Of these I am the foremost. ¹⁶Yet mercy was shown me for this reason, that in me, as the foremost, Jesus Christ might display his patience to the full, as a pattern for those who, in the future, were to repose their faith in him and gain eternal life. ¹⁷Now to him who is the king of the ages, immortal and invisible, to him who alone is God, be ascribed honour and glory for ever and ever. Amen.

¹⁸This is the charge which I am laying before you, Timothy, my son, in accordance with the prophecies made concerning you in former times—that you are to fight the good fight led by their spirit, ¹⁹holding on to the faith and keeping your conscience free from guilt, the very thing certain people have refused to do, thus making shipwreck of their faith. ²⁰Hymenaeus and Alexander are of their company, men whom I have consigned to Satan, that they may be taught to desist from their blasphemies.

2 First of all, then, I urge you that supplications, prayers, intercessions, and thanksgivings are to be offered on behalf of all mankind, and in particular ²on behalf of kings and all those occupying a high position, so that we may be enabled to lead a tranquil and undisturbed life, one that is godly in every way and fully deserving of respect. ³This is what is right and finds acceptance in the sight of God our Saviour, ⁴whose will it is that all men should find salvation and arrive at knowledge of the truth. ⁵For there is only one God, one mediator between God and men, the man Christ Jesus, ⁶who gave himself as a ransom paid on behalf of all, bearing his testimony at the time fixed for this purpose. ⁷And as for myself, I have been appointed to be his herald and apostle for the proclamation of these very things (I am speaking the truth; I am telling no falsehood), that I might become a teacher serving the Gentiles, urged on by my faith and my love of the truth.

⁸In consideration of all this, it is my desire that, wherever men may be, they should offer prayer lifting up their hands in a spirit of consecration, never giving way to angry impatience or wanting to argue for argument's sake. ⁹The conduct of women is to be in conformity

with this. They are to adorn themselves modestly and soberly, with befitting apparel, not with braided hair, not with gold, pearls, or costly attire, [10]but with good deeds, as becomes women who profess reverence for God. [11]In learning something a woman should do so in silence, showing herself submissive in every way. [12]No woman shall have leave from me to engage in teaching or to have authority over a man. No, her part is to keep silent. [13]It was Adam who was formed first, not Eve. [14]Besides, it was not Adam who was led astray; it was the woman who allowed herself to be led astray, and so fell into sin. [15]Still, a woman will attain to salvation in virtue of becoming the mother of children, so long, that is, as women take their stand by the side of faith, love, and holiness, all linked with sobriety.

3 How faithful to the truth are the words, 'If any man is desirous of holding the office of a bishop,* it is a noble work that he aspires to.' [2]Now a bishop* must be above reproach, married but once, temperate, sober-minded; his conduct must be dignified, he must be hospitable and have a gift for teaching. [3]He must not be addicted to wine or be a quarreller but instead be fair-minded, peaceable, and not given to covetousness. [4]He must manage his own household well, keeping his children under proper control with all the dignity at his command. [5]If a man does not know how to manage his own household, how will he be able to take proper care of God's church? [6]He ought not to be a man who has only recently accepted the faith, lest, led on by self-conceit, he might let the devil tempt him, thus incurring a judgment of condemnation. [7]He must have a good reputation with those outside the church, to prevent him from falling into disgrace and becoming a victim of the snares of the devil.

[8]Deacons in the same way must be dignified. They must not engage in double-talk, not be addicted to drinking overmuch, nor be greedy for gain. [9]No, what is incumbent on them is to keep a hold, with a conscience free from all guilt, on the deep truth of our faith. [10]Besides, these men should first of all be subjected to a test; then, if they prove themselves blameless, let them serve as deacons. [11]The women, too, must be dignified, not given to slander, but sober-minded and trustworthy in every respect. [12]Deacons should be married but once, and should rule their children and their households well. [13]Those who have proved their worth by the way they have performed the office of a deacon win a high standing for themselves, and besides, it is with great confidence in their hearts that they will be proclaiming the faith which has its source in Christ Jesus.

* [Or 'pastoral leader', or 'church leader'.]

[14]I am writing these things to you even though it is my hope that I shall be coming to see you before long; [15]and in order that, should I be delayed, you might know what one's conduct ought to be in the household of God, the church of the living God, which is the pillar and bulwark of the truth. [16]And indeed—there is no denying it—it is a great and profound mystery which is the object of our worship.

> 'It is he who was manifested in the body,
> vindicated as righteous by the Spirit,
> who was seen by angels,
> proclaimed to the Gentiles,
> believed in throughout the world,
> taken up in glory.'

4 Now the Spirit expressly declares that in later times there will be some who will be falling away from the faith, giving heed to spirits which work deception and to teachings inspired by demons, [2]all this coming about through the activity of men who, urged on by their lack of straightforwardness, resort to telling lies, their consciences being branded as though with a hot searing-iron. [3]These are the very men who seek to prevent people from getting married and who insist that they must abstain from certain foods, which God has created to be partaken of—and that with thanksgiving—by those who have faith in their hearts and have arrived at full knowledge of the truth. [4]Indeed, everything created by God is good, and everything is to be accepted so long as it is received with thanksgiving, [5]consecrated as it is by the word of God and by prayer.

[6]If these are the teachings you put before the brothers, you will be a good servant of Christ Jesus, nourished on the words of the faith and the wholesome doctrine you have made your own. [7]Yet you must refuse to have anything to do with old wives' tales which have their root in nothing but impiety. No, train yourself for godliness; [8]for while bodily training avails but little, godliness is all-availing, holding out as it does a promise for this life and the next. [9]How faithful to the truth, how deserving of our full acceptance, are these words: [10]'If we toil, if we struggle, that is because we have come to repose our hope in the living God, who is the Saviour of all mankind, and above all of those who have learned to believe in him.'

[11]Let this be the content of your instructions and teaching: [12]Do not permit anyone to look down on you because of your youthfulness, but instead show yourself a model for the believers in speech and in conduct, taking love, faith, and innocence for your guides. [13]Give

heed to the public reading of scripture, to exhortation, and to instruction till my arrival, [14]and do not neglect that gift in your soul which was so graciously bestowed upon you, amidst prophesyings, when the hands of the elders were laid upon you. [15]Occupy yourself with these matters, be involved in them, so that your progress may be manifest to all. [16]Take pains with yourself and with the teaching, remaining true to it all, for by so doing you will obtain salvation both for yourself and for those who are listening to you.

5 Never administer a sharp rebuke to an older man, but appeal to him as though he were your father. Treat the younger men as brothers, [2]the older women as mothers, and the younger women—and that in all innocence—as sisters. [3]Pay honour to widows who really deserve that name. [4]But if a widow has children or grandchildren, they should learn first of all that it is their duty to show piety towards their own, and to make a return to those from whom they are descended. For this is the very thing which finds acceptance in the sight of God. [5]The widow who really deserves that name and who has been left solitary is a woman who has come to place her hope in God and who continues in her prayers and supplication night and day. [6]A widow who is self-indulgent, on the other hand, is dead even while she is still alive. [7]Warn them of that, so that they may learn to live without incurring reproach. [8]If anyone fails to make provision for those who belong to him, particularly his own family, that amounts to his having renounced the faith and being worse than an unbeliever. [9]A widow, to be enrolled, should be no less than sixty years of age, have been a faithful wife to her one husband, [10]and stand in high repute for her good works. Moreover, she should have reared children, shown hospitality to strangers, washed the feet of those consecrated to God, reached out a helping hand to those in distress, and devoted herself to good deeds in every way. [11]As for the younger widows, refuse to have anything to do with them; for once their cravings make them turn away from Christ, they wish to marry again, [12]incurring the censure of having renounced the pledge they originally gave. [13]At the same time they learn to be idlers, gadding about from house to house, and not only idlers but gossips and busybodies who say things which are unbecoming. [14]As for myself, I would have the younger women marry again, have children, and keep house, leaving our enemies with no opportunity of pouring abuse upon us. [15]Already there are some who have turned away, becoming Satan's followers. [16]Meanwhile, if a woman who is a believer has widows dependent on her, it is for her to assist them, so that the church should not be burdened by them, but instead be enabled to help widows who really deserve that name.

¹⁷Let the elders who do well while acting as leaders be counted worthy of a double stipend, in particular those who labour in preaching or in giving instruction. ¹⁸For, this is what scripture says: ^{*a*}'**You shall not muzzle an ox when it is treading out the corn.**' And then there are the words, 'The labourer has a right to his maintenance.'

¹⁹Do not entertain a charge against a presbyter, unless it be ^{*b*}**supported by two or three witnesses.** ²⁰Rebuke those who have fallen into sin in front of the whole company, thus putting fear into the rest. ²¹I adjure you, in the sight of God, of Christ Jesus, and of those whom he has chosen as his angels, to observe these instructions, never prejudging any issue and with no showing of partiality. ²²Do not, in the case of anyone, proceed hastily to the imposition of hands, so as not to become a sharer in the sins of others. Keep yourself in a state of innocence. ²³Do not confine yourself any longer to drinking nothing but water, but take a little wine as well on account of your digestion and because you suffer so often from bouts of ill health. ²⁴Some men's sins are known to all, and they run ahead of them, being brought to judgment, while with other men the position is that their sins are lagging behind them. ²⁵In the same way, there are good works which are known to all, while, where it is otherwise, there is no way of their remaining hidden for ever.

6 All those who are under the yoke of slavery ought to think of their masters as being worthy of all honour, to prevent God's name, and the doctrine which proclaims him, from falling into disrepute. ²Those whose masters are believers must not treat them disrespectfully, because they are members of the brotherhood. On the contrary, they are to serve them the more readily, because those who derive benefit from their service share with them a common bond of faith and love.

Let what you teach men, what you exhort them to do, be the things which I have mentioned. ³If, however, there be anyone who teaches otherwise, paying no heed to wholesome words, those which have their source in our Lord Jesus Christ and in the teaching which accords with godliness, ⁴he is simply moved by the empty conceit which he has of himself. No real understanding of anything is to be found in him, but instead he has a morbid craving for disputes and wordy battles which result in envy, strife, slander, mutual suspicions— ⁵all such encounters as are bound to arise between men whose minds are corrupted, who are bereft of the truth, and who suppose that godliness is a profitable occupation. ⁶And indeed, godliness yields great profit, but only in the sense that one is at the same time satisfied with

^{*a*}Dt 25:4   ^{*b*}Dt 19:15

having but few possessions. [7]After all, [c]we have brought nothing into the world, neither can we take anything out of it. [8]If we have food, then, and means of shelter, let us rest content with these. [9]But those who are intent on acquiring riches are led into temptation and caught in a snare, being at the mercy of many foolish and harmful desires such as plunge men into ruin and perdition. [10]Indeed, greed for money is the very root of whatever evil things there are, the craving for money being the cause why certain men have strayed from the faith, inflicting many a grievous wound on themselves.

[11]You, however, a man given up to serving God, must shun all this, striving after righteousness, godliness, faith, love, steadfastness, and a spirit of gentleness. [12]Fight the good fight in defence of the faith; lay hold of eternal life, that life to which you were called, making a noble confession of this in the presence of many witnesses. [13]I appeal to you, in the sight of God who is the source of life of whatever there is, and in the sight of Christ Jesus who bore witness, making his noble confession before Pontius Pilate, [14]to keep the charge entrusted to you unblemished and irreproachable till the appearance of our Lord Jesus Christ, [15]who will be shown forth, at the time appointed for it, by him who is the sole Sovereign, ever-blessed, who is [d]King of kings and Lord of lords. [16]To him alone immortality belongs; unapproachable light is his dwelling place; and it is he whom no human eye has ever seen, nor can see. Let honour and everlasting dominion be ascribed to him. Amen.

[17]Urge those who are rich with this world's riches that they must not be haughty in mind, and that they are to place their hope not in riches, uncertain as they are, but in God, who bestows everything richly upon us for our enjoyment. [18]It is the duty of these rich men to give themselves up to well-doing, to be rich in the performance of good deeds, to be generous givers, to share things with their fellows, [19]so storing up for themselves a sure foundation for the future, that they may lay hold of the life which is truly life.

[20]Keep guard over the charge which has been entrusted to you, my dear Timothy, holding yourself aloof from profane and empty talk, from the self-contradictory quibbles which have their source in what is knowledge only in name, [21]the knowledge which some have laid claim to, with the result that, as far as the faith is concerned, they went altogether off the mark.

May grace be by the side of you all.

[c][Job 1:21; Ps 49:17; Ec 5:15]   [d][Dt 10:17]

PAUL'S SECOND LETTER
TO TIMOTHY

1 From Paul, by the will of God an apostle of Christ Jesus, in pursuance of God's promise of the life there was to be, the one led in union with Christ Jesus. ²I am sending my greetings to you, Timothy, my well-loved son. May grace, mercy, and peace be by your side, brought to you by God the Father and our Lord Jesus Christ.

³I give thanks to God, to whom, after the manner of my forefathers, I render service, with a conscience free from all guilt, while I keep you unceasingly in remembrance during the prayers which I offer by day and by night. ⁴Meanwhile, there arises in me, as I call to mind the tears which you shed, a great longing to see you face to face, so that I may be filled with joy by your presence. ⁵Moreover, there is being brought back to my mind the recollection of that faith of yours, so free from all pretence, the very faith which dwelt first of all in your grandmother Lois and your mother Eunice, and which now, I am fully convinced, dwells within you.

⁶In view of all this, I would remind you to fan into fresh life that special grace coming to you from God which became yours through my laying my hands upon you in blessing. ⁷And indeed, the spirit which God has bestowed upon us is not one that makes us shrink back in fear. No, it is a spirit which results in our being filled with power, with love, as well as with an ability to discipline ourselves. ⁸Be not ashamed, therefore, to bear witness for our Lord, nor of me who has been cast into prison for serving him. No, what you must do instead is take upon you your share of suffering on behalf of the gospel, doing so in the exercise of that power which God has given you, ⁹God who has brought us deliverance, summoning us to his side through the call towards holiness which he sent out to us. However, if he did so, that was not on the strength of any works we ourselves had performed; no, it was by virtue of his own design, by virtue of the grace which he bestowed upon us from all eternity, namely, that we were to be united to Christ Jesus. ¹⁰And it is this very grace which has now been made manifest by the appearing of our deliverer, Christ Jesus, who has

broken the power of death and has, through the gospel, brought life and immortality to light.

[11] As for myself, I have been appointed to herald that gospel, to proclaim it, and to teach it, [12] and this indeed is the reason why I am undergoing these sufferings. However, there is nothing in this of which I am ashamed, since I know full well who it is in whom I have placed my confidence, and I am persuaded that he has the power to keep guard over that which I have put in his charge until the coming of that Day. [13] Keep before your mind an outline of the wholesome words of preaching which you heard from me, and let yourself be guided by that faith and that love which are grounded in Christ Jesus. [14] Keep guard over the charge committed to your hands by the Holy Spirit which dwells within us.

[15] As you are aware, those in Asia have, one and all, turned away from me, Phygelus and Hermogenes being of their number. [16] But as for the household of Onesiphorus, may the Lord's mercy rest upon them. He has brought refreshment to my spirit many a time. Besides, he found nothing in my imprisonment to be ashamed of. [17] On the contrary, no sooner had he arrived in Rome than he made a diligent search for me, and succeeded in finding me. [18] The Lord grant that he may obtain mercy from his Lord when that Day comes. As for the services which he rendered at Ephesus, you do not need me to tell you about these.

2 You, then, my dear son, must draw your strength from the grace which is to be found in Christ Jesus, [2] and you must hand on to men worthy of trust the very things which you have heard me say in the presence of many witnesses, who, in their turn, will be competent to give instruction to others. [3] Take upon yourself your share of suffering, like a good soldier of Christ Jesus. [4] No one serving as a soldier becomes entangled in the pursuits of everyday life; his aim is to please the man who has enlisted him. [5] Again, if there be anyone taking part in an athletic contest, there will be no prize coming to him unless he has kept the rules of the contest. [6] The first share in the harvest ought to go to the tiller of the soil who has bestowed his labour upon it. [7] Turn over in your mind what I am saying to you. The Lord will endow you with an ability to understand all things.

[8] Be ever mindful of Christ Jesus, raised to life from the dead, descended from the line of David, as is declared in the gospel which I preach, the gospel for the sake of which I suffer misfortune, [9] to the point even of finding myself bound in prison, as though I were an evildoer. [10] Yet the word of God is not bound, and so it is that I endure it all, doing so for the sake of those chosen by God, with this end in

view, that they, too, may attain to the salvation to be found in Christ Jesus, and the never-dying glory which goes with it. [11]How faithful to the truth are the words,

'If we have died with him, we shall also live by his side.
[12]If we are steadfast, we shall also reign by his side.
If we disown him, he in turn will disown us.
[13]If we are faithless, he, for his part, remains faithful.
He cannot disown his own nature.'

[14]Let these be the things you put men in remembrance of, solemnly urging them, as though you were standing in God's sight, not to engage in battles about words, an enterprise which is profitless and can only bring ruin upon those who are listening.

[15]Make every effort to present yourself before God as a man of whom he will approve, a workman who need not be ashamed of anything he does, a man who, without ever turning aside, paves the way for the spreading of the message of truth. [16]But as for profane and empty talk, keep yourself entirely aloof from that; for those who indulge in it will be falling into greater and ever greater impiety, [17]their doctrine meanwhile spreading like a cancerous growth. Hymenaeus and Philetus are to be counted among these, [18]men who have gone altogether off the mark where the truth is concerned, alleging as they do that our resurrection has already taken place. They are, it is true, successful in subverting the faith of certain people. [19]All the same, the firm foundation which God has laid remains unshakable, this being the impress which it bears: [a]'**The Lord knows those who belong to him.**' And then this: 'May those who [b]**invoke the Lord's name** keep away from all wickedness.' [20]As for the vessels to be found in a large house, they are not all made of silver and gold. No, some of them are made of wood, others of earthenware; some of them are valued, while others are not valued at all. [21]Now it is precisely by avoiding contact with what has no value that a man will make of himself a vessel which is valued, which is consecrated, which is serviceable to the master and made ready for honourable use of every kind. [22]But you must shun the cravings of youth, striving after righteousness, faith, love, and peace, in fellowship with those who, with innocence ruling in their hearts, invoke the name of the Lord. [23]As for discussions which have their root in foolishness and a want of proper education, you must refuse to have anything to do with them. You know well enough that they only lead to quarrelling. [24]But the man who is in the Lord's service must not engage in quarrels. No, he must be kind to everybody, he must be skilled in teaching, and a man who bears injury with

[a]Nm 16:5   [b]Is 26:13

patience, 25one who corrects in a spirit of gentleness those who oppose him. After all, there is always the possibility that God will grant them a change of heart, enabling them to arrive at knowledge of the truth, 26so that by coming to their senses they will escape from the snare of the devil, by whom so far they are being held captive, so as to be obedient to his will.

3 Of this you may rest assured, that grievous times will set in when days are about to vanish, 2men conducting themselves in ways such as these: they will be lovers of self, lovers of money, braggarts, full of arrogance, given to slander, disobedient to their parents, without gratitude, without a sense of the holy, 3without affection, incapable of forgiving, maligning others, intemperate, savage, with no love for the good, 4treacherous, reckless, bloated with conceit, their concern not being with God but rather with their own pleasures. 5They will, it is true, hold on to the outward trappings of godliness, yet at the same time they will be the living denial of its efficacy. But you, for your part, have the duty to shun men such as these. 6And indeed, they count among their number those who worm their way into people's houses, getting feeble women into their clutches, women who find themselves overwhelmed by the burden of their sins, being impelled by a whole medley of desires, 7and who, while ever occupied with learning something or other, are yet never able to arrive at knowledge of the truth. 8 cJust as Jannes and Jambres offered resistance to Moses, so these men offer resistance to the truth, being creatures corrupted in mind and wholly worthless in matters of faith. 9However, they will make no further progress; their folly will become manifest to all, just as did that of those other men.

10But as for yourself, you have made yourself acquainted in every way with my teaching, my conduct, my purposes, my faith, my patience, my love, and my steadfastness. 11You know of the persecutions and sufferings I endured, of the things which befell me at Antioch, Iconium, and Lystra. You are aware of the kind of persecutions I underwent, and how the Lord delivered me out of all this. 12And indeed, all those who are resolved to lead a godly life, in obedience to Christ Jesus, will find themselves made the victims of persecution, 13while wicked men and mountebanks—at once impostors and dupes —will go from bad to worse. 14As for yourself, on the other hand, your duty is to keep true to what you have learned, to what you have become firmly convinced of, knowing as you do what manner of men your teachers were, 15and how, from when you were but a child, you

c[Ex 7:11.22; 8:7; 9:11]

became acquainted with the sacred writings. It is these which have the power to endow you with wisdom and to lead you on your way to salvation, the faith which is grounded in Christ Jesus being the means of accomplishing this. [16] As for scripture, it is all divinely inspired, being serviceable for teaching, for convicting men of their errors, for showing them the right way, for training them for a righteous life, [17] the aim of it all being that the man in the service of God should become a master of his craft, being fully equipped to do good works of every kind.

4 I adjure you in the sight of God and of Christ Jesus, who is to be judge of the living and the dead, in the name of his appearing and of his kingdom: [2] proclaim the word of God, press on, not taking into account whether the time is convenient or inconvenient. Convict men of their errors, reprove them, appeal to them, showing the utmost patience and exercising care in your teaching. [3] For the time will surely come when men will refuse to tolerate wholesome teaching, when in obedience to their own appetites, and wishing to have their ears tickled, they will provide themselves with a never-ending succession of teachers, [4] turning away from the truth and wandering off to give their attention to mere fables. [5] You, on the other hand, must be sober-minded in all things, bearing with hardship, doing the work of an evangelist, discharging the duties of your ministry to the full. [6] As for myself, I am like a drink-offering already poured out upon the altar, and the time of my departure from life is at hand. [7] The good fight has already been fought by me; I have reached the end of my course; I have kept guard over the faith. [8] What remains is only the garland, in token of a righteous life, which is laid up for me, and which the Lord, the all-just judge, will award to me when that Day comes—and not only to me but to all who have learned to love the thought of his appearing.

[9] Make every effort to come to me as soon as possible; [10] for this is how things stand. Demas has deserted me, having become a man in love with this present world, and has gone off to Thessalonica; Crescens has gone to Galatia, Titus to Dalmatia. [11] Luke alone is by my side. Get hold of Mark and bring him along here when you come. He is most serviceable to me in the matter of the ministry. [12] Tychicus I have left behind at Ephesus. [13] Bring with you, when you come, the cloak which I left behind at Troas in the house of Carpus; and the books as well, especially the parchments.

[14] Alexander the coppersmith has wronged me in many ways. [d]**The Lord will requite** him **according to what his deeds deserve.** [15] And

[d]2 Sm 3:39; Ps 28:4; 62:12; Pr 24:12

you, too, must be on your guard against him, seeing that he opposed himself with great vehemence to everything I said. [16]There was no one who stood by me the first time I had to offer my defence. May it not be laid to their charge. [17]Yet the Lord stood by my side, endowing me with strength, that the proclamation of the gospel might attain its full scope, and that all the Gentiles might hear it. And so it was that I was rescued *out of the jaws of the lion.* [18]Yes, the Lord will protect me against any evil-doing at the hands of men, bringing me safely into his heavenly kingdom. To him may glory be ascribed for ever and ever. Amen.

[19]My greetings to Prisca and Aquila, as well as to Onesiphorus and his household. [20]Erastus has stayed on at Corinth. Trophimus fell ill, and I left him behind at Miletus. [21]Do everything you can to be here before winter sets in. Eubulus, Pudens, Linus, and Claudia send their greetings, and so do all the brothers who are with me here.

[22]May the Lord hold his protecting hand over your spirit. May grace be by the side of you all.

*Ps 22:21; Dn 6:20

PAUL'S LETTER TO TITUS

1 From Paul, a servant of God and made an apostle of Jesus Christ to lead people to the faith which is to be embraced by those who have been chosen by God, to cause them to have knowledge of the truth as it is discovered by those who follow God, ²the hope of eternal life being the foundation of it all. A promise of this life was held out countless ages ago by God, who is a stranger to all falsehood. ³But now, at the time fixed by himself, he has made his meaning perfectly clear through the message he sent out, the message which has been entrusted to me to proclaim, at the command of God, the bringer of our salvation. ⁴I am sending greetings to Titus, my true son by virtue of a common faith uniting us. May grace and peace be by your side, brought to you by God the Father and Christ Jesus our Saviour.

⁵If I left you behind in Crete, this was so that you might set right the things which still needed to be remedied. In conformity with the directions I gave you, you were to appoint elders in each town, ⁶always looking for a man free from all blame, married but once, his children being believers, while at the same time not open to any charge of profligacy or found to be wanting in obedience. ⁷A bishop,* after all, seeing that he is God's steward, ought to be free from all blame. He must not be self-willed, or of a violent temper, or addicted to wine, or a quarreller, or a man greedy for gain. ⁸No, he must be hospitable, a lover of the good, sober-minded, just, devout, and self-controlled. ⁹In other words, he must hold fast to what accords with what he has been taught, to the message which is deserving of all trust, so that he may be able to bring encouragement to others by putting wholesome teaching before them, while he must have the power of convicting those who oppose themselves to him of their errors.

¹⁰For there are many—especially among those who are converts from Judaism—who are rebellious, who are given to idle talk and lead others into error. ¹¹People of this sort ought to have silence imposed on them, being the very men who subvert whole households, teach-

* [Or 'pastoral leader', or 'church leader'.]

ing things which are opposed to all decency, and doing it all with an eye to their own sordid gain. [12]Why, there is one of their own number, a prophet of theirs, who has spoken these words, 'The men of Crete were ever liars, beasts full of malice, gluttons with nothing to do.' [13]And indeed, this account of them is no more than the truth. In view of this, then, it is your duty to convict them of their errors with all severity, so that they may become soundly established in the faith, [14]paying no attention to Jewish legends or to injunctions coming from those who have turned their backs on the truth. [15]Nothing is looked upon as impure by those whose own minds are pure, while for those who are defiled, who are devoid of faith, there is nothing which retains its purity. No, defilement has entered their very thoughts, their very conscience. [16]They claim to be giving recognition to God, but in fact they disown him by everything they do, being men who deserve nothing but loathing, who refuse to render obedience, who are unfit for the performance of any good deed.

2 Yet, as for yourself, may the words which you address to others be such as to be in conformity with sound doctrine. [2]Charge the old men to be temperate, dignified, sober-minded, and to be soundly established in faith, love, and patience. [3]And so with the old women. They are to comport themselves in a manner which befits those called to a holy life. They are not to be slanderers, not to be at the mercy of a desire to drink a great deal of wine, but instead they should be teachers of everything that is good, [4]so that they may be a living example to the younger women, showing them how to love their husbands and their children, [5]to be sober-minded, to keep themselves pure, to manage their households well, to be gentle, submitting themselves to their husbands—all this to ensure that God's message should not fall into disrepute.

[6]Urge the young men likewise to be sober-minded. [7]And as for your own duty, you must show yourself in all respects a model for the performance of good deeds, while your teaching is to show forth integrity and dignity. [8]May you deliver your message in a way which is wholesome, and not open to any reproach, so that the man opposing you may be put to shame, finding that there is nothing evil he can say about us. [9]Slaves are to be obedient to their masters, seeking to please them in every way. There is to be no answering back, [10]no misappropriation of things. No, it is for them to show their good faith in everything, so that in every respect they may do credit to the teaching which has its source in God, the bringer of our salvation.

[11]For the grace of God has dawned upon the world, the very grace which brings salvation to everyone, [12]schooling us to live soberly,

justly, and devoutly in the midst of this present world, renouncing impiety and all worldly desire, [13]while waiting for the fulfilment of that blessed hope of ours, for the appearing in glory of him who is the great God, our Saviour Jesus Christ, [14]who gave himself up on our behalf, so that he might [a]**set us free from all lawlessness,** and, [b]**cleansing** us, might provide for **himself a people entirely his own possession,** a people in eager pursuit of noble deeds of every kind. [15]Let this be your message; let it be with this in view that you exhort the people, and convict them of their errors, doing this with all the impressiveness at your command. Do not allow anyone to treat you slightingly.

3 Remind the people to be submissive to rulers and authorities, and to render obedience to them, while standing ready for the performance of good works of every kind. [2]They are not to slander anyone but instead ought to be peaceable, of a forbearing disposition, and display gentleness in their attitude towards everyone. [3]After all, there was a time when we ourselves were without sense, when we were rebellious, misguided, at the mercy of a whole medley of desires and appetites, passing our lives in malice and envy, when we were loathsome and living in hatred of one another. [4]However, when the time came for God our Saviour to let his kindness and his love for mankind dawn upon the world, [5]it was not by reason of any righteous acts which we ourselves had performed that he acted. No, if he brought us salvation, that was in virtue of his own mercy, the means of accomplishing it being the bathing in water which brings about regeneration and the renewal which has its source in the Holy Spirit. [6]And it was this Spirit which he lavishly poured out upon us, through Jesus Christ our Saviour, [7]so that, being accepted as righteous by virtue of his grace, we might gain possession of the inheritance, with the hope of eternal life held out to us. [8]These words are worthy of all trust.

I would have you insist most strongly on the points which I have made, so that those who have come to place their faith in God may be at pains to occupy themselves with the performance of good works. For that is an excellent thing and one by which men will find themselves greatly benefited. [9]As against this, you must keep yourself entirely aloof from foolish disputes, from genealogical researches, from controversy, and from wranglings over the law. These are futile and of no benefit to anyone. [10]As for a man who is given to factiousness, you may give him one warning and then another. If this remains unheeded, you should have nothing further to do with him, [11]since you

[a]Ps 130:8   [b]Ezk 37:23; Ex 19:5; Dt 14:2

are well aware that this sort of man has a distorted mind, has fallen into sin, and stands self-condemned.

[12]Make every effort, after my sending Artemas or Tychicus to you, to come to see me at Nicopolis; for this is where I have decided to spend the winter. [13]Give Zenas the lawyer and Apollos their send-off on their travels, doing the best you can, so that they may want nothing. [14]And may our own people be taught that they must engage in honest work for the supply of necessities, to prevent them from being of no use to anyone.

[15]All that are with me here send their greetings. My greetings to those who hold us dear by virtue of the faith we share with one another.

May grace be by the side of you all.

PAUL'S LETTER TO PHILEMON

From Paul, held prisoner for his allegiance to Christ Jesus, and from your brother Timothy. We send our greetings to Philemon, that well-loved fellow worker of ours, [2]to Apphia our sister in the faith, to Archippus our comrade-in-arms, as well as to the congregation which meets at your house, Philemon. [3]May grace and peace be by your side, brought to you by God our Father and the Lord Jesus Christ.

[4]I give thanks to God at all times, making mention of you while I am engaged in prayer, [5]because of what I hear of the faith and the love you show forth towards the Lord Jesus and, indeed, to all those who have consecrated themselves to God. [6]And this is the supplication which I make, that your participation in the faith may become effective in your coming to have a deeper and ever deeper understanding of all the blessings which are ours in virtue of our union with Christ. [7]And indeed, I have derived much joy and comfort from the love to be found in you, my brother, seeing that, because of it, you have been the means of bringing refreshment to the hearts of those who have dedicated themselves to God's service.

[8]It is in consideration of all this that, although I might well have given you an order to do what duty demands by reason of the great confidence I call my own as a man united to Christ, [9]yet for love's sake I would rather make an appeal to you: I Paul, an ambassador for Christ Jesus, and now a prisoner also for serving his cause. [10]I am appealing to you on behalf of my child whose father I have become because of my imprisonment, on behalf of Onesimus, [11]who was once of so little use to you, but who now lives up to his name, being of great use both to you and to me.

[12]I am sending him back to you, sending my very heart. [13]I should have been glad to keep him by my side, that he might serve me in your stead during my imprisonment on behalf of the gospel. [14]Yet I did not wish to do anything without your consent, so that this kindness of yours might be done not under compulsion but of your own free will. [15]After all, it was perhaps for this reason that he was parted from you for a while, so that you might keep him for ever; [16]no longer a slave but something much more than a slave, a well-loved brother, most

specially to me, and how much more so to you, now that you are tied together both by his natural condition and his allegiance to the Lord.

[17]If, then, you look upon me as a man united to you in fellowship, make him welcome as you would myself. [18]And if he has wronged you in any way, or is in your debt, make me answerable for it. [19]I, Paul, am writing this with my own hand; I shall compensate you in full—to say nothing of the fact that you owe me your very self. [20]Well then, my brother, let me, under the inspiration of the Lord, be the recipient of a great benefit from you. Refresh my heart, with Christ standing over us.

[21]I am writing this being fully confident that you will be obedient to my wishes; indeed, I know full well that you will do even more than I ask. [22]At the same time, I would urge you to prepare a guest room for me; for my hope is that, through your prayers, I shall be restored to you.

[23]Epaphras, my fellow prisoner on behalf of the cause of Christ Jesus, sends his greetings. [24]So do Mark, Aristarchus, Demas, and Luke, my fellow workers.

[25]May the grace of the Lord Jesus Christ hold its protecting hand over your spirits.

A LETTER ADDRESSED TO
READERS OF HEBREW DESCENT

1 God having spoken, in times of old, to our forefathers by the mouth of the prophets—and that on many an occasion and in many different ways— ²has now, at the close of these days of ours, spoken to us in the person of one who is his Son, whom he has appointed to possess all things as his inheritance, just as it was through him that he created whatever there has been throughout the ages. ³It is he who radiates forth God's glory, who is the precise counterpart of his very being, who sustains all things by his mighty word of command. Moreover, having accomplished the purging away of sins, *ᵃ*he took his seat at the right hand of the divine Majesty on high, ⁴being as highly exalted above the angels as the title which he has inherited is more excellent than theirs.

⁵And indeed, what angel is there to whom God has ever said, *ᵇ*You are my Son; today I have become your Father'; or again, *ᶜ*I shall be Father to him; and he shall be Son to me'? ⁶And then, there is this, that when, in his turn, he brings his firstborn into the inhabited world, he speaks thus: *ᵈ*And may all the angels pay homage to him.' ⁷In referring to the angels he says, *ᵉ*He who makes winds of his angels, and a fiery flame of those who serve him'; ⁸while, when referring to the Son he says, *ᶠ*It is God who is your throne for ever and ever; and the sceptre showing forth the uprightness which you bear is the sceptre of God's kingdom. ⁹You have loved righteousness and hated lawlessness. And so it is that God, who is your God, has anointed you with the oil of gladness, giving you a greater share of it than to any of your fellows.'

¹⁰Then there are these words: *ᵍ*You, Lord, laid the foundations of the earth when it first took its rise, and the heavens are the works of your hands. ¹¹They shall perish, while you endure. They shall all grow old like a garment, ¹²and you will roll them up like a cloak.

---

*ᵃ*Ps 110:1   *ᵇ*Ps 2:7   *ᶜ*2 Sm 7:14   *ᵈ*Dt 32:43 LXX; Ps 97:7   *ᵉ*Ps 104:4   *ᶠ*Ps 45:6f
*ᵍ*Ps 102:25-27

They shall undergo change, as does any piece of clothing. **But you remain ever the same, and there never will be an end to the years of your life.'**

[13] Moreover, to which of the angels has God ever spoken words such as these: [h]**"Take your seat at my right hand until I make your enemies a footstool for your feet'**? [14]Is not the nature of angels this, that they are all spirits whose business it is to render service, being sent forth on behalf of those who are to obtain salvation as their inheritance?

2 In consideration of this, it is all the more essential for us to pay close attention to what we have been told, to avert all danger of our drifting away from our course. [2]And indeed, if the message delivered at the hands of the angels established its own validity, every transgression and every act of disobedience meeting with the penalty it deserved, [3]how are we to escape if we neglect a deliverance so great as this, which took its rise by being proclaimed by the Lord himself, and then was guaranteed to us at the hands of those who heard it from his own lips, [4]God adding his witness by signs and wonders and by apportioning to us the gifts of the Holy Spirit, just as he chose?

[5]For this is how the matter stands. As for the world to come which is our theme, it is not to the angels that God has subjected it. [6]And indeed, there is a place where witness is borne by someone uttering these words, [i]**"What is man that you should be mindful of him? Or the son of man that you should hold him in your regard? [7]For a short time you have placed him lower than the angels. You have crowned him with glory and honour. [8]You have put all things in subjection underneath his feet.'**

What is meant by **'to subject all things'** to him is that he left nothing that was not made subject to him. But then we note, as an actual fact, that things have not as yet **been all subjected** to him, [9]while we perceive at the same time that Jesus, who **for a short time was placed lower than the** angels, has, by virtue of his suffering death, **been crowned with glory and honour,** so that, by God's gracious will, he might taste death on behalf of everyone.

[10]And indeed, it was clearly fitting that God, for whom and through whom all things exist, in leading many sons to glory, should bring the author of their salvation to perfection by virtue of his sufferings, [11]the truth being that he who bestows the hallowing and those who are being hallowed derive their origin, one and all, from the One. And that is why the Son is not ashamed to call them his brothers,

[h]Ps 110:1   [i]Ps 8:4-6 LXX

[12]saying, [j]'I shall proclaim your name to my brothers; in the midst of the congregation I shall sing your praises'; [13]and again, [k]'I shall repose my confidence in him'; and yet again, 'Here am I, and the children whom God has given me.' [14]Now since it was flesh and blood which **these children** shared, he too, in like manner, partook of these, so that, through undergoing death, he might bring to nought the one who held death in his power, that is to say, the devil, [15]and might set free those who because of their fear of death were throughout their lives subject to servitude. [16]The truth is that it is not to the angels but to the [l]**descendants of Abraham** that **he holds out his helping hand.** [17]And that being so, it was necessary that he should, in every way, be made like these [m]**brothers** of his, so as to become a merciful and faithful high priest in all matters pertaining to God, for the expiation of the sins of the people. [18]For inasmuch as he himself has undergone suffering, and has been put to the test, he is in a position to come to the aid of those who are being tested.

3   Therefore, my brothers, marked out for a holy life, who have been made partakers of a call from heaven, fix your minds on Jesus, on him who was sent forth to make known the faith which we profess and to be its high priest. [2]He was [n]**faithful** to him who appointed him, just as **Moses** was faithful **in God's household.** [3]Indeed, he was held worthy of greater renown than was Moses, in the same way as the founder of a house is held in greater honour than is his household. [4]And indeed, every house is founded by someone, while it is God who is the founder of all things. [5]Moreover, true though it is that Moses was faithful throughout the whole of **God's household**, he was so while holding the position of a **servant;** and the testimony which he was called upon to bear concerned things which were to be revealed in the future. [6]Christ, on the other hand, is set over **God's household** as a son. And we are that household, so long, that is, as we hold on firmly to the confidence we have and to the hope in which we find our glory. [7]In view of this, then, let us go by these words spoken by the Holy Spirit:

[o]'If you hear his voice today,
   [8]Do not harden your hearts as you did at the time of the
     rebellion,
   During the days when you put me to the test in the desert,
   [9]Where your forefathers subjected me to their trials,

[j]Ps 22:22   [k]Is 8:17 LXX; 2 Sm 22:3; Is 8:18   [l]Is 41:8f   [m]Ps 22:22   [n]Nm 12:7 LXX
[o]Ps 95:7-11

Even though [10]**for forty years they saw the works which I
performed.
And so it was that I was filled with indignation against this
generation,
And said to myself, "They ever go astray in their hearts,
They, the men who keep themselves in ignorance of my ways.**
[11]**And so things will be in accordance with the oath I have
sworn in my anger:
They shall never enter my rest." '**

[12]Take care, then, my brothers, that in none of you there should be
an evil heart making you lose your faith, so as to fall away from the
living God. [13]On the contrary, exhort one another day by day, so long
as there is still something to be given the name **today**, that none of
you should **become hardened** by sin and its deceitfulness. [14]For what
we have become are men who have been given a share in Christ, so
long, that is, as we hold on, to the very end, to the firm confidence
with which we set out.

[15]Now when it is being said, *P*'**If you hear his voice today, do not
harden your hearts as you did at the time of the rebellion,**' [16]who, I
ask, were those who heard and yet **rebelled?** Was it not all those who
went out of Egypt under Moses' leadership? [17]And who were they,
against whom *q***he was filled with indignation for forty years?** Was
it not those whose **dead bodies** lay where they **had fallen in the
desert?** [18]And who were they concerning whom *r***he swore on oath
that they would never enter his rest?** Was it not those who refused
to believe? [19]And indeed, it was through their unbelief that they were
prevented from entering.

4 Let us then stand in anxious dread, seeing that God's promise of
entry into his rest is a promise which still remains open, lest one or
the other among you might somehow be found to have forfeited his
opportunity. [2]We, too, have had good news proclaimed to us, just as
these others had. But the message preached to them did not benefit
them in any way, because no faith through which they might make it
their own was to be found in those who heard the message. [3]And indeed, it is we ourselves—the ones who have faith—who *s***enter the
rest** to which reference is made in the words, '**And so things will be
in accordance with the oath which I have sworn in my anger: They
shall never enter my rest.**' And this was said even though God's own
works were complete ever since the creation of the world. [4]For scrip-

*P*Ps 95:7f   *q*Nm 14:29   *r*Nm 14:22f   *s*Ps 95:11

ture speaks thus of the seventh day: ^t'**God rested on the seventh day from all his works.**' [5]On the other hand, there are these words in the above passage, ^u'**They shall never enter my rest.**' [6]Seeing, then, that the sole alternative left is that some should **enter** that rest, those who formerly had good news preached to them not **having entered** it by reason of their lack of faith, [7]God, for his part, fixes another day— 'today' as he calls it—saying through the mouth of David, after the lapse of so many years, in the words already cited: ^v'**If you hear his voice today, do not harden your hearts.**' [8]And indeed, if Joshua had given them rest, God would not, after this, be speaking of another day. [9]It follows, then, that there remains a sabbath rest for the people of God, [10]the truth of the matter being this: ^w'**He who entered God's rest has found rest from his work,** just as **God** found rest from his.' [11]Let us make every effort, then, **to enter** that **rest,** making certain that no one should, through lack of faith, suffer a fall in the same way as happened to men in former times.

[12]And indeed, the word of God is imbued with life and full of power. It cuts more sharply than any two-edged sword, penetrating so deeply as to separate soul and spirit, joints and marrow. It pronounces judgment upon the purposes and the thoughts of the heart. [13]No creature is hidden from God's sight. On the contrary, everything is open and laid bare to the eyes of the one to whom we have to render our account.

[14]Now since we have a great high priest who has traversed the heavens, Jesus the Son of God, let us hold fast to the faith we profess. [15]For we do not have a high priest unable to feel for us in our weaknesses, but one tested in every way like ourselves, while yet free from sin. [16]Let us draw near, therefore, in confidence to the throne from which grace flows, so that we may receive mercy and find grace coming to our aid in time of need.

5 Now the nature of a high priest's office is invariably as follows. A man is taken from among his fellow men and on their behalf, being appointed to act for them in all matters pertaining to divine worship. He is called upon to present offerings and sacrifices to atone for sins, [2]while at the same time, seeing that he himself is beset by weakness, he has the capacity for dealing gently with those who find themselves in a state of sinful ignorance and who are apt to be led into error. [3]He is under obligation—and that because of this weakness—to make sin offerings not only on behalf of the people but on his own behalf as well. [4]Moreover, the honourable office he holds is not one which a

^tGn 2:2   ^uPs 95:11   ^vPs 95:7f   ^wGn 2:2

man just takes for himself. No, he is called to it by God, *just as Aaron was. ⁵And indeed, in a manner corresponding to this, Christ likewise did not bestow upon himself the glory of becoming high priest. No, he had it bestowed upon him by the one who addressed to him the words, *'You are my Son; today I have become your Father'; ⁶just as in another place we find it said, *'You are a priest for ever in the succession of Melchizedek.' ⁷As for Christ himself, he offered up, during the days of his earthly life, prayers and supplications addressed to him who had the power to save him from death, doing so with a loud outcry and amidst tears. And he found a hearing by reason of his reverent submission. ⁸Son though he was, he learned obedience by the sufferings which he endured, ⁹and, once perfected, he became the source of *eternal salvation for all those rendering obedience to him, ¹⁰being designated by God as high priest *in the succession of Melchizedek.

¹¹About this matter we shall have a great deal to say, but it will be hard to explain by reason of your having become so dull of hearing. ¹²Indeed, while by this time you ought to be teachers, you once again stand in need of someone to give you instruction in the very rudiments of God's revelation. What has happened is that it is milk, not solid food, which suits your needs. ¹³But then, anyone who lives on milk must, seeing that he is no more than an infant, be a person with no experience of what the doctrine about righteousness stands for, ¹⁴while solid food is for grown men, for those who have had their perceptions trained by practice, so as to be able to distinguish between good and evil.

6 Let us take leave, then, of the rudimentary teachings about Christ, and, being borne on towards perfection, let us refrain from once again laying the foundation, occupying ourselves with such matters as coming to repent deeds which have no life in them, with faith in God, ²with instructions about ablutions and the laying on of hands, with the resurrection of the dead, or with eternal judgment. ³And indeed, God willing, that is the course we propose to take.

⁴Moreover, when people have once had the light shed upon them, when they have come to taste of the gift from heaven and have become partakers of the Holy Spirit, ⁵when they have come to taste of God's word in all its goodness as well as of the power of the age to come, ⁶and when, after all this, they fall away, there is no possibility of restoring them, so as to lead them to repentance. For what they in fact do is that, with their own hands, they crucify the Son of God a

*[Ex 28:1]   *Ps 2:7   *Ps 110:4   *Ps 45:17   *Ps 110:4

second time, holding him up to contempt. [7]Likewise, when a piece of ground drinks up the rain which falls upon it on many an occasion, when it produces [c]**vegetation** which is serviceable to those for whose benefit it is being cultivated, it partakes of a blessing from God. [8]But when it is [d]**thorns and thistles which are brought forth,** then the piece of ground is rejected as worthless. It is almost as though there were a **curse** upon it, and the fate which awaits it is that it is burned up.

[9]Yet, dearly-loved ones, even though we speak in this manner, we are fully convinced that much better things are in store for you, things which make for salvation. [10]After all, God is not so unjust as to care nothing about the work you have done and the love you have shown for his name's sake, having rendered service, and still rendering it, to those who are consecrated to him. [11]And as for ourselves, our desire is that each one of you may persist in showing forth the same zeal, retaining your hope in all its fullness to the very end, [12]so that you might not become sluggish but instead take for your model those who by reason of their faith and patience obtain the promises as their inheritance.

[13]When God made his promise to Abraham, [e]**he swore by himself** since there was no one greater to swear by, [14]saying, '**Of a certainty I shall exceedingly bless you, and exceedingly shall I multiply your descendants.'** [15]And so it came about that Abraham, having waited patiently, obtained what had been promised to him. [16]Men do indeed swear by something greater than themselves, and in their case an oath, putting an end to all disputing, serves as a final confirmation. [17]And it was taking this into consideration that God, being determined to signify with even greater clarity to the inheritors of the promise that in this matter his purpose was unchangeable, provided a further guarantee by the swearing of an oath, [18]so that, in virtue of two things incapable of being changed and about which it was impossible that God should play us false, we should find ourselves powerfully encouraged—we, who are seeking our safety by holding fast to the hope set before us. [19]And this hope is indeed ours, like an anchor of the soul firm and sure. [f]**It enters the inner sanctuary behind the curtain,** [20]the place which Jesus has entered ahead of us, and in our behalf, having become a high priest [g]**for ever in the succession of Melchizedek.**

7 Now it was this [h]**Melchizedek, king of Salem, priest of God most high, who went to meet Abraham on his return, after he had utterly defeated the kings, and who bestowed a blessing upon him.** [2]And it was he to whom **Abraham** apportioned **the tenth part of**

[c]Gn 1:11f   [d]Gn 3:17f   [e]Gn 22:16f   [f]Lv 6:2.12   [g]Ps 110:4   [h]Gn 14:17-20

everything. As for his name, the current rendering of it is 'king of righteousness,' and moreover, he is **king of Salem,** which means 'king of peace.' ³There is no father or mother, no genealogy tracing back his origin, nothing about the beginning of his days or the end of his life. Thus, bearing a likeness to the Son of God, he remains a priest for ever.

⁴Consider, then, how great a man he must be, he to whom **Abraham** the patriarch gave a **tenth** out of the booty he had made. ⁵And then there is this: those who belong to the family of Levi, on receiving the priesthood, are enjoined in accordance with what is said in the law to tithe the people, that is to say, their own kinsmen—and this notwithstanding the fact that the people, like themselves, are descendants of Abraham. ⁶On the other hand, what happened in the case of the man where there was no genealogy tracing his descent to these Levites was that he tithed Abraham, and, moreover, **bestowed a blessing** upon him, upon the man who had received the promises. ⁷But then, it is beyond all dispute that, if a blessing is bestowed, it is always the lesser that is blessed by the greater. ⁸Besides, in the one instance it is men subject to death who receive the tithe, while in the other it is one of whom it is testified that he is alive. ⁹Indeed, the case might be put by saying that Levi, the man who receives tithes, was himself tithed through Abraham being tithed; ¹⁰for he was still in his forefather's loins at the time when **Melchizedek went to meet Abraham.**

¹¹In view of all this, there arises the following question. If perfection had been attainable through the Levitical priesthood (and it is on the basis of that priesthood that the people received the law), what need was there that another priest should make his appearance, one standing ⁱ**in the succession of Melchizedek,** in the place of one reckoned **in the succession** of Aaron? ¹²When there is a change of priesthood, the necessary consequence is that a change of law should likewise take place. ¹³And indeed, we find that the one spoken of here belongs to a different tribe, no member of which has ever had any dealings with the altar; ¹⁴for it is evident that our Lord takes his origin from Judah, a tribe in connection with which Moses said nothing whatever about priests.

¹⁵The true state of affairs is made even more evident if, **in a manner** resembling what happened in the case of **Melchizedek,** a new **priest** makes his appearance, ¹⁶one who has become priest not by virtue of a system of law laying down injunctions about purely outward matters but by virtue of a power arising from an indestructible life, ¹⁷testimony being borne to him in the words, ʲ**'You are a priest for ever in the succession of Melchizedek.'** ¹⁸So now the previous in-

ⁱPs 110:4   ʲPs 110:4

junctions are set aside because of their feebleness and uselessness [19](for the law brought nothing to perfection), and something of much greater value is being introduced instead, namely, a hope providing us with the means of drawing near to God.

[20]Moreover, it remains that, when these men were made priests, no oath was sworn, [21]while, when he became priest, this was accompanied by the swearing of an oath coming from the one who said to him, [k]**'The Lord has sworn and will not go back on his word: you are a priest for ever.'** [22]And to the extent that the swearing of an oath was not dispensed with in the case of Jesus, he has become the guarantor of a covenant of much greater value. [23]Besides, in the one case it was many men who became priests, death precluding it that they should remain in office, [24]while he, seeing that he endures **for ever**, holds his priesthood in perpetuity. [25]Thus, in bringing salvation to those who approach God through him, he has the power of accomplishing this to the uttermost, being ever alive to plead on their behalf.

[26]For indeed, it fitted our condition to have a high priest such as this: one who is holy, free from all guile and defilement, entirely separated from sinful men, and exalted to a height greater than the very heavens. [27]He has no need, as had the high priests, to offer sacrifice day by day, first for his own sins and then for those of the people; for everything that had to be done in this matter he accomplished once and for all through the offering up of himself. [28]As for the law, it appoints as high priests men beset by weakness, while it is the [l]**Son** perfected **for ever** who is chosen, at a time subsequent to the law, by the declaration in which recourse is had to the swearing of an oath.

8 Now the main point of what we are expounding is this. Such a high priest we do indeed call our own, one who [m]**has taken his seat on the right hand** of the throne occupied by the divine majesty in the heavens, [2]one who, in performing his ministry in the sanctuary, does so in the [n]**tabernacle**, properly so-called, **the one set up by the Lord** and not by human hands. [3]Now every high priest is appointed for the purpose of presenting offerings and sacrifices; and so it was necessary that he, too, should have something to present. [4]But then, if he were on earth, he would not be a priest at all, there already being others who present offerings in accordance with what the law prescribes. [5]These men, while performing their ministry, are surrounded by things which are no more than copies and mere shadows of the

[k]Ps 110:4   [l]Ps 2:7; 110:4   [m]Ps 110:1   [n]Nm 24:6 LXX

heavenly realities, a matter confirmed in these words which God addressed to Moses when he was setting up the tabernacle: *ᵒ*See to it that you make everything according to the pattern shown you on the mountain. ⁶As for Christ, on the other hand, the position is this: he has obtained a ministry surpassing the other in excellence, to the same extent as the covenant of which he is the mediator is of greater value, enacted as it is on the basis of more valuable promises.

⁷Now had that first covenant been faultless, there would have been no occasion to seek another to take its place. ⁸However, what we find is that God addresses these words to the people, finding fault with them,

> *ᵖ*Of a certainty the days are coming, says the Lord,
> When I shall conclude a New Covenant with the house of
>   Israel and the house of Judah.
> ⁹It will not be like the covenant which I made with their
>   forefathers
> At the time when I took them by the hand and led them out of
> the land of Egypt.
> *ᑫ*For they did not hold by my covenant,
> And I became unconcerned about them, says the Lord.
> ¹⁰So then, this is the covenant which I shall establish with the
>   house of Israel,
> When that day comes, says the Lord.
> I shall put my laws into their minds
> And write them upon their hearts.
> I shall be their God,
> And they will be my people.
> ¹¹And they shall by no means teach one another,
> Each saying to his fellow citizen,
> Each saying to his brother, "Know the Lord."
> For they shall all know me,
> From the least among them to the greatest.
> ¹²And that will be because I shall deal mercifully with them, as
>   regards their evil deeds,
> And because I shall by no means hold their sins in
>   remembrance.'

¹³In speaking of a *ʳ*new covenant, he implies that the first one has grown old. But then, if a thing is growing old and is aging, it is not far from vanishing altogether.

---

*ᵒ*Ex 25:40   *ᵖ*Jr 31:31-34   *ᑫ*[2 M 2:1-8]   *ʳ*Jr 31:31

413

9 The first covenant did indeed have its ordinances for dealing with divine worship, and its sanctuary—a sanctuary, however, which had its home in this world. ²And this is what happened. A tabernacle—the outer one—was set up in which there was the lampstand as well as the table with the bread of the Presence upon it. This is called the Holy Place. ³And beyond the second curtain was a tabernacle called the Holy of Holies, ⁴containing the golden altar of incense and the ark of the covenant, covered with gold on all sides; and placed in this ark was the golden jar with the manna in it, as well as Aaron's staff—the one that budded—and the tablets with the covenant inscribed upon them, ⁵while above the ark were the cherubim, showing forth God's glory and overshadowing the place where expiation is to be found. But then, these are matters which we cannot at present discuss in detail. ⁶Now the procedure adopted, once things have been set up in the manner described, is that the priests go continually into the outer tabernacle to perform their services, *⁷while it is the high priest alone who goes into the inner tabernacle, doing so once a year; and even he does not omit to take blood with him, offering it to atone for the sins of ignorance committed by himself and the people. ⁸What is signified by the Holy Spirit in this manner is that, so long as the outer tabernacle is still in existence, it has not yet been revealed how the way into the sanctuary is to be found. ⁹In fact, it all amounts to a symbolic representation pointing to the present time. The lesson it teaches is this: the offerings and the sacrifices which are being presented here are incapable of perfecting the worshipper in respect of his conscience, ¹⁰seeing that their sole reliance is on foods, drinks, and various kinds of ablution—outward ordinances imposed only until the new order arrives by which things are set aright.

¹¹But now Christ has made his appearance, a high priest concerned with blessings already won. The tabernacle of which he made use was the greater and more perfect one, the tabernacle not fashioned by any human hand, that is to say, the one which does not belong to this order of creation at all. ¹²Moreover, if he has entered the sanctuary once and for all, securing a deliverance which lasts for ever, it was his own blood, not that of goats and calves, which was his means of accomplishing this. ¹³And indeed, if the blood of goats and bulls and the ashes of a heifer sprinkled upon those who have suffered defilement hallows them, so as to restore their outward purity, ¹⁴how much more effective will be the blood of Christ, who, by virtue of the eternal spirit which was his, offered himself up to God, as a sacrifice free from all blemish; how much more effective, I say, will be Christ's

---

*[Ex 30:10; Lv 16:2.14]

blood in cleansing our conscience, so that we turn our backs on actions without any life in them and instead give ourselves up to the service of the living God.

15 And so it is that he is likewise the mediator of a new covenant, or let us say, testament, the aim of all this being that, since a death has occurred to bring about deliverance from the sins committed when the first covenant was in force, those called by God might receive the eternal inheritance promised to them. 16 And indeed, when it is a last will or testament which is in question, it is necessary first of all that the death of the testator should be established. 17 For a will is operative only after a death, and it cannot possibly have any force while the testator is still alive. 18 And that is also the reason why, even when the first covenant was inaugurated, this did not take place without the use of blood. 19 For after Moses had recited to all the people each one of the commandments, as the law enjoined them, he took the blood of calves and goats, along with water, scarlet wool, and hyssop, and besprinkled the lawbook itself as well as all the people, 20 saying, *t*'**This is the blood used on behalf of the covenant which God has enjoined upon you.**' 21 Moreover, in the same manner he sprinkled blood on the tabernacle as well as on all the vessels used for divine service. 22 Indeed, where the law is concerned, it might almost be said that there is nothing which is not cleansed by blood, and that, without the outpouring of blood, there can be no such thing as forgiveness of sins.

23 Now while it was requisite that these things, which are in fact nothing more than copies of the heavenly things, should be cleansed in the manner described, the heavenly things themselves had to be cleansed by virtue of a sacrifice of a much greater value. 24 After all, the sanctuary into which Christ made his entry was not a mere representation of the sanctuary, truly so-called. No, he made his entry into heaven itself, so that he might now—and that for our sakes—make his appearance before the very face of God. 25 On the other hand, his purpose was not to offer himself up repeatedly, in the way that the high priest enters the sanctuary year by year, bringing with him blood other than his own. 26 Were that so, he would have had to suffer time and again ever since the foundation of the world. No, this is what has in fact happened. He has once and for all—and that at the close of the ages—revealed himself as what he really is through offering himself up in sacrifice, his aim being that sin should be brought to nought. 27 And just as it is the appointed lot of men to die once, and after that comes the judgment, 28 so Christ, having been offered up once and for all to *u***take away the sins of a multitude of men, will**

*t*Ex 24:6-8   *u*Is 53:12

appear a second time—sin having been done away with—to those who are waiting for him to obtain their salvation.

10 The law contains what is but the shadow of the blessings to come, not the true image of the realities themselves. Thus it is quite incapable of making perfect for all time those who draw near to God by virtue of the same sacrifices which are being offered year after year. ²Were it otherwise, would not the offering of these sacrifices have been done away with before now, because in that case the worshippers, cleansed once and for all, would no longer have any consciousness of sin? ³The truth, however, is that in these sacrifices sins are brought to remembrance year after year; ⁴for there is no possibility at all that the blood of goats and bulls should have the effect of freeing people of their sins. ⁵And so it is that, on coming into this world, he speaks these words,

> ᵛ**You did indeed have no desire for sacrifices and offerings,**
> **But you have prepared a body for me.**
> ⁶**Holocausts* and sin offerings are things you take no delight**
> **in.**
> ⁷**Then I said, "Here I am,**
> **As it is written of me in the scroll of the book;**
> **I have come, God of mine, to do your will."'**

⁸Saying first of all, ʷ**'Sacrifices and offerings, holocausts and sin-offerings are things you had no desire for, nor did you take any delight in them'**—these being the very things offered in obedience to what is laid down in the law— ⁹he **thereupon** says, '**Here I am: I have come to do your will.'** He does away with the first to establish the second. ¹⁰And indeed, it is in conformity with that will of God that we have received our consecration, and that by virtue of the **offering up,** once and for all, of the **body** of Jesus Christ.

¹¹Moreover, every priest takes up his stand day after day, performing his services and offering over and over again the same sacrifices, these having no power at all to take away sins. ¹²As against this, Christ, having offered a single sacrifice for the atonement of sins which is effective for ever, ˣ**took his seat at the right hand of God,** ¹³waiting from that time onward **until the time that** his **enemies** should be **made a footstool for** his **feet,** ¹⁴the truth being that by a single sacrifice he has made perfect for ever those who are receiving

---

ᵛPs 40:6-8　　ʷPs 40:6; [1 Sm 15:22]　　ˣPs 110:1

* I.e., whole burnt offerings.

his consecration. [15]And the Holy Spirit likewise bears witness to us in this matter. For having spoken these words first of all,

> [y][16]**'This is the covenant which I shall establish** with them
> **When the time comes, says the Lord.**
> **I shall put my laws into their hearts**
> **And write them upon their minds,'**

[17]it is then added,

> [z]**'And I shall by no means hold their sins** and their lawless
> deeds **in remembrance.**

[18]But then, where forgiveness of sins has been granted, there is no longer any room for a sin offering.

[19]So, my brothers, since we are full of confidence that, by virtue of the blood of Jesus, we can enter the sanctuary, [20]this being the new and living way of approach through the curtain which he has opened up for us—the curtain here standing for his body of flesh and blood—, [21]and since we have [a]**a great priest set over God's household,** [22]let us draw near in sincerity of heart and full assurance of faith, having had our hearts sprinkled clean and freed from all guiltiness of conscience, having had our bodies washed in pure water. [23]And let us hold on, without wavering, to the hope which we profess, for he who has given us his promise deserves to be trusted. [24]Moreover, let us be mindful of each other, stirring each other up to the uttermost to love and to the performance of noble deeds, [25]making sure at the same time that we do not, as is customary with certain people, fail to be present at the gatherings which are held by us. No, let us rather encourage one another in this, all the more so because, as you can see for yourselves, the great day is drawing near.

[26]Indeed, if we fall into deliberate sin after having obtained knowledge of the truth, no sacrifice for the atonement of sins remains any longer; [27]all that is left is the terrifying expectation of Judgment and of the [b]**fury of a fire** which will **consume** God's **adversaries.** [28]Anyone who sets the law of Moses at defiance is [c]**put to death** without mercy **on the evidence of two or three witnesses.** [29]How much more severe a punishment do you suppose a man will be thought to deserve if he tramples the Son of God underfoot, looking upon the [d]**blood of the covenant,** which was the means of his consecration, as a thing with no holiness in it, and offering outrage to God's Spirit, the source of grace? [30]We know well enough who it is that spoke the words, [e]**'Vengeance is mine; I will repay';** and again,

[y]Jr 31:33   [z]Jr 31:34   [a]Zc 6:11-13; Nm 12:7   [b]Is 26:11 LXX   [c]Nm 35:30; Dt 17:6
[d]Ex 24:8   [e]Dt 32:35f; Ps 135:14

'**The Lord will judge his people.**' ³¹And indeed, it is a terrible thing to fall into the hands of the living God.

³²Remember the former days, when the light was first brought to you, when you had to endure a great struggle, being called upon to face your sufferings, and bore it all with fortitude. ³³At times you were made a public show of, having abuse poured on you and being made to suffer affliction; at other times again, you made common cause with those suffering such a fate. ³⁴Indeed, you became one in feeling with those held in prison, and besides, you cheerfully accepted the seizure of your possessions, knowing as you do that you call your own a possession which is of much greater value and one which at the same time endures. ³⁵See to it, then, that you do not throw away that confidence of yours which carries a great reward with it. ³⁶It is endurance you stand in need of, so that, having done what is in accordance with God's will, you may obtain what has been promised to you. ³⁷In the words of scripture, ᶠ'**There is a little while, a very little while** still to wait; **and then he who is to come will come, making no delay. ³⁸It is by his faith that the righteous man who follows me shall gain life.** And indeed, **if anyone shrinks back, my soul finds no pleasure in him.**' ³⁹We, however, are not the ones to **shrink back** to be led into ruin; no, we take our stand upon **faith,** and so preserve our souls alive.

11 Now faith is that which provides us with confident assurance with regard to things which we hope for; it serves by way of convincing us about things which cannot be seen.

²It was by reason of their faith that the men of old found themselves highly praised.

³It is faith which makes us apprehend that everything there ever has been throughout the ages has been fashioned by the word of God, the visible coming forth from something that does not outwardly appear.

⁴It was because of his faith that Abel offered up to God a richer sacrifice than did Cain and found himself highly praised as a man of righteousness, ᵍ**God** testifying **in favour of the offerings** which he had made. And it is on account of that faith of his that he is still speaking to us, even though he is dead.

⁵It was because of his faith that Enoch, without experiencing death, was taken away to another place. In the words of scripture, ʰ'**If no trace of him could be found anywhere, that was on account of his having been taken away by God.**' As for the time before he was taken away, testimony is borne to him that **he had pleased God.** ⁶But then, it is impossible that, in the absence of faith, there should be any such thing as

ᶠHab 2:3f LXX   ᵍGn 4:4   ʰGn 5:24

pleasing God; for if anyone is to make his way towards God, it is necessary first of all that he should believe that God exists, and secondly that God has a recompense in store for those who are seeking him.

[7]It was because of the faith he had that Noah, being divinely warned concerning happenings which as yet were not visible, took heed and built an ark, to serve as a place of safety for his household. And so it was that, in doing what he did, he showed up the whole world as deserving of condemnation, while at the same time he was acknowledged to be a possessor of that righteousness which comes through faith.

[8]It was by virtue of his faith that Abraham rendered obedience, when he received the call, and [i]**went forth** to the place which he was destined to receive as his inheritance, while yet he had no knowledge, as he went forth, of where his journey would take him. [9]It was guided by faith that he [j]**took up residence as a stranger,** and there he was, as though in a foreign land, living in tents with Isaac and Jacob, who were inheritors of the same promise. [10]And that came about because he was in expectation of the city resting on proper foundations, the city which has God for its designer and its maker.

[11]It was by reason of her faith that Sarah received the power to conceive a child, even though she was past the age, because she was convinced that he who had made the promise would keep true to it. [12]And so it was that from one man, and him as good as dead, there sprang descendants as many in number [k]**as the stars of heaven and the grains of sand upon the seashore, which cannot be counted.**

[13]All these died guided by faith, not obtaining what had been promised them but seeing it from afar, while acknowledging at the same time that they were [l]**strangers and passing travellers upon earth.** [14]Now those who use language such as this make it plain enough that what they are seeking is a land of their own. [15]But if what they had had in mind here were the land from which they originally came, the opportunity of returning to it was, after all, left open to them. [16]As it is, however, it is a better land which they are longing for, namely, one in heaven. That is why God is not ashamed to be called their God. Indeed, there is a city he has made ready for them to be their home.

[17]It was because of the faith which was in him that [m]**Abraham, when he was put to the test, was prepared to offer up Isaac,** and why this man who had received the promises made ready to sacrifice his **only son,** [18]concerning whom it had been said to him, [n]**'it is through the line of Isaac that you are to have your descendants.'** [19]What he was reckoning with was that God even had the power to raise up the

[i]Gn 12:1.4   [j]Gn 23:4; 26:3; 35:12   [k]Gen 15:5; 22:17; 32:12; [Ex 32:13]   [l]Ps 39:12; [119:19]; 1 Ch 29:15   [m]Gn 22:1f   [n]Gn 21:12

dead; indeed, the matter being considered symbolically, it was thus that he had him given back to him.

²⁰ It was by reason of his faith that Isaac, being concerned with what the future was to bring, bestowed his blessing upon Jacob and Esau. ²¹ It was guided by faith that Jacob, as he was dying, called down a blessing upon each of the sons of Joseph; and *o*he paid homage to God, leaning over the head of his staff. ²² It was because of his faith that Joseph, when he was nearing his end, made mention of the departure of the Israelites from Egypt and gave directions as to what was to be done with his bones.

²³ Faith was the reason why Moses, after he was born, was *p*hidden by his parents for three months. They saw how well-pleasing a child he was, and they were not afraid of the king's edict. ²⁴ It was because of his faith that Moses, *q*when he reached manhood, refused to be called the son of Pharaoh's daughter. ²⁵ choosing rather to receive cruel treatment along with the people of God than to enjoy the fleeting pleasures of sin, ²⁶ and looking upon the *r*revilings suffered by God's anointed as riches greater than all the treasures of Egypt. He had eyes firmly fixed on the time when he would receive his recompense. ²⁷ It was his faith, not his fear of the king's anger, which accounted for his departure from Egypt. And indeed it was as a man seeing him who is invisible that he preserved his steadfastness.

²⁸ It was because of his faith that he celebrated the *s*Passover and sprinkled the blood, to make sure that the destroying angel would not touch the firstborn of Israel's people. ²⁹ It was in faith that they crossed the Red Sea as though it were dry land, while the Egyptians, when they made the attempt, were swallowed up by the water.

*t*³⁰ It was faith which made the walls of Jericho fall down after seven days spent in marching round them. ³¹ It was because of her faith that *u*Rahab the harlot, having given a peaceable welcome to the spies, did not perish along with those who would not submit themselves.

³² And what more can I say? For time would fail me if I set out to tell of Gideon, Barak, Samson, and Jephthah, of David, Samuel, and the prophets. ³³ It was through their faith that they overthrew kingdoms, established justice, obtained what had been promised them, stopped the mouths of lions, ³⁴ quenched the fury of fire, escaped the edge of the sword, turned weakness into strength, became mighty in war, hurled back the armies of the foe.

³⁵ Women received back their dead through their being resurrected. On the other hand, there were those who, when they were having cruel torture inflicted on them, declined to purchase their release,

*o*Gn 47:31 LXX *p*Ex 2:2 *q*Ex 2:10f *r*Ps 89:50 *s*Ex 12:12f *t*[Jos 6:20] *u*[Jos 6:17.25] their aim being that they should be made partakers of a better resurrection. [36]Others, again, experienced mockery and scourging; and on top of this, they found themselves put in chains and confined to prison. [37]They were stoned; they were sawn in two; they died, slain by the sword. They went about dressed in skins made of sheep or goats, being in want, suffering affliction, being maltreated. [38]It was to men whom the world was not worthy to contain that these things happened; and there they were, roaming about in deserts and on the hills, or hidden away in caves and holes in the ground. [39]Yet all these, highly praised as they were for the faith which was in them, did not obtain what they had been promised, [40]God, bearing us in mind, having made an even better provision—that it was only in company with us that they were to attain to perfection.

12 Well then, as regards ourselves, seeing that we have so great a host of witnesses encompassing us like a cloud, let us clear every obstacle out of our way, divesting ourselves of sin by which we are so prone to be ensnared; and let us, without faltering, run the race which is set before us, [2]having our eyes fixed on him who is the founder of our faith and the one who brings it to perfection, on Jesus, who, bearing in mind the joy in store for him as his recompense, endured the cross, looking upon the disgrace it brought as a thing to be held in contempt, and who has now [v]**taken his seat at the right hand** of God's throne. [3]Well then, let your minds dwell on him who has borne up patiently with so much hostility [w]**against himself** on the part of **sinful men.** That will prevent your growing weary or suffering discouragement in your hearts. [4]For in your struggle against sin, you have not as yet been called upon to offer resistance to the point of having to shed your blood. [5]In fact, you have become altogether forgetful of the encouragement to be found in words from scripture in which you are addressed as sons:

> [x]**'My son, do not think lightly of the Lord's discipline,**
> **Neither be discouraged when you are corrected by him.**
> [6]**For the Lord disciplines those whom he loves,**
> **And he chastises everyone who is acknowledged by him as a son.'**

[7]If you are called upon to endure, that is because you are being disciplined. God is dealing with you as **sons** of his, and what **son** is there whom his father does not **discipline?** [8]But if you are held exempt from **discipline,** then you are in fact nothing more than bastards, not **sons** at

[v]Ps 110:1   [w]Nm 17:2f LXX   [x]Pr 3:11f; [Dt 8:5]

all. [9]Besides, there were our earthly fathers imposing discipline upon us, and we paid due respect to them. Shall we, then, not submit ourselves with much greater readiness to him whose fatherhood is one over a world of spirits, and so lay hold of life? [10]After all, these earthly fathers of ours disciplined us for but a short time, at their discretion, while God does so having our true welfare in mind, intending that we should come to partake of his holiness. [11]All discipline, it is true, seems, at the time when it is being applied, not to be a matter of feeling joy but of feeling pain. At a later time, however, it yields for those who have been trained by it a harvest making for peace, that of an upright life.

[12]See to it, then, that your [y]**drooping hands and palsied knees are set aright,** [13]and [z]**make straight paths for** your **feet,** so that the limb which has been crippled may not be put out of joint even further, but rather be healed. [14][a]**Strive after peace** with all men and after a life of holiness, for unless a man pursues such a course he will never see the Lord. [15]And take care that there should be no one who forfeits the grace of God, [b]**that no root** bearing **bitter** fruit **should spring up and be the cause of trouble,** many suffering defilement as the result of it, [16]that there should be no one given over to fornication, no impious person like [c]**Esau,** who **sold** his **birthright** for a single meal. [17]For you know that when subsequently he made an effort to obtain the blessing, as being his by right of inheritance, he was repudiated. He failed in his plea that he should be given a second chance, and that notwithstanding the fact that he strove for the blessing to the point of shedding tears.

[18]As for yourselves, it is not a tangible object before which you stand at the end of your journey. It is not Mount Sinai with the [d]**flaming fire,** the **darkness,** the **gloom** and the **whirlwind,** [19]the **sounding of the trumpet, and the voice uttering words** of such a kind that those who heard them begged that no further message should be addressed to them. [20]That happened because they found past all endurance this injunction which had been given: [e]**'If even a beast touches the mountain, it shall be stoned.'** [21]Indeed, so terrifying was the spectacle that Moses said, [f]**'I am frightened** and seized by trembling.'

[22]No, you stand before Mount Zion, before the city of the living God, the heavenly Jerusalem, before myriads of angels in festal gathering, [23]before an assembly consisting of firstborn sons who have their names recorded in heaven, before God, the judge of all, and the spirits of righteous men made perfect, [24]before Jesus, the mediator of a new covenant; and there is his blood to be used for sprinkling which holds out a better promise than Abel's did.

[25]See to it that you do not refuse to listen to him who is speaking

[y]Is 35:3   [z]Pr 4:26 LXX   [a]Ps 34:14   [b]Dt 29:18 LXX   [c]Gn 25:33f   [d]Dt 5:23; Ex 19:12.16.18   [e]Ex 19:12f   [f]Dt 9:19

to you. And indeed, if these other men, when they were on earth, did not escape when they refused to listen to the one who was giving them warning, still less shall we escape if we turn a deaf ear to him when he is addressing us from heaven. 26 It was his voice that shook the earth on that former occasion. But now he has made us a promise in these words: *g*'**Yet once more shall I shake** not the **earth** alone but **heaven** also.' 27 But then, what the words '**Yet once more**' signify is this, that there will be a removal of the things which can be shaken, as these are things which have been created, the aim of it all being that it is to be the unshakable things which alone remain. 28 Thus, since the kingdom of which we have been made possessors is one which is unshakable, let us give thanks, worshipping God in a manner which meets with his approval: in a spirit of reverence and of awe. 29 And indeed, that *h***God** of ours is a **fire devouring all.**

13 May you ever love one another like brothers. 2 As for hospitality, this is something which you must never neglect. After all, there were those who found that, through the exercise of it, they had been receiving angels as their guests, even though at the time they had not been aware of this.

3 Have a loving concern for those bound in prison, just as though you were there with them as their fellow prisoners; and also for those who are being maltreated, bearing in mind that your life, like theirs, is still lived in this mortal body.

4 Let the marriage tie be held in honour in every way; and may the marriage bed ever remain inviolate. God's judgment will fall on those who are given over to fornication or adultery.

5 See to it that there is no love of money in your lives, and be content with what you have. For it is God himself who has said, *i*'**I will never desert you, never abandon you.**' 6 And so, taking courage, we can say, *j*'**The Lord is my helper; I shall not be afraid: what can man do to me?**'

7 Keep your leaders in mind, the men who first proclaimed God's message to you; and, while contemplating what the outcome of their lives has been, let it be their faith which you take for your model.

8 Jesus Christ is ever the same: yesterday, today, and to all eternity. 9 See to it that you are not swept off your course by a whole variety of out-of-the-way teachings. That our hearts should find themselves strengthened by grace is indeed a good thing. Rules about food, on the other hand, count for nothing, and no benefit has been received by those who have taken account of them in the conduct of their lives.

10 There is an altar which is ours, from which those who place

*g*Hg 2:6   *h*Is 33:14; Dt 4:24; 9:3   *i*Dt 31:6.8; Jos 1:5   *j*Ps 118:6

reliance on the tabernacle when offering divine service have no right to eat. [11]For those animals whose [k]**blood is carried** by the high priest **into the sanctuary** as a **sin offering** have their bodies **burned outside the camp,** [12]this being likewise the reason why Jesus, so that he might sanctify the people with his own blood, underwent his sufferings outside the gate. [13]Let us go forth to him, then, **outside the camp,** bearing the ignominy which he bore. [14]After all, the city in which we are to make our permanent home is not to be found anywhere here on earth. No, what we seek is the city which is to come into being in the future. [15]And this being so, [l]**let** it be through Jesus that **we offer up,** without ceasing, **a sacrifice of praise to God.** For this is the **harvest** yielded by the **lips** of those who acknowledge the name of Jesus. [16]Do not be neglectful of doing good or of sharing your possessions with others, these being the kind of sacrifices in which God finds his delight. [17]Render obedience to your leaders and give way to them. They are making tireless efforts on behalf of your souls, being men who will be called upon to render an account of what they have done. See to it, then, that they should perform their task joyfully and not in a manner grievous to them; for if the latter were the case, it would only be to your own disadvantage.

[18]Pray for us, for we are convinced that there is nothing our conscience has to reproach us with, and we are resolved in all circumstances to acquit ourselves in an honourable manner. [19]And I make this request for your prayers with all the greater urgency, because it is my hope that, through them, I shall be restored to you all the sooner.

[20]Now may God, the giver of peace, he who [m]**has brought back** from the realm of the dead the great [n]**shepherd of the sheep,** our Lord Jesus, doing so [o]**by virtue of the blood** shed in token of the **eternal covenant,** [21]equip you to perfection with everything that is good, so as to make you act in conformity with his will; and may he bring forth in us that which is well pleasing in his sight through Jesus Christ, to whom glory be ascribed for ever and ever. Amen.

[22]I appeal to you, my brothers, to give a ready hearing to the words of exhortation which I have been addressing to you. It is, after all, but in brief that I have written to you. [23]Be informed that our brother Timothy has been released from prison. Should he arrive here without delay, it is in his company that I shall be coming to see you.

[24]Give my greetings to each of your leaders and to all who are consecrated to God. Those who come from Italy send their greetings to you.

[25]May God's grace be by the side of each and every one of you.

[k]Lv 16:27   [l]Lv 7:12; Ps 50:14.23; Hos 14:2   [m]Is 63:11   [n]Zc 9:11   [o]Is 55:3; Jr 32:40; Ezk 37:26

THE LETTER OF JAMES

1 James, God's servant, and servant of Jesus Christ, sends his greetings to the members of the twelve tribes who live scattered all over the world.

²You will, it is true, my brothers, find yourselves beset by trials of the most varied sort, but you should look upon this as the very source of extreme joy, ³while being aware at the same time that the very genuineness of your faith creates the power to endure. ⁴Still, it is essential that this endurance should manifest itself to perfection in what you do, to make of you men who are mature, complete in themselves, and lacking in nothing. ⁵If, however, there be someone of your number who is still lacking in wisdom, let him make an appeal for it to God, who will bestow it upon him, seeing that his nature is to give generously to all men, never grudging them anything. ⁶(Only he must make his appeal as a man having faith, with no doubt filling his mind. For he who doubts resembles the surf of the sea, which is driven to and fro by the wind. ⁷Moreover, let no man of that sort imagine that he will receive anything from the Lord, ⁸he, a man divided in mind and lacking in steadiness in everything he does.)

⁹If some member of the brotherhood finds himself in a lowly position, he should at the same time make his boast in how highly placed he is, ¹⁰while in the case of a rich man, it may turn out that he has nothing to boast about apart from his lowliness, seeing that he is bound to vanish away, ^a**like the flower of the field.** ¹¹For this is what scripture says: 'The sun came up with its scorching heat, **drying up the field, while the flower** which was on it **fell to the ground,** and all the loveliness of its appearance vanished away.' In the same way the rich man will be made to fade away, and all his enterprises with him.

¹²The man who ^b**stands up** under trials is to be counted **happy** indeed; for, having shown himself tried and true, he will receive the crown of life, which God has promised to those who love him. ¹³Let no one who finds himself subject to temptation say, ^c'It is God by

---

^aIs 40:6f; 49:10 LXX; Hos 12:1 LXX; Jr 18:17 LXX   ^bDn 12:12   ^c[Ec'us 15:11-20]

whom I am being tempted.' For God cannot be tempted to do evil, and he himself tempts no one. [14] On the contrary, it is the desire to be found in each man that tempts him, enticing him and dragging him off. [15] And what happens next is that the desire is made to conceive and that it gives birth to sin, while sin, for its part, having run its course, brings forth death. [16] Dearly-loved brothers of mine, do not allow yourselves to be deceived in this matter.

[17] Every benefit which is to be valued highly, and every gift which has perfection about it, is given to us from above. It comes down from him who is the Father of everything that gives light, from him who is a stranger to all change, and in whom there can be no variation due to the casting of a shadow. [18] It was he whose will it was to bring us to birth by virtue of the message proclaiming the truth, while he meant us to be the first fruits of all his creation.

[19] There is one thing you do know, my dearly-loved brothers, [d] that it is the duty of each man to be a ready listener, while yet being himself slow to speak, and slow in being moved to anger. [20] Indeed, human anger is not the sort of thing which promotes the uprightness which God requires of us. [21] Now since this is so, you must rid yourselves of everything that defiles a man, and of every trace of evil which may still remain with you, and instead must accept God's word in all humility, the word which is implanted in you and which has the power of bringing salvation to your souls.

[22] Moreover, you must see to it that you become men who carry out God's commandment in what they do, and who are not mere listeners to it. If you were the latter, you would simply be deceiving yourselves. [23] Indeed, if a man be a listener to God's commandment, without carrying it out in what he does, he is not unlike a man who examines in a mirror the face nature has given him: [24] he has examined himself, and then gone off, forgetting immediately what he looked like. [25] But a man who has had a close look at the law which is perfect, that is to say, [e] the law which brings freedom with it, and who has persisted in this course, not becoming a mere listener who forgets again, but a doer who achieves what he sets out to do—such a man, I say, will indeed be blessed in everything he does.

[26] Should anyone suppose that he is a worshipper of God, while yet he lets his tongue run away with him unbridled, he is deceiving himself in his own mind, and the service he engages in is futile. [27] For this is what a pure and undefiled service, [f] in the eyes of God the Father, consists in: that a man should take care of the orphans and widows in their distress, and that he should keep himself uncontaminated by this world in which we live.

[d] [Pr 14:17; Ec'us 5:11.13]   [e] [Ps 19:7]   [f] [1 Ch 29:10 LXX; Wis 2:16]

2   My brothers, you have faith in our Lord Jesus Christ, the fount of all glory. However, it is your duty to make sure that you do not at the same time exhibit ⁸partiality in your treatment of men. ²Let us assume, for instance, that a certain man enters your place of worship who is adorned with golden rings and clad in splendid apparel, and that another, a poor man, enters at the same time, clad in shabby apparel. ³Suppose, further, that you pay special attention to the one splendidly dressed, saying to him, 'Take your seat here in this place which is a good one.' But to the poor man you say, 'You can stand here if you like, or else sit down on the floor by my footstool.'

⁴What is one to make of all this? Is it not true that you are at odds with yourselves, and that you are influenced by the wrong standards in the decisions you make? ⁵Listen to what I have to say, my dearly-loved brothers. Is it not true that God has made the very ones who are beggars in the eyes of the world the objects of his special choice, causing them to be rich in faith and to be inheritors of the kingdom which he has promised to those who love him? ⁶Yet you have seen fit to treat the poor man in an insulting manner. Moreover, is it not true that the rich lord it over you? Is it not they who drag you before their law courts? ⁷Is it not they who revile the noble name which you had called over you when God claimed you as his own?

⁸If, on the other hand, you fulfil the law which you received from your king, and act in conformity with the commandment laid down in scripture, ʰ'**You shall love your neighbour as much as you love yourself,**' you will do well indeed. ⁹But all you will achieve by treating people with partiality is that you will be committing a sin; and then you will be convicted by the law as a transgressor. ¹⁰And indeed, anyone who fulfils the law in its entirety, while failing only in one particular respect, makes himself liable to be treated as one who has broken the whole of it. ¹¹Surely, he who has said, ⁱ'**Do not commit adultery,**' has also said, '**Do not commit murder.**' Well then, this is what has happened, when, not committing adultery, you yet commit murder: you have become a transgressor of the law. ¹²Always speak and act in such a way as befits those destined to be judged by a law whose aim is freedom. ¹³And in that judgment there will be no mercy for one who has shown no mercy, while it is true at the same time that mercy will always be able to boast that it has nothing to fear from judgment.

¹⁴What good does it do, my brothers, if a man claims to have faith, while yet there are no deeds to substantiate such a claim? Is it to be supposed that faith has the power of bringing him salvation? ¹⁵To

⁸[Lv 19:15; Dt 1:17; Pr 24:23]   ʰLv 19:18   ⁱEx 20:14.13; Dt 5:18.17

take an example, let us put the case that there are fellow believers, whether men or women, who have insufficient clothing and are in want of their daily food, 16and someone out of your midst comes along, saying, 'You have my best wishes. Go forth, keep yourselves warm, and have your fill.' And let us suppose further that nothing is in fact done to supply them with the bare necessities which their bodily needs require. 17So it is with faith. Left to itself it is nothing but a dead thing.

18This is the proper way of dealing with people of that sort: 'You have faith,' you allege, 'while I, for my part, have deeds to point to.' Well then, show me this faith of yours which operates divorced from good deeds, and I will show you my faith by my good deeds. 19Moreover, your belief is that there is one God and one God only. Well and good; but the demons believe the very same thing, and they shudder with fear. 20When will the time come, you shallow men, when you will be ready to acknowledge that faith divorced from deeds is worth nothing at all? 21Was it not on the strength of the deeds which he had performed that our forefather *j*Abraham was accepted as a righteous man, **when he offered up his son Isaac on the altar?** 22 You will realize, then, that his faith and his deeds performed a common task, and that it was by virtue of the works he performed 23that fulfilment came to the following passage from scripture: *k*Abraham **put his faith in God, and this was reckoned to him as righteousness.'** And elsewhere he is given the title of *l*God's friend.' 24You will thus perceive that, if a man is accepted as righteous, this is by reason of the deeds which he has performed, and that faith by itself is incapable of achieving such a result. 25Moreover, is it not true, in accordance with this, that, if Rahab the harlot was accepted as righteous, this happened because of the deed she had performed, welcoming the strangers into her house as she did, and sending them away by a different route? 26And indeed, as the body is a dead thing but for the presence of the spirit in it, so faith is a dead thing if no account be taken of the deeds to be performed.

3   See to it, my brothers, that there are not too many among you who wish to become teachers; for you are aware, surely, that those among us who are engaged in teaching must expect to be treated with greater severity. 2We are indeed, all of us, betrayed into many a fault, while he who is never thus betrayed in respect of what his tongue utters must be a man who had reached maturity, and who has the capacity for putting a curb on every aspect of his bodily existence. 3In a similar

*j*Gn 22:9.10.12   *k*Gn 15:6   *l*Is 41:8; 2 Ch 20:7

way, if we put a bridle into the mouths of our horses to make them obedient to our will, we are then in a position to turn their entire bodies this way or that. [4]Or look at ships, how huge they are, and how they are driven to and fro by gales of the greatest severity. And yet a tiny rudder will turn them in this direction or that, according to what course is chosen by the man who has the steering under his control. [5]Just so the tongue is but a tiny organ; yet there are great things it may rightly boast of.

How vast a forest is set ablaze by a small fire! [6]And that is what the [m]tongue is: a fire. Indeed, among all the parts of the body the tongue represents a world of its own, a world representing the sum-total of wickedness. It defiles the whole body, and catching fire from hell itself, it sets aflame the very driving-wheel of our existence. [7]Moreover, all creatures can be subdued and have been subdued by those partaking of the nature of man, whether they are four-footed animals, birds, reptiles, or inhabitants of the sea. [8]But no human being is capable of subduing the tongue, never-resting evil that it is, and filled as it is with a death-bringing poison. [9]With the tongue do we offer praise to him who is our Lord and Father; and it is with the tongue that we invoke curses upon our fellow men, who have been created [n]in God's image. [10]It is the same mouth which brings forth praises and curses. Yet there is no need, my brothers, that things should happen in this way. [11]Does a spring gush forth both fresh water and salt water out of the same opening? [12]Is it possible, my brothers, for a fig tree to bring forth olives? Can a vine bring forth figs? In the same way, no salt spring has the power to bring forth fresh water.

[13]Which among you is a wise man, a man of discernment? Let him give proof of it by his noble-minded conduct and by the deeds which he performs; and let him show forth that spirit of lowliness which characterizes true wisdom. [14]As against this, if what is in your hearts are feelings of bitter jealousy and selfish ambition, are you not then mere braggarts, and telling falsehoods to the detriment of the truth? [15]Wisdom of that sort is not the true kind which descends to us from above. No, such wisdom belongs to this earth; it is unspiritual, it is the work of demons. [16]For where bitter jealousy and selfish ambition manifest themselves, restlessness makes itself felt, and, indeed, everything that is evil. [17]The wisdom which comes from above, on the other hand, is in the first place free from any stain, while at the same time it is peaceable, [o]fair-minded, compliant, full of compassion as well as yielding a harvest of noble deeds, not given to doubting, and free from all pretence. [18]Moreover, the harvest which righteousness yields is sown in a spirit of peace, and comes from those who establish peace.

[m][Pr 16:27]   [n]Gn 1:27   [o][Wis 7:22f]

4 How is it that there are conflicts, that there are quarrels among you? Surely, what they spring from is this, that the appetites which are active in the various parts of your bodies are on the warpath? [2] An appetite arises in you, and you are incapable of satisfying it. And so it is that you resort to murder, that you give vent to feelings of envy. You are still not in a position to reach your goal, and so get involved in quarrelling and controversy. However, the real reason why you fail is that you do not pray for what you desire; [3] or if you do, your requests are not granted on account of your praying from what is in fact an evil motive, namely, that you should be provided with the means for satisfying your appetites. [4] You, to whom faithfulness is a stranger, are ignorant of the fact that to be on terms of friendliness with the world as it is at present implies that your attitude towards God is one of hostility. And indeed, anyone who sets out to be a friend of the world becomes, by so acting, an enemy of God. [5] Or do you suppose that scripture speaks to no purpose when it employs these words, 'God watches jealously over the Spirit which he has implanted in us.' [6] On the other hand, there are the words, *p*'**He bestows** his **grace** upon us,' which is something of still greater value. And this is why it is said in scripture, *q*'**He opposes himself to the arrogant, but to the humble he gives of his grace.'**

[7] It is to God, then, that you must submit yourselves, while offering resistance to the devil, who, if you do, will depart from you and take to flight. [8] Draw near to God, and he will draw near to you. Wash your hands clean, you sinners; keep your minds pure, you doubters. [9] Lament, mourn, and burst out crying. May your laughter turn into grief, your joy into gloom. [10] Humble yourselves before the Lord, and he will raise you up.

[11] *r*'Do not slander one another, my brothers. For he who slanders his fellow believer or passes judgment on him does in fact slander the law, and passes judgment on it. But then, if you pass judgment on the law, you are no longer a man carrying out the law, but one who occupies himself with judging it. [12] In truth, however, there is only one who is the giver of the law, and at the same time called upon to pass judgment on it; and he it is who has the power to bring salvation to men or to destroy them. So who are you that you should claim the right to pass judgment on your fellow man?

[13] Further, what is one to make of you who use words such as these: 'Today or tomorrow we shall set out for such and such a place, spending a year there, engaging in trade and making a profit'? [14] The truth is that you *s*do not even know what the next day will bring. This is

*p*Pr 3:34 LXX   *q*Pr 3:34 LXX; Job 22:29   *r*[Lv 19:16]   *s*[Pr 27:1] what your life is like, *that you are nothing more than a vapour which appears for but a short time and then vanishes away. ¹⁵Well then, instead of speaking the way you do, you should express yourselves thus: "If it be the Lord's will, we shall find ourselves alive to do this thing or another." ¹⁶As things are, however, you resort to boasting and conduct yourselves as braggarts. All such boasting is, surely, a bad thing; ¹⁷for if one knows how to accomplish that which is good yet fails to accomplish it, such conduct will be imputed to him as something sinful.

5 Come now, then, you rich men. Let the tears flow freely, and bemoan the miseries which are coming upon you. ²These riches of yours have melted away, and as for the garments you wear, they have become moth-eaten. ³The gold and silver which you possess have suffered corrosion, and the rust which is in them will bear witness against you and will consume your flesh as though it were a flame of fire. You have heaped up riches, and have done so during what are in fact the days when everything is to come to an end. ⁴You have—mark my words—kept back in your own hand **the wages** due to the labourers who mowed your fields, and it is these very wages withheld by you which **cry out against you;** while the shouts of distress coming from the reapers have found entry **into the ears of the Lord of hosts.** ⁵You have led a life of luxury on earth and have indulged yourselves. You have gorged yourselves full to your heart's content at the very **time** when the great **slaughter** is to come. ⁶You have condemned, and in fact murdered, the righteous one; and he offers you no resistance.

⁷Arm yourselves with patience, my brothers, until the day of the Lord's coming. Keep before your minds the farmer and how he gets ready to obtain the precious fruit of the earth. He waits patiently for the **early and the late rain** to fall before the harvest can be brought in. ⁸And you, too, must be patient, and it is your duty to fortify your minds, seeing that the coming of the Lord is indeed close at hand. ⁹My brothers, you ought not to find fault with one another, in a spirit of peevish complaining, lest you yourselves be brought to judgment. And as for the judge, he does indeed stand close at the door. ¹⁰If, my brothers, you would have an example to model yourselves on, an example of men persevering in evil conditions and displaying their patience, you should call to mind the prophets who spoke in the name of the Lord. ¹¹And remind yourselves, too, that those **who have displayed fortitude** are ever thought of as enjoying blessedness. You

*[Ps 39:6] *Lv 19:13; Dt 24:14f; Mal 3:5; Job 31:38-40 *Is 5:9 LXX *Jr 12:3 LXX
*Dt 11:14; Jl 2:23; Zc 10:1; Jr 25:4 *Dn 12:12

have heard of the fortitude which Job showed, and are likewise aware what treatment he received from the Lord in the end. And if the Lord acted in this way, that was because of his ^z**tender-heartedness and compassion.**

¹² Above all things, my brothers, you must refrain from ^aswearing oaths, whether they are sworn by heaven, by earth, or by anything else. If you mean 'Yes,' let it be a plain 'Yes'; if you mean 'No,' let it be a plain 'No.' And act in this manner for fear that you yourselves should become liable to condemnation.

¹³ Is there someone among you who suffers misfortune? Let him offer prayer. Is there someone who is in good heart? Let him sing a psalm of thanksgiving. ¹⁴ Is there someone among you who is ill? Let him call the elders of the church to his side, and let them say prayers over him, while at the same time anointing him with oil in the Lord's name. ¹⁵ And the result of this will be that the prayer offered in faith will restore the sick man, the Lord making him rise from his bed. And even if he has committed sins, they will be forgiven him. ^b¹⁶ Confess your sins to one another, then, and pray on each other's behalf, so that you may be healed of your distress. The prayer of an upright man proves by its effectiveness how great is the power of prayer. ¹⁷ Elijah was a man with the same frail power as ourselves. And yet, when he offered prayer that rain should cease, no rain fell on the earth for three years and a half. ¹⁸ Then he prayed again, and the sky poured forth rain, and the earth yielded its fruit.

¹⁹ My brothers, should any of you stray from the truth, while another succeeds in making him turn back to it, ²⁰ let it be known to you that he who has made the sinner turn back from the misguided course he had taken will, in fact, bring salvation to the sinner's soul. And at the same time he ^c**will move out of sight** a whole host of **sins.**

^zPs 103:8; 111:4   ^a[Ec'us 23:9]   ^b[Pr 28:13]   ^cPr 10:12

THE FIRST LETTER OF PETER

1 Peter, an apostle of Jesus Christ, sends his greetings to God's chosen ones who live scattered and as aliens in the lands of Pontus, Galatia, Cappadocia, Asia, and Bithynia. [2] Chosen you were, by virtue of the foreknowledge of God the Father, to be sanctified by the Spirit, so that, having Jesus Christ's sacrificial blood sprinkled upon you, you may give your allegiance to him. May grace and peace be yours in abundance.

[3] Praise be to him who is the God and Father of our Lord Jesus Christ, who out of the fullness of his compassion caused us to be born anew by kindling in us a life-giving hope through the resurrection of Jesus Christ from the dead. [4] He has made us sharers in an inheritance which is imperishable, free from all blemish, and which can never fade, an inheritance stored up in heaven for your benefit, [5] for the benefit of those who, by virtue of their faith, are being kept under the protection of God's power, in readiness for a work of deliverance which is waiting to be disclosed at the end of time.

[6] This being so, you feel overjoyed, even though, if it has to be, you may find yourselves saddened for a short time by various trials. [7] And there is a purpose in this, namely, that the genuineness of your faith having been established—your faith which is more precious than gold, which, perishable as it is, is yet tested by the assayer's fire—you will be seen to have praise redounding to you, when the time comes for Jesus Christ to reveal himself.

[8] Him you do indeed love, although you have never seen him. And even now, though you still do not see him, you exult by reason of your believing in him, and are filled with a joy ineffable and all-glorious, [9] because you are obtaining possession of what is the supreme end of your faith, the salvation of your souls. [10] It was this very salvation the prophets were so seriously searching after and enquiring into. In fact, it was the wealth which was to become yours which was the object of their prophecies. [11] They tried to discover the circumstances and the time pointed to by the Spirit of Christ which was in them, as it predicted the sufferings in store for Christ as well as the splendours

which were to follow. [12] And what was disclosed to them was this, that they were serving not themselves but you when they concerned themselves with the things which have now been proclaimed to you by those who brought you the Good News in the power of the Holy Spirit sent down from heaven. These things are such that even the angels long to catch a glimpse of them.

[13] Put your minds in readiness, therefore, as a man girding up his loins. Learn to be self-controlled, and fix all your hopes on the gift of grace which is to be yours when Jesus Christ reveals himself. [14] Submission to God should be the very expression of your nature, and nothing you do ought in any way to conform to the desires which shaped your lives when you were in your former state of ignorance. [15] He who has sent out his call to you is holy, and you, too, modelling yourselves on him, should become holy in all your conduct. [16] For, as scripture says, [a] **'You shall become holy because I am holy.'**

[17] Moreover, if he who judges impartially and who treats everyone according to what his deeds have deserved is [b] **invoked** by you as your **father**, you must, in ruling your conduct, ever stand in awe of him during all the time that you are leading the life of strangers here on earth. [18] For you know that, if you have been redeemed so as to turn away from the futile way of life handed down to you by your forefathers, [c] **the ransom has not been paid** in perishable things such as **silver** or gold. [19] No, it has been paid by the precious blood of one who, like a lamb, was without stain or blemish, that is to say, by Christ. [20] He it was who, although predestined from before the creation of the world, has been revealed only in these last days. And this was done for your sakes, [21] you being the ones who, through him, have learned to repose their faith in God, who raised him from the dead and bestowed glory upon him, with the result that your hope and your faith have come to rest in God alone. [22] If, then, through your submission to the truth your souls have been made pure so as to engender in you an unfeigned love, let the love you bear one another be one that comes from the heart and is ever fervent. [23] You have indeed been born anew. Yet that birth of yours did not originate in any perishable seed, but in an imperishable seed-bed: the life-giving and ever-enduring word of God. [24] As scripture has it, [d] **Whatever partakes of flesh is like grass, and all the splendour** of it **is like the flower of the field. The grass has withered and the flower has fallen,** [25] **but the word** of the **Lord endures for ever.'** What is meant by [e] **word** here **is the good news which you have had proclaimed to you.**

---

[a] Lv 11:44; 19:2; 20:7   [b] Ps 89:26; Jr 3:19; Mal 1:6   [c] Is 52:3   [d] Is 40:6f   [e] Is 40:8

2 These, then, are the evil things which you must banish from your hearts: all maliciousness and guile, every kind of pretence or jealousy, and all slander. [2]Instead of being ruled by these, you must, like newborn babes, long for spiritual milk, the milk, that is, which is wholly pure. And this is why you must partake of it, so that you may, through it, grow more and more in stature and in the end obtain your salvation. [3]*f***Since you have had a taste of the goodness of the Lord,** [4]you must draw near to the one who is the life-giving *g***stone** which has been spoken of—the stone, I mean, which men have **rejected,** while to God it is something specially **chosen** by him and to be looked upon as **precious** indeed. [5]As for yourselves, being, as it were, stones which live and breathe, let yourselves be built up into a spiritual temple, so as to become a holy priesthood offering up spiritual sacrifices which, through Jesus Christ, are made most acceptable to God. [6]And it is because of all this that the following words are to be found in scripture: *h*'**Look,** how I am laying **in Zion a choice stone, a precious cornerstone. And he who rests his faith in it will indeed not suffer disappointment.'** [7]This stone, then, is a thing held in honour by you who have faith, while what it signifies to those who have no faith is this: *i***the very stone which the builders rejected as unworthy has become the cornerstone.** [8]Moreover, it has been found to be a *j***stone causing men to stumble, a rock which will make them fall.** It is those who repudiate God's message who stumble; that, indeed, is their appointed lot. [9]You, however, are a *k***nation specially chosen, a royal priesthood, a people consecrated to God and claimed by him as his own, so that you should proclaim the excellencies of him** who called you out of darkness into his wonderful light. [10]There was a time when you were *l***not a people;** now you are **God's people.** Once you were **outside the scope of his mercy.** Now, however, **mercy has been granted to you.**

[11]Dearly-loved ones, I would appeal to you that, since you have *m***no permanent home on earth and live here as mere strangers,** you should keep away from those appetites which originate in the flesh-bound part of our nature. For these are ever at war with the true human soul. [12]Let the lives you lead among the Gentiles be wholly free from blame, so that, when they observe how noble your deeds are—and this precisely with regard to those things which now make them malign you as evildoers—they may come to a different opinion, and give praise to God on the *n***day** when he comes to hold his **assize.**

[13]Render obedience to every institution duly established, and act

---

*f*Ps 34:8 *g*Is 28:16 LXX; Ps 118:22 *h*Is 28:16 LXX *i*Ps 118:22 *j*Is 8:14f *k*Is 43:20f; Ex 19:6; 23:22 LXX *l*Hos 1:6.9; 2.1.23 *m*Ps 39:12 *n*Is 10:3

in this way for the Lord's sake. Submit yourselves to the king as the one most highly placed, [14]and to those who are governors because they have been commissioned by the Lord to punish evildoers and to bestow praise upon those who have done well. [15]For this is God's intention, as regards the men in question, that, doing what is right, they should silence the ignorant talk of foolish men.

[16]As for your conduct, let it be that of free men, not that of men to whom freedom is nothing more than a cloak for their own malicious disposition. Be nobody's servants but God's. [17]Pay honour to everyone; hold the brotherhood dear; [o]**stand in awe of God; honour the king.**

[18]You who are slaves must hold your masters in the highest regard. Act in this way not only towards the masters who treat you with kindness, but also towards those who deal with you harshly. [19]For it is a thing most gratefully acknowledged if a man, because God is in his thoughts, bears the pain of undeserved suffering. [20]And indeed, if a man has done wrong, and then, when a beating is inflicted on him, bears it with fortitude, what credit is that to him? But if, after doing what is right he finds himself enduring sufferings, and endures them with fortitude, this is a thing most acceptable in the sight of God. [21]This, indeed, was the goal which was set before you when you received your summons. For Christ, too, suffered, and did so for your sakes, leaving you a model for imitation: you were to follow in his footsteps. [22][p]**He never committed** a sin, **nor was any guile to be found in any of his utterances.** [23]When he was reviled, he did not revile in return. When he suffered, he uttered no threats but committed himself to him who judges in justice. [24]In his own body [q]**he carried our sins** up to the cross, so that, our sins having been done away with, we should spend our lives in the pursuit of righteousness. [r]**His wounds were the means through which we received healing.** [25]There was a time when you were [s]**like sheep who had lost their way.** But now you have turned to him who is the shepherd and guardian of your souls.

3   You who are wives must act in a similar way, submitting yourselves to the authority of your husbands, so that if any among them reject God's word and disbelieve it, they may be won over, without a word being spoken, [2]simply by observing the purity and respectfulness of their wives' conduct. [3]The beauty to be found in you ought not to reside in any outward adornment—the braiding of the hair, the putting on of golden trinkets, or the dresses which you wear. [4]No, it

[o]Pr 24:21   [p]Is 53:9   [q]Is 53:4.12.5   [r]Is 53:5   [s]Is 53:6

ought to lie in what are hidden features of the human being which have their dwelling place in the heart, in a possession which can never be lost, that of a gentle and tranquil spirit. And this indeed is a treasure beyond price in the eyes of God. [5]It was thus that the holy women of olden times used to adorn themselves, those who reposed all their hopes in God and rendered obedience to their husbands. [6]Call to mind how obedient Sarah was to Abraham, and how [t]**she referred to him** as her **master.** And it is Sarah's children that you have now become, provided you lead honest lives, refusing to allow yourselves to be [u]**intimidated** by anything.

[7]In the same way, you who are husbands, in sharing your lives with your wives, must treat them in a manner which accords with true knowledge; bestow all due honour to woman as a weaker sex than your own, while being aware at the same time that God's life-giving grace is a possession you both share, and that your prayers must not suffer interruption.

[8]To sum up: be one in thought and feeling, each and every one of you. Be filled with brotherly love, be compassionate, be humbleminded. [9]Do not repay injury with injury or abuse with abuse. On the contrary, pay back with a blessing. For if the call has come to you, that was so that you should become sharers of a blessing. [10]As scripture says, [v]**Whoever has a desire to lead a life he can enjoy and to see happy days, let him restrain his tongue from speaking evil and his lips from uttering deceit. [11]Let him turn away from that which is evil, and let him do only that which is good. Let him strive for peace and be in pursuit of it. [12]For the eyes of the Lord look upon the upright with favour, and his ears are attentive to their pleading, while, as regards those who do evil things, they have the Lord's countenance frowning upon them.'**

[13]For who can seriously harm you so long as your ambitions are inspired only by that which is good? [14]And even though you should have to undergo suffering for the cause of uprightness, you may rightly count yourselves blessed. [w]**Do not allow yourselves to become frightened by their threats; neither become confused in your own minds.** [15]On the contrary, you must **enthrone** Christ as **Lord** in your hearts, being ready at all times, whenever you are asked by anyone to give an account of the hope which you cherish, to rise up in its defence. [16]Your manner, however, should be considerate and respectful, and you should keep your conscience free from guilt, so that when you are made the victims of calumny, grievous disappointment should be suffered by those who defame the holy lives which you lead as men united to Christ. [17]It is better, should that be God's will, to endure suf-

[t]Gn 18:12 LXX   [u]Pr 3:25   [v]Ps 34:12-16   [w]Is 8:12f

fering for well-doing than for doing wrong. [18] After all, Christ himself went to his death, paying a ransom once and for all to atone for our sins, he the just on behalf of the unjust; and he did so in order to bring us into God's presence.

In his mortal nature he was put to death, but in respect of his spirit, he had new life given to him. [19] And it was indeed by virtue of his spirit that he went on his way preaching to the spirits kept captive in the world below, [20] the same as had refused obedience at the time when God in his patience still held back his hand, at the time of Noah and of the building of the ark. This ark, in which only a small number of persons, eight in all, found refuge as they passed through the waters, [21] prefigured the baptism which is now our means of securing salvation, this baptism of ours not being the removal of any outward defilement, but, in truth, an appeal to God proceeding from an untroubled conscience, an appeal made in reliance on the resurrection of Jesus Christ, [22] who, having entered heaven, is now *at the right hand of God*, all the angelic authorities and powers having declared their submission to him.

4　Since Christ endured bodily suffering, it is your duty to equip yourselves with the same disposition as he had, seeing that, if a man be ready to face bodily suffering, this means that he has parted company with sin, [2] and that he will spend the rest of his life ruled not by human appetites but by the will of God. [3] And indeed, ample time was spent by you in the past in doing what the Gentiles would have you do, following a course of debauchery and of inordinate desires, being given over to drunken bouts, to revels, to carousals, and to wanton idolatries. [4] In view of all this, people are greatly surprised that you are no longer prepared to act as they do, rushing along recklessly and pouring out their profligacies. And so it comes about that they take to vilifying you. [5] However, they will have to render their account to him who stands ready to pronounce judgment on both the living and the dead. [6] Moreover, if the gospel was also proclaimed to the dead, its purpose was that, while receiving their judgment in respect of the bodily aspect of their being, as is the fate of all mankind, they should yet, in respect of their spirit, live on, fashioning themselves after the divine life.

[7] The end of all things is at hand. Learn to be reasonable and soberminded, this being the frame of mind which will help you with your prayers. [8] Above all, keep the love you bear to one another at the highest pitch, for *ylove cancels out* a host of **sins**. [9] Behave hospitably

towards one another, and let there be no grumbling. ¹⁰Whatever precious gift each of you may have received, you must use it in serving one another, as befits those who are competent stewards of a God who bestows his gifts in so lavish a manner. ¹¹One man preaches: let him keep in mind that it is God's utterances that he is dealing with. Another performs acts of mercy: let him keep in mind that it is God who supplies him with whatever strength he possesses. And the ultimate goal of it all is that God may be glorified in all things. To him all glory and strength belongs for ever and ever. Amen.

¹²Dearly-loved ones, do not let it be a matter of surprise to you, as though something unheard of were coming upon you, that you should find yourselves beset by so fiery an ordeal, meant to put you to the test. ¹³On the contrary, inasmuch as you are sharers in Christ's sufferings, let this be to you a matter for rejoicing, so that, when Christ's glory stands revealed, you may likewise rejoice and be full of exultation. ¹⁴If people revile you for your allegiance to Christ's cause, you are fortunate, for the truth is that, if such be the case, you have ᶻ**resting** upon you all that pertains to glory, in fact, the very **Spirit of God.** ¹⁵May it never happen that any of you has to endure suffering because he is a murderer, a thief, a criminal, or an informer. ¹⁶But if there be one who has to suffer for being a Christian, he has no need to be ashamed of it. On the contrary, he should, by virtue of invoking Christ's name, give glory to God.

¹⁷The time has come for God's judgment to ᵃ**start,** and to **make a beginning with** God's own household. But then, if it makes a beginning with you, what will be the fate of those who reject God's Good News? ¹⁸Moreover, if the ᵇ**upright can obtain their salvation only with difficulty, what will be the position of the impious and sinful?** ¹⁹So, then, let those who suffer because it is God's will that they should do so commend their souls to their Creator, who will be true to his word; and let them devote their lives to doing good.

5 Now I appeal to those among you who hold the position of elders, since I am their fellow elder, as well as a witness of the sufferings of Christ, and, moreover, am to be a sharer of the splendour which is to be revealed. ²Be shepherds of God's flock in whose midst you are; and in performing this task you must not act under compulsion but of your own free will, as God would have it, not for sordid gain but most eagerly, ³not as men lording it over their charges but as men who become models of imitation for their flock. And if this is the way in which you proceed, ⁴then at the time when the shepherd who is set

ᶻIs 11:2   ᵃEzk 9:6; Jr 25:29   ᵇPr 11:31 LXX

over all other shepherds manifests himself, you will receive your reward: the never-fading garland which is the sign of glory.

⁵In the same way you, the younger men, ought to submit yourselves. Indeed, all of you must, in your dealings with one another, wrap yourselves in the garment of humility. As scripture has it, *c*'**God, while setting his face against the arrogant, bestows his favour upon the humble.**'

⁶Bow down, then, beneath God's mighty hand, and he will lift you up at the appointed time. ⁷*d***Cast** all your **anxieties** upon him, because he is concerned about you.

⁸Be sober-minded, be watchful; for your enemy, the devil, roams about like a *e*roaring lion, looking for a victim to devour. ⁹You, however, who are strong in faith must offer resistance to him, while being aware that the same sufferings as you are enduring are laid upon the brotherhood all over the world. ¹⁰And God, the source of all grace, who has summoned you to his side, so that, after a brief time of suffering, you may be granted entry into his eternal realm of glory, will set you to rights, give you steadiness and strength, and establish you securely. ¹¹May all power be assigned to him for ever and ever. Amen.

¹²I have written you a brief account, by the hand of Silvanus, who, as I reckon, is one of the brothers who are deserving of all trust. At the same time I would insist and bear testimony that the grace in which you are so firmly established is indeed the true grace of God.

¹³Greetings from her who dwells in Babylon* and who has been chosen by God, just as you have; and greetings also from Mark, who is a son to me. ¹⁴Greet one another with the kiss of love.

Peace to you all who belong to Christ.

---

*c*Pr 3:34 LXX; [Job 22:29]   *d*Ps 55:22   *e*[Ps 22:13]

* [Possibly a nickname for Rome.]

THE SECOND LETTER OF PETER

1 Symeon Peter, a servant and apostle of Jesus Christ, sends his greetings to those who have been granted the privilege of being sharers with us in the same precious faith, all this being due to the righteousness shown forth by Jesus Christ, by him who is our God and our Saviour. ²Grace and peace be yours in ever greater measure, as you gain fuller knowledge of God and of Jesus our Lord.

³His divine power has bestowed upon us everything that makes for a true life and for devotedness, precisely the things which we have had granted to us through the knowledge we possess of him who, by virtue of his majesty and excellence, has sent out his summons to us. ⁴And it is through these things that he has made us promises of true worth and greatness, the purpose of it all being that by their means you should come to be partakers of the very nature of God, you, the men who have succeeded in escaping from the corruption which has infected the world through the lustful passions which it cherishes.

⁵And this is why you, for your part, must bring the greatest efforts into play, crowning your faith with virtue, your virtue with discernment, ⁶your discernment with self-control, your self-control with fortitude, your fortitude with godliness, ⁷your godliness with brotherly affection, and your brotherly affection with love.

⁸For if you have these excellent qualities, and they are present with you in ever greater abundance, the last thing which will happen is that they will make you idle and useless when it comes to your acquiring a thorough knowledge of our Lord Jesus Christ. ⁹And indeed, it is the one who is devoid of these excellent qualities who is the one having defective eyesight, to the point of being wholly deprived of sight, forgetful as he is of the time when he was purged of his former sins. ¹⁰In view of all this, my brothers, it is all the more essential that you should do your utmost to make God's call to you, and his choice of you, into something that is firmly established. For in that case you will find yourselves with ample support, ¹¹and there will be granted to you entry into the eternal kingdom of our Lord and Saviour Jesus Christ.

[12]In consideration of all this, my purpose will ever be to remind you of these things, notwithstanding the fact that you know them already, and that you are firmly rooted in the teaching of the truth which has reached you. [13]Still, it seems to me only right that, so long as I remain in this impermanent dwelling of mine, I should keep stirring you up by way of a reminder, [14]while I know full well that my leave-taking from it will not long be delayed. Indeed, our Lord Jesus Christ has made it plain to me that it must be so. [15]Moreover, I shall take great pains to make certain that, even after my departure, you will at all times have the opportunity of having these things called to mind.

[16]After all, if we told you about the power possessed by our Lord Jesus Christ and his future return, our procedure was not that we followed up artfully designed fables. On the contrary, we were placing reliance on the fact that we ourselves had become eyewitnesses of his majesty. [17]Such honour, such glory was bestowed upon him by God the Father that a voice, issuing from the very presence of the divine majesty, was borne on to him, exclaiming, 'This is [a]**my Son**, my **dearly-loved one; it is he on whom my favour rests**'! [18]And this is the very voice we ourselves heard borne forth from heaven at the time when we were in his company on the holy mountain.

[19]Moreover, we possess the message of the prophets as something altogether reliable, and you yourselves will do well to attend to it, while looking upon it as a lamp, as it were, which shines forth in a gloomy place until the day breaks and the morning star rises to illumine our minds.

[20]But first take note of this. There is no prophecy in scripture which should be considered a matter of private interpretation. [21]For never at any time was it man's initiative that gave rise to prophecy. Men gave it utterance, but they were impelled by the Holy Spirit, and what they said had its source in God.

2   But there were other men, the false prophets, who made their appearance among the people of God. And in the same way teachers of falsehoods will be found in your midst; they will be introducing wayward opinions which can lead to nothing but ruin, disowning the very master to whom they owe their redemption. And so it will happen that they bring swift ruin upon themselves. [2]Moreover, there will be many ready to follow them, embracing their views, which are contrary to all decency, and it is through them that [b]**disrepute will be brought** on that way which alone leads to the truth. [3]They will seek

[a]Ps 2:7; Is 42:1   [b]Is 52:5

to make you their property, their means of achieving this being their deceitful utterances which have their root simply in their greed.

However, their condemnation, decreed from old, will not remain idle, and their doom makes its way unrestingly towards them. [4]For God did not even spare the angels when they made themselves guilty of sin. On the contrary, he consigned them to murky pits in the nethermost world, and there they were kept to await their sentence. [5]He did not spare the world he had first made [c](only Noah, that herald of an upright life, he preserved, along with seven others), at the time when he brought the deluge upon the world of impious men. [6]The cities of [d]Sodom and Gomorrah he condemned to utter ruin, reducing them to ashes, so as to set a warning example to those who might be tempted to commit impious deeds in future days. [7]Lot, on the other hand, he rescued, that upright man who found himself greatly oppressed in mind by the profligate ways in which his neighbours, who acknowledged no law, conducted themselves. [8]For that seeker after righteousness, who lived in their midst, felt greatly tortured day by day in his upright soul, as he became witness, by both sight and ear, to the lawless deeds which they perpetrated. [9]The Lord knows full well how to rescue the godly out of their trials, while keeping the wicked in readiness, that they might receive their punishment on the Day of Judgment.

[10]He will deal particularly severely with those who, in obedience to their carnal nature, conduct themselves in such a way as to be ruled by their appetite for a corrupt life. They have nothing but contempt for authority, and, headstrong and audacious as they are, they are not afraid to shower blasphemies on celestial beings, [11]while angels, with all their superior strength and might, refrain from offering insults to them in seeking to obtain from the Lord that he should pronounce a defaming judgment against them.

[12]These men are like irrational animals, driven on by their natural instincts, destined to be caught and to perish, certain to destroy themselves by their own work of destruction, [13]and suffering injury for the injury they have inflicted. Their notion of pleasure is that they should take part in revels in broad daylight. What a stain they are, what disfigurement, as they feast with you at table, feeding on their own deceptions!

[14]They have eyes that ever look for an occasion for adultery, and they give themselves over unceasingly to committing sinful deeds. They throw out a bait for the catching of those whose souls have no steadiness about them. They have minds trained for greediness. They are the offspring of a curse. [15]They have left the straight path and have

[c][Gn 8:18]   [d][Gn 19:24f]

wandered off to follow the path of *e*Balaam son of Beor, the man who did not have the least scruple in taking payment as a recompense for doing wrong. 16However, he was rebuked and told to desist from his perversity when the dumb beast of burden spoke with a human voice to put a stop to the insane conduct of the prophet.

17These men are springs which yield no water, misty clouds chased away by a storm, and the place reserved for them is darkness of the deepest hue. 18Their utterances are full of bombast and futility, and carnal appetites and debaucheries are to them a bait for the catching of those who have but lately escaped from the clutches of those who are bent on deceiving others in whatever they do. 19The promise they make to these people is that they will obtain their freedom, while in fact they are slaves, with corruption as their master. And indeed, if anyone allows himself to succumb to any thing, he is its slave. 20For if, having escaped from the corrupting influences of the world by virtue of gaining knowledge of our Lord and Saviour, Jesus Christ, they then find themselves once again enmeshed in these influences and ruled by them, that only goes to show that their *f*condition is, in fact, worse than it was at first. 21How much better it would have been for them never to have known the way which leads to righteousness than, having discovered it, to turn back and abandon the holy command once handed down to them. 22What has befallen them confirms the truth of the proverb, *g*'**The dog returns to its own vomit**', as well as that of another: 'The sow, once washed, rolls about in the mud again.'

3 　　This, my well-loved friends, is already the second letter I am addressing to you, my purpose in both of them being to stir you up by way of a reminder, so that, freed from any trace of insincerity, 2you may recall in your minds the predictions made in times past by God's holy prophets, and remind yourselves, too, of the command laid down by the Lord and Saviour at the hands of his apostles.

3Now the first thing you must take note of is this. During the days of the end mockers will appear with their mocking, men whose conduct will be wholly ruled by their appetites. 4And this is what they will say. "What can have become of that promised return of his? After all, ever since our fathers have been laid to their rest, everything has remained as it always has been from the beginning of the world."

5However, there is one thing which has escaped the notice of those who would be self-assertive in this manner, namely, that there were heavens a long, long time ago, and that there was also an earth, brought into being by God's word of command, with water for its

e[Nm 22:28-33; Dt 23:5; Neh 13:2] 　*f*[Ezk 3:20] 　*g*Pr 26:11

origin and water for its frame, [6]water likewise being the means by which the world, as it then was, met with destruction, when it was enveloped by floods at the time of the deluge. [7]As for the present heaven and the present earth, they have, in virtue of the same word of command, been saved up to be consumed by flames, and have been kept in being until the day comes when the godless will be judged and suffer destruction.

[8]However, my well-loved friends, there is one thing you must ever be mindful of, that with the Lord a day can mean a thousand years, and a [h]**thousand years** are **like one day.** [9]The Lord is by no means [i]tardy in fulfilling his promise, in the sense in which certain people understand tardiness. No, what is really happening is that he exhibits the patience he has with us, his intention being that there should be enough time that[j]none should perish, but that there should be enough time for everyone to be brought to a change of heart.

[10]But the Day of the Lord will come, and when it comes, it will be upon us like a thief; and then the heavens will vanish away with a great rushing sound; the elements, all aflame, will dissolve into nothingness, no trace being left of the earth or of anything contained in it.

[11]Since all things are destined to suffer annihilation in this way, it is clear what sort of people we ought to be, that our conduct should be one conforming to holiness, and that devotion to God should determine us in whatever we do. [12]We should look eagerly for the coming of the Day of God, and play our part in the hastening on of that day on which the heavens will be burned up and annihilated, and the elements, all aflame, will be melting away. [13]However, what we may expect, in accordance with the promise which God has made, is this, that there will be [k]**new heavens** and a **new earth,** righteousness having its dwelling place in them.

[14]So then, my dearly-loved ones, with such a prospect to look forward to, you must do your utmost to be found without blemish, innocent, and at peace in the sight of God. [15]Moreover, look upon our Lord's patience as a means of obtaining your salvation, a matter concerning which Paul, that brother so dear to my heart, has also written to you, doing so by virtue of the special wisdom which he has had bestowed upon him. This is the subject with which he dealt in the letter you had from him, [16]as he does in all his other letters, some of the points he makes being somewhat hard to grasp, with the result that the ignorant and unsteady are led to distort what he says, just as they distort the rest of scripture, proceeding in this way to their own undoing.

[17]But as for yourselves, dearly-loved ones, you are forewarned.

[h]Ps 90:4   [i][Hab 2:3]   [j][Ezk 18:23]   [k]Is 65:17; 66:22

You must see to it that you are not led astray by the illusory beliefs of these unprincipled men, thus letting your native steadiness fall by the wayside. [18]No, your aim must be that the grace bestowed on you by our Lord and Saviour Jesus Christ, and the knowledge you have of him, should ever increase. May all the glory be his, now and to the Day of Eternity.

THE FIRST LETTER OF JOHN

1 That which existed from the very beginning: we have heard it; we have seen it with our own eyes; we have fixed our gaze upon it; our very hands have touched it. The life-giving word is our subject. ²It manifested itself, and we have seen it and bear witness to it. What we are making known to you is the life which is eternal, the life which was first by the Father's side and then manifested itself to us. ³That which we ourselves have seen and heard we are making known to you as well, so that you, too, may share in our fellowship, this fellowship being one which we have with the Father and with his Son, Jesus Christ. ⁴Moreover, if we are writing these things to you, this is because of our desire that the joy of all of us should attain to its full measure.

⁵The message from him which has reached us, and which we are making known to you, is that God is light, no admixture of darkness being found in him. ⁶If we maintain that we are in fellowship with him, while yet our lives are conducted in the sphere of darkness, this simply means that we are telling a falsehood and that we do not act as the truth would have us act. ⁷On the other hand, if we lead our lives in the sphere of light, as he himself dwells in light, we have fellowship with one another, and the result will be this, that the blood of his Son, Jesus Christ, makes us clean of all sin.

⁸If we assert that no sin is to be found in us, we should be deceiving ourselves, truth being a stranger to us. ⁹But if we confess our sins, he is the one to be true to his word and to act justly, the result being his forgiving our sins and making us clean of all unrighteousness. ¹⁰In maintaining that no sin has ever been committed by us, we are making him out to be a liar, and this would simply mean that no room for his message was to be found in our hearts.

2 Little children of mine, in writing to you in this manner, my purpose is to keep you clear of sin. Meanwhile, even though someone should fall into sin, we have an intercessor, Jesus Christ the Righteous

One, who stands by our side pleading our cause with the Father. [2]He, in his own person, is the sin-offering atoning for our sins—in fact, not only for our sins but for the sins of the whole world. [3]And this is the test through which we can know for certain that we have come to know him truly, that we keep the commandments he has laid down. [4]Should there be a man who maintains that he has come to know him, while yet he disobeys his commandments, that man is a liar, and no truth is to be found in him. [5]On the other hand, if there be a man who is truly obedient to his word of command, it follows that in such a man the divine love has been brought to the highest perfection. This is how we can know that we have our being in him. [6]He who makes the claim that he dwells in him is under obligation to conduct his life in the very same manner as Christ conducted his.

[7]Dearly-loved ones, the commandment of which I am writing to you is not a new commandment; it is an old commandment which you had given you from the first. That old commandment is the very message which reached your ears. [8]And yet, it is a new commandment which I am writing to you about, a commandment which had its truth confirmed in him as well as in yourselves. And what it signifies is this, that darkness is passing away and that the light which is truly light already shines.

[9]He who maintains that the sphere in which he moves is that of the light, while at the same time he feels hatred for his brother, does in fact still move in the sphere of darkness. [10]It is the man who loves his brother who has the light for his dwelling place, and with such a one there is no danger that he might stumble. [11]The man who feels hatred for his brother, on the other hand, dwells and moves in darkness, and has no knowledge of where he is going. Darkness has fallen and has blinded his eyes.

[12]If I am writing to you, dear children, this is because you have had your sins forgiven you for his name's sake. [13]If I am writing to you, fathers, it is because you have come to the true knowledge of him who existed from the very beginning. If I am writing to you, young men, that is because you have already gained mastery over the evil one. I have been writing to you, dear children, because you have come to have knowledge of the Father. [14]I have been writing to you, fathers, because you have come to have knowledge of him who existed from the very beginning. I have been writing to you, young men, because you are strong, because God's word has made its home within you, and because you have already gained mastery over the evil one.

[15]You must have no love for the world or for anything in the world. And indeed, if anyone loves the world, he cannot but be a stranger to the love which is found in the Father, [16]since whatever has its home

in the world, whether it be the appetites deriving from our carnal nature, or the lustful eye, or pride in one's possessions, has an existence the origin of which is to be traced not to the Father but to this present world. 17 And as for the world, it is passing away, and all the desires bound up with it. But he who carries out the will of God continues the same for ever and ever.

18 My children, the last hour is upon us. You were told that the Antichrist must needs come, and now several antichrists have in fact already appeared—and indeed, this is how we know that the last hour has arrived. 19 True enough, it was from our midst that these men went forth on their way. Yet, for all that, they did not belong to us. Had they done so, they would have remained by our side. Indeed, if things went the way they did, this was to make it evident that it is not everybody that belongs to our company.

20 As for yourselves, you have had an anointing bestowed upon you by the Holy One, with the result that each one of you has come to have knowledge. 21 Indeed, I have written to you not because you did not know the truth, but because you did know it, and because you are aware likewise that the truth can never give birth to a lie.

22 Who, then, is the arch-liar but he who denies that Jesus is the Christ? Indeed, anyone who would argue thus is the very Antichrist. He who denies the Father denies the Son. 23 Whoever denies the Son has no grasp of the Father, while he who acknowledges the Son has at the same time a grasp of the Father. 24 As for yourselves, let that which you were told at the very beginning remain within your hearts. For if that which you heard at the outset still dwells within you, you will dwell in the Son and also in the Father. 25 And this is the promise which he himself made us, that everlasting life is to be ours.

26 These are the things I have written to you, bearing in mind those who are intent on deceiving you. 27 As for yourselves, the anointing which you have received remains with you, and there is no need for you to go to any other teacher. On the contrary, just as it is true that the anointing you have received from him is capable of serving as your teacher in everything, and true likewise that it embodies the truth, with no admixture of falsehood, and, moreover, that it is by him that you have been taught, so it is your duty to make him your dwelling place.

28 Even now, dear children, you must make him your dwelling place, so that, when he manifests himself, we can approach him with boldness, there being no need to shrink away from him in shame on the day of his coming again. 29 If you are aware that it is he who is the Righteous One, you will know also that anyone who does what is righteous is in fact his offspring.

3 Consider the nature of the love which God the Father has displayed towards us. So great indeed it was that we are rightly spoken of as God's children! And that in fact is what we are! Moreover, if the world does not acknowledge us, the reason is that it did not acknowledge him either. ²Dearly-loved ones, it is true that we are God's children even at the present time. Still, what we shall be hereafter has as yet not been disclosed. But one thing we do know, that when the time comes for him to reveal himself, we shall be found to be like him, for we shall see him as he really is. ³Moreover, anyone having this hope before his eyes is bound to set out to purify himself, even as Christ is pure.

⁴Whoever commits a sin is at the same time a lawbreaker. In fact, sin is nothing else than a breaking of the law. ⁵Moreover, you know that, if Christ manifested himself, this was so that he should be enabled to bring sin to nought, and you know likewise that no sin whatever is to be found in him. ⁶No one who has him for his dwelling place ever commits a sin. He who sins, on the other hand, has in fact never set eyes on him or come to know him in any way.

⁷Do not allow yourselves to be misled, my children. It is the man who is in pursuit of righteousness who is righteous in the sense in which Christ is righteous, ⁸while the sinful man is an offspring of the devil, the devil having been a sinner from the very beginning. Moreover, if the Son of God revealed himself, he did so with this end in view, that he should be able to destroy the works of the devil.

⁹No one who is God's offspring commits a sin, because he has the seed of the divine remaining within him. Indeed, he is incapable of sinning, on the ground that it is as God's offspring that he has come into being. ¹⁰And this is how the children of God and those of the devil are clearly distinguished from one another. No one who in what he does ignores the claims of righteousness can trace his origin to God, that is to say, no man who is devoid of love towards his brother. ¹¹For the message we had proclaimed to us from the beginning was this, that we were to love one another. ¹²We were to be the opposite of what Cain was, the man who, being an offspring of the evil one, slaughtered his brother. And for what reason did he slaughter him? It was that his own actions were evil, while those of his brother were the outcome of his righteousness.

¹³Do not be surprised, my brothers, if the world hates you. ¹⁴We know that we have passed out of the sphere of death and have entered that of life, being certain of this because we love the brothers; whereas anyone who is devoid of love remains within the realm of death. ¹⁵Whoever hates his brother is a manslayer, and we are indeed aware that no manslayer can have eternal life bestowed upon him as a per-

manent possession. [16] We have come to know what love really is, and have done so by way of grasping that Christ laid down his life on our behalf. And so we in turn are in duty bound to lay down our lives on behalf of our brothers. [a][17] Further, if a man has a sufficiency of worldly goods, and yet, on encountering a brother who is in want, withholds all feelings of compassion for him, how can it be said that the divine love still retains possession of his heart?

[18] My children, do not let our love be one that is merely a matter of words and of utterances of the tongue. No, let it be a love which issues in action and is in conformity with the truth. [19] This is the way in which we can come to know for certain that we belong to the realm of the truth, and that we are entitled to set our minds at rest in God's sight. [20] We must come to realize that, even though our minds should still raise accusations against us, God can see further than our minds can, and that nothing is unknown to him.

[21] If, on the other hand, my dear friends, the position be that we find nothing in our minds to raise any accusation against ourselves, then we can approach God with full confidence, [22] receiving from him whatever we ask for. It could not be otherwise, seeing that we keep his commandments and never do anything but what finds acceptance in his sight. [23] And what we have been commanded to do is this, that we should place all our confidence in the name of his Son Jesus Christ, and that we should love one another, in obedience to the commandment laid down by him.

[24] Moreover, whoever keeps his commandments dwells in God, and God dwells within him. And the instrument by which we can know for certain that God dwells within us is his Spirit, which he has bestowed upon us.

4 Dear friends, you must not make the mistake of placing confidence in every spiritual utterance. On the contrary, you should test the various spirits to find out whether or not they have their source in God. This is necessary because many false prophets have gone forth into the world. [2] The proper way of recognizing the Spirit of God is this. Every spirit which acknowledges Jesus Christ as having made his appearance in bodily form is a spirit that has its source in God, [3] while every spirit which disowns Jesus is one that does not have God for its source. This, indeed, is the course taken by the Antichrist, of whom you have been told that he was to make his appearance. And here he is in the world already.

[4] Yet as for yourselves, my dear children, you derive your origin

[a][Dt 15:7.11]

from God. And if you have gained the mastery over these false prophets, that is because the power at work within you is greater than that possessed by him whose field of operation is in this world. 5 They themselves belong to the world, and that is why their utterances bear the mark of having their home in the world, and why the world listens to them. 6 We, on the other hand, belong to God, and so it is that those to whom God is properly known listen to us, while those who do not belong to God refuse to listen. It is in this way, then, that we are enabled to distinguish between the spirit of truth and the spirit of falsehood.

7 Dear friends, let us love one another, seeing that love has its source in God, and that anybody who loves is God's offspring and has true knowledge of him. 8 He who is devoid of love, on the other hand, has never come to know God at all, because God is love. 9 Moreover, this was the way in which God's love toward us was manifested, that he sent his only Son into the world, so that through him we should have life given to us. 10 And the essential nature of such love lies in this: not that we came to love God, but that he, loving us, sent forth his Son, that he might be the means of expiating our sins. 11 Dear friends, if God has borne such love to us, it is incumbent on us that we, too, should love one another. 12 No one has ever seen God. And yet, if we love one another, God does in fact dwell within us, and his love has been brought to perfection in our hearts.

13 If we know for certain that we dwell in him, and that he dwells in us, the reason is this—that he has imparted to us a portion of his Spirit. 14 Besides, there is one circumstance about which we have the assurance of our own eyes, and are thus willing to bear testimony to it, namely, that the Father has sent forth his Son to be Saviour of the world. 15 And so, if anyone acknowledges that Jesus is the Son of God, he in fact has God dwelling in him, and he himself dwells in God. 16 Moreover, we ourselves have come to know, and to have faith in, the love which God displays towards us.

God is love, and he to whom love is the sphere within which he dwells, dwells in God, and God dwells in him. 17 As for the way in which love is in our case brought to its fullest expression, this shows itself in our being entitled to be filled with confidence on the Day of Judgment, and such a confidence we can have on the ground that even in this world we are like-minded with him. 18 No admixture of fear is to be found in love. On the contrary, perfect love banishes all fear, and this must be so because, wherever there is fear, the notion of punishment is bound up with it, the conclusion to be drawn from this being that he who is still afraid has as yet not attained to love in its perfection. 19 If we love God, it is because he loved us first. 20 But should someone say that he loves God, while yet hating his brother, he is nothing but a liar. And indeed, if he has no love for his brother, whom he has seen, there is no way in which he can love God, whom he has not seen. [21]Besides, there is this commandment enjoined upon us by himself, that he who loves God must also love his brother.

5 Whoever believes that Jesus is the Christ has God for his parent; moreover, to love the parent means to love the child that owes his existence to him. [2]Besides, there is only one way in which we can know for certain that we love God's children, namely, if we love God and do what he has commanded us to do. [3]And indeed, this is what loving God consists in, that we should keep his commandments. *b*Now these commandments are not difficult to fulfil— [4]and that is because anyone who has God for his parent is set on gaining victory over this present world, while, on the other hand, it is our faith which signifies that the victory over the world is being won. [5]Who, indeed, can be a victor over the world but he who believes that Jesus is the Son of God? [6]It was he, Jesus Christ, whose coming was borne witness to by water and blood; not with water only, but with water and blood. [7]The Spirit likewise adds its testimony, and it can be relied on because the Spirit is in fact the embodiment of truth. [8]And so it is that there are three which bear testimony, the Spirit, the water, and the blood, all three being in complete agreement. [9]We willingly accept human testimony, but surely divine testimony is much weightier. Moreover, this is what God's testimony amounts to: he has borne testimony in behalf of his Son. [10]He who believes in the Son of God has this testimony in his very heart, but he who disbelieves God makes him out to be a liar, since he refuses to trust the testimony which God has borne concerning his Son. [11]And that testimony consists precisely in this: that God has bestowed eternal life upon us, and that that life is to be found in his Son. [12]Anyone who has a grasp of the Son has a grasp also of that life, while anyone to whom the Son of God is something he cannot grasp will also find the life in question beyond his grasp.

[13]I am writing these things to you to make you comprehend that everlasting life has been granted to you, to you who have come to rest your faith in the name of the Son of God and all it stands for. [14]As for the confidence with which we approach God, we have it because we are aware that, if we ask him for anything, and do so conformably to his will, he will lend his ear to us. [15]And knowing as we do that, whatever we ask, he will listen to us, we know at the same time that we have already been granted that which we asked of him.

b[Dt 30:11]

[16]Should anyone see his brother committing a sin which is not a deadly sin, he should pray on his behalf, and then the other shall have life granted to him. I am not here thinking of those who fall into deadly sin, and the point I am making is not that prayer should be offered on behalf of a sin of that sort. [17]Whenever an unrighteous action is performed, sin is indeed present, but this does not imply that there can be no sin except deadly sin.

[18]We know that no true child of God ever sins, this being so on the ground that he is under the protection of him who has God for his Father, and thus he cannot be touched by the evil one.

[19]We know that we have our origin in God, whereas the whole of this world is in bondage to the evil one. [20]Moreover, we are well aware that the Son of God has made his appearance, and has provided us with insight such as enables us to have knowledge of the true God. Indeed, our very existence is one having its dwelling place in the true God, and this by virtue of the fact that we dwell in his Son, Jesus Christ. It is he who is the true God, who is eternal life. [21]My children, be on your guard against gods, falsely so-called.

THE SECOND LETTER OF JOHN

The Elder sends his greetings to the august Lady specially chosen by God, and also to her children, whom I love in very truth. But not only I love her, but all those who have attained to knowledge of the truth. [2]And if we do love her, that is for the sake of the truth which is ever alive in us and which will remain with us to the very end. [3]Grace, mercy, and peace shall be our companions, coming as they do from Jesus Christ, the Father's Son, in a spirit of truthfulness and of love.

[4]On encountering some of those who are children of yours, I was overjoyed to find that in the conduct of their lives they were guided by the truth, in strict accordance with the commandment we have received from God the Father. [5]And now, august Lady, I have a request to lay before you. It is not as though we were enjoining a new commandment. No, what we are concerned with is the commandment we have had by our side from the very beginning. And this is what it says, that we are to love one another. [6]Moreover, the essence of love is that we should lead our lives in obedience to God's commandments. This is the very commandment of which you have heard from the beginning, that in the conduct of your lives you should be ruled by love.

[7]Keep all this in mind, for many deceivers have gone forth into the world, who refuse to acknowledge that Jesus Christ has appeared in bodily form. He who would argue thus is the arch-deceiver, the Antichrist. [8]Take the greatest care not to suffer the loss of all we have worked for, so that, instead, you may receive your [a]reward in full.

[9]If anyone is not satisfied to keep within the teaching about Christ, but goes beyond it, he is no longer in touch with God. He, on the other hand, who stands by the teaching concerning Christ is in touch with both the Father and the Son. [10]Should anyone come along bringing a different doctrine with him, you must not receive him into your house or bid him welcome in any other way. [11]For he who does bid him welcome becomes, by so doing, a sharer in his wicked deeds.

[12]Although I have many things to tell you, I do not wish to convey

[a][Rt 2:12 LXX]

them to you in black and white. Instead, I am hoping that I shall be able to visit you; then it will be possible to communicate with you by word of mouth, so that the joy which we feel will reach its fullest measure. [13]Greetings to you from the children of her who is your sister, the one chosen by God.

THE THIRD LETTER OF JOHN

The elder sends his greetings to the dearly-loved Gaius, the man whom I love in very truth.

2Dearly-loved one, my prayer is, above all, that all may go well with you and that you may be in good health, certain as I feel that everything goes well with your soul. 3I was greatly delighted when some of our fellow believers arrived here and bore witness to your loyalty to the truth, as indeed it is a fact that in your whole life you are guided by the truth. 4There is, I would have you know, no greater joy I can have than when I am told that it is the truth which guides the lives of my children.

5Dearly-loved one, you furnish convincing proof of your loyalty in everything you do on behalf of these fellow believers of ours, strangers as they are to you. 6They have indeed borne witness to your great kindness to them, and have done so in front of the congregation here; and you will do well if you give them their send-off in a manner worthy of God. 7If these men went forth into the world, it was in support of Christ's cause; at the same time, they refused to accept any help from the pagans. 8It is for us, then, to lend our assistance to men such as these, so that we, too, may play our part in supporting the truth.

9There is a message which I sent to the congregation. However, Diotrephes, who would seem to be determined to play a leading role, refuses to acknowledge our authority. 10And this being so, the course I shall adopt when I come to see you will be that I shall be bringing up the things which he does. For he speaks evil of us, accusing us in a frivolous manner; and not being satisfied with this, he not only refuses to receive these fellow believers of ours as guests, but over and above this he puts obstacles in the way of those who wish to receive them, and expels them from the congregation.

11Dearly-loved one, let the good, not the evil, serve you as your model. He who does good is a child of God; the evil-doer has never set eyes on God. 12Demetrius is well spoken of by everybody. Indeed, truth itself vouches for him. We, too, bear testimony on his behalf; and you know that this testimony of ours is in accordance with the truth.

[13]I have many things to write to you about, but I have no mind to convey them by resorting to paper and ink. [14]I am hoping to visit you in the near future; and then it will be possible for us to communicate with one another by word of mouth. [15]May peace be by your side. Your friends here send you their greetings. Convey greetings to our friends, to each of them by name.

THE LETTER OF JUDE

Jude, servant of Jesus Christ and brother of James, sends his greetings to those who are most dear in the eyes of God the Father, and who, after receiving the call, have been kept safe for the sake of Jesus Christ, to whom they belong. ²May mercy, peace, and love be by your side in ever-increasing measure.

³My dearly-loved ones, as one who is ever making the greatest efforts to address himself to you in writing about the salvation we all share, it has become necessary that I should be writing to you now, urging you to take your share in the strenuous fight on behalf of the faith which has been entrusted, once and for all, to those who have consecrated themselves to God.

⁴The present position is that certain fellows have wormed their way into our company, indeed, the very people whom scripture marked out long ages ago for the doom which they have in fact brought upon themselves. Impious men that they are, they have seen fit to pervert the life of grace which our God has bestowed upon them, turning it into a life of dissipation, while at the same time they have repudiated him who is our only Lord and Master, Jesus Christ.

⁵Now, even though you are men to whom everything has been made known once and for all, there are certain matters I would wish to put you in remembrance of. The Lord God, having first saved his people out of the hands of the Egyptians, none the less saw fit on a later occasion to destroy all those who had refused to put their trust in him. ⁶Moreover, there were angels who were not content to keep to the sphere of influence assigned to them but who abandoned their proper domain. And the way the Lord dealt with these was that he confined them to a dark place, binding them with everlasting chains, and reserving them to receive their judgment on the Great Day. ⁷Remember Sodom and Gomorrah, and with them their neighbouring cities, how they made themselves guilty of the same debauchery as the angels had, pursuing their unnatural lusts. And now they lie before our eyes, serving as a warning, and suffer the punishment of being consumed by an everlasting fire.

⁸However, in spite of it all, the conduct of these men is of precise-

ly the same nature. They give themselves over to idle dreams, and so it is that they defile their bodies, set all authority at nought, and pour abuse on glorious angelic beings. [9]As against this, the archangel [a]**Michael,** when he found himself engaged in controversy with the devil, arguing with him over the possession of Moses' body, did not presume to condemn him by way of having recourse to blasphemous language, and all he said was, [b]'**Let the Lord correct you.**' [10]Yet, as regards these fellows, they pour abuse on what they cannot understand, while things which they are capable of understanding—through an instinctive grasp, after the fashion of unreasoning animals—are the very things by which they are led to their ruin. [11]Woe betide them, seeing that they have chosen the path which Cain trod; that they rushed headlong into the very same error as Balaam fell into, for the sake of gain; and that they were destroyed because of their rebellious spirit, which was like that which prompted the doings of Korah.

[12]They are the men who, when you celebrate your love feasts, hold festival with you without the least compunction, although in truth they are nothing more than blots on your society. They are like clouds which yield no rain, carried away by the winds, like trees bare of fruit, standing there at the height of the autumn season. Dying not one death but two, they find themselves pulled up by the roots. [13]Like angry waves of the sea they cast up their own shameless deeds, just as though they were foam. They are like stars which have wandered from their course, and the place for ever reserved for them is blackest darkness.

[14]It was they whom Enoch, the seventh in descent from Adam, had in mind when he uttered these prophetic words: 'I have seen the Lord come with his myriads of angels [15]to call everyone to judgment, and to convict the impious of all the deeds of impiety which they have perpetrated and of all the callous words spoken by them against the Lord, impious and sinful men that they are.' [16]They are a set of grumblers, ever dissatisfied with their lot. In the conduct of their lives they are wholly led by their own appetites, and from their [c]**mouths** there ever proceeds **talk** which is nothing but **bombast.** Moreover, it is a policy of favouritism they resort to whenever that happens to suit their ends.

[17]But you, dearly-loved ones, must remind yourselves of the predictions made in times past by the apostles of our Lord Jesus Christ [18]when they spoke these warning words to you: 'At the time of the end mockers will appear who will lead their lives in obedience to their own impious appetites.'

[19]These are the sowers of dissension, persons to whom only animal

[a]Dn 10:13; 12:1   [b]Zc 3:2   [c]Dn 7:8.20

nature is known, and who are wholly devoid of the Spirit. [20]But you, dearly-loved ones, must make your most holy faith the foundation of your lives, offering prayer impelled by the power of the Holy Spirit, [21]keeping yourselves within the compass of God's love, and waiting for the mercy which our Lord Jesus Christ will exhibit towards you, eternal life being the goal.

[22]There are some wavering souls for whom you should feel nothing but pity. [23][d]**Snatch them from the fire** and bring them salvation. With others, again, your pity should have an admixture of fear. You must hold them in abhorrence, and learn to shun even the outward trappings of those contaminated by sensuality.

[24]There is one who has the power to keep you from stumbling and to bring you, amidst great exultation, unreproved, face to face with his glorious presence. [25]To him, to the only God who is our deliverer, be ascribed, through Jesus Christ our Lord, all glory, majesty, might, and authority, before time ever began, now, and to all eternity. Amen.

[d]Am 4:11; Zc 3:2

THE REVELATION
WHICH JOHN RECEIVED

1 A revelation: it comes from Jesus Christ, who had it bestowed upon him by God, that he might show forth to his servants the things which are ^a**destined to take place** very soon. Christ made it known by way of sending a message through his angel to his servant John, ²who, for his part, has set down everything he saw, thus bearing testimony on behalf of the word of God and of the testimony borne by Jesus Christ. ³A blessing rests on him who reads this, on those who, in hearing the words of the prophecy, attend to what is written in it. For indeed, the time is close at hand.

⁴John sends his greetings to the seven churches in Asia. Grace and peace be yours from him who is, who ever was, and who is yet to come, from the seven spirits which stand in his presence before his throne, ⁵and from Jesus Christ, from him who is the ^b**faithful witness, the firstborn** of the dead, the one who is ruler over the **kings of the earth.** It is he who loves us, who, by virtue of his own blood, ^c**has set us free from** our **sins.** ⁶ ^d**A company of kings** he has made of us, men that are **priests** in the service of him who is his **God** and Father. To him be ascribed glory and might for ever and ever. Amen.

^{7e}**Look, here he is making his appearance in the midst of the clouds,** seen by every eye, seen by the very men who **pierced him through.** ^f**And indeed, all the nations on earth shall make lamentation over him.** So shall it be! Amen.

^{8g}**"I am** the Alpha and the Omega," says the **Lord God,** he **who is,** who ever was, and who is yet to come, **the Almighty One.**

⁹I, John—the man who is your brother, who is in fellowship with you by virtue of the tribulation, the royal dignity, the power of endurance which are ours as having our being in Jesus—found myself on the island called Patmos, being there on behalf of the word of God and of the testimony borne by Jesus. ¹⁰There it was that, on the Lord's

---

^aDn 2:28f   ^bPs 89:37.27   ^cPs 130:8; Is 40:2   ^dEx 19:6; Is 61:6   ^eDn 7:13   ^fZc 12:10ff   ^gEx 3:14; Is 41:4; Am 3:13 LXX

Day, the Spirit took possession of me, and what I heard was a power-ful voice, like the call of a trumpet, [11] addressing me thus: "Write down in a book whatever you see, and send it to the seven churches, to that in Ephesus, in Smyrna, in Pergamum, in Thyatira, in Sardis, in Philadelphia, and that in Laodicea." [12] I turned round to see who it was whose voice was speaking to me, and what I saw, on turning round, were seven golden lampstands, [13] and surrounded by these lampstands a figure [h]**like one of the sons of men.** He was clad in a [i]**garment reaching right down to his feet,** and round his breast[j]**he was girt** with a **golden girdle.** [14][k]**As for his head,** the **hair** on it was **white, like** white **wool, like snow, and his eyes were like** a flame of **fire.** [15]**His feet bore a likeness to burnished bronze** melted in the furnace. [l]**His voice had the sound of waters in full flood.** [16] In his right hand he held seven stars, and from his mouth there jutted out a sharp two-edged sword. His face was like the [m]**sun** shining forth **in all its power.** [17] When I saw him, I fell down at his feet as though I were dead. But he laid his right hand upon me and addressed me thus: [n]**"Banish all fear. I am** the **first and also the last.** [18] I am the Living One; for I was dead, and here I am being alive for evermore! It is I that hold the keys of death and the realm of death. 19 So then, write down what you have seen, the things which are, and [o]**those which will be hereafter.**

[p][20] "The hidden meaning of the seven stars which you saw in my right hand and of the seven golden lampstands is this: The seven stars are the angels in charge of the seven churches, and the seven lampstands are the seven churches.

2   "This is what you are to write to the angel in charge of the church at Ephesus:

"'These are the words of him who holds the seven stars firmly in his right hand, who moves about from place to place in the midst of the seven golden lampstands: [2]"I am aware of your deeds, of your toil, and of your power of endurance. I am aware also that you can-not abide evil men, that you have put to the test those who make them-selves out to be apostles while in fact they are not, and that you have found them false. [3] A power to endure you *do* have, and you have borne up firmly for the sake of my name without ever flagging. [4] Still, there is this I have against you, that you have let go the love which you showed at first. [5] Call to mind, then, what height you have fallen from, be led to repentance, and let the things you do be of the same kind as those which you did at first. Otherwise, if you fail to repent,

[h]Dn 7:13; Ezk 1:26   [i]Ezk 9:2.11 LXX   [j]Dn 10:5   [k]Dn 7:9; 10:6   [l]Ezk 1:24; 43:2   [m]Jg 5:31   [n]Is 44:2.6; 48:12   [o]Is 48:6 LXX   [p][Dn 2:28.29]

I shall be coming to you and will take your lampstand away from its place. [6]However, there is this to be said in your favour, that you loathe what is done by the Nicolaitans, just as I loathe it." [7]Let him who has ears listen to what the Spirit is saying to the churches. As for the man who is victorious, I shall give him to [q]**eat from the tree of life,** which grows **in the paradise of God.**'

[8]"And this is what you are to write to the angel in charge of the church in Smyrna:

"'These are the words of him who is [r]**first and also last,** of him who was dead and came to life again: [9]"I am aware of your distress, of your poverty. But in truth you are rich. And I am aware, too, of the slander heaped upon you by those who make themselves out to be Jews, while in fact they are members of Satan's synagogue. [10]Do not be afraid of the things you are about to suffer. Mark my words: the devil is indeed about to cast some of you into prison, so that you [s]**may be put to the test,** and you will have hardship to endure for **ten days.** Still, show yourselves faithful to the point of being ready to die, and then I shall bestow the crown of life upon you." [11]Let him who has ears listen to what the Spirit is saying to the churches. As for him who is victorious, the second death will never have the power of injuring him.'

[12]"And this is what you are to write to the angel in charge of the church at Pergamum:

"'These are the words of him who is in possession of the sharp, two-edged sword: [13]"I know where you have your dwelling place; it is in the place where Satan has his throne. You hold fast to my name, and you did not repudiate your faith in me, not even in Antipas' time, my faithful witness who was killed in your city, the place where Satan has his dwelling. [14]However, there are a few matters I have to bring against you, inasmuch as there at Pergamum you have those among you who hold to the teaching of [t]**Balaam,** the man who taught Balak to put temptation in the way of the **Israelites, enticing them to eat food sacrificed to idols and to commit fornication.** [15]In the same way you, too, have in your midst those who hold to the doctrine of the Nicolaitans. Be led to repent, then! [16]Otherwise I shall be coming soon, waging war against them with the sword which is in my mouth." [17]Let him who has ears listen to what the Spirit is saying to the churches. As for him who is victorious, I shall [u]**give** him some of **the manna** hidden from sight. Moreover, I shall let him have a white stone with a **new name** written on it, a name not understood by anyone except the man who receives it.'

---

[q]Ezk 31:8 LXX; Gn 2:9; Pr 3:18   [r]Is 44:6; 48:12   [s]Dn 1:12.14   [t]Nm 31:16; 25:1f   [u]Ps 78:24; Is 62:2; 65:15

¹⁸ "And this is what you are to write to the angel in charge of the church at Thyatira:

"'These are the words of the Son of God, of him who has ᵛeyes like a flame of fire, and whose feet are like burnished bronze: ¹⁹"I am aware of your deeds, of your love, of your faith, of your good service, and of your power of endurance; and I am aware, too, that of late you have done even more good deeds than you did before. ²⁰However, I have this against you, that you let the woman Jezebel have free rein, the one who makes herself out to be a prophetess, while in fact she lures my servants, by her teaching, into ʷcommitting fornication and partaking of food sacrificed to idols. ²¹I have given her time to repent, but she refuses to be repentant of her fornication. ²²Well then, I shall be throwing her on a bed of woe, and, as for those lending themselves to adulterous relations with her, I shall bring great distress upon them, unless they come to be repentant of practices such as she engages in. ²³As for her children, I shall kill them outright, and then all the churches will know that I am the one who ˣsearches the hearts and the thoughts of men, and that ʸI shall requite every one of you according to what your deeds have deserved. ²⁴And this is what I have to say to the rest of you at Thyatira who do not accept this teaching, who know nothing of the deep mysteries of Satan, as they are called. I have no wish to impose any further burdens upon you. ²⁵Only hold fast to what you have, until the very day that I make my appearance. ²⁶As for him who is victorious, who to the end takes my deed for his model, I shall ᶻbestow upon him authority over the Gentiles, ²⁷and he shall rule them with an iron rod, breaking them as pieces of earthenware are broken. I shall endow him after the fashion in which I have been endowed by my Father, ²⁸and I shall bestow the Morning Star upon him." ²⁹Let him who has ears listen to what the Spirit is saying to the churches.'

3 "And this is what you are to write to the angel in charge of the church at Sardis:

"'These are the words of him who has in his keeping the seven spirits of God and the seven stars: "I am aware of your doings: how you have the reputation of being alive, while in fact you are nothing more than a corpse. ²So see to it that you wake up, strengthening that which still remains: it is on the point of death. And indeed, what I have found is that, in the eyes of my God, none of the works you do have any perfection about them. ³Call to mind, then, how the message came to you and you lent your ear to it. Hold on to that and be

ᵛDn 10:6   ʷNm 25:1f   ˣJr 17:10; 11:20   ʸPs 62:12; Jr 17:10   ᶻPs 2:8f

led to repentance. I shall come upon you like a thief if you do not wake up, you being wholly ignorant of the hour at which I shall be coming to deal with you. [4]Still, there are a few among you at Sardis who have not soiled their garments. They will be walking by my side dressed in white clothing. For that is what they deserve. [5]As for him who is victorious, he will thus clothe himself in white garments. Never shall I [a]**strike out** his name **from the book of life,** and I shall acknowledge it in my Father's presence and that of his angels." [6]Let him who has ears listen to what the Spirit is saying to the churches.'

[7]"And this is what you are to write to the angel in charge of the church at Philadelphia:

"'These are the words of him who is all holiness and truth, who holds [b]**the key of David,** so that, **when he opens none can close, when he closes none can open:** [8]"I am aware of the works you have accomplished. Look out, then; I have thrown open before you a door which no one has the power of closing. And this I have done because, although you have indeed but little power, you have held fast to what I have commanded and have not repudiated my name. [9]Mark my words: this is what will happen to those who belong to Satan's synagogue, to those who claim to be Jews, while in fact it is all a lie and they are nothing of the sort. I shall make them [c]**come and fall down at your feet,** and make them acknowledge that it is **you upon whom I have bestowed my love,** [10]because you have held fast to my lesson of endurance. And indeed, I shall keep you safe in the hour of trial which is about to come upon the whole world, to put to the test those who dwell on earth. [11]I am coming soon. Hold on to what you have, that no one may be able to rob you of your crown. [12]As for him who is victorious, I shall make him a pillar in the temple of my God. He shall never leave it. Moreover, I shall inscribe him with the name of my God and with the [d]**name of the city** of my God, that of the new Jerusalem which comes down out of heaven from my God. And with my own [e]**new name** I shall inscribe him as well." [13]Let him who has ears listen to what the Spirit is saying to the churches.'

[14]"And this is what you are to write to the angel in charge of the church at Laodicea:

"'These are the words of the Amen, of him who is the ever [f]**faithful** and truthful **witness,** who is **the ultimate source of** God's **creation:** [15]"I am aware of the things done by you: how you are neither cold nor hot. How I wish that you were either cold or hot! [16]But, as it is, you are lukewarm, not either hot or cold. What will happen to you is that I shall spit you out of my mouth. [17]And this I will do because

[a]Ps 69:28; Ex 32:32f　　[b]Is 22:22; Job 12:14　　[c]Is 60:14; 49:23; 45:14; Is 43:4　　[d]Ezk 48:35
[e]Is 63:2; [65:15]　　[f]Ps 89:37; Pr 8:22

of your saying to yourself, 'I am rich; *8***I have amassed riches;** there is nothing I am in need of.' What you are not aware of is that you are in fact in a wretched and pitiful condition, that you are poor, blind, and without covering. [18] My advice to you is that you are to buy from me gold refined by fire so as to become rich, that you are to buy white garments from me to put them round you so that your disgraceful nakedness may be hidden, that you are to buy eye ointment to put on your eyes, so that you may be able to see properly. [19] As for myself, *h***I correct and discipline all those whom I love.** Be zealous, then, and come to repent. [20] Here I am, standing at the door and knocking. If anyone hears my voice and opens the door, I shall come in and have my meal with him, and he with me. [21] As for him who is victorious, I shall grant it to him that he is to sit by my side on my throne, just as I have been victorious and have sat down by my Father's side upon his throne." [22] Let him who has ears listen to what the Spirit is saying to the churches.'"

4 Then I had a vision. There was a door opened up in heaven, and there was the same voice as I had heard before, the one like a *i***trumpet,** addressing me and saying, *j***"Come up** here, and I shall show you **the things which are destined to happen."** [2] At that I was caught up by the Spirit in an instant, and this is what I saw. There was a throne set up in heaven, and *k***there was one sitting upon the throne.** [3] And he who was sitting there was similar in appearance to the gleam of a jasper stone or a cornelian stone. There was a *l***rainbow round the throne,** being like an emerald in appearance. [4] Moreover, there were twenty-four other thrones placed round the throne, and upon them there were sitting twenty-four elders dressed in white garments with golden crowns upon their heads. [5] *m***Out of the** throne **there came forth flashes of lightning, certain kinds of sound,** and lastly, **claps of thunder.** Further, there were burning before the throne seven flaming torches — they are the seven spirits of God — [6] and right in front of the throne there was something like a sea of glass, something that *n***bore a resemblance to crystal.**

*o***In the centre, grouped round the throne itself,** there were **four living creatures covered with eyes** both in front and on their backs. [7] The *p***first** creature was like a **lion,** the **second** creature like an **ox;** the **third** creature had a **face** like a man; the **fourth** creature was like an **eagle** in flight. [8] *q***Each and every one** of the four living creatures had

---

*8*Hos 12:8   *h*Pr 3:12   *i*Ex 19:16.24   *j*Dn 2:29   *k*Is 6:1; Ps 47:8; Ezk 1:26   *l*Ezk 1:28.27.26   *m*Ezk 1:13; Ex 19:16   *n*Ezk 1:22.26   *o*Ezk 1:4f.18; 10:1; Is 6:1   *p*Ezk 1:10; 10:14   *q*Is 6:2; Ezk 1:18

six wings. **They were covered** with **eyes all the way round,** as well as on the inside. And without ever resting, either day or night, they cried out, *ʳ***"Holy, Holy, Holy** is the **Lord God, the Almighty,** he who ever was, who *ˢ***is,** and who is yet to come."

⁹And every time the living creatures ascribe glory and honour *ᵗ***to him who sits on the throne and who lives for ever** and ever, and give thanks to him, ¹⁰the twenty-four elders fall down before the one **who sits on the throne,** and pay homage to him **who lives for ever** and ever. Moreover, they lay down their crowns in front of the throne, exclaiming:

¹¹"You are worthy, you who are our Lord and our God, to have ascribed to you all glory, honour, and power! For you have created all things; and it is by your will that they were created and have their being."

5 And this is what I saw on the right hand side of the one who *ᵘ***sat on the throne.** A **scroll** was there, inscribed **both on the inside and the outside;** and it was **sealed up** with seven seals. ²Moreover, I saw a mighty angel, and he made an announcement in a powerful voice. "Who is there," he exclaimed, "worthy to open the scroll and break its seals?" ³However, neither in heaven nor on earth nor under the earth was there anyone capable of opening the scroll or of looking inside it. ⁴As for myself, I burst into copious tears because no one was to be found worthy to open the scroll or to look inside it. ⁵However, one of the elders addressed me in these words: "Cease from weeping. Here he is, the *ᵛ***lion** that comes from the tribe of **Judah,** the **scion** of the house of David. He has prevailed, thus winning the right to open the scroll and break the seven seals." ⁶And this is what I saw in the centre of the throne, with its four living creatures and its circle of elders. Standing there was a *ʷ***lamb,** one which had the appearance of **having been offered in sacrifice.** It had seven horns and *ˣ***seven eyes,** these being the seven spirits sent forth by God **all over the world.** ⁷The Lamb drew near to take what it was to receive from the right hand of the one *ʸ***sitting on the throne.** ⁸And as he was taking the scroll, the four living creatures and the twenty-four elders threw themselves to the ground in front of the Lamb, each holding a harp as well as golden bowls filled with *ᶻ***incense** — this incense being **the prayers** offered up by those consecrated to God. ⁹Moreover, *ᵃ***they were singing a new song,** these being their words:

ʳIs 6:3   ˢEx 3:14   ᵗIs 6:1; Ps 47:8; Dn 4:34; Dn 6:26   ᵘIs 6:1; 29:11; Ps 47:8; Ezk 2:9f
ᵛGn 49:9f; Is 11:1.10   ʷIs 53:7   ˣZc 4:10   ʸIs 6:1; Ps 47:8   ᶻPs 141:2   ᵃPs 33:3; 144:9

"You are worthy to take the scroll and to break its seals, because you have been slain in sacrifice, and, by virtue of your blood, have purchased, on behalf of God, men of every tribe, every language, every people, and every nation. 10 You have made them members of a *b*kingdom in the service of our **God**. You have made them his **priests**, and they shall rule upon earth."

11 Moreover, this happened in the course of my vision. I heard the voice of countless angels. They stood round the throne, round the living creatures, and the elders. *c***Myriads upon myriads, thousands upon thousands** they were in number. 12 And this is what they ex-claimed in a powerful voice:

"Worthy is the *d***lamb which has been slain in sacrifice** to have ascribed to it power, riches, *e***wisdom, might,** honour, glory, and praise!"

13 Then I heard every created thing, whether in heaven, upon the earth, under the earth, or in the sea—all that is in them—calling out:

"To him*f***who sits on the throne** and to the Lamb be ascribed praise, honour, glory, and power for ever and ever!"

14 "Amen!" exclaimed the four living creatures, and the elders threw themselves to the ground and did homage.

6 Then I looked on as the Lamb was breaking the first of the seals, while at the same time I heard one of the living creatures calling out in a voice sounding like thunder, "Come forth!" 2 And suddenly there was before my very eyes a *g***white horse,** and there was a man sitting on it. He was holding a bow and had a crown handed to him. And so he went on his way, a conqueror, one intent on conquest.

3 Then, as the Lamb was breaking the second seal, I heard the second of the living creatures calling out, "Come forth!" 4 And there appeared another *h***horse,** a **flame-red** one. And he who was sitting on it had granted him the right to remove peace from the earth, *i*men slaughtering one another. Moreover, he had a sword of great size given to him.

5 And, as the Lamb was breaking the third seal, I heard the third of the living creatures calling out, "Come forth!" I looked, and here, all of a sudden, there was a *j***black horse,** and the one riding it held a pair of scales in his hand. 6 Then I heard what sounded like a voice com-ing from amidst the four living creatures, calling out, "A silver piece for a quart of grain, a silver piece for three quarts of barley! But as for the olive orchard and the vine, you must not harm them in any way."

*b*Ex 19:6; Is 61:6   *c*Dn 7:10   *d*Is 53:7   *e*Dn 2:20   *f*Is 6:1; Ps 47:8   *g*Zc 1:8; 6:1-3
*h*Zc 1:8; 6:1-3   *i*[Ex 21:14-16]   *j*Zc 1:8; 6:1-3

7 And, as the Lamb was breaking the fourth seal, I heard the voice
of the fourth of the living creatures calling out, "Come forth!" 8 I
looked, and here, all of a sudden, there was a [k]**horse,** deathly pale in
colour. [l]**Death** was the name of the man who rode on it, with Hades
following close behind. They were invested with authority over one
fourth of the inhabitants of the earth, being given the right [m]**to put to
death by the sword, by famine, by pestilence, and through the wild
beasts of the earth.**

9 And this is what I saw when the Lamb broke the fifth seal. Underneath the altar there were the souls of those who had been slaughtered
on behalf of the word of God and of the testimony which they had
borne. 10 And this is what they cried out in a mighty voice: [n]**"How
much longer is it to be, Sovereign Lord,** you who are all holy and
true, that you will fail to **pass sentence, taking vengeance for** our
blood at the hands of those who dwell on earth?" 11 At that, each of
them had a white robe given to him, and they were told to be patient
a little while longer until the tally of their fellow servants and brothers
who were destined to be put to death, just as they themselves had
been, should be complete.

12 And these are the things I witnessed as I watched the Lamb breaking the sixth seal. There was a violent earthquake. [o]**The sun** went
black like sackcloth made of hair. The [p]**moon** turned red all over like
blood. 13 **The stars fell down** upon the earth **from the sky,** as a fig tree
sheds its unripe fruit when it is shaken by a mighty wind. 14 [q]**The sky**
was split open **after the fashion of a scroll rolled up;** and there was
no mountain, no island, that was not moved from its place.
15 Moreover, [r]**the kings of the earth, the notables,** the commanders,
the rich, the powerful, in fact every man, whether slave or free, took
to the mountains to [s]**hide in caves and in rocks.** 16 And these were
their [t]**words to the mountains and to the rocks: "Fall on us** and **hide
us** from sight, to remove us from the presence of him who [u]**sits on the
throne** and from the anger of the Lamb. 17 For [v]**the great day** of their
anger has come; and [w]**is there anyone who has the power to stand
firm** in the face of it?"

7

What I saw after this was four angels taking their stand [x]**at the
world's four corners.** And what they did was hold back [y]**the four
winds** of the world, that no wind should blow on either land or sea

[k]Zc 1:8; 6:1-3 [l]Hos 13:14 [m]Ezk 5:12; 14:21; 33:27; Jr 14:12; 15:3; Ezk 29:5 [n]Zc 1:12; Ps 79:5; Dt 32:43; 2 K 9:7; Gn 4:10 [o]Ezk 32:7f [p]Is 13:10; Jl 2:30f [q]Is 34:4 [r]Ps 48:4 LXX; 2:2; Is 24:21; 34:12 [s]Jr 4:29; Is 2:10.19.21 [t]Hos 10:8 [u]Ps 47:8; Is 6:1 [v]Jl 2:11.31; Zp 1:14.18 [w]Mal 3:2 [x]Ezk 7:2; 37:9 [y]Jr 49:36; Zc 6:5; Dn 7:2

or on any of the trees. ²Then I saw another angel ascending from the place where the sun rises. He had with him the seal of the living God, and with a mighty voice he cried out to the four angels that had been granted the right to bring harm to both land and sea. ³And these were his words: "Do not harm either land or sea or any of the trees until ᶻwe have put the seal on the foreheads of those who are servants of our God." ⁴Then I heard what the number of the sealed was: a hundred and forty-four thousand, taken from members of every tribe of Israel. ⁵From the tribe of Judah twelve thousand were sealed; from the tribe of Reuben twelve thousand; from the tribe of Gad twelve thousand; ⁶from the tribe of Asher twelve thousand; from the tribe of Naphtali twelve thousand; from the tribe of Manasseh twelve thousand; ⁷from the tribe of Simeon twelve thousand; from the tribe of Levi twelve thousand; from the tribe of Issachar twelve thousand; ⁸from the tribe of Zebulun twelve thousand; from the tribe of Joseph twelve thousand; from the tribe of Benjamin twelve thousand.

⁹And what I saw next was this. There was a vast crowd of people, which no one was able to count, taken from all nations, tribes, peoples, and speaking every sort of language. There they stood before the throne in the presence of the Lamb. They were clothed in white robes and were holding branches of palms in their hands. ¹⁰And these are the words they cried out in a mighty voice: "Victory belongs to our God, ᵃwho sits on the throne, and to the Lamb."

¹¹And all the angels stood round the throne, round the elders, and the four living creatures. They fell upon their faces in front of the throne, did homage to God, and exclaimed:

¹²"Amen! Praise, glory, wisdom, thanksgiving, honour, might, and strength be ascribed to our God for ever and ever. Amen."

¹³And one of the elders turned to me and said, "These people who are clothed in white robes: who are they, and where do they come from?" ¹⁴"It is you that know," was my reply to him. At that he addressed me in these words: "These are the ones who have come here from the great ᵇtribulation. ᶜThey have washed their robes, making them white in the blood of the Lamb. ¹⁵That is why they are here now before the throne of God, rendering service to him night and day in his temple. And so it is that he who ᵈsits on the throne will take them under his wings. ¹⁶ᵉNo longer shall they suffer either hunger or thirst. The sun shall not beat down on them, nor any scorching heat, ¹⁷because the Lamb that is seated in the very centre of the throne will be their shepherd and will guide them to the springs of the water of life. And ᶠGod will wipe away every tear from their eyes."

ᶻEzk 9:4.6   ᵃIs 6:1; Ps 47:8   ᵇDn 12:1   ᶜGn 49:11   ᵈIs 6:1   ᵉIs 49:10; Ezk 34:23; Ps 23:1; 36:9; Jr 2:13   ᶠIs 25:8; Jr 31:16

8 And what happened when the Lamb broke the seventh seal was that there was silence in heaven for the space of about half an hour. ²I looked, and here there were the seven angels that stand in the presence of God, and they had seven trumpets given to them.

³Then another angel came forth. ᵍ**He took his stand by the altar,** having with him a golden censer. And ʰ**incense** was given to him, a great deal of incense, that he might cause it to pass over **the prayers** of all those consecrated to God, making an offering of it all upon the golden altar which stands before the throne. ⁴And so the smoke **of the incense,** along with **the prayers** of the consecrated ones, went up from the angel's hand into the presence of God. ⁵And after that the angel seized ⁱ**the censer, filled** it with **fire taken from the altar,** and threw it down upon the earth. Then there were peals of ʲ**thunder,** there were other **sounds** coming forth; there were flashes of **lightning;** and there was an earthquake.

⁶As for the seven angels that had the seven trumpets, they made themselves ready to blow upon them.

⁷The first angel blew upon his trumpet. And there came ᵏ**hail and fire** mingled with **blood** thrown down **upon the earth.** Moreover, a third of the earth was burned up; a third of the trees were burned up; and all the green grass was burned up.

⁸The second angel blew upon his trumpet. Then something that ˡ**had the appearance** of a great **mountain,** all **aflame with fire,** was thrown into the sea. A third of the sea ᵐ**turned into blood.** ⁹A third of the creatures that live in the sea died, and a third of all ships were wrecked.

¹⁰Then the third angel blew upon his trumpet. And a ⁿ**star** of great size **fell down from the sky,** all aflame like a torch. It fell upon a third of the rivers and upon the water springs. ¹¹'Wormwood' was the name borne by the star. A third of the waters turned into wormwood. And a large number of men died from the waters, so bitter had they become.

¹²The fourth angel then blew upon his trumpet, and a third of the sun, a third of the moon, and a third of the stars were struck, with the result that a third of them were shrouded in darkness, no light appearing during a third of the day, and things being the same during the night.

¹³And this is the next thing which happened in the course of my vision. I heard an eagle flying in mid-heaven and crying out in a powerful voice, "Woe, woe, woe upon those that dwell upon earth

ᵍAm 9:1　ʰPs 141:2　ⁱLv 16:12; [Ps 11:6; Ezk 10:2]　ʲEx 19:16　ᵏEzk 38:22; Jl 2:30; Ex 9:23-26　ˡJr 51:25　ᵐEx 7:20　ⁿIs 14:12; Dn 8:10

for what will befall them from the remaining trumpet blasts which the three angels are about to blow."

9 And the fifth angel blew upon his trumpet. And this is what I saw. A star had fallen down from the sky upon the earth, and it had given to it the key that gives entry to the shaft leading down to the abyss. [2]The star opened up the shaft which leads down to the abyss with the key. And [o]**smoke rose** up from the shaft, **like the smoke** coming from a huge **furnace,** the [p]**sun** and the air **being darkened** by the smoke coming out of the shaft. [3]Moreover, out of the smoke there came down [q]**upon the earth locusts** which were given powers such as are possessed by the scorpions that live on the earth. [4]And this was the command given to them. They were to inflict no injury [r]**on the grass of the earth,** or **any plant,** or **any tree.** All the harm they were intended to do was to injure the men who failed to have [s]**the seal** of God **upon their foreheads.** [5]Moreover, they were not granted the right to put them to death, but only that they might torture them for five months, this torture being like that inflicted by scorpions when they sting a man. [6]At the time when this happens, men [t]**will be looking for death, without ever** finding it; they will be longing to die, but death shall make its escape from them.

[u][7]**In appearance** the locusts resembled **horses** got ready **for battle.** On their hands they had what looked like crowns made up of something like gold. Their faces seemed like human faces, [8]and their hair was like women's hair. [v]**Their teeth** were **like lions' teeth.** [9]What they had as covering for their breasts looked like breastplates made of iron. The sound their wings made was [w]**like the noise of chariots,** like that of many horses **rushing into battle.** [10]They had tails resembling those of scorpions, with stings in them, and it was in these tails that there resided their power of inflicting injury on men for five months. [11]They have the angel of the abyss set over them as king, his name being [x]**Abaddon** in Hebrew, while in Greek his name is Apollyon, that is to say, the Destroyer.

[y][12]The first woe has now passed. Yet there are two more—keep it in mind—to come after it.

[13]And the sixth angel blew upon his trumpet. Then I heard a voice coming from the four corners of the golden altar, the one that stands right opposite the place where God is. [14]And this is what the voice said to the sixth angel who stood there with his trumpet: "Loosen the four angels which are held bound at [z]**the great river Euphrates.**" [15]At

---

[o]Gn 19:28; Ex 19:18 [p]Jl 2:2.10 [q]Jl 1 & 2 [r]Ex 10:12.15 [s]Ezk 9:4 [t]Job 3:21 [u]Jl 2:4.5 [v]Jl 1:6 [w]Jl 2:5 [x]Job 26:6; 28:22 [y][Ezk 7:5f] [z]Gn 15:18; Dt 1:7; Jos 1:4

that the four angels were let loose, they who had been held in readiness for this very hour, this very day, this very month, this very year, that they might destroy one third of mankind. 16 As for the number of the host of horsemen, they were twice ten thousand times ten thousand. The number was mentioned in my hearing.

17 This is the way in which I saw the horses and those riding on them in my vision. They wore breastplates that were fiery red, hyacinth blue, and sulphurous yellow. The heads of the horses were lions' heads, and out of their mouths there came fire, smoke, and sulphur. 18 By these three plagues, that is to say, by the fire, the smoke, and the sulphur that came from their mouths, a third of mankind was destroyed. 19 The power of the horses resided in their mouths but also in their tails. For their tails resembled snakes with heads, and it was with these, too, that they inflicted injuries.

20 As for the rest of mankind—those who were not destroyed by these plagues—they failed to be repentant of the *a***things which they had made with their own hands,** so as to turn away from their worship of **demonic spirits,** from worshipping **idols** made of **gold, silver, bronze, stone, or wood,** which have no power of **either seeing, hearing,** or **walking.** 21 Moreover, they failed to be repentant of their murders, their *b***witchcraft,** their **fornication,** or their stealing.

10 After that I saw another mighty angel coming down from heaven. He had a cloud wrapped round him, and there was a rainbow over his head, his face being like the sun and his feet like pillars of fire. 2 In his hand he had a small scroll unrolled, while he had his right foot on the sea and his left foot on the land. 3 He cried out in a mighty voice, sounding like a *c***lion that roars.** And as he was crying out, seven claps of thunder made themselves heard. 4 And after the seven thunderclaps had given utterance, I made myself ready to write. However, there came a voice from heaven addressing these words to me: *d***"Seal up** what the seven thunderclaps have said; do not write it down." 5 And then the angel whom I saw standing on the sea and the land *e***lifted up his right hand towards heaven,** 6 **and swore by him who lives for ever** and ever, **by him who created heaven, earth, the sea, and everything in them.** And this is what he said: "There will be no more delay! 7 But when the time comes for the voice of the seventh angel to be heard, when he shall be blowing his trumpet, then *f***God's secret purpose** will have been fulfilled, this

---

*a*Is 17:8; 2:8.20; Ps 135:15; 115:4; Dn 5:4.23   *b*2 K 9:22   *c*Jr 25:30; Am 1:2; 3:8   *d*Dn 8:26; 12:4.9   *e*Dt 32:40; Dn 12:7; Gn 14:22.19; Neh 9:6; Ps 146:6; Ex 20:11   *f*Am 3:7; Dn 9:6.10; Zc 1:6

being precisely the good news which he proclaimed **to his servants, the prophets."**

8 After that the voice from heaven which I had heard before spoke to me again, addressing these words to me: "Go forward and take the scroll which lies open in the hand of the angel who is standing on the sea and the land." 9 And I went forth to the angel, asking him to give me *g***the little scroll. And this is what he said to me:** "Take it **and eat** it. It will turn **your stomach** sour, although in **your mouth** it will be as sweet as honey." 10 And I took **the little scroll** from the hand of the angel **and ate it, and in my mouth it tasted as sweet as honey.** But when I had eaten it, my stomach turned sour.

11 Then there was another thing I was told: "You are destined *h***to utter prophecies** once again **concerning peoples, nations, languages, and kings** in large numbers."

11 The next thing which happened was that there was handed to me a *i***measuring rod,** one that bore a resemblance to a staff. And what was said to me was this: "Be on your way and measure the temple of God and the altar, and, moreover, make a reckoning of those who offer worship in the place. 2 However, as for the outer court, leave it out of account and do not measure it, for it has been made over to *j***the Gentiles,** who will be **treading** the holy city underfoot for forty-two months. 3 Still, I shall assign a task to my two witnesses, and they will prophesy for twelve hundred and sixty days, being clothed in sackcloth. 4 And this is who these are: they are the *k***two olive trees,** the two **lampstands that stand before** him who is **the Lord of the earth.** 5 If anyone sets about doing an injury to them, *l***fire comes forth from** their **mouth** and **consumes** their **enemies.** Indeed, if anyone sets about injuring them in any way, that is the way in which he is bound to find his death. 6 The power which has been given to them is that of closing up the doors of heaven, *m***rain ceasing to fall** during the days of their prophetic ministry. Moreover, they have been given the power *n***to turn water into blood,** as well as **to strike** the earth **with every kind of plague,** whenever they desire to do so. 7 However, when the time comes for them to have completed their witnessing, *o***the beast that comes up from the abyss will wage war** on them, **defeat them,** and put them to death. 8 And their corpses shall be in the main street of the city which, when things are looked upon in a spiritual way, is known by the names of Sodom and Egypt—the very place

gEzk 2:8; 3:1-3   hJr 1:10; 25:30; Dn 3:4; 7:14   iEzk 40:3; Zc 2:1   jZc 12:3 LXX; Ps 79:1.6; Is 63:18   kZc 4:2f; 11–14   l2 K 1:10; 2 Sm 22:9; Jr 5:14   m1 K 17:1   nEx 7:17.19f; 1 Sm 4:8   oDn 7:3.7.21

where their Lord was put on a cross. ⁹For three days and a half men from all peoples and tribes, speaking every sort of language, and coming from all nations, will be gazing on their corpses, not permitting them to receive burial. ¹⁰Those who dwell on earth will be glad on account of what has happened to these men; they will be *P*full of joy; they will be **sending presents to one another.** Such a torment were these two prophets to all that dwell on earth. ¹¹However, after three days and a half a *q*life-giving spirit from God **entered into them, they rose to their feet,** and a great *r*dread took possession of those that saw them. ¹²Then they heard a mighty voice from heaven saying to these men, "Come up here." And they went up *s*into heaven in a cloud, their enemies looking on. ¹³At that very instant there arose a *t*violent earthquake, a tenth of the city falling to the ground. Seven thousand souls found their death in the earthquake, while the rest, filled with terror, paid due honour to the *u*God of heaven.

¹⁴The second woe has now passed. *v*The third woe—keep it in mind— will soon be making its appearance.

¹⁵Then the seventh angel blew upon his trumpet. And at that powerful voices were heard in heaven, exclaiming:

w"Royal power over the world has been assumed by our Lord and his anointed; and he will reign for ever and ever!"

¹⁶And the twenty-four elders, they who are seated on their thrones before God, fell upon their faces and did homage to God, their words being these:

¹⁷"We give thanks to you, Lord God Almighty, you *x*who are and who ever were, because, laying hold of your great power, you have entered upon your *y*royal rule. ¹⁸The nations were filled with anger, but now your anger has been displayed. The time has come for the dead to be judged, for the recompense to be received by *z*your servants the prophets, indeed, by all consecrated to you, by those *a*standing in awe of your name, both great and small; the time for the destruction of those who are the destroyers of the earth."

¹⁹At that, God's temple in heaven was thrown open, and *b*within this temple of his there was seen the ark of his covenant. And then there followed *c*flashes of lightning, sounds in the sky, claps of thunder, an earthquake, and a *d*violent hailstorm.

12 Next a great portent made its appearance in heaven. *e*There was a woman clothed with the sun. The moon was underneath her feet,

*P*Ps 105:38; [Est 9:18f]　　*q*Ezk 37:5　　*r*Gn 15:12　　*s*2 K 2:11　　*t*Ezk 38:19f　　*u*Dn 2:19
v[Ezk 7:5]　　*w*Dn 2:44; 7:14.27; Zc 14:9; Ex 15:18; Obd 21; Ps 2:2; 10:16; 22:28　　*x*Ex 3:14
*y*Ps 99:1; Ps 2:1.5.12; 46:6　　*z*Am 3:7; Dn 9:6.10; Zc 1:6　　*a*Ps 115:13　　*b*1 K 8:1.6; 2 Ch
5:7; 2 M 2:4-8　　*c*Ex 9:16　　*d*Ex 9:24　　*e*[Gn 37:9; Sg 6:10]

and upon her head she wore a crown made up of twelve stars. *f2*She was with child, and in the **torment** of her **birth pangs she cried out to be delivered.** ³Then a second portent appeared in heaven, and, all of a sudden, there was seen a huge dragon coloured red. He had seven heads and *8***ten horns;** and upon his heads there were seven diadems. ⁴With his tail he swept away a third part *h***of the stars from the sky, flinging** them **to the earth.** Moreover, the dragon took up his stand in front of the woman who was about to give birth, so that, as soon as she would be giving birth to her child, he might devour it. ⁵What happened was that *i***she gave birth** to a son, to a **male** child destined to rule over all the *j***Gentiles with an iron rod.** This child of hers was caught up to God, right before his throne, ⁶while the woman fled into the wilderness, where she has a place prepared for her by God, that she might be given sustenance there for twelve hundred and sixty days.

⁷And now war broke out in heaven, *k***Michael** and his angels **engaging in war** against the dragon. The dragon and his angels, for their part, fought back. ⁸But they did not prevail, and *l***no longer could place for them be found** anywhere in heaven. ⁹And so the huge dragon was hurled down, *m***the serpent** of old, he who is called 'Devil' or *n*'**Satan,**' the deceiver of the whole world. Hurled down he was to the earth, and his angels with him.

¹⁰Then I heard a mighty voice in heaven exclaiming, "This is the very hour when our God has won his victory, when he has assumed power and entered upon his royal rule, when his Anointed One has been given his rights! For what has happened is this. The accuser of our brothers has been overthrown, he who accused them day and night before our God. ¹¹But they have triumphed over him by virtue of the Lamb's spilled blood, because of the words they uttered by way of bearing testimony, and because they did not cling to life to the extent of holding on to it till death should claim it.

¹²*o*"**Rejoice,** then, you **heavens,** and you who have your dwelling in them. But woe upon the earth and upon the sea, for the devil has come down to you filled with violent rage, and knowing full well that he has but little time."

¹³When the dragon found that he had been hurled down upon the earth, he pursued the woman who had given birth to the male child. ¹⁴But the woman received as a gift two great *p***eagles' wings,** so that she could fly into the wilderness, to the place prepared for her, where she was to be given sustenance *q***for a year, twice a year, and half a**

---

f[Gn 3:16;] Is 66:7; [21:3;] Mic 4:10   *8*Dn 7:7   *h*Dn 8:10   *i*Is 66:7; Jr 20:15   *j*Ps 2:9
*k*Dn 10:13.21; 12:1   *l*Dn 2:35   *m*Gn 3:1.14   *n*Zc 3:1.2   *o*Is 44:23; 49:13   *p*Ex 19:4;
Is 40:31   *q*Dn 7:25; 12:7

year, out of reach of the serpent. [15] The dragon spewed water out of his mouth, like a river, after the woman, so that he might overwhelm her by its flood. [16] But the [r]**earth** came to the aid of the woman, **opened its mouth, and swallowed** the river which the dragon had spewed out of his mouth. [17] At that the dragon flew into a rage with the woman and went off to wage war against the rest of her offspring, against those who keep God's commandments and who hold fast to the testimony borne by Jesus. [18] And there the dragon was, having taken his stand upon the seashore.

13 The next thing I saw was this. [s]**A beast came up out of the sea.** It had **ten horns** and seven heads. Diadems were found on its horns, while on its heads it bore names giving vent to blasphemy. [2] Moreover, the [t]**beast** that I was seeing **bore a resemblance to a leopard.** Yet its feet were **like** those of a **bear,** its mouth being like the mouth of a **lion.** The dragon bestowed upon it all his might, his dominion, and his great authority. [3] One of its heads had the appearance of having received a deadly blow. Yet this mortal wound had in fact been healed. And so it was that the whole of the world went after the beast, filled with admiration, [4] while men at the same time were paying homage to the dragon for having bestowed his authority upon the beast. And as they were paying homage, they exclaimed the words, "Who is equal to the beast and has the power to wage war against it?"

[5] Moreover, the beast had bestowed upon it a [u]**mouth uttering bombast** and blasphemies; and besides, there was conceded to it the right to [v]**pursue its course** for forty-two months. [6] It opened its mouth and made blasphemous attacks on God, reviling his name and his dwelling place, reviling in fact all those who have their dwelling in heaven. [7] Likewise, it was given permission [w]**to make war on those consecrated to God and to defeat them,** having conferred on it authority over every tribe and people, tongue and nation. [8] And in fact homage will be paid to the beast by all dwellers on earth except those whose name the [x]**lamb has recorded** in his **book of life,** the **lamb slain** in sacrifice ever since the beginning of the world.

[9] Let him who has ears listen to these words. [10][y]**If anyone is marked out for captivity, into captivity** he goes. **If anyone** should kill **by the sword,** he is destined to be killed **by the sword.** This is where the power of endurance and the faithfulness of those consecrated to God have their place.

[11] After that I saw another beast, one coming up out of the earth. It

[r]Nm 16:32   [s]Dn 7:3.7   [t]Dn 7:4-6   [u]Dn 7:8.11   [v]Dn 7:25   [w]Dn 7:21   [x]Dn 12:1; Ps 69:28; Is 53:7   [y]Jr 15:2

had two horns like those of a lamb, but it spoke like a dragon. [12]It had all the authority of the first beast, exercising it before its very eyes. It caused the world and those that dwell in it to pay homage to the first beast, the one whose mortal blow had been healed. [13]It performed great miracles, to the extent even of making fire come down from heaven to the earth in the sight of men. [14]It led astray those who dwell on earth by virtue of the miracles which it had been permitted to perform, and it gave to those that dwell on earth the order to set up an image in honour of the beast which had received a wound by the sword and yet had lived. [15]Moreover, it had conferred on it the power of breathing life into the image of the beast, enabling the image of the beast to speak and to bring it about that those [z]**who were not doing homage to the image** of the beast were all to be put to death. [16]Further, it caused everyone, great or small, rich or poor, free or slave, to be branded with a mark on his right hand or his forehead. [17]And there was another thing it effected, that no one should be allowed to buy or to sell anything except those bearing the mark of the beast, be it its name or its number. [18]This is where ingenuity comes into play. Let anyone endowed with true understanding reckon up the number of the beast, this number representing a certain man. And this is what his number is: six hundred and sixty-six.

14 Then I looked on intently, and this is what I saw. There was the Lamb standing on [a]**Mount Zion,** and with him were a hundred and forty-four thousand who had his name and that of his Father inscribed [b]**upon** their **foreheads.** [2]Then I heard a sound from heaven, a [c]**sound like that** made **by a great quantity of water** rushing forth, a sound like that given out by a violent clap of thunder. In fact, the sound I heard came from harpers playing on their harps. [3]There they were, [d]**singing a new song** before the throne in the hearing of the four living creatures and of the elders. And there was no one who was able to learn the song except the hundred and forty-four thousand upon whom redemption from the world had been bestowed. [4]These are the men who have not defiled themselves with women, who have kept their chastity; these are the men who follow the Lamb wherever he may go. These are the men who have been redeemed as the firstfruits of humanity for God and the Lamb. [5][e]**No falsehood was ever found upon** their **lips.** They are wholly free from blame.

[6]Then I saw another angel flying in mid-heaven, who had a gospel to proclaim—one of eternal import—to all the dwellers on earth, to

[z]Dn 3:5–7:15   [a]2 K 19:31; Jl 2:32; Obd 17   [b]Ezk 9:4   [c]Ezk 1:24; 43:2   [d]Ps 33:3; 40:3; 96:1; 98:1; 144:9; Is 42:10   [e]Ps 32:2; Is 53:9; Zp 3:13

every nation, tribe, tongue, and people. [7]And this is what he cried out in a powerful voice: "Stand in awe of God and give due honour to him, for the hour when he pronounces judgment has come. Pay homage to him who *f*has created heaven, the earth, the sea, and the water springs."

[8]Then I saw in my vision yet another angel, who followed him and cried out these words: *g*"The great Babylon has fallen, has fallen, she who has made all the nations drink from the wine of her reckless profligacy!"

[9]Yet a third angel followed them, exclaiming in a mighty voice, "If anyone pays homage to the beast or its image, and receives its mark upon his forehead or his hand, [10]he, for his part, *h*shall drink of the wine of God's indignation, poured undiluted into the cup of God's fury. Sulphurous flames shall torment him in the sight of the holy angels and the Lamb. [11]*i*Moreover, the smoke coming from the fire tormenting such men goes up for ever and ever. And no rest is to be found night or day by those who pay homage to the beast and its image, and who receive the mark bearing its name. [12]This is where the power of endurance in those consecrated to God is to be found—in those who keep God's commandments and hold fast to their faith in Jesus."

[13]Moreover, I heard a voice from heaven exclaiming, "Set it down: a blessing rests from henceforth on those who die united to the Lord." "Yes," says the Spirit, "they may rest from their toil; for the records of what they have done follow on after them."

[14]Then, as I *j*looked, there appeared all at once a white cloud, and on that cloud was seated one that bore resemblance to a son of man. Upon his head he wore a golden crown, and in his hand he held a sharp sickle. [15]Then another angel came forth from the temple, crying out in a mighty voice to him who was sitting on the cloud, *k*"Put in your sickle and reap, for the hour of harvesting has come, the earth's crop being over-ripe." [16]Thereupon he who was sitting on the cloud set his sickle to work on the earth, and the earth's harvest was reaped.

[17]Then another angel came forth from the temple in heaven, and he, too, had a sharp sickle. [18]And then there came from the altar yet another angel—the one who has authority over fire—and he called out in a mighty voice to the one having the sharp sickle, *l*"Put in your sharp sickle and gather in the clusters of the vine of the earth, for its grapes are ripe." [19]And the angel set his sickle to work on the earth. He gathered the vintage of the earth and put it into a winepress of great size, that of God's anger. [20]*m*The winepress was trodden out-

---

*f*Ex 20:11; Ps 146:6　*g*Is 21:9; 51:17; Jr 25:15; 51:7f; Dn 4:30　*h*Is 51:17; Ps 75:8; Jr 25:15　*i*Is 34:10　*j*Dn 7:13; 10:16　*k*Jl 3:13　*l*Jl 3:13　*m*Jl 3:13; Is 63:3

side the city, and blood gushed forth from the winepress to a distance of sixteen hundred furlongs, reaching as high as the horses' bridles.

15 Then my eyes fell upon another portent in heaven, one of great significance and of an astonishing nature. There were seven angels bringing with them *n*seven plagues—the last of all—because in them God's anger has found its final expression. [2]Moreover, I saw something that had the appearance of a sea of glass suffused all through with a glow of fire. And beside the sea of glass, holding harps in their hands given to them by God, there were standing those who had won the victory over the beast, over its image, and over the number of its name. [3]They were *o*singing the song of Moses, God's servant, and the song of the Lamb. And these were their words:

p"Great and wonderful are your works, Lord God Almighty. All your ways accord with justice and with truth. You are the king of the nations. [4]*q*Who would fail to stand in awe of you, Lord? Is there any one who will not give due praise to your name? For you alone are holy. And indeed, *r*all the nations shall come prostrating themselves before you, seeing that your just dealings stand revealed."
[5]And this is what I saw after that. The sanctuary of the heavenly *s*tent of testimony was thrown open, [6]and out of it there came forth the seven angels with the *t*seven plagues, clothed in fine linen, spotless and shining forth, and girded with golden girdles round their breasts. [7]And one of the four living creatures handed to the seven angels seven golden bowls filled with what came of the anger of God, of him who lives for ever and ever. [8]At that *u*the sanctuary was filled with smoke by virtue of God's glory and power, and no one was able to enter the sanctuary until the time that the *v*seven plagues in the hands of the seven angels would have been fully dealt out.

16 Next I heard a mighty *w*voice from the sanctuary, addressing the seven angels in these words: "Go forth and *x*pour out upon the earth the seven bowls provided by the anger of God." [2] Then the first angel went on his way and poured out his bowl upon the earth. And what *y*happened was that a malignant and virulent sore appeared on those men who bore the mark of the beast and were worshippers of its image.

*n*Lv 26:21　*o*Ex 15:1; Jos 14:7　*p*Ex 15:11; Dt 32:4; Ps 111:2　*q*139:14; 145:17; Ex 34:10; Jr 10:6f; Ps 111:9　*r*Ps 86:9; Mal 1:11　*s*Ex 40:34　*t*Lv 26:21; [Ezk 28:13]　*u*Ex 40:34f; 2 K 8:10; Is 6:4; [Ezk 40:4]　*v*Lv 26:21　*w*Is 66:6　*x*Ps 69:24; Jr 10:25; Zp 3:8　*y*Dt 28:35; Ex 9:10f

³And the second angel poured out his bowl upon the sea, and it ᶻturned into blood, like the blood from a corpse, every living creature in the sea being killed.

⁴The third angel poured out his bowl on the rivers and the water springs. And they turned into blood.

⁵Then I heard the angel who is in charge of the waters exclaiming, "You have displayed how ᵃjust you are in giving these judgments, you who are and ever were, you who are holy! ⁶These people have ᵇshed the blood of those consecrated to you, of your prophets, and you have given them blood to drink. It is what they deserve." ⁷Then I heard the altar uttering these words: "So it is, ᶜLord God Almighty: Your judgments accord with truth and with justice."

⁸The fourth angel poured out his bowl over the sun, and it was given leave to scorch men with its fiery heat. ⁹However, all that men did when they found themselves scorched by this fierce heat was that they reviled the name of God, who had the power to inflict such plagues. They would not repent, giving due praise to him.

¹⁰The fifth angel poured out his bowl on the throne of the beast. Thereupon the beast's kingdom ᵈwas shrouded in darkness. Moreover, men bit their tongues because of the pain they felt, ¹¹and reviled ᵉthe God of heaven because of their pains and the sores they had upon them. And they were not led to be repentant of the deeds which they had perpetrated.

¹²The sixth angel poured out ᶠhis bowl over the great river Euphrates. Its ᵍwater was dried up, so that the way might be free for the coming of the kings ʰfrom the east.

¹³The next thing I saw in my vision was this. There came forth from the mouth of the dragon, from the mouth of the beast, and from that of the false prophet three tarnished spirits having the appearance of ⁱfrogs. ¹⁴They were the spirits of demonic beings, having the power to work miracles. What they did was to go out to all the kings of the world, to assemble them for the battle which is to be waged on the Great Day of God Almighty. ¹⁵(This is how it will be: I shall be coming like a thief. A blessing rests on the man who stays awake, who keeps his clothing on him, so that he does not have to go about naked, his disgrace being exposed to the eyes of others.) ¹⁶So these creatures assembled the kings at a place which in Hebrew goes by the name of Armageddon.*

¹⁷Then the seventh angel poured out his bowl into the air. At that

---

ᶻEx 7:19.24; Ps 78:44　　ᵃPs 119:137; 145:17; Ex 3:14; Dt 32:4　　ᵇIs 49:26; Ezk 35:6; Ps 79:3　ᶜPs 19:9; 119:137　　ᵈEx 10:21f; Is 8:21f　　ᵉDn 2:19　　ᶠGn 15:18; Dt 1:7; Jos 1:4　　ᵍIs 11:15f; 44:27; Jr 50:38　　ʰIs 41:2.25　　ⁱEx 8:3

* 'The use of Hebrew and absence of interpretation are in the style of apocalyptic.'— J. Jeremias, *Theological Dictionary of the New Testament*, I, 468.

there sounded forth *j*out of the sanctuary a powerful **voice**, coming from the throne, which exclaimed, "It is done!" [18] Then there were flashes of *k*lightning, peals of **thunder,** and other **sounds.** Moreover, there was a violent earthquake, *l*such as there never has been since there have been men upon the earth, so violent an earthquake it was. [19] The great city split into three parts, while the cities inhabited by the nations of the world collapsed in ruin. As for the *m*great Babylon, God did indeed remain mindful of her, and he handed her the *n*cup containing the **wine** which is the product **of the fierceness of his** anger. [20] Every island vanished, and as for the mountains, none of them was to be found any longer. [21] *o*Huge hailstones, each about a hundred-weight heavy, fell down on men from the sky. And men reviled God for the plague of hail, so *p*very terrible a plague it was.

17   And one of the seven angels with the seven bowls approached me and addressed me in these words: "Come to my side; I will show you the judgment of condemnation visited upon the great whore. She has her place of residence *q*near an abundance of waters. [2] *r*The kings of the earth have committed fornication with her, and men all over the *s*world have made themselves drunk with the wine which accompanies her fornication." [3] At that the angel lifted me up, under the impulse of the Spirit, and carried me off into the wilderness. And this is what I saw there. There was a woman mounted on a beast which was coloured scarlet. This beast was covered all over with names giving expression to blasphemy, and it had seven heads and *t*ten horns. [4] As for the woman, she was clothed in purple and scarlet. She was adorned with gold, with precious stones, and with pearls; and in her hand she held a *u*golden cup which was filled to the brim with her fornications, with the foul practices attending her in her abominations. [5] Moreover, she had the cryptic title inscribed upon her forehead: *"BABYLON THE GREAT ONE, THE MOTHER OF WHORES AND OF THE ABOMINABLE THINGS OF THE WORLD."* [6] And there was this. I saw that the woman was drunk, drunk with the blood of those consecrated to God, with the blood of those who had borne testimony on behalf of Jesus.

I was struck with great amazement when I saw this. [7] However, the angel addressed me in these words: "Why are you so amazed? I shall explain to you the hidden meaning that lies behind the woman and the beast she is riding on, the one that has seven heads and ten horns. *v*[8] The beast you saw was once and is no longer. Still, it is destined to

*j*Is 66:6   *k*Ex 19:16   *l*Dn 12:1f   *m*Dn 4:30   *n*Is 51:17; Jr 25:15   *o*Ex 9:23f   *p*Ex 9:23f   *q*Jr 41:12; 51:13   *r*Is 23:17   *s*Jr 25:15f; 51:7   *t*Dn 7:7   *u*Jr 51:7   *v*Dn 7:3

come up from the abyss, and it is only then that it will go on its way to perdition. The inhabitants of the world will be full of wonder, all those, I mean, regarding whom it was decided, before the world ever began, that their names were not to be [w]**inscribed in the book of the living**. They will be full of wonder when they see the beast which once was, which is no longer, and which is yet to appear.

9 "It is here that ingenuity is called for, that there is a call for a man of true understanding. The seven heads are seven hills, with the woman sitting on them. They also represent seven kings. 10 Five of them have already fallen; one is here now; another has not yet appeared; and when he does appear, he is destined to appear for but a little while. 11 As for the beast which once was, and no longer is, he is an eighth king, and yet he is one of the seven, and he is going to perdition. 12[x]**The ten horns** you saw **represent ten kings**. They have not as yet assumed their royal rule, but have been granted the right to exercise authority as kings for one hour, sharing that authority with the beast. 13 They have but a single purpose among them and will confer their power and authority upon the beast. 14 It is these that will be waging war against the Lamb, but the Lamb will win victory over them because he [y]**is Lord of lords and King of kings**. And his associates—the ones who have been called, who have been chosen, who have proved their faithfulness—will share that victory."

15 And he addressed these further words to me. [z]"**The waters** which you saw in the place where the whore has her place of residence represent peoples, populations, nations, and tongues. 16 Moreover, as for the horns which you saw, they—and the beast along with them—will come to hate the whore. They will lay her waste and [a]**strip her naked**. They will batten on her flesh and will burn her down. 17 For what has happened is that God has put it into their minds that they should carry out his purpose, and that they themselves should have but one purpose—to bestow their royal power upon the beast, until the time when the words God has spoken should have found their fulfilment. 18 Moreover, the woman whom you saw is the great city which exercises kingly rule over [b]**the kings of the earth**."

18   The next thing I saw in my vision was another angel coming down from heaven. He had great power bestowed upon him. [c]**And the earth was illumined by his glorious presence.** 2 Crying out in a powerful voice he exclaimed, "[d]**The great Babylon has fallen, has**

[w]Dn 12:1; Ps 69:28   [x]Dn 7:20.24   [y]Dt 10:17; Dn 2:47   [z]Is 8:7; Jr 47:2; 51:13   [a]Ezk 16:37.39; 23:26.29   [b]Ps 2:2; 89:27   [c]Ezk 43:2   [d]Is 21:9; Jr 51:8; Dn 4:30

fallen. She has become *e***a dwelling place of demons,** the abode of every tarnished spirit, the abode of every unclean and loathsome bird. [3] And the reason why this has come about is that *f***all nations have drunk deep from the heady wine** of her fornication, that *g***the kings of the earth have committed fornication with her,** and that the traders of the earth have enriched themselves by her wealth which she has so wantonly acquired."

[4] Then I heard another voice from heaven. And this is what was said: *h***"Come out of her, my people,** so as not to be led to make common cause with her in her sins, being given your share in the plagues which she has had to endure. [5] And indeed, *i***her sins have piled up as high as heaven;** and God is mindful of the crimes which she has committed. [6] *j***Pay her back in her own coin: she is to be dealt with according to the deeds she has done,** and, indeed, must be made to disgorge twice of what she has exacted. In the very cup where she provided the mixture she dealt out to others a double portion is to be mixed for her. [7] To the extent that she has taken pride in herself, that she has played the wanton, she is to have torments and wretchedness inflicted upon her. For this is what she is telling herself *k***in her own heart:** 'Here **I sit enthroned like a queen. Widowhood is not for me, and I shall never know what it is to be wretched.'** [8] It is precisely because that is her way of thinking that her plagues *l***will come upon her in a single day:** pestilence, wretchedness, and famine. She shall be burned to the ground, for the *m***Lord** God who has **condemned** her is **mighty** indeed.

[9] *n***The kings of the earth who have committed fornication with her,** who have shared with her in her life of wanton luxury, *o***shall weep and wail over her** as they see the smoke rising from the fire consuming her. [10] They will be standing at a distance for horror at her torment, and this is what they will say: " Alas, alas, for *p***the great** city, for **Babylon, the powerful city.** Your doom has come upon you in a single hour."

[11] Moreover, the *q***traders** of the earth **will be weeping and mourning** over her because there is no longer anyone ready to buy their cargo, [12] cargo of gold, silver, precious stones, and pearls, of fine linen, purple cloth, silks, scarlet cloth, all kinds of scented woods, of articles made of ivory, of articles made of wood of great worth, bronze, iron, or marble; [13] cinnamon and spice, incense, perfume, and frankincense; wine, oil, fine flour, and wheat; stocks of cattle, sheep, horses, chariots, and slaves—*r***human** cargo. [14] 'All the fruit your heart longed for,'

---

*e*Is 13:21; 34:11.14; Jr 50:39 *f*Jr 25:15 *g*Is 23:17; Nah 3:4 *h*Is 48:20; 52:11; Jr 50:8; 51:6.9.45 *i*Gn 18:20f; Jr 51:9 *j*Ps 137:8; Jr 50:15.29 *k*Is 47:7f *l*Is 47:9 *m*Jr 50:34 *n*Ezk 26:16f; 27:30.33.35 *o*Ps 48:4 LXX; Is 23:17 *p*Dn 4:30; Is 21:9; Jr 51:8 *q*Ezk 27:36.31 *r*Ezk 27:13

they will say, 'has departed from you. All the dainties, all the glittering things, are lost to you, never to be yours again.' 15The *traders in these wares will be standing at a distance for horror at her torment. And this is what they will say, **weeping and mourning:** 16"Alas, alas, for the great city, for her who is clothed in fine linen, in cloth of purple and scarlet, who is adorned with gold, with precious stones, and with pearls! 17Alas, that such great wealth should have been brought to ruin within a single hour."

And all the steersmen, all the voyagers, *t*the sailors, those who make their living by the sea, took up their stand at a distance, 18exclaiming, when they saw the smoke rising from the fire consuming her, "Was there ever a city *u*like the great city?" 19They threw dust on their heads and cried out amidst weeping and mourning, "Alas, alas for the great city by whose lavish way of living riches were provided for all who had ships on the sea. Alas, because she *v*has been laid waste in a single hour.

20*w*"But let heaven exult over her. And you who are consecrated to God, who are apostles, who are prophets, exult likewise. For if God has given his judgment, that was to vindicate your cause against her."

21Then an angel endowed with great strength lifted up a boulder which looked like a large millstone and *x*threw it into the sea, with these words: "So may Babylon, the great city, be hurled down with violence, never to be seen again." 22*y*No longer shall the sound of harpists, of minstrels, of flute players, of trumpeters, be heard in you. No longer shall any craftsman, of whatever trade, be found in you. No longer shall the *z*sound of the mill be heard in you; 23no longer shall the light of a lamp shine forth in you; no longer shall the voice of the bridegroom and of the bride be heard in you. *a*The great ones of the earth were your traders; and it is by *b*your magic arts that all the nations were led astray.

24"And indeed, it was in her that there was to be found the blood of the prophets, of those consecrated to God; in fact, the blood of *c*all those who were butchered on earth."

19 After that I heard what sounded like the voices raised high of a vast throng in heaven exclaiming:

d"Alleluia! Victory, glory, and power belong to our God, 2for *e*his judgments accord with truth and with justice. And indeed, he has

---

*s*Ezk 27:36.31   *t*Is 23:14; Ezk 27:27-29   *u*Ezk 27:30-34   *v*Ezk 26:19   *w*Dt 32:43; Is 44:23; Jr 51:48   *x*Jr 51:63f; Ezk 26:21; Dn 4:30   *y*Is 24:8; Ezk 26:13   *z*Jr 25:10; 7:34; 16:9   *a*Is 23:8   *b*Is 47:9   *c*Jr 51:49   *d*Ps 104:35; Tb 13:18   *e*Ps 19:9; 119:137

pronounced judgment on the great whore who corrupted the earth with her fornication, and he *f*has avenged on her the blood of his servants."

³Then they resumed and exclaimed, *g*"Alleluia! The smoke rising from her will go up for ever and ever." ⁴At that the twenty-four elders and the four living creatures prostrated themselves and did homage to God—to him who is *h*seated upon the throne. "Amen! Alleluia!"

⁵Then a voice came from the throne which said: *i*"Give praise to our God, everyone that is his servant, all those who stand in awe of him, whether great or small."

⁶And again I heard what sounded *j*like voices coming of a vast crowd, like the sound made by a great quantity of water rushing forth, like the sound given forth by mighty peals of thunder. And this is what they cried out:

k"Alleluia! For the Lord our God, he who is sovereign over all, has entered on his reign. ⁷Let us be glad, let us exult! And we shall indeed give due praise to him. For the Lamb's wedding day has come. His bride has made herself ready for it, ⁸and she has been granted the right to clothe herself in fine linen, shining and spotless."

(What is signified by the fine linen is the righteous deeds of those consecrated to God.)

⁹Then the angel spoke to me thus: "Set it down: A blessing rests on those who are invited to the Lamb's wedding banquet." And he added, "These, in very truth, are the words of God." ¹⁰At that I threw myself down at his feet to worship him. But he said, "Be careful not to do that! I am nothing more than a fellow servant of yours and of your brothers who bear testimony to Jesus. It is God that you must worship! And indeed, testimony borne to Jesus and the spirit of prophecy are essentially the same."

¹¹After that *l*I saw heaven opened up wide, and right before me there was a white horse and one riding upon it. 'The Faithful One,' 'The True One' is what he was called; and indeed, it is in a spirit of *m*justice that he pronounces judgment, that he engages in conflict. ¹²*n*He had eyes like a flame of fire, and on his head he wore many diadems. He had a name inscribed upon him known to no one but himself. ¹³He was clothed in a garment soaked in blood, and the name by which he was known was 'The Word of God.' ¹⁴The armies of heaven followed him on white horses clothed in fine linen, white and spotless. ¹⁵From his *o*mouth there jutted out a sharp sword with

*f*Dt 32:43; 2 K 9:7   *g*Ps 104:35; Is 34:10   *h*Is 6:1; Ps 47:8; Ps 104:35   *i*Ps 22:23; 134:1; 135:1; 115:13   *j*Dn 10:6; Ezk 1:24; 43:2   *k*Ps 104:35; 93:1; 97:1; 99:1; Ps 118:24   *l*Ezk 1:1   *m*Ps 96:13; Is 11:4   *n*Dn 10:6   *o*Is 11:4; 49:2

which he was to **strike down the nations.** He is the one who *P*will
rule them with an iron rod, who will *q*tread the winepress containing the wine which comes of the indignation and the anger of God Almighty. 16 And on his robe as well as on his thigh this title was written: '*KING OF KINGS AND LORD OF LORDS.*'

17 The next thing I saw in my vision was an angel standing in the
sun and *r*crying out these words to all the birds flying in mid-heaven:
"To my side. Gather yourselves together for the great feast that God
is giving. 18 Gorge yourselves full with the flesh of kings, with the
flesh of commanders, with the flesh of fighting men, with the flesh
of horses and of those riding on them, with the flesh of all men, free
and slave, small and great." 19 Then I saw the beast and *s*the kings of
the earth with their armies, assembling themselves together against
the rider and his army. 20 The beast was taken prisoner, and so was
the false prophet, he who had worked miracles in the sight of the
beast, thus leading astray those who had accepted the mark of the
beast and who were worshippers of its image. The two of them were
thrown alive into the fiery lake, the lake *t*aflame with sulphur. 21 As
for all the rest, they were put to death by the sword of that horseman,
the sword that jutted out from his mouth. And *u*all the birds devoured
their flesh and had their fill.

20 Then I saw an angel coming down from heaven, having with
him the key which gives access to the abyss, and holding a long chain
in his hands. 2 He laid hold of the dragon, *v*that serpent of old, the
devil, or Satan, and chained him up for a thousand years. 3 He cast
him into the abyss, shut the entrance, and sealed it up above him, to
make certain that he would no longer lead the nations astray until the
thousand years had run their course. After that he is destined to be let
loose for a short while.

4 *w*Thrones were the next thing that appeared to me in my vision,
and taking their seats on them were those to whom the right to judge
had been committed. Moreover, I could see the souls of those who
had been beheaded on behalf of the word of God and of the testimony
borne by Jesus, those who had not worshipped the beast and its
image, and who had not received its mark on their foreheads or hands.
It was they who came to life again, and reigned with Christ for a
thousand years, 5 while there was no coming back to life for the rest
of the dead until after the thousand years had run their course. This
is the first resurrection. 6 A blessing rests on those who, consecrated

*P*Ps 2:9   *q*Jl 3:13; Is 63:3   *r*Ezk 39:4.17-20   *s*Ps 2:2   *t*Dn 7:11; Gn 19:24; Is 30:33; Ezk
38:22   *u*Ezk 39:17.20   *v*Gn 3:1; Zc 3:1   *w*Dn 7:9.22.27

to God, have a share in the first resurrection. The second death is without any power over them; instead, they shall be *x*priests of God and of Christ, reigning with him for the said thousand years.

7When the thousand years shall have run their course, Satan will be loosed from his dungeon, 8and he will go forth to mislead the nations in *y*the four quarters of the world—the enterprise of Gog and Magog—and will assemble them for battle, numbers past counting like the sand of the sea. 9And so they will come up swarming over the whole *z*breadth of the earth, laying siege to the place where those consecrated to God have their encampment, the city of his *a*love. However, *b*fire came down on them from heaven and consumed them. 10And the devil—the one that leads them astray—was cast into the lake of fire and sulphur, where the beast and the false prophet likewise are. And there they shall be tormented night and day for ever and ever.

11Next *c*I saw a white throne of great size and him who was seated on it, *d*from whose presence heaven and earth fled away, no place for them being found any longer. 12Moreover, I saw the dead, both great and small, standing before the throne. Then the *e*books dealing with them were opened, and another book was opened, the book of life. The dead were judged on what was recorded in these books, judged *f*in accordance with the deeds they had done. 13The sea gave up the dead who were in it, and Death and Hades gave up the dead in their keeping. And each person was judged *g*in accordance with the deeds he had done. 14As for Death and Hades, they were flung into the lake of fire. (What the lake of fire signifies is the second death.) 15And if someone's name *h*was not found recorded in the book of life, he was flung into the lake of fire.

21 Then I saw *i*a new heaven and a new earth, for the first heaven and the first earth had vanished, and there was no longer any sea. 2Moreover, I saw coming out of heaven, from God, *j*the holy city, the new Jerusalem, made all ready *k*like a bride adorned for her husband. 3Then I heard a powerful voice making this proclamation from the throne: *l*"It has come about: God has his dwelling place with men. They shall be his own people, and he, God himself, will be right among them. 4He will wipe away every tear from their eyes. Death

*x*Is 61:6   *y*Ezk 7:2; 38:2.9.16   *z*Hab 1:6 LXX   *a*Jr 11:15; 12:7; Ps 87:2; 78:68   *b*2 K 1:10; Zc 12:9; Gn 19:24; Ezk 38:22   *c*Is 6:1; Dn 7:9   *d*Ps 114:7.3   *e*Dn 7:10; Ps 69:28 *f*Ps 28:4; 62:12; Jr 17:10   *g*Pr 24:12   *h*Ps 69:28; Dn 12:1   *i*Is 65:17   *j*Is 52:1   *k*Is 61:10   *l*Zc 2:10; Ezk 37:27; 48:35; Is 25:8; 35:10; 65:19; Jr 31:16

will be no longer. No longer will there be **grief, cries of distress,** or any pain at all. For the old order of things has passed away."

[5] Then the one [m]**sitting on the throne** said to me, "Now is the time: [n]**I am making** all things **new.**" Then he said to me: "Set it down: these things are trustworthy and in accordance with the very truth." [6] And he spoke these further words to me: "It is already accomplished. I am the Alpha and the Omega, the beginning and the end. [o]**As for him who is thirsty,** I shall let him have, as a **free gift,** a draught of the spring which gives forth the [p]**water of life.** [7] It is the man who proves victorious who shall obtain all this for his inheritance; and [q]**I shall be his God, and he shall be my son.** [8] But this is what is in store for the cowards, those devoid of belief, those who lend themselves to loathsome practices, the murderers, the fornicators, those practising magic, the idolaters, and all who tell falsehoods. The second death will be their lot, and they will find themselves in the lake which is [r]**aflame with sulphurous fire.**"

[9] Then there appeared one of the seven angels in charge of the seven bowls filled with the [s]**seven** last **plagues,** and he addressed these words to me: "To my side, I shall show you the bride, the wife of the Lamb." [10][t]**And he carried me away,** under the impulse of the Spirit, to the top of a **high mountain,** showing me the [u]**holy city** of **Jerusalem,** as she was coming down out of heaven from God. [11] It was shining with [v]**God's glory,** and its radiance was like that of some priceless jewel, one like a jasper stone, as clear as crystal. [12] It had a wall great in extent and raised high, and it had twelve [w]**gates.** There was an angel at each of these gates which had **names** inscribed upon them, the names of the **twelve tribes of Israel.** [13]**There were three gates to the east, three gates to the north, three gates to the south, and three gates to the west.** [14] The wall of the city had twelve foundation stones, and on these were written the names of the twelve apostles of the Lamb.

[15] As for him who was talking to me, he had with him a golden [x]**measuring-rod,** to measure the city, its gates, and its wall. [16] The city was laid out as a [y]**square,** being as long as it was wide. He measured the city with the rod, and it came to twelve thousand furlongs, length, width, and height being the same. [17][z]**Moreover, he measured the wall** of the city. It was one hundred and forty-four cubits high, according to the human measurement which was what the angel was using. [18] The material the **wall** was built of was **jasper,** while the city consisted of pure gold, bright as glass of perfect clarity. [19][a]**The founda-**

---

[m]Is 6:1; Ps 47:8　　[n]Is 43:19　　[o]Is 55:1　　[p]Zc 14:8　　[q]2 Sm 7:14; Ps 89:26f; Zc 8:8　　[r]Gn 19:24; Is 30:33; Ezk 38:22　　[s]Lv 26:21　　[t]Ezk 40:2　　[u]Is 52:1　　[v]Is 58:8; 60:1.2.19　　[w]Ezk 48:31-35; Ex 28:21; 39:14　　[x]Ezk 40:3.5　　[y]Ezk 43:16　　[z]Ezk 48:16f　　[a]Is 54:11f

tion stones of the wall of the city were adorned with all kinds of **precious stones.** The first foundation stone had a jasper stone upon it; the second lapis lazuli; the third chalcedony; the fourth emerald; [20] the fifth sardonyx; the sixth cornelian; the seventh chrysolite; the eighth beryl; the ninth topaz; the tenth chrysoprase; the eleventh turquoise; and the twelfth amethyst. [21] As for the twelve gates of the city, they were twelve pearls. Each of the gates is made up of a single pearl. The main street of the city consists of pure gold, like glass of perfect transparency.

[22] I saw no temple in the city. The Lord God Almighty is its temple, and so is the Lamb. [23] Moreover, the city had no need of either the [b]**sun or the moon** to **shine** upon it. It was the **glory of God that gave** it **light;** and it was the Lamb who served it as a lamp. [24]**The nations shall walk by its light, and the kings of the earth shall bring** their **treasure** into it. [25][c]**The gates** of it **will never be closed by day;** and there will be no night there. [26] They will come and **bring** the **treasure** and the wealth **of the nations** into it. [27][d]**Nothing unclean shall ever come into it,** and no one with loathsome or deceitful ways shall enter. No one shall be there except those [e]**inscribed** in the Lamb's **book of life.**

22 Then he showed me a [f]**river,** that of the **water of life,** gleaming like crystal, which **flowed out** from **the throne of God** and of the Lamb [2] down **the middle** of the city's main street. [8]**On either side of the river there stand trees of life** which yield twelve crops of fruit, bringing forth [h]**fruit** every **month** of the year. As for the **leaves** of the trees, they serve for bringing **healing** to the nations. [3][i]**Nothing accursed shall be in the city any longer,** but the throne of God and of the Lamb shall be there. God's servants shall worship him there; [4][j]**they shall see his face;** they shall have his name inscribed upon their foreheads. [5]There shall be no more night. [k]**No** light of a lamp, no **light of the sun,** shall be needed by them, for **the Lord God will shine** upon them, and they [l]**will reign as kings for ever and ever.**

[6] And he spoke to me thus: "These words are deserving of all trust; they are in accordance with the truth. And the Lord—the God who imparts their spirits to the prophets—has sent forth his angel to show to his servants the things which are [m]**destined to come about,** and come about shortly. [7] And [n]**remember,** I am **coming** soon."

A blessing rests on whoever gives heed to the prophecies in this

---

[b]Is 24:23; Ps 60:1.6.10.13.19.20; 89:27; Is 60:3.5   [c]Is 60:11   [d]Is 35:8; 52:1   [e]Dn 12:1; 69:28   [f]Ezk 47:7.1; Zc 14:8; Jl 3:18; Jr 3:17   [8]Gn 2:9f; 3:22   [h]Ezk 47:12   [i]Zc 14:11 [j]Ps 17:15; 42:2   [k]Is 60:19; Ps 139:12   [l]Dn 7:18.27   [m]Dn 2:28   [n]Is 40:10

book. [8]As for myself, John, the man who heard and saw these things, I threw myself down to the ground when I heard and saw them, at the feet of the angel showing me these things, meaning to worship him. [9]But this is what he said to me: "Be careful not to do that! I am nothing more than a fellow servant of yours and of your brothers the prophets, and, moreover, of those that take heed of the words contained in this book. It is God that you must worship!"[10]And he addressed these further words to me: o"**Do not seal up** the words of prophecy found in this **book,** seeing that the **appointed time** is drawing near. [11]Meanwhile, let the [p]evil-doer go on doing evil; let the filthy-minded wallow in his filth; let the righteous man go on pursuing righteousness; let the holy man go on keeping himself holy.

[12]q"**I shall be coming** soon—mark my word—and I shall bring my [r]**recompense** with me, **rewarding each man according to** what **his deeds** have deserved. [13]s**I am** the Alpha and the Omega, **the first and the last,** the beginning and the end."

[14]A blessing rests on those who [t]**wash** their **robes** clean, securing their right to feed on the [u]**tree of life** and to make their entry into the city by its gates. [15]But these must stay outside: those leading the lives of dogs, those practising magic, the fornicators, the murderers, the idolaters, as well as everyone who loves deceit and practises it.

[16]"I, Jesus, have sent my angel to lay my testimony before you on behalf of the churches. I am the [v]**scion,** the offspring of the house of David. I am the Morning Star shining forth."

[17]The Spirit and the Bride say, "Come!" "Come!" let each hearer reply. [w]**Let him who is thirsty come forward.** Let all who want it accept the [x]**water of life as a free gift.**

[18]This is the testimony which I lay before every hearer of the [y]**words** of prophecy contained in this book. If anyone **brings in any addition to them,** God will bring **upon him** all the plagues **written about in this book.** [19]And if anyone **takes away anything** from the words found in this book of prophecy, God will take away from him all share in the [z]**tree of life** and in the holy city of which a description has been given in this book.

[20]These are the words of him who testifies to these things: "Yes, indeed, I shall be coming soon." So be it; do come, Lord Jesus.

[21]May the grace of the Lord Jesus be with you all.

[o]Dn 8:26; 12:4   [p][Dn 12:10]   [q]Is 40:10   [r]Ps 28:4; 62:12; Jr 17:10   [s]Is 44:6; 48:12; [41:4]   [t]Gn 49:11   [u]Gn 2:9; 3:22   [v]Is 11:1.10   [w]Is 55:1   [x]Zc 14:8   [y]Dt 4:2; 12:32; 29:20   [z]Gn 2:9; 3:22

APPENDIX

The Emotional and Spiritual Categorical Headings under Which
the Translator Initially Divided the Content of St. Paul's Letters

Circumcision and Uncircumcision
Disease
Divisions within the Church Lead to Fatal Results
Enthusiasm (St. Paul's strictures on uncontrolled enthusiasm:
   tongues, etc.)
Faith
Flesh
Freedom and Bondage
Gentiles
God Abandons
Grace
Handwriting
Heresies (heretical doctrines lead to character defects on the
   part of those propounding them)
Humility
Ignorance (Culpable/Wilful ignorance)
Judaism
Knowledge and Love
Law, Law and Sin, Law and the Flesh
Love
Maturity
Morality (Natural morality in its positive and negative aspects)
Mortification
New Life, New Man, etc.
Personal (Expression of personal attitudes)
Responsibility to Oneself before God
Righteousness by Faith
Salvation (Universal salvation)
Sarcasm

Self-esteem; Domineering
Separate Existence (A Christian has no longer separate existence:
    he lives in and for Christ; he lives in and for others)
Sin
Sobriety
Spirit, Spiritual
Sufferings
Sufferings and Comfort
Sympathy, all-embracing
Tension (Spiritual tension in those still in the flesh)
Tolerance (Every possible sacrifice to be made on behalf of the
    over-scrupulous)
Truth
Unity (Combining Divisions, Separate Existence, and Spirit)
Wisdom and Foolishness